National Geographic
Picture Atlas of
OUR FIFTY STATES

PUBLISHED BY
THE NATIONAL GEOGRAPHIC SOCIETY
MELVIN M. PAYNE, *Chairman of the Board*
ROBERT E. DOYLE, *President*
OWEN R. ANDERSON, *Secretary*
MELVILLE BELL GROSVENOR, *Editor Emeritus*
GILBERT M. GROSVENOR, *Editor*

PREPARED BY
NATIONAL GEOGRAPHIC BOOK SERVICE
JULES B. BILLARD, *Director*

Staff for this Book
MARGARET SEDEEN, *Editor*
CHARLES O. HYMAN, *Art Director*
ANNE DIRKES KOBOR, *Illustrations Editor*
ROBERT C. FIRESTONE, *Production Manager*
THOMAS B. ALLEN
ROSS BENNETT
JULES B. BILLARD
WENDY W. CORTESI
SEYMOUR L. FISHBEIN
MARY SWAIN HOOVER
EDWARD LANOUETTE
CAROL BITTIG LUTYK
ELIZABETH L. NEWHOUSE
DAVID F. ROBINSON
SHIRLEY L. SCOTT
VERLA LEE SMITH
KAREN HOFFMAN VOLLMER
ANNE ELIZABETH WITHERS
Editorial Staff
CONNIE BROWN BOLTZ, *Design*
KAREN F. EDWARDS
Assistant Production Manager
MOLLY KOHLER
LINDA BRUMBACH MEYERRIECKS
BARBARA G. STEWART
Illustrations Research
SUZANNE P. KANE, *Assistant*
JOHN T. DUNN, *Engraving and Printing*
JOHN D. GARST, JR.
PETER J. BALCH
VIRGINIA L. BAZA
CHARLES W. BERRY
SUSANAH B. BROWN
GEORGE COSTANTINO
MARGARET DEANE GRAY
VICTOR J. KELLEY
MILDA R. STONE
KATHERINE TUERR
ALFRED ZEBARTH
Map Design, Research, and Production
ANNE McCAIN, SARAH WERKHEISER, *Index*
MICHAELINE A. SWEENEY, *Style*
Contributions by
BETTIE DONLEY, DIANE S. MARTON,
MAUREEN PALMEDO

*659 Illustrations in full color,
including 94 maps*

National Geographic Picture Atlas of
OUR FIFTY STATES

Contents

Maps and Your Atlas 6

America's Many Faces 10

Our Nation's Capital 28

America at Work 56

Weather and Climate 106

The Wonders of Agriculture 166

Energy and Its Uses 202

City Places, Country Places 252

Facts at Your Fingertips
Populations of U. S. Cities 286
U. S. Super Facts
World Super Facts
Largest U. S. Metropolitan Areas
U. S. Forest Areas 288
Top Products/Top States
U. S. Territories and Outlying Areas 289

Copyright © 1978 National Geographic Society, Washington, D. C. All rights reserved. Reproduction of the whole or any part of the contents without written permission is prohibited.
First edition 525,000 copies
Library of Congress CIP data page 304

New England 30
Connecticut 32
Maine 36
Massachusetts 40
New Hampshire 44
Rhode Island 48
Vermont 52

Mid-Atlantic States 62
Delaware 64
Maryland 68
New Jersey 72
New York 76
Pennsylvania 80

Appalachian Highlands 84
Kentucky 86
North Carolina 90
Tennessee 94
Virginia 98
West Virginia 102

The Southeast 114
Alabama 116
Arkansas 120
Florida 124
Georgia 128
Louisiana 132
Mississippi 136
South Carolina 140

Great Lakes States 145
Illinois 146
Indiana 150
Michigan 154
Ohio 158
Wisconsin 162

The Heartland 173
Iowa 174
Kansas 178
Minnesota 182
Missouri 186
Nebraska 190
North Dakota 194
South Dakota 198

The Southwest 208
Arizona 210
New Mexico 214
Oklahoma 218
Texas 222

Mountain States 226
Colorado 228
Idaho 232
Montana 236
Nevada 240
Utah 244
Wyoming 248

Pacific Coast States 261
California 262
Oregon 266
Washington 270

Alaska, Hawaii and Distant Shores 274
Alaska 276
Hawaii 280
Distant Shores 284

Books to Know About 290
Abbreviations Used in this Book 292
Index 292
Map supplement in back of book

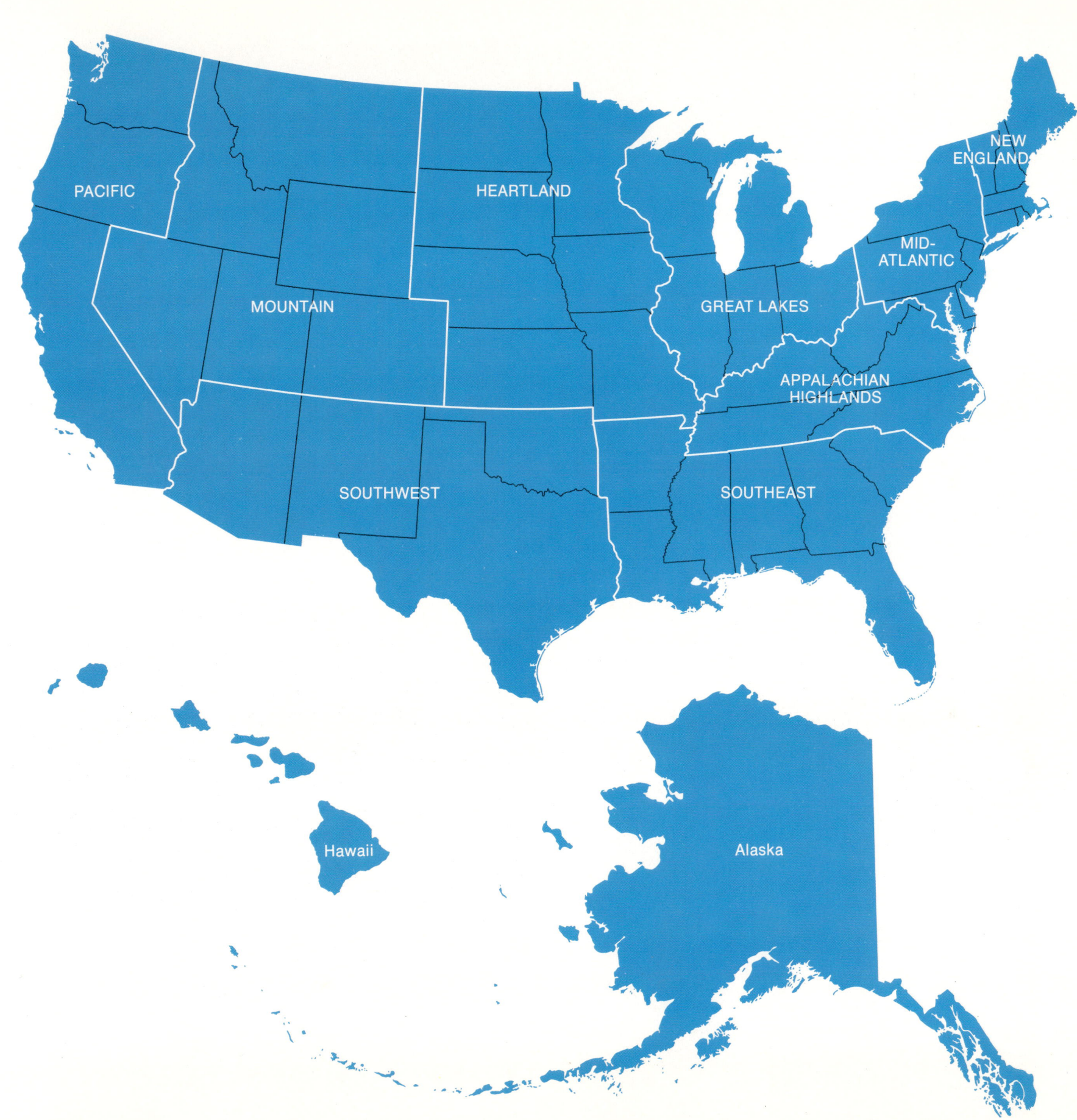

Maps and Your Atlas

What kind of book will tell you enough to fill a library if you can figure out its code? The answer: an atlas. The first person to name a book of maps an "atlas" was Gerhardus Mercator, a Flemish mapmaker of the 1500's. This early map of America is from a Mercator atlas. Mercator was also one of the first mapmakers to call the New World "America," after the explorer Amerigo Vespucci. The name stuck.

Early maps were often fanciful drawings based on legend and guesswork. But Vespucci, Christopher Columbus, and other explorers changed cartography—the art of mapmaking. Maps became better pictures of the earth's geography. The age of exploration has been called "unrolling the map."

Today, airplanes, satellites, and computers make cartography a science too. Look at the photograph of Harpers Ferry, West Virginia, taken from a plane. Then compare it to the map on page 7. Does that give you an idea of how a modern map is made?

Mapmakers draw only the things they want to tell you about. How much they show depends partly on how large the map's scale or size is. On page 7, the maps are drawn to three different scales. In the map of Harpers Ferry, you can see the land, rivers, and roads. In the smallest scale map, you can't even see where the town is. On a map, a small length—an inch or a centimeter, for example—stands for a large distance on the ground. The map's scale bar tells you what relationship the mapmaker used.

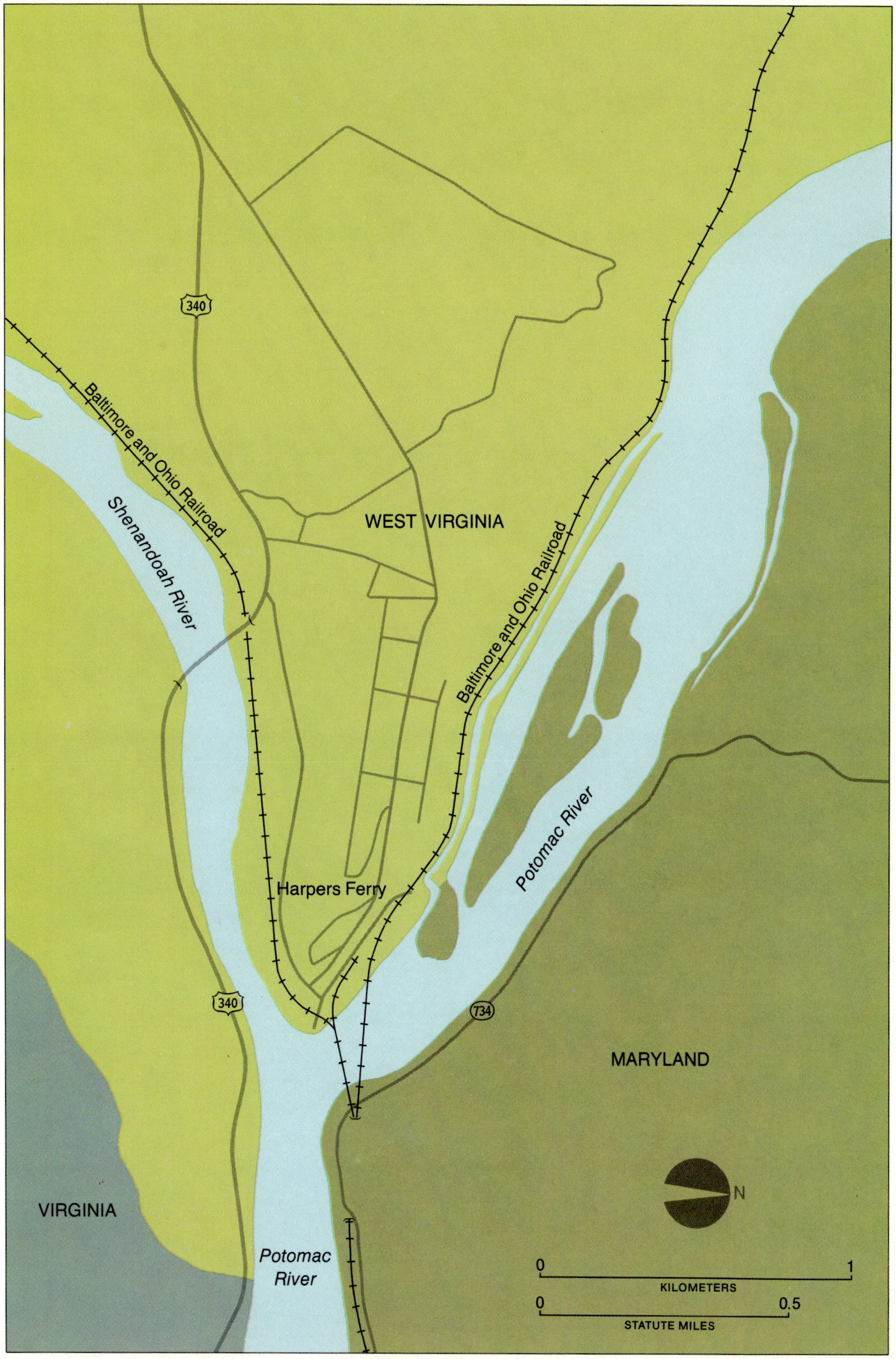

Maps also show you where a place is in relation to other places. A glance at the maps on this page will tell you about the location of Harpers Ferry quicker than a string of words can. We see that it sits on a tip of land in West Virginia where the Potomac and Shenandoah rivers meet, near the Maryland-Virginia border. And we see that West Virginia is in the eastern United States, about 141 miles (227 km) from the ocean.

Don't confuse "up" with north or "down" with south. Up means straight into the sky, and north means toward the North Pole. Maps can't always be placed on a page so that north is at the top. That's why there is usually a compass or an arrow to

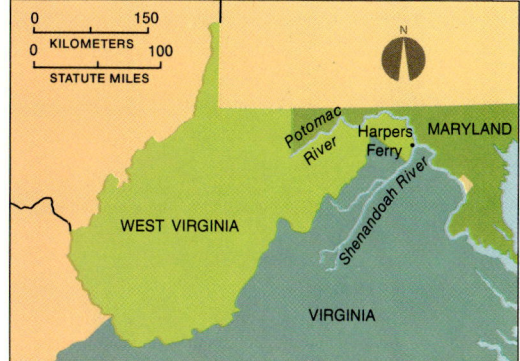

In smaller scale, Harpers Ferry is just a dot.

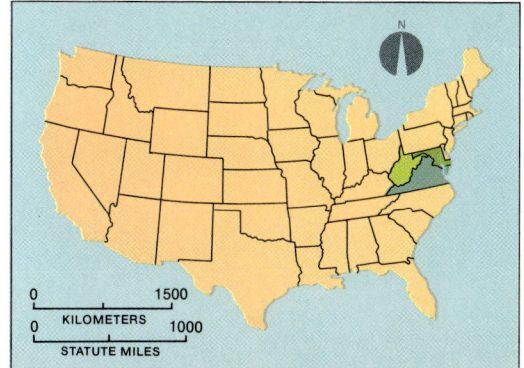

From this distance, we can't see it at all.

We look straight down at Harpers Ferry, West Virginia, on a map but not in the photograph.

What the Type Size Shows about Cities and Towns

★ **OLYMPIA** *is the capital*
• **Seattle** *has over 100,000 people*
• Bellevue *has between 50,000 and 100,000*
• Redmond *has under 50,000 people*

What Color Shows

Dark green *is for national parks and big national monuments, seashores, and recreation areas.*

Yellow *stands for Indian reservations.*

Red *is for hiking trails like the Pacific Crest and the Appalachian trails.*

Gray shading shows hilly or mountainous areas.

How to Find a Place

Look up Davenport, Washington in the index. You'll find **271 F16***. Turn to page* **271***. Place a finger on the number 16 on the grid at the top of the map, and another on the letter F along the side. Then follow the imaginary lines across the page until the fingers meet. There you'll find Davenport.*

8

show which direction north is on the map.

Maps can tell you much more about a place than just its location, direction, and how far it is from other places. Look at the drawing of the railroad tracks on the map of Harpers Ferry. On maps we call this kind of drawing a symbol. Symbols *stand for* something; they make up the code of the map. Some maps, like most in this book, have symbols that resemble what they stand for. But other maps don't. That's why a key is a very important feature of a map. A key explains the code.

In your *National Geographic Picture Atlas*, all 50 state maps have keys like the one on page 8. From these maps you can find out a lot about the geography of each state even though there wasn't room to include every town, river, lake, and road. Color can also be used as a symbol on maps. The notes on the Washington map on page 8 tell you how. The size of the names and of the dots for towns and cities means something too—about how large or small their population is.

Your atlas also has more than 30 special-purpose maps that give a range of useful information. In the back of the book there's an extra-special one—a Landsat map—which shows you a picture of the country "taken" by satellite 570 miles (917 km) above the earth. You'll be surprised at the things you can see on it if you look closely—from tiny offshore islands to lakes and rivers right near your home. Scientists use Landsat pictures to pick out sick crops, find polluted water, explore for oil and minerals.

With the map of each state, there is a state story and a quick summary of economic facts. In your atlas there are also drawings, photographs, and graphs. You'll see that an atlas can sometimes be much more than just a plain book of maps.

Maps are amazing—*there's no end to the things they can show. These special-purpose maps give one kind of information. They answer questions such as: What types of trees grow in Florida? Which areas of the country raise cattle? Compare several maps of a place and you'll have a good idea of what it's like, even if you've never been there.*

What do our farms grow? See pages 170-71.

Where are all the people? See pages 20-21.

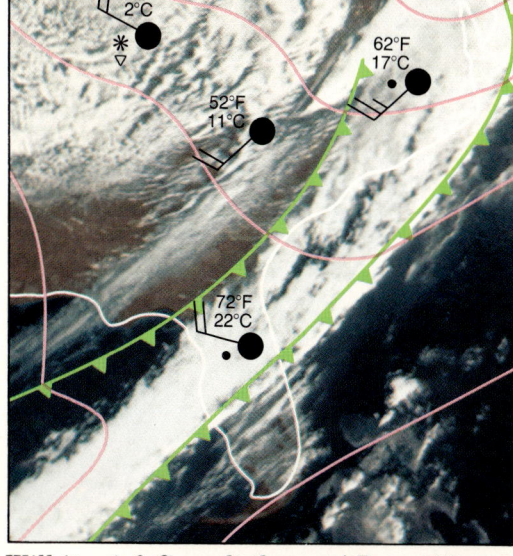
Will it rain? Consult the map! Page 109.

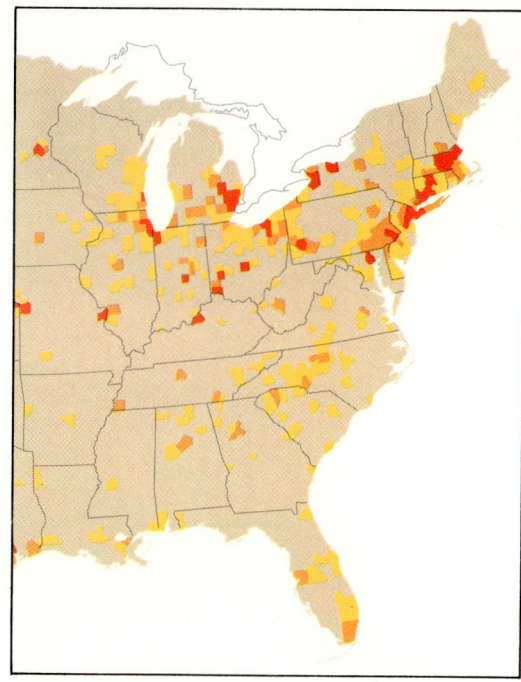
Made in America! But where? See page 59.

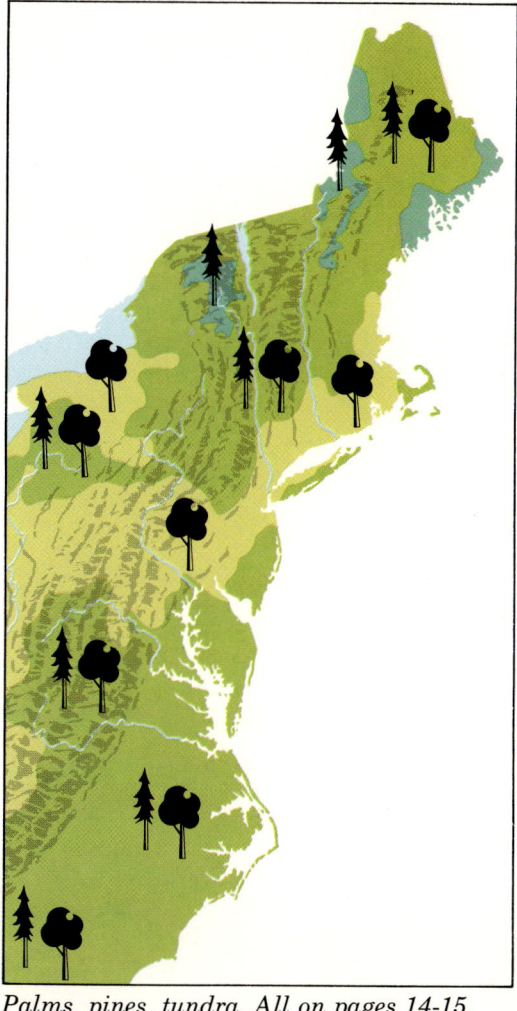
Palms, pines, tundra. All on pages 14-15.

America's Many Faces

Drifting up and away, the big balloon floats high above the land. Imagine yourself aboard, with an eagle's-eye view of our huge country. It stretches 2,807 miles (4,517 km) from the Atlantic to the Pacific Ocean and covers enough space for nearly two billion football fields. The land wears many faces. There are glaciers in Montana, sand dunes in California, barren salt flats in Utah, and soil so fertile in Iowa you can hear the corn growing. Kansas is flat, and Colorado is an up-and-down state: Some 50 peaks rise 14,000 feet (4,267 m) or higher— more major mountains than are found in Switzerland. The land is home to a wonderful variety of animals, including the human kind. But sprawling cities, farms, and factories mean less unspoiled land and vanishing wildlife. This too is part of the story.

The sun sparkles on the Golden Gate Bridge and San Francisco Bay. As our balloon lifts off, the ground drops away and we sail eastward past plump green hills and rolling farmland to the crest of the Sierra Nevada. On the other side lies a harsh brown desert.

Look down there: an old mine shaft and a few ramshackle buildings. Gold and silver prospectors struck it rich and then moved on when the mine played out. Only a ghost town is left, the wind sighing through broken windows. Ahead of us rise the snow-clad summits of the Rocky Mountains.

Through long ages, the earth was torn by exploding volcanoes, heaved up by great pressures, and carved by rushing rivers. Slowly it was pushed and squeezed into all the shapes we know today.

Before the West was settled, pioneer scouts and trappers roamed the Rockies. They found reminders of those long-ago days when the earth gushed hot lava. Some brought back tales of the wonders they had seen. People laughed when told of a galloping river that leaped over a cliff, a mountain of glass, and spouts of hot water that came roaring out of the ground.

Anyone who has visited Yellowstone National Park knows that many of the old yarns were true. We know the galloping river as Yellowstone Falls, the glass mountain as Obsidian Cliff—a chunk of black volcanic glass. The geyser, Old Faithful, shoots hot water a hundred or more feet (30 m) into the air every hour or so.

An underground "furnace" heats Yellowstone's pools and geysers. About two miles (3.2 km) under the park lies a dome of hot,

Our land, *with its many familiar faces, has seen vast change in the last 600 million years. The dry plains once lay under water, and dinosaurs roamed Utah. Sprouting in warm swamps were the ancestors of pine and fir trees. As wind and rain grind away mountains, and rivers carry tons of soil down to the sea, new chapters are written in earth's history book. What will the land look like in another 600 million years?*

Waterways soak Louisiana's delta country.

Cathedral Spires tower in the Alaska Range.

12

Wind molds the desert in Arizona.   *Shooting stars blossom on an Iowa prairie.*   *Maples and birches light a Maine forest.*

molten rock. It measures about 30 miles (48 km) across and descends perhaps four miles (6.4 km) into the earth. Cold groundwater seeps downward and heats up. Under great pressure it rises again, and boiling water and steam explode as a geyser eruption.

Animals gather around the steam-heated pools like hikers around a campfire. Elk and buffalo graze near geysers where the ground is free of snow. Grizzly bears curl up in back-country dens, but they don't truly hibernate. Sometimes they tramp grumpily through the forest in the dead of winter.

Thousands of grizzlies once roamed the West, from Kansas to California. Hunted by settlers and trappers, they retreated farther and farther into the wilderness. Today only a few hundred exist outside Alaska.

Exploring the Rockies would take a long time. The mountains zigzag 1,900 miles (3,058 km) from Canada to New Mexico. An imaginary line called the Continental Divide runs north and south along the high rims and ridges. It separates the streams that flow eastward toward the Atlantic from those that flow westward to the Pacific. A hiker who stayed on the divide, so the story goes, could walk from Canada almost to Mexico without getting his feet wet.

If instead he followed one of the westward streams—the Colorado River—he would see

From the cold, *dry Arctic to the hot, moist tropics, our country unfolds as a patchwork quilt of landscapes. This map serves as a guide to the natural vegetation: If there were no one to farm the land, cut down the trees, and build cities and suburbs, this is the way our garden would grow. Climate, soil, and altitude draw rough boundaries around these realms; the color key tells what the most important vegetation is. Many other trees and plants grow in each domain.*

Trees of the Western needleleaf forests include many kinds of conifers—pines, firs, spruces, and junipers.

Alaska is bordered by stretches of tundra— a cold, treeless plain where mosses and lichens grow.

Arid lands range from dry cactus deserts to scrub and sagebrush country that receives more rainfall.

Hawaii lies within the tropics. Palm trees and other tropical plants also grow in Florida.

14

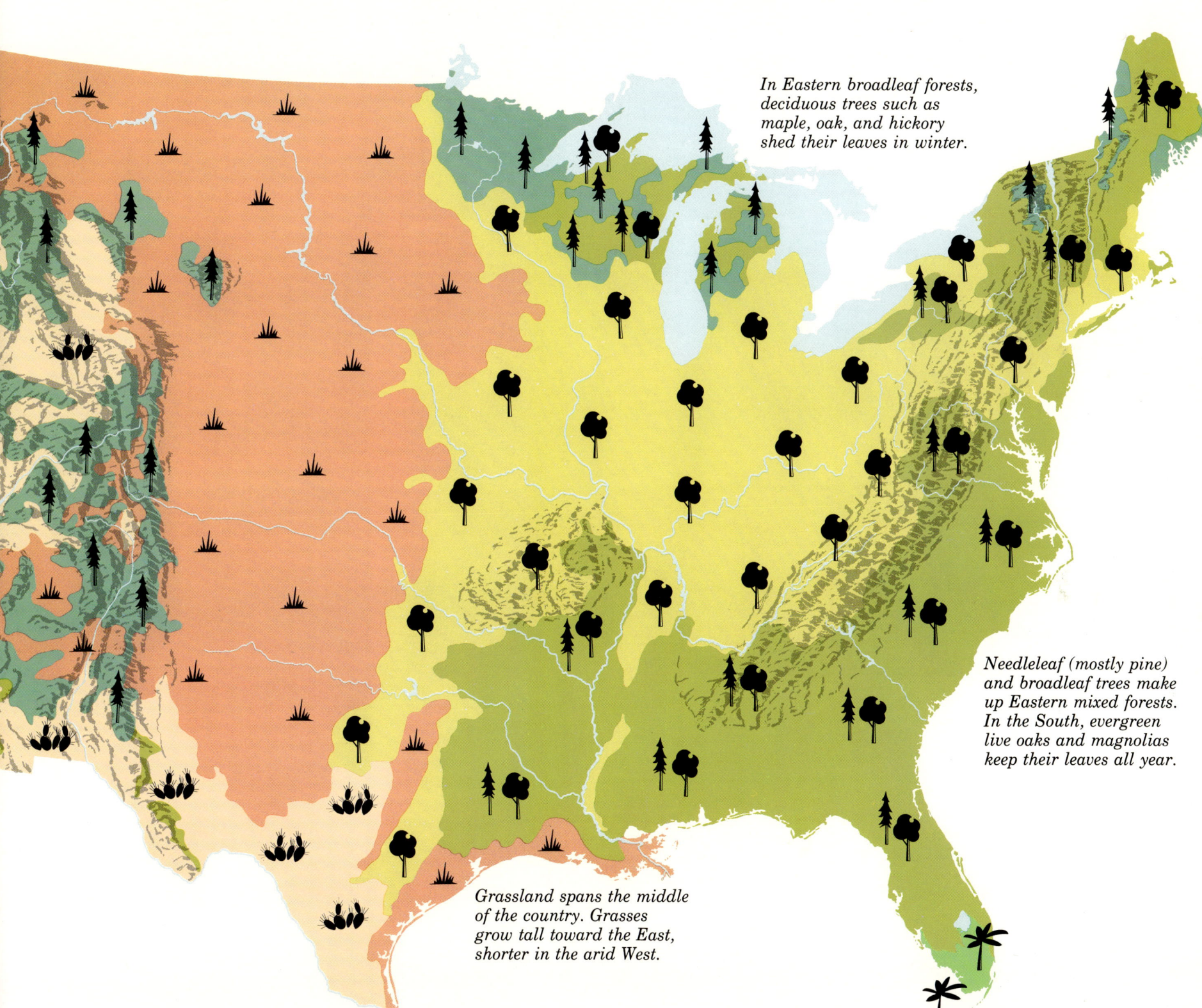

The sidewinder, a desert rattlesnake

Polar bears on Alaska's pack ice

Egrets in a South Carolina refuge

Buffalo on a Montana range

Shy deer in an eastern woodland

Born free, *animals dwell in wild kingdoms across the land. In the desert where everything either "sticks, stings, or stinks," a rattlesnake slithers on the hot sand. It can swallow a lizard whole. Polar bears follow the scent of seals, killing with a single blow of a huge paw. These wading birds in a southern marsh eat frogs and insects; they stir up small fish and crabs, then grab them with daggerlike beaks. Buffalo travel in family bands, often joining others to form large herds.*
At home in the woods, many deer live near people, but the bighorn sheep hides away on the craggy slopes of its mountain home.

Rocky Mountain bighorn sheep

a strange thing: sailboats and water-skiers in the middle of the desert. One stretch of the river, trapped behind Glen Canyon Dam, forms Lake Powell. The dam generates electricity, and the lake is a playground for fishermen and boaters.

The boats are sailing on a desert plateau, a high shelf of land slashed by the Grand Canyon and smaller gorges. Weird and colorful stone shapes decorate part of the plateau, where cowboys and Indians ride again, filmed by Hollywood moviemakers. The Navajos own a corner of the stony wilderness. Centuries ago, ancestors of the Pueblo Indians lived in cliff cities built on narrow ledges. You can still see the ruins.

Desert country blankets the Southwest and even pokes fingers into Oregon and Idaho. The sun beats down on shrubby flatland and sand dunes. Half the area gets less than ten inches (254 mm) of rain a year, and sometimes this evaporates before it hits the ground. Old desert dwellers say that even the jackrabbits have to carry canteens!

Why is the desert dry? Moist winds blow in from the Pacific Ocean. The Sierra Nevada and the Cascade Range rob the winds of their moisture. Little rain falls east of these high mountains.

As we soar above the sunbaked desert, it looks still and empty. But hikers and campers know that it teems with life. Hundreds of birds live or visit there. Bobcats and coyotes hunt mice and rabbits. Look out for the pack rat—it likes shiny things and may steal a camper's coins or jewelry.

Where the desert has a barren look, humans must often take the blame. Bulldozers scar the countryside, and too many cattle graze the sparse grasses. No one knows if this land will ever recover. Some people want to build up and cultivate the desert, to make it "bloom." Others believe the wild lands are beautiful as they are.

Drifting east again, we're on the other side of the Rockies. The world is flat. Once the Great Plains from Canada to Texas were grasslands where Indians hunted buffalo. Now they're a checkerboard of wheat fields, dotted with giant harvesters and grain elevators. Ahead lies the Mississippi, a winding ribbon of silver. Once the grass that grew nearest the river was so tall a horseman had to stand in his stirrups to see over it. Homesteaders boarded prairie schooners to cross this ocean of grass.

In time, the grasses were plowed under and the Midwest and Great Plains became the nation's breadbasket. But farmers on the dry western plains were in for trouble. Grass had been the "glue" that held the soil together. Now when winds swept the land and there was little rain, the plowed fields crumbled and blew away.

After a long dry spell in the 1930's, howling winds stirred up dust clouds from the Dakotas to Texas. Tons of topsoil were blown eastward into the Atlantic Ocean. Dust settled on the decks of ships 300 miles (483 km) at sea. During these Dust Bowl days, many families left their ruined farms. Those who stayed had to learn new ways of managing the land.

Many plains animals suffered when the settlers came. Take the prairie dog. Billions of these little rodents scampered across the grasslands a hundred years ago. In Texas, a single prairie-dog town housed about 400 million animals. Because they competed with cattle for grazing land, ranchers nearly wiped out the prairie dogs.

About 50 million buffalo still grazed the plains in pioneer days. In 1871, near Fort Hays, Kansas, a troop of the Sixth Cavalry faced an enormous herd. The black sea of animals took several days to pass.

Then the railroad came to Indian country, bringing hide hunters who killed buffalo by the millions. Buffalo Bill Cody alone slaughtered 4,120 animals in 18 months. By 1900, less than a thousand were left. Protection in wildlife refuges has saved the buffalo from extinction.

We'll see no free-roaming buffalo east of the Mississippi. But we will see mountains more ancient than the Rockies. We're skimming the Appalachians, tree-clad ranges that stretch from Canada to Alabama.

The Appalachians began to take shape about 400 million years ago. Much later,

glaciers crept down from the north, digging out lakes and sawing off rocks. In the eastern United States, the last ice sheet moved south as far as present-day Philadelphia. Ice half a mile (.8 km) thick topped the Presidential Range in New Hampshire and the Berkshires in Massachusetts.

The southern Appalachians escaped the glaciers and gave refuge to northern plants and animals. In Great Smoky Mountains National Park, you can see more than 150 different kinds of trees.

From the mountains, the land slopes gently to the coastal plain and the Atlantic beaches. A little farther on and we land— bumpily—on Blackbeard Island off the coast of Georgia. On this island look for gold the pirate Blackbeard is said to have buried here. There's another kind of treasure too. Loggerhead turtles swim ashore to lay their eggs, huge bull alligators roar in the marshes, the flapping wings of thousands of wild ducks fill the air.

The bald eagle *needs help to keep flying. People crowd our national bird, chemical poisons kill it. Scientists study the eagles, hoping they can be saved. A squawking eaglet from the nest weighs in (below).*

In the 1600's sailing ships brought settlers to the Atlantic's wild shores. The newcomers looked upon a coast unspoiled and filled with wildlife. The land was like Blackbeard Island. More and more people came. Most of them lived in what would become the thirteen original colonies.

By the time our country was born in 1776, nearly everyone lived in a farmhouse somewhere between the Atlantic coast and the Appalachians. The mountains were like a big stone wall that forced people to stay on the edge of the continent.

But a way was found through the mountains. Daniel Boone and his frontiersmen carved the Wilderness Road along a pass in the Appalachians. Soon pioneers were walking the road to the other side of the mountains. By the 1790's about 100,000 people were living in new settlements scattered beyond the mountain wall. They soon were planning new states.

Most of the pioneers moved out of the East because they wanted to find a new place for a new start. That was also the reason most people gave later, when they headed west and spread out across the continent.

We are still on the move. Many families are leaving the North to live in what is called the "sun belt." This booming part of the country runs from Florida through the South and Southwest to California, which now has more people than any other state.

At the very beginning, no one really knew how many people lived in the United States. Indians weren't counted. A slave was counted as three-fifths of a person. (In real numbers, about 20 percent, or one-fifth, of the non-Indian population was black.)

People were too busy making a nation to stop and count themselves in 1776. But in the Constitution they wrote orders for a regular count of the people. The count is called the decennial (every ten years) census.

Our first official census in 1790 counted 3,900,000 people. About half of them were no older than 16. We were a young nation and growing fast. Many people came to the United States. Most of them were from Europe. That was the Old World — and ours

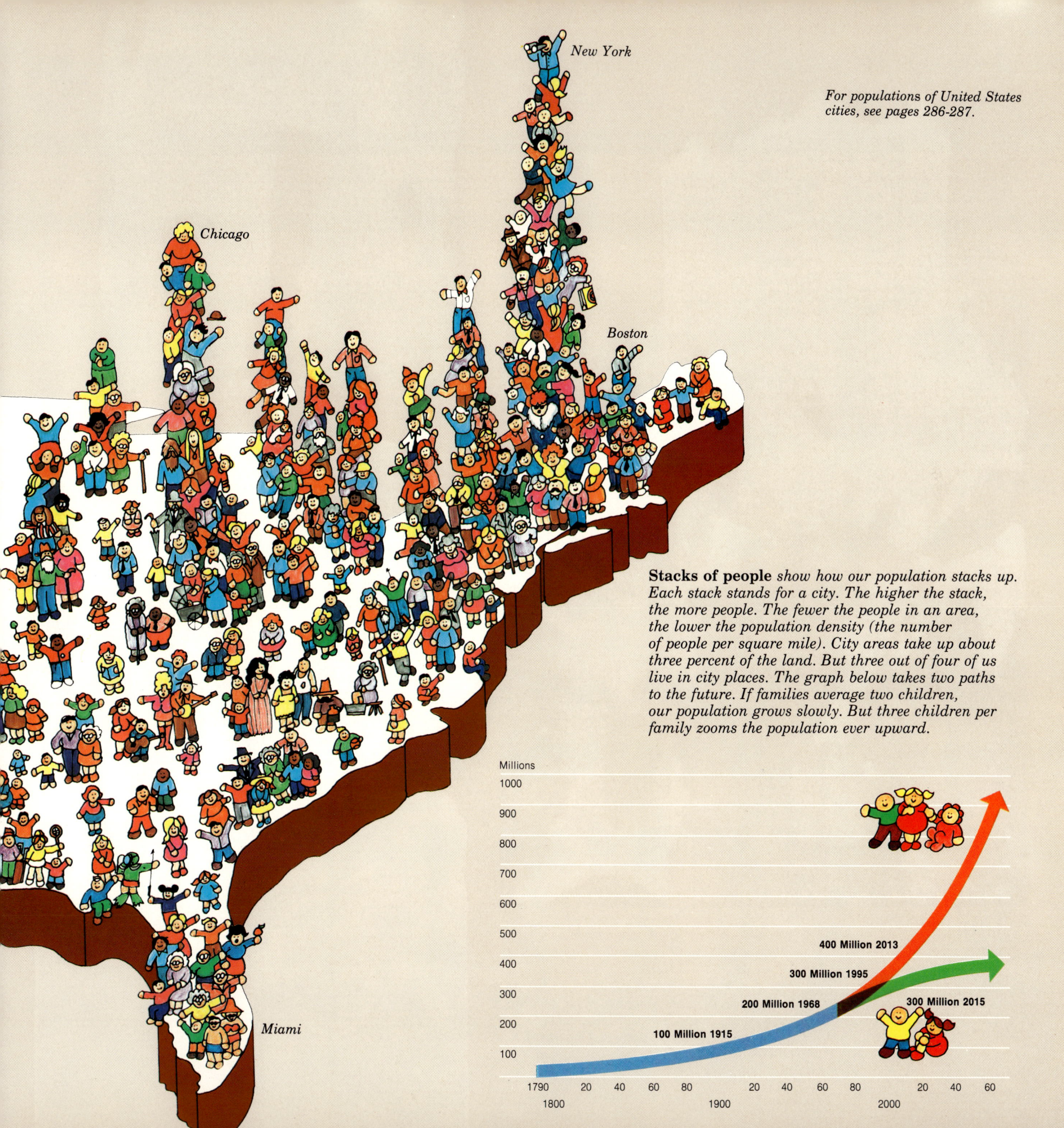

This high-rise apartment is for retirees only.

Where we live: *High-rise apartment, farm, inner city... Americans call many places home. Most of our ancestors lived on farms. Now farm population is getting smaller; in some farm areas there are more deaths than births. Houses cost so much that mobile homes make up about 16 percent of new one-family housing. They usually stay put, even if they do have wheels.*

Some houses don't need much land!

Suburbs are home to about 27 percent of us.

22

Mobile homes: 63,000 built in 1950—and 277,000 a year now.

About 26 percent of us live in country places.

Only about 15 percent of us live in small towns.

Central cities: home for 31.5 percent of us.

was the New. Ours was a big, rich, promising land. The country needed only one more natural resource: settlers.

Our greatest growth came between 1880 and 1920, when more than 21 million Europeans entered the country. Many of them passed through Ellis Island, the place in New York harbor that became the gateway to America. The Statue of Liberty stands there. A poem on the statue's base tells why America welcomed so many people: "Give me your tired, your poor, Your huddled masses yearning to breathe free...."

By 1890 about four out of every ten people in New York, Chicago, and other big cities had been born in foreign countries. America became "a nation of nations." In 1910 there were twice as many Irish in New York City as in Dublin, Ireland. And there were more Italians in New York than there were in Naples, Italy. Only the big German cities of Berlin and Hamburg had more Germans than our own city of Chicago. In such factory cities as Cleveland and Milwaukee, more than 30 percent of the people had been born in other countries.

Many of the newcomers looked for places like home. People from northern countries, such as Iceland and Norway, went to our Upper Midwest—to Minnesota and North Dakota. Dutch farmers found marshes in Michigan—and drained them, as they had in the Netherlands. Italians and Armenians went to southern California to find warm farm country. Spanish shepherds became shepherds in the mountains of the West. Greek sponge divers went to Tampa, Florida, and dived for American sponges. Portuguese fishermen made a living catching fish off Massachusetts.

As the nation grew, the job of counting everybody got much harder. The federal government had to hire census takers (also called enumerators). In every year ending in "0," the census takers went around and counted heads. One special day—Census Day—was picked. On that day, all the numbers were added up for the grand total.

On Census Day in 1970 there were 203,211,926 people living in the 50 states

and the District of Columbia. That figure is the Official Census. (If you add soldiers, sailors, government workers, their families, and other Americans living outside our country, then the total was 204,949,762.)

Our population (from *populus,* a Latin word for people) is not just a number added up on Census Day. Our population keeps changing. Between censuses, we need a way to *estimate* that change.

You can see the most up-to-date estimates in the Department of Commerce building in Washington, D. C. There you will find a big clock. But it does not tell time. It is called the Census Clock. It figures how many of us are living here at any certain minute.

If you had stood in front of the clock at 8 a.m. on July 4, 1976, for instance, the clock would have told you that there were 215,667,979 of us at America's 200th birthday. (Just compare that to the 1970 Official Census figure and see how fast we grew!)

The Census Clock's long number has a sign under it: "Our Changing Population." The number is a string of nine digits. It looks like a readout on a calculator. In fact, the clock is a huge calculator. Its ever-changing number is made up by putting facts into the clock, the way you put numbers into a pocket calculator to get a readout.

The facts help tell what makes the population of the United States keep changing.

Workers line up *to show how Americans make a living. People grouped above stand for 44,791,000 "white-collar" workers. The name came from what males wore in offices. Now women outnumber men. "Blue collar" and service workers (next page) total 41,773,000. Two out of three are men. About 2,060,400 men and women are in the armed services. Farms employ 2,694,000.*

7% under 5

22% 5 to 17 years old

40% 18 to 44 years old

20% 45 to 64 years old

11% 65 and over

The march of life *begins with babies, in 1978 our smallest age group. As they grow up, they make changes in our society. Out of school, they look for jobs and start families. After 45, they probably won't add babies to the population. At 65, most will retire, and others will take their jobs.*

They are facts about births and deaths, and about the numbers of immigrants (people coming *into* the country) and emigrants (people going *out* of the country).

We get these facts from demographers—which means people who study not *geo*-graphy but *demo*-graphy. (And *demo* comes from the same Greek word that gives us *demo*-cracy. Demo = People.)

The demographers say that the population changes in these four ways: Every ten seconds someone is born somewhere in the United States. Every 16 seconds a person dies in the United States. Every 81 seconds a new immigrant arrives in the United States. And every 15 minutes an American leaves the country.

When all of these facts are fed into the Census Clock's calculator, it figures out the rate of our population change. The Census Clock tells us that we gain another American just about every 21 seconds!

The Constitution orders the government to have censuses. This is because the number of people in each state must be known so the states can send the right number of lawmakers to the House of Representatives. The number of representatives is based on a state's population.

For instance, look at the difference between the number of representatives from Alaska and from California. Alaska, with

about 407,000 people, has only one Congressman in the House of Representatives. California, with almost 22,000,000 people, has 43 representatives.

After each census, some states gain or lose representatives. Take the census of 1970. California gained five representatives, Florida gained three, and Texas, Colorado, and Arizona gained one each. Pennsylvania and New York each lost two.

The gains and losses show that the old part of the country is losing people to the new. For instance, between 1967 and 1977, about 500,000 newcomers moved into the Sonoran Desert of young Arizona, which is one of our fastest-growing states.

The South is also booming. Northerners began moving to Southern states about the time that air-conditioning became cheap enough for a family — or a factory — to afford. Northerners found they could live comfortably in the South. And they could get jobs in factories that either moved to or sprang up in the sun belt.

Back in 1940, about 70 percent of America's factory workers lived in the North. By 1970 only about half of our factory workers lived in the North. The rest were enjoying warm winters and the outdoor way of life in the sun-belt states.

Many older people head for the warm places when they retire. That's why a visit to grandma and grandpa often means heading south. In the old days, grandparents usually stayed put. Now they move, and so do many of the rest of us.

Each year about one out of every five Americans moves from one home to another. If you watched the moves for a long time, you would notice they were mostly from east to west and from farm to city.

In 1860, about four out of every five Americans lived on a farm or a ranch. By 1900, when the population was 76,000,000, about 30,000,000 lived in cities. One out of every 12 persons lived in New York City, Philadelphia, or Chicago. By 1930, only about 21 percent of our people lived on farms. Almost half of them did not own the farms.

The end of World War II in 1945 is the time when the next big change began in America's "human geography." The men who fought in the war returned, got married, found places to live, and started families. From 1947 to 1957, about 43,000,000 babies were born.

Their needs — from food and shoes to houses and schools — would produce jobs, services, and even inventions. The sudden increase in population would also produce problems for a long time.

The "baby boom" became a big bump or bulge in our population, and as the years passed, so did the bulge: The babies of the 1940's and 1950's produced the "school boom" of the 1950's and 1960's — and many of the job seekers of the 1970's. Early in the 21st century, still a bulge in the population, they'll make a "senior citizen" boom.

With the bulge came the need to make more things. Factories became automated. Advertising became more important than ever, telling more and more people about more and more things to buy. Television, a new way to advertise, became a big part of just about everybody's life.

More families meant more houses. The cheapest land to build on was outside the city: the suburbs. People might still work in the city. But they lived and shopped in the suburbs. So they needed shopping centers and more cars. And more highways, and more energy. More and more needs. More and more changes.

The men and women we elected to run our towns, states, and nation, along with the people who run our businesses, began to realize that all these changes were causing problems. And one of the biggest problems was how they could keep track of all the changes that were happening.

The planners had to invent a new name for a place so big that "city" wasn't enough. The new name: Standard Metropolitan Statistical Area — SMSA for short. *Standard* just means a way to measure so that what

is true for one place is true for another. *Metropolitan* meant "mother city" to the Greeks. To us, the word means a big city that has a lot of other communities around it. *Statistical* has to do with numbers, and *Area* is the amount of land in an SMSA.

The planners defined an SMSA as a place that includes a central city or twin cities of 50,000 or more people—plus nearby communities connected with the central city. Most Americans live in or next to an SMSA. Not all the area in an SMSA is full of people. Part of the Mojave Desert in California is in the San Bernardino-Riverside SMSA. The Duluth-Superior SMSA in Minnesota includes a wilderness. For a list of metropolitan areas, see page 288.

Sixty percent of us live on about one percent of the land. Most of us live in or close to a city. More than 85 percent of us live close enough to an SMSA so that we can make a living in a city. Very few workers live within walking distance of their jobs.

We've come a long way from the farms of the 13 original states. You don't have to be a demographer to know that we, the people, keep changing where and how we live.

Time flies *across the country from east to west. Time zones keep all clocks in an area ticking to the same time. Until railroads laid out time zones in 1883, most places set their own time. Philadelphia's clocks were five minutes behind New York's, 19 minutes ahead of Pittsburgh's. The time zones are about 900 miles (1,448 km) wide. The zones are based on a worldwide system that uses longitudes as zone borders. But the borders bend to tie together natural areas, such as the Mountain states. And the borders zigzag in some places so that neighboring communities can be neighbors in time too.*

Our Nation's Capital
The District of Columbia

People who live in Washington really live in two cities. Outsiders see only one, the Federal City, with its government buildings and monuments. Most visitors never see the second, the home of about 690,000 Washingtonians. That means houses, schools, stores, hospitals, police and fire departments—everything a big American city needs to be a city.

But for most of its history Washington could not have what every other city in America had: self-government. The Founding Fathers thought of the Capital as a special place, not as a regular U. S. city. Finally, in 1974, Washingtonians elected their mayor for the first time in more than 100 years. The District of Columbia (Washington's other name) also elects to Congress a representative who can work on bills but cannot vote them into law.

More than 70 percent of Washington's population is black. Many black families can trace their roots to the Capital's earliest days. Then, a poet wrote, the city had two kinds of people—"Slaving blacks and democratic whites." Today, by their votes and in City Hall, blacks govern Washington.

About 350,000 people in and around the District work in its major industry: the federal government. The second biggest industry is tourism. So many visitors crowd the streets in summer that Washingtonians often feel lost. Some wear T-shirts that say: "I'm not a tourist. I live here."

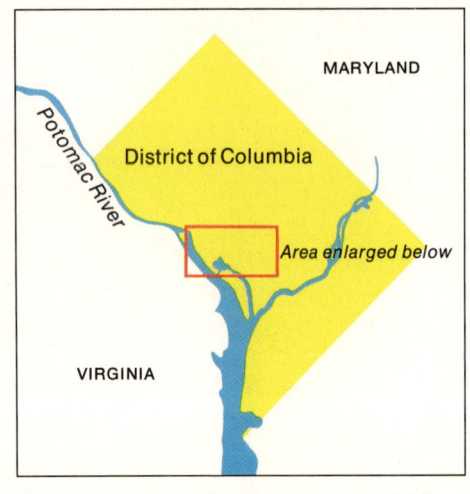

The District of Columbia began as 100 square miles of land, donated mostly by Maryland. In 1846, Virginia's gift—about a third—was given back.

New Metro subway lines snake through Washington's street plan, which dates to 1792.

The motto over the pillars tells what happens in the Supreme Court: "Equal Justice Under Law."

Light bathes the Capitol Dome, the Washington Monument, and the Lincoln Memorial.

Newly-chosen Vice President Ford speaks to both the House of Representatives and the Senate.

Under special glass and filters at the National Archives can be seen the Bill of Rights, the Constitution, and the Declaration of Independence.

New England

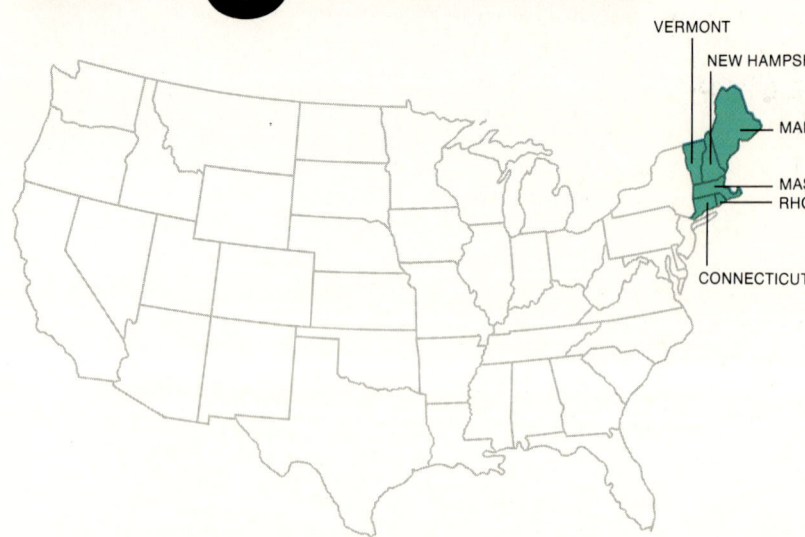

Glaciers formed many New England lakes. But movements in the earth created 107-mile-long (172 km) Lake Champlain.

New England: A wrinkle of mountains. A blanket of forests. Lakes by the thousands, sparkling across the land. Silver threads of rivers twisting down the valleys, hurrying to the sea.

The sea, reaching in through the sheltered waters of Long Island Sound, laps gently against Connecticut. The sea cuts deep into Rhode Island, rubs against the sandy arm of Cape Cod, pounds into the rocky edge of Maine.

As with the sea, so with New England's highlands. They begin gently with the Connecticut hills, climb to the Berkshires and the cold northern peaks—the Green Mountains of Vermont, the White Mountains of New Hampshire, mile-high Mount Katahdin in Maine.

Half of New England was once in farmland. Now the forest has returned, and covers four-fifths of the land.

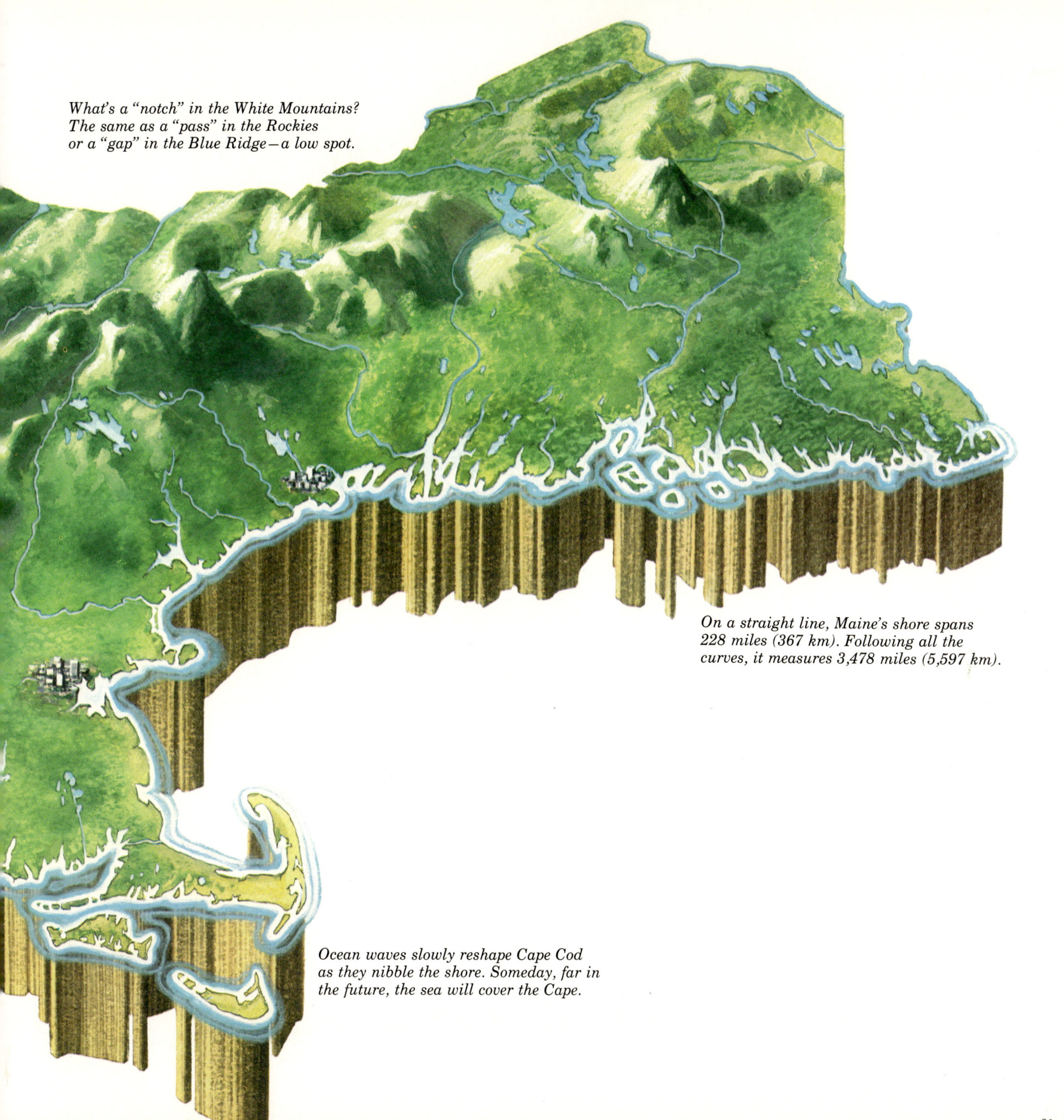

What's a "notch" in the White Mountains? The same as a "pass" in the Rockies or a "gap" in the Blue Ridge—a low spot.

On a straight line, Maine's shore spans 228 miles (367 km). Following all the curves, it measures 3,478 miles (5,597 km).

Ocean waves slowly reshape Cape Cod as they nibble the shore. Someday, far in the future, the sea will cover the Cape.

Mountain Laurel

Robin

CONNECTICUT

Connecticut seems to "connect" the Middle Atlantic and New England regions. But that's not why it's called Connecticut. The name comes from an Indian word meaning "long tidal river." The Connecticut River flows 410 miles (660 km), the longest river in New England. It begins in northern New Hampshire, forms the entire border between that state and Vermont, splits Massachusetts and then Connecticut, and empties into Long Island Sound.

In its fertile valley, tobacco and vegetables and other crops grow. Tobacco? Visitors driving along Interstate 91 do a double take when they see this southern plant growing in Massachusetts and Connecticut.

Yet this has been tobacco country since Indian days. Today it produces prime wrapper leaf for cigars—and prime money, too. Per pound, this tobacco is among the most valuable cash crops in the country.

Beyond the valley, much of Connecticut is rocky and hard to farm. Early on, settlers had to use their wits to make a living. They built ships and went to sea from the fine natural harbors on Long Island Sound. They built mills and began making things.

Soon Yankee peddlers spread across the land. On their backs they hauled packs stuffed with pins, hats, tin cups, combs, clocks, brass kettles. Some of them sold fake nutmegs, carved from wood, instead of the spice itself. That's how Connecticut came to be known as the Nutmeg State.

The peddlers needed new things to sell. Yankee ingenuity supplied them. Connecticut is also the "Gadget State." It produced the first copper coins, the first stone crusher, the first football tackling dummy, the first submarine torpedo boat (in 1775!), and the first American-made steel fishhook.

"From the Latest Observations and best Authorities." So boasted Abel Buell of Connecticut in 1784, when he produced the first American-made map of the new nation.

Area: the 48th largest state, 5,009 sq mi (12,973 sq km). **Population:** 3,108,000. Ranks 24th. **Major Cities:** Bridgeport, 142,960; Hartford, 138,152; New Haven, 126,845. **Manufacturing:** transportation equipment, non-electrical machinery, fabricated metals, electronic equipment, chemicals. **Agriculture:** dairy products, eggs, nursery and greenhouse products, tobacco. **Mining:** stone, sand and gravel. **Fishing:** lobsters, flounder, oysters. **Other Important Activities:** insurance companies, tourism. **Statehood:** the fifth state. Ratified Constitution on Jan. 9, 1788.

In 1886 Everett Horton of Bristol invented a telescoping fishing rod. He wanted to be able to hide it when he went fishing on the Sabbath. (Connecticut's Puritan heritage made for some strict laws. In early New Haven a child over 16 years of age could be put to death for cursing a parent.)

Women made new things too. In 1801 a Mrs. Prout of South Windsor made the first American cigars. A few years later Mary Kies became the first American woman to win a patent for an invention, a machine for weaving silk and straw.

Eli Whitney manufactured his cotton gins in New Haven. He and Samuel Colt the gunmaker and Eli Terry the clockmaker were among the Connecticut men who developed ways of making things by machine instead of by hand. Such techniques would lead to today's mass production industries.

From Colt's gun factory came Francis Pratt and Amos Whitney. Their names live on today in the Pratt & Whitney jet engines made at Hartford. Nearby, Igor Sikorsky built his pioneering helicopter. The first nuclear submarine was launched at Groton.

The tradition that began with tin cups and brass pots still lives. Nearly three out of four Connecticut factory workers make metal products, from handguns and silverware to helicopters and submarines.

Yet much of the state preserves the old New England look...neat white houses and steepled churches...towns like Litchfield, with its historic village green.

The "long tidal river," fouled by human and industrial wastes, was one of the first of our rivers to become polluted. Now there is a cleanup under way. Parts of it are swimmable again—for people as well as fish. By about 1988, if the cleanup continues, all of the river will be swimmable.

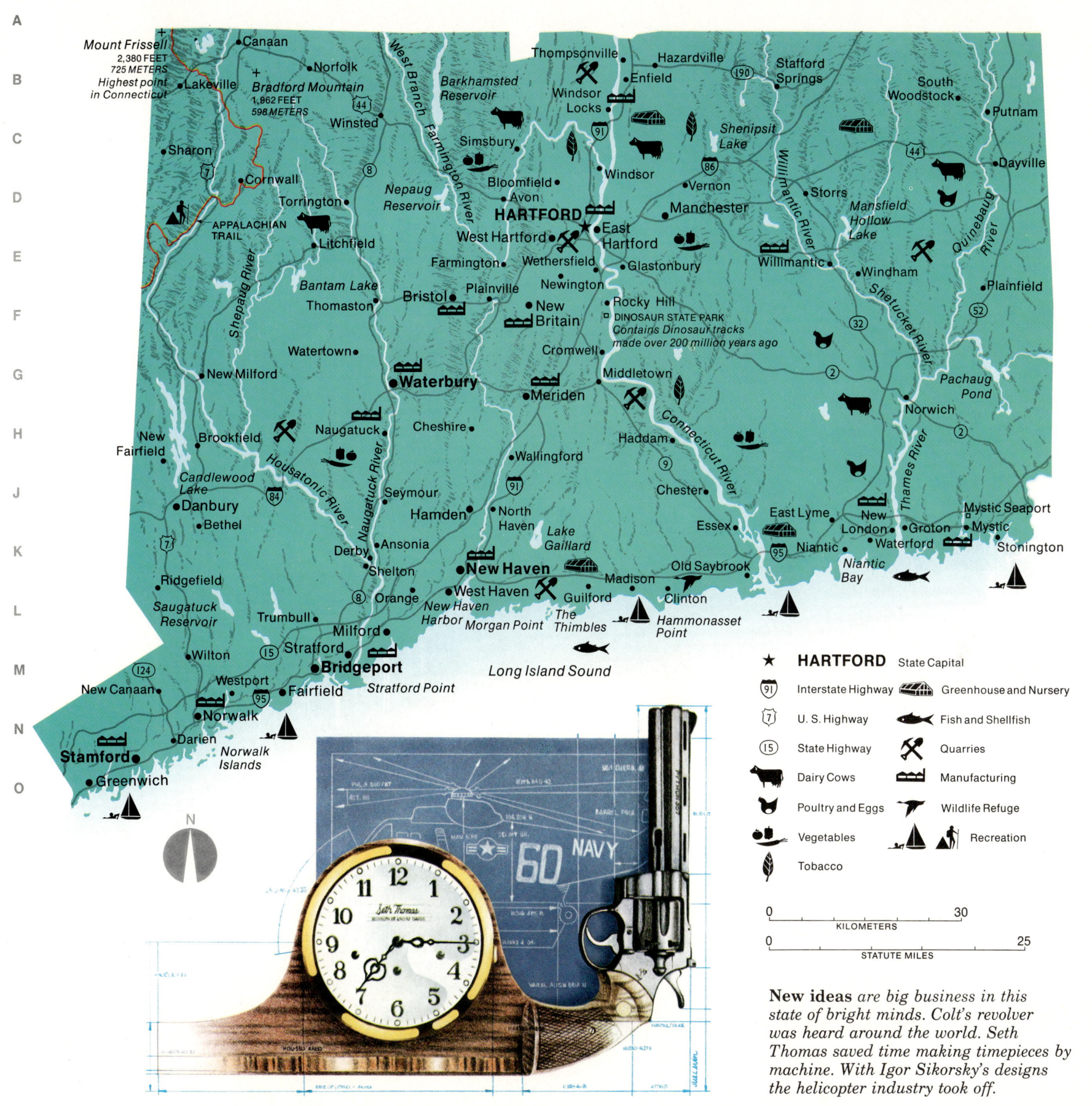

Connecticut Map

Grid coordinates
1 2 3 4 5 6 7 8 9 10 11 12 13 14 15 16 17 18

Rows: A–O

Map Labels

- Mount Frissell, 2,380 FEET, 725 METERS, Highest point in Connecticut
- Canaan
- Lakeville
- Norfolk
- Bradford Mountain, 1,962 FEET, 598 METERS
- Barkhamsted Reservoir
- Thompsonville
- Hazardville
- Stafford Springs
- South Woodstock
- Winsted
- Windsor Locks
- Enfield
- Putnam
- Sharon
- West Branch Farmington River
- Simsbury
- Shenipsit Lake
- Cornwall
- Bloomfield
- Windsor
- Dayville
- Appalachian Trail
- Torrington
- Nepaug Reservoir
- Avon
- Vernon
- Mansfield Hollow Lake
- Litchfield
- HARTFORD
- Manchester
- West Hartford
- East Hartford
- Storrs
- Quinebaug River
- Shepaug River
- Farmington
- Wethersfield
- Willimantic
- Windham
- Bantam Lake
- Plainville
- Newington
- Glastonbury
- Plainfield
- Thomaston
- Bristol
- New Britain
- Rocky Hill
- DINOSAUR STATE PARK, Contains Dinosaur tracks made over 200 million years ago
- Shetucket River
- Watertown
- Cromwell
- Willimantic River
- New Milford
- Waterbury
- Middletown
- Meriden
- Pachaug Pond
- Housatonic River
- Naugatuck
- Norwich
- New Fairfield
- Brookfield
- Cheshire
- Candlewood Lake
- Haddam
- Thames River
- Danbury
- Seymour
- Wallingford
- Bethel
- Hamden
- Chester
- Connecticut River
- Derby
- Ansonia
- North Haven
- Lake Gaillard
- East Lyme
- New London
- Mystic Seaport
- Ridgefield
- Essex
- Groton
- Mystic
- Shelton
- Niantic
- Waterford
- Saugatuck Reservoir
- New Haven
- Old Saybrook
- Stonington
- Orange
- West Haven
- Madison
- Niantic Bay
- Trumbull
- Guilford
- Clinton
- New Haven Harbor
- Morgan Point
- The Thimbles
- Hammonasset Point
- Milford
- Wilton
- Stratford
- Bridgeport
- New Canaan
- Westport
- Fairfield
- Long Island Sound
- Norwalk
- Stratford Point
- Stamford
- Darien
- Greenwich
- Norwalk Islands

Legend

- ★ **HARTFORD** State Capital
- 91 Interstate Highway
- Greenhouse and Nursery
- 7 U.S. Highway
- Fish and Shellfish
- 15 State Highway
- Quarries
- Dairy Cows
- Manufacturing
- Poultry and Eggs
- Wildlife Refuge
- Vegetables
- Recreation
- Tobacco

0 — 30 KILOMETERS
0 — 25 STATUTE MILES

New ideas are big business in this state of bright minds. Colt's revolver was heard around the world. Seth Thomas saved time making timepieces by machine. With Igor Sikorsky's designs the helicopter industry took off.

33

Sailors aloft in the square-rigger Joseph Conrad *look down over Mystic Seaport and the* Charles W. Morgan, *last of the wooden whalers.*

Black duck leads her hungry brood. Connecticut marshes offer snails, mussels, water plants.

Fishermen line the Connecticut River in spring, to hook the shad running upstream to spawn.

"**A**ll hands topside!" rings out at Mystic Seaport. As visitors stroll the cobbled streets, they expect to see sailors of old scurrying about the tall-masted ships anchored here.

But teenagers answer the call, pouring out of their bunks on the *Joseph Conrad*. In this re-created seaport, at a town which sent whalers and clippers to earth's far corners, young people study the lore of the sea. Aboard small dinghies they learn the ancient ways of wind and sail.

Not far from Mystic, the Age of Sail meets the 20th century. Coast Guard Academy cadets in New London train on a sailing ship. Groton, next door, claims the title of submarine capital of the world.

Displaying skill that has made Connecticut a leader in metalworking since colonial days, this silversmith in Wallingford puts finishing touches on an elegant coffeepot.

Tobacco, shielded from hot sun by gauzy tents, thrives in the Connecticut River Valley. Hauled in baskets to curing sheds, the leaves later wrap America's finest cigars.

35

MAINE

The Maine you hear about is a breath of fresh air, a summer delight of cool seashore and quaint old sailing towns. True enough. But that's only a sliver of Maine. This state is mostly forest. Evergreens and leafy trees cover 90 percent of the land, a greater percentage of forest land than any other state.

For 300 years the trees have provided the raw material for Maine's biggest industry. Felling those trees and hauling them out of the forest has never been an easy job. Maine folk are hardy and hardworking; the forest has helped make them so.

Loggers still go into the forest in the dead of winter, with temperatures way below freezing, sometimes way below zero. Until a few years ago the felled trees were piled up by frozen rivers. With the spring thaw began the great log drives down the "liquid conveyor belts"—swollen streams such as the Androscoggin, Kennebec, and Penobscot. Loggers rode the floating timber, breaking up jams, keeping it moving.

A misstep, a sudden jolt, and the woodsman's life was in peril. There was danger to the rivers too. A pileup of sunken, rotting logs could pollute the streams.

Today, trucks haul the logs to mills and factories, where they are made into furniture, boats, skis, toothpicks (100 million a day), and tons upon tons of paper. Pulp and paper companies own about a third of the land of Maine. The water power that moved the logs also powered the mills. At towns like Westbrook, Rumford, and Millinocket, you can see the tree trunks being stripped of bark, chopped up, cooked to pulp, and dried and pressed into paper.

From the woodland heart of Maine rises Mount Katahdin, almost exactly a mile high, veined with hiking trails. On the longest days of the year that mark the beginning of summer, the flat rays of the rising sun light Katahdin's peak at around 3:30 a.m.

Just to the northwest begin the 98 miles (158 km) of river, lake, and rapids known as the Allagash Wilderness Waterway, one of the great canoe trips of our country. Much of the Allagash flows through Maine's famous potato county, Aroostook, so big that all of Connecticut and Rhode Island could fit within its borders. Here youngsters go to school in August so they can help dig the harvest in autumn. Out of Aroostook's rich red soil comes one out of every dozen potatoes grown in the United States.

In bygone days, when Maine sailing ships came home from Boston, they ran eastward along the coast. When a wind at their back sped them along, they ran "downwind." So the Maine coast became known as "Down East." Here fishermen go out for herring and cod and haddock and scallops. Lobstermen tend their traps in the cold dark waters. On the tidal flats diggers rake the mud for clams and for the marine worms that bring a pretty penny from the sport fishermen.

Here, too, come artists to paint the seascapes, and flocks of sailboats to explore rocky bays and "secret coves." Here come summer folk to clambakes and lobster feasts and blueberry festivals. Do they come to swim? Depends where they're coming from. A Marylander might dip a toe and shiver. But many a Canadian will plunge right into these warm "southern" waters.

In the forest or on the coast Maine people have known hard times. Some, seeking jobs or softer climate, drifted away. Nowadays, more and more people drift into Maine, seeking to share its enduring riches: a beautiful, unspoiled land and an unhurried, independent way of life.

From Maine mud flats comes our biggest supply of bloodworms and sandworms. Prime bait for saltwater sport fishing, the worms are shipped as far as California.

Area: the 39th largest state, 33,215 sq mi (86,026 sq km). **Population:** 1,085,000. Ranks 38th. **Major Cities:** Portland, 59,857; Lewiston, 41,045; Bangor, 32,262. **Manufacturing:** paper and paper products, leather products, food products, lumber and wood products. **Agriculture:** potatoes, eggs, broilers, dairy products, apples, beef cattle. **Fishing:** lobsters, clams, sardines, ocean perch. **Mining:** sand and gravel, cement, zinc, stone, copper, gemstones. **Other Important Activities:** tourism. **Statehood:** the 23rd state. Admitted March 15, 1820.

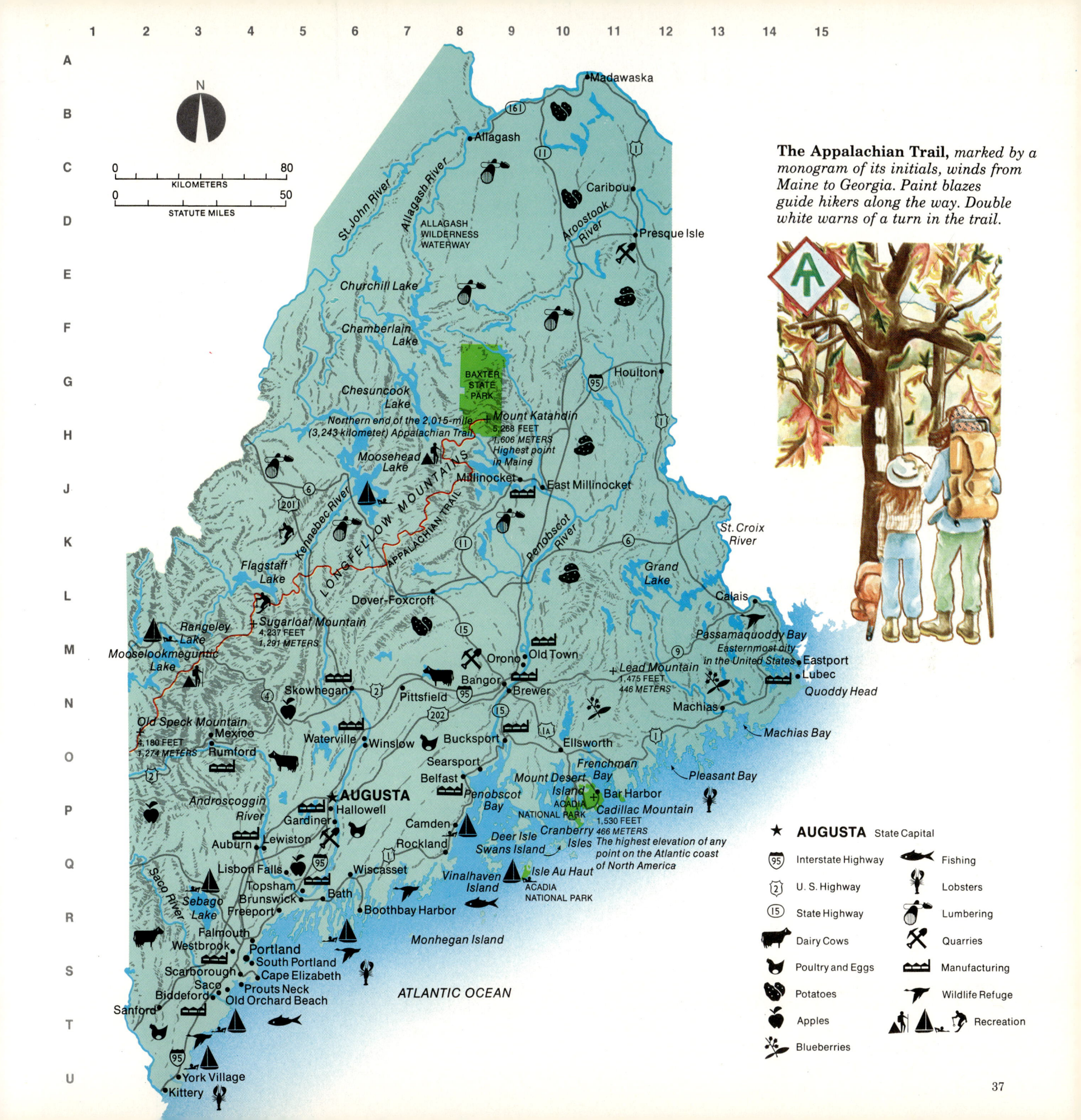

Maine

The Appalachian Trail, marked by a monogram of its initials, winds from Maine to Georgia. Paint blazes guide hikers along the way. Double white warns of a turn in the trail.

Map Labels

- Madawaska
- Allagash
- St. John River
- Allagash River
- Allagash Wilderness Waterway
- Caribou
- Aroostook River
- Presque Isle
- Churchill Lake
- Chamberlain Lake
- Baxter State Park
- Chesuncook Lake
- Houlton
- Northern end of the 2,015-mile (3,243 kilometer) Appalachian Trail
- Mount Katahdin 5,268 FEET / 1,606 METERS / Highest point in Maine
- Moosehead Lake
- Millinocket
- East Millinocket
- Longfellow Mountains
- Kennebec River
- Penobscot River
- St. Croix River
- Appalachian Trail
- Flagstaff Lake
- Grand Lake
- Calais
- Dover-Foxcroft
- Rangeley Lake
- Sugarloaf Mountain 4,237 FEET / 1,291 METERS
- Mooselookmeguntic Lake
- Passamaquoddy Bay / Easternmost city in the United States
- Orono
- Old Town
- Lead Mountain 1,475 FEET / 446 METERS
- Eastport
- Lubec
- Skowhegan
- Bangor
- Brewer
- Quoddy Head
- Machias
- Old Speck Mountain 4,180 FEET / 1,274 METERS
- Mexico
- Waterville
- Winslow
- Bucksport
- Ellsworth
- Machias Bay
- Rumford
- Searsport
- Frenchman Bay
- Pleasant Bay
- Androscoggin River
- Belfast
- ★ AUGUSTA
- Hallowell
- Penobscot Bay
- Mount Desert Island
- Bar Harbor
- Gardiner
- Camden
- Acadia National Park
- Cadillac Mountain 1,530 FEET / 466 METERS / The highest elevation of any point on the Atlantic coast of North America
- Auburn
- Lewiston
- Rockland
- Cranberry Isles
- Lisbon Falls
- Wiscasset
- Deer Isle / Swans Island
- Topsham
- Bath
- Vinalhaven Island
- Isle Au Haut / ACADIA NATIONAL PARK
- Sebago Lake
- Brunswick
- Freeport
- Boothbay Harbor
- Saco River
- Falmouth
- Westbrook
- Portland
- Monhegan Island
- South Portland
- Scarborough
- Cape Elizabeth
- Saco
- Prouts Neck
- Biddeford
- Old Orchard Beach
- Sanford
- ATLANTIC OCEAN
- York Village
- Kittery

Legend

- ★ **AUGUSTA** State Capital
- (95) Interstate Highway
- (2) U.S. Highway
- (15) State Highway
- Dairy Cows
- Poultry and Eggs
- Potatoes
- Apples
- Blueberries
- Fishing
- Lobsters
- Lumbering
- Quarries
- Manufacturing
- Wildlife Refuge
- Recreation

37

Maine rivers that floated logs downstream provided power for sawmills and gristmills. Many of today's cities grew from hamlets located at good dam sites or natural falls.

The force of earth's gravity makes the rivers rush downstream. But along the coast moon power pushes the tides in and out. As the moon circles our planet, the force of the moon's gravity pulls against the earth, creating high and low tides.

In Passamaquoddy Bay, thundering tides rise 26 feet (7.9 m). People have dreamed of feeding this enormous power into turbines to make electricity. As the energy shortage goes on, we know the sun will help. Perhaps the moon can help too.

Meet Ethel and Leroy, moose residents of Baxter State Park. Its name honors a governor who donated the land, to keep it wild forever.

Fishing off the coast, the puffin eats at sea. Fish in its gaudy beak means there are young to feed.

Log drives, old and new— Once timber rode the spring melt out of Moosehead Lake and down the Kennebec River. Today the log drives are on wheels. Trucking is faster—and pollution laws keep logs off the streams.

Eastport fishermen clean the day's catch of cod, which they'll sell in Portland. Gulls crowd in for the scraps tossed overboard.

Potatoes roll out of northern Maine to supply 8 percent of the nation's harvest. Wild blueberries, pollinated by bees imported from out-of-state, flourish near the coast. From the forest comes wood for paper products, houses—and custom-made canoes.

Chickadee

Mayflower

MASSACHUSETTS

We can read part of the story in the map. Toward the coast the roads weave into a pattern, like a spiderweb, or a wheel. At the hub lies Boston. Hub City. Hub of a hundred surrounding cities and towns.

In recent years Boston has had its share of big-city problems—crime, poor housing, school disturbances. Yet it has become one of the most exciting cities in the country.

You have to be there to see it and feel it. You have to hear the music—rock and jazz, the symphony, the opera company. You have to see the street life on the Common, the science and art museums, the student scene at Harvard and the Massachusetts Institute of Technology.

You have to walk along the Charles River and take in the gleaming skyline of tall buildings. And on a hot summer day, cool off in the fountains at the new city hall.

How this city loves its sports teams! When the Red Sox are hot and banging baseballs against the fence, Fenway Park is heaven—and all New England hangs by the TV.

What of the old red-brick Boston, city of history? It's still there. Red lines on the sidewalks mark the Freedom Trail to landmarks of the Revolution—Faneuil Hall, where Sam Adams spoke fighting words; Paul Revere's house; and Old North Church. Out in the suburbs you'll find the battlefields of Lexington and Concord.

Harvard, born in 1636, is our oldest college and one of our best, located in a great center of learning. You can get a degree from 61 institutions in the Boston area. Hundreds of companies along Route 128—the beltway that circles the city—draw on the brainpower of the universities.

Yet even without the Boston area, Massachusetts could boast of its fine colleges. Out in the western reaches of the state stand Amherst and Williams, Smith and Mount Holyoke, and the big main campus of the University of Massachusetts.

This is different country—farming country, and hiking and camping country. To Tanglewood in the beautiful Berkshire Hills come hundreds of thousands of music lovers for the summer Berkshire Festival. Deerfield will show you the charm of a colonial village, and some of the scars left by Indian raids. There's industry, too. Springfield's historic armory made guns and ammunition for our soldiers from George Washington's time to Viet Nam. Dalton makes most of the paper for our dollar bills.

Across the state Cape Cod juts into the ocean like an arm bent to make a muscle. This is where the adventure of New England began. The Pilgrims first landed at the "fist." Then they sailed across the bay to "Plimoth." Today, at Plymouth, the stockaded community of Plimoth Plantation keeps the Pilgrim world alive for us.

Out of that world, the English settlers and their descendants spread into the region that was rightly called New England. For hundreds of years these people, the Yankees, made up most of the population. From them came the leaders in government and business. There are still plenty of old Yankee families in Massachusetts and the rest of New England. But there are others, too. Since early in the 1800's people from many lands have come in—Irish, French Canadians, Italians, Jews, Poles, Portuguese.

In some places their descendants now make up most of the population. From these new Yankees have come leaders as well, with such names as Grasso and St. Germain and Muskie. From the Irish of Massachusetts came President John F. Kennedy.

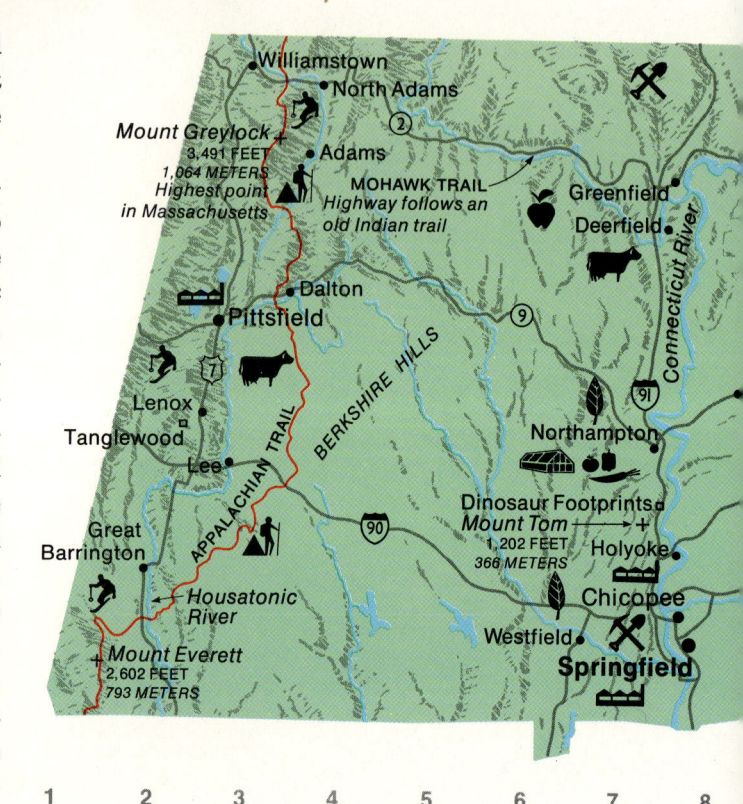

Area: the 45th largest state, 8,257 sq mi (21,385 sq km). **Population:** 5,782,000. Ranks 10th. **Major Cities:** Boston, 636,725; Worcester, 171,566; Springfield, 170,790. **Manufacturing:** machinery, electrical equipment, instruments, fabricated metals, printing and publishing, food products, paper products, rubber and plastics, transportation equipment, chemicals. **Agriculture:** dairy products, greenhouse and nursery products, eggs, cranberries, tobacco, apples, beef cattle, hogs. **Fishing:** scallops, flounder, lobsters, cod, haddock, pollock. **Mining:** stone, sand and gravel. **Other Important Activities:** tourism, education. **Statehood:** the sixth state. Ratified Constitution on Feb. 6, 1788.

Map Legend

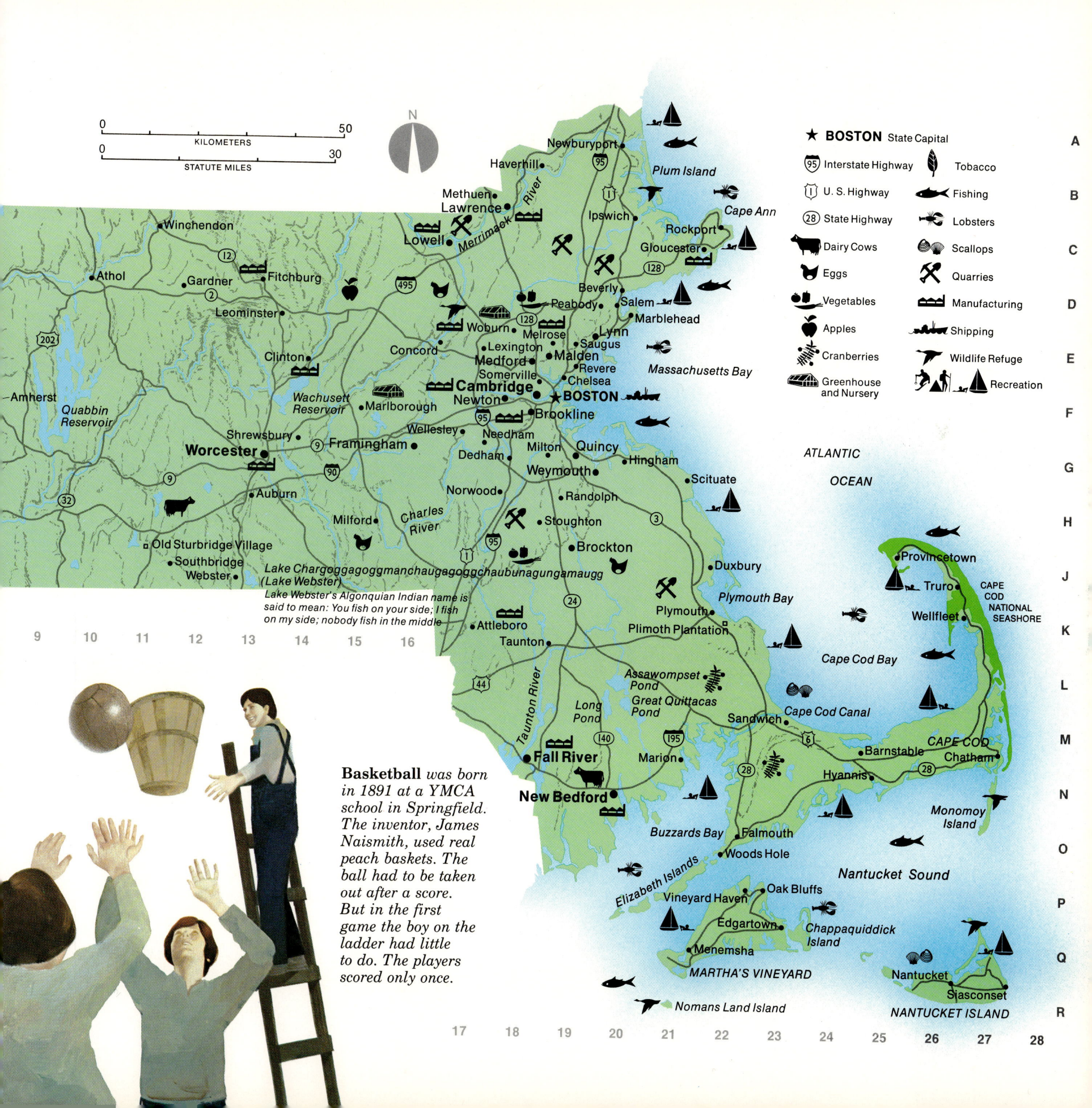

★ **BOSTON** State Capital
- 🛣 (95) Interstate Highway
- 🛣 (1) U.S. Highway
- 🛣 (28) State Highway
- Dairy Cows
- Eggs
- Vegetables
- Apples
- Cranberries
- Greenhouse and Nursery
- Tobacco
- Fishing
- Lobsters
- Scallops
- Quarries
- Manufacturing
- Shipping
- Wildlife Refuge
- Recreation

Map of Massachusetts

Cities and Towns: Newburyport, Haverhill, Methuen, Lawrence, Ipswich, Rockport, Cape Ann, Gloucester, Plum Island, Winchendon, Athol, Gardner, Fitchburg, Lowell, Merrimack River, Beverly, Peabody, Salem, Marblehead, Leominster, Woburn, Melrose, Lynn, Saugus, Medford, Lexington, Malden, Revere, Concord, Somerville, Chelsea, Amherst, Quabbin Reservoir, Clinton, Wachusett Reservoir, Cambridge, Newton, BOSTON, Brookline, Marlborough, Massachusetts Bay, Shrewsbury, Framingham, Wellesley, Needham, Worcester, Dedham, Milton, Quincy, Weymouth, Hingham, Auburn, Norwood, Randolph, Scituate, Milford, Stoughton, Old Sturbridge Village, Charles River, Brockton, Southbridge, Webster, Duxbury, Lake Chargoggagoggmanchaugagoggchaubunagungamaugg (Lake Webster), Provincetown, Truro, Plymouth, Plymouth Bay, Wellfleet, CAPE COD NATIONAL SEASHORE, Attleboro, Taunton, Plimoth Plantation, Cape Cod Bay, Assawompset Pond, Great Quittacas Pond, Cape Cod Canal, Long Pond, Sandwich, Barnstable, CAPE COD, Chatham, Fall River, Marion, Hyannis, New Bedford, Buzzards Bay, Falmouth, Monomoy Island, Woods Hole, Nantucket Sound, Elizabeth Islands, Vineyard Haven, Oak Bluffs, Edgartown, Chappaquiddick Island, Menemsha, MARTHA'S VINEYARD, Nantucket, Siasconset, Nomans Land Island, NANTUCKET ISLAND, ATLANTIC OCEAN, Taunton River

Lake Webster's Algonquian Indian name is said to mean: You fish on your side; I fish on my side; nobody fish in the middle

Basketball was born in 1891 at a YMCA school in Springfield. The inventor, James Naismith, used real peach baskets. The ball had to be taken out after a score. But in the first game the boy on the ladder had little to do. The players scored only once.

The seashore vacationland we know as Cape Cod began as an Ice Age dump. A glacier moved down from the north, pushing a pile of soil and rock before it. About 12,000 years ago the ice stopped and began to melt. The heap of debris remained. Geologists call it a moraine. That's what Cape Cod is.

Wind and sea changed its shape some. Plants and wildlife took root. The result: a fine sweep of beach and sea cliff, of bog and salt marsh, of dunes covered with heath and bayberry. Where tourist places and summer people crowd up, the Cape today looks a bit dumpy. But much of its "forearm" has been set aside as a national seashore, to keep the look of the glorious dump the glacier created.

Cranberries grow in soggy soil of bogs. Massachusetts, Wisconsin grow the most.

Herring gulls flap down on a Cape Cod weather vane—a carving of the fish for which the Cape was named. Massachusetts folk have fished for cod since Pilgrim days. Gulls' heads are dark in winter, white in summer.

Cape Cod National Seashore offers 12 miles (19.3 km) of bikeways, nature trails, clam digging and surf casting, and sun and sand for tanning.

A bronze Paul Revere sits "ready to ride" behind Boston's Old North Church. From its steeple in 1775 lanterns signaled the British route to Concord.

Onto Plymouth Rock, it is said, the Pilgrims stepped off the Mayflower. *The 1620 date was carved in 1880.*

Mayflower II, tied up at Plymouth, was built in modern times. She resembles the ship that bore the Pilgrims.

Boats on the Charles sail into evening below downtown Boston and the domed State House on Beacon Hill.

43

NEW HAMPSHIRE

Flatlanders in southern New England sniff spring in the air. Up here in the mountains chair lifts will soon grind to a halt. Good skiing is getting hard to find. New Hampshire folk know at least one good place to look: high on Mount Washington, the only New England peak to top 6,000 feet (1,829 m).

There, in a huge natural bowl called Tuckerman Ravine, the best is yet to come. All winter long, snow has drifted into the bowl. By early March the drifts blanket the bouldery slopes. Time for downhill skiing.

This grand run measures some 3.5 miles (5.6 km), with a vertical drop of 3,000 feet (914 m). But whoever skis down must first hike up, lugging the gear. No ski lifts climb the monarch of the White Mountains.

The best time is April, when the snow has packed down and the sun's warmth has turned the surface to grainy "corn snow." Even then Mount Washington may spring a surprise. For one such April surprise, see the sketch on this page.

Some years the skiing may last into June. By then the auto road has opened; skiers can drive up. By then, too, the cog railway has started running again, chugging up the mountain with warm-weather tourists.

You can find good farmland among the mountains of the Granite State—for dairying, growing apples, raising cattle or hogs. But not all that much. New Hampshire realized this long ago, and began to promote industry when the American Revolution ended. Mills grew along racing rivers. "Cobblers' towns," where men made shoes by hand, turned into shoe-factory towns. Early in the 1800's, Manchester was named for a famous industrial city of England, with the hope of gaining similar fame.

In time, the new city's visions came true.

On April 12, 1934, Mount Washington was hit by the strongest wind ever measured on earth's surface—231 mph (372 kmph).

Area: the 44th largest state, 9,304 sq mi (24,097 sq km). **Population:** 849,000. Ranks 42nd. **Major Cities:** Manchester, 83,417; Nashua, 61,002; Concord, 29,321. **Manufacturing:** electrical equipment, non-electrical machinery, paper products, instruments, rubber and plastics, leather products. **Agriculture:** dairy products, eggs, apples, greenhouse and nursery products. **Mining:** sand and gravel, stone. **Fishing:** lobsters, cod, pollock, flounder. **Other Important Activities:** tourism. **Statehood:** the ninth state. Ratified Constitution on June 21, 1788.

Here along the banks of the Merrimack River rose the Amoskeag Mill, in its time the biggest textile plant in the world. It wove 147,000 miles (236,574 km) of cloth each year. Then, in this century, came the sad tale you hear all over New England. Factories moved south, or just closed down.

Like so many others, Amoskeag is gone. Some of its red-brick buildings still stand, busy with other kinds of manufacturing. The state continues to welcome industry, and has recently had an increase in electronics and metals production.

Hiking, climbing, and skiing trails in the White Mountains...more than a thousand lakes...grand old Mount Monadnock in the south, where on a clear day you can see all six New England states. All this gives New Hampshire the image of a rural state. Yet it is also one of our most highly industrialized states. It has a bigger percentage of its working population in factory jobs than does New York or Massachusetts.

Every four years New Hampshire's Presidential primary election makes the news. It is the first in the nation, when Democrats and Republicans pick party candidates to run for President. It comes in late winter, a custom that arose when most roads were unpaved. People went to vote before the spring thaw turned the roads to mud.

The news stories tell of wintry mountain towns, of people slow to change. They dislike high taxes here, and try extra hard to keep them low. This has lured business from neighbor states. New Hampshire gets a lot of advice about changing its ways, especially from Massachusetts. Not everyone here disagrees. Yet the population has kept growing, faster than that of any other New England state. The flatlanders keep coming, especially from Massachusetts.

Legend

- ★ **CONCORD** State Capital
- (93) Interstate Highway
- (2) U.S. Highway
- (28) State Highway
- Cattle
- Dairy Cows
- Eggs
- Greenhouse and Nursery
- Recreation
- Apples
- Fish and Shellfish
- Lumbering
- Quarries
- Manufacturing
- Wildlife Refuge

Scale: 0–50 Kilometers / 0–30 Statute Miles

Map Labels

Third Lake, Second Lake, First Connecticut Lake, Lake Francis, Colebrook, Dixville Notch, Blue Mountain 3,723 FEET / 1,135 METERS, Umbagog Lake, Groveton, Androscoggin River, Mount Cabot 4,160 FEET / 1,268 METERS, Berlin, Connecticut River, Littleton, PRESIDENTIAL RANGE, WHITE MOUNTAINS, Ammonoosuc River, Bretton Woods, Mount Washington 6,288 FEET / 1,917 METERS, Highest point in New England, Old Man of the Mountains — Face formed naturally by five separate rock ledges, APPALACHIAN TRAIL, Lincoln, KANCAMAGUS HIGHWAY, Conway, Pemigewasset River, Mount Chocorua 3,475 FEET / 1,059 METERS, Madison, APPALACHIAN MOUNTAINS, Squam Lake, Ossipee Lake, Plymouth, Hanover, Newfound Lake, Lebanon, Weirs Beach, Lake Wentworth, Winnisquam Lake, Lake Winnipesaukee, Laconia, Franklin, Lake Sunapee, Claremont, Newport, Mount Sunapee 2,743 FEET / 836 METERS, Merrimack River, Bow Lake, Rochester, Somersworth, **CONCORD** ★, Dover, Piscataqua River, Hillsboro, Suncook, Durham, Little Bay, Great Bay, New Castle, Newmarket, Portsmouth, Rye, Isles of Shoals, Massabesic Lake, Exeter, Hampton, ATLANTIC OCEAN, Keene, Manchester, WAPACK NATIONAL WILDLIFE REFUGE, East Derry, Mount Monadnock 3,165 FEET / 965 METERS, Peterborough, Derry, Hampton Harbor Inlet, New Ipswich, Milford, Nashua, Hudson, Salem

Mount Washington Plant Zones

- **Above 4,800 feet (1,463 m)** — Heath-tundra plants: Diapensia, Labrador tea
- **3,500–4,800 feet (1,067–1,463 m)** — Coniferous forest: Balsam fir, black spruce
- **2,600–3,500 feet (792–1,067 m)** — Mixed forest: Red spruce, red maple, paper birch
- **2,000–2,600 feet (610–792 m)** — Hardwood forest: Beech, sugar maple, white ash

Climbing *a mountain is like traveling north. The air gets colder, plant life changes. See how it varies here, as we move up Mount Washington. At low levels we find mostly leafy hardwood trees. Higher, cone-bearing evergreens — coniferous trees — join the mix, then take over. They stand the cold better. At 4,800 feet the trees are tiny. Above that level it's treeless heath and tundra plants, as in the far north.*

45

Great Stone Face, 40 feet (12 m) of weathered rock, symbolizes the Granite State. Mount Washington (top, at right) looms above all others in New England.

Skyline siding eases traffic jams on the Mount Washington Cog Railway. Each "Puffin' Devil" pushes a passenger car uphill. On the downhill run the engine rides in front to serve as a brake.

Anglers await nibbles at Streeter Pond, one of about 1,300 lakes in the state. Created by glaciers, many lie nestled in the foothills south of the White Mountains.

Want a challenge that can last a lifetime? Forty-seven peaks in the White Mountains top 4,000 feet (1,219 m). Climb them all and you can join the Four Thousand Footer Club. It has some 2,000 members, including a collie, according to the Appalachian Mountain Club. The oldest to qualify was a man in his 70's; the youngest, a boy of 6.

Some 600 kept climbing—12 more tall peaks in Maine, 5 in Vermont. Scaling all 64 made them members of the exclusive New England Four Thousand Footer Club.

Snow delights skiers. But it was rough on wooden bridges. The covering that protected them now delights sightseers. This covered bridge crosses a gorge at Franconia Notch.

47

RHODE ISLAND

Rhode Island Red

Violet

Once in a while, as our country grew, a new state would claim to be No. 1 in size. The smallest never changed. This is it, No. 50. It measures 48 by 37 miles. Going metric would boost the numbers a bit—77 by 60 kilometers. Either way, it can fit 200 times into Texas, nearly 500 times into Alaska. Alas, you can almost fit two Rhode Islands into No. 49, Delaware. On the other hand, Alaska would have to double its population to match Rhode Island's.

Something really important about the way we live happened in this little corner of land. In colonial days the Puritans who ran Massachusetts set up religious rules for settlers. You had to follow them—or else. Roger Williams opposed that. He moved south and started the new settlement of Providence. The rules for governing it kept away from religion. People had a nice phrase for this idea: "soul liberty." Rhode Island welcomed Jews, Quakers, Catholics—people who did not always find a welcome elsewhere. In time the Rhode Island way became the American way. Today we go to the church we choose, or to none. No government decides for us.

Roger Williams's settlement was named Providence Plantations. Soon after it began, Newport was founded on an island later called the Isle of Rhodes. Eventually the colony took the name Rhode Island and Providence Plantations. That is still the state's name—the longest of the 50 states. You can fit nearly six "Alaska"s in it.

Providence became a busy port. Today it is one of New England's biggest cities. You can drive to it from anywhere in the state in no more than 60 minutes, except from Block Island—add 75 minutes for the 14-mile (22.5 km) ferry ride from Point Judith.

*There was a young lady in Providence
Whose talent right here is in evidence.
In 1798 Betsey Metcalf's braided creation
Became the first straw hat in the nation.*

Area: the 50th largest state, 1,214 sq mi (3,144 sq km). **Population:** 935,000. Ranks 39th. **Major Cities:** Providence, 167,724; Warwick, 85,875; Cranston, 74,381. **Manufacturing:** jewelry and silverware, fabricated metals, primary metals, electrical equipment, non-electrical machinery, textiles, rubber and plastics. **Agriculture:** greenhouse and nursery products, dairy products, vegetables. **Fishing:** flounder, lobsters, clams, scup. **Other Important Activities:** tourism. **Statehood:** 13th state. Ratified Constitution on May 29, 1790.

Some of Rhode Island's industries are almost as old as the United States. In Pawtucket the Old Slater Mill museum shows us how the American factory system was born. Built in 1793, the wooden mill with its bell tower looked more like a New England schoolhouse. But it represents America's first successful attempt to spin cotton by machine. Making cloth out of cotton or wool became the biggest industry in Rhode Island. By the 1920's some 90,000 people were making such textiles. Today only about a sixth of that many work in textile plants, but the industry remains important. Of all the lace produced in the United States, about half is made here.

Just about the time the cotton machines started rolling, a Providence jeweler named Nehemiah Dodge figured out how to make jewelry that lots of people could buy. Instead of using only silver or gold, he put just a coating of these precious minerals on cheap metal. He built a good business, and to this day inexpensive jewelry—called costume jewelry—is a big business here. The Providence area makes more of it than any other place in America.

One of Dodge's helpers, Jabez Gorham, started another big industry making silver spoons. Today the Gorham company of Providence is one of the biggest manufacturers of sterling silver products in the world.

Rhode Island sounds like all work and no play. Far from it. Sailor and swimmer and fisherman enjoy the Atlantic Ocean and Narragansett Bay, which spread cooling summer breezes across the state. At Newport, historic sites from colonial times and spectacular mansions add to the pleasures of the seashore. Little No. 50 lists 95 bathing beaches, 69 on salt water. How's the swimming up there in big No. 1?

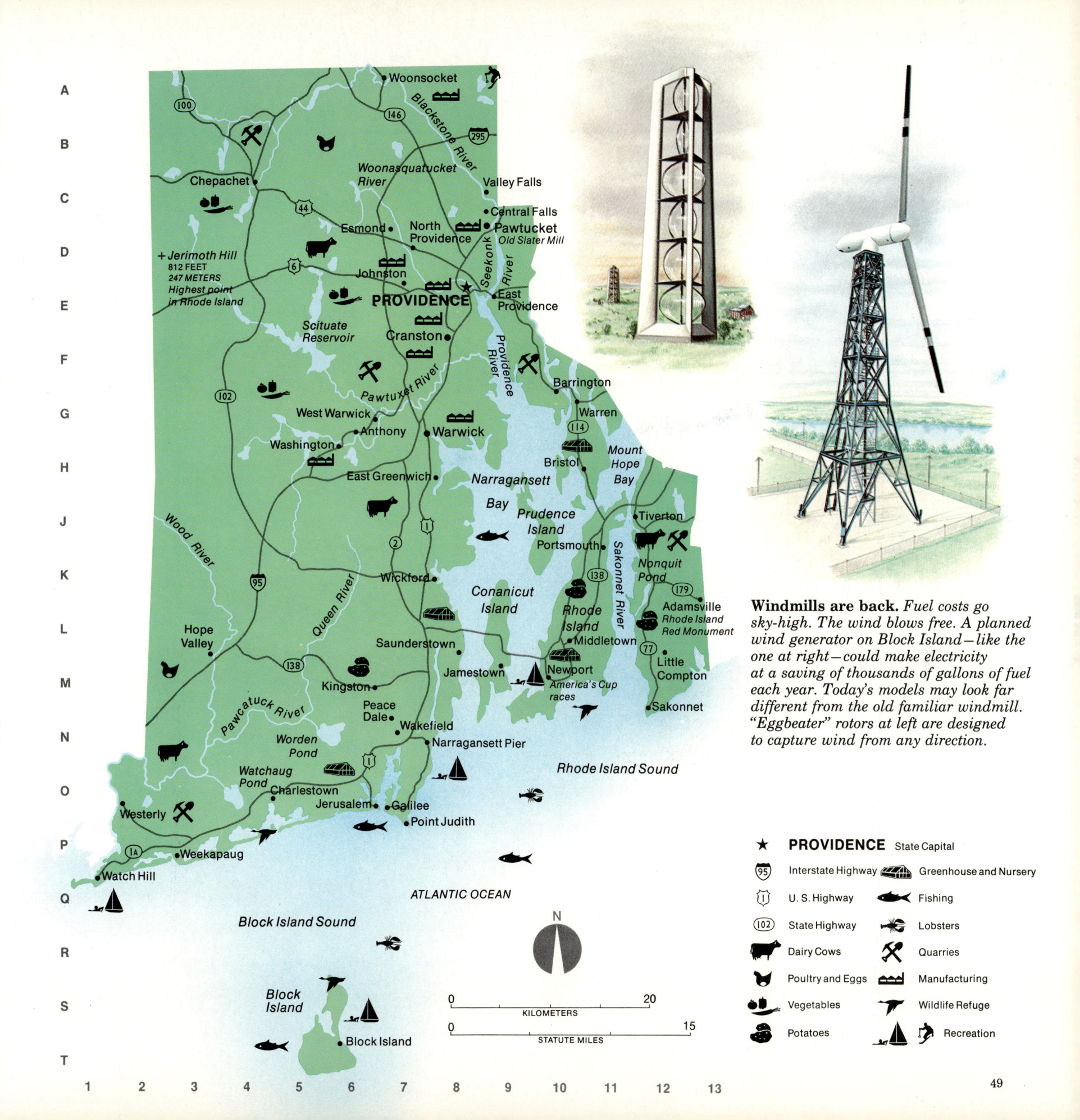

Windmills are back. *Fuel costs go sky-high. The wind blows free. A planned wind generator on Block Island—like the one at right—could make electricity at a saving of thousands of gallons of fuel each year. Today's models may look far different from the old familiar windmill. "Eggbeater" rotors at left are designed to capture wind from any direction.*

★ **PROVIDENCE** State Capital
- Interstate Highway
- U.S. Highway
- State Highway
- Dairy Cows
- Poultry and Eggs
- Vegetables
- Potatoes
- Greenhouse and Nursery
- Fishing
- Lobsters
- Quarries
- Manufacturing
- Wildlife Refuge
- Recreation

49

Harvesters pile pumpkins and squash. Little Rhode Island finds room for growing things.

Block Island lighthouse sits atop wave-scarred bluffs that lose 2.5 feet (.8 m) to erosion each year. The light could topple by the year 2000.

Rhode Island calls itself America's "first vacationland." The claim goes way back to 1524, when the Italian explorer Giovanni da Verrazano sailed the coast. He found Narragansett Bay so pleasant that he stayed a fortnight—the first two-week vacation on record.

Two hundred years later, rich southerners began spending summers in the cool seaside city of Newport. And there, after the Civil War, some of America's wealthiest families built "summer cottages" that looked like European palaces. They cost a fortune to build, and a fortune to live in.

That life is gone. Some of the palaces remain, inviting tourists to wander through and imagine the days when a hostess spent $300,000 to entertain her summer guests.

This 15-pounder eluded lobster traps for 20 years until caught off Galilee. Rhode Island follows Maine and Massachusetts as a lobster producer.

Newport's breathtaking Cliff Walk wanders past millionaires' homes and rocky headlands. At center stands the Breakers, a 70-room "cottage."

Tame mute swan graces a Block Island pond. When migrating birds pause here, island schoolchildren flock outdoors to study them.

Sails line up for a start during Block Island's Race Week. Hundreds of East Coast sailors compete. Across Rhode Island Sound, off Newport, yachtsmen race for the most famous prize of all—the America's Cup.

51

VERMONT

If you set out to design a fit place to live in, you might come up with Vermont. The Green Mountain State looks right—mountains and valleys, farms and villages arranged just so. But it doesn't always look the same. The landscape may change sharply with the seasons. On the other hand there are years when the old saying comes true: Vermont is "nine months snow and three months poor sledding."

In almost any year snow still covers the ground in March. As the days warm up, pussy willows burst, a few brave robins sing, and the sap buckets hang in the sugar bush. Bush? Right. That's what New Englanders call a grove of tall sugar maple trees. Little pipes tapped into the trunks draw the sap. Then it's boil and boil and boil until what's left is sweet, golden syrup. Vermont makes more than any other state. It's cold, rugged work, but a great treat rewards the workers: "sugar on snow." Thick, hot syrup ladled on snow makes a delicious, chewy "maple wax." You can't buy it in a store.

Not until April does spring really come to the Green Mountains. Then water music echoes in the valleys as snowmelt fills the brooks and makes the air thick with mist. Mayflowers, violets, and ferns pop through the fallen leaves. Near Lake Champlain the apple orchards bloom. In a few months the trees will hang heavy with crisp McIntosh apples that crackle when you bite in.

Vermont is the only New England state that doesn't touch the sea, but it has a county almost entirely surrounded by water. Grand Isle County consists of islands in Lake Champlain plus a small peninsula hanging down from Canada. You meet the lake country again and again in history books. It's hard to think of another place that's been fought over in so many of our wars. There were battles here in the French and Indian War, the Revolution, and the War of 1812. Even a Civil War skirmish. In 1864 Confederates dashed down from Canada and raided the town of St. Albans.

As summer comes on, lilac bushes bloom in farmyards and villages. Lilac and many kinds of fern prefer a limestone soil. Vermont has lots of limestone, and marble and granite as well. It leads the nation in producing these building stones. In Barre, you can visit the world's largest granite plant.

They used to say that Vermont had more cows than people. It was true—until 1963. Even so, dairy farming is still important, and Vermont is still a rural state. Across the nation three out of four people live in city places. In Vermont two out of three live in country places—farms and little towns. Look at the city dots on the map. All are small, the smallest size used. This means that no city has more than 50,000 people. Only Burlington comes anywhere close. Yet industry is important, too. In "Precision Valley" the towns of Windsor and Springfield make machine tools that shape parts for many of the cars we drive.

Autumn leaves blaze with color, yellow in the birches, scarlet in the sugar maples. Winter drapes the mountains with snow and skiers. The first chair lift in the East began hauling skiers in 1940 on Mount Mansfield, highest peak in the state.

It was on Killington Peak, today a major ski center in the East, that a preacher claimed to have christened the land "Verd-Mont" in 1763. The two French words mean "green mountain." In time the "d" was dropped. That ruined it, said the preacher, because "ver" is a French word for "maggot." Nobody paid much mind. The Maggot Mountain State? That's not Vermont!

Snow on July 4th? Old almanacs say snow fell in July and August in 1816—known as "eighteen hundred and froze to death."

Area: the 43rd largest state, 9,609 sq mi (24,887 sq km). **Population:** 483,000. Ranks 48th. **Major Cities:** Burlington, 37,133; Rutland, 19,019; Bennington, 15,889. **Manufacturing:** electrical equipment, non-electrical machinery, fabricated metals, paper products, printing and publishing, stone, clay, and glass products. **Agriculture:** dairy products, beef cattle, eggs, apples, forest products, maple products, hay. **Mining:** stone, asbestos, talc, sand and gravel, gemstones. **Other Important Activities:** tourism. **Statehood:** the 14th state. Admitted March 4, 1791.

Vermont

Map Legend

★ **MONTPELIER** State Capital
- 89 Interstate Highway
- 302 U.S. Highway
- 102 State Highway
- Cattle
- Dairy Cows
- Eggs
- Apples
- Maple Syrup
- Lumbering
- Mining
- Quarries
- Manufacturing
- Wildlife Refuge
- Recreation

Scale: 0–50 Kilometers / 0–30 Statute Miles

Map Locations

- Richford
- Swanton
- Isle La Motte
- Saint Albans
- Fairfield
- Lake Memphremagog
- Jay Peak — 3,861 FEET / 1,177 METERS
- Newport
- Norton
- Gore Mountain — 3,330 FEET / 1,015 METERS
- Orleans
- Missisquoi River
- Long Trail — Hiking path from Massachusetts to Canada along crest of mountains
- South Hero Island
- Lake Champlain
- Lamoille River
- Smugglers Notch
- Mount Mansfield — 4,393 FEET / 1,339 METERS — Highest point in Vermont
- Morrisville
- Winooski
- Burlington
- Essex Junction
- South Burlington
- Stowe
- Green Mountains
- Saint Johnsbury
- Shelburne
- Waterbury
- Winooski River
- ★ MONTPELIER
- Barre
- Waitsfield
- Vergennes
- Sugarbush Valley
- Northfield
- Warren
- Weybridge
- Morgan Horse Farm
- Middlebury
- Appalachian Mountains
- Salisbury
- Strafford
- Connecticut River
- Otter Creek
- White River
- Appalachian Trail
- Lake Bomoseen
- Proctor
- Rutland
- White River Junction
- Fair Haven
- West Rutland
- Killington Peak — 4,241 FEET / 1,293 METERS
- Woodstock
- Poultney
- Plymouth
- Windsor
- Danby
- Springfield
- Bromley Mountain — 3,260 FEET / 994 METERS
- Mount Equinox — 3,816 FEET / 1,163 METERS
- Manchester
- Bellows Falls
- Batten Kill River
- Stratton Mountain — 3,936 FEET / 1,200 METERS
- Townshend
- Mount Snow — 3,556 FEET / 1,084 METERS
- Haystack Mountain — 3,462 FEET / 1,055 METERS
- Bennington
- Wilmington
- Brattleboro
- Marlboro
- Whitingham
- Vernon
- West River

From the Vermont stallion, Justin Morgan, came the Morgan horse, first breed developed in America. Other U.S. breeds include the Standardbred harness racer; the Appaloosa, bred by Nez Perce Indians; and the golden Palomino, prized for its color.

Standardbred

Palomino

Appaloosa

Morgan

53

Vermont marble traces its origins back 350 million years, when a sea reached from the St. Lawrence River to the Gulf of Mexico. Tiny animals took calcium from the water to form shells. As they died, the shells piled up. The weight of the layers pressed everything into limestone. Movements in the earth pushed up the stone. It came under great heat and pressure. As it cooled, it changed into marble. Sometimes in a slab of marble you can see traces of the ancient sea creatures.

Marble takes a high polish. Sculptors and architects like to work with it. The Supreme Court and the Lincoln and Jefferson Memorials in Washington are marble buildings. Some marble is ground into white powder, for filler in toothpaste and chewing gum.

Filing makes the shoe fit. Old skills, old ways find a welcome in Vermont.

Wind whips iceboats on Lake Champlain. Ice, up to two feet (.6 m) thick, makes a winter road for Champlain folk.

Autumn's brilliance bathes Strafford's white clapboard homes and churches. Such charm draws out-of-staters, who now own about a third of Vermont.

Marble rises from a Danby quarry, a man-made cave dug into a mountain. Vermont quarries 50 varieties, from pure white to black veined with gold.

Sugarin' time. In late winter, when nights freeze and days thaw, sap rises in the maples. It drips out through spouts placed in the trunks. Forty gallons (151 l) yield a gallon (3.8 l) of maple syrup after excess water is evaporated by boiling.

America at Work

Back in the winter of 1790, nine years after the American Revolution ended, a young mechanic named Samuel Slater helped start another kind of revolution. In a small building beside a river in Pawtucket, Rhode Island, Slater put together some hand-made machinery. Connecting the apparatus to a waterwheel for power, he watched the cylinders, gears, and spindles automatically comb and spin fibers of cotton into yarn. Until then, Americans had done this tiresome job by hand.

Slater's mill not only helped mechanize the manufacture of textiles. It speeded up our country's industrial revolution. Over the next 200 years a nation of farmers grew into an industrial giant as more and more entrepreneurs—people who take the risk of starting a business—went into manufacturing. (The youngsters above with the lemonade stand are entrepreneurs.)

Today more than 300,000 manufacturing companies turn out 11,500 different kinds of products, from paper clips to jumbo jet liners. In one year factories can deliver huge quantities: 7 million passenger cars, a billion light bulbs, 150 million tons (134 million metric tons) of steel.

We have paid a price for all this. Feeding and fueling the manufacturing machine chews up the land and devours our limited natural resources like iron, coal, and oil. Waste byproducts pollute lakes and streams and the air we breathe. Products that we throw away turn into junk, which litters the landscape. Even workers themselves suffer, often doing robot-like jobs eight hours a day.

Yet manufacturing creates many of the jobs in America and keeps our standard of living one of the highest in the world.

From its beginning in the 18th century, the industrial revolution meant change in the way machines and science worked to meet the needs of people. At different times the revolution was called by different names—the machine age, the age of steam, the age of electricity, the nuclear age, the computer age. These names suggest how one technology built on top of another. The industries that grew out of those ages affect what we eat and wear, and how we work, play, travel, and communicate.

Most manufacturing industries are located in the northeastern part of our country. There, in the early days, the geography of the land provided energy or raw materials. Textile mills sprang up in New England, for example, because waterpower was abundant in plunging rivers. Iron and steel mills were concentrated in western Pennsylvania because raw materials (coal and iron ore) were close at hand. Vast coalfields lay south of Pittsburgh. And iron ore mined in Wisconsin and Minnesota could move easily down the Great Lakes in giant ore boats.

Today geography is not so important in deciding where an industry will grow. Electricity supplies most of our power. It can be generated on the spot or sent over long distances by wires. Swift planes, trains, and trucks move materials where they are needed. Pipelines transport fuels, like oil and natural gas, halfway across the country, from Texas and Oklahoma to industries in the East. Coal is even sent through pipes in the form of slurry, a combination of crushed coal and water. When it reaches its destination, the slurry is drained of water and the powdered coal is ready to be burned.

Many types of manufacturing keep our country strong and economically healthy. Three important businesses are steel, autos, and oil. Steel gives our industrial giant muscle, autos give it flexibility, and oil gives it fuel and lubrication. Each depends on the other. Like textiles and Slater's mill, each of these businesses experienced a "revolution" in its growth.

Before 1851 it took two weeks to make 50 pounds (22.7 kg) of steel. But in that year, near Eddyville, Kentucky, a man named William Kelly hid in the woods to experiment with a furnace. He hoped it would make larger amounts of steel quicker. His neighbors thought his ideas were strange, and they called him Crazy Kelly. But he had stumbled onto an important fact: You could make steel quickly by burning most of the carbon out of molten iron with a blast of air.

People think *of Detroit when they speak of cars. But auto parts may come from widely distant places to assembly plants all over the country. This make-believe car could be made with a vinyl top and a fender from Ohio, a muffler from North Carolina, a bumper from Georgia, a radiator from New York, a coil spring from Pennsylvania.*

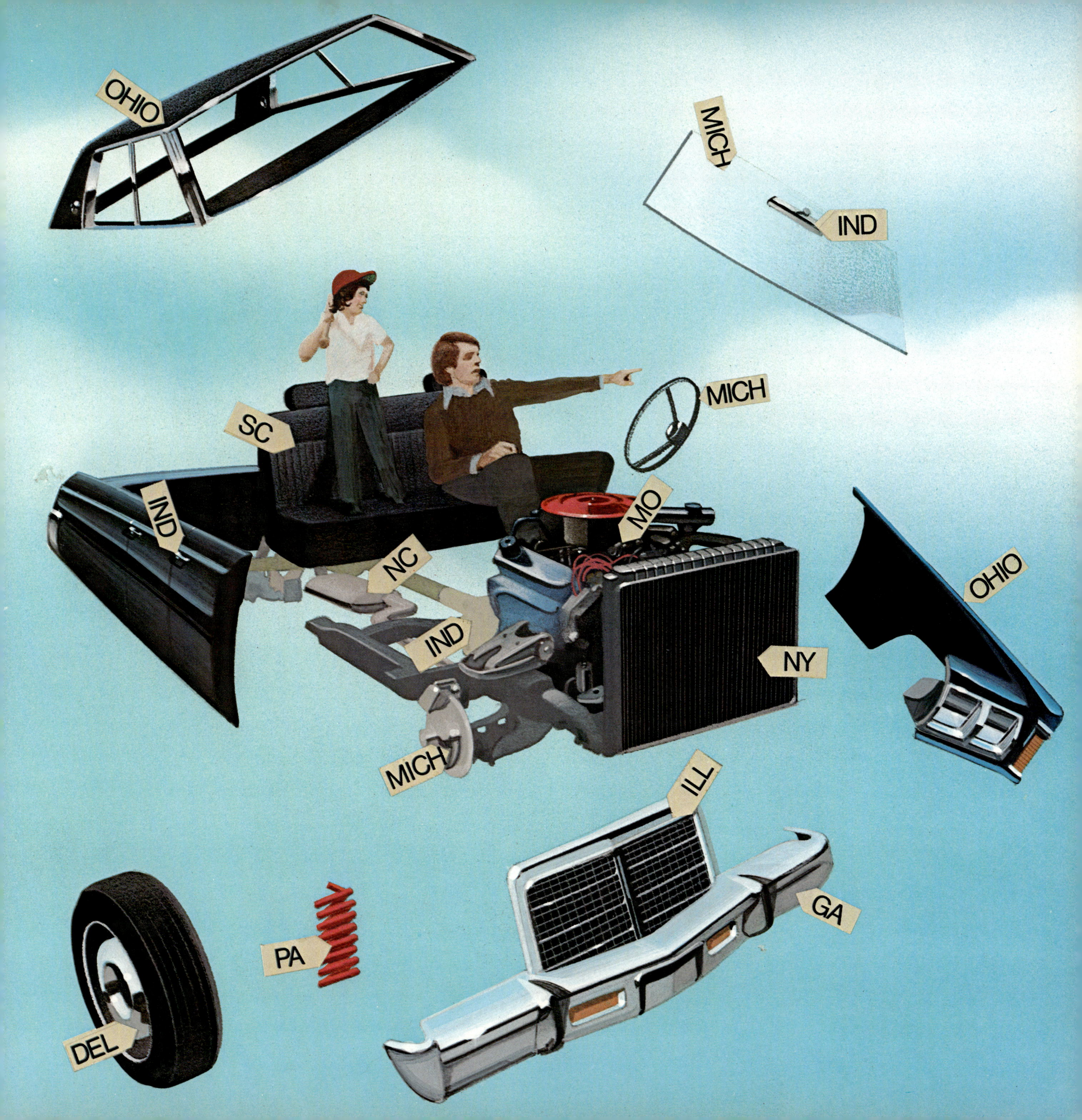
OHIO
MICH
IND
MICH
SC
IND
MO
NC
OHIO
IND
NY
MICH
ILL
GA
PA
DEL

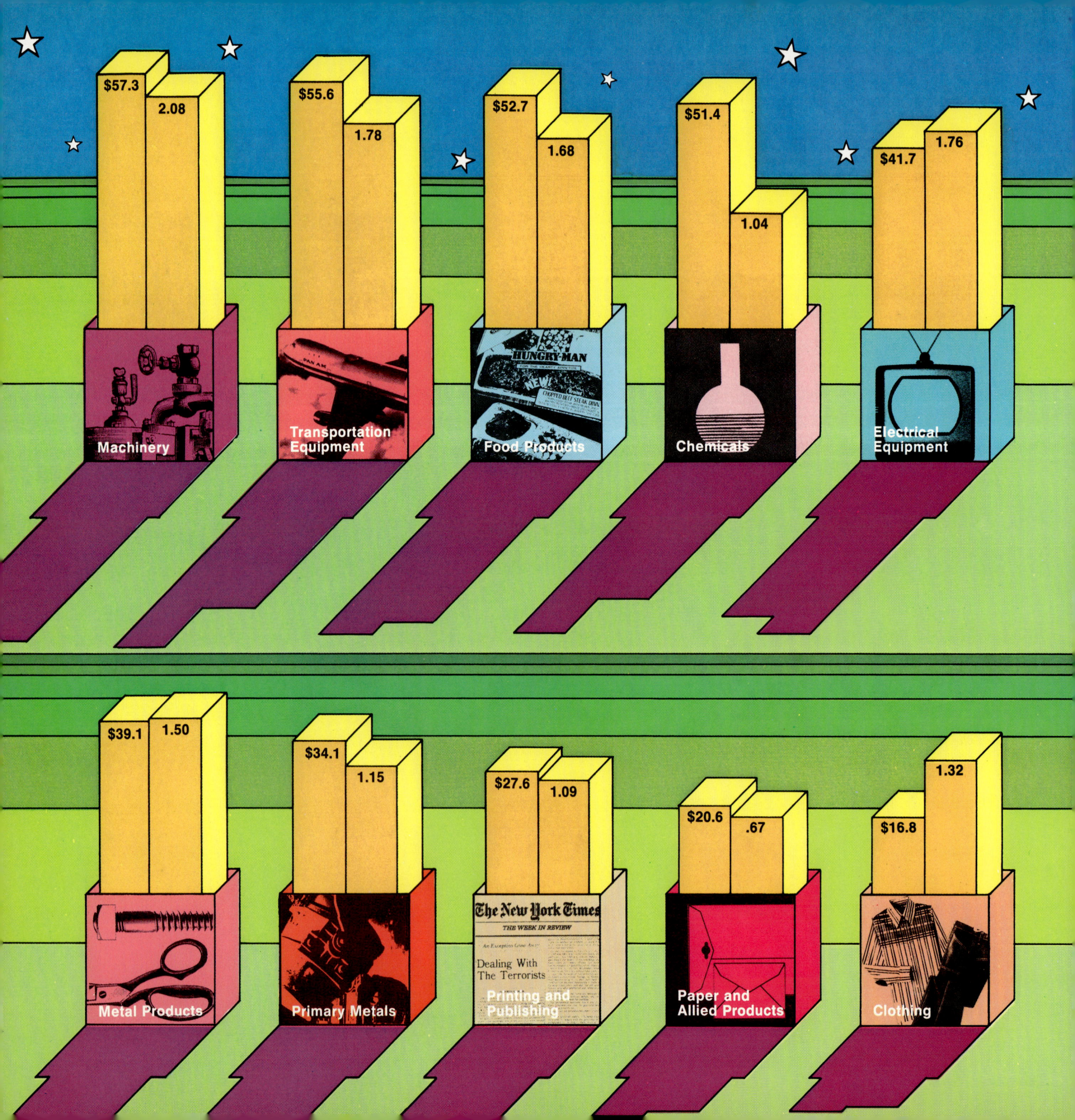

Category	$	Value
Machinery	$57.3	2.08
Transportation Equipment	$55.6	1.78
Food Products	$52.7	1.68
Chemicals	$51.4	1.04
Electrical Equipment	$41.7	1.76
Metal Products	$39.1	1.50
Primary Metals	$34.1	1.15
Printing and Publishing	$27.6	1.09
Paper and Allied Products	$20.6	.67
Clothing	$16.8	1.32

Kelly's method was later called the Bessemer process after an Englishman who discovered it about the same time. Theirs was the revolution that would make it possible for America's steel industry to produce *17,000 tons of steel in one hour.*

Today the manufacture of iron and steel is a basic industry. It makes possible nearly all other industries. If steel does not go directly into a product, it usually is used to make the machines that make the product.

First, steel is rolled into usable shapes called blooms, billets, and slabs. These are taken to finishing mills which press, roll, and cut them into sheets, rods, pipes, rails, and girders. Other manufacturers stamp the sheets into auto bodies and bend the pipes into bicycle frames. Still others cut rods into the nuts and bolts that hold our world together and grind out the ball bearings that keep it moving.

Half a century after Kelly hid in the woods, we Americans suddenly changed the way we traveled about our neighborhoods. Just outside Detroit, Michigan, in 1913, automaker Henry Ford improved the moving assembly line. He began mass-producing Model T's. Before that, a team of workers would build one car at a time. Now the frame of each car was pulled along a line of workers. As the growing car passed, each worker added another part.

Ford's assembly line cut the time to put the parts of a car together from 12 hours to 1½ hours. That cut the cost, which cut the price. It eventually fell to around $260 in the 1920's. Nearly everyone could afford a "tin lizzie." Today the assembly line, which revolutionized the auto industry, rolls out a car a minute. There are 135 million cars on the roads of America, at least one for every two people in the country.

Industries often reach crossroads. Development may go in one direction or another. Around the turn of the 20th century, the young automobile industry reached such a crossroads. Steam drove 40 percent of all U.S. cars, electric batteries 38 percent, and the gasoline engine only 22 percent. Which would the industry choose—steam, electricity, or gasoline? We know it chose gasoline. Nearly all cars are powered by the gasoline in the internal-combustion engine.

But why did the industry choose gasoline? Two main reasons: The gas engine developed a lot of power for its weight, and it ran on cheap, available fuel.

For years, people had been lighting their homes with lamps that burned kerosene. The oil industry made kerosene by refining crude oil, the name given to the petroleum pumped out of wells. But in 1879 Thomas Edison invented a long-burning light bulb. People began switching from kerosene to electricity, and that hit the oil industry hard. It couldn't sell as much kerosene.

What was worse, in making kerosene from crude oil, gasoline was left over as a useless by-product, 11 gallons (41.6 l) for every 100 gallons (378 l) of crude oil. So refineries threw it away—until the demand of the gas engine made gasoline useful.

Now the oil industry set out to convert more of its crude oil into gasoline. Along the way, company chemists revolutionized the refining process. Today the industry can squeeze as much as 45 gallons (170 l) of gasoline out of 100 gallons of crude oil.

Oil refineries can be found all across the country, from New Jersey to Wyoming and California. Have you ever wondered what goes on in those tall, pipe-laced towers? First you have to learn a few simple things about crude oil.

Crude oil is made up of parts, or fractions. Each part is composed mainly of two chemical elements, hydrogen and carbon. These

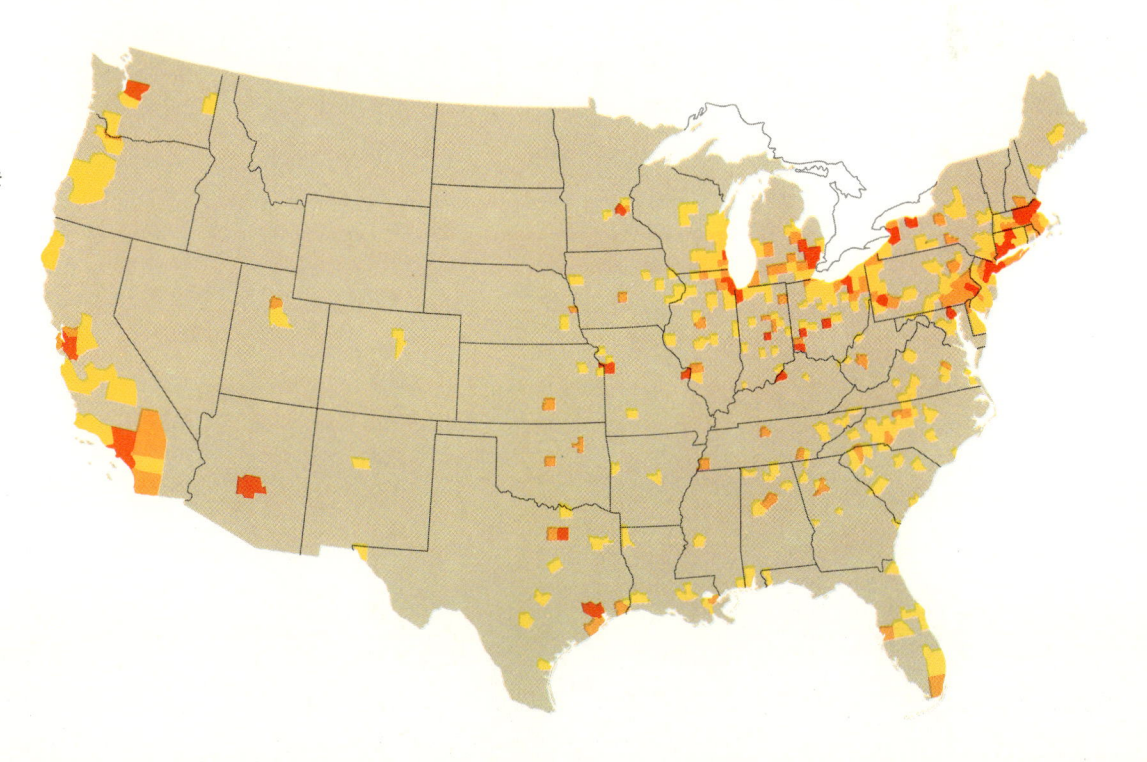

Factories grow *in numbers where the population is the thickest. Men and women in a region serve both as a labor pool and as a consumer market: they work in the factories and then buy the products that come out of those factories. The map at right shows important industrial areas, based on the value of the products made there. Red areas produce the highest value; then comes orange, then yellow. Note that most of the spots are where most of the people live—east of the Mississippi and along the West Coast.*

The illustration opposite shows the top ten kinds of products manufactured, in both the value created (in billions of dollars) and the number of workers in that industry (in millions). Since we still live in the age of machines, it is not surprising that the manufacture of non-electrical machinery leads all other industries, with $57,300,000,000 value produced by 2,080,000 workers.

two elements come in many combinations, but all are called hydrocarbons. They can help people—or kill. One by-product of a hydrocarbon, left over after gasoline is burned, comes out of a car's exhaust pipe. This is deadly carbon monoxide.

When oil is heated, different fractions boil and turn to vapor at different temperatures. The first fraction to vaporize is gasoline. Next comes kerosene, then diesel oil, then lubricants like grease. As the vapors rise in the fractionating towers, they are caught in separate chambers and cooled. This causes them to condense back into a liquid.

In the early days of refining, much of the crude oil was wasted. Today, every part of the oil is made into something useful. Even the sludge left in the bottom of the fractionating tower helps us live better. We turn it into asphalt to pave roads and to make roof shingles and floor tiles.

One of industry's most recent revolutions took place in the 1950's when scientists learned to harness light waves to produce the laser. The word *laser* is made up of the first letters of the words Light Amplification by Stimulated Emission of Radiation. In other words, intensified light.

One way to create a laser is with a ruby crystal rod. One end of the rod is painted silver to make a mirror. The other end is partially mirrored to allow the laser beam to escape. Around the ruby rod a powerful corkscrew-shaped light bulb is set in place. When the light is turned on and shines in through the sides of the ruby rod, certain atoms in the rod become "excited." Each excited atom releases energy in the form of darts of light called photons.

As the photons bounce around inside the ruby rod and bang into the mirrors, they bump into other atoms. This excites more atoms and releases more photons. Energy builds up to such an intensity that the photons begin to flow in one direction. They escape out the partially closed end of the ruby rod as a laser beam.

Unlike the rays of a flashlight that fan out in the dark, laser rays remain parallel. This concentration of colorless light creates intense heat, as much as 10,000°F (5,538°C). Have you ever focused the sun's rays through a magnifying glass into a pinpoint of heat that could burn paper? Laser light has the same effect. It can burn a hole in a diamond, the hardest substance known.

As a tool, the laser is barely out of the laboratory. But industry already has it hard at work. The magic beam can weld transistor wires as small as one-thousandth of an inch in diameter, cut cloth for garments, and operate a switch at one-trillionth of a second. Someday, when you talk on the telephone your voice will be one of thousands riding the same laser through hair-thin fibers, causing a revolution in communication.

In years to come the laser may burn a path to unnamed industrial ages. But for the present, let's call this period in the industrial revolution the age of wonders.

Manufacturing creates a lot of business in the United States. But more than half of America's workers earn their living in jobs that provide a service for the community—schoolteacher, auto mechanic, architect, barber, lawyer, airline pilot, government file clerk. In this picture, see how many of the numbered occupations you can name. Answers appear below.

1. Librarian 2. Music teacher 3. Maid 4. Waitress 5. Doorman 6. Palmist, or Fortune-teller 7. Journalists 8. Newspaper photographer 9. Seamstress 10. Painters 11. Dentist 12. Bank guard 13. Veterinarian 14. Barber 15. Postman 16. Welder 17. Carpenter 18. Bricklayer

Lake Erie's waters plunge 193 feet (59 m) over Niagara Falls to feed Lake Ontario.

Lake Ontario, 802 feet (244 m) at its deepest point, is the smallest of the Great Lakes.

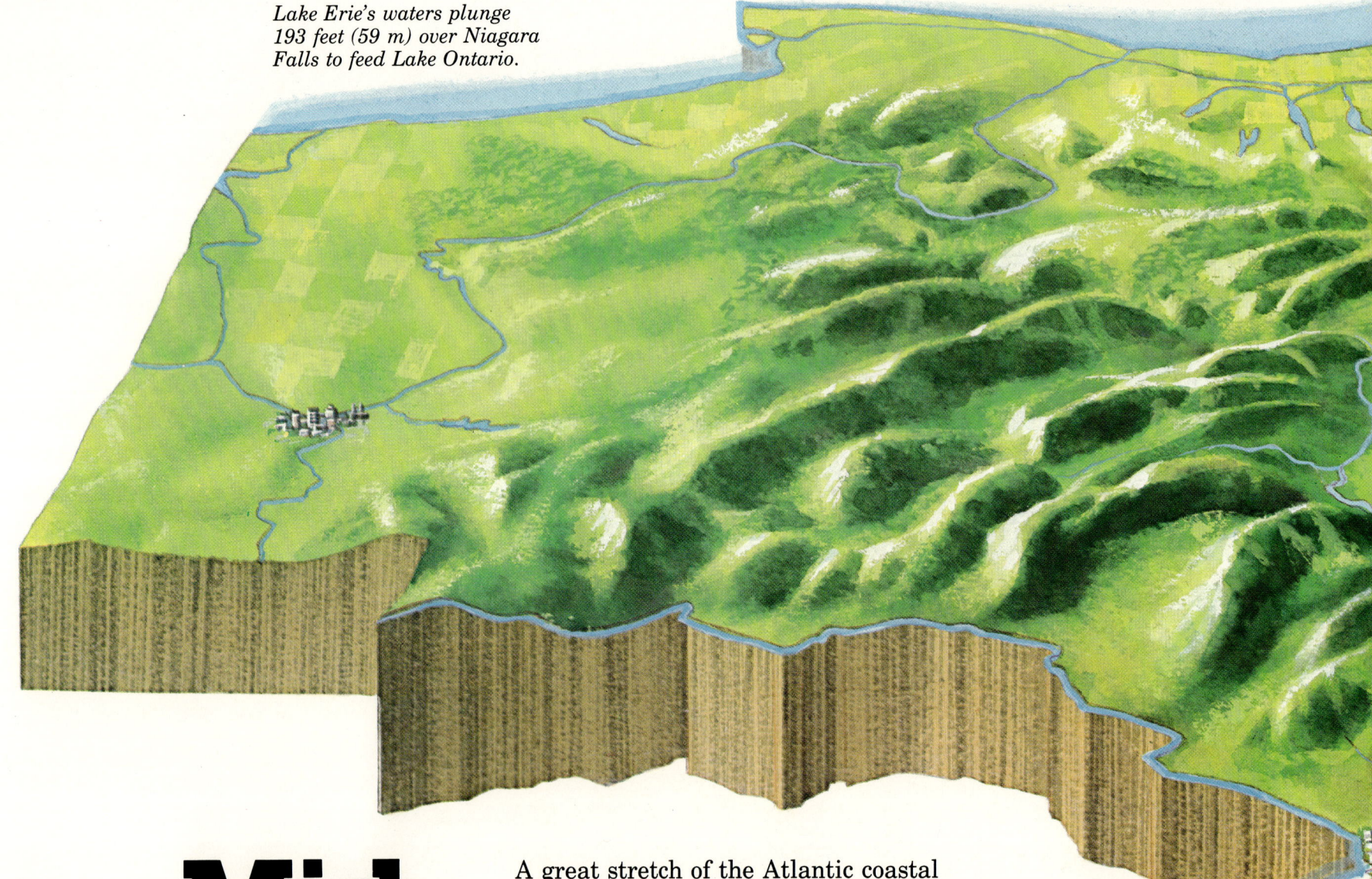

Mid-Atlantic States

A great stretch of the Atlantic coastal plain sweeps toward the mountains. Then the land slopes upward, forming the piedmont ("mountain feet"). Old, hard rock lies under the piedmont. Softer rock blankets much of the plain. The boundary between is the fall line, where rivers tumble over falls and rapids. Many cities were built at the fall line, for here was water power to turn mill wheels. Here too was often a fine upriver port. Early roads that linked the cities followed the fall line. So did railroad tracks—and, in our day, U. S. Interstate 95.

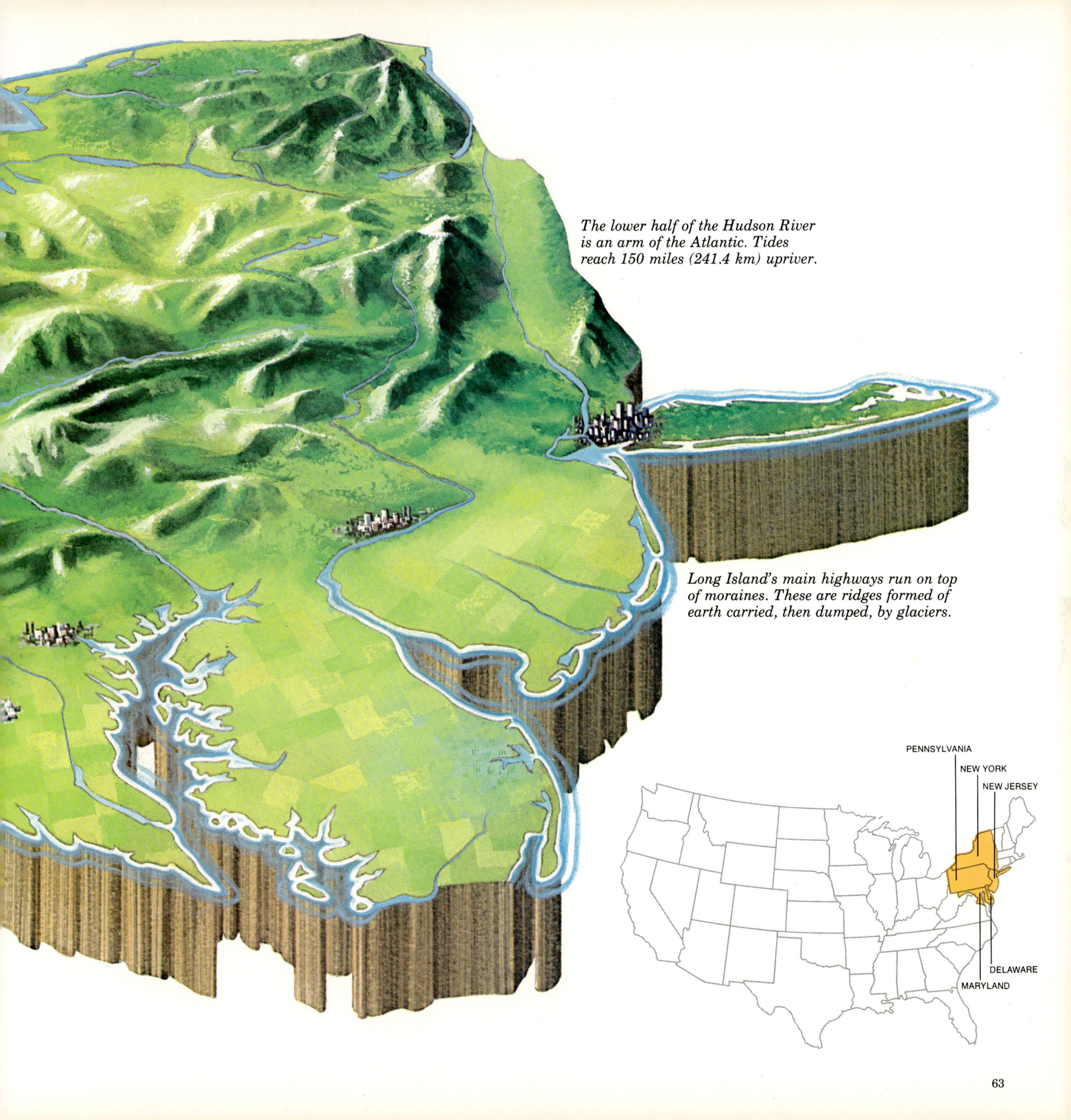

The lower half of the Hudson River is an arm of the Atlantic. Tides reach 150 miles (241.4 km) upriver.

Long Island's main highways run on top of moraines. These are ridges formed of earth carried, then dumped, by glaciers.

PENNSYLVANIA
NEW YORK
NEW JERSEY
DELAWARE
MARYLAND

DELAWARE

Peach Blossom

Blue Hen Chicken

Delaware may be tiny, but it's packed with so much that a description of our second-smallest state looks like a description of the whole United States. There are factories in the north and farms in the south, rivers and an ocean coast, big city and little towns, poor city neighborhoods and rich suburbs, a major industry (chemicals) and a major agricultural product (chickens).

In fact, the state is so like a small-scale U.S.A. that pollsters—people who make surveys by asking other people questions—sometimes go just to Delaware to look for answers. By finding out what citizens in Delaware are thinking, the pollsters can get a pretty good idea what people all over the United States are thinking.

The flags of three nations had flown over the Delaware Bay colony before it became our "First State." The colony began as a Dutch settlement. Next it became New Sweden. Eventually, the English took it over: King Charles II included it in the land that he gave to William Penn.

The biggest piece of the king's grant was named Pennsylvania, and Penn paid most of his attention to it. The folks in little Delaware felt they were being ignored. So they decided to go on their own. In 1704 Delaware became a crown colony. People there again showed they liked liberty when the state earned a nickname by being the first state to ratify—approve—the U. S. Constitution.

The First State is the only state with a round border. The neat bite out of Pennsylvania happened in William Penn's day. To measure off a northern boundary, mapmakers drew an arc of a circle from the end of the "Horse Dyke at New Castle." Later measurers used the spire of the courthouse there to mark a 12-mile (19.3 km) radius.

America's first log cabins were built in Delaware in the 17th century. Swedish settlers brought the idea with them.

Area: the 49th largest state, 2,057 sq mi (5,328 sq km). **Population:** 582,000. Ranks 47th. **Major Cities:** Wilmington, 76,152; Newark, 26,645; Dover, 22,480. **Manufacturing:** chemicals and related products (synthetic yarn, plastic, dye, paint), food and food products, leather goods, transportation equipment (including autos and ships), textiles, machinery. **Agriculture:** broiler chickens, corn, soybeans, dairy products. Also hogs, mushrooms, potatoes, nursery and greenhouse products. **Mining:** sand, gravel, clay. **Fishing:** clams, crabs, oysters, menhaden, flounder, shad. **Statehood:** the first state. Ratified Constitution on Dec. 7, 1787.

*De*laware, *Mary*land, and *Virginia* gave parts of their names to the area where they meet: the Delmarva Peninsula. Delaware's share of Delmarva's coast includes a string of beaches and wildlife refuges. At one of them, more than 300 species of birds have been spotted. Delaware protects its beautiful coast with the nation's first tough save-the-seashore law. According to the law, no steel mills, oil refineries, or other pollution-threatening plants can be built within two miles (3.2 km) of the coast.

The sandy-shored town of Lewes, near Cape Henlopen, lies 17 miles (27.3 km) across the water from Cape May, New Jersey. These capes stick out like gates, guarding Delaware Bay and forming the mouth of a great harbor.

Ships from around the world sail up the bay to Wilmington, "the chemical capital of the world." In Wilmington are made not only chemicals but also things made of chemicals. These things include such everyday materials as the nylon for bristles on your toothbrush, the Teflon "no-stick" lining of frying pans, and the Dacron and Orlon in shirts and blouses.

Du Pont, the largest chemical company in the world, makes these substances. Du Pont began as a gunpowder mill by a river near Wilmington. The company now has plants in many places. But Wilmington is still home. Research scientists work there.

The state is famous for producing fine broilers (chickens between nine and 12 weeks old). But the state bird, the Blue Hen Chicken, is famous as a brawler—not a broiler. Back in the days when people raised birds for fighting, a certain blue hen hatched great battlers. In the Revolution, Delaware soldiers were called "The Blue Hen's Chickens," and the name lived on.

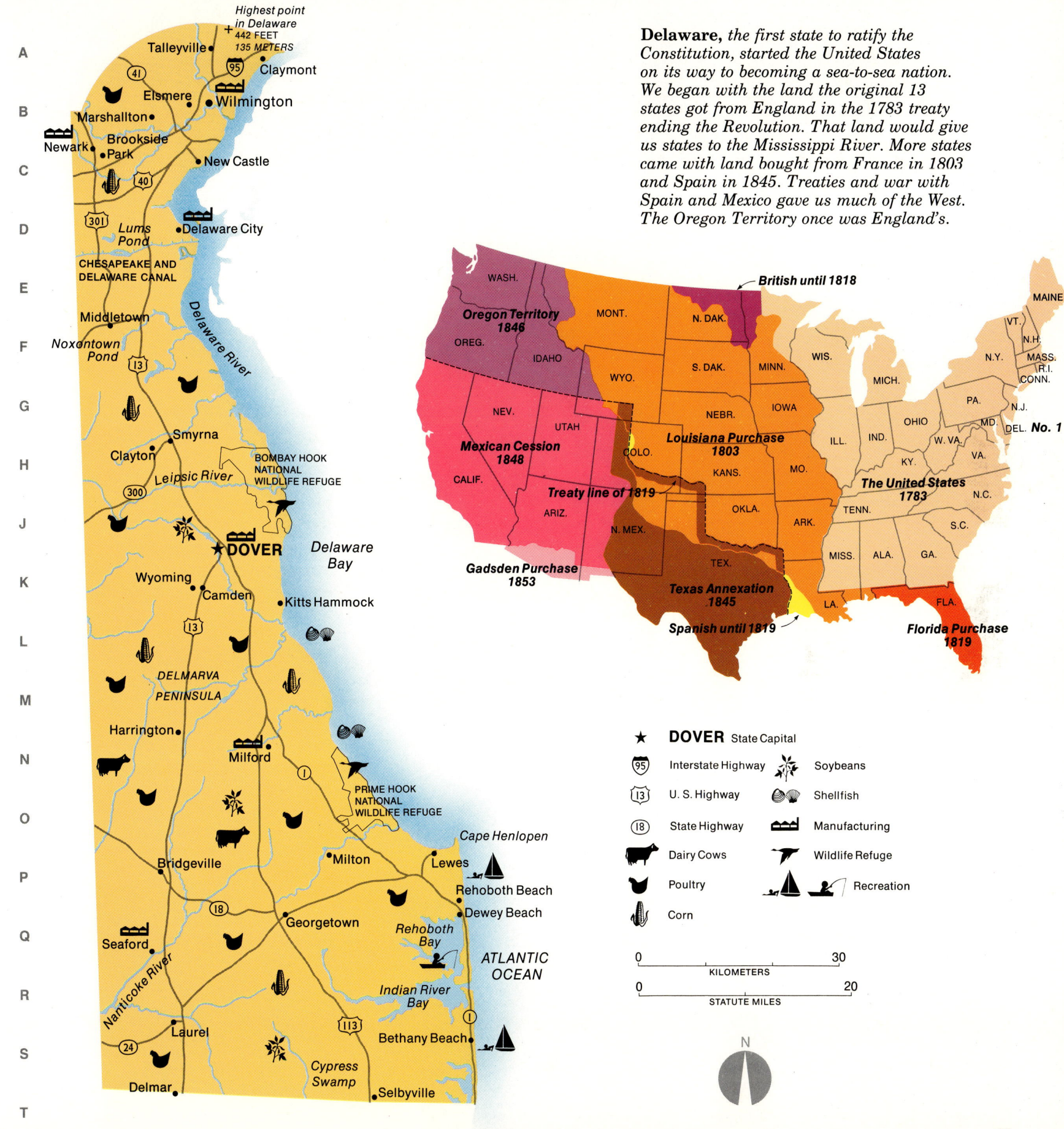

Delaware, *the first state to ratify the Constitution, started the United States on its way to becoming a sea-to-sea nation. We began with the land the original 13 states got from England in the 1783 treaty ending the Revolution. That land would give us states to the Mississippi River. More states came with land bought from France in 1803 and Spain in 1845. Treaties and war with Spain and Mexico gave us much of the West. The Oregon Territory once was England's.*

Delaware map labels

- Highest point in Delaware 442 FEET 135 METERS
- Talleyville
- Claymont
- Elsmere
- Wilmington
- Marshallton
- Newark
- Brookside Park
- New Castle
- Lums Pond
- Delaware City
- CHESAPEAKE AND DELAWARE CANAL
- Delaware River
- Middletown
- Noxontown Pond
- Smyrna
- Clayton
- Leipsic River
- BOMBAY HOOK NATIONAL WILDLIFE REFUGE
- ★ DOVER
- Delaware Bay
- Wyoming
- Camden
- Kitts Hammock
- DELMARVA PENINSULA
- Harrington
- Milford
- PRIME HOOK NATIONAL WILDLIFE REFUGE
- Cape Henlopen
- Bridgeville
- Milton
- Lewes
- Rehoboth Beach
- Dewey Beach
- Seaford
- Georgetown
- Rehoboth Bay
- ATLANTIC OCEAN
- Nanticoke River
- Indian River Bay
- Laurel
- Bethany Beach
- Delmar
- Cypress Swamp
- Selbyville

U.S. territorial acquisitions

- Oregon Territory 1846
- British until 1818
- Mexican Cession 1848
- Treaty line of 1819
- Louisiana Purchase 1803
- The United States 1783 — DEL. No. 1
- Gadsden Purchase 1853
- Texas Annexation 1845
- Spanish until 1819
- Florida Purchase 1819

Legend

- ★ **DOVER** State Capital
- 95 Interstate Highway
- 13 U.S. Highway
- 18 State Highway
- Dairy Cows
- Poultry
- Corn
- Soybeans
- Shellfish
- Manufacturing
- Wildlife Refuge
- Recreation

0 — 30 KILOMETERS
0 — 20 STATUTE MILES

N

We've rounded Cape Henlopen on our voyage up the bay to Wilmington. Our skipper is from Lewes, "saltiest town in Delaware," and he's telling us a yarn. "Captain Kidd did dock in Lewes, you know. It's in the books. Traded his pirate loot for our merchants' goods...." Near Bombay Hook refuge, the skipper points toward shore. "On the chart it's Kitts Hammock. A hammock? Some folks call it a hummock, a high bit of land in a marsh. Anyhow, should be *Kidd's* Hammock, because that's where they say he buried a chest of his treasure. Now, I know folks dug there, but as to findin'...."

Redwinged blackbirds pepper the sky over a Delaware thicket. Bird watchers also flock to the state, which lies on the "migratory flyway" used by birds that winter in the south.

Waves of sand sweep across Cape Henlopen State Park. The dunes creep inward 5 to 14 feet (1.5 to 4.2 m) a year.

In a Du Pont laboratory near Wilmington, a technician tests a plastic for packaging. The company pioneered nylon in Delaware.

A Liberian tanker, passing an empty (left), enters the Chesapeake and Delaware Canal.

The Delaware Memorial Bridge, with towers 440 feet (134.1 m) high, opened in 1951. A twin (left) arrived in 1968 with towers a foot higher.

MARYLAND

Sounds of honking come from far above. A great, fluttering V appears in the gray fall sky. The Canada geese have come back to Chesapeake Bay! In spring, they will fly to their nesting grounds in the north. By then, the bay will welcome another flock: sailboats. Life follows the seasons in the bay.

The map of Maryland looks like a jigsaw puzzle. The big blue piece in the middle is Maryland's share of Chesapeake Bay: 1,726 square miles (4,470.3 sq km). Maryland could be named Water-land!

The rest of the pieces in the puzzle got their shapes from geography and history. The straight northern border, for instance, is part of what became known as the Mason-Dixon Line. Charles Mason and Jeremiah Dixon, surveyors from England, drew it in the 1760's. They thus settled a border fight that had gone on for years between Maryland and Pennsylvania. Now look at that piece stamped out of the western border. Here is where the state donated land that helped make the District of Columbia.

For years the geography of the bay split the state. On what is called the Eastern Shore, people lived on their own. They had little to do with the Marylanders across the bay. That was where the city folks lived. They had row houses in Baltimore. Or they were people who lived in suburbs around their work place, Washington.

Then in 1952 Maryland built the world's longest all-steel bridge over salt water. The bridge united the two pieces of Maryland and opened the Eastern Shore to new industries. The bridge also gave Marylanders a faster trip to the state's 30 miles (48.3 km) of Atlantic shore on the Delmarva Peninsula.

In summertime the bridge was clogged by cars carrying families to Ocean City's beaches and boardwalk, and to the campsites, surf fishing, and swimming at Assateague Island National Seashore. A second bridge has eased the traffic jams.

The bridges have to be high enough over the water so that oceangoing ships can pass under on their way to and from Baltimore. The city's 45 miles (72 km) of waterfront have made it one of the busiest ports in the country. During a bombardment of Baltimore Harbor in 1814, Francis Scott Key wrote "The Star-Spangled Banner." And it was in Baltimore that Edgar Allan Poe wrote many of his poems and stories.

Big ships pass by the snug harbor of Annapolis—but history doesn't. One of our first planned cities, Maryland's capital keeps its old look. Right after the Revolution it was the nation's capital. Its residents claim to be outnumbered by boats. One sailboat fleet belongs to the U. S. Naval Academy, which was established here in 1845.

Farmers make a living raising chickens on the Eastern Shore, growing tobacco in the south, and harvesting apples and peaches in central and western counties. Watermen in the bay harvest oysters and crabs. But in the area around the District of Columbia the biggest crop has been houses and apartments. More than 1,000,000 people live in the Maryland suburbs that spread on three sides of Washington.

Beyond, in what planners call a "corridor," about 63,000 people live where there were only 10,000 in 1960. The corridor is lined with research companies and federal agencies. It lies along 35 miles (56 km) of highway north of the Maryland-D. C. border. Planners hope to make the area into a kind of checkerboard, with squares for clusters of homes or offices—and some squares for the old green land of Maryland.

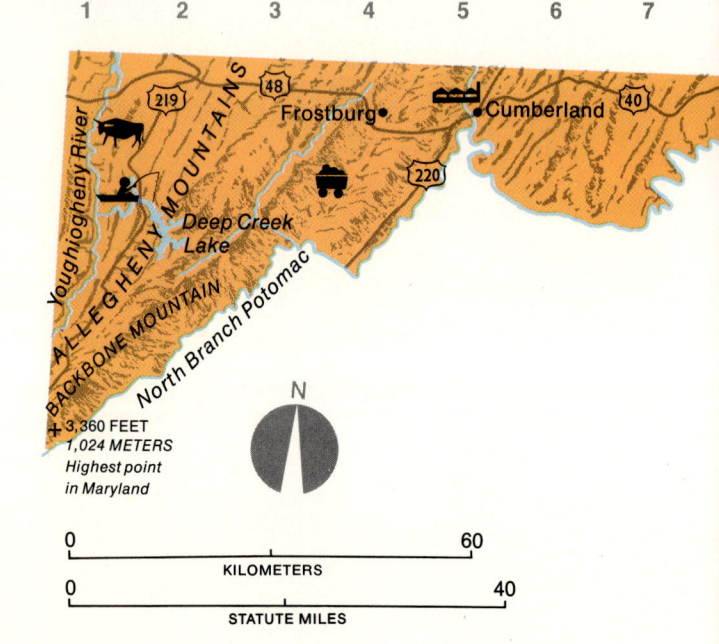

Area: the 42nd largest state, 10,577 sq mi (27,394 sq km). **Population:** 4,139,000. Ranks 18th. **Major Cities:** Baltimore, 851,698; Rockville, 44,299; Bowie, 37,323. **Manufacturing:** food and food products (meat packing, vegetable processing, packing and distribution of spices and sugar), steel, smelting of copper and aluminum, transportation equipment, shipbuilding and repairing, electrical equipment, chemicals, fabricated metals. **Agriculture:** broiler chickens, dairy products, corn, soybeans, beef cattle, vegetables, tobacco. Also hogs, wheat. **Mining:** coal, stone, cement, sand, gravel. **Fishing:** oysters, crabs, clams, striped bass. **Other Important Activities:** work of federal agencies and research firms; printing and publishing, tourism. **Statehood:** the seventh state. Ratified Constitution on April 28, 1788.

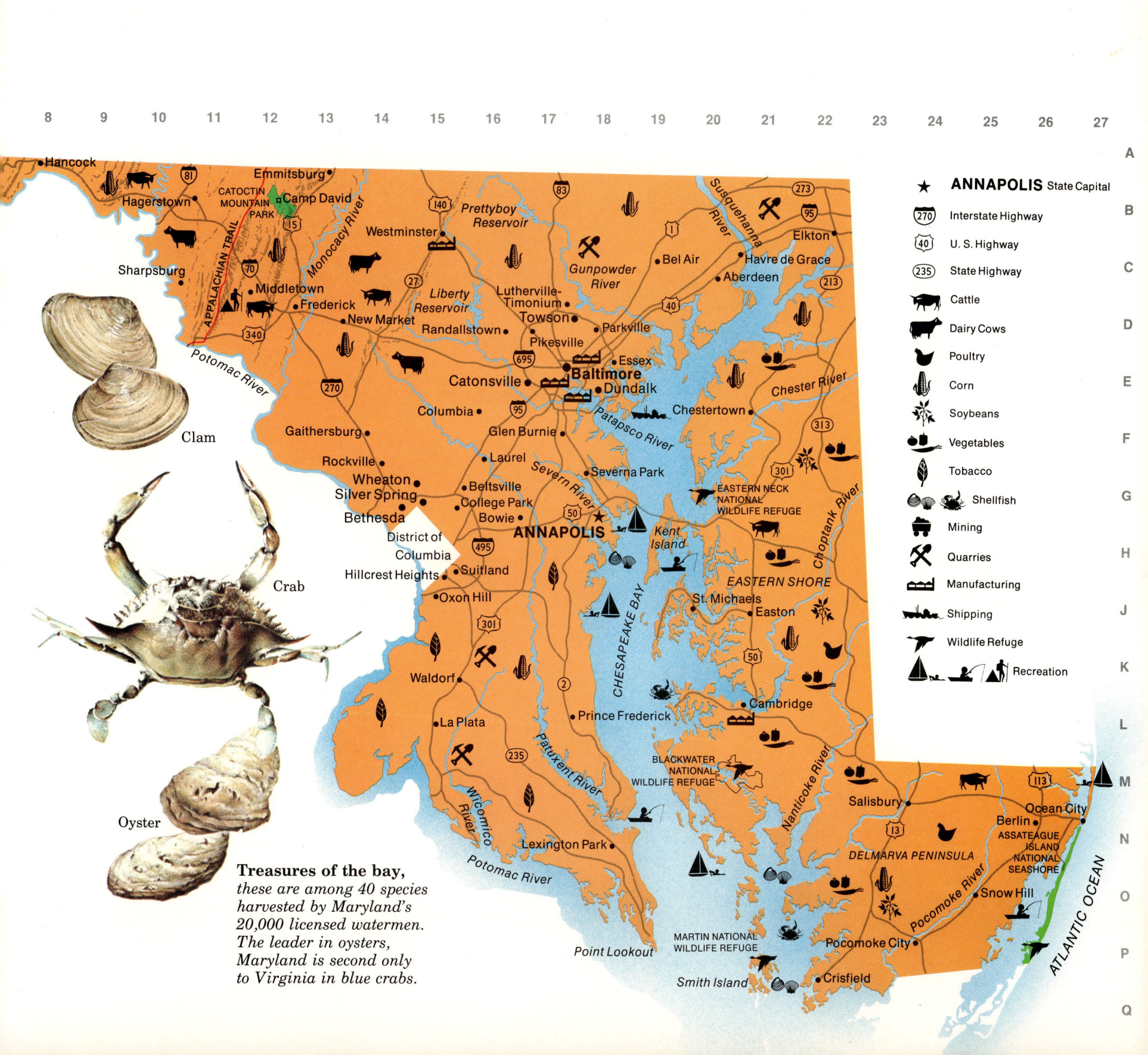

Maryland

Map Legend

★	**ANNAPOLIS** State Capital
(270)	Interstate Highway
(40)	U.S. Highway
(235)	State Highway
🐂	Cattle
🐄	Dairy Cows
🐔	Poultry
🌽	Corn
🌱	Soybeans
🥬	Vegetables
🍃	Tobacco
🦪🦀	Shellfish
⛏	Mining
⚒	Quarries
🏭	Manufacturing
🚢	Shipping
🦅	Wildlife Refuge
⛵🎣🏕	Recreation

Locations shown on map

Hancock, Emmitsburg, Hagerstown, Catoctin Mountain Park, Camp David, Westminster, Prettyboy Reservoir, Elkton, Sharpsburg, Middletown, Frederick, New Market, Liberty Reservoir, Lutherville-Timonium, Towson, Bel Air, Havre de Grace, Aberdeen, Randallstown, Pikesville, Parkville, Gunpowder River, Catonsville, Baltimore, Essex, Dundalk, Chestertown, Chester River, Columbia, Gaithersburg, Glen Burnie, Patapsco River, Rockville, Laurel, Severna Park, Wheaton, Beltsville, Silver Spring, College Park, Bethesda, Bowie, ANNAPOLIS, Kent Island, Eastern Neck National Wildlife Refuge, District of Columbia, Hillcrest Heights, Suitland, Oxon Hill, St. Michaels, Easton, Eastern Shore, Choptank River, Waldorf, La Plata, Prince Frederick, Cambridge, Lexington Park, Blackwater National Wildlife Refuge, Salisbury, Berlin, Ocean City, Assateague Island National Seashore, Snow Hill, Delmarva Peninsula, Martin National Wildlife Refuge, Point Lookout, Smith Island, Pocomoke City, Crisfield, Potomac River, Wicomico River, Patuxent River, Nanticoke River, Pocomoke River, Susquehanna River, Monocacy River, Severn River, Chesapeake Bay, Atlantic Ocean, Appalachian Trail

Caption

Treasures of the bay, *these are among 40 species harvested by Maryland's 20,000 licensed watermen. The leader in oysters, Maryland is second only to Virginia in blue crabs.*

Clam

Crab

Oyster

Writer H. L. Mencken lived (and ate) in Baltimore. He called Chesapeake Bay a "protein factory." The protein he loved comes from the shellfish and finfish that thrive in the bay. In a typical year, the bay will put about $75 million worth of seafood on restaurant and dining room plates.

Chesapeake Bay is the nation's largest estuary. In such a body of water, salty seawater mixes with fresh river water. The blend is just right for the many living things in the estuary. Minerals and salts, underwater plants, and tiny animals become the chowder for bigger animals to eat. They start what ecologists call the "food chain." Fishes, oysters, crabs, and clams become links in it. The chain ends at our tables.

Watermen of Chesapeake Bay haul in a dredgeful of oysters. As the boat, a skipjack, sails over an oyster bed, the dredge drags across it. Watermen also catch crabs. Marylanders steam them to eat by the plateful.

Crewmen risk a dunking to keep an odd boat from capsizing in the bay. A sailing canoe, its hull is made of logs.

U.S. Department of Agriculture experts study apples to zucchini in Beltsville laboratories.

A foal is born! Central and upper-bay counties form the state's horse country. Breeders raise Thoroughbreds and trotters. Many racing champs hail from here.

Skyscrapers blaze over Baltimore's busy harbor. The port can handle 175 oceangoing ships at one time. Much of what we import—such as these cars from West Germany—enters here. In foreign tonnage, the port is topped only by New York, Philadelphia, and Norfolk.

American Goldfinch

Purple Violet

NEW JERSEY

Put a finger on New Jersey's map near Newark. You'll cover about 20 square miles (51.8 sq km). In that area under your fingertip live more than 320,000 people! The counting of the number of people per square mile is a way to measure an area's population density. New Jersey has the greatest population density of all the states: about 975 men, women, and children per square mile.

You put your finger on an area where people live so close to each other that the density in some places is 50,000 persons per square mile. If they spaced themselves out like checkers, each would get a square about 20 by 26 feet (6 by 8 m).

Now move your finger to the area around Chatsworth. It's labeled "Pine Barrens." Here the density is about 15 people per square mile. Houses are often miles apart. Here you could wander through 1,000 square miles (2,590 sq km) of wilderness.

In fact, in this state so full of people, you'd sometimes have to walk a long way to find *anybody*. Forests, farms, and small towns cover about 75 percent of New Jersey.

A flat plain makes up the south-central part of the state. The soil is so fertile that more than 60 kinds of vegetables grow there. In summer most of the fresh produce eaten by people in New York City and Philadelphia comes from New Jersey.

The harvest begins as early as May in the asparagus fields, where workers bend low to cut the plump green stalks. In summer, machines roll in to harvest lima beans, string beans, and other vegetables raised mostly for canning and freezing. "Jersey tomatoes" usually find their way into soup. They're canned not far from where they are grown.

In 1930 New Jersey's harvest came from about 25,000 farms. The "Garden State" had some of the most fertile farms in the country. They produced more vegetables per acre than did many farms in the Midwest. Then factories, shopping centers, and suburbs began gobbling up land. To save small farms, special tax laws were passed. They help family farms stay in business.

A scientist in 1858 identified fossils from Haddonfield, New Jersey, as the first dinosaur skeleton found in North America.

Area: the 46th largest state, 7,836 sq mi (20,295 sq km). **Population:** 7,329,000. Ranks ninth. **Major Cities:** Newark, 339,568; Jersey City, 243,756; Paterson, 136,098; Elizabeth, 104,405. **Manufacturing:** chemicals (including drugs and paints), household appliances, telephones, food and food products, non-electrical machinery, fabricated metals, transportation equipment. **Agriculture:** dairy products, vegetables, nursery and greenhouse products, eggs. **Mining:** sand, gravel, stone, zinc. **Fishing:** clams, lobsters, oysters, menhaden. **Statehood:** the third state. Ratified Constitution on Dec. 18, 1787.

Of the 75 largest industrial companies in the country, more than 60 have branches in New Jersey. Nearly every kind of thing that is made in the United States—from automobiles to telephones—is manufactured somewhere in this hardworking state.

And, as the head of the state's department of environmental protection once put it, New Jersey also "has more things per square mile that make the air and water dirty than any other state."

The state is trying hard to improve its environment. But some of its industries produce pollution along with their products. The New Jersey Turnpike carries traffic through the worst pollution belt. Here are refineries that can produce more than 500,000 barrels of oil a day. With the refining come smells and smoke.

The turnpike is the busiest toll road in the United States. Alongside much of the turnpike run other highways and railroad tracks. The turnpike is part of the "transportation corridor" in what has been called the East Coast's "megalopolis," a city that seems to go on and on. The megalopolis goes from Richmond, Virginia, to Boston, Massachusetts. About 40 million people live in it.

In summer many of those people head for New Jersey's 130-mile (209 km) coastline. They cross saltwater bays and grassy marshes that link the mainland to a long sandbar. Here are Atlantic City and other resorts. They manufacture another New Jersey product: fun by the sea.

Boxes of cargo, *hauled to dockside by truck or train, go aboard a containership. Giant traveling gantry cranes load boxes, saving time and labor costs. New York-New Jersey Port District's container terminals handle nearly all shipping entering New York Harbor.*

Legend

- ★ **TRENTON** State Capital
- (287) Interstate Highway
- (40) U.S. Highway
- (72) State Highway
- Dairy Cows
- Poultry and Eggs
- Grain
- Vegetables
- Fruit
- Greenhouse and Nursery
- Fishing
- Oysters, Clams, Scallops
- Quarries
- Manufacturing
- Shipping
- Wildlife Refuge
- Recreation

Scale: 0–60 Kilometers / 0–40 Statute Miles

Map Labels

Grid columns 1–11, rows A–U

- High Point, 1,803 FEET, 550 METERS, Highest point in New Jersey
- Delaware Water Gap National Recreation Area
- Appalachian Trail
- Kittatinny Mountains
- Wanaque Reservoir
- Lake Hopatcong
- Dover
- Ridgewood
- Paterson
- Paramus
- Hudson River
- Clifton
- Hackensack
- Montclair
- Passaic
- Morristown
- Bloomfield
- Union City
- East Orange
- Hoboken
- Irvington
- Newark
- Jersey City
- Phillipsburg
- Great Swamp National Wildlife Refuge
- Elizabeth
- Bayonne
- Plainfield
- Raritan River
- Perth Amboy
- New Brunswick
- Sandy Hook Bay
- Sayreville
- Gateway National Recreation Area
- Hopewell
- Delaware and Raritan Canal
- Princeton
- Red Bank
- Eatontown
- Long Branch
- Mercerville
- Asbury Park
- TRENTON ★
- Neptune
- White Horse
- New Jersey Turnpike
- Lakewood
- Point Pleasant
- Delaware River
- Willingboro
- Toms River
- Pennsauken
- Camden
- Haddonfield
- Cherry Hill
- Barnegat Bay
- ATLANTIC OCEAN
- Chatsworth
- Pine Barrens
- Garden State Parkway
- Glassboro
- Killcohook National Wildlife Refuge
- Barnegat National Wildlife Refuge
- Supawna Meadows National Wildlife Refuge
- Mullica River
- Atlantic City Expressway
- Great Egg Harbor River
- Beach Haven
- Vineland
- Brigantine National Wildlife Refuge
- Bridgeton
- Millville
- Great Bay
- Maurice River
- Atlantic City
- Ventnor City
- Ocean City
- Delaware Bay
- Avalon
- Cape May
- Wildwood

New Jersey's city people have a backyard half as big as Grand Canyon National Park. The wilderness is the Pine Barrens. Colonial settlers gave the area its name. Pine trees covered soil too poor to farm. It didn't seem to be worth much. Today, though, city dwellers go to the Pine Barrens to get away from crowded cities. Canoeists can paddle along unpolluted rivers (below) and enjoy a living marshland. Rain falling on the Pine Barrens goes down into an aquifer, a natural underground reservoir. Pollution does not reach it. Clean water from the aquifer feeds the countless streams.

Fresh-picked New Jersey peas slide from a wagon to a conveyor belt for processing. In 20 minutes they will be quick-frozen.

Pine Barren explorers find wonders, such as the sundew, an insect-eating plant. This trapped ant will supply nitrogen and protein to its captor.

74

Atlantic City's fir-plank Boardwalk stretches five miles. This pioneer resort shares its street names with Monopoly players.

About 17,000,000 people a year flee to the fun at Atlantic City.

Drivers on the New Jersey Turnpike see miles of oil refineries. Chemicals—from perfume to vitamins—lead all state products.

NEW YORK

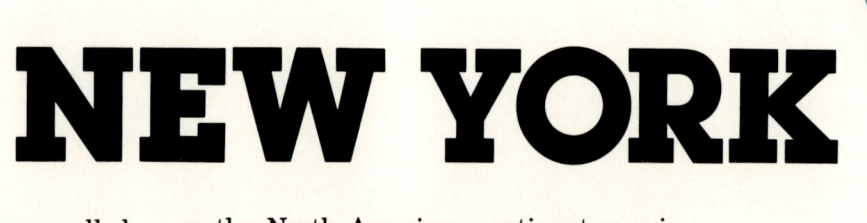

Bluebird
Rose

George Washington once called New York the "Seat of Empire"—the place from which the country would be run. The nickname stuck. So did the idea behind it: New York State is still the place where big and important decisions are made.

Most of the decisions are made in New York City. Television networks' managers there decide what we'll see on TV. The advertising agencies there decide on television commercials—and they give us ideas about what we'll buy. Clothing designers tell us what we will wear.

The great banks of New York City decide what to do with billions of dollars: Should a factory in Ohio get a loan? Should a utility company in New Hampshire get money to start work on a nuclear power plant?

At the New York Stock Exchange, people make another kind of decision: Shall I buy or sell shares in a corporation? The Stock Exchange handles about 70 percent of the shares traded in the U.S. Other New York City exchanges buy and sell such commodities (goods) as cotton, sugar, butter, cocoa, and animal hides for leather.

Another place where decisions are made is the United Nations. UN headquarters is in New York City. So, in a way, the city is the capital of the world!

Ever since our country started, New York State has led all the other states in manufacturing. New York workers couldn't have made the things they made without some source of power. They got that power from water, the natural resource that helped build the Empire State.

At first, fast-moving streams powered the flour mills and the early factories. Then people figured how waterpower could be turned into electricity. The first use of this energy on the North American continent was in New York. This form of energy is called hydroelectric power.

Water has also helped New York by giving manufacturers a way to ship goods to customers outside the state. Rivers and canals connect many parts of the state with the Atlantic Ocean, the Great Lakes, and the St. Lawrence Seaway. This transport system of canals, rivers, and lakes connects the Atlantic Ocean with the Great Lakes. Upstate cities on the lakes, such as Rochester and Buffalo, now welcome oceangoing ships from all over the world. About 25 percent of the manufactured goods exported from the United States passes through one of New York's busy ports.

Imagine a trip on New York's water highways. You begin at New York City's great harbor and sail 145 miles (233 km) up the Hudson to Albany, the capital. Your freighter can't go any farther because the river is too rocky and shallow. So you bear west on the Mohawk River, passing Schenectady, site of General Electric's first plant. It still works, making electrical equipment.

To go westward toward Buffalo by water, you must board a barge. You'll be following much of the route of the Erie Canal, a wonder when it opened in 1825.

You won't really need a barge to go from New York City to Buffalo. The New York Thruway, longest toll expressway in the world, follows the Hudson-Mohawk-Erie route. In the "population belt" around these big fertile valleys live about 85 percent of the state's people.

Even in these modern, big-city days, two-thirds of New York is covered by forests, mountains, parks, meadows, and farms. George Washington would still know his way around the Empire State.

Area: 30th largest state, 49,576 sq mi (128,401 sq km). **Population:** 17,924,000. Ranks second. **Major Cities:** New York City, 7,481,613; Buffalo, 407,160; Rochester, 267,173. **Manufacturing:** scientific instruments and clocks, clothing, textiles, household appliances, radios and TV sets, electrical equipment. **Agriculture:** dairy products, vegetables, cattle. **Mining:** cement, stone, salt. **Fishing:** shellfish. **Other Important Activities:** printing and publishing, banking and finance, tourism. **Statehood:** the 11th state. Ratified Constitution on July 26, 1788.

Map of New York State

Grid coordinates: 5, 6, 7, 8, 9, 10, 11, 12, 13, 14, 15, 16, 17, 18, 19, 20, 21, 22, 23 (columns); A, B, C, D, E, F, G, H, I, J, K, L, M, N, O, P, Q, R, S, T, U (rows)

Legend
- ★ **ALBANY** State Capital
- (81) Interstate Highway
- (219) U.S. Highway
- (23) State Highway
- Cattle
- Dairy Cows
- Poultry and Eggs
- Ducks
- Vegetables
- Fruit
- Quarries
- Manufacturing
- Shipping
- Wildlife Refuge
- Recreation

Labels on Map

The St. Lawrence Seaway connects the Great Lakes to the Atlantic Ocean

- Massena
- ST. REGIS INDIAN RESERVATION
- Ogdensburg
- Potsdam
- Plattsburgh
- Lake Champlain
- St. Lawrence River
- Thousand Islands
- Saranac Lake
- Whiteface Mountain 4,867 FEET 1,483 METERS
- Lake Placid
- Tupper Lake
- Mount Marcy 5,344 FEET 1,629 METERS Highest point in New York
- Watertown
- ADIRONDACK PARK
- ADIRONDACK MOUNTAINS
- Ticonderoga
- Lake George
- LAKE ONTARIO
- Oswego
- Glens Falls
- Oneida Lake
- Rome
- Great Sacandaga Lake
- Rochester (ERIE CANAL)
- Syracuse
- Oneida
- Utica
- Mohawk River
- Saratoga Springs
- Amsterdam
- Genesee River
- NEW YORK STATE BARGE CANAL
- Geneva
- Auburn
- ONONDAGA INDIAN RESERVATION
- NEW YORK STATE THRUWAY
- Rotterdam
- Schenectady
- Troy
- Finger Lakes — *Glaciers dug deep basins for lakes*
- APPALACHIAN MOUNTAINS
- Cooperstown
- ALBANY ★
- Hornell
- Ithaca
- Susquehanna River
- Corning
- Elmira
- Binghamton
- CATSKILL MOUNTAINS
- Hudson River
- CATSKILL PARK
- Kingston
- Hyde Park
- Poughkeepsie
- Delaware River
- Newburgh
- Middletown
- West Point
- APPALACHIAN TRAIL
- Peekskill
- New City
- LONG ISLAND SOUND
- Montauk Point
- White Plains
- Port Chester
- Yonkers
- New Rochelle
- Mount Vernon
- Glen Cove
- Riverhead
- Sag Harbor
- NEW YORK CITY
- Levittown
- Brentwood
- Deer Park
- LONG ISLAND
- Southampton
- Staten Island
- Hempstead
- Babylon
- FIRE ISLAND NATIONAL SEASHORE
- GATEWAY NATIONAL RECREATION AREA
- ATLANTIC OCEAN

United Nations *headquarters opened in New York City in 1952. UN emblem's olive branches symbolize peace.*

Scale: 0 — 120 KILOMETERS / 0 — 80 STATUTE MILES

N (compass)

Happy harvesters take home one of New York's leading crops. Others: pears, grapes, cherries, potatoes, maple syrup.

New-made paper fills a pulp warehouse in Ticonderoga, historic town on Lake Champlain. The state, a leader in papermaking and printing, publishes about 40 percent of U.S. books.

Symbols of freedom and business soar in New York's busy harbor. The Statue of Liberty, 151 feet, 1 inch (46.05 m) tall, was given to our people by the people of France in 1884. Towers of the World Trade Center rise 110 floors. Export and import firms rent most center offices.

Think of New York and you imagine skyscrapers and the Statue of Liberty. But drive through the traffic jams of Manhattan to Long Island and you can find duck farms. Or head north from the Big City and in about 4½ hours you'll be in the Big Woods—Adirondack Park, largest wilderness in the eastern United States.

State laws keep the area "forever wild," even though about 125,000 people are scattered through it. Many of them make their living off the land. Some are guides. Some work as trappers. They catch beavers, raccoons, and other furry animals, then sell the pelts. In the skyscraper state, some people still live the way their ancestors did in the days of log cabins.

Long Island ducklings waddle around a farm near Riverhead. About 6,000,000 are raised in this top duck-producing area each year.

Niagara Falls, on the Canada-New York line, spills about 4,000 bathtubs of water a second.

79

Mountain Laurel

Ruffed Grouse

PENNSYLVANIA

If a helicopter set you down somewhere in Pennsylvania, you could use your senses to figure out where you landed. Smell chocolate? You're in Hershey, home of the candy kiss. Feel fiery heat? You're in one of the steel plants in Pittsburgh. The taste of shoofly pie welcomes you to Lancaster and the land of the "Pennsylvania Dutch." The sight of the Liberty Bell tells you that you've found Philadelphia, birthplace of our independence. And the sound "Play ball!" means you've arrived in Williamsport, birthplace of Little League baseball, in time for the world series.

Pennsylvania has such a variety of people and places because of its size and geography. The state is about 300 miles (480 km) wide, from Pittsburgh on the west to Philadelphia on the east. The state's geography makes Pennsylvania the nation's link between the Northeast and the Midwest. Its rivers bear ships to the ocean, carrying Pennsylvania's many products to other parts of the world. The state also has rich farmland and huge deposits of minerals.

Pittsburgh, the "Steel City," rises where the Allegheny and Monongahela rivers come together. They form the Ohio River, which carries goods to the Mississippi River and on to the Gulf of Mexico. The hills around Pittsburgh contain billions of tons of soft, or bituminous, coal. Soft coal is easily baked into coke, the fuel for the blast furnaces in which steel is made. Pennsylvania also has plenty of limestone, another mineral used in making steel.

Iron ore arrives in Pennsylvania from other places. Canadian iron is hauled in big ore boats across the Great Lakes to Erie. South American iron ore comes by ship to Philadelphia. Railroads carry iron to the state's steelmaking cities. Pittsburgh's rival is Bethlehem, where the Bethlehem Steel Corporation plant stretches more than four miles (6.4 km) along the Lehigh River.

No river flows across the state from east to west. So railroads and highways do the job of stitching Pennsylvania together. The Pennsylvania Turnpike, which opened in 1940, became the model for toll superhighways. The turnpike paved the way for our high-speed highways: slight curves, no traffic lights, and no railroad crossings. The turnpike tunnels through Appalachian mountain ridges as it crosses the state, connecting Pennsylvania with the New Jersey and Ohio turnpikes.

If you drive on the turnpike from Philadelphia to Pittsburgh, you'll soon see a turnoff for Valley Forge. Here 3,000 of George Washington's 10,000 soldiers died in the winter of 1777-78.

At the Reading/Lancaster exit is another gateway to the past. On the back roads you'll see few telephone or power-line poles. Here live people known as the Amish. Most of them believe that God does not want them to use electricity or cars. But with mules and horses they work farms that are among the nation's most valuable.

Pennsylvania has about 60,000 farms. The crops they produce are worth about $1 billion a year. The state, though, still has wilderness. Forests and mountains cover about half the state. Ski runs and hiking trails lure families from the cities.

William Penn would be pleased. When he first saw this land he called it "Sylvania" for its beautiful woodlands. Then, when he laid out Philadelphia, he put trees in the names of the city's streets: Chestnut, Walnut, Spruce, Pine. The idea caught on, and in many other American cities tree names sprouted on street signs.

America's first successful oil well was drilled near Titusville, Pennsylvania, in 1859. It produced over 7,000 barrels a year.

Area: the 33rd largest state, 45,333 sq mi (117,412 sq km). **Population:** 11,785,000. Ranks fourth. **Major Cities:** Philadelphia, 1,815,808; Pittsburgh, 458,651; Erie, 127,895. **Manufacturing:** iron and steel, non-electrical machinery, food and food products (including pretzels and chocolate), fabricated metals, chemicals. **Mining:** anthracite and bituminous coal, cement, stone, lime, natural gas, sand and gravel, petroleum. **Agriculture:** dairy products, cattle, eggs, mushrooms, corn, vegetables, fruits. **Other Important Activities:** tourism. **Statehood:** the second state. Ratified Constitution on Dec. 12, 1787.

80

Pennsylvania

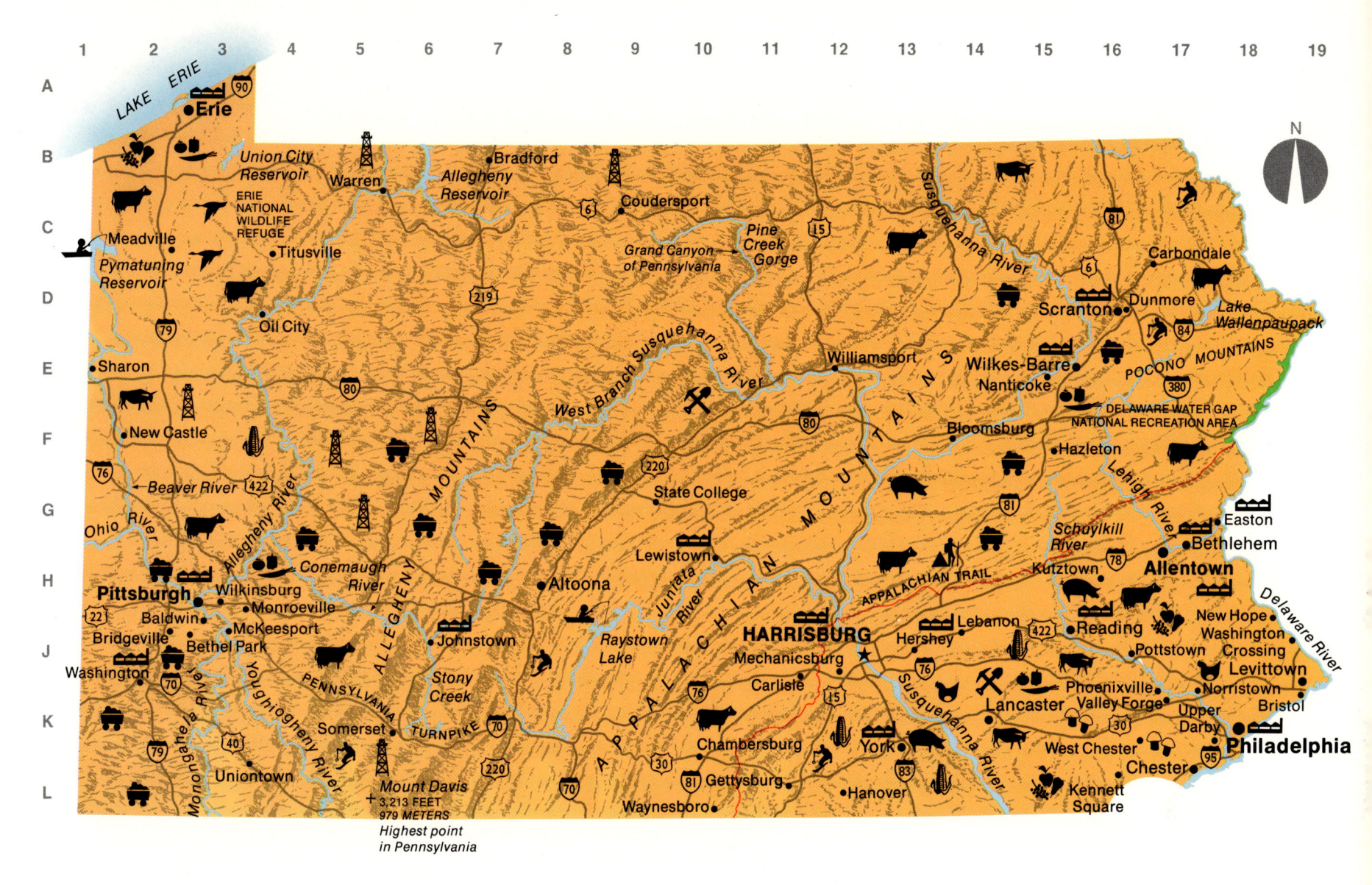

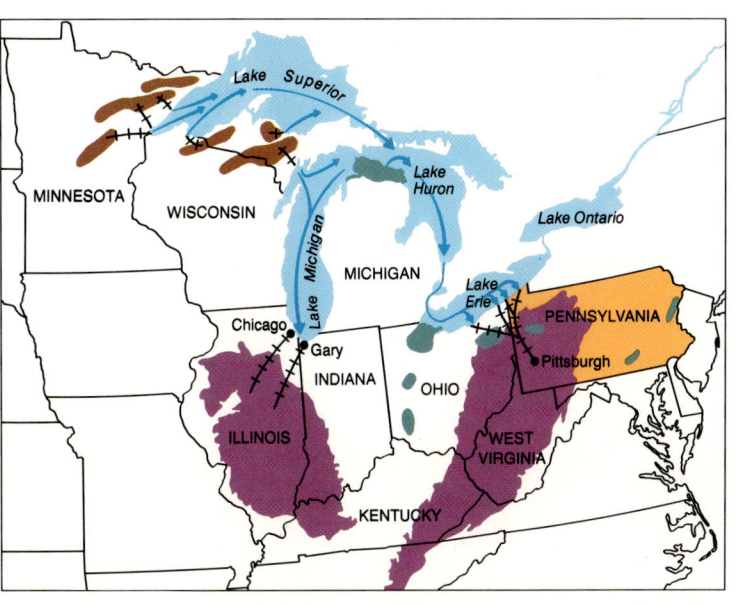

Map Grid
Columns 1–19, Rows A–L

Map Labels

Row A–B: Lake Erie, I-90, Erie

Row B: Union City Reservoir, Warren, Bradford, Allegheny Reservoir

Row C: Meadville, Erie National Wildlife Refuge, Titusville, Coudersport, Grand Canyon of Pennsylvania, Pine Creek Gorge, US-15, Susquehanna River, US-6, Carbondale

Row D: Pymatuning Reservoir, I-79, Oil City, US-219, Scranton, Dunmore, I-84, Lake Wallenpaupack

Row E: Sharon, I-80, Williamsport, Wilkes-Barre, Nanticoke, Pocono Mountains, I-380

Row F: New Castle, West Branch Susquehanna River, Bloomsburg, Hazleton, Delaware Water Gap National Recreation Area

Row G: I-76, Beaver River, US-422, State College, US-220, I-80, Lehigh River, Schuylkill River, Easton

Row H: Pittsburgh, Wilkinsburg, Allegheny River, Conemaugh River, Allegheny Mountains, Lewistown, Juniata River, Appalachian Mountains, I-81, Appalachian Trail, Kutztown, I-78, Bethlehem, Allentown

Row J: Baldwin, Monroeville, McKeesport, Altoona, Harrisburg, Hershey, Lebanon, Reading, New Hope, Washington Crossing, Delaware River

Row J–K: Bridgeville, Bethel Park, Johnstown, Raystown Lake, Mechanicsburg, Carlisle, I-76, Pottstown, Phoenixville, Valley Forge, Norristown, Levittown, Bristol

Row K: Washington, I-70, Pennsylvania Turnpike, Stony Creek, Susquehanna River, US-422, Lancaster, Upper Darby, US-30, West Chester, Chester, I-95, Philadelphia

Row L: I-79, US-40, Uniontown, Somerset, Mount Davis +3,213 FEET 979 METERS Highest point in Pennsylvania, US-220, I-70, US-30, Chambersburg, York, US-83, Hanover, Kennett Square, Monongahela River, Youghiogheny River, I-81, Gettysburg, Waynesboro

Legend

- ★ **HARRISBURG** State Capital
- Interstate Highway (I-80)
- U.S. Highway (US-30)
- Cattle
- Dairy Cows
- Hogs
- Eggs
- Corn
- Oil and Natural Gas
- Vegetables
- Mushrooms
- Fruit
- Mining
- Quarries
- Manufacturing
- Wildlife Refuge
- Recreation

Scale: 0–60 Kilometers / 0–60 Statute Miles

Inset Map

Coal (purple): Illinois, West Virginia, Kentucky, Pennsylvania
Iron ore (brown): Minnesota, Wisconsin, Michigan
Limestone (teal): Michigan, Ohio

Cities shown: Chicago, Gary, Pittsburgh

Text

Pittsburgh started as a trading post because nearby rivers gave traders a way to move their goods. Location later made Pittsburgh our leading steel city. Great Lake ore boats deliver iron and limestone; coal lies all around. Chicago and Gary, other steelmaking cities, get two of the raw materials just the way Pittsburgh does. But it has a big advantage—and so outranks the others—because its coal is in its own backyard.

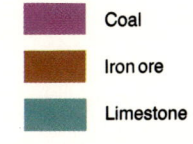

81

Some Americans choose to live in the past. They form their own communities. They keep to themselves. And they almost always have some deep belief that helps hold them together, generation after generation. The Amish, the "Plain People" of Pennsylvania, are Americans who live that way.

They trace their roots to Germans and Swiss who fled to America to practice their religion without fear. The newcomers were called the "Pennsylvania Dutch" because Americans did not correctly pronounce *Deutsch*, which means "German."

Other Pennsylvania Dutch are not plain. They call themselves "fancy." They love to dance and paint brightly colored "hex" signs on their barns. To bring good luck? Well, at least the sign painters think so.

Green pastures and golden shocks of corn surround Amish houses and barns near Lancaster. At 14, Amish children can cut back school time to do farm work.

A giant pretzel welcomes you to the Pennsylvania Dutch festival in Kutztown. Don't miss the shoofly pie: sugar and molasses in a crumb-covered shell.

Amish, in their horse and buggy and old-fashioned clothes, are showing what they believe. "Horses and hard work," one says, "keep us nearer to God."

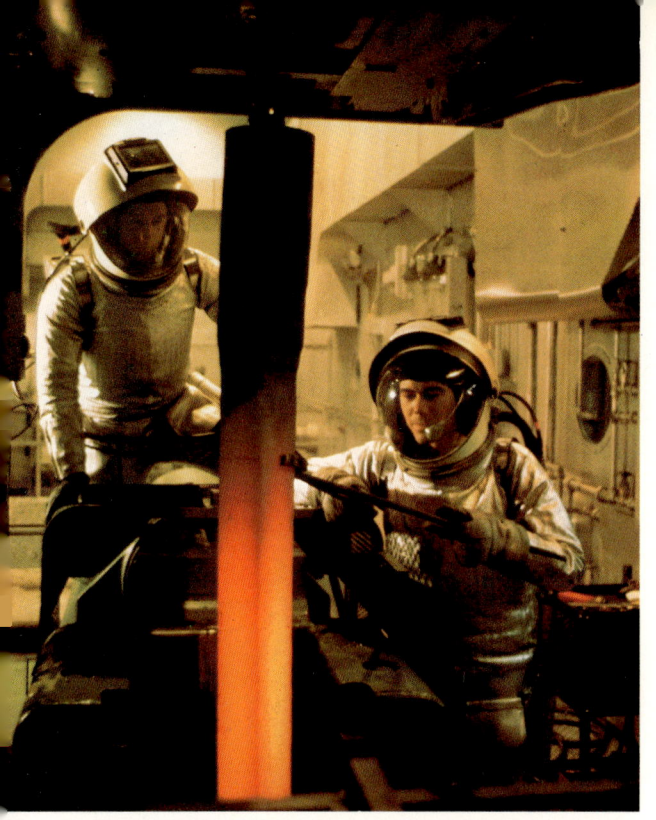

Workers handle a bar of molybdenum steel in an airless room at a Bridgeville plant. Oxygen would pollute the molten metal.

Cleaned, polished, and waiting to be stamped, penny blanks pile up at Philadelphia's Mint.

The Liberty Bell hangs at Independence Mall in Philadelphia, where it rang out the news of the Declaration of Independence. It last rang on Washington's Birthday in 1846.

Independence Hall in Philadelphia holds memories of Franklin, Jefferson—and the Declaration "that all Men are created equal...."

In brushy green waves, the peaks of the Appalachian Mountains reach northeast to southwest. In places, on the long folds of valley and ridge, you can see forests the first Indians saw. Rivers on the east side of the backbone flow to the Atlantic Ocean.

From a sandy sea rim, the coastal plain rises gradually, stepping west toward the rolling farm and forest land at the foot of the mountains.

To go westward across the wall, Indians, pioneers, and modern road builders all looked for the gaps cut by running streams. Once over, they saw wrinkled slopes, high tableland, and fertile valleys. They saw rivers rush down out of the mountains on their way west to the Mississippi.

Appalachian Highlands

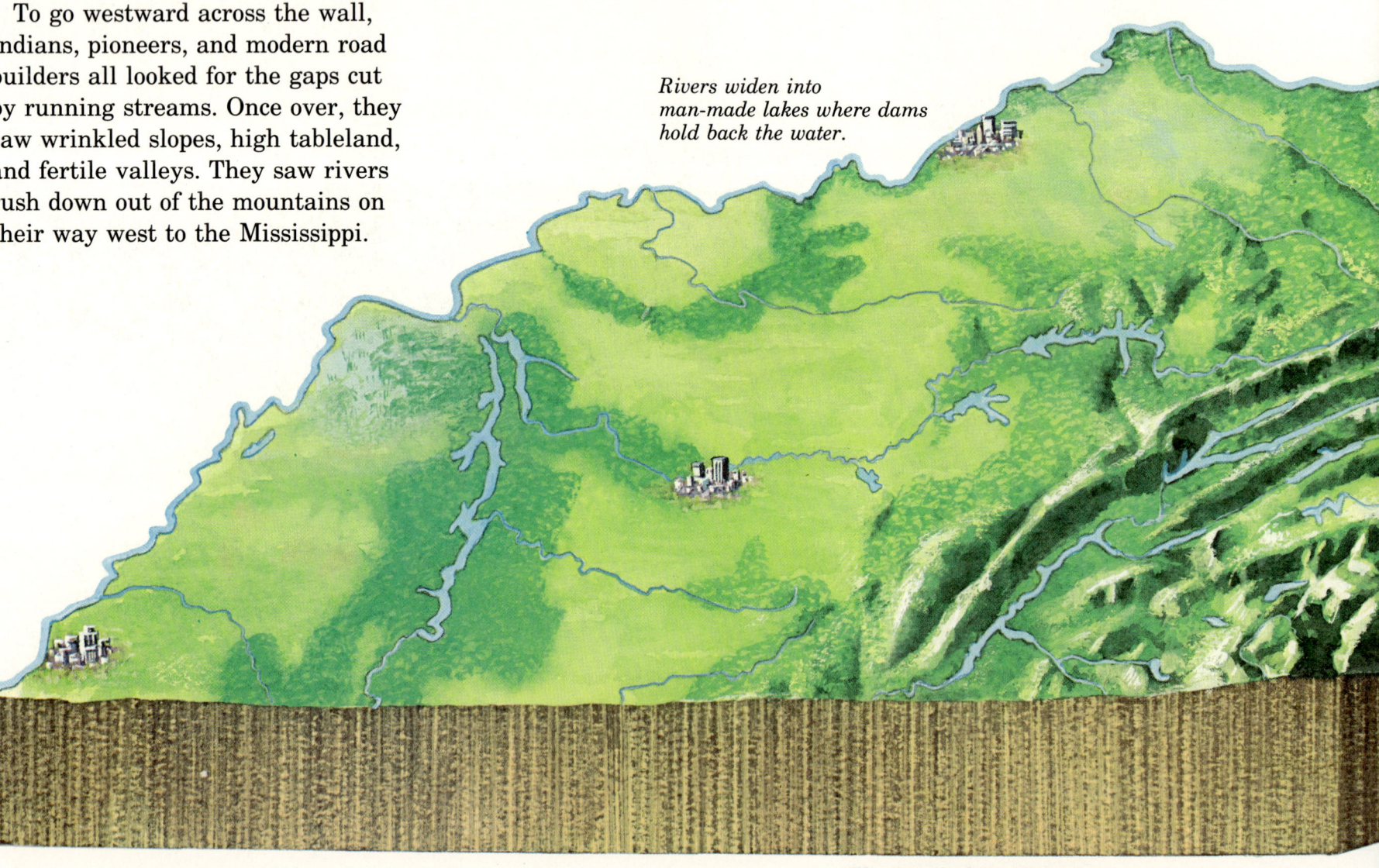

Rivers widen into man-made lakes where dams hold back the water.

The Appalachian Mountain chain—under many names—stretches from Canada to northern Alabama.

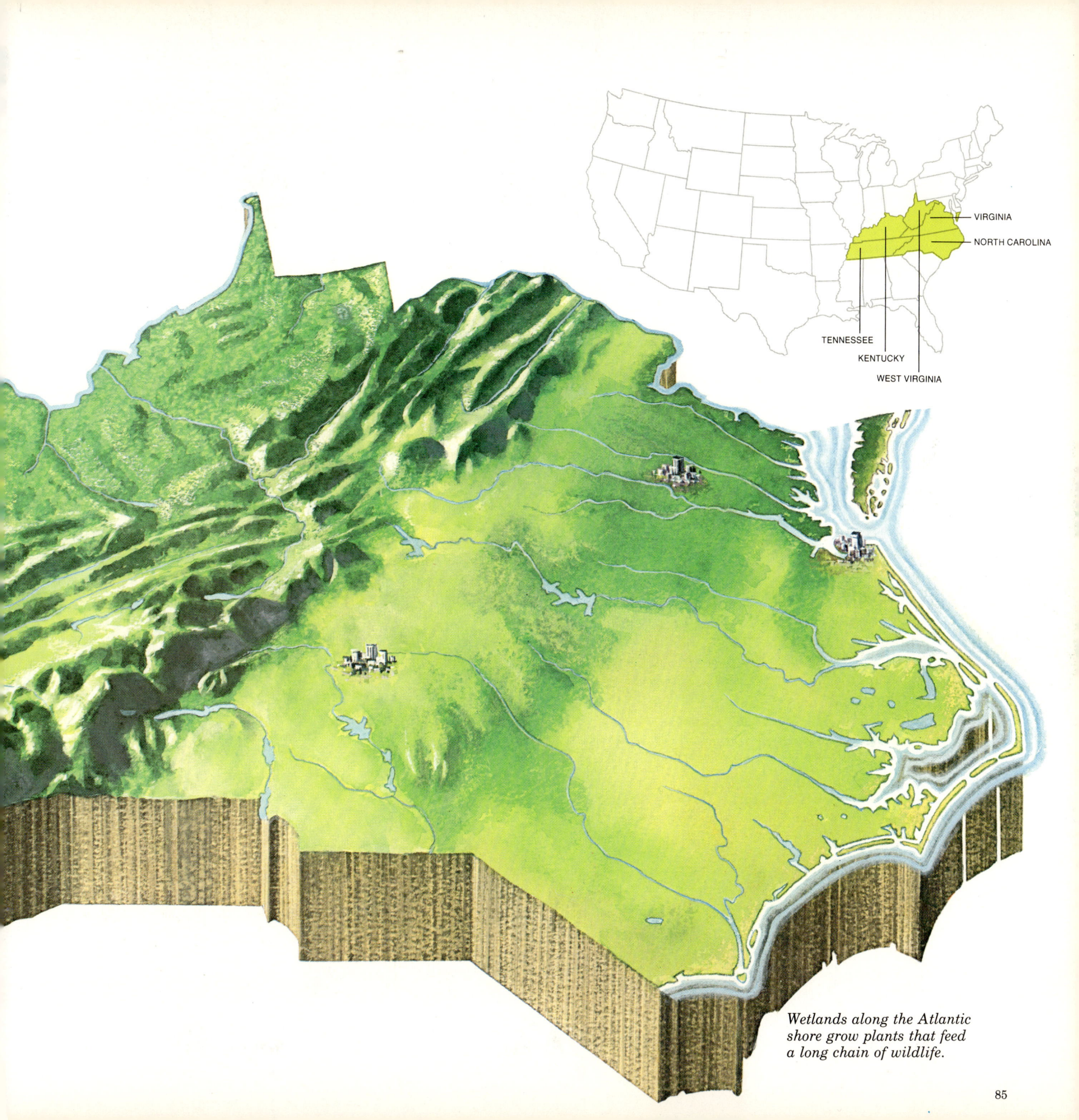

Wetlands along the Atlantic shore grow plants that feed a long chain of wildlife.

KENTUCKY

On a cool spring evening, a newborn foal takes its first, shaky steps. Soon it will romp with other Thoroughbreds in the bluegrass pastures of a Kentucky horse farm. As a three-year-old it may even run in the Kentucky Derby and wear the winner's roses.

Around Lexington, the heart of the Bluegrass country, the work of hundreds of people depends on horses. Veterinarians care for them; auctioneers sell them; grain dealers feed them; trainers and an army of grooms live with them every day.

Bluegrass isn't blue—it's green. But in May its tiny flowers give it a bluish tint. It is full of minerals from the rich deposits of limestone in the area. Seeping water puts the minerals into the soil, and grazing puts them into the bones of the horses.

Southwest of the Bluegrass country, few streams flow. Instead, rainwater sinks into the ground and slowly eats out the limestone far below the surface. Caves form. One geologist calls central Kentucky "a land of caves." Mammoth Cave, the largest one, sprawls like a giant subway system.

Eastern Kentucky and the mountainous areas of neighboring states are known as "Appalachia." The name comes from the Appalachian Mountains. Some of the pioneers who poured across these mountains came to America from western Europe. Others left homes in Virginia, the Carolinas, Maryland, and Pennsylvania. Many headed west, but some stayed in the hills and hollows, and their descendants live there today.

These independent people kept to themselves, cut off from the rest of the world. One girl who grew up in the mountains wrote that "to stand in the bottom of any of the valleys is to have the feeling of being down in the center of a great round cup."

From the great forests of oak, chestnut, and tulip poplar, mountain folk cut the logs for their houses. From cherry and walnut, they carved furniture and whittled animals. Children played with cornhusk dolls.

Many mountaineers worked deep underground in the dark tunnels of coal mines. But big machines took the place of many workers. For instance, a "continuous miner" operated by just two men can dig out 12 tons (10.9 t) of coal a minute. It scoops up loosened coal and loads it onto shuttle cars. They carry the coal to the shaft where man-sized buckets lift it to the surface.

Beginning in the 1950's, thousands of out-of-work miners and their families left Appalachia. But now the nation demands more coal for energy. There is new life in the industry. Many people who left their mountains for factory jobs in northern cities are coming home. While new houses go up in the hollows, suburbs spread around towns. All over the state factories are busy. Tobacco products are big business, and Kentucky is our leading producer of bourbon whiskey.

Kentuckians have been traders for a long time. By the early 1800's, freight traffic on the Ohio River had already made Louisville a bustling place. Then, boats going upstream or downstream stopped at Louisville because of the Falls of the Ohio, a two-mile (3.2 km) stretch of dangerous rocks and rapids. The cargo was unloaded, carried through town beyond the falls, and loaded on another boat to finish the trip.

In 1830 a canal was built around the falls. Hundreds of boats every year began carrying products north and south. The little settlement of Louisville, where the first pioneer families had listened to the howl of the wolves and the roar of the falls, grew into Kentucky's largest city.

Area: the 37th largest state, 40,395 sq mi (104,623 sq km). **Population:** 3,458,000. Ranks 23rd. **Major Cities:** Louisville, 335,954; Lexington, 186,048; Owensboro, 50,788. **Manufacturing:** machinery, electrical equipment, food products (includes whiskey), chemicals, transportation equipment, tobacco products, primary metals, fabricated metals, clothing, printing and publishing, paper and paper products, rubber products. **Mining:** coal, petroleum, stone, natural gas, sand and gravel. **Agriculture:** tobacco, beef cattle, dairy products, corn, soybeans, hogs. Also eggs and wheat. **Other Important Activities:** tourism, horse breeding. **Statehood:** the 15th state. Admitted June 1, 1792.

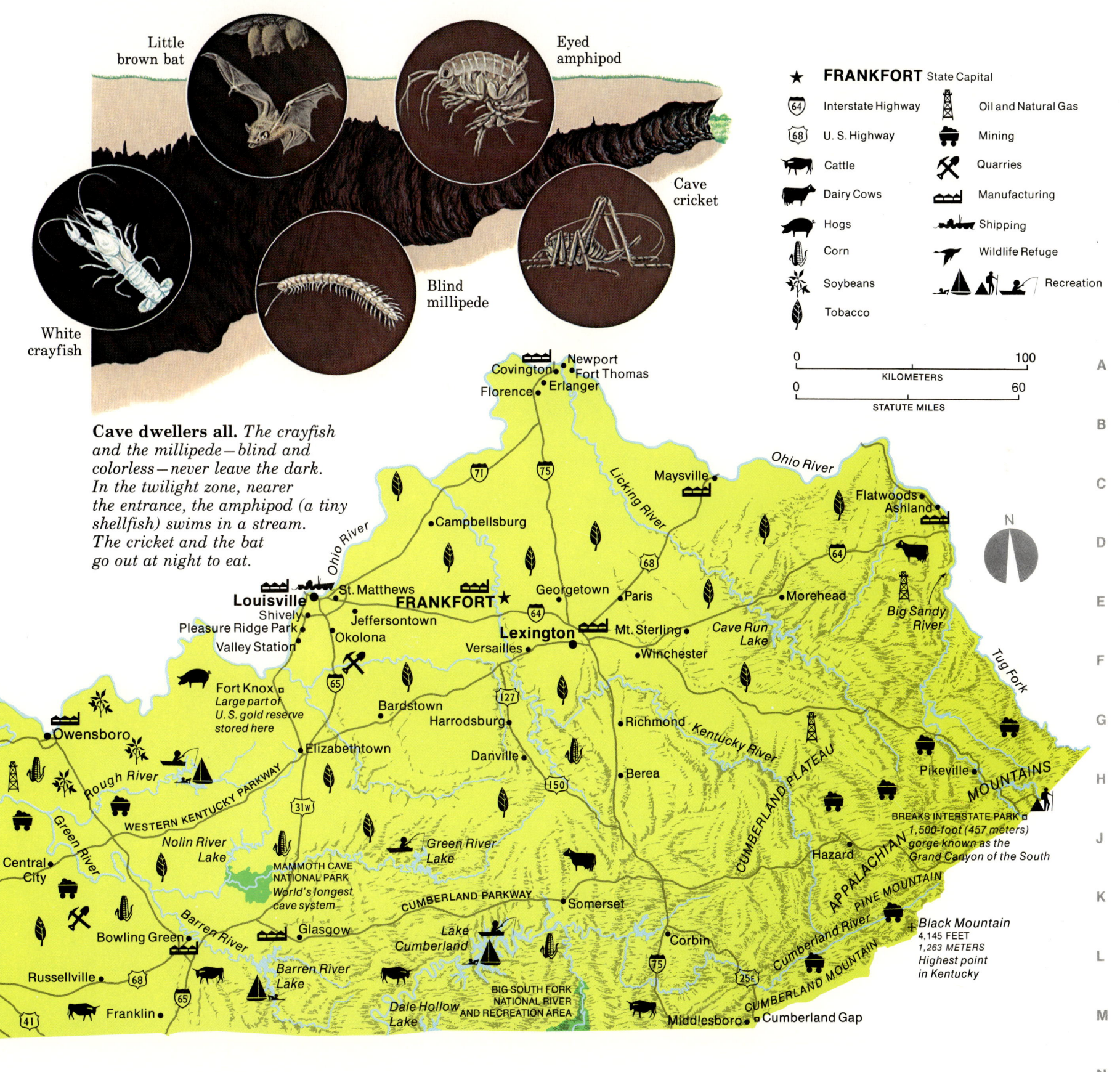

Little brown bat
Eyed amphipod
Cave cricket
Blind millipede
White crayfish

Cave dwellers all. *The crayfish and the millipede — blind and colorless — never leave the dark. In the twilight zone, nearer the entrance, the amphipod (a tiny shellfish) swims in a stream. The cricket and the bat go out at night to eat.*

★ **FRANKFORT** State Capital
- Interstate Highway
- U. S. Highway
- Cattle
- Dairy Cows
- Hogs
- Corn
- Soybeans
- Tobacco
- Oil and Natural Gas
- Mining
- Quarries
- Manufacturing
- Shipping
- Wildlife Refuge
- Recreation

0 — 100 KILOMETERS
0 — 60 STATUTE MILES

Covington, Newport, Fort Thomas, Florence, Erlanger
Maysville
Ohio River
Flatwoods, Ashland
Campbellsburg
Licking River
Louisville, St. Matthews, Shively, Pleasure Ridge Park, Valley Station, Jeffersontown, Okolona
FRANKFORT ★
Georgetown
Paris
Morehead
Big Sandy River
Lexington, Versailles, Mt. Sterling, Winchester
Cave Run Lake
Tug Fork
Fort Knox — Large part of U.S. gold reserve stored here
Bardstown
Harrodsburg
Danville
Richmond
Berea
Kentucky River
Owensboro
Rough River
Elizabethtown
Pikeville
CUMBERLAND PLATEAU
APPALACHIAN MOUNTAINS
WESTERN KENTUCKY PARKWAY
Green River
Nolin River Lake
MAMMOTH CAVE NATIONAL PARK — World's longest cave system
Green River Lake
Hazard
BREAKS INTERSTATE PARK — 1,500-foot (457 meters) gorge known as the Grand Canyon of the South
Central City
CUMBERLAND PARKWAY
Somerset
PINE MOUNTAIN
Black Mountain 4,145 FEET 1,263 METERS Highest point in Kentucky
Bowling Green
Barren River
Glasgow
Lake Cumberland
Corbin
Cumberland River
CUMBERLAND MOUNTAIN
Russellville
Barren River Lake
Dale Hollow Lake
BIG SOUTH FORK NATIONAL RIVER AND RECREATION AREA
Middlesboro, Cumberland Gap
Franklin

Busy as bees, kids on a shade-covered wagon pollinate tobacco flowers by hand to produce hybrid seed.

Like a flag unfurled, bars of soil and early spring grass ripple across a farmer's hillside near Lexington. Strip plowing helps prevent erosion.

Tight squeeze tickles a caver. A scramble in Mammoth Cave may require head lamps, hard hats, and kneepads.

Playful yearlings frisk across a sun-dappled pasture in the Bluegrass region. Kentucky has more than 350 Thoroughbred horse farms.

Hidden treasure, buried 300 million years ago, underlies nearly half of Kentucky. It isn't gold—it's coal. Coal began to form when swamp plants died. As the plants decayed, heat and pressure from deposits of mud and sand slowly dried and hardened them into coal.

Bituminous, or soft, coal formed in neat horizontal beds near the earth's surface. Where the earth's crust folded, the beds were upended and pressed further. Anthracite, or hard coal, resulted. Its oddly-angled seams thrust deep into the earth, making it difficult to mine. Soft coal has more pollutants than hard coal, but it is plentiful and easier to mine. To an energy-hungry nation, coal is as good as gold.

Scrappy raccoon fights to keep his log perch during coon dog trials.

Rock layers record earth's ancient history. Black coal shows where swamps existed. Crumbly shale is mud squeezed dry. Red sandstone was delta sand.

NORTH CAROLINA

From its fringe of sandy beaches on the east to its towering mountain border on the west, North Carolina is a wide state. Across its 503-mile (809 km) stretch, different climates and soils create a great variety of plant communities—natural combinations of plants suited to a particular place. Near Wilmington, on a pleasant January afternoon, you can stroll under palm trees and admire moss-draped live oaks hundreds of years old. At the same time of year, in the Great Smoky Mountains, you trudge along a snowy trail and sniff the fragrant spruce on some of the highest peaks of eastern North America.

North Carolina farmers profit from the variety of growing conditions because they can grow many kinds of crops. Sweet potatoes and soybeans grow well in the coastal plain. Peach orchards do best on the rolling hills of the piedmont. Farmers grow one kind of tobacco in the eastern part of the state and another in the mountains where the air is cooler. Tobacco used to bring more than half North Carolina's agricultural income. Now its share has fallen to one-third, and growers are faced with scientists' warnings that smoking is harmful to health.

Late summer means harvest on a tobacco farm. By machine or by hand, workers strip huge leaves from stalks that may stand taller than a man. The leaves then hang in heated barns, where several days of "curing" improves their taste and smell. Soon it's time to sell the crop. Off to market it goes.

To the ears of a tobacco farmer, nothing is more pleasant than the hubbub of a market town at auction time. The rafters of the big tobacco warehouses ring to the singsong chatter of the auctioneer as he sells the bundles of "brown gold" to export dealers and buyers from cigarette factories.

North Carolina has the nation's fifth largest farm population, but it is also a busy industrial state. Many factories are spread across the state in medium-sized towns instead of being concentrated in a few large cities. In fact, North Carolina has no really large cities. About half of North Carolina's farmers also work at jobs off the farm. They do their plowing, milking, and other chores outside working hours and on weekends.

North Carolina manufactures more tobacco products than all the other states together, but the textile industry has long been the state's biggest money-maker. Once nearly every small town in the piedmont had a mill to knit or weave cloth. Most of the mills are still at work. In Greensboro the largest denim mill in the world turns out enough denim each year to wrap twice around the globe.

From pioneer skills grew a furniture industry now first in the nation. Wood—the raw material—once grew abundantly in coastal and western forests. Now it's bought from many places. Upholstery comes from nearby textile mills. From other piedmont factories, furniture makers get glue, paint, mirrors. Furniture buyers from around the country and the world come to factory towns such as High Point and Hickory.

But life in North Carolina is not all tobacco, textiles, and furniture. Within an area known as the Research Triangle—between the University of North Carolina in Chapel Hill, Duke University in Durham, and North Carolina State University in Raleigh—almost 5,000 scientists are at work. They study problems related to the industrial development of North Carolina and the rest of the South. Laboratories there conduct research in forestry, in the chemistry of synthetic fibers, in computer technology, and in health and medicine.

Area: the 28th largest state, 52,712 sq mi (136,560 sq km). **Population:** 5,525,000. Ranks 11th. **Major Cities:** Charlotte, 281,417; Greensboro, 155,848; Winston-Salem, 141,018. **Manufacturing:** textiles, tobacco products, chemicals, machinery, furniture, food products, electrical equipment, clothing, paper, fabricated metals, lumber and wood products. **Agriculture:** tobacco, poultry, hogs, corn, dairy products, soybeans. Also eggs, peanuts. **Mining:** stone, phosphate rock, sand and gravel. **Other Important Activities:** tourism, fishing. **Statehood:** the 12th state. Ratified the Constitution on Nov. 21, 1789.

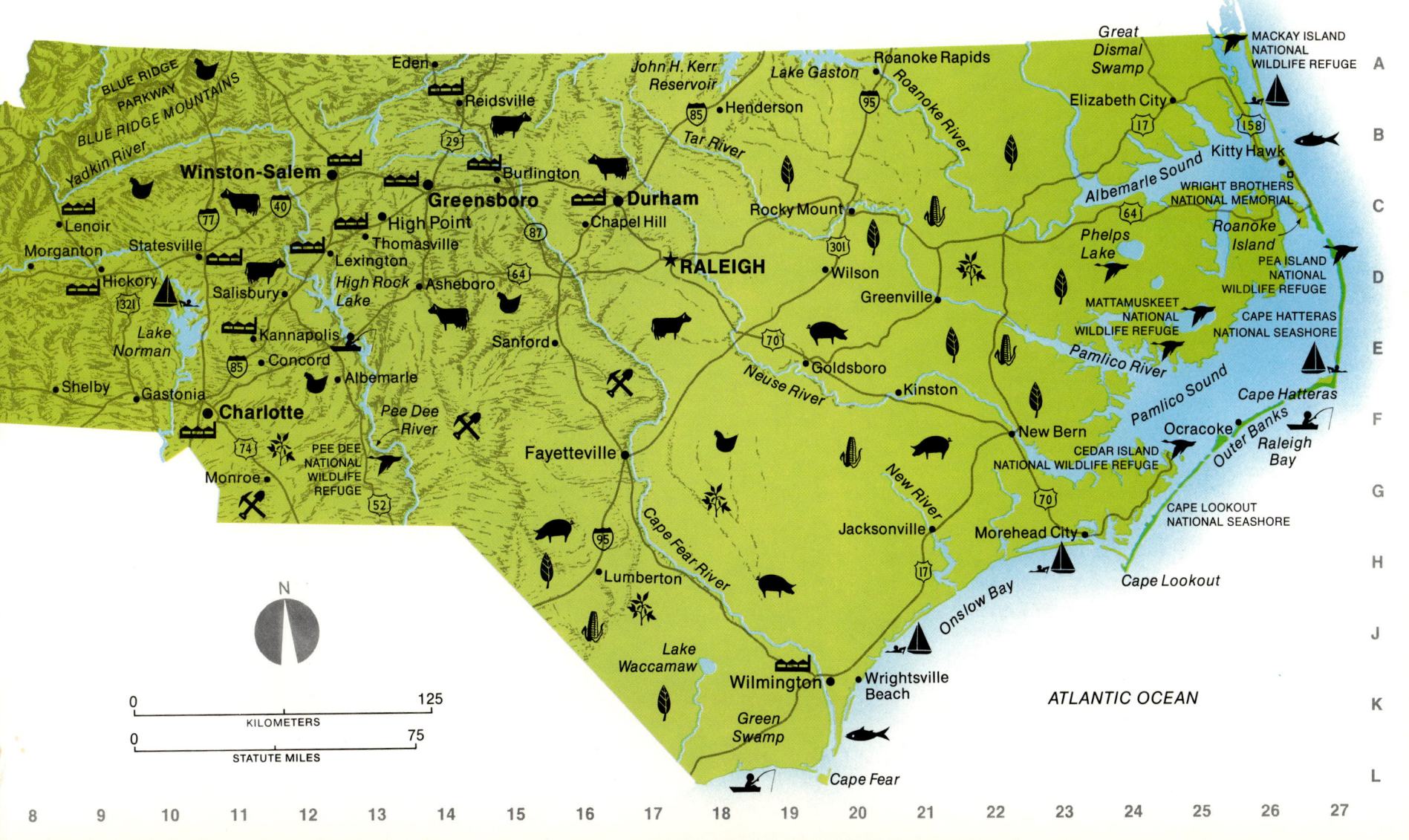

Man flies! *Orville and Wilbur Wright changed our lives forever. On December 17, 1903, their flying machine stayed aloft for 12 seconds above the sands at Kitty Hawk, North Carolina.*

Legend

- ★ **RALEIGH** State Capital
- (40) Interstate Highway
- (70) U.S. Highway
- (87) State Highway
- Dairy Cows
- Hogs
- Poultry
- Corn
- Soybeans
- Tobacco
- Fishing
- Quarries
- Manufacturing
- Wildlife Refuge
- Recreation

No headstones mark the "Graveyard of the Atlantic." Instead, broken hulls and rotting timbers dot the Outer Banks. Some 700 vessels—sailing ships, steamers, even submarines—have foundered off these hazardous islands.

Wind and waves continually reshape this sandy chain. Storms can cut an island in two overnight. Shorelines change so fast that charts can't keep up. Before radar, only lighthouses and foghorns warned of danger.

Most sailors fear the Banks, but pirate Edward Teach—Blackbeard—used them as a hideout. He terrorized Carolina ships. The British killed him on Pamlico Sound in 1718, but his treasure was never found.

Rainy-day hikers in the Great Smokies find the Appalachian Trail leads to wet feet.

Buyers trail a roving auctioneer to bid for stacks of tobacco at a warehouse in Wilson. North Carolina grows 43 percent of the U.S. tobacco crop. Nearly all of it goes up in smoke.

A Smokies trademark, black bears also roam near the coast.

Newly spun rayon threads pass inspection at a factory in Enka. North Carolina has more than 1,150 textile plants.

The lighthouse at Cape Hatteras is the nation's tallest. Visitors climb 257 steps to the balcony.

Like a sheltering arm, the barrier islands of the Outer Banks wrap around the coast, protecting the mainland from the Atlantic.

Laughing gulls, named for their chuckling calls, wait for the ferry at Ocracoke.

TENNESSEE

Climb the Great Smokies and hike on west. You'll come down in East Tennessee. As you journey over thickly wooded hills and past lonely houses, someplace deep in a hollow your ear may catch the twang of a mountain fiddle. At the same time, in a city near the middle of the state, a famous singer steps before an audience to belt out a country western hit. And in West Tennessee, near the Mississippi River, a jazz group plays the mournful "Memphis Blues."

Tennesseans see their state in thirds: East, Middle, and West. East Tennesseans live in the Appalachian Mountains. Small isolated farms contrast with the factories and shopping centers of cities such as Knoxville and Kingsport. East Tennessee has Oak Ridge, an "atomic city." In the 1940's, during World War II, our government needed a place to produce uranium for atomic bombs. They chose these sparsely settled mountains because nearby Norris Dam gave them a source of electric power. A nuclear plant, laboratories, and a new town sprang up almost overnight, all top secret—young strangers amid the proud old mountain culture. Today, Oak Ridge scientists, once known for destruction, study peaceful uses for nuclear energy.

A coal-bearing area lies under about half of eastern Tennessee, much of it close to the surface of the ground. The simplest way to get it out is strip mining—huge machines strip earth and rock off the coal and then blast it out and dig it with power shovels. Big parts of East Tennessee bear ugly scars from old strip mines, which still cause erosion and polluted streams. But now, new laws protect the land. Coal companies must put it back into usable, attractive shape.

To Middle Tennesseans, home is a land of rolling pasture for cattle and fine horses, of tobacco fields, of 150-year-old plantation homes, of little towns and family farms. The Tennessee River loops around the whole region. In its heart, Nashville nestles in a fertile, bowl-shaped valley.

Both Middle and West Tennessee have ties to the South of the days before the Civil War. (Eastern mountaineers stayed loyal to the Union.) Both Middle and West, until the mid-20th century, depended on agriculture. Now it's industry, but in West Tennessee cotton still grows on huge, plantation-like farms. The land is flat and slopes gently to bluffs overlooking the swampy lowlands along the Mississippi. Here on the bluffs sits Memphis, Tennessee's largest city.

In 1811, when western Tennessee was mostly Chickasaw Indian land, violent earthquakes raged there. Before terrified settlers, the ground rose and fell like a sea. Great cracks tore it open. Hillsides crashed into the Mississippi River. The water surged back and forth, thick with uprooted trees. Pieces of land sank, making long, narrow holes. In rushed the swirling river to fill them up. One of these earthquake-born areas is Reelfoot Lake. A few years later, when Davy Crockett went hunting around there, he called it the "Shakes Country."

East, Middle, West. They're different geographically, they're different culturally. But they all love music. Field hands sang as the sun beat down: "Cotton needs pickin' so bad, I'm gonna pick all over this world." Mountain pioneers sang about their troubles and about the animals in their woods. They poked fun at themselves with words like "Groundhog gravy all over my chin." Such songs began the country music that now makes Nashville famous.

Area: the 34th largest state, 42,244 sq mi (109,411 sq km). **Population:** 4,299,000. Ranks 17th. **Major Cities:** Memphis, 661,319; Nashville, 423,426; Knoxville, 183,383. **Manufacturing:** chemicals, food products, machinery, clothing, electrical equipment and supplies, fabricated metals, paper and paper products, transportation equipment, rubber products, printing and publishing, primary metals. **Agriculture:** beef cattle, soybeans, dairy products, tobacco, hogs, cotton, eggs, poultry. Also corn. **Mining:** coal, stone, zinc, cement, sand and gravel, phosphate rock. **Other Important Activities:** fishing; country, folk, and western music. **Statehood:** the 16th state. Admitted June 1, 1796.

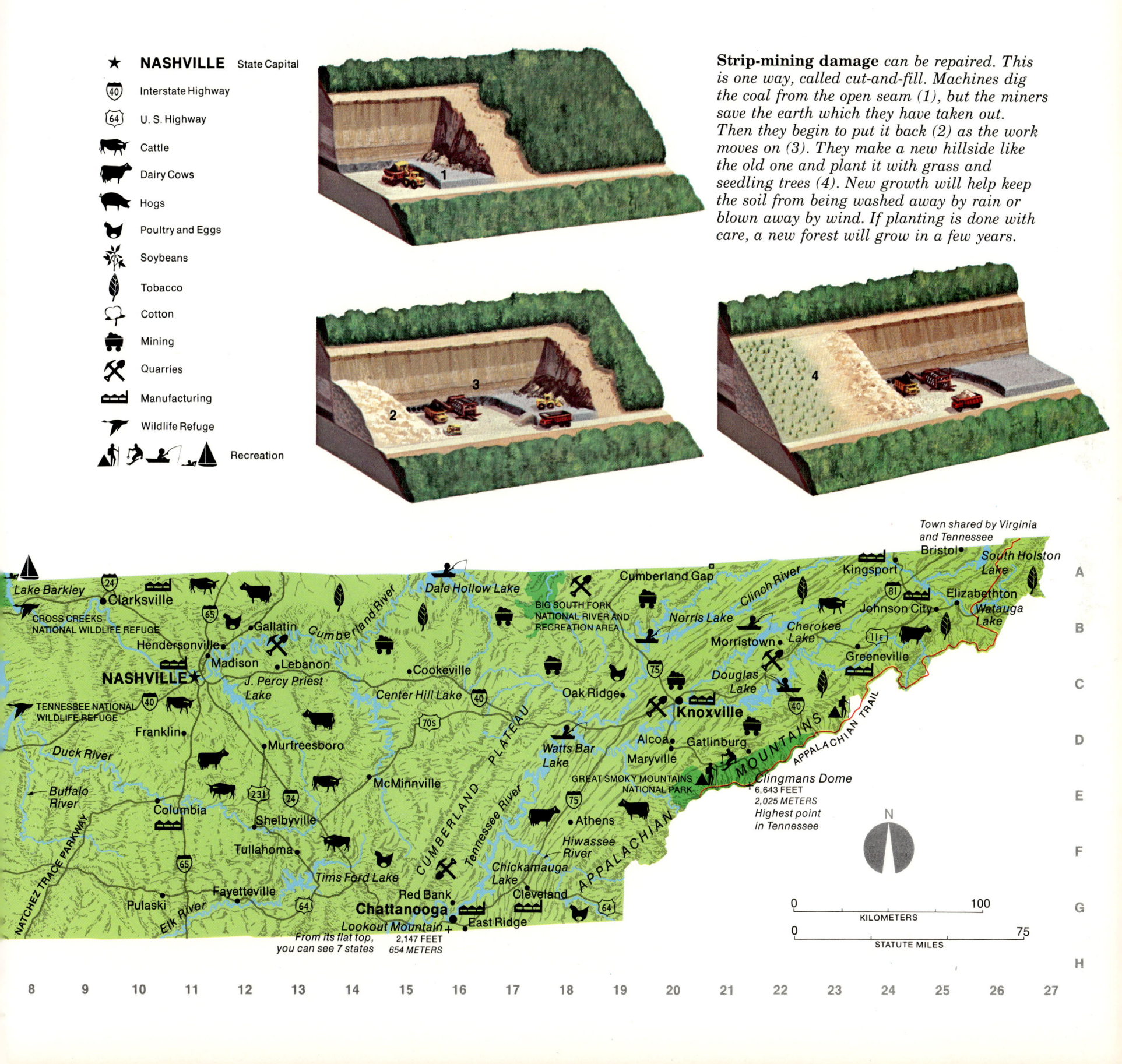

★ **NASHVILLE** State Capital
🛣(40) Interstate Highway
🛣(64) U. S. Highway
🐄 Cattle
🐄 Dairy Cows
🐖 Hogs
🐓 Poultry and Eggs
🌱 Soybeans
🍃 Tobacco
☁ Cotton
⛏ Mining
⚒ Quarries
🏭 Manufacturing
🦅 Wildlife Refuge
⛺🎿🛶🎣⛵ Recreation

Strip-mining damage *can be repaired. This is one way, called cut-and-fill. Machines dig the coal from the open seam (1), but the miners save the earth which they have taken out. Then they begin to put it back (2) as the work moves on (3). They make a new hillside like the old one and plant it with grass and seedling trees (4). New growth will help keep the soil from being washed away by rain or blown away by wind. If planting is done with care, a new forest will grow in a few years.*

Town shared by Virginia and Tennessee

Clingmans Dome 6,643 FEET 2,025 METERS Highest point in Tennessee

From its flat top, you can see 7 states
Lookout Mountain 2,147 FEET 654 METERS

0 — 100 KILOMETERS
0 — 75 STATUTE MILES

In March 1867 a steamboat chugged down Chattanooga's main street. Water buried the city 28 feet (9 m) deep. The wild Tennessee River had flooded again. Finally, in the 1930's and 1940's the Tennessee Valley Authority—TVA—tamed the river and brought electricity to its valley. Today 34 major dams on the Tennessee and its tributaries act as brakes.

TVA engineers study rainfall and the amount of water flowing down from the mountains. If a flood threatens, they can close upriver dams to hold the water while they drain the lakes farther down to make room. The flood crest is delayed and lowered. And valley residents sleep a lot better.

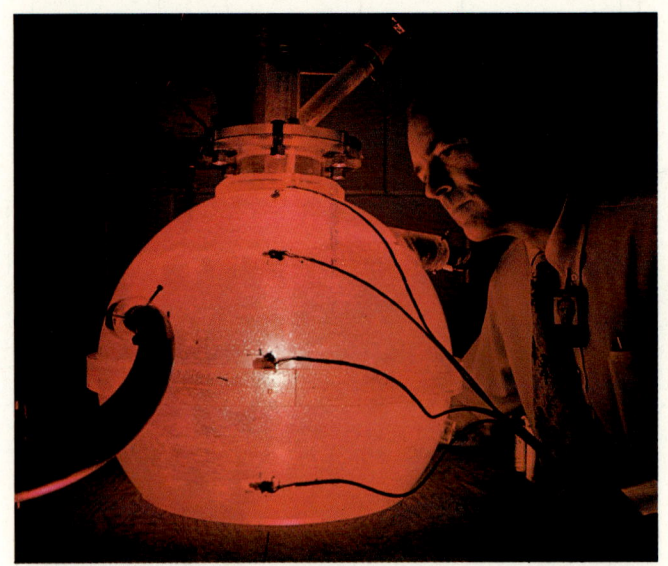

At Oak Ridge National Laboratory, scientists develop a new form of nuclear energy to make electricity.

Shivers go with the showers at Grotto Falls in the Smokies.

Ernest Tubb performs at the Grand Ole Opry. Country music is big business in Nashville.

Lightning rips the sky over downtown Memphis as car lights streak along the Mississippi River. This busy port is the nation's largest trading center for cotton and hardwood lumber.

Rebel guns on Lookout Mountain helped trap Union troops in Chattanooga during the Civil War. Unable to receive supplies, Union soldiers starved until General Grant broke the siege.

Created by TVA dams, a maze of lakes spreads over seven states. Really reservoirs, the 28 "Great Lakes of the South" and their rivers delight outdoorsmen. When dam engineers lower the level of lakes like Norris (below), streams rise, drawing canoeists. Fishermen know trout bite better when dams are closed and rivers low.

VIRGINIA

Gulls wheel in the sky over Assateague Island, at the northern tip of Virginia's Eastern Shore. Small herds of wild ponies gallop in and out of the piney woods and graze on the marsh grass along the beach. A boy and girl stroll across the sand, watching for an otter to pop its head from a pool.

From northern Virginia, office workers stream across the Potomac River into Washington, D. C. Twice a day they make the trip, to or from high-rise apartments or suburban houses in Arlington, Alexandria, or Fairfax. Some commuters live in Reston, a planned "new town" 18 miles (29 km) from the nation's capital. Here children walk to school without crossing streets.

Virginians follow different ways of life, but as they go to work or to school they find their heritage all around them. George Washington's "hometown" was Alexandria, a few miles north of Mount Vernon. He too was a commuter, between his country home and his town house. As an army officer he drilled his troops in the Alexandria streets. Near Roanoke, the great black leader Booker T. Washington was born a slave. He studied and taught at Hampton Institute. In Richmond worshipers still attend St. John's Church, where Patrick Henry cried out, "Give me liberty or give me death!"

Virginia was settled early because of its natural harbors, moderate climate, and fertile soil. Four rivers—the Potomac, Rappahannock, York, and James—empty into a huge waterway, Chesapeake Bay. The flat coastal plain is called the Tidewater region, because ocean tides ebb and flow in the rivers. Settlers cleared land here and planted tobacco which they sold in England. Some wealthy planters built mansions of brick made from the red clay soil.

Where the James River meets the bay is the harbor of Hampton Roads. It got its name from an old meaning of *road:* a sheltered body of water where ships can *ride* at anchor. Hampton, Newport News, Portsmouth, and Norfolk export coal, tobacco, and other goods—in all, about 15 percent of United States exports. The U. S. Navy installation at Norfolk is the largest naval base in the country. In the Newport News shipyards, workers build everything from tugs to missile-launching submarines.

Across the bay is the Delmarva Peninsula, the Eastern Shore. Many people here make their living raising food for the cities. Once a trip to the Eastern Shore meant a long ferry ride. But in 1964 the Chesapeake Bay Bridge-Tunnel opened to carry cars over the water and under shipping lanes. When you leave Norfolk by the bridge-tunnel, you are only a few miles from Cape Henry. That's where the first permanent English settlers in the New World landed in April 1607 on their way to Jamestown.

South of the James River, near Smithfield, peanuts and soybeans thrive on the coastal plain. Many farmers also tend small woodlots of loblolly pine. They sell their wood to mills that grind it into pulp for paper or rayon. The first rayon factory in the country opened in Roanoke in 1917, and today the world's largest is in Front Royal.

Near Front Royal is a gateway to yet another Virginia—the Shenandoah National Park. Millions of Americans every year seek out Shenandoah's mountains and valleys. On Skyline Drive they follow the ridge through the forests. They hike trails into the hollows and camp near the streams of Shenandoah's "gentle wilderness." A haven of peace and natural beauty, the park was a gift, in 1935, from Virginians to the nation.

Area: the 36th largest state, 40,815 sq mi (105,738 sq km). **Population:** 5,135,000. Ranks 13th. **Major Cities:** Norfolk, 286,694; Richmond, 232,652; Virginia Beach, 213,954. **Manufacturing:** chemicals, tobacco products, food products, textiles, electrical equipment, paper and paper products, fabricated metals. **Mining:** coal, stone, lime, sand and gravel, zinc, natural gas. **Agriculture:** dairy products, tobacco, beef cattle, broilers, hogs, corn, peanuts, eggs. Also soybeans, apples. **Other Important Activities:** tourism, fishing (menhaden and shellfish). **Statehood:** the 10th state. Ratified Constitution on June 25, 1788.

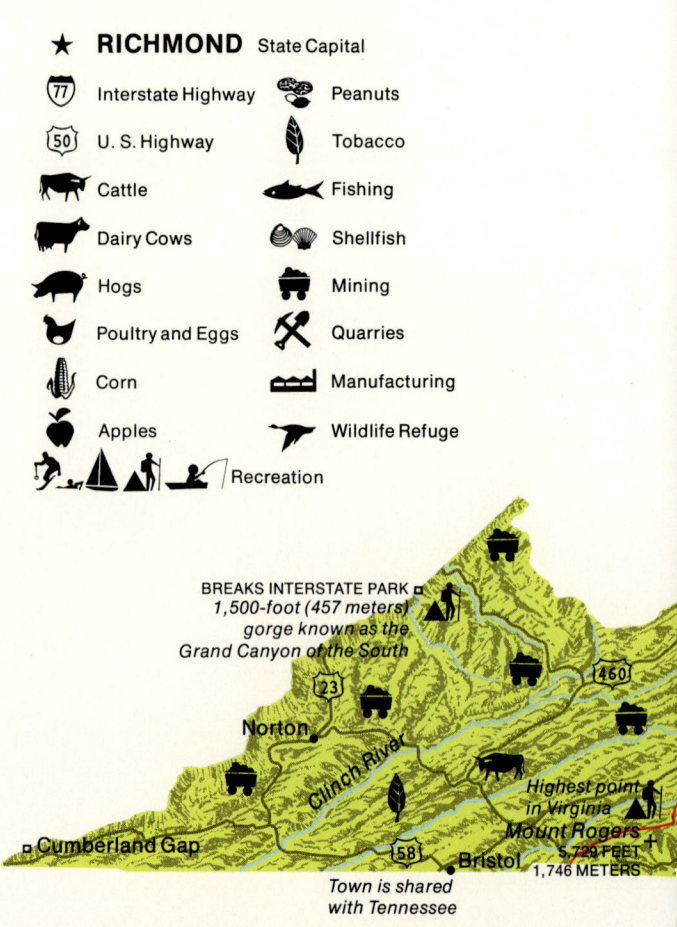

★ **RICHMOND** State Capital
- Interstate Highway
- U. S. Highway
- Cattle
- Dairy Cows
- Hogs
- Poultry and Eggs
- Corn
- Apples
- Peanuts
- Tobacco
- Fishing
- Shellfish
- Mining
- Quarries
- Manufacturing
- Wildlife Refuge
- Recreation

BREAKS INTERSTATE PARK
1,500-foot (457 meters) gorge known as the Grand Canyon of the South

Norton

Cumberland Gap

Clinch River

Bristol

Highest point in Virginia
Mount Rogers
5,729 FEET
1,746 METERS

Town is shared with Tennessee

Witch hazel for soothing lotion

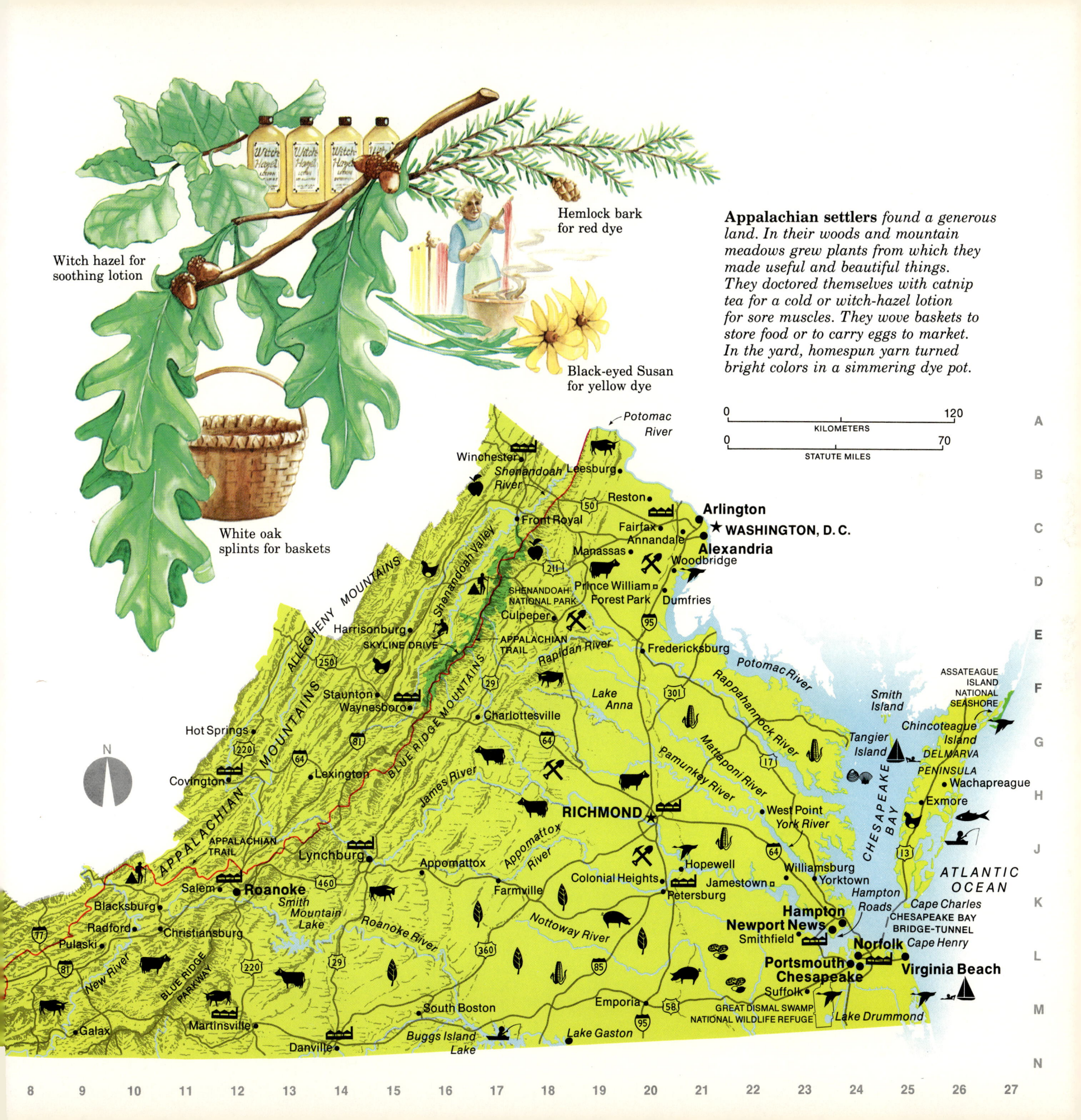

Hemlock bark for red dye

Black-eyed Susan for yellow dye

White oak splints for baskets

Appalachian settlers *found a generous land. In their woods and mountain meadows grew plants from which they made useful and beautiful things. They doctored themselves with catnip tea for a cold or witch-hazel lotion for sore muscles. They wove baskets to store food or to carry eggs to market. In the yard, homespun yarn turned bright colors in a simmering dye pot.*

0 120
KILOMETERS
0 70
STATUTE MILES

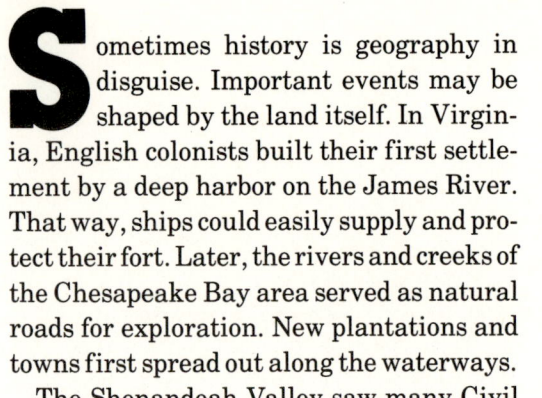

Sometimes history is geography in disguise. Important events may be shaped by the land itself. In Virginia, English colonists built their first settlement by a deep harbor on the James River. That way, ships could easily supply and protect their fort. Later, the rivers and creeks of the Chesapeake Bay area served as natural roads for exploration. New plantations and towns first spread out along the waterways.

The Shenandoah Valley saw many Civil War battles. Both sides wanted control over it because it gave the South a good route for invading Washington, D. C.

Mountains, rivers, and valleys are shown on maps. To understand a history book, sometimes it helps to read a map.

Mountain of flavor from a valley of mist, these apples will be milled for vinegar. The fertile Shenandoah Valley produces half of Virginia's apples.

Tiny ships like these moored at Jamestown brought English colonists across the Atlantic to the New World in 1607.

"Up periscope!" A heron chick peers from a nest near Wachapreague. Only four weeks old, it can't fly yet. Instead, it hops from bush to bush and practices flapping its wings. It will soon learn to stalk the marsh as its parents do, snatching small fish to eat.

Patriots on parade recall the sights and sounds of colonial days in Williamsburg.

Men use a saw to trim logs at James Fort, a copy of the colonists' first camp. Settlers built huts of sticks and mud.

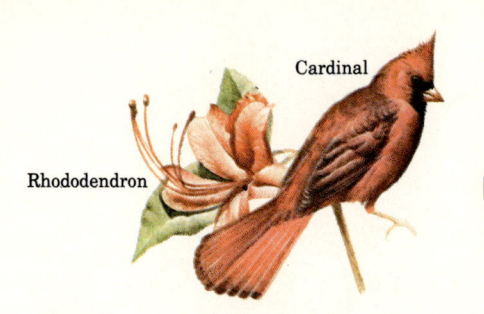

WEST VIRGINIA

In mountainous West Virginia, they tell a story about a farmer who farmed on a hillside so steep that he kept falling out of his cornfield. And—if you can believe it—his neighbor had an orchard that went straight up the mountain behind his house. At harvest time, he just shook the trees, and ripe apples rolled right into the cellar. Between the mountains are valleys so narrow that people say the dogs there wag their tails up and down.

The truth is that except for river valleys, West Virginia has almost no flat land. The state has two panhandles and a border that mostly winds like a snake, along rivers and up and down mountains. At one point the state is less than five miles (8 km) wide, but, all in all, it stretches farther south than Richmond, Virginia; farther north than Pittsburgh, Pennsylvania; farther east than Buffalo, New York; and farther west than Port Huron, Michigan.

Once a little part of West Virginia was a bathtub for George Washington. You can see it if you go to Berkeley Springs in the eastern panhandle. Here, warm water gushes from several spots at the foot of a mountain. These mineral springs became famous for their healthful qualities. To Indians they were sacred places. Even warring tribes put aside their weapons to sit together in the comforting pools and soothe their aching joints. During colonial days Berkeley Springs was a fashionable resort. Ladies and gentlemen took turns bathing in the warm springs behind a screen of evergreens. And George Washington soaked in a natural stone hollow—his own private tub.

Big old houses in eastern West Virginia may remind you of Tidewater Virginia. Six mansions in the Charles Town area were built by Washington kin. In one, the family still lives—descendants of settlers who came here some 200 years ago. Other settlers who went farther west founded towns that today depend on trade and manufacturing and on the coal mines.

The most productive bituminous coal beds in the United States lie beneath parts of West Virginia and Kentucky. But machines have taken over more than half the jobs that West Virginia miners once held. Now more West Virginians work in industry than in the mines or hillside farms and apple orchards. Factories and cities dot the valleys of the Ohio and Kanawha rivers in the west and the Monongahela in the north. Factories in Beckley make coal-mining machinery.

A steel company in Weirton is the largest single employer in West Virginia. Here, as in many places in the country, steel is made in new clean-burning basic oxygen furnaces instead of by the old pollution-producing open-hearth method. West Virginia's glass industry grew because the state has plenty of fine silica sand, with natural gas to fuel the furnaces. Some factories specialize in hand-blown glass. Others make plate glass, tubing, and building blocks.

City-dwelling West Virginians head for the woods on weekends. They hunt and fish and climb challenging rock formations. They run the wild rapids of rivers such as the Cheat and the New—which isn't new at all. (Many millions of years ago, a river flowed in the same bed.)

Before the Civil War there was no West Virginia. The state of Virginia went all the way to the Ohio River. But the people in the western counties wanted to support the Union. They separated from Virginia, and in 1863 at the height of the war West Virginia became a state.

Knuckle down! Shoot for keeps. All the marbles you win, if they were made in the United States, came from West Virginia.

Area: the 41st largest state, 24,181 sq mi (62,628 sq km). **Population:** 1,859,000. Ranks 34th. **Major Cities:** Huntington, 68,811; Charleston, 67,348; Wheeling, 44,369. **Mining:** coal, natural gas, petroleum, stone, sand and gravel. **Manufacturing:** chemicals, primary metals, stone, clay and glass products, fabricated metals, machinery, electrical equipment, food products. **Agriculture:** dairy products, beef cattle, apples, broilers, eggs. Also turkeys, hogs. **Other Important Activities:** tourism. **Statehood:** the 35th state. Admitted on June 20, 1863.

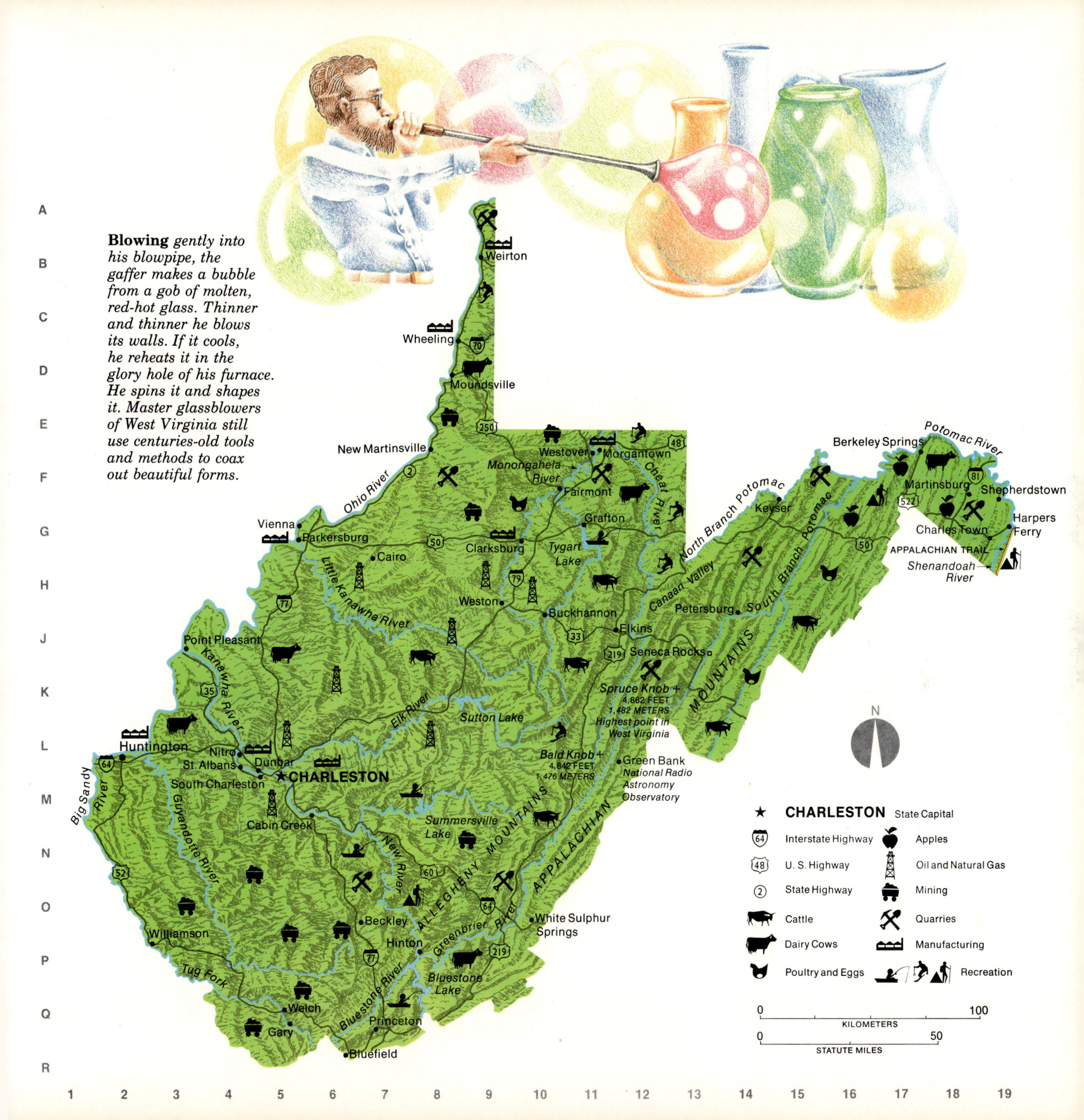

Blowing gently into his blowpipe, the gaffer makes a bubble from a gob of molten, red-hot glass. Thinner and thinner he blows its walls. If it cools, he reheats it in the glory hole of his furnace. He spins it and shapes it. Master glassblowers of West Virginia still use centuries-old tools and methods to coax out beautiful forms.

★ **CHARLESTON** State Capital
- Interstate Highway
- U.S. Highway
- State Highway
- Cattle
- Dairy Cows
- Poultry and Eggs
- Apples
- Oil and Natural Gas
- Mining
- Quarries
- Manufacturing
- Recreation

West Virginia, the Mountain State, could also be called the White Water State. White water is the frothy, fast water churned up as mountain streams tumble over rocks. West Virginia has lots of mountains, and it has lots of roaring rivers.

Many people enjoy the excitement of canoeing in these wild waters. Some compare running the rapids to riding a bucking bronco. Their canoes, though made of new materials such as aluminum and fiberglass, still follow a traditional design: the birch-bark canoe of the American Indian.

West Virginia hosts canoe and kayak meets with downriver and slalom races. The sport is very "democratic"; everyone has an equal chance of getting splashed!

The oldest river in North America, the New, flows past Hinton. The New River is known for its rapids.

A kayaker competes on the rough North Fork River. Racers must wear helmets and life preservers.

This hand-made flower garden grew from cloth scraps and wool yarns.

A coal miner uses a 5-foot (1.5 m) bolt to anchor the coal ceiling in solid limestone.

Snaggleteeth of the Alleghenies, the Seneca Rocks test climbers. This sandstone formation rises 1,000 feet (305 m) from the forest floor.

Coal cars at Gary are ready to roll. Many electric power plants need coal for fuel.

105

Weather and Climate

Bears at the zoo in Anchorage, Alaska, wouldn't hibernate because the air was too warm. Colorado ski resorts had to close when it didn't snow. And Miami, Florida, saw its first snowfall in history. That was the wacky winter of 1977.

Severe cold in the East and a long dry spell in the West brought hardship to millions of Americans. From Florida to California, crops were ruined, and thousands of farm workers lost their jobs. Snowbound cars, frozen pipes, and frostbitten ears and fingers were common east of the Rockies, while Westerners looked in vain for a good blizzard to refill their rivers with melted snow.

That winter of '77 was a sharp reminder of how the weather can affect our lives. But we don't need unusual conditions. We think about weather every day. When dressing in the morning and planning outdoor activities, we always look at the weather. Even our feelings are affected by it: Sunshine can brighten our spirits, dark clouds can make a day seem gloomy.

Whatever the weather may be, it is likely to change before long. That's one way weather differs from climate. While weather is constantly changing, climate is steady and dependable. Weather is the condition of the atmosphere right now. Climate is the weather of a place over many years. Weather affects what we do each day. Climate influences long-range plans such as how we build our houses, when we plant our crops, and where we take our vacations.

Until about a hundred years ago, people relied on weather signs to tell them what kind of weather was on the way. Many old sayings have been handed down, and some work pretty well as guides:

Evening red and morning gray
Sets the traveler on his way;
Evening gray and morning red
Brings down rain upon his head.

Other sayings are more doubtful: "When ants travel in a straight line, expect rain; when they scatter, expect fair weather." With no better forecasts than that, farmers often lost crops that might have been saved by hasty harvesting before a storm.

Today forecasting is more scientific, and our lives are better and safer for it. Weather stations all over the country, airplanes, ships at sea, and weather satellites and balloons send reports to the National Meteorological Center, a part of the U. S. Weather Service, near Washington, D. C.

There, computers make weather maps and transmit them back across the country to the Weather Service's 52 Forecast Offices. Meteorologists, the scientists who study weather, prepare forecasts for their areas with the help of these maps. Most television and radio weather reports are based on these forecasts. Climatologists, the people who study climate, use the data to figure out average yearly temperature, humidity, rain and snowfall.

What makes the weather and climate that are so much a part of our way of life? The sun is the driving force. That blazing furnace sends out huge amounts of solar energy. Most of it is lost in space, but some heats the atmosphere and the earth's surface. Earth's heat from the sun also warms the surrounding air. Clouds and gases in the atmosphere act like a blanket to keep the warmth close to earth. The glass panes of a greenhouse trap heat this way too.

The security blanket we call *atmosphere* measures more than 60 miles (100 km) thick. In the part closest to earth, the bottom 10 miles (16 km), our weather is made.

The sun heats the earth unevenly. Where it shines straight down—on the Equator—the air is hot; where its rays hit the earth at an angle, near the poles, the air is cold. In between, there is much variation in temperature. We measure how hot or cold the air is with a thermometer.

The latitude of a place—its location between the Equator and the poles—greatly influences its weather and climate. Because the United States (excluding Alaska and Hawaii) lies in the middle latitudes (halfway between the Equator and the poles), it falls in the temperate zone. But that doesn't mean our climate is the same from coast to coast—far from it.

Like temperatures of other countries in the middle latitudes, our own range from very hot to very cold. Even so, average temperatures here are not nearly as hot as at the Equator or as cold as at the poles. To our temperate climate we owe part of our great success in agriculture.

A cold front *noses in under warm air, shoving it up fast into a thundercloud— a cumulonimbus. Colder air will sweep in and clear the sky. Fronts—where different air masses meet—bring weather changes. If a warm air mass bumps into a cold one, rain often lingers. A barometer (left) measures air pressure, indicates change.*

Cirrus clouds
Cumulonimbus clouds
Warm air mass
Warm air mass
Cold front
Cumulus clouds
Cold air mass

Air has weight although we don't usually notice it. The weight of air as it pushes down on the earth is called *air pressure.*

The difference in air pressure between one place and another causes wind. This is what often happens: Warm air is light and thin. Since cool air is heavier, it exerts greater pressure than the same amount of warm air does. Cool air flows toward the warm air and pushes it out of the way. That movement of air is wind. From a sea breeze to a dangerous tornado, wind itself is an important part of weather. It's also important because it moves clouds and warm or cool air from one place to another.

There are so many temperature and pressure differences around the globe that most of the earth's air moves most of the time. As air warms at the Equator and cools at the poles, it continually circulates around the earth on regular paths. In the United States winds generally travel from the West Coast to the East Coast, bringing much of our weather with them.

Local winds are caused by temperature and pressure differences over small areas. You'll notice these winds if you're at the beach on a summer day. Land heats up faster than water does, so the warmer air over the beach is pushed upward and replaced by cool air coming in off the ocean. That is why being outdoors in summer is often more comfortable at the seashore than it is farther inland.

More than just wind comes from the difference between cool and warm air. That difference can also cause clouds and rain. All air contains water in the form of a gas called *water vapor.* In light, warm air the tiny air particles are far apart. There's room for more vapor. So warm air can hold more water vapor than cold air can. When air cools it may reach a point where it can't hold all of its vapor. Then the extra vapor changes—or condenses—to liquid droplets. And a cloud forms.

Clouds are made of microscopic droplets of water or crystals of ice. They bring the water we need in the form of rain and snow. It takes millions of cloud droplets to make a single raindrop or snowflake.

There is another ingredient too: Specks of dust or some other tiny particles must be present in the atmosphere for a cloud to grow. The water droplets collect around these particles. When the droplets grow big and heavy enough, we get rain if they fall through warm air, or snow if the air is cold.

So clouds are visible patches of water in the sky. The way a cloud looks depends on the way it forms. The familiar puffy ones, for example, which are called *cumulus* (meaning "piled up"), form when warm air rises and cools enough to make the clouds. They usually mean fair weather. Those layers of grayish clouds that often hang over us are called *stratus.* They form when clouds develop under a lid of warm air that makes them spread out.

Most changes in the weather are brought about by large traveling bodies of air called *air masses.* An air mass contains only one kind of air. It is called "warm" or "cold" depending on whether the air in it is warmer or colder than the air around it.

Air masses take their temperature and moisture from the land or ocean over which they form. An air mass born over land in the Arctic will be cold and dry because the temperature and humidity are very low there. Moving southeastward over Canada, this air mass will bring us clear, dry weather. This means relief on a hot summer day and freezing temperatures in winter.

An air mass may move thousands of miles from where it formed. Different air masses travel across the United States all the time. For instance, cool humid air comes from the Pacific Ocean. These air masses make the Pacific Coast drizzly and foggy, and they drop snow on the western mountain ranges. A warm, moist air mass forms over a warm body of water such as the Gulf of Mexico. When this air moves in, watch out! It's likely to cause a lot of rain. The kinds of air masses that regularly sweep over an area determine its climate.

Most weather changes take place when an air mass collides with another one of a different kind. Along the place where the two

Reading the Weather

With numbers and symbols used worldwide, a map pictures our weather. See how an April day looks from a satellite 23,000 miles (37,015 km) up. Then lower the plastic and "read" what's going on. Rain or drizzle falls from Florida to Maine, and it's snowy and windy over the Great Lakes states. Elsewhere, skies are mostly clear and breezes light.

Like the newspaper weather map, this is a simplified version of the Weather Service computer map. Forecasters study maps and tell us what the weather will be like.

Curving isobars connect places where air pressure is the same, as shown by numbers on the lines. Closed isobars encircle the "highs" and "lows." Fronts are marked by lines with "teeth" or half-moons (or both) pointed the way the front is heading. Stationary fronts hardly move at all. Occluded fronts form when a cold front catches up with a warm one. The circles mark places reporting their weather. Shading inside the circles tells how cloudy it is there. Other symbols and numbers show wind speed and direction, temperature and precipitation.

Weather Map Symbols

▲▲▲▲▲	Cold Front
●●●●●	Warm Front
▲●▲●▲	Stationary Front
▲●▲●▲	Occluded Front
~~	Isobar
••	Continuous Rain
•	Scattered Showers
,,	Drizzle
※	Snow Showers
∞	Haze
≡	Fog

Cloud Cover

| ○ Clear | ◔ One quarter | ◑ One half |
| ◕ Three quarters | ● Completely overcast | ⊗ Sky obscured |

Wind Direction And Speed

West ○   ○ East

─○	1-2 mph (1.6-3 kmph)	╲○	3-8 mph (5-13 kmph)
╲○	9-14 mph (14-23 kmph)	╲╲○	15-20 mph (24-32 kmph)
╲╲○	21-25 mph (34-40 kmph)	╲╲╲○	26-31 mph (42-50 kmph)
╲╲╲○	32-37 mph (51-58 kmph)	╲╲╲╲○	38-43 mph (61-69 kmph)

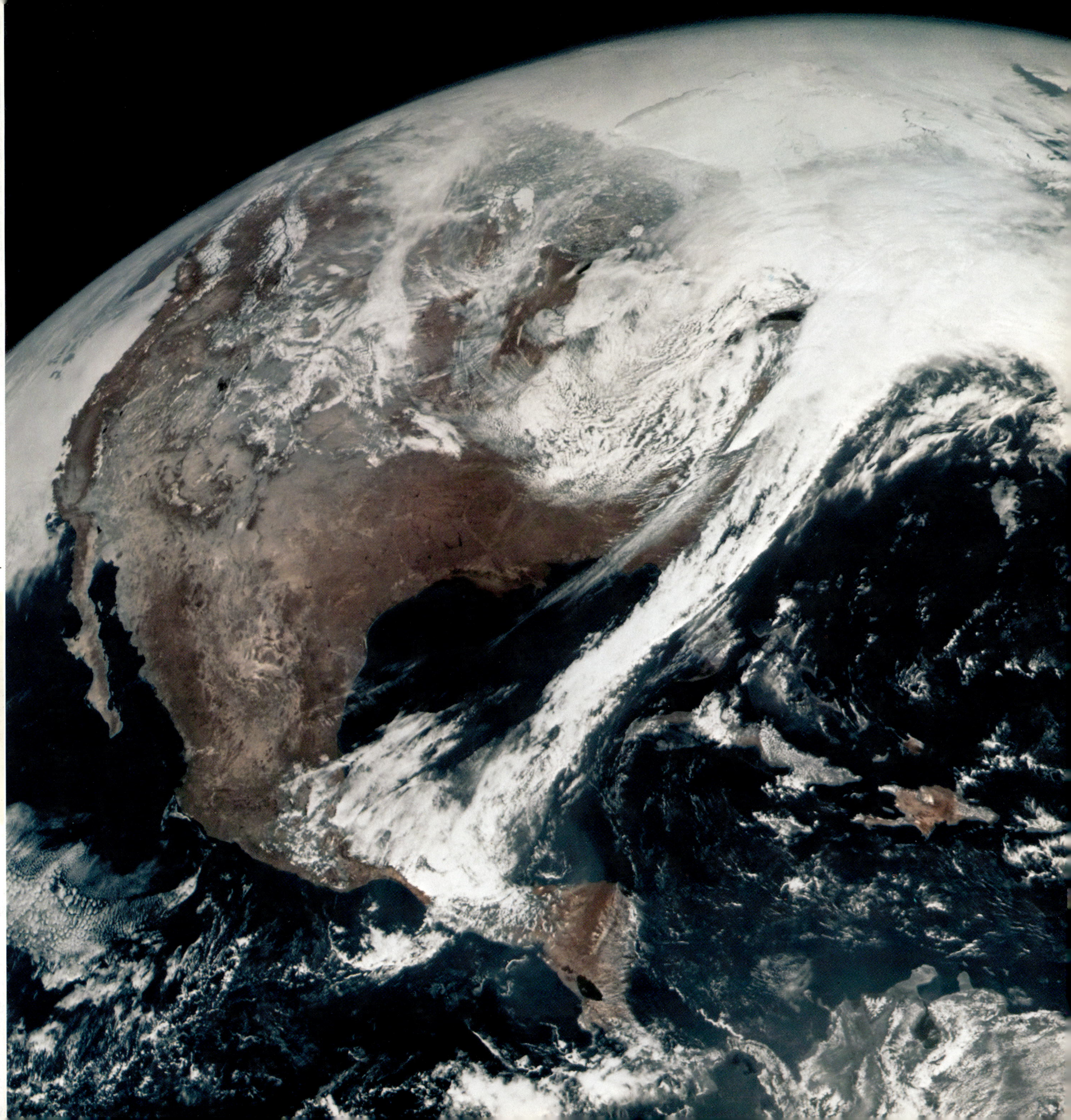

This was a piano until a tornado hit it.

meet, a sharp zone or *front* may form as one pushes up against the other.

Wind, thick clouds, and rain or snow often go with a front. The greater the differences in temperature and moisture content between the colliding air masses, the stormier the weather will be. Some of our most violent storms take place in the Middle West as a cold Canadian air mass bumps up against a warm, moist air mass flowing north from the Gulf of Mexico.

The uneven heating and cooling of the earth, together with its rotation, create the high and low pressure areas (or "highs" and "lows") that the television forecaster talks about. A high is an area of generally good weather. A low is an area of generally bad weather. Lows often bring strong winds and rising air currents that cause rain or snow. The low that brings bad weather in the winter almost always forms along a front.

Fronts sometimes bring thunderstorms, but thunderstorms can also grow right over your head when there are large temperature differences in the atmosphere. Winds will lift the warm, moist air very rapidly into a tall, dark threatening cloud called

A "twister" roars across an Oklahoma field.

Severe drought turned a Minnesota cornfield into this.

When weather goes wild, *look out! It means danger. A tornado's twisting winds slam into the ground, destroying buildings, uprooting trees, hurling people and animals through the air. The U. S. gets hit the most—148 times in less than a day set the record. Blizzards and other winter storms paralyze large areas. They ruin crops, close factories, cut off supplies, and cause accidents. Their icy winds can swirl snow into huge drifts that bury cars and fences, and sometimes people. Unlike most storms, drought creeps up on you, but its effect on the land is just as mean. Each year our extreme weather kills about 1,200 people and causes $1 billion or more in damage. Advance warning is still our best defense, but scientists are searching for ways to tame storms and relieve severe water shortages.*

Frozen orange juice? Florida had it in January 1977.

Buffalo, New York, will never forget the blizzard of '77.

111

cumulonimbus—the familiar "thunderhead." Lightning crackles and thunder booms as electrical charges built up in the cloud are released. Wispy *cirrus* clouds way up in the sky often mean a storm is coming.

Meteorologists think that at any moment about 2,000 thunderstorms are rumbling around the earth. They can hit nearly anywhere in our land, most often in summer. Central Florida sees the most—on an average of 100 days a year. Places along the West Coast, on the other hand, get many fewer, less than five a year.

Tornadoes sometimes accompany severe thunderstorms. Tornadoes are whirlpools of winds that spin violently around a center of extreme low pressure. The winds often look like funnels as they descend from black clouds to hit the ground with terrific force. People who have lived through them say they "roar like a thousand freight trains."

In an average year, over 600 tornadoes strike the country, most often in the Middle West and South. Fortunately, the majority skip along a narrow path for less than 16 miles (26 km) and then die out.

Even in a short time, their savage winds can cause frightful damage. A tornado in Minnesota once sent an 83-ton (75 metric ton) railroad car and its 117 passengers flying through the air and dropped them in a ditch 80 feet (24 m) away!

But hurricanes win the title of "the greatest storms on earth." These giant low-pressure areas form in the hot, humid air over tropical oceans. Averaging several hundred miles across, with torrential rains and winds gusting to 200 miles (322 km) an hour, hurricanes swirl around a center called the "eye." In the eye, winds are light and skies are mostly clear.

Hurricanes affecting the United States usually develop in late summer and early fall. At the Weather Service's National Hurricane Center in Miami, their paths are carefully watched. When hurricanes move over colder northern waters, they're likely to die out. But when one strikes land, its winds can wreck houses and tear up trees.

The surging waves that sweep the coast like giant bulldozers do the greatest damage. In August 1969 Camille, one of our most destructive hurricanes, churned storm tides up to 24 feet (7 m). Camille took more than 300 lives and caused $1.4 billion in property losses. But because of the Weather Service's early warnings, 75,000 people escaped to safety and many lives were saved.

Can we do anything to tame these terrifying forces of nature? So far no one has learned how to control a tornado, but experiments to calm down hurricanes have had some success. The government's Project Stormfury is testing a way to sap the power of a hurricane. It's called "cloud-seeding." This same method is sometimes used to make rain when there is a drought.

Remember those tiny solid particles that must be in the air for a raindrop to form? We can put them into a cloud. Dry ice or silver iodide (chemical crystals resembling ice) is dropped by planes into cumulus

Pacific Ocean

Coast Ranges

Great Central Valley

clouds. If enough moisture is present, rain may fall. In Project Stormfury, planes will seed the outer walls of a hurricane to encourage the clouds in them to grow. That may shift the storm's energy away from the area around the center and slow down the winds.

Think of a spinning figure skater. In some ways she's like a hurricane. With her arms in close to her body, she spins faster and faster, like the winds near a hurricane's center. With her arms slightly extended, the skater's spin slows just as the hurricane's winds will slow down when some of its energy is shifted outward.

However, many problems go with efforts to change the weather. Seeding clouds in one place may cheat another place of rain. Who is to say which place needs the moisture more? If we weaken a hurricane's winds, we may also cut down the rain that goes with it. Some parts of the world may need that water supply. Tampering with nature is a tricky business.

Many scientists think that people's activities may affect weather and climate in another, more damaging way. Countless particles of dust, smoke, and other wastes are blown into the air each year. They may be warming the atmosphere by holding in more heat. Or they may be having the opposite effect. Possibly they are cooling down the earth by reflecting more and more sunlight back into space.

When fuels are burned, carbon dioxide (CO_2) is released into the air in great quantities. Growing plants use carbon dioxide from the air and give back oxygen for people and animals to breathe. But we are now burning so much fuel that there is more CO_2 in the air than our plants can use. Instead of planting more trees to absorb the additional CO_2, the world is cutting down more and more forests.

The build-up of carbon dioxide in the atmosphere could cause a warming trend. Carbon dioxide is one of the principal gases in the air that trap the sun's heat.

If the amount of CO_2 keeps increasing as it has, the world may be several degrees warmer in the next century. Good agricultural land would become scarcer. More people would go hungry.

Climate changes slowly over the centuries. Scientists don't know very much about why this happens. But they worry that in the 20th century, people may be causing changes that will make earth's climate less hospitable to life in the future.

A slice of the Far West *shows how mountains wring moisture from ocean air. Our great western ranges block Pacific air on its way eastward. As the air is forced up the mountainside, it cools quickly. Clouds form. Heavy rain or snow falls on the mountains' western slopes and thick forests grow. But on the eastern slopes and between ranges, the dried-out air creates a "rain shadow" with little moisture.*

The sun evaporates ocean water, adding moisture to the air. When the moisture condenses it makes clouds, and flows to the sea as rain or snow to begin the cycle again.

Sierra Nevada

Great Basin Desert

Rocky Mountains

Great Plains

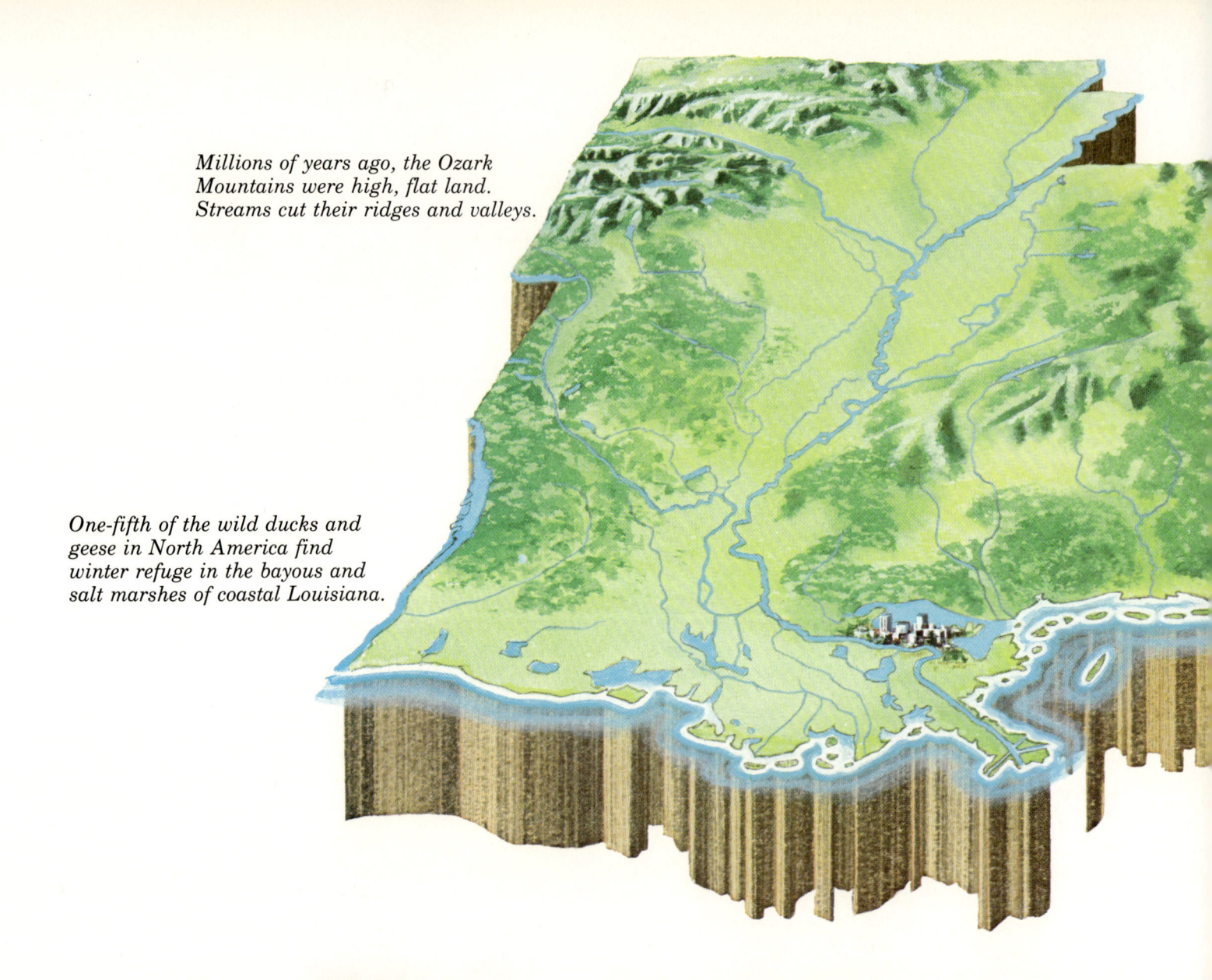

Millions of years ago, the Ozark Mountains were high, flat land. Streams cut their ridges and valleys.

One-fifth of the wild ducks and geese in North America find winter refuge in the bayous and salt marshes of coastal Louisiana.

The Southeast

The Mississippi, mightiest of all North America's rivers, here ends its journey from Minnesota. It divides into four "passes" as it empties into the Gulf of Mexico, pouring out some 461,000 cubic feet (13,054 cu m) of water per second. From 31 states and parts of Canada the Mississippi carries sand and mud. Once it piled enough of these into the gulf to move Louisiana's shoreline six miles (9.6 km) farther to sea every century. Now the silt sweeps off the continental shelf into the ocean depths. New Orleans stands on land about 1,000 years old—some of the youngest in the U. S.

Islands and sandbars fringe the coast. Waterways thread among them, offering small boats protection from ocean storms.

The Florida Keys are islands built up mainly of coral reefs—the skeletons of tiny sea animals that live and die in clusters.

SOUTH CAROLINA
GEORGIA
ALABAMA
FLORIDA
MISSISSIPPI
LOUISIANA
ARKANSAS

ALABAMA

Common Flicker

Camellia

Build a statue to a beetle—a bug that chewed its way through everybody's cotton fields? That's what the people of the little town of Enterprise did in 1919. They built a monument to their enemy, the boll weevil. The statue: A silver-painted goddess holds above her head the ugliest, snoutiest creature you'll find outside a science-fiction movie.

The boll weevil, you see, turned out to be a blessing in disguise. When the hungry pest rampaged through the state's cotton fields in the early 1900's, the disaster forced farmers and planters to turn to other crops for a living—crops the boll weevil wouldn't eat. They began to grow vegetables and peanuts and to raise hogs and cattle and chickens. Enterprise soon prospered on peanuts (today the town calls itself the "Peanut Capital of the World"), and the grateful farmers put up their memorial.

Alabama still grows cotton, but the days of "King Cotton" are gone forever.

Alabama has lots of piney woods and grand old oak and magnolia trees. Its summer climate is hot and humid, but breezes cool the coast near the Gulf of Mexico. Along the coast lie bayous and marshes inhabited by birds, snakes, and alligators.

Bayou La Batre, a fishing village near the sea, is known for its shrimp boats and for its "blessing-of-the-fleet" festival in July. If you lived here along the coast, you would pay attention to weather reports. Squalls and hurricanes roar in from the gulf and you might have to head for high ground—fast.

At the head of Mobile Bay sprawls the city of Mobile, a bustling seaport filled with ships from all over the world. Graceful old homes with lacy ironwork balconies along streets named Dauphin, Conception, and Joachim recall a time when French and Spanish pioneers settled here. Newly discovered oil fields in the area are creating jobs and expanding the economy.

Plant scientist George Washington Carver developed more than 300 products from the peanut—from ink to instant "coffee."

Area: the 29th largest state, 51,609 sq mi (133,667 sq km). **Population:** 3,690,000. Ranks 21st. **Major Cities:** Birmingham, 276,273; Mobile, 196,441; Montgomery, 153,343. **Manufacturing:** primary metals, paper and paper products, textiles, chemicals, food products, clothing, fabricated metals, rubber products, lumber products. **Agriculture:** poultry, beef cattle, soybeans, eggs, cotton, peanuts, hogs, dairy products. **Mining:** coal, petroleum, cement, stone, natural gas, lime, sand and gravel, clays. **Other Important Activities:** tourism, fishing. **Statehood:** the 22nd state. Admitted Dec. 14, 1819.

Birmingham, Alabama's biggest and richest city, lies among hills red with iron ore, at the southern end of the Appalachian Mountains. People sometimes call it the "Pittsburgh of the South" because of its many steel mills and heavy industries (everything from cast-iron pipe to railroad cars). It used to be one of the grimiest cities in the South, choked with smoke and smog. But tough new pollution laws, strictly enforced, have helped bring fresh air back to Birmingham.

The city got its start as an industrial center in the late 1800's when enormous deposits of coal, iron ore, and limestone—the raw ingredients for making iron and steel—were found in the hills nearby. Today, the city is also noted for its pioneering work in health and medical research. Its University Hospital, for example, is world-famed as a center for developing open-heart surgery.

Northwest of Birmingham, in the rolling green hills below the Tennessee River, lies a state you won't find on any map—the Free State of Winston. The people who lived here around the time of the Civil War, mostly poor white farmers, didn't like the slave-owning cotton planters of the rest of the state. When the war began, these stubborn hillfolk threatened to set up their own state. They never actually did. But they did muster a regiment that fought for three years—on the Yankee side!

In 1955 another stubborn person, this time a tired black woman named Rosa Parks, refused to give up her bus seat to a white man in Montgomery, the capital city. Her refusal stirred the civil rights movement that led the nation into a struggle to make *all* its people free and equal.

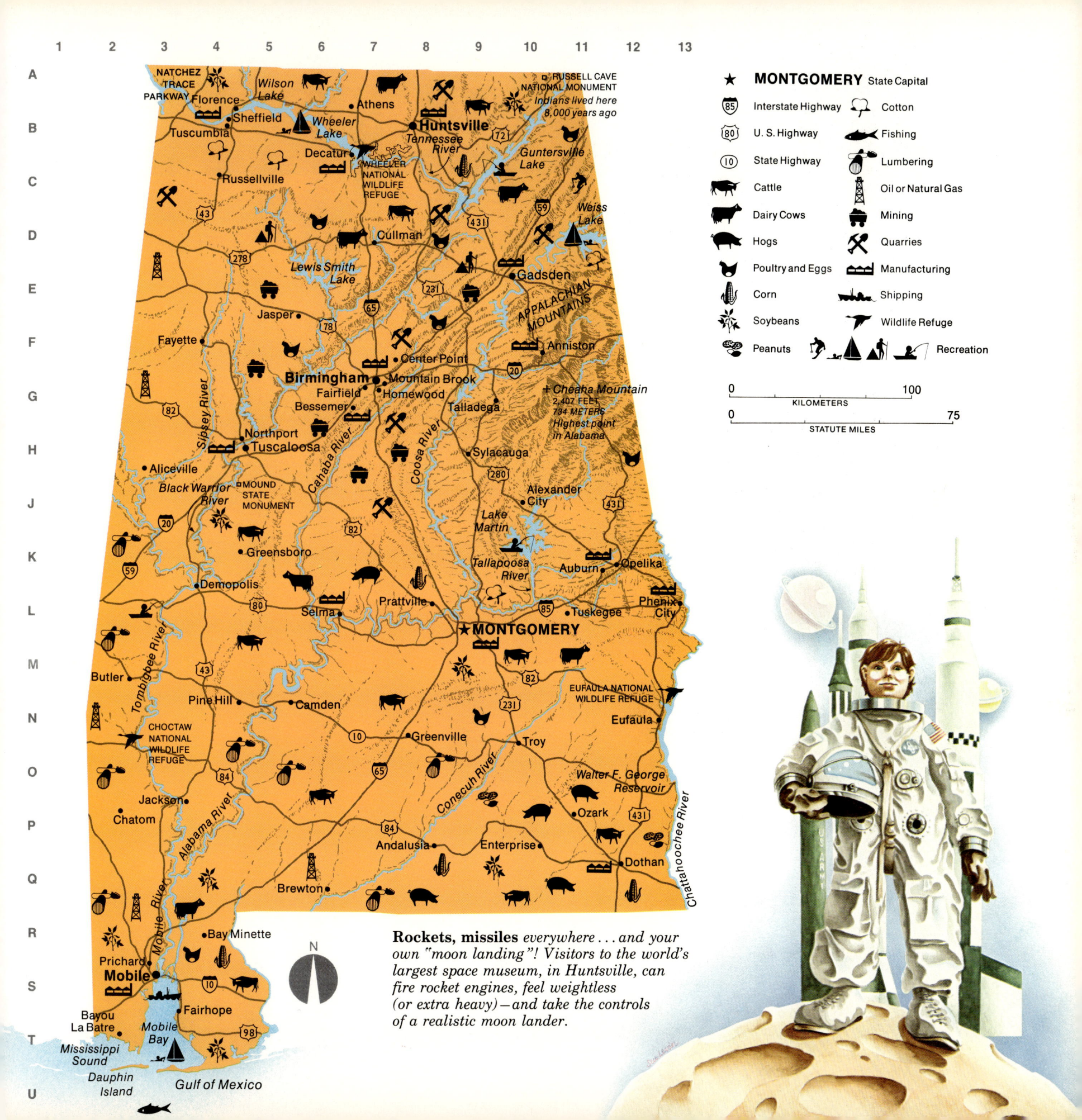

Alabama

Map Legend

★ **MONTGOMERY** State Capital
- 🛣 85 Interstate Highway
- 🛣 80 U.S. Highway
- 🛣 10 State Highway
- Cattle
- Dairy Cows
- Hogs
- Poultry and Eggs
- Corn
- Soybeans
- Peanuts
- Cotton
- Fishing
- Lumbering
- Oil or Natural Gas
- Mining
- Quarries
- Manufacturing
- Shipping
- Wildlife Refuge
- Recreation

Scale: 0–100 Kilometers / 0–75 Statute Miles

Map Labels

Cities and Towns: Florence, Sheffield, Tuscumbia, Athens, Huntsville, Decatur, Russellville, Cullman, Gadsden, Jasper, Fayette, Anniston, Center Point, Birmingham, Mountain Brook, Fairfield, Homewood, Bessemer, Talladega, Northport, Tuscaloosa, Aliceville, Sylacauga, Alexander City, Greensboro, Auburn, Opelika, Demopolis, Selma, Prattville, Tuskegee, Phenix City, Butler, MONTGOMERY, Pine Hill, Camden, Eufaula, Greenville, Troy, Jackson, Chatom, Ozark, Andalusia, Enterprise, Dothan, Brewton, Bay Minette, Prichard, Mobile, Bayou La Batre, Fairhope

Water features: Wilson Lake, Wheeler Lake, Tennessee River, Guntersville Lake, Weiss Lake, Lewis Smith Lake, Sipsey River, Black Warrior River, Cahaba River, Coosa River, Lake Martin, Tallapoosa River, Tombigbee River, Alabama River, Conecuh River, Walter F. George Reservoir, Chattahoochee River, Mobile River, Mobile Bay, Mississippi Sound, Dauphin Island, Gulf of Mexico

Points of Interest: NATCHEZ TRACE PARKWAY, RUSSELL CAVE NATIONAL MONUMENT — Indians lived here 8,000 years ago, WHEELER NATIONAL WILDLIFE REFUGE, APPALACHIAN MOUNTAINS, Cheaha Mountain 2,407 FEET / 734 METERS Highest point in Alabama, MOUND STATE MONUMENT, EUFAULA NATIONAL WILDLIFE REFUGE, CHOCTAW NATIONAL WILDLIFE REFUGE

N (compass)

Rockets, missiles everywhere... and your own "moon landing"! Visitors to the world's largest space museum, in Huntsville, can fire rocket engines, feel weightless (or extra heavy)—and take the controls of a realistic moon lander.

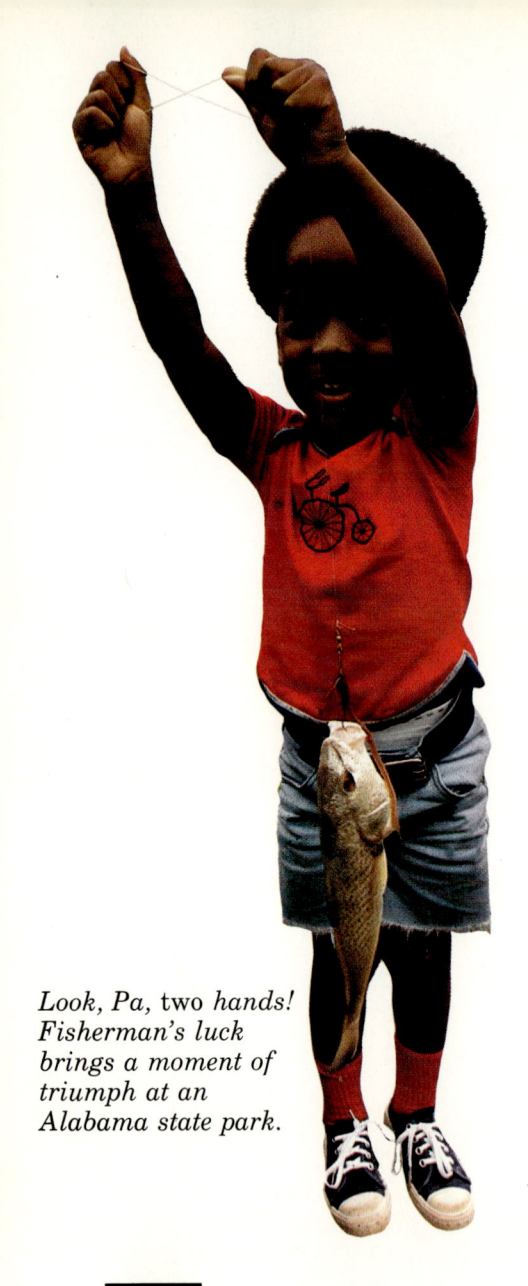

Look, Pa, two hands! Fisherman's luck brings a moment of triumph at an Alabama state park.

Up the shaft goes debris from a Tuscaloosa mine. Coal is the state's biggest mineral resource.

Mother 'possum tends her crew in a hollow tree. As babies they lived in her stomach pouch.

The Black Belt, a tongue of dark, rich soil that curves across the middle of Alabama, looks very different from the red clays that cover the northern part of the state. White settlers quickly recognized the black earth's remarkable fertility. They soon turned the Black Belt into Alabama's chief cotton-producing region. Slaves worked the land, and fine, pillared mansions sprouted like mushrooms after a rain.

Cahaba, a town built where the Alabama and Cahaba rivers meet, became the state's first capital (1819-1826). But it was doomed from the beginning. Floods and diseases regularly swept the city. People moved away. Today Cahaba is a ghost town — moss-grown and choked with vines and memories.

Dawn plays tag with wisps of night near Demopolis in the heart of the Black Belt. Beef and dairy cattle now fatten in fields once given to cotton.

Chomp...snip...and away goes another tree to a paper mill in Pine Hill (top). Forest products rank as the state's second biggest industry. From trees like this come everything from plastics to grocery bags (above).

119

ARKANSAS

Pick and shovel in hand, you enter Crater of Diamonds State Park. You head for the 78-acre (32 hectare) field where visitors bend over on hands and knees. Stooping down, you sift loosely packed earth, looking for a souvenir from North America's only public diamond field. Whatever you dig up, you can keep. Not everyone is lucky, but park officials say an average of one diamond a day is found.

These gems hide in kimberlite, a volcanic rock that cuts "pipes" as it erupts to the earth's surface. In 1906, the story goes, an Arkansas farmer plowed up a strange, shiny stone from his field. The field turned out to be the crater of an ancient volcano. More than 100 kinds of minerals and stones lay buried in its pipe—including diamonds! Commercial mining proved unprofitable, but the 40-carat "Uncle Sam" stone, unearthed in 1924, remains the largest diamond ever found on our continent. Visitors have turned up some prizes too.

And other riches come from Arkansas. If you place a ruler diagonally across the map, from St. Francis to Texarkana, the edge will follow U. S. 67 and Interstate 30. These routes divide the state into two natural triangles, the lowlands and the highlands.

Rugged mountains and hills almost fill the northwest triangle. Here farmers raise poultry, cattle, and hogs. Commercial forests provide jobs for many people. Under this area flow streams that contain dissolved minerals. Where hot or cold springs trickle out of hillsides, resort towns like Hot Springs and Eureka Springs now stand. The soothing water is piped into large indoor pools called baths, where people come to soak aching backs and stiff joints.

Across the north wanders the only sizable free-flowing stream left in the Arkansas Ozarks—the Buffalo National River. All the others have been dammed. To preserve the Buffalo's wild beauty, Congress named it a national river in 1972. Now the federal government protects the river and the land along its banks from dams and development.

Arkansas's southeast triangle contains oil and bauxite, the ore aluminum comes from. Here too lie fertile farmlands that yield cotton, soybeans—and watermelons, some as heavy as grown men!

Throughout the eastern river valleys, low dirt walls, called dikes or levees, crisscross miles of flat, flooded fields. Farmers grow rice here—for soup, cereal, your dinner plate, and for export. Arkansas produces more rice than any other state.

Young rice plants must stay wet. So farmers build the dikes around their fields, then pump in water to flood the fields. The pumps keep the plants covered with 2 to 6 inches (5 to 15 cm) of water until the grain begins to ripen. Then the water is drained.

In autumn, flocks of Canada geese and mallard ducks, tired from their long trip, glide into the rice and soybean fields. Many winter at the White River National Wildlife Refuge. Some rest, feed in the fields, then fly farther south toward the Gulf of Mexico.

Little Rock and Fort Smith remain the leading industrial areas, but factories now dot many parts of the Arkansas River banks. Arkansas workers process all kinds of food products, from animal feed to canned fruits and soft drinks. Plants make refrigerators, air conditioners, television sets, paper bags, tissues, and towels.

In the southwest corner stands Texarkana, a town built across the border of Arkansas and Texas. Here you can go to school in one state and drink a milkshake in another just by crossing State Line Avenue.

Human quacks fill the air each autumn at the World Championship Duck Calling Contest in Stuttgart, a rice center.

Area: the 27th largest state, 53,104 sq mi (137,539 sq km). **Population:** 2,144,000. Ranks 33rd. **Major Cities:** Little Rock, 141,143; Fort Smith, 66,663; North Little Rock, 61,768. **Manufacturing:** food products, electrical equipment, paper products, lumber and wood products, chemicals, fabricated metals, rubber products, machinery. **Agriculture:** soybeans, poultry, rice, cotton, beef cattle. Also eggs. **Mining:** petroleum, bromine, natural gas, cement, stone. Also bauxite. **Other Important Activities:** tourism, fishing. **Statehood:** the 25th state. Admitted June 15, 1836.

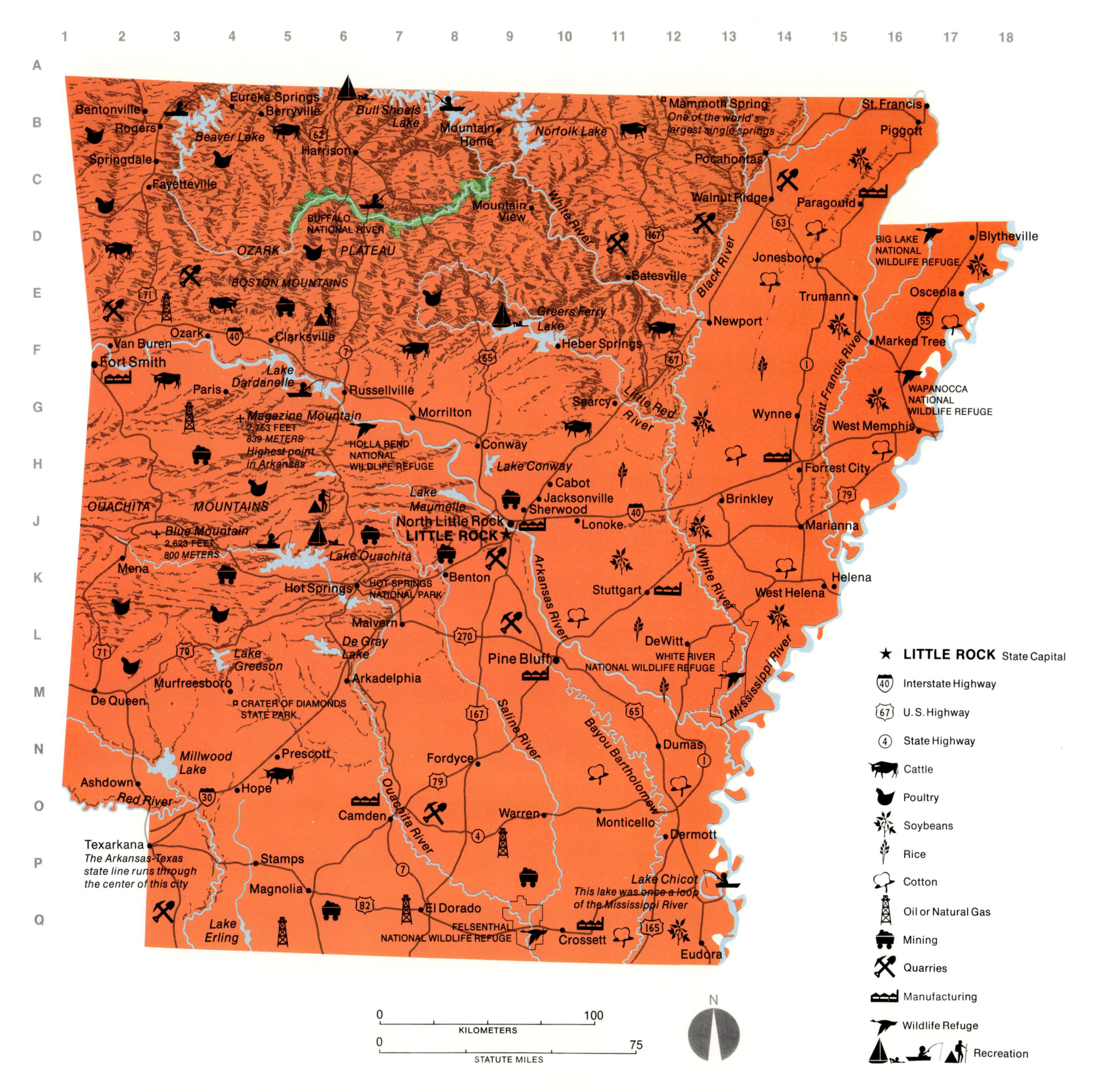

Arkansas

Map Legend

★ **LITTLE ROCK** State Capital
- 🛣 40 Interstate Highway
- 🛣 67 U.S. Highway
- ④ State Highway
- 🐂 Cattle
- 🐓 Poultry
- 🌱 Soybeans
- 🌾 Rice
- ☁ Cotton
- 🛢 Oil or Natural Gas
- ⛏ Mining
- ⚒ Quarries
- 🏭 Manufacturing
- 🦅 Wildlife Refuge
- ⛵🎣⛺ Recreation

Notable locations and features

- Bentonville, Rogers, Springdale, Fayetteville
- Eureka Springs, Berryville, Bull Shoals Lake, Mountain Home
- Norfolk Lake, Mammoth Spring (One of the world's largest single springs)
- St. Francis, Piggott, Pocahontas
- Beaver Lake, Harrison
- Walnut Ridge, Paragould
- Ozark Plateau, Boston Mountains
- Buffalo National River
- Mountain View, Batesville
- Big Lake National Wildlife Refuge, Blytheville
- Ozark, Clarksville, Van Buren, Fort Smith
- Jonesboro, Trumann, Osceola
- Greers Ferry Lake, Heber Springs, Newport
- Marked Tree, Wapanocca National Wildlife Refuge
- Lake Dardanelle, Paris, Russellville
- Searcy, Little Red River
- Wynne, West Memphis
- Magazine Mountain 2,753 FEET 839 METERS Highest point in Arkansas
- Morrilton, Holla Bend National Wildlife Refuge
- Conway, Lake Conway, Cabot, Jacksonville, Sherwood
- Forrest City, Brinkley, Marianna
- Ouachita Mountains
- North Little Rock, LITTLE ROCK ★, Lonoke
- Blue Mountain 2,623 FEET 800 METERS
- Mena, Lake Ouachita, Hot Springs, Hot Springs National Park, Benton
- Stuttgart, Helena, West Helena
- Malvern, De Gray Lake
- DeWitt, White River National Wildlife Refuge
- Murfreesboro, Arkadelphia, Pine Bluff
- Lake Greeson
- De Queen, Crater of Diamonds State Park
- Millwood Lake, Prescott, Fordyce, Saline River
- Bayou Bartholomew, Dumas
- Ashdown, Hope, Red River
- Texarkana — The Arkansas-Texas state line runs through the center of this city
- Camden, Warren, Monticello, Dermott
- Stamps, Ouachita River
- Lake Chicot — This lake was once a loop of the Mississippi River
- Magnolia, El Dorado, Felsenthal National Wildlife Refuge, Crossett, Eudora
- Lake Erling

Scale: 0–100 Kilometers / 0–75 Statute Miles

121

Arkansas leads the nation in producing broilers, nine-week-old chickens. In this house alone, 16,000 scientifically fed birds await shipment to market.

Back-porch music ends a busy day. Ozark musicians often make their own fiddles, banjos, and guitars.

Arkansas hills harbor many skilled wood-carvers.

Finders keepers! For a fee, visitors can hunt for gems like these in a diamond field near Murfreesboro.

Twisting through wooded hills and remote meadowland, past tumbling waterfalls and hidden caves, the Buffalo National River etches a watery playground into Arkansas' Ozark Plateau. Local folks and tourists alike come here to swim, canoe, fish for bass, and shoot the rapids.

Since pioneer days, the Ozarks have sheltered resourceful mountain people. Log cabins and split rail fences built by early settlers still stand. Poor roads made it hard to get to stores, and money was scarce. People learned to make things themselves—soap from wood ashes, banjos from gourds, dolls from apples or corn husks. The Ozark Folk Center at Mountain View now preserves the area's unique music, crafts, and folklore.

Adventurers scale limestone cliffs that rise from the Buffalo's banks. Over the centuries the river has cut steep canyons into the soft-layered rock.

The Buffalo National River threads through 132 miles (212 km) of Ozark woods and countryside.

123

FLORIDA

Swamps...alligators...pirate ships and rocket ships...orange groves, mangroves, and palm groves... Indians...Disney World...islands of coral...land cows—and sea cows, too! For being just plain *different,* Florida takes the cake. Even the land is different—mostly a green mat poking 400 miles (644 km) into the Atlantic and the Gulf of Mexico.

A huge limestone ledge, full of holes like a Swiss cheese, lies beneath the state. Most of the holes and passageways are filled with water, giving Florida some 300 springs and beautiful rivers and recreation areas. The holes in the ledge also form lakes and ponds—some 10,000 altogether.

Florida has no mountains. But it does have 1,350 miles (2,173 km) of coastline and all kinds of coves, inlets, and skinny barrier islands along the shore. Protected harbors and channels that now shelter fleets of pleasure boats once hid pirate ships.

Fine beaches line much of the coast. Thousands of winter visitors flock to them to escape the snow and ice of the North, making tourism the state's No. 1 industry. Florida's sun also makes it a favorite place for people to retire. No other state has such a big proportion (15 percent) of old folks.

Many a kid who strolls a Florida beach hopes to find a gold coin glittering on the sand—a souvenir from some old Spanish treasure ship smashed to pieces in a storm. But few people know of a *real* treasure that washed ashore in 1878, when the *Providencia* went down off Palm Beach. Stuffed in her hold were tons of coconuts. They took root in the sand, and that's how Palm Beach got its name. It went on to become one of the fanciest, richest resorts on the Atlantic coast.

Hilly central Florida is the heart of the citrus industry but some growers are moving south, around Lake Okeechobee, where winters are a little warmer. A hard freeze can kill trees, and frozen fruit will rot when it thaws. If a frost threatens, growers act quickly. They set oil heaters among the trees. They start tall, gasoline-powered windmills to stir up the warmer air above ground. And once they've saved their crop, they turn right around and freeze most of it anyway—as orange juice concentrate.

Fort Lauderdale is a city so carved by canals that people often hop into their boats to go shopping or visiting. Miami, a bustling city near the tip of the state, is now home to hundreds of thousands of refugees who fled from Communist Cuba. Two languages are officially used in Miami—Spanish and English—and the city's newest citizens give it a lively, often festive spirit.

Curving 125 miles (201 km) out to sea below Miami lies a chain of coral-fringed islands—the Florida Keys. Some of them have plants found nowhere else in the U.S.—Jamaica morning-glory, wild dilly, and West Indies satinwood trees. The Keys and their coral reefs are favorite haunts for fishermen and scuba divers, as well as botanists and bird-watchers from all over the world.

West of Miami, covering the lower fourth of the state, stretch Big Cypress Swamp and the Everglades—a great saw grass river dotted with clumps of tropical trees. Here lurk alligators, wildcats, snakes, lizards, hundreds of kinds of birds, and billions of biting bugs! Mangrove trees, land plants that can live in salt water, grow in the Everglades. Their tangled roots trap sand and leaves to make new land. So Florida really is a growing state! And in quiet channels you'll find lovable manatees—sea cows—peacefully nibbling water plants.

Tarpon Springs is the nation's leading producer of sponges—sea creatures whose rubbery skeletons soak up water.

Area: the 22nd largest state, 58,560 sq mi (151,670 sq km). **Population:** 8,452,000. Ranks eighth. **Major Cities:** Jacksonville, 535,030; Miami, 365,082; Tampa, 280,340. **Manufacturing:** food products, electrical equipment, chemicals, transportation equipment, printing and publishing, fabricated metals, paper products. **Agriculture:** oranges, dairy products, beef cattle, sugarcane. **Mining:** phosphate rock, petroleum, cement, stone, natural gas. **Other Important Activities:** tourism, fishing. **Statehood:** the 27th state. Admitted Mar. 3, 1845.

Orange Blossom

Mockingbird

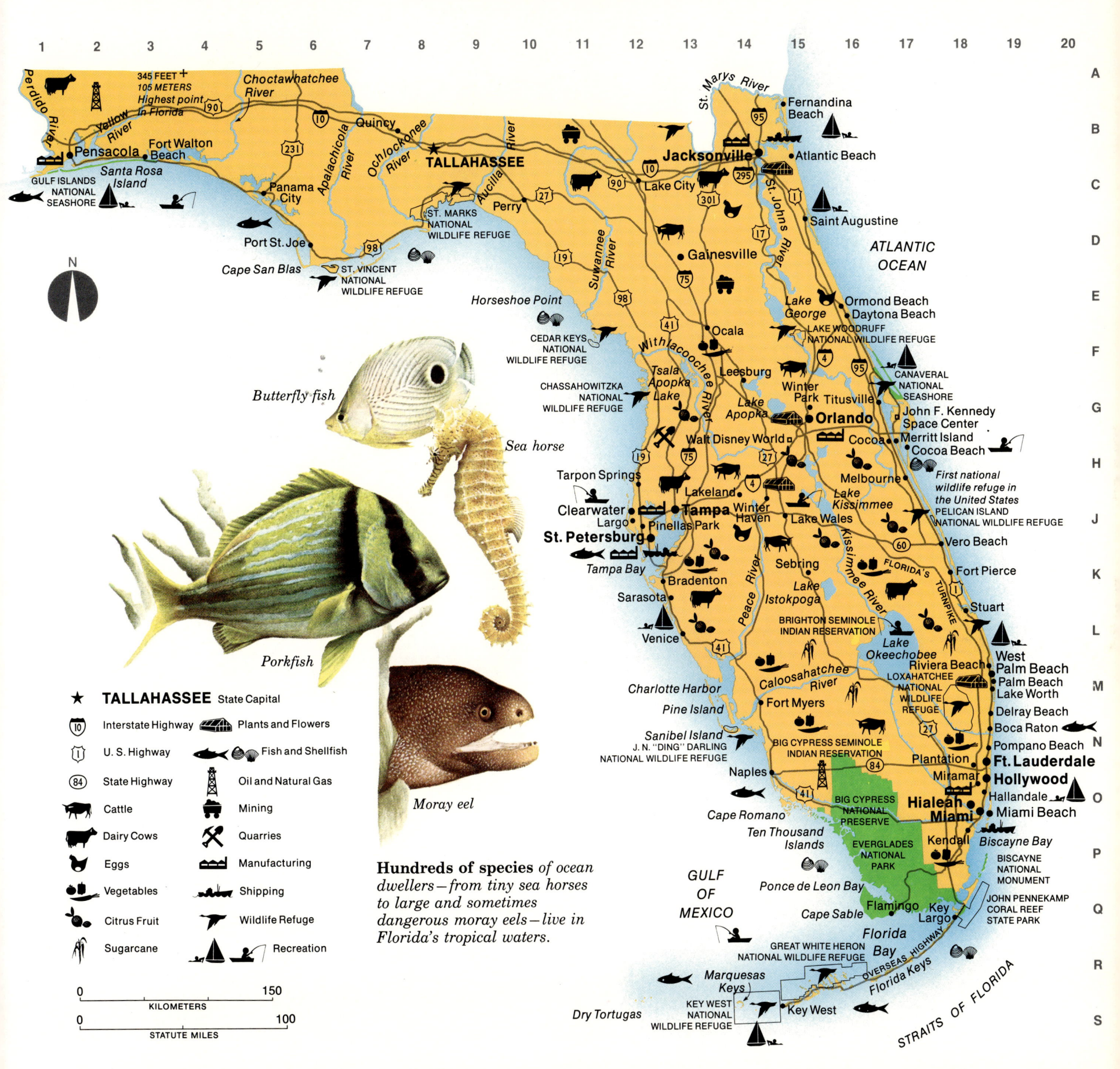

Florida

Map Grid
Columns: 1–20
Rows: A–S

Key Locations and Features

TALLAHASSEE ★ (State Capital)

Cities
- Pensacola
- Fort Walton Beach
- Panama City
- Port St. Joe
- Perry
- Quincy
- Lake City
- Fernandina Beach
- Jacksonville
- Atlantic Beach
- Saint Augustine
- Gainesville
- Ocala
- Ormond Beach
- Daytona Beach
- Leesburg
- Winter Park
- Titusville
- Orlando
- Cocoa
- Cocoa Beach
- Tarpon Springs
- Clearwater
- Largo
- Pinellas Park
- Tampa
- Lakeland
- Winter Haven
- Lake Wales
- Melbourne
- Vero Beach
- St. Petersburg
- Bradenton
- Sarasota
- Venice
- Sebring
- Fort Pierce
- Stuart
- Fort Myers
- Riviera Beach
- West Palm Beach
- Palm Beach
- Lake Worth
- Delray Beach
- Boca Raton
- Pompano Beach
- Naples
- Plantation
- Ft. Lauderdale
- Miramar
- Hollywood
- Hialeah
- Hallandale
- Miami
- Miami Beach
- Kendall
- Flamingo
- Key Largo
- Key West

Physical Features
- Perdido River
- Yellow River
- Choctawhatchee River
- Apalachicola River
- Ochlockonee River
- Aucilla River
- St. Marys River
- Suwannee River
- St. Johns River
- Withlacoochee River
- Kissimmee River
- Peace River
- Caloosahatchee River
- Santa Rosa Island
- Cape San Blas
- Horseshoe Point
- Lake George
- Lake Apopka
- Tsala Apopka Lake
- Lake Kissimmee
- Lake Istokpoga
- Lake Okeechobee
- Charlotte Harbor
- Pine Island
- Sanibel Island
- Cape Romano
- Ten Thousand Islands
- Ponce de Leon Bay
- Cape Sable
- Florida Bay
- Biscayne Bay
- Florida Keys
- Marquesas Keys
- Dry Tortugas
- Tampa Bay
- Gulf of Mexico
- Atlantic Ocean
- Straits of Florida

Highest Point
345 FEET + 105 METERS — Highest point in Florida

National Parks, Refuges, and Monuments
- Gulf Islands National Seashore
- St. Marks National Wildlife Refuge
- St. Vincent National Wildlife Refuge
- Cedar Keys National Wildlife Refuge
- Chassahowitzka National Wildlife Refuge
- Lake Woodruff National Wildlife Refuge
- Canaveral National Seashore
- John F. Kennedy Space Center
- Merritt Island
- Pelican Island National Wildlife Refuge — First national wildlife refuge in the United States
- Walt Disney World
- Brighton Seminole Indian Reservation
- Loxahatchee National Wildlife Refuge
- J.N. "Ding" Darling National Wildlife Refuge
- Big Cypress Seminole Indian Reservation
- Big Cypress National Preserve
- Everglades National Park
- Biscayne National Monument
- John Pennekamp Coral Reef State Park
- Great White Heron National Wildlife Refuge
- Key West National Wildlife Refuge
- Overseas Highway

Highways
- Interstate 10, 75, 95, 295, 4
- U.S. 1, 17, 19, 27, 41, 90, 98, 231, 301
- Florida's Turnpike
- State Highway 60, 84

Map Legend
- ★ **TALLAHASSEE** State Capital
- 🛣 Interstate Highway
- 🛣 U.S. Highway
- 🛣 State Highway
- 🐄 Cattle
- 🐄 Dairy Cows
- 🐔 Eggs
- 🥬 Vegetables
- 🍊 Citrus Fruit
- 🌾 Sugarcane
- 🌷 Plants and Flowers
- 🐟 Fish and Shellfish
- 🛢 Oil and Natural Gas
- ⛏ Mining
- ⚒ Quarries
- 🏭 Manufacturing
- 🚢 Shipping
- Wildlife Refuge
- ⛵ Recreation

Scale: 0–150 Kilometers; 0–100 Statute Miles

Hundreds of species of ocean dwellers — from tiny sea horses to large and sometimes dangerous moray eels — live in Florida's tropical waters.

Butterfly fish
Sea horse
Porkfish
Moray eel

125

Florida's Everglades and Big Cypress Swamp are home to the only Indians never to surrender while fighting the U. S. Army. They are the Seminoles, whose name means "frontiersman."

At one time the Seminoles lived in Georgia and were members of the Creek tribes. They moved to Florida in the 1700's, and when white settlers later tried to push them off their land, they fought back. Many Indians died or were captured, but about 150 of them went so far and so deep into the swamps that the army gave up the chase.

Today the Seminoles live much like anyone else. They rent land to builders for shopping centers. Some raise cattle. Others act as guides or sell handmade dolls and souvenirs. Some still hunt and fish and trap. Youngsters go to school. Civilization is taming the "wild" Seminoles.

A Seminole Indian grandmother and youngsters in tribal costume attend a festival near Lake Okeechobee. Some 1,600 Seminoles live in Florida.

Hotels and apartments crowd Miami Beach, luring a million winter visitors.

Egrets, pelicans, wood storks, and spoonbills flock to an Everglades breakfast.

Shlurp! Florida produces a quarter of the world's oranges and other citrus fruits.

Mighty Saturn readies for countdown at Cape Canaveral, the U.S.'s leading launchpad.

A cockleshell prize comes from the waters off Sanibel Island, a Gulf Coast paradise for shell collectors big and little.

Porkfish, grunts, and a gray angelfish cruise the John Pennekamp Coral Reef State Park.

Angry alligators hiss like this— but roar with their jaws closed.

GEORGIA

The Goober State? The Peach State? Empire State of the South? Georgia lawmakers have never given their state an official nickname. Georgia leads the nation in so many products and industries, perhaps it wouldn't be easy to choose a name.

For instance, Georgia is our No. 1 grower of peanuts—goobers. This name for peanuts came from Africa with the slaves. Peanuts aren't nuts. They are a kind of pea which thrives in the coastal plain's sandy soil. Georgia farmers harvest more than 750,000 tons (680,389 t) of peanuts each year. Some are roasted or crushed for oil. About half turn into peanut butter at one of the world's largest peanut butter plants, at Dawson. The peanut vine can be used as hay for livestock. Even the shells can be used, powdered, in plastics and wallboard. And the growing plant enriches the soil with nitrogen.

Georgia peaches usually get to northern markets early, ahead of other states. Georgia is third in peach production. What are some other ways that Georgia is at or near the top? Poultry—more broilers than any state except Arkansas. Pecans. Tobacco. Marble—the statue of Lincoln in the Lincoln Memorial, in Washington, D. C., is of Georgia marble. Granite—Georgia quarries more of it than any other state. And kaolin, a clay which becomes part of fine china and gives the gloss to high quality magazine and book paper. That's only part of the list.

Georgia is the largest state east of the Mississippi. It slopes, Georgians say, "from Rabun Gap to Tybee Light"—from the mountainous northeast almost a mile (1.6 km) high to sea level. Tybee Lighthouse has guided ships at the mouth of the Savannah River most of the last two centuries. South along the coast there are hundreds of "sea islands." They range from exclusive vacation resorts to nature laboratories where ecologists study wildlife. The highest point in the state, near Rabun Gap, is a bare-topped mountain called Brasstown Bald.

Rabun Gap is a Georgia name known in all 50 states and more than a dozen foreign countries. High school students living near this narrow pass through the Blue Ridge publish a magazine and a series of best-selling books called *Foxfire*. In them the area's oldest mountaineers tell in their own words how they lived close to the land. If you want to build a log cabin or sharpen a millstone or roast bear meat, *Foxfire* will tell you how. *Foxfire* preserves old tales and customs that might have been lost.

The highlands reach south into the state almost to where Stone Mountain rises 683 feet (208 m) above the piedmont plateau. This one-and-one-half-mile-long (2.4 km) smooth, gray dome is a kind of rock "iceberg"—geologists think that only a small part of it is seen above ground. It is the world's largest isolated block of granite.

Almost in its shadow is Atlanta. Nearly two million people live in and around this metropolis of the South. Atlanta began as a railroad town and is still a transportation center—and a banking center, a convention site, a manufacturing city, and a distribution center for products of the region. Construction is always going on as its sparkling towers rise.

The city of Atlanta represents the modern South in yet another way—it was the home of the great black civil rights leader Martin Luther King, Jr. Dr. King is buried in Atlanta. On his tombstone are the words from one of his most famous speeches, "Free at Last, Free at Last, Thank God Almighty, I'm Free at Last."

Meet Jackson Oak, Jr. of Athens, Georgia. The tree has a legal paper that says it owns itself. Jackson Oak, Sr. inherited the little plot when its human owner died.

Area: the 21st largest state, 58,876 sq mi (152,488 sq km). **Population:** 5,048,000. Ranks 14th. **Major Cities:** Atlanta, 436,057; Columbus, 159,352; Macon, 121,157. **Manufacturing:** rugs and other textiles, transportation equipment, food products, paper products, chemicals, clothing, electrical equipment, lumber and wood products. **Agriculture:** poultry, peanuts, eggs, corn, soybeans, hogs, beef cattle, tobacco, dairy products, vegetables, cotton, fruit and nuts, lumbering. **Mining:** clays, stone, cement. **Statehood:** the fourth state. Ratified Constitution Jan. 2, 1788.

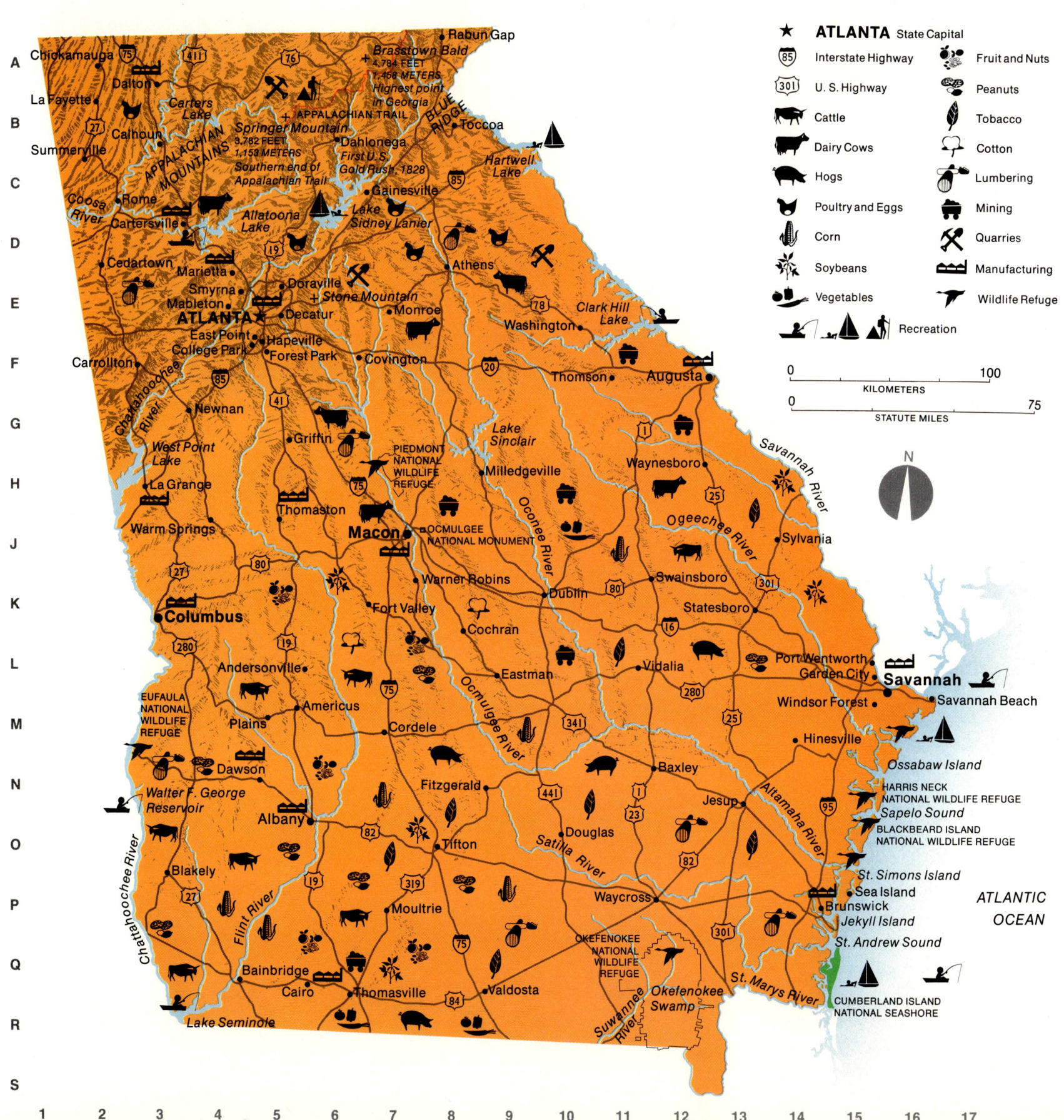

Georgia

Map Legend

★ **ATLANTA** State Capital
🛣 85 Interstate Highway
🛣 301 U.S. Highway
Cattle
Dairy Cows
Hogs
Poultry and Eggs
Corn
Soybeans
Vegetables
Fruit and Nuts
Peanuts
Tobacco
Cotton
Lumbering
Mining
Quarries
Manufacturing
Wildlife Refuge
Recreation

Scale: 0–100 Kilometers / 0–75 Statute Miles

Locations (by grid)

- Chickamauga (A1)
- Rabun Gap (A7)
- Dalton (A3)
- Brasstown Bald 4,784 FEET 1,458 METERS Highest point in Georgia (A6)
- La Fayette (B2)
- Toccoa (B8)
- Summerville (B2)
- Calhoun (B3)
- Carters Lake (B4)
- Springer Mountain 3,782 FEET 1,153 METERS Southern end of Appalachian Trail (C4)
- Dahlonega First U.S. Gold Rush, 1828 (C6)
- APPALACHIAN TRAIL
- APPALACHIAN MOUNTAINS
- BLUE RIDGE
- Coosa River (C2)
- Rome (C3)
- Hartwell Lake (C8)
- Cartersville (D3)
- Allatoona Lake (D4)
- Gainesville (D6)
- Lake Sidney Lanier (D6)
- Cedartown (E2)
- Marietta (E4)
- Smyrna (E4)
- Mableton (E4)
- Doraville (E5)
- Stone Mountain (E5)
- Athens (E7)
- ATLANTA ★ (F4)
- Decatur (F5)
- Monroe (F6)
- Washington (F8)
- Clark Hill Lake (E9)
- East Point (F4)
- Hapeville (F4)
- College Park (F4)
- Forest Park (F5)
- Covington (F6)
- Carrollton (F2)
- Chattahoochee River (F2)
- Thomson (F9)
- Augusta (F10)
- Newnan (G4)
- Griffin (G5)
- Lake Sinclair (G8)
- Waynesboro (G11)
- Savannah River
- West Point Lake (H2)
- PIEDMONT NATIONAL WILDLIFE REFUGE (H7)
- Milledgeville (H8)
- La Grange (H3)
- Thomaston (H5)
- Ogeechee River
- Warm Springs (J3)
- Macon (J6)
- OCMULGEE NATIONAL MONUMENT (J7)
- Oconee River
- Sylvania (J12)
- Warner Robins (K7)
- Dublin (K9)
- Swainsboro (K11)
- Columbus (K3)
- Fort Valley (K6)
- Cochran (K8)
- Statesboro (K12)
- Vidalia (L11)
- Port Wentworth (L14)
- Garden City (L14)
- Savannah (L15)
- Andersonville (L5)
- Americus (L5)
- Eastman (L8)
- Windsor Forest (L14)
- Savannah Beach (L15)
- EUFAULA NATIONAL WILDLIFE REFUGE (M2)
- Plains (M4)
- Cordele (M7)
- Hinesville (M13)
- Ossabaw Island (M15)
- Dawson (N3)
- Walter F. George Reservoir (N2)
- Fitzgerald (N7)
- Baxley (N10)
- Jesup (N12)
- HARRIS NECK NATIONAL WILDLIFE REFUGE (N15)
- Sapelo Sound (N15)
- BLACKBEARD ISLAND NATIONAL WILDLIFE REFUGE (O15)
- Albany (O4)
- Tifton (O7)
- Douglas (O10)
- Satilla River
- Altamaha River
- Blakely (P3)
- Moultrie (P5)
- Waycross (P11)
- St. Simons Island (P15)
- Sea Island (P15)
- Brunswick (P15)
- Jekyll Island (P15)
- Chattahoochee River
- Flint River
- OKEFENOKEE NATIONAL WILDLIFE REFUGE (Q12)
- St. Andrew Sound (Q15)
- Bainbridge (Q4)
- Cairo (R4)
- Thomasville (R5)
- Valdosta (R8)
- Okefenokee Swamp (R12)
- St. Marys River
- CUMBERLAND ISLAND NATIONAL SEASHORE (R15)
- Lake Seminole (R3)
- Suwannee River
- ATLANTIC OCEAN

Spanish moss curtains Sea Island oak trees. Rain gives moisture to this moss and dissolves minerals for it from the tree's dead cells.

Georgians tap pine trees for gum that goes into printing ink, paint, and shiny paper finishes.

Long summers with lots of rain help Georgia grow juicy peaches, apples, and many other fruits.

"Goodness! how delicious, Eatin' goober peas," sang Civil War soldiers of Georgia's protein-rich peanuts.

This bobcat shares Okefenokee Swamp with 300 kinds of wildlife—bears, turtles, otters, birds, raccoons, opossums.

Tea-colored water, floating fields of grass and flowers—that's Okefenokee Swamp. It covers 681 square miles (1,764 sq km) in southeastern Georgia and northern Florida. Its spongy mats of plant life look like islands. Walk on one. It shivers under your feet. Even the cypress trees might tremble, shaking their gray beards of Spanish moss. Some birds, animals, and insects that live here have not changed for millions of years. The alligator is one. Its roar (like a lion's but louder) booms over Okefenokee during the mating season or in answer to a crash of thunder. And now the 12-foot (3.7 m) giants have a new "thunder" to stir them. When an airplane breaks the sound barrier, the 'gators bellow back.

De Soto Falls, near the Appalachian Trail, plunges 600 feet (183 m) in one-third of a mile. Spanish explorer Hernando de Soto and his soldiers crossed this wilderness in 1540.

LOUISIANA

A haunted river? Perhaps the Mississippi is. A legend says that in an old cutoff part of the river north of Baton Rouge, the ghost of a paddle-wheel steamboat chugs back and forth, trapped forever. On foggy nights, they say, you can hear the signal bell clang and the pilot shout in anger at the trick the big river played on him.

By the time the Mississippi River reaches Louisiana it has made a 2,350-mile (3,782 km) journey from its source in Minnesota. Now it is what geologists call an old river. An old river, instead of running briskly in a rather straight course, wanders and loops. In *Life on the Mississippi*, Mark Twain showed how hard it was for river pilots to follow the river during the mid-1800's. It turned so often, he said, that if you "throw a long, pliant apple-paring over your shoulder, it will pretty fairly shape itself into an average section of the Mississippi."

He wouldn't know his river today. Engineers have straightened it and deepened its channel. They have walled it with levees — banks of dirt and gravel — or concrete walls. Many towns have been cut off from their former riverbank setting. Floodways have been built so that floodwater can drain into the Gulf of Mexico.

At Baton Rouge the river rolls by the largest oil refinery in the United States. Louisiana is second only to Texas in oil and gas production. Petroleum comes to Baton Rouge from oil fields throughout the state and from offshore oil rigs in the gulf. The refinery's maze of storage tanks, towers, and laboratories produces jet fuel and gasoline as well as waxes, oils, and hundreds of other petrochemical products.

For 130 miles (209 km) from Baton Rouge to New Orleans, the Mississippi's banks are lined with industries. They locate near the river for a water supply and good transportation. Many stand on land which grew cotton and sugarcane until about 20 years ago. Louisiana still grows both, though soybeans and rice give the state its largest agricultural income.

The city of Lafayette has grown with the oil and gas industry. Lafayette is also the heart of "Acadian country," a part of southern Louisiana settled 200 years ago by French Canadians. The Acadians, or Cajuns, have kept many of their old ways. They speak French. Some are rubber-booted cowboys, raising cattle near the coast. Many work by the seasons, fishing in summer and fur trapping in winter. Muskrat, nutria, and mink keep Louisiana a leader in furs.

From December to March, Cajun trappers work in the bayous. "Sleeping water," settlers called these slow-moving streams concentrated where the Mississippi nears the end of its journey. On the water, tiny duckweed plants make floating green carpets. Cypress trees, hung with Spanish moss, tower from bulging, bottle-shaped bases.

Moss picking used to be another bayou industry. From boats people gathered the moss with hooks, and sold it for furniture stuffing. Now synthetics are replacing this ghostly-gray "Spaniard's beard," as the Cajuns call it, and moss pickers are rare.

French and Spanish colonists settled New Orleans; their descendants are called Creoles. With people of many other heritages, they make New Orleans one of America's most colorful cities. Every year merrymakers flock there for the celebration known as Mardi Gras. In the history-rich French Quarter, with 19th-century houses and shops, is a blacksmith shop that may have belonged to the pirate Jean Laffite.

Jean Laffite, bayou buccaneer, fighting on the American side in the War of 1812, helped beat the British at New Orleans.

Area: the 31st largest state, 48,523 sq mi (125,674 sq km). **Population:** 3,921,000. Ranks 20th. **Major Cities:** New Orleans, 559,770; Baton Rouge, 294,394; Shreveport, 185,711. **Mining:** natural gas, petroleum, natural gas liquids, sulfur, salt. **Manufacturing:** chemicals, petroleum and coal products, food products, paper products, transportation equipment, fabricated metals. **Agriculture:** soybeans, rice, cotton, beef cattle. **Other Important Activities:** tourism, fishing, fur trapping. **Statehood:** the 18th state. Admitted April 30, 1812.

BATON ROUGE State Capital
Interstate Highway
U. S. Highway
State Highway
Cattle
Dairy Cows
Soybeans
Rice
Cotton
Sugarcane
Recreation
Pelts
Fishing
Shellfish
Oil and Natural Gas
Mining
Quarries
Manufacturing
Shipping
Wildlife Refuge
0 125
KILOMETERS
0 75
STATUTE MILES
N
A
B
C
D
E
F
G
H
J
K
L
M
N
O
P
Q
1 2 3 4 5 6 7 8 9 10 11 12 13 14 15 16 17 18 19
Springhill
Vivian
Caddo Lake
Shreveport
Bossier City
Bayou Dorcheat
Homer
Minden
Bayou D' Arbonne
Ruston
Bastrop
West Monroe
Monroe
Lake Providence
Tallulah
Lake Bistineau
Driskill Mountain
535 FEET
163 METERS
Highest point in Louisiana
Jonesboro
Ouachita River
Bayou Macon
Winnsboro
Mansfield
Winnfield
Saline Lake
Natchitoches
Tensas River
Mississippi River
Ferriday
Vidalia
Red River
Catahoula Lake
Black River
Toledo Bend Reservoir
Alexandria
Pineville
Leesville
Bunkie
De Ridder
Oakdale
Sabine River
Calcasieu River
Ville Platte
Atchafalaya River
Jackson
Bogalusa
Hammond
Covington
Pearl River
Scotlandville
BATON ROUGE
Ponchatoula
Opelousas
Eunice
Slidell
Plaquemine
Lake Maurepas
Lake Pontchartrain
Sulphur
Lake Charles
Jennings
Crowley
Lafayette
Donaldsonville
Lake Borgne
LACASSINE NATIONAL WILDLIFE REFUGE
St. Martinville
Metairie
New Orleans
Kenner
Chalmette
Westwego
Gretna
Marrero
Kaplan
New Iberia
Lac des Allemands
Chandeleur Sound
Sabine Lake
Calcasieu Lake
Abbeville
Avery Island
Grand Lake
A huge salt dome that rises in the coastal marsh
Six Mile Lake
Thibodaux
Lake Salvador
SABINE NATIONAL WILDLIFE REFUGE
Cameron
White Lake
Franklin
Morgan City
Lafitte
BRETON NATIONAL WILDLIFE REFUGE
Houma
Breton Sound
West Cote Blanche Bay
Atchafalaya Bay
Barataria Bay
East Cote Blanche Bay
GULF OF MEXICO
DELTA NATIONAL WILDLIFE REFUGE
Grand Isle
Caillou Bay
Terrebonne Bay
Timbalier Bay
Mississippi River Delta

In the Mississippi's snaking curves lies New Orleans, our second busiest port.

Flames of waste gas light the sky above a petrochemical plant near New Orleans.

The grinning figure of Rex, King of Carnival, heads this Mardi Gras parade in New Orleans.

The trumpet of jazzman Kid Valentine spices nightlife in New Orleans's French Quarter.

As misty dawn breaks in Alligator Bayou, fishermen cast for bass. Cypress trees draped with Spanish moss grow out of the swamps.

Crimson crawfish await the finishing touch of a Cajun chef in Lafayette. Freshwater cousin of the lobster, the crawfish may be fried, baked in juicy patties, or simmered in fragrant gumbos. Backcountry Cajuns and city Creoles brew dishes that show southern Louisiana's rich mix of people and cultures. Cajuns and Creoles combine a French love for delicate recipes and a Spanish taste for strong spices. Dishes made with local fish and meats use an African thickener—okra—and sassafras, an American Indian herb.

The bayous of Atchafalaya Swamp crawl with crawfish. They provide fishermen with a $10 million industry each year—and the Cajuns honor the crawfish with dances and parades. They also celebrate the sugarcane harvest and rice, yams, and shrimp.

Delta Queen, the last wooden steamboat on the Mississippi, rolls down to New Orleans. In the 1800's, ships like this moved tons of goods and people from port to port.

MISSISSIPPI

Old Prentiss was a town three times. In the early 1800's it rose on the banks of the Mississippi River, near where Cleveland is today. Then the Civil War came. Mississippians living in Old Prentiss took so many potshots at Union gunboats on the river that Union troops burned the village. The people built it again. Then the Mississippi changed its course, drowning the town. For years, stores and houses lay under water. In the 1950's, the river level lowered and Old Prentiss reappeared. People came to hunt souvenirs there but the contrary river covered it once more. Now Old Prentiss is extinct. It doesn't exist any longer.

Along the Mississippi there are dozens of extinct towns. Many began because of river traffic. Then, by the late 1800's, a network of railroads covered the state. People and freight traveled inland. The river landings weren't used as much and many little towns died. Others, like Old Prentiss, were conquered by the river itself.

But Vicksburg fooled the river. This historic port city rose on bluffs overlooking a sweeping loop of the Mississippi. In 1876 the river straightened its course and left Vicksburg high and nearly dry on an oxbow lake. To get the city back on the river, U. S. Army Engineers dug channels north and south from the ends of the oxbow and put Vicksburg back in business.

Over the years, industries that had to move bulk cargo—like gravel, coal, and grain—discovered that barges did the job cheaply and well. River ports began to thrive again. Now Vicksburg is one of three in the state that can handle ocean vessels as well as barges. The largest port in Mississippi, both in the number of vessels served and in tons of cargo shipped, is Pascagoula, on the Gulf of Mexico. Oil refining and shipbuilding have made this port one of the state's fastest growing cities.

Those whiskerlike barbels of the catfish contain feelers and taste buds—very handy for finding food on muddy river bottoms!

Area: the 32nd largest state, 47,716 sq mi (123,584 sq km). **Population:** 2,389,000. Ranks 29th. **Major Cities:** Jackson, 166,512; Biloxi, 46,407; Meridian, 46,256. **Manufacturing:** transportation equipment, clothing, chemicals, food products, lumber and wood products, electrical equipment, paper products, machinery, furniture. **Agriculture:** cotton, soybeans, poultry, beef cattle, eggs, dairy products, rice. Also lumbering. **Mining:** petroleum, natural gas, sand and gravel, clays. **Other Important Activities:** tourism, fishing (menhaden, shrimp, catfish, oysters). **Statehood:** the 20th state. Admitted Dec. 10, 1817.

A little more than half of Mississippi's population lives in rural areas, but the state—like the rest of the nation—becomes more urbanized each year. People are moving to its northwestern corner to be near the factories and stores of Memphis, Tennessee, just across the state line. Jackson, Mississippi's capital and largest city, is an industrial and trade center. In the southern and southeastern parts of the state, lumbering and the manufacture of wood products employ many people who, a generation ago, probably would have been farmers.

The Gulf Coast lures tourists to its sand beaches and warm, sunny winters. People who live there know that summer or fall may bring them a hurricane. Year-round ice-free harbors and waters rich in fish and shellfish make Mississippi a leading fishing state. One of the most important catches, menhaden, is processed into fish meal and added to poultry and livestock feed.

Some of the state's most profitable commercial fishing is done on farms! Far from the gulf, catfish are grown in ponds and fed and cared for like livestock. Catfish ponds can yield as much as 5,000 pounds (2,268 kg) of high-protein meat per acre.

Mississippi ranks third to Texas and California in cotton and is high among states east of the Mississippi River in beef cattle. The state's richest farmland was a gift of the muddy, mighty Mississippi before the days of modern dams and flood control. As it looped along, the river once carried sand and earth brought by its branches from as far west as Montana and as far east as New York. In flooding, it spread this fertile silt on land along its banks.

Mockingbird

Magnolia

136

The looping Mississippi River *used to cut into its banks to take a more direct route. Earth, sand, and stone from the river built up at both ends of the old loop, eventually blocking it off from the main stream. Left behind — a crescent-shaped oxbow lake.*

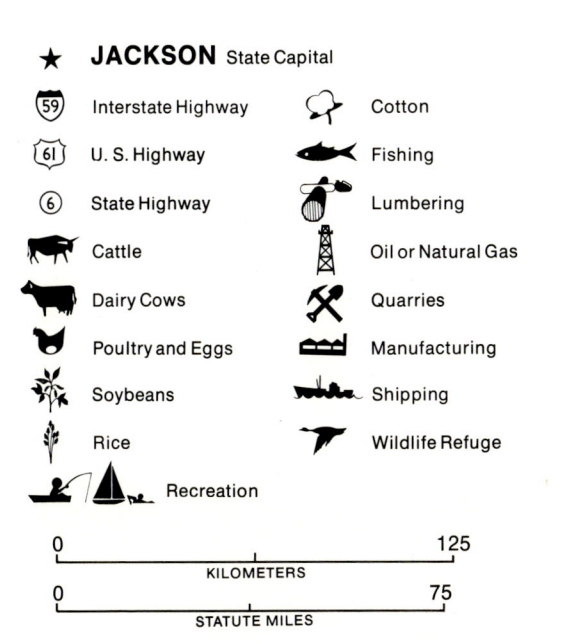

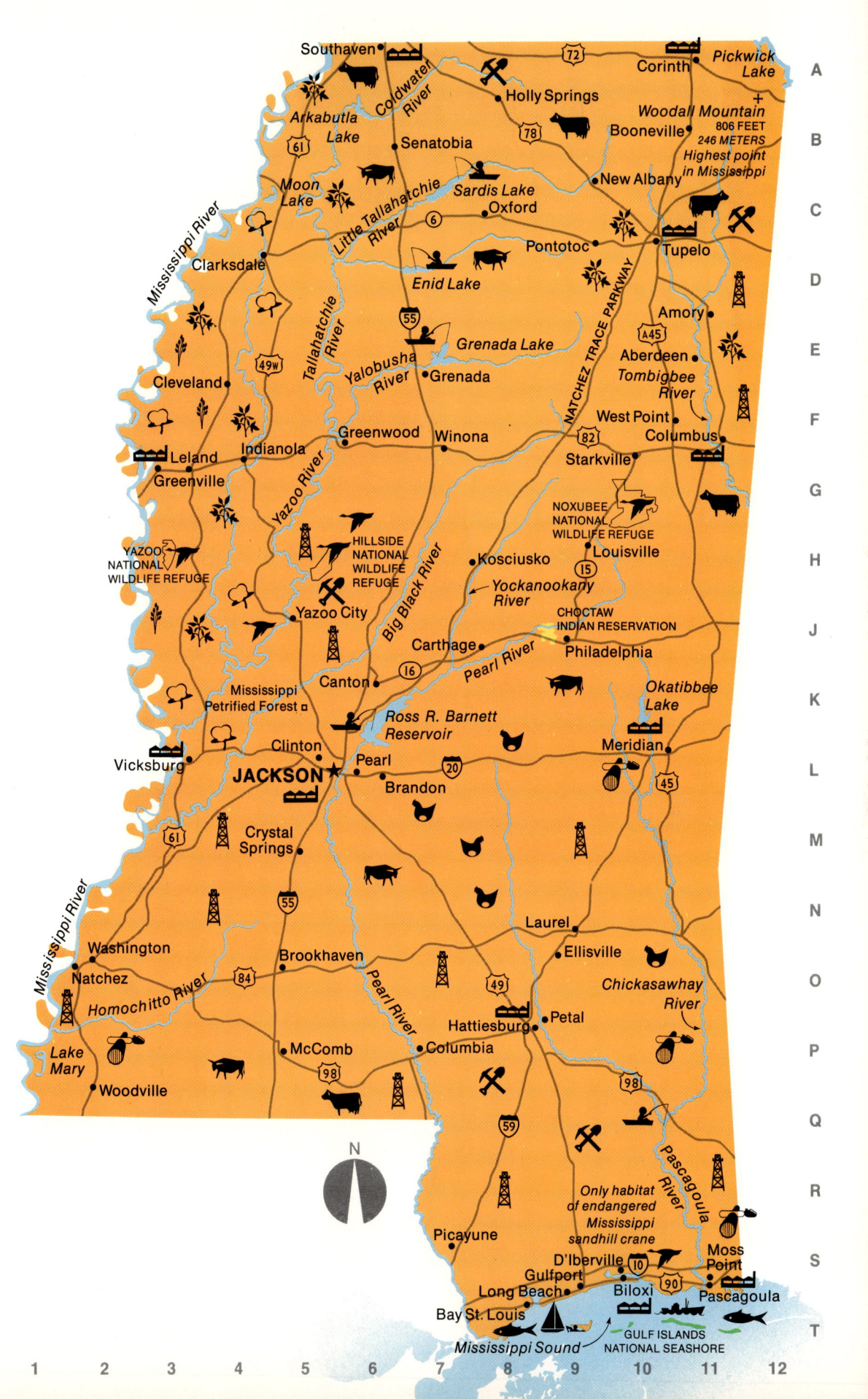

Legend

★ **JACKSON** State Capital

- (59) Interstate Highway
- (61) U.S. Highway
- (6) State Highway
- Cattle
- Dairy Cows
- Poultry and Eggs
- Soybeans
- Rice
- Recreation
- Cotton
- Fishing
- Lumbering
- Oil or Natural Gas
- Quarries
- Manufacturing
- Shipping
- Wildlife Refuge

0 — 125 KILOMETERS
0 — 75 STATUTE MILES

Annual stickball championships, held in Philadelphia, Mississippi, preserve a favorite Indian sport. About 4,000 Choctaws live here.

The Natchez Pilgrimage honors Old South roots. Costumed guides show visitors through The Elms and other stately mansions.

In the early 1800's, traders and settlers tramped Mississippi's first road, an Indian trail called the Natchez Trace.

Ghosts of Mississippi's past linger along the river and trail that shaped her history. Frontiersmen floated flour, tobacco, hemp, and livestock down the Mississippi to market in Natchez. Rather than pole their flatboats upstream, they sold them for lumber and walked back north. Most took the Natchez Trace. Today, the Natchez Trace Parkway, a two-lane scenic route, runs through remaining parts of the trace—an old French word meaning "line of footprints."

Cotton kingdoms thrived on the rich black soil. White-columned mansions lined the riverbanks while back-road shanties housed the slaves who worked the fields. Crippled by the Civil War, plantations gave way to tenant farming.

The Mississippi twists along the state's western border—once a changeable one. Old tales claim that Mississippians sometimes woke up in the morning to find their land in Louisiana!

No longer "king," cotton remains an important Delta crop. Machines replace more cotton pickers each year. The field hand tossing his pickings onto a trailer has become a rare sight.

SOUTH CAROLINA

Carolina Jessamine
Carolina Wren

"I lived the cotton life," said writer Ben Robertson of his farm boyhood near Clemson. "The fields blossomed like islands in the South Seas... the white and red hibiscus-like cotton flowers on the green cotton plants that spread away in long curving rows...." Farming in South Carolina's "up country" was hard work. But he said, "I liked to plow cotton, to stand between the swerving handles of the plow... and to walk barefooted in the fresh earth."

This was the early 1900's in the rolling red clay hills of the piedmont plateau. The Robertson family owned their land. However, thousands of farmers all over the South worked land that they rented. Many of these tenants were sharecroppers—this means that cash from the *crop* is *shared* between the worker and the landowner. Often tenant farmers are poor. Most, in those days, depended for income on the South's main crop, cotton.

Land can get tired. Tired land needs more and more fertilizer. Also, the soil planted year after year in cotton lost its ability to hold moisture. It eroded in deep gullies. The plants grew spindly and produced less cotton. Then, around 1920, the boll weevil came along and began destroying the fields.

South Carolina farmers found new crops that would help to improve the soil. Now the state ranks second to California in its harvest of peaches. Some farmers plant worn-out cotton land with loblolly pine seedlings. These trees grow so fast that they are ready to be cut for wood pulp in 15 to 20 years. Many old cotton fields have become lush pasture by being planted in grasses on which beef cattle graze.

"Cotton's going west, cattle's coming east," a saying goes. South Carolina doesn't grow much cotton anymore, but it buys a lot for its textile industry from states to the west. Spartanburg, Greenville, and many smaller towns turn out more than $66 billion worth of textile-mill products a year.

The "Best Friend of Charleston," a little engine that could—and did—pull the first scheduled steam train in America, in 1830.

Area: the 40th largest state, 31,055 sq mi (80,432 sq km). **Population:** 2,876,000. Ranks 26th. **Major Cities:** Columbia, 111,616; North Charleston, 58,544; Greenville, 58,518; Charleston, 57,470. **Manufacturing:** textiles, chemicals, clothing, machinery, paper products, electrical equipment, fabricated metals, food products, lumber and wood products. **Agriculture:** tobacco, soybeans, corn, eggs, hogs, dairy products, beef cattle, cotton, peaches. Also poultry. **Mining:** cement, stone, clays, sand and gravel, vermiculite. **Statehood:** the eighth state. Ratified Constitution on May 23, 1788.

The first textile mills grew up along a line of low hills which runs diagonally across the state. The line divides the "up country" from the "low country"—the coastal plain and the sandy barrier islands that border South Carolina from Georgetown south. Where rivers cross the hills, at the fall line, waterfalls and rapids created power. One of the first public hydroelectric plants in the United States began making electricity by waterpower near Anderson in 1897.

South Carolina has changed from an agricultural state to an industrial one. Besides textile mills, the turnaround brought garment factories, steel plants, nuclear technology. It also brought in money and jobs from foreign countries. South Carolinians manufacture tires in plants built by a French company. West Germans own a factory near Spartanburg that makes textile machinery.

South Carolina began with a mixture of cultures. Spanish settlers brought the seeds of orange trees. Landowners from Barbados, in the West Indies, settled on island and coastal plantations to raise rice and a valuable long-fibered "sea-island" cotton. With the slaves from Africa came the okra loved by Southern cooks today. In the 1700's, colonists living in and around Charleston were English, Scots, Dutch, German, French.

Charleston sits on a narrow peninsula in a natural harbor. Since colonial days it has been a major port. Now factories in the area produce chemicals, fertilizer, petroleum. Military bases and shopping centers give a 20th-century look to this historic region. But at the peninsula's southern tip, old Charleston has been lovingly preserved.

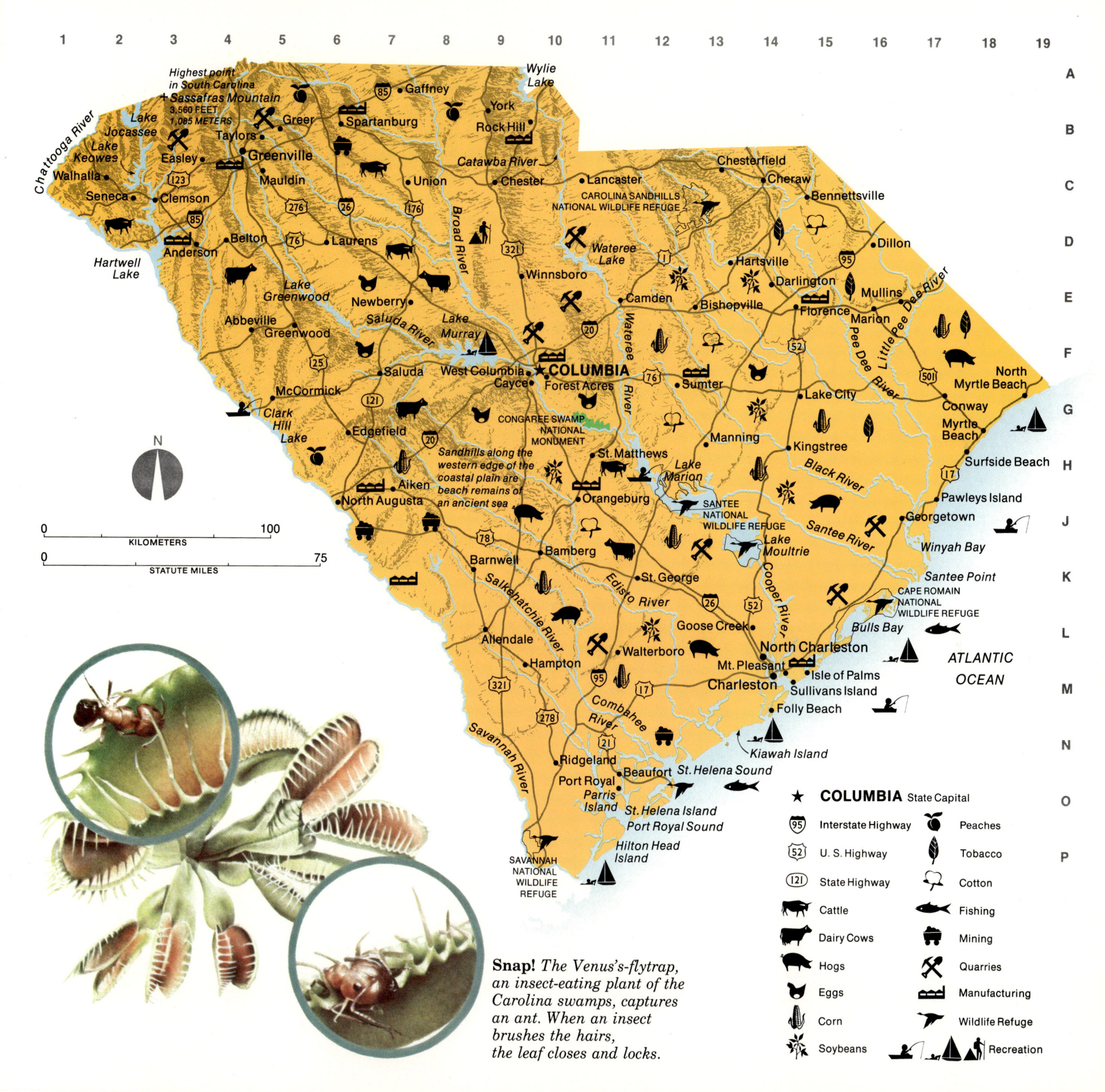

Snap! *The Venus's-flytrap, an insect-eating plant of the Carolina swamps, captures an ant. When an insect brushes the hairs, the leaf closes and locks.*

COLUMBIA State Capital
- 95 Interstate Highway
- 52 U.S. Highway
- 121 State Highway
- Cattle
- Dairy Cows
- Hogs
- Eggs
- Corn
- Soybeans
- Peaches
- Tobacco
- Cotton
- Fishing
- Mining
- Quarries
- Manufacturing
- Wildlife Refuge
- Recreation

141

This deer roams an 18th-century garden, Middleton Place, near Charleston.

An Atlantic loggerhead turtle comes out of the sea to a Cape Romain shore. She finds a site, digs a hole with her rear flippers, and lays eggs. After covering her nest, she returns to the water. Wildlife workers are moving some eggs to other beaches.

Once upon a time, in the colony of South Carolina, there was a busy little town named for a king—Charles Town. (Today we call it Charleston.) A cruel pirate, Stede Bonnet, wanted the riches of its trade for himself. Charles Town's snug harbor bristled with guns as merchant ships sailed in and out. But before Bonnet's bold crew, no ship was safe. Finally, in 1718, Col. William Rhett gave chase. After a desperate battle at the mouth of the Cape Fear River, the rascals surrendered. Kept under guard at Charles Town, Bonnet begged for mercy. But the colonists were firm. Hang he must and hang he did.

Grand old Charleston houses crowd the city's historic harbor area. A carriage drives along Rainbow Row. No high-rises allowed.

As in colonial days, street vendors sell flowers from the gardens of sunny Charleston.

143

Lake Superior—1,333 feet (406 m) deep. This is the largest body of fresh water in the world.

144

Great Lakes States

Lake Michigan — 923 feet (281 m) deep — is the only one of the Great Lakes wholly within the U.S.

Lake Huron — 750 feet (229 m) deep. Next to Superior, Huron has the least pollution.

Lake Erie — 210 feet (64 m) deep. Wind can whip its shallow coastal waters into high waves.

WISCONSIN
MICHIGAN
ILLINOIS
INDIANA
OHIO

Almost an island in the heart of the nation—that's the Great Lakes states. Four of the Great Lakes and the Ohio and Mississippi rivers wrap around them. Along the blue boundary, beaches, cliffs, hills, and woods edge the land—except where cities grow mile upon mile. The glaciers that covered much of North America left deep layers of rich soil here. Where the pioneers cleared the forests or found prairie, a corn-yellow checkerboard marks off fertile cropland.

So big are the five Great Lakes that they hold one-fourth of all the fresh water in the world—enough to cover the United States 12 feet (3.7 m) deep. In summer they usually look as peaceful as ponds. But hot-weather squalls can blow up bad seas. And gray-waved winter storms roar down out of the north.

ILLINOIS

The biggest city in Illinois almost wasn't in Illinois at all. The territory that became the state of Illinois reached from the Mississippi River only to the southern tip of Lake Michigan. In 1818, when statehood was near, an Illinois leader, Nathaniel Pope, asked Congress for an extra strip of land on the north. On the shore of the lake a tiny village called Chicago grew into the greatest inland port in the world. Thanks to Pope's foresight, it grew in Illinois and not in Wisconsin.

Chicago is the only place in North America where the Great Lakes link with the Mississippi River system. From Chicago you can even sail to Europe in two directions. The city has spent billions of dollars to dig harbors and build docks where ships load with grain, machinery, and automobiles "made in America." On a Chicago dock a ship's captain from Germany might meet a captain from Japan.

More than half the people of the state live in this small northern strip. But at its western end, about 100 miles (161 km) from Chicago, is some of the most rugged land in the Midwest. Steep limestone cliffs rise above the river in a region called the Mississippi Palisades. Forested hills offer a refuge to many kinds of wildlife. Bald eagles, hawks, and wood ducks winter here and move north in the spring.

Mostly-flat-as-a-pancake Illinois was scraped almost level by the ice sheets that covered the region thousands of years ago. But the glaciers skipped one area—the Mississippi Palisades and they didn't reach another: In the south are the state's only other high hills, the Illinois Ozarks. Generally less than 1,000 feet (305 m) high, they're almost mountains but not quite.

Southern Illinois calls itself "the land between the rivers." On the western border, at Cairo, the muddy Mississippi meets the Ohio. Along the east border the quiet Wabash flows south, carrying mostly pleasure boats and fishermen. Above Shawneetown it joins the Ohio, busy with freight traffic. Just below Shawneetown, Cave-in-Rock, a huge cavern in a bluff, opens over the river. In frontier days outlaws hid in the cave, waiting to rob boat crews and pioneers.

In the small towns between the rivers, the courthouse or a bandstand sits shaded by tall trees. Along the main street there may be a roof over the sidewalk in front of the stores. It protects shoppers from sun, and from rainstorms so heavy that local folks call them "gully washers."

Townspeople work at meat packing, quarrying, milling, mining. Southern Illinois factories turn out everything from comic books to pipe organs. Farmers raise livestock, feed grains, and timber.

Rich, deep, black soil covers more than three-fourths of Illinois. This soil lured the pioneer family of young Abe Lincoln. As you drive north, fields of corn and soybeans stretch to the horizon, crisscrossed by roads straight as an arrow. Under the fields and pastures lies enough coal to last the entire world 100 years. Illinois is fourth among the states as a miner of coal, and eighth as producer of petroleum products. More steel and machinery come from factories around Chicago than from any other area in the world.

Steel made Chicago rich. It also made it tall. The skyscraper—which depends on a steel frame—was invented in Chicago in the 1880's. Now Chicago has the tallest building in the world, the Sears Tower. From the observation deck on the 103rd floor of the 110-story building, you can see all the way to Wisconsin.

Up we go on the world's first and biggest Ferris wheel. George Ferris's new idea thrilled Chicago at the 1893 world's fair.

Area: the 24th largest state, 56,400 sq mi (146,075 sq km). **Population:** 11,245,000. Ranks fifth. **Major Cities:** Chicago, 3,099,391; Rockford, 145,459; Peoria, 125,983. **Manufacturing:** machinery, food and food products, fabricated metals, electrical equipment, chemicals, clothing, transportation equipment, musical instruments. **Agriculture:** corn, soybeans, hogs, beef cattle, dairy products. **Mining:** coal, petroleum, stone. **Other Important Activities:** finance, transportation. **Statehood:** the 21st state. Admitted Dec. 3, 1818.

Illinois

Charles Mound 1,235 FEET +376 METERS Highest point in Illinois

The northwestern corner of Illinois was untouched by the glaciers

UPPER MISSISSIPPI RIVER WILDLIFE AND FISH REFUGE

GREAT RIVER ROAD

ILLINOIS & MISSISSIPPI CANAL

MARK TWAIN NATIONAL WILDLIFE REFUGE

CRAB ORCHARD NATIONAL WILDLIFE REFUGE

Southern limit of North American glaciation

LAKE MICHIGAN

Cities and places:
- Freeport
- **Rockford**
- Zion
- Waukegan
- North Chicago
- Highland Park
- Arlington Heights
- Wilmette
- Evanston
- Elgin
- Des Plaines
- Oak Park
- **Chicago**
- De Kalb
- Elmhurst
- Wheaton
- Cicero
- Aurora
- Downers Grove
- Harvey
- Calumet City
- Joliet
- Chicago Heights
- Park Forest
- Morris
- Ottawa
- Seneca
- Kankakee
- Rock Island
- Moline
- Monmouth
- Galesburg
- Pontiac
- Nauvoo
- Macomb
- **Peoria**
- Pekin
- Normal
- Bloomington
- Dickson Mounds
- Rantoul
- Danville
- Champaign
- Urbana
- Quincy
- Beardstown
- Decatur
- **SPRINGFIELD** ★
- Jacksonville
- Lake Shelbyville
- Charleston
- Mattoon
- Effingham
- Alton
- Edwardsville
- Carlyle Lake
- Lawrenceville
- East St. Louis
- Belleville
- Centralia
- Mt. Vernon
- Du Quoin
- Rend Lake
- Carmi
- Carbondale
- Crab Orchard Lake
- Marion
- Shawneetown
- Cairo

Rivers:
Rock River, Fox River, Kankakee River, Spoon River, Illinois River, Mississippi River, Sangamon River, Kaskaskia River, Little Wabash River, Wabash River, Big Muddy River, Ohio River

---

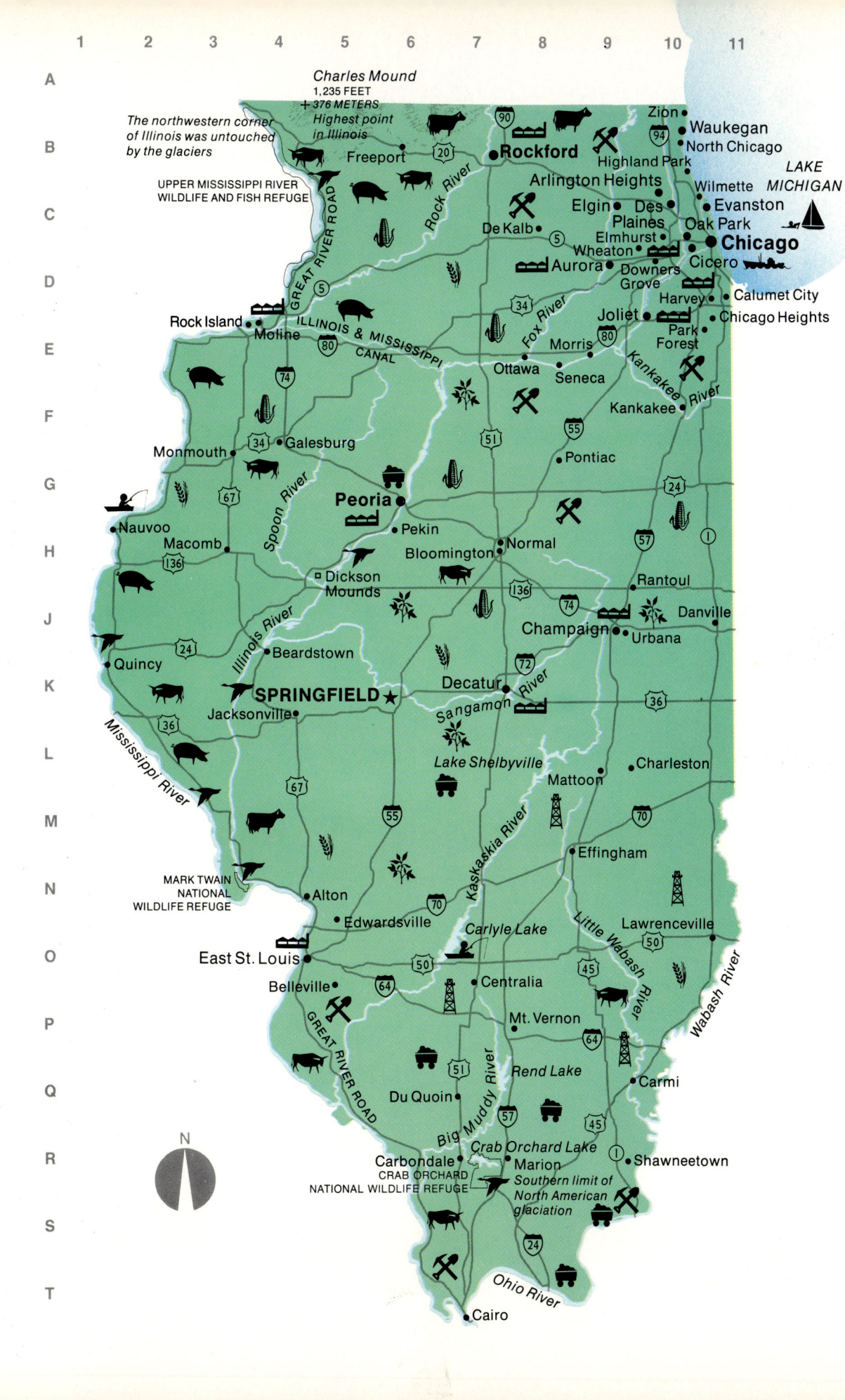

The Illinois Waterway links two of North America's most important shipping routes, the Mississippi River and the Great Lakes–St. Lawrence Seaway system. Part river, part canal, it makes a water road between the Gulf of Mexico and the Atlantic Ocean, used by oceangoing ships or strings of barges.

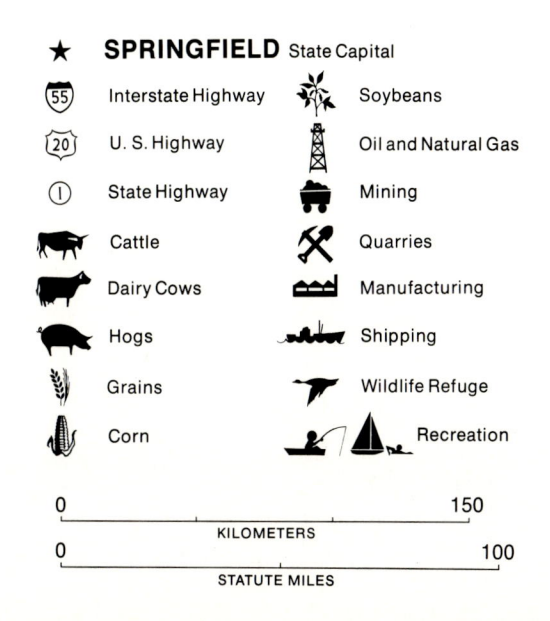

CANADA — St. Lawrence Seaway — Great Lakes — Hudson River — Erie Canal — Chicago — New York — Illinois Waterway — UNITED STATES — Mississippi River — Atlantic Ocean — New Orleans — Gulf of Mexico

---

Legend:
- ★ **SPRINGFIELD** State Capital
- 55 Interstate Highway
- 20 U.S. Highway
- 1 State Highway
- Cattle
- Dairy Cows
- Hogs
- Grains
- Corn
- Soybeans
- Oil and Natural Gas
- Mining
- Quarries
- Manufacturing
- Shipping
- Wildlife Refuge
- Recreation

0 — 150 KILOMETERS
0 — 100 STATUTE MILES

147

Towboats don't always tow. They often push. Long ago they did pull barges behind them. They haven't changed their name, but they have changed their habits. Modern towboats, with diesel engines up to 9,000 horsepower (6,714 kwt), can push a fleet of barges longer than an ocean liner. If such a heavy load were pulled, it would whip out of control. The barges are lashed together to make a raft.

On the Illinois Waterway and the Ohio and Mississippi rivers, the barges carry grain, soybeans, coal, salt, ore, limestone, petroleum, steel — the products of Midwest farms and industries. Along the rivers, electric power plants wait for coal. More coal, iron ore, and limestone go to steel mills. Huge elevators store the grain. Much of the cargo will travel to ports where it will be loaded on ocean-bound ships.

A tough towboat pushes grain barges on the Illinois Waterway. The load passes through an open railroad bridge.

Canada geese winter near Crab Orchard Lake. They eat corn, soybeans, and wheat.

Rugged hills of southern Illinois rise where Ice Age glaciers did not reach.

Big city beach. Chicagoans sunbathe on a calm summer day. But on stormy days Lake Michigan can send 10-foot (3 m) waves thundering against the shoreline.

Freshly smoked loops of bologna wait to be sealed in plastic at a Du Quoin factory.

In Joliet spinning spools of steel wire feed machines that can cut 3,000 kinds of nails.

INDIANA

Bumper-to-bumper traffic is nothing new to Indiana. One of the first highways in the United States, the National Road, went through Indianapolis in the 1830's. A little boy lived in the woods near the rutted track. Later he wrote a book. He remembered "the rumbling of the wheels, the noise of the animals, and the chatter of the people," as a stream of covered wagons and stagecoaches moved westward. In our day the National Road is Route 40, one of several broad transcontinental highways that make Indiana a crossroads of the nation.

Indiana's love for cars began on the Fourth of July in 1894. That was when Elwood Haynes cranked up a strange contraption called an automobile and drove it seven miles an hour along Pumpkinvine Pike in Kokomo. He had invented the first automobile with a clutch and an ignition system. Only a few years later, in 1909, cars began racing on the now world-famous Indianapolis Motor Speedway. Many classic American automobiles, as writer Jean Shepherd said, were born "in dusty Indiana hamlets and came together every spring in the dawn of automobiling to battle it out."

Now, every Memorial Day, almost half a million fans flock to Indianapolis to watch the battles between the powerful racers. The cars we drive on our highways owe much to safety improvements tried out on those early Indy autos. Rearview mirrors, aluminum pistons, modern spark plugs, balloon tires, disc brakes, and streamlined styling first appeared on the Indy track.

Without steel there would be no automobiles, and steel is Indiana's second-biggest business. In fact, beginning in 1906, the city of Gary was built in a sandy wilderness on the shore of Lake Michigan just for the purpose of making steel. Gary sits between the great iron ranges to the north and the coalfields to the south—the steel industry needs both. Today Gary is part of a jungle of steel mills, factories, and power plants that line the lakeshore, forming one of the most important industrial regions in the world.

Some of that sandy wilderness is still there: the Indiana Dunes. These huge hills build up as sand sweeps in from the lake. Dunes never rest, but these creep so slowly over the years that you can't see them move. As they shift they sometimes uncover forests dead and buried thousands of years ago.

Near the big cities, truck farms grow vegetables. From Indiana's rich farmland come corn, wheat, oats, and soybeans that help feed the country and the world.

A lot of the soybean crop goes to feed the millions of turkeys Indiana farmers raise every year. A baby turkey, gobbling away at soybean meal, fish meal, and corn, can fatten to 20 pounds (9 kg) from spring to fall—when it goes off to market.

Turkey eaten in the U.S. amounts to about nine pounds (4 kg) per year for each of us, some at holiday celebrations. In Indiana the turkeys celebrate too. Every fall Daviess County holds a turkey race. The fastest bird gets to stay off the platter.

Holidays are not the only reason for festivals in Indiana towns. Chicken dinners and fish fries raise money to buy uniforms for the high school band or a new fire engine. People dress in old-fashioned clothes to honor early settlers. Growing up in a small Midwestern town means getting together with your neighbors for harvest celebrations. Boys and girls march in parades or decorate their bikes and ride with flags flying. The band plays. Floats crawl down the street. Everybody has a good time.

A lawn mower clips along in a yearly race at Twelve Mile. First to finish 12 miles (19 km) is hailed champ.

Area: the 38th largest state, 36,291 sq mi (93,993 sq km). **Population:** 5,330,000. Ranks 12th. **Major Cities:** Indianapolis, 714,878; Fort Wayne, 185,299; Gary, 167,546. **Manufacturing:** electric and electronic equipment, primary metals, transportation equipment, machinery, chemicals, fabricated metals, food and food products, rubber and plastics. **Agriculture:** corn, soybeans, hogs, beef cattle, dairy products, wheat, eggs, vegetables, turkeys. Also tobacco. **Mining:** coal, cement, limestone, petroleum, sand and gravel. **Statehood:** the 19th state. Admitted Dec. 11, 1816.

A glacier made our "inland seas." It plowed down from the north about 14,000 years ago and made deep holes. It melted some 10,500 years ago and filled the holes: five Great Lakes.

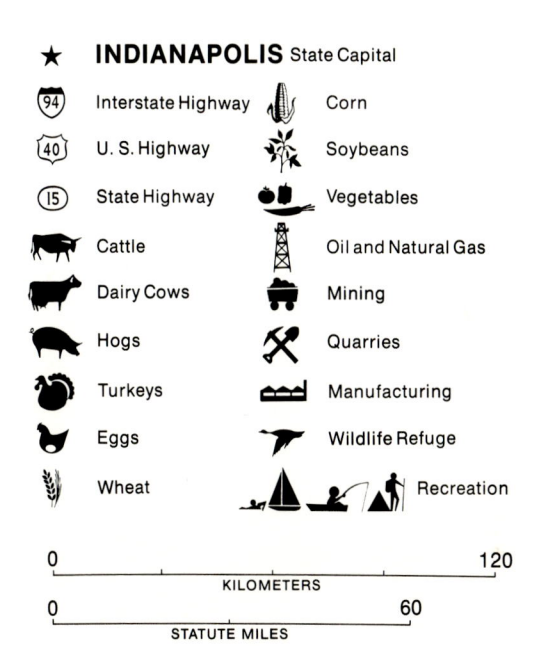

Legend

- ★ **INDIANAPOLIS** State Capital
- (94) Interstate Highway
- (40) U.S. Highway
- (15) State Highway
- Cattle
- Dairy Cows
- Hogs
- Turkeys
- Eggs
- Wheat
- Corn
- Soybeans
- Vegetables
- Oil and Natural Gas
- Mining
- Quarries
- Manufacturing
- Wildlife Refuge
- Recreation

0 — 120 KILOMETERS
0 — 60 STATUTE MILES

Ever been to Beanblossom? How about Gnaw Bone? Or Stoney Lonesome? They're southern Indiana villages that the rest of the world—or most of it, anyway—has forgotten. And in the hills around them, the people, "uplanders," seem to prefer it that way. A lot of them live in log cabins, some old, some brand new with television antennas. Many of the rocky slopes refuse to grow crops, and the farmers have turned them into pasture. Artists and craftsmen have left noisy cities to make their homes in these quiet hills. Uplanders are a self-reliant lot, growing their own vegetables, canning food for the winter, keeping a cow, chopping wood. There are weavers, beekeepers, gunsmiths. You could make a living as a hunter or a trapper if you knew all the good spots.

Smoky glow...Lake Michigan mirror...A forest of steel-mill stacks smudges the Hammond sky.

Machines cut limestone. Indiana quarries high-quality stone which America likes to use for important buildings and statues in the park.

A southern Indiana craftsman, stone carver Jake Peterson, chisels a limestone model of A. J. Foyt's winning car in the 1967 Indianapolis 500.

In the hilly southern Indiana "uplands," cornfields sometimes twist and turn. This one curves around a pocket of marsh and between hardwood forests.

Unwanted leaves in Bloomington steam as they turn into good, cheap fertilizer for city gardens and lawns.

Swimmers head across dunes on the shore of Lake Michigan. Plants try to root in the windblown hills.

Music goes 'round and 'round and comes out at an Elkhart band-instrument factory.

153

MICHIGAN

Is Michigan shaped like a mitten? Some people say so, but that's only the lower peninsula. There's also the upper peninsula. It is mostly forest, with iron mines in the west and, on its eastern end, the great shipping lanes known as the Soo Canals. They carry ships around the rapids of the St. Marys River.

And then there's the watery part of the state, two square miles (5.2 sq km) of it for every three square miles (7.8 sq km) of land. Four of the five Great Lakes give Michigan more than 3,100 miles (4,989 km) of shoreline. That's longer than the distance from Maine to Florida. Michigan also has some 11,000 smaller lakes. Nobody in the state lives more than a few minutes' drive from at least one of them.

Just inland, along the east shore of Lake Michigan, cherry, peach, and apple orchards make a springtime fringe of blossoms. Air, cooled by the lake, helps to slow blooming of the trees in the spring. That lessens the danger of damaging frost. In the fall, the lake water warms up the air that passes over it before coming ashore. This makes the growing season a little longer, and helps give pie-lovers more sour cherries than come from any other state.

Michigan's rivers are among the most important waterways in the world. The St. Marys River on the north and the Detroit and St. Clair on the southeast connect the three upper Great Lakes with the St. Lawrence Seaway and the Atlantic Ocean. They make international ports of inland cities.

Detroit, Michigan's largest city, has suffered from racial tension and neglect of its downtown area since the 1940's. In 1967 violent riots broke out. Many people thought Detroit was a dying city. But now there is a new spirit of hope sparked by better race relations and by downtown renewal. Projects range from the sparkling skyscrapers that tower over the riverfront to housing that lures suburbanites back to the city.

Think "Michigan" and you think "automobile," and rightly so. More than 85 percent of all the motor vehicles produced in the nation are made by Michigan-based companies. Transportation equipment equals one-third the value of Michigan's manufactured goods. High in importance are the "primary" and "fabricated" metal industries. The Ford Motor Company's huge factory complex in Dearborn shows how these are related to auto manufacturing. Iron ore is made into finished iron and steel—the primary metal—which are then made into car and truck parts—the fabricated metal.

Southern Michigan is an industrial beehive: Grand Rapids furniture, Kalamazoo paper, Battle Creek cereal, Ann Arbor space vehicles, Fremont baby food.

The state's second most important "work" is *play*—a billion-dollar tourism and recreation industry. In Michigan almost 35,000 businesses and about 350,000 people provide everything from snowmobiles to motel rooms to paper cups—all for tourists. Michigan residents use more of their land for recreation than for anything else.

Every year 100,000 people come to the Seney National Wildlife Refuge, a waterfowl breeding area on the upper peninsula. Michigan tourists play in one of the world's biggest sandpiles, the 600-acre (243 hectare) Sleeping Bear Dune. Around the state are zoos, beaches, tiny city parks, and huge forests for campers and hikers. Resort villages sprout where cherry orchards grew just a few years ago. And a part of Detroit's riverfront, once run-down stores and warehouses, now boasts a sports arena.

Salt sellers sell salt from a salt cellar. It's under Detroit. The mine, with miles of roads, has been there for 70 years. The salt's been there about 300 million.

Area: the 23rd largest state, 58,216 sq mi (150,779 sq km). **Population:** 9,129,000. Ranks seventh. **Major Cities:** Detroit, 1,335,085; Flint, 174,218; Warren, 172,755. **Manufacturing:** transportation equipment, machinery, fabricated metals, primary metals, chemicals, food and food products, electrical equipment. **Agriculture:** dairy products, corn, vegetables, beef cattle. **Mining:** oil, iron, cement, natural gas, sand and gravel, stone, salt. **Other Important Activities:** tourism. **Statehood:** the 26th state. Admitted Jan. 26, 1837.

1 2 3 4 5 6 7 8 9 10 11 12 13 14 15 16 17 18
A B C D E F G H J K L M N O P Q R S T U
Rock Harbor Lodge
Isle Royale
ISLE ROYALE NATIONAL PARK
Largest island in Lake Superior
LAKE SUPERIOR
Copper Harbor
Keweenaw Peninsula
Hancock
Portage Lake
Keweenaw Bay
Mt. Curwood
1,980 FEET
604 METERS
Highest point in Michigan
L'ANSE INDIAN RESERVATION
Erosive action of waves, rain, and frost has carved cliffs, caves, and arches in the colorful sandstone
PICTURED ROCKS NATIONAL LAKESHORE
GOGEBIC RANGE
Ontonagon River
Lake Gogebic
Ironwood
Grand Island
Marquette
Ishpeming
Munising
SENEY NATIONAL WILDLIFE REFUGE
Tahquamenon River
Whitefish Bay
Sault Ste. Marie
Soo Canals
BAY MILLS INDIAN RESERVATION
St. Marys River
Manistique Lake
Drummond Island
Escanaba River
Brule River
Iron Mountain
Manistique
Mackinac Island
Straits of Mackinac
Bois Blanc Island
Big Bay de Noc
Escanaba
Cheboygan
Beaver Island
Mullett Lake
Burt Lake
Menominee River
Green Bay
Little Traverse Bay
Black Lake
Alpena
Manitou Islands
Grand Traverse Bay
Torch Lake
SLEEPING BEAR DUNES NATIONAL LAKESHORE
Glaciers pushed rock, sand and silt from the far north to create huge dunes, some as high as 480 feet (146 meters)
Elk Lake
Hubbard Lake
LAKE HURON
Traverse City
Kalkaska
Grayling
Au Sable River
Oscoda
Manistee River
Higgins Lake
Houghton Lake
Manistee
Ludington
Pere Marquette River
Muskegon River
Saginaw Bay
Harbor Beach
Midland
Bay City
Cass River
LAKE MICHIGAN
Mt. Pleasant
Saginaw River
Saginaw
Fremont
Flint River
Muskegon Lake
Muskegon
Owosso
Flint
Port Huron
Grand Rapids
Grand River
Kentwood
Wyoming
East Lansing
Holland
LANSING
Troy
Sterling Heights
Roseville
St. Clair River
Pontiac
Warren
Lake Saint Clair
St. Clair Shores
Kalamazoo River
Royal Oak
East Detroit
Livonia
Detroit
South Haven
Battle Creek
Dearborn Heights
Dearborn
Kalamazoo
Ann Arbor
Portage
Jackson
Ypsilanti
Wyandotte
Trenton
Benton Harbor
St. Joseph
St. Joseph River
Raisin River
Detroit River
Adrian
Monroe
Coldwater
LAKE ERIE
Niles
2 45 41 141 77 2 75 41 23 22 31 131 75 10 31 27 23 25 96 75 94 96 196 69 127 94 131 12 12
N
LANSING State Capital
Interstate Highway
U. S. Highway
State Highway
Cattle
Dairy Cows
Hogs
Wheat
Corn
Soybeans
Vegetables
Fruit
Oil and Natural Gas
Mining
Quarries
Manufacturing
Shipping
Wildlife Refuge
Recreation
0 150
KILOMETERS
0 100
STATUTE MILES

Isle Royale National Park seems to drift like a tattered green leaf on Lake Superior. Copper mining, lumbering, and forest fires made a wasteland of the main island in earlier days, but now it is again densely forested. Isle Royale is the scene of an unusual experiment. Moose and their natural enemies, timber wolves, live there with no interference from man. The moose eat the vegetation, in ponds and along the shorelines. The wolves eat the moose, mainly old or sick animals. The population of each stays fairly steady. Is there a balance? Only time will tell.

Coho salmon, imported from the Pacific, now thrive in Lake Michigan. By eating harmful species they balance fish life.

Every Labor Day you can take a five-mile (8 km) walk over Mackinac Bridge—"Big Mac"—world's longest suspension bridge.

On Isle Royale, hiking trails wind through a wilderness where, about 4,000 years ago, Indians mined copper with stone hammers and fire.

Beware! That's more than 1,600 pounds (726 kg) of unpredictable bull moose, 8 feet (2.4 m) at the shoulder. About 1,200 moose live in Isle Royale National Park.

At the huge Ford plant in Dearborn, sparks shower from the torch as an auto worker welds a frame.

Why flip flakes in the cornflake factory? Flipped flakes fly for testing the toasting.

157

OHIO

It might happen some day that you would be hiking a woodsy Ohio path when you'd see, almost hidden in the undergrowth, the tangled branches of an old apple tree. Would you dare to think that Johnny Appleseed had planted it? He *was* real. From 1801 until the late 1830's, John Chapman (the pioneers called him Johnny Appleseed) tramped central Ohio. He carried apple seeds he got from cider presses of Pennsylvania, and hunted for fertile spots along a stream or in a clearing.

Johnny was a religious man. He believed that he had a holy mission to provide growing fruit for frontier families. People say that you can still find Johnny's orchards but his wild countryside is long gone. In its place is a modern Ohio that has been called "the most American state."

If Ohio is "most American," possibly that's because it's a mixture. There's a little bit of New England in Ohio's northeast corner. Here, villages founded by transplanted Yankees have a central green, or common, surrounded by white, colonial-style houses.

In western Ohio, settlements grew up as farmers' markets. Even today, in some, the grain elevator is the tallest thing in town. These little communities sit flat on the fields, as though they'd blown in off the Illinois prairie. In hilly southeastern Ohio you find coal mining towns. Here former Virginians or West Virginians cluster around a country crossroad, making new homes like those they left behind in the mountains. In Cincinnati and Columbus, neighborhoods where Polish or German immigrants settled look like parts of old New York.

Cincinnati, Ohio's oldest large city, prospered because of the Ohio River, with its trade and passenger traffic. Today the Ohio carries more tonnage than the St. Lawrence Seaway or the Panama Canal. Cincinnati, midway between coalfields of West Virginia and of Kentucky, is the largest inland coal distribution center in the world.

For its 436 miles (702 km) along the southern border of the state, the Ohio River is lined with the tall smokestacks of power plants, factories, and steel mills—all with their mountains of coal. But around the bend from many of these grimy spots, you can still find wild stretches. In these clumps of sycamore and willow, the ghost of Johnny Appleseed might wander.

Cincinnatians learned the hard way to keep the river clean. By the 1930's it had taken in so much sewage and industrial waste that it began to kill fish and spread disease through the valley. In 1948, along with seven other states, Ohio formed a group to clean up the river.

Other Ohio regions also are cleaning up pollution. In 1969 many Americans read in their newspapers that a northern Ohio river, the Cuyahoga, had caught fire! Its dirty, oil-slicked waters burned for an entire day, so furiously that the fire almost destroyed two railroad bridges.

Waste from Cleveland and other cities had so polluted Lake Erie that until recently it was called "dead." Almost nothing could live in it. But people are paying attention now. The lake is coming back to life.

Ohioans take a lot of kidding. People say they're like the shape of their state—kind of square. It may be true that some Ohioans think a big town is one with more than four stoplights, but a couple of Ohio boys went pretty far. John Glenn, of New Concord, was the first American to orbit in space. Neil Armstrong, of Wapakoneta, took mankind's first steps on the moon. They leaped from their small towns right off the planet Earth.

Thanks to Johnny Appleseed,
The Middle West is apple-treed.
A bag of seeds in either hand,
He planted orchards in the land.

Area: the 35th largest state, 41,222 sq mi (106,764 sq km). **Population:** 10,701,000. Ranks sixth. **Major Cities:** Cleveland, 638,793; Columbus, 535,610; Cincinnati, 412,564. **Manufacturing:** transportation equipment, machinery, fabricated metals, primary metals, electric and electronic equipment, chemicals, food and food products, rubber and plastics, stone, clay, and glass products. **Agriculture:** soybeans, corn, dairy products, beef cattle, hogs. Also wheat, poultry, vegetables, oats, apples. **Mining:** coal, petroleum, stone, lime, natural gas, sand and gravel, cement. **Statehood:** the 17th state. Admitted March 1, 1803.

1 2 3 4 5 6 7 8 9 10 11 12 13 14 15 16
A B C D E F G H J K L M N O P Q R
LAKE ERIE
CEDAR POINT NATIONAL WILDLIFE REFUGE
OTTAWA NATIONAL WILDLIFE REFUGE
Kelleys Island
Toledo
Oregon
Maumee
Bryan
Defiance
Maumee River
Bowling Green
Fremont
Sandusky
Fostoria
Tiffin
Sandusky River
Blanchard River
Findlay
Van Wert
Lima
Ottawa River
Kenton
Scioto River
Marion
Olentangy River
Celina
Wapakoneta
Grand Lake
Indian Lake
Campbell Hill 1,550 FEET 472 METERS Highest point in Ohio
Bellefontaine
Sidney
River
Great Miami River
Piqua
Greenville
Troy
Springfield
Marysville
Delaware Lake
Delaware
Alum Creek Lake
Hoover Reservoir
Upper Arlington
Worthington
Whitehall
Reynoldsburg
COLUMBUS
Fairborn
Dayton
Kettering
Xenia
Little Miami River
Middletown
Hamilton
Fairfield
North College Hill
Sharonville
Reading
Cheviot
Norwood
Cincinnati
Wilmington
Washington Court House
Paint Creek
Rocky Fork Lake
GREAT SERPENT MOUND
Circleville
Ancient Indians shaped mounds from the earth to cover their dead
MOUND CITY GROUP NATIONAL MONUMENT
Chillicothe
Scioto River
Jackson
Portsmouth
Ohio River
Ironton
Gallipolis
Athens
Hocking River
Belpre
Marietta
Muskingum River
Lancaster
Buckeye Lake
Newark
Dillon Lake
Zanesville
New Concord
Cambridge
Senecaville Lake
Mt. Vernon
Coshocton
Mohican River
New Philadelphia
Mansfield
Ashland
Shelby
Norwalk
Lorain
Elyria
Cleveland
East Cleveland
Euclid
Willoughby
Lakewood
North Olmsted
Parma
Brunswick
Cuyahoga River
Cuyahoga Falls
Akron
Barberton
Tuscarawas River
Massillon
Canton
North Canton
Alliance
Kent
CUYAHOGA VALLEY NATIONAL RECREATION AREA
Wickliffe
South Euclid
Cleveland Heights
Shaker Heights
Garfield Heights
Mentor
Painesville
Ashtabula
Mosquito Creek Lake
Warren
Niles
Austintown
Youngstown
Boardman
Struthers
East Liverpool
Atwood Lake
Leesville Lake
Steubenville
Martins Ferry
Ohio River
90 11 6 80 76 77 30 250 7 70 36 71 33 35 50 23 68 52 32 75 127 224 24 33 275 271
N
★ COLUMBUS State Capital
Interstate Highway
U. S. Highway
State Highway
Cattle
Dairy Cows
Hogs
Poultry and Eggs
Wheat
Corn
Soybeans
Oil and Natural Gas
Mining
Quarries
Manufacturing
Wildlife Refuge
Recreation
0 100 KILOMETERS
0 80 STATUTE MILES

The Great Serpent Mound uncoils along a hilltop in southern Ohio. About 2,000 years ago, Adena Indians built this religious monument of earth. Hopewell Indians buried the 3-inch (7.6 cm) clay head in another mound.

A blur of Cincinnati Bengals and a stadium full of fans at a Cleveland Browns game show that football is big in Ohio.

160

With everything from light bulbs to airplanes to artificial hearts, Ohio industries touch nearly every part of our lives. But products begin with new ideas. Harvey Firestone, of Akron, found a way to make safe, inflatable tires. Now Akron leads the world in rubber and plastic products. Akron workers made the first space suits for our astronauts. Dayton's output of modern business machines— like the buzzing computers you see in department stores— began in 1879 with the invention of the cash register. But in Cincinnati, one day in 1878, some soapmakers daydreamed. They mixed in too many air bubbles and "invented" floating soap.

Hard hat and goggles protect a worker as he rolls pipe in a Lorain steel mill.

In Cincinnati the careful hand of a chemist tests the purity of detergent.

Tires flow through an Akron assembly line. They've been stamped out like big waffles.

WISCONSIN

Wisconsin never had a gold rush, but it had a lead boom, which is just about the same thing. And there are ghost towns to remind us. In the 1830's and 1840's our growing country needed paint and ammunition. Lead was used for both. Wisconsin was frontier then but the southwestern corner of the state had rich lead deposits. Miners and their families poured in. Some didn't take time to build houses. Instead they found shelter in caves or in the lead mines, burrowing like badgers. (And giving Wisconsin its nickname, the Badger State.) The town of Mineral Point (you can tell how *it* got its name) began as a mining center.

By 1850 the lead was worked out. Most people left as fast as they had come. And the ghost towns? You can find them by their abandoned trash dumps and the telltale pits from the mining operations. Miners who stayed behind when the boom ended turned to farming, at first wheat, then dairying.

Wisconsin owes its dairy industry to a newspaperman who later became governor, William Hoard. In 1870 Hoard began shouting a message to farmers of the state: DAIRY. He showed them that dairying would make money and that the crops they grew to feed their herds—clover and alfalfa—were better for the soil than wheat. And Hoard had a high opinion of cows. "Speak to a cow as you would to a lady," he advised, because a cow is "the foster mother of the human race."

Wisconsin dairymen looked for new products and new ways to market their milk. In 1887 a Racine man invented the malted, using dried milk. Because cheese was easier to store and ship than liquid milk, Wisconsin began the industry that made it the Big Cheese of all the states.

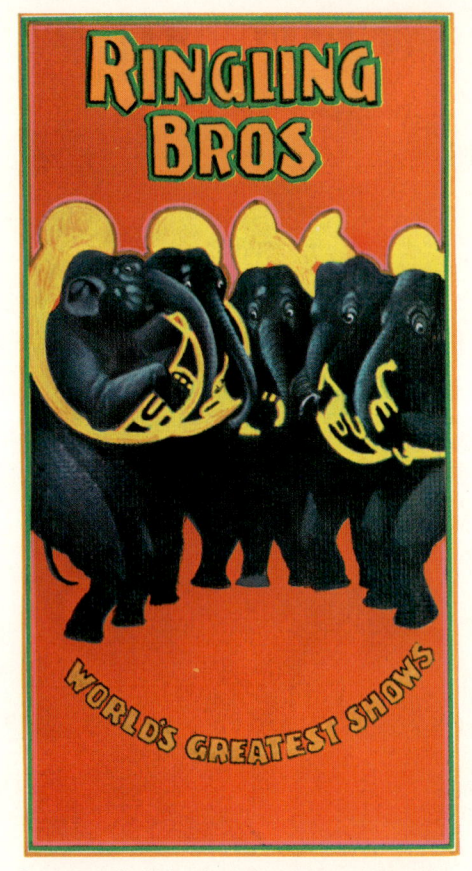

In 1884 the Ringling brothers of Baraboo started their world-famous circus. The elephant brass band really played—loud.

Area: the 26th largest state, 56,154 sq mi (145,438 sq km). **Population:** 4,651,000. Ranks 16th. **Major Cities:** Milwaukee, 665,796; Madison, 168,196; Racine, 94,744. **Manufacturing:** machinery, food and food products, paper and allied products, fabricated metals, transportation equipment, electrical equipment, primary metals, chemicals, lumber and wood products. **Agriculture:** dairy products, beef cattle, hogs, corn, vegetables. **Mining:** sand and gravel, stone, iron, cement, lime. **Statehood:** 30th state. Admitted May 29, 1848.

Almost two million cows work hard to protect their state's first place in the production of milk and cheese.

From southwestern Wisconsin you can look far back in time. Thousands of years ago, as glaciers moved south over the continent, they came to high ground (Timms Hill and Rib Mountain) and parted to go around it. In a sea of ice they left an island of land—this quarter of Wisconsin, plus a strip of Minnesota, Iowa, and Illinois. Here we can see what the whole northeastern U. S. must have looked like before the glaciers.

But what they gave to Wisconsin! When the ice sheets melted for the last time, they left behind thousands of low places that filled with water. Northern Wisconsin became a land of lakes—today loved by vacationers. Lake Winnebago, the largest, covers 215 square miles (557 sq km). Under the summer sun, sailboats skim its waves. Motorboats buzz. Swimmers crowd its beaches.

Winter used to scare away the tourists but now they love winter sports too. One of the oldest and coldest is fishing through the ice with a spear. You walk or drive out onto the frozen lake, cut a hole, put up a small shelter. Spear in hand, you wait for your fish to swim by. Your prize catch is a sturgeon, which can weigh from 30 to more than 150 pounds (14 to 68 kg).

Forests cover almost half of Wisconsin. They provide wood pulp for paper mills. If you've heard of Paul Bunyan, the giant lumberjack, you've heard of the logging camp where the cookstove measured 1,760 steps from end to end. Little boys greased the pancake griddle by skating on it with bacon slabs tied to their shoes. Paul's big Blue Ox, Babe, used to get very thirsty. So that Babe could drink, they say, Paul took his shovel and scooped out all those lakes.

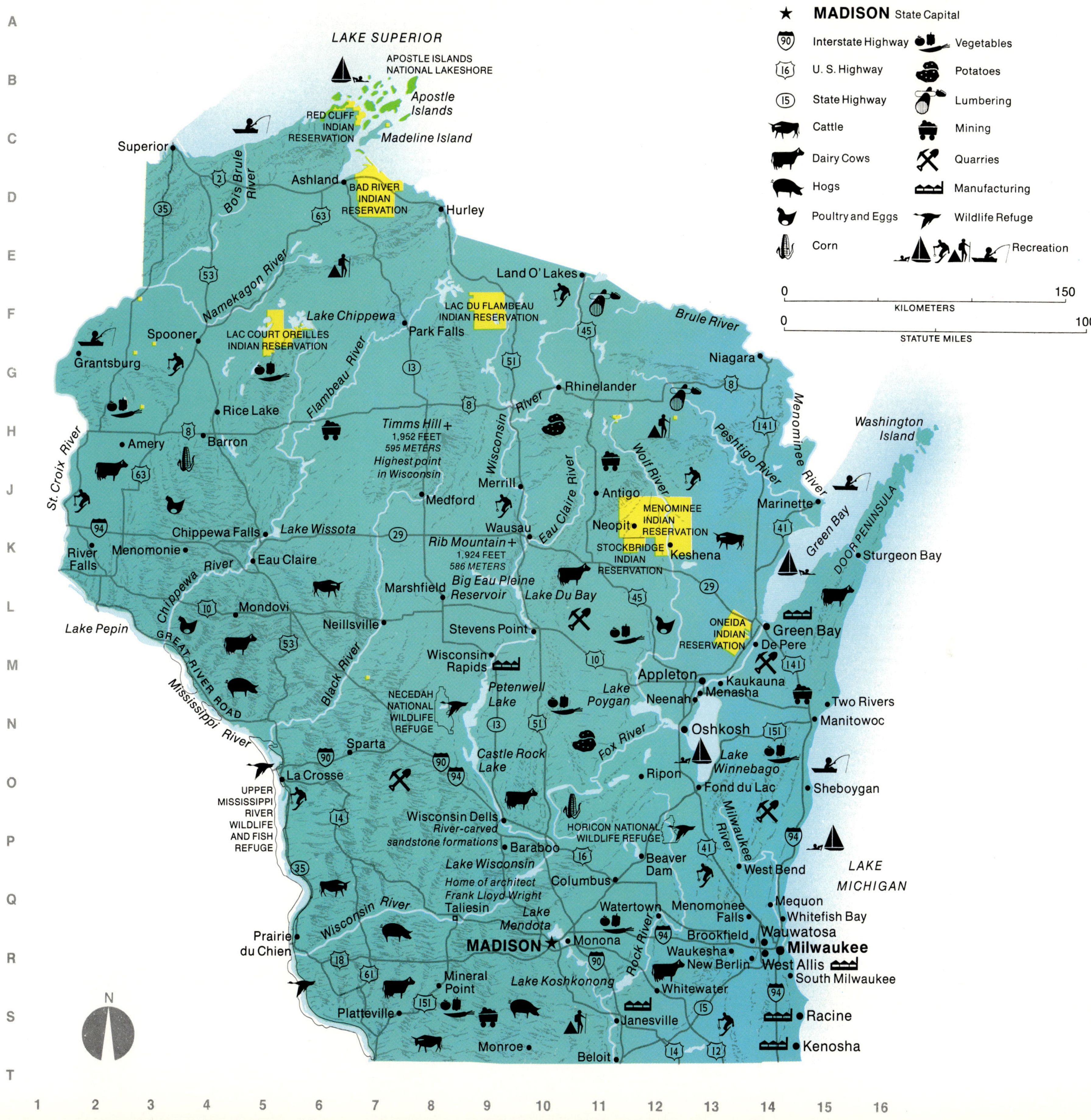

MADISON State Capital
Interstate Highway
U. S. Highway
State Highway
Cattle
Dairy Cows
Hogs
Poultry and Eggs
Corn
Vegetables
Potatoes
Lumbering
Mining
Quarries
Manufacturing
Wildlife Refuge
Recreation
0 150
KILOMETERS
0 100
STATUTE MILES
LAKE SUPERIOR
APOSTLE ISLANDS NATIONAL LAKESHORE
Apostle Islands
RED CLIFF INDIAN RESERVATION
Madeline Island
Superior
Ashland
BAD RIVER INDIAN RESERVATION
Hurley
Bois Brule River
Namekagon River
Land O' Lakes
LAC DU FLAMBEAU INDIAN RESERVATION
Brule River
Lake Chippewa
Spooner
LAC COURT OREILLES INDIAN RESERVATION
Park Falls
Grantsburg
Flambeau River
Niagara
Rhinelander
Rice Lake
Wisconsin River
Menominee River
Washington Island
Timms Hill
1,952 FEET
595 METERS
Highest point in Wisconsin
Amery
Barron
Peshtigo River
St. Croix River
Wolf River
Eau Claire River
Merrill
Antigo
Medford
MENOMINEE INDIAN RESERVATION
Marinette
Green Bay
DOOR PENINSULA
Neopit
Wausau
Chippewa Falls
Lake Wissota
Rib Mountain
1,924 FEET
586 METERS
STOCKBRIDGE INDIAN RESERVATION
Keshena
Sturgeon Bay
River Falls
Menomonie
Eau Claire
Chippewa River
Big Eau Pleine Reservoir
Marshfield
Lake Du Bay
Mondovi
Lake Pepin
Neillsville
Stevens Point
ONEIDA INDIAN RESERVATION
Green Bay
De Pere
GREAT RIVER ROAD
Wisconsin Rapids
Black River
Appleton
Kaukauna
Menasha
Neenah
Mississippi River
NECEDAH NATIONAL WILDLIFE REFUGE
Petenwell Lake
Lake Poygan
Two Rivers
Manitowoc
Oshkosh
Fox River
Sparta
Castle Rock Lake
Lake Winnebago
La Crosse
Ripon
Fond du Lac
Sheboygan
UPPER MISSISSIPPI RIVER WILDLIFE AND FISH REFUGE
Wisconsin Dells
River-carved sandstone formations
HORICON NATIONAL WILDLIFE REFUGE
Milwaukee River
Baraboo
Beaver Dam
Lake Wisconsin
West Bend
LAKE MICHIGAN
Home of architect Frank Lloyd Wright
Taliesin
Columbus
Wisconsin River
Watertown
Menomonee Falls
Mequon
Whitefish Bay
Lake Mendota
Prairie du Chien
MADISON
Monona
Rock River
Brookfield
Wauwatosa
Waukesha
Milwaukee
New Berlin
West Allis
South Milwaukee
Mineral Point
Lake Koshkonong
Whitewater
Platteville
Janesville
Racine
Monroe
Beloit
Kenosha
N

Milking's done. Dairy farmer Bill Thull (right) collects milk in a portable tank. In one of Wisconsin's 368 cheese factories (below), a worker takes loaves of brick from their forms. Today Wisconsin does $1.8 billion worth of dairy business a year.

On the reservation, Menominee Indians sometimes hunt and fish for food.

Motor-driven metal arms pick cherries, shaking ripe fruit onto twin canvas aprons. On the Door Peninsula, cherry growing can be risky. A late-spring cold spell can cut a crop in half.

"Menominee Indians are sometimes called the Rice Eaters," wrote Suzanne DeMontigny one day at school on the reservation. She was explaining her tribe's name in the Menominee language. Long ago these Indians gathered wild rice as their main food. "The Indians used to shoot wild game," wrote Suzanne's classmate, Michelle Keshena. "But now we buy food in stores." About 2,500 Indians live on the wooded, 360-square-mile (932 sq km) reservation. Most of the men work at the tribe's sawmill on the Wolf River. "It is very good to be a Menominee," wrote Greg Jacobs, "because there is no smog and no big buildings here." Pam Grignon said, "There are very few Menominees left but my Grandma is a full blooded Menominee.... I am proud to be a Menominee."

Hello, mink! How do you like it on your mink farm? Better in the wild, you say?

Summer skiing at Green Bay means fun for Wisconsin college students year after year.

165

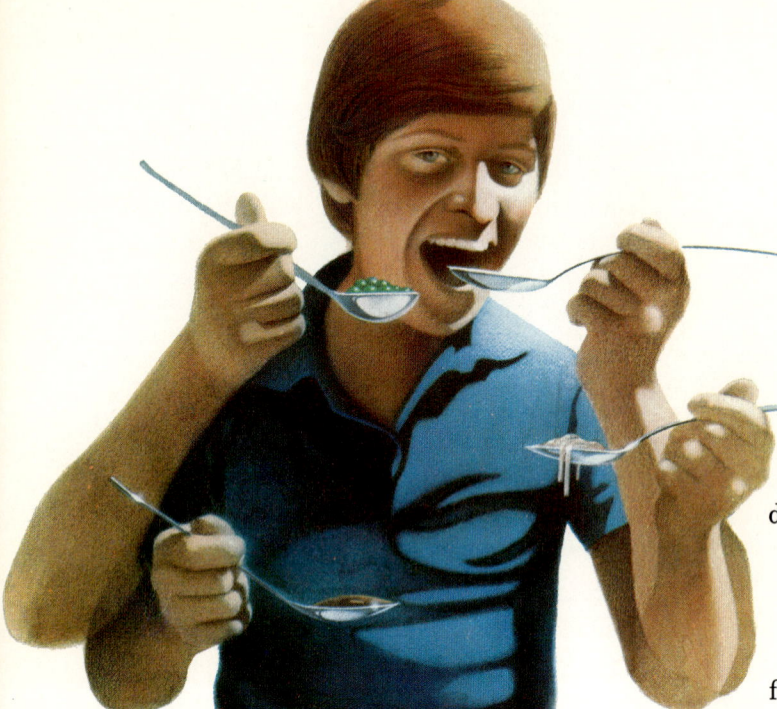

The Wonders of Agriculture

Have you ever wondered how much food you eat? And where it all comes from? Experts at the U. S. Department of Agriculture figure that the average teenage American boy puts away 5.3 pounds (2.4 kg) of food a day. That's nearly a ton—1,917 pounds—every 12 months! The average teenage girl eats about 200 pounds less. Counting together men, women, and children, the average per person is 1,450 pounds (658 kg).

Now multiply these 1,450 pounds by the 219,000,000 people in our nation. You'll get an idea of the tremendous food production that comes from our farms. But that's only the beginning. The biggest share of some of our most important crops—corn, for example—isn't eaten by people. It goes into feed for pigs, poultry, cattle, and other animals. Farmers and ranchers also produce fibers that become the clothes we wear. And raw materials for items we have in our medicine cabinets—even for paints and plastics.

Farmers in the United States also grow things for sale in other countries—agricultural products rank as our number one export. Two facts show what this can mean: (1) As much U. S. wheat goes overseas as is marketed here at home. (2) The number of acres in the United States growing food for Japan is greater than all the cropland in that little island country.

Once most of the people in our nation were farmers. Only a hundred years ago three-fourths of the population lived on farms, one-fourth in cities. Today it is just the reverse. Yet the one-fourth that now live in rural areas aren't all farmers. Actually, only about one person in twenty makes a living today by raising crops or animals. It is this small group that supplies food and fiber for the rest of us. Since we don't have to grow our own, we can live as secretaries or lawyers or schoolteachers or policemen.

Or as fertilizer manufacturers and tractor salesmen and butchers and supermarket clerks. For estimates suggest that one out of every five jobs in the nation depends in some way on farming—providing supplies to farmers or processing and bringing farm products to us.

At the time of the Civil War one person on the farm grew enough to support himself and three other people. Today it is himself and 56 others. What has made this leap possible? Among the major things: machinery, specialization, scientific advances.

Today's farmer has machine power that would amaze the Civil War plowman with his horses. Motorized giants that can plow in an hour six times as much as the old-timer could do in a day. Planters that put seeds into the ground in a swath half as wide as a football field. Mechanical cotton pickers that can snatch up 21,000 pounds (9,525 kg) of cotton a day—50 times as much as could be done by a top field hand.

Tractors that pull modern farm machines may have air-conditioned cabs, stereo sets, and two-way radios to keep in touch with other people on the farm. But even without such driver comforts those tractors can sell for as much as $50,000 each. A tire may cost $1,000 to replace. Today's farmer has mighty machines, but he also needs a lot of capital—money—to equip his place. Many owners have hundreds of thousands of dollars invested. They even buy such things as airplanes to sow seeds, spread fertilizer, and spray fields more efficiently. They use computers to help solve management problems. For running a farm today is as complicated as running a small factory or business.

Farmers need a lot of land. It doesn't pay to have a big tractor just to work a few acres. So operators try to buy or rent enough land to put their machines to best use. Thus over the years farms have gotten bigger. Once the saying "40 acres and a mule" told what it took to make a living as a farmer. Now farms may spread over hundreds, even thousands, of acres.

People with small farms may have trouble making ends meet. Without money to get machines or land, they can't produce very much. Incomes then may not be enough to keep them going. Many small farmers have had to sell out to more successful neighbors. That has played a part in the movement of people from farms to cities. Villages have also become "ghost towns" as stores dependent on farmer customers have had to close their doors.

From field *to elevator to mill to bakery to you—with trucks and trains, machinery and handling in between. That's how wheat becomes the bread you buy. Each processing or transportation step adds to the cost. Similar things happen with other foods— one reason the farmer gets only 39 cents out of every grocery dollar you spend.*

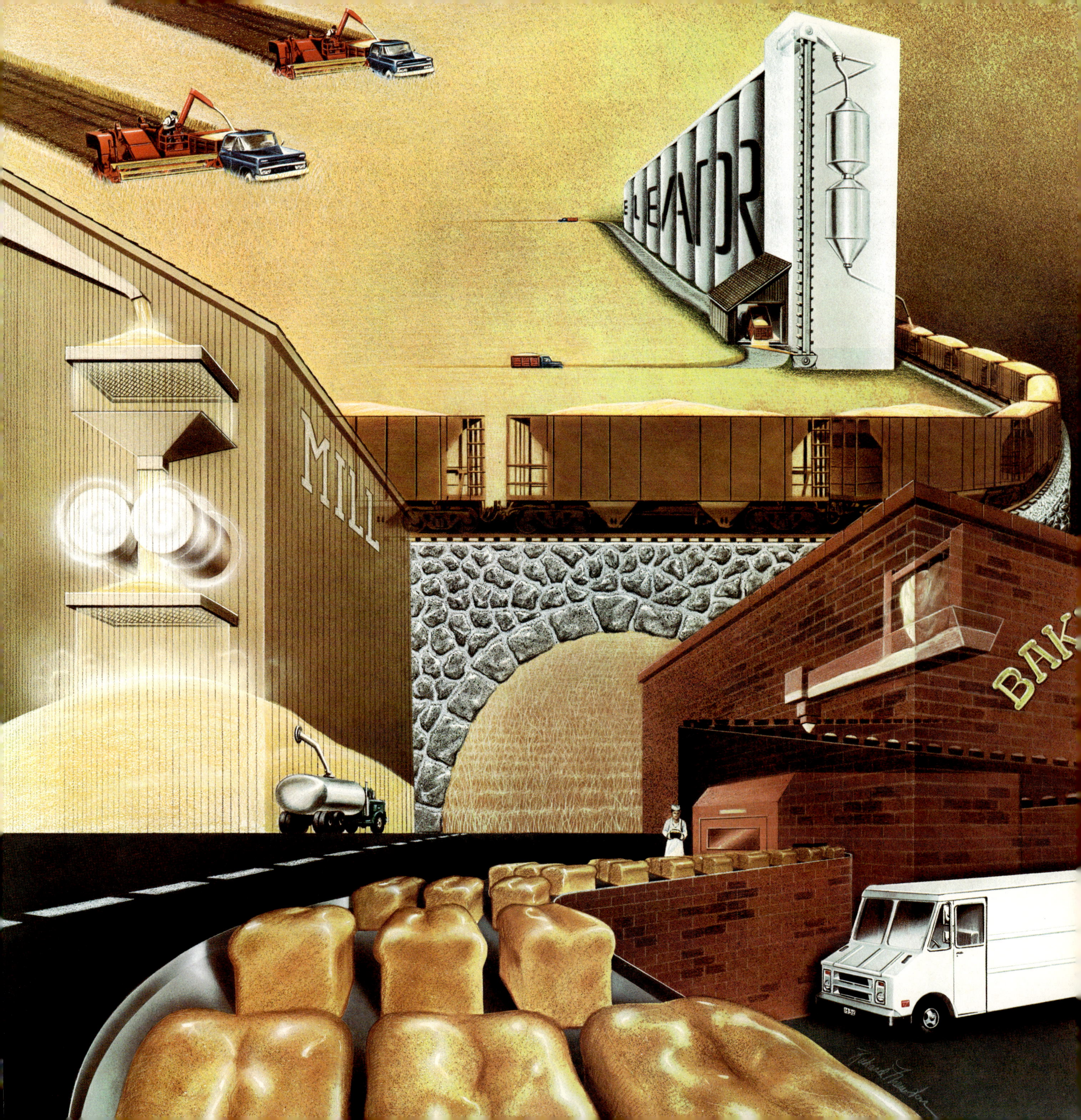
ELEVATOR
MILL
BAK

Farming in the United States is mainly a family-run business. Only a fraction of our acres are operated by big corporations. Family farms can compete because they can be more flexible—with fewer bosses, they can make decisions faster, for example.

The bounty of our farms makes us the best-fed nation in all the world. Their efficiency keeps prices low enough for the average U. S. family to spend a smaller share of its income on food than any other people in history. Our farms and our marketing system let us dine without an eye to the calendar—having berries in midwinter, oranges and lettuce the year around, for example. Not so long ago everyone had to eat mostly what happened to be in season.

Specialization has played an important part in these changes. It's easy to understand why warmth-loving oranges thrive in Florida but not in frigid Alaska. Or why rice, which needs lots of water, does well in the wetlands of Louisiana but not in the dry canyons of Utah. Farmers concentrate on growing things best suited to the weather and geography where they live.

Millions of years ago, wild short-stem grasses adapted to the growing conditions of the plains that sprawl across such states as Kansas, the Dakotas, and Montana. When farmers came, they found that a tame, short-stemmed grass—wheat—would do well there. Now fields of the grain stretch as far as the eye can see. Farmers produce an average of 32 bushels per acre—enough to make 2,200 loaves of bread.

On the rolling prairie of such states as Iowa and Illinois, tall grasses once grew wild. Today the farmer's tamed tall grass—corn—marches for miles in rows across the land. More acres are planted in corn than any other crop. On them our farmers produce as much corn as all the rest of the world's farmers put together.

Other combinations of geography and man and machines make other areas tops in their own ways. Cranberries thrive in the cool, wet bogs of Wisconsin and Massachusetts, for example. Peanuts like the sandy soil of Georgia's coastal plain. U. S. olives come from sunny groves in California.

Roots and Tubers

Potatoes

Radish

Sugar beet

Fruits

Cotton

Pears

Strawberries

Eggplant

Seeds

Cacao

Corn

Lima beans

Peanuts

168

Thus we have wheat farmers and peanut growers and cattlemen and poultry raisers and dozens of other farming specialists. Even tree farmers. In many places around the nation, land not very good for food crops is planted with trees. Farmers raise them for harvest as fence posts, lumber, decorative greenery—and Christmas trees.

But having acre upon acre of one crop in one location carries risks. Harmful insects can multiply rapidly and cause great damage. Plant diseases can spread like wildfire; in 1970 a disorder called blight threatened to destroy a great part of the nation's corn crop. Weather also can bring widespread ruin. Not enough rain, or too much at the wrong time, or hail, or windstorms may wipe out big areas. In a way, the farmer has to be a gambler; he plants, and works, and prays that no disaster strikes. And he hopes that when he finally gets his crop to market he'll get a decent enough price to repay him for his efforts and his risks.

Modern science is helping the farmer with some of his problems. Long-range weather forecasting aids in planting and harvesting decisions. New developments provide ways of boosting crop yields or of producing better quality items with more efficiency. Research helps in the battle against plant diseases and insect pests.

Take insect control, for example. Technicians grow ladybug beetles that eat destructive aphids, or raise wasps that kill harmful caterpillars. These are among promising ways of replacing sprays that pollute the environment. Scientists work on methods of flashing light over a field to fool unwanted insects into coming out of hibernation in freezing weather. They use the insects' own scents to draw pests to their deaths; one female moth's chemical "perfume" is so

In colonial days *most people grew their own food. Even city folk often had cows and gardens. They ate what was in season, or what they had preserved. Now farming and marketing methods give us great variety. And we use many parts of plants. Samples below may hold surprises. Did you know that onions are kinds of leaves, or potatoes are fat underground stems called tubers?*

Flowers

Rose
Broccoli
Cauliflower

Leaves

Parsley
Peppermint
Lettuce
Onion

Stalks and Stems

Sugarcane
Pine tree
Celery
Asparagus

Orchard and forest in the rainy north, wide variety in the drier south—that's Far West farming.

Irrigated acres, mostly west of the Mississippi, grow a fifth of our harvest on a tenth of our farmland.

Giant garden—*that's how the nation looks in this pictorial map showing where things grow. And compared with most countries, the United States really is an agricultural giant. Few others have the many kinds of soil or climate we do. These make it possible for us to produce almost anything—except some of the spices, fruits, and vegetables of the tropics.*

Where a farmer lives influences what he raises. Rugged land and weather in Alaska, for example, limit crops. Hawaii, far from mainland markets, turns to things that can stand shipping. So it goes across the U.S., where half the land is in farms, half in woods, parks, swamps, deserts, cities, and towns.

Agriculture means wheat and livestock in the Plains and Mountain states, where ranches can average 2,000 acres (809 ha).

Rain in America's midsection—30 inches (762 mm) or more a year—nourishes bumper yields of rice, sugarcane, cotton, corn.

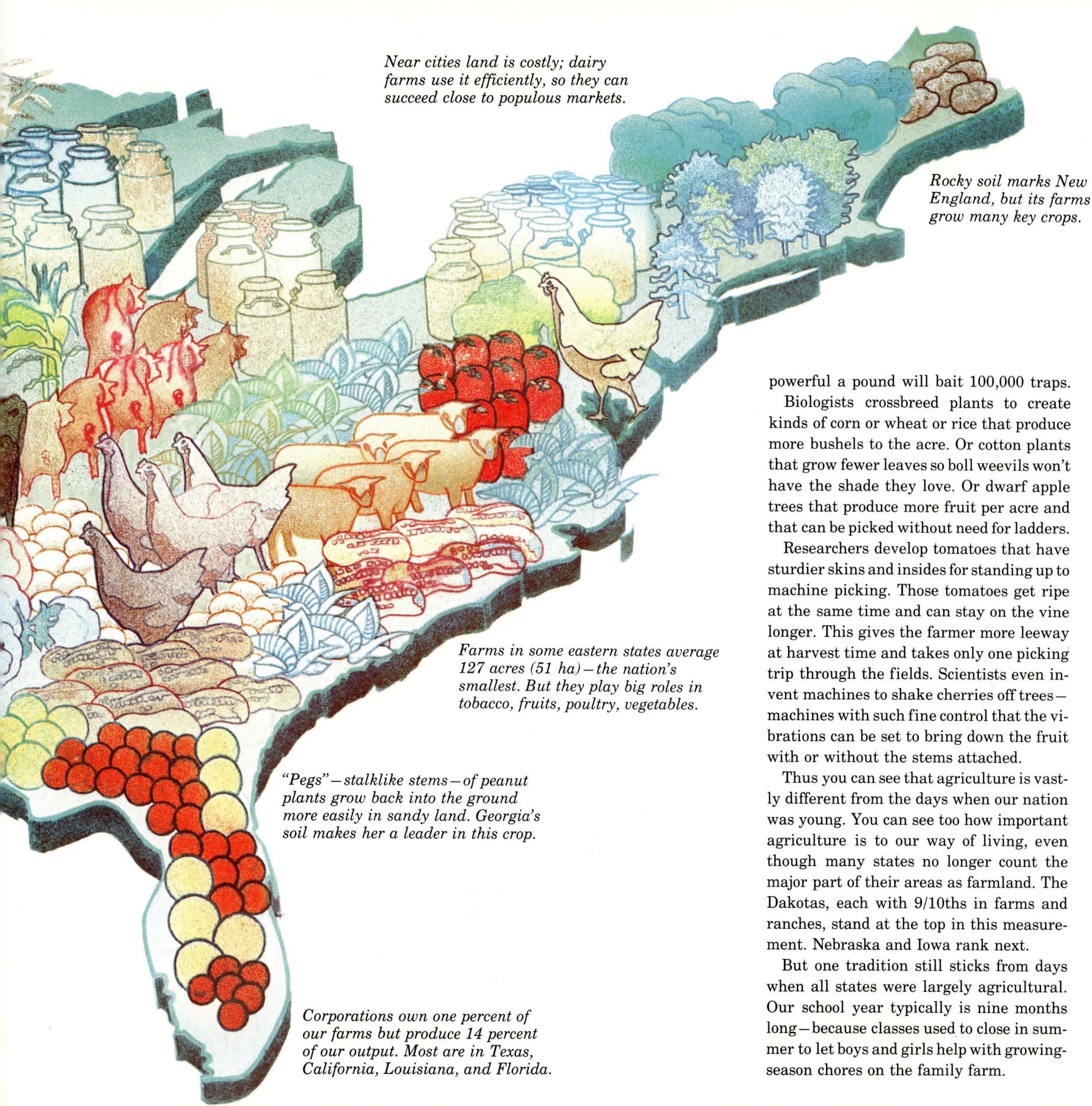

Near cities land is costly; dairy farms use it efficiently, so they can succeed close to populous markets.

Rocky soil marks New England, but its farms grow many key crops.

Farms in some eastern states average 127 acres (51 ha)—the nation's smallest. But they play big roles in tobacco, fruits, poultry, vegetables.

"Pegs"—stalklike stems—of peanut plants grow back into the ground more easily in sandy land. Georgia's soil makes her a leader in this crop.

Corporations own one percent of our farms but produce 14 percent of our output. Most are in Texas, California, Louisiana, and Florida.

powerful a pound will bait 100,000 traps.

Biologists crossbreed plants to create kinds of corn or wheat or rice that produce more bushels to the acre. Or cotton plants that grow fewer leaves so boll weevils won't have the shade they love. Or dwarf apple trees that produce more fruit per acre and that can be picked without need for ladders.

Researchers develop tomatoes that have sturdier skins and insides for standing up to machine picking. Those tomatoes get ripe at the same time and can stay on the vine longer. This gives the farmer more leeway at harvest time and takes only one picking trip through the fields. Scientists even invent machines to shake cherries off trees—machines with such fine control that the vibrations can be set to bring down the fruit with or without the stems attached.

Thus you can see that agriculture is vastly different from the days when our nation was young. You can see too how important agriculture is to our way of living, even though many states no longer count the major part of their areas as farmland. The Dakotas, each with 9/10ths in farms and ranches, stand at the top in this measurement. Nebraska and Iowa rank next.

But one tradition still sticks from days when all states were largely agricultural. Our school year typically is nine months long—because classes used to close in summer to let boys and girls help with growing-season chores on the family farm.

Pressure from below can raise bumps in earth's crust called dome mountains. The Black Hills are an example.

The Heartland

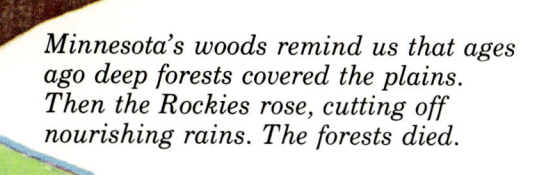

Minnesota's woods remind us that ages ago deep forests covered the plains. Then the Rockies rose, cutting off nourishing rains. The forests died.

An island when seas drowned the Midwest, the Ozarks expose rocks 1.3 billion years old.

NORTH DAKOTA
MINNESOTA
SOUTH DAKOTA
IOWA
NEBRASKA
KANSAS
MISSOURI

Far-apart patches of highlands and hills emphasize the wavy flatness of the nation's heart. Here is plain and prairie land, covered ages ago by great seas. It slopes up gently from the Mississippi River that forms the eastern border of the heartland states. As the land rises it gets drier and drier the closer it comes to the rain-robbing Rockies. But the peaks give something in turn. Half of the Rockies' original mass has washed onto the old sea bottoms, carried by river systems like the Missouri's that threads this map. On the drier plains, short grasses grew. On the wetter prairie, tall grasses thrived. That's the main difference between these look-alike flatlands. Settlers tamed the region. Now farms make the heartland a horn of plenty.

IOWA

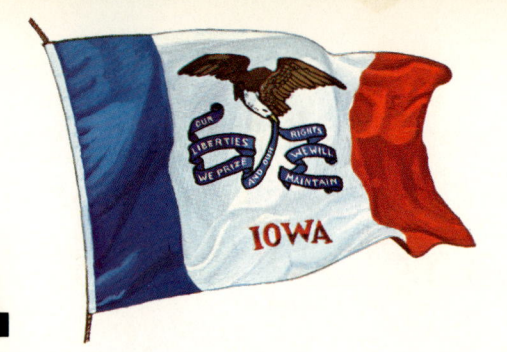

When August nears its end in Iowa, excitement stirs in the air. Soon families will be traveling to Des Moines and the Iowa State Fair. Teenagers try to win blue ribbons for raising the best calves and pigs. Grown-ups compete for prizes awarded the best ears of corn, or the best pickles, jams, and preserves. Half a million people come to see the fair and relax after working hard through the hot summer days.

Gentle, rolling prairies, deep, fertile soil, and 26 to 36 inches (660 to 914 mm) of rain—most of it during the growing season—make Iowa an ideal state for farming. Poet Robert Frost once said that Iowa's soil looked "good enough to eat."

You can see on the map that Iowa has big rivers for its eastern and western borders. It also is drained by more than 1,200 smaller rivers and streams. Although most of the state is nearly level land, hills covered with oaks, maples, and birches rise from the river valleys. The northeastern part, near the town of Marquette, is sometimes called "Little Switzerland." Here buttes and cliffs of limestone—some as high as a 30-story building—poke above the rivers.

You can also find strange mounds of stone and earth in Iowa and the Midwest. Ancestors of American Indians—called "Mound Builders"—made them. Many were used as burial places. Others were erected as flat-topped hills on which temples stood. Some were raised in the shapes of giant men and animals. One, a bear, measures half again as big as a basketball court!

The ancient people who put together such shapes carried the earth for them a basketful at a time. Think how much work it must have been. Yet we can only guess why they built the figures. Effigy Mounds National Monument preserves some of them. It attracts both tourists and archeologists—scientists who study the mounds to learn about these long-ago settlers.

One of the first white settlers in Iowa was Julien Dubuque, a French Canadian who got permission from the Indians to mine lead. Lead was needed for ammunition and printing type. The city of Dubuque grew from this early mining operation. Another city on the Mississippi, Muscatine, grew because of buttons. People discovered that they could make "pearl" buttons from clam shells found in the river, and factories rose. Today this port city of the corn belt manufactures plastic buttons as well.

In eastern Iowa lie the Amana Colonies. The community began in the 1880's as a religious society in which all land, buildings, and machinery belonged to everyone as a group. It worked that way until the 1930's when its property was divided and sold to individuals. The founders planned seven villages with homes and barns clustered together. This left the rest of their land uncluttered and easier to farm. Gradually the Amana villagers began producing woolen cloth, furniture, sausages, and wine. A workshop that turned out beverage coolers has developed into a factory making refrigerators, freezers, and microwave ovens. These industries employ many persons who don't live in the villages.

Iowa remains famous for its agriculture, and people come from all over to visit its universities, seed houses, plant nurseries, and farms. Iowans have experimented for years with new kinds of corn, better feed for livestock, improved breeds of animals. Because of such research, an average Iowa hen, for example, lays 238 eggs a year. Half a century ago the average was 100.

The nation's biggest popcorn plant is in Sioux City, Iowa. Popcorn "pops" when heat turns its moisture to steam, swelling the kernel's size as much as 35 times.

Area: the 25th largest state, 56,290 sq mi (145,790 sq km). **Population:** 2,879,000. Ranks 25th. **Major Cities:** Des Moines, 194,168; Cedar Rapids, 108,998; Davenport, 99,941. **Manufacturing:** farm and garden equipment and other non-electrical machinery, meat packing, grain processing, chemicals, electrical equipment, fabricated metal products. **Agriculture:** hogs, cattle, corn, soybeans, milk, oats. **Mining:** cement, stone, sand and gravel, gypsum, coal. **Statehood:** 29th state. Admitted Dec. 28, 1846.

Iowa Map

Grid coordinates: 1–18 (columns), A–M (rows)

Cities and Features

- Ocheyedan Mound, 1,670 FEET, 509 METERS, Highest point in Iowa
- Spirit Lake
- East Okoboji Lake
- Spencer
- Union Slough National Wildlife Refuge
- Clear Lake
- Algona
- Mason City
- Decorah
- Effigy Mounds National Monument — Animal-shaped Indian mounds up to 2,500 years old
- Marquette
- Le Mars
- Upper Mississippi River Wildlife and Fish Refuge
- Storm Lake
- Sioux City
- Fort Dodge
- Cedar Falls
- Waterloo
- Dubuque
- Onawa
- Denison
- Carroll
- Boone
- Ames
- Marshalltown
- Cedar Rapids
- Marion
- Clinton
- Newton
- Amana
- Coralville Lake
- Urbandale
- West Des Moines
- DES MOINES
- Sac and Fox Indian Reservation
- Coralville
- Iowa City
- Davenport
- Bettendorf
- Muscatine
- Lewis and Clark Trail
- Council Bluffs
- Indianola
- Pella — Tulip growing center
- Red Rock Reservoir
- Oskaloosa
- Mark Twain National Wildlife Refuge
- Red Oak
- Creston
- Mormon Trail
- Chariton
- Ottumwa
- Rathbun Lake
- Burlington
- Shenandoah
- Fort Madison
- Keokuk

Rivers
Big Sioux River, Missouri River, Little Sioux River, Boyer River, Raccoon River, Iowa River, Cedar River, Wapsipinicon River, Maquoketa River, Mississippi River, Shellrock River, Skunk River, Des Moines River, Great River Road

Highways
75, 18, 20, 29, 35, 30, 71, 63, 80, 61, 67, 65, 34

Legend

- ★ **DES MOINES** State Capital
- Interstate Highway (80)
- U.S. Highway (63)
- Cattle
- Dairy Cows
- Hogs
- Oats
- Corn
- Soybeans
- Seed Houses and Nurseries
- Mining
- Quarries
- Manufacturing
- Wildlife Refuge
- Recreation

Scale: 0–150 Kilometers / 0–100 Statute Miles

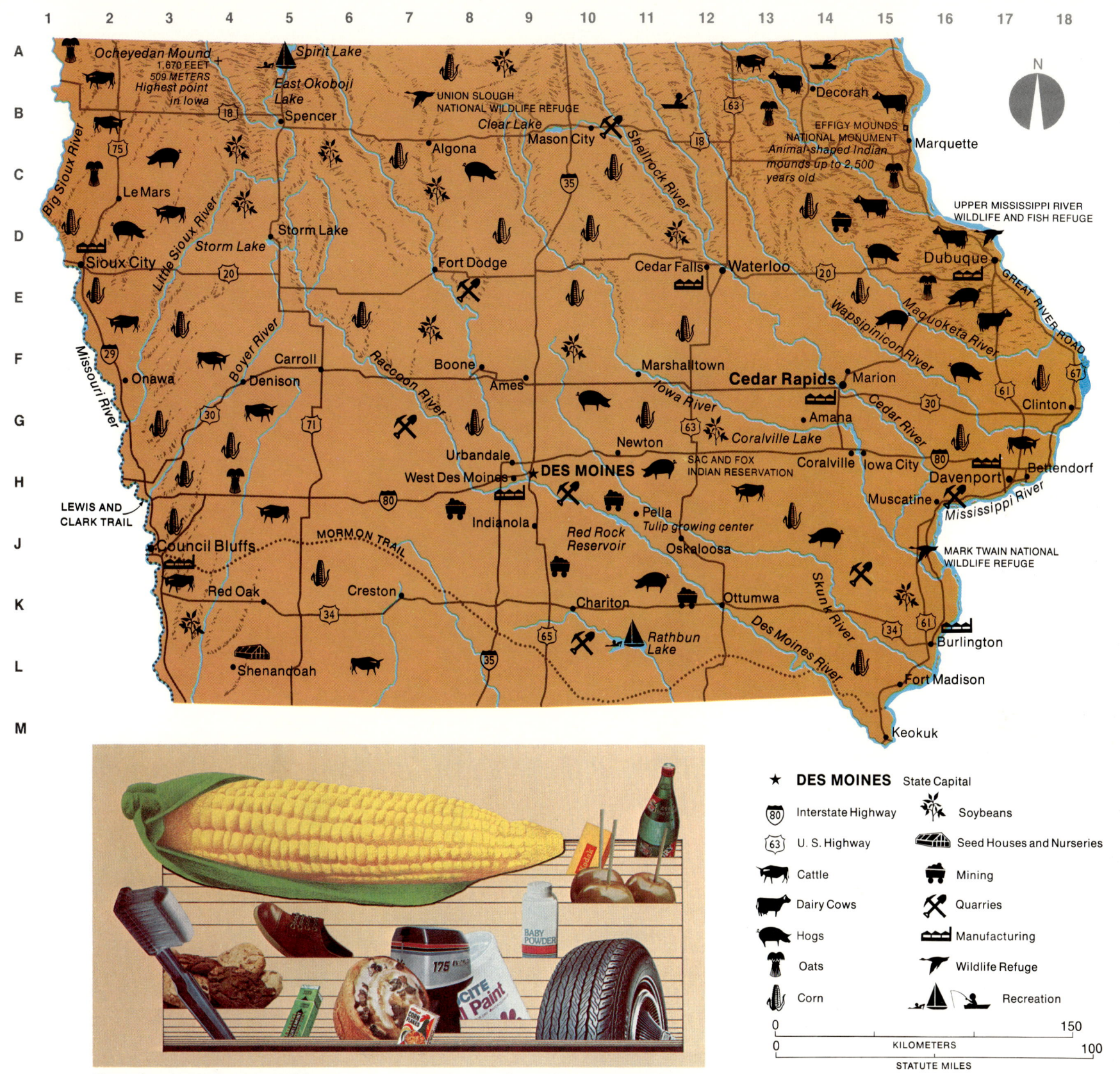

Corn is more than something to eat. It also goes into things as different as tires, plastics, and explosives. From kernels and cobs come corn sugars, starches, oils, and alcohols. These corn chemicals find many uses. In your supermarket alone more than 2,400 items have corn products in them.

"**B**iggest cornfield on earth"—that's what people often say about Iowa. They're joking, but there's truth in the remark. On fertile soil where grass once grew tall as a man, farm after farm now stretches. Most raise corn. Three out of every four bushels grown in the U. S. "walk" to market—as corn-fattened animals. Much of the rest is used by industry.

Roads run arrow straight in the flat region. That's because they follow a plan set out by our government in 1785, dividing new Midwest lands into square-mile pieces. Each could be cut into plots of 40 acres (16.2 hectares)—putting the expression "plowing the south 40" into our language.

Iowa farm buildings nest behind a pine windbreak. Today's farmer needs lots of equipment—like this combine that can pick, husk, shell, and load corn, all in one trip.

Showcase for champions and things people do—that's an agricultural fair. Iowa's is one of the U.S.'s largest.

Fairs mean fun, too—scary rides, shows, games of chance, hot dogs, buttery popcorn.

Hot loaves slide from a wood-fired oven in an Amana village that trades on old-time ways.

Pedigreed pigs and prize roosters hint at how research touches farming. Among advances: piglets that go to market sooner, chickens that have meatier breasts, bigger drumsticks.

KANSAS

You can see them rolling down the highways, five big trucks at a time. Carrying combines for harvesting wheat, the caravans of trucks travel up from Texas in early summer and move from one huge wheat farm to another. The crews work night and day to cut the ripened grain. They must do their work quickly, because sudden thunderstorms or hail can destroy the valuable crop. A spark may set off a fire which sweeping winds can spread out of control.

Once the wheat is cut, the combines thresh the grain from the stalks. Then trucks speed the grain to storage in nearby towns. The exhausted workers—some in their teens—fall into bed, ready to move to wheat fields farther north in the morning.

Once these golden fields in western Kansas were considered part of the "Great American Desert." Early explorers gave this name to the heartland region of flat, grass-covered plains. They thought crops would not grow because so little rain (18 inches—457 mm) fell each year. But Russian settlers brought seeds of hard red winter wheat from their homes near Turkey. That country has a dry climate much like Kansas'. The hard wheat did well in Kansas and now grows from Texas into Nebraska.

Many western Kansas farmers practice "dry" farming, a method of growing crops in a semiarid climate. They plow across sloping ground so the furrows will act like dams and hold the rain. They let some plots go unplanted for a year so the soil can store up water. They destroy weeds that would use the moisture needed for crops.

Farmers also have dug thousands of wells to pump water from as far as 600 feet (183 m) underground. This makes it possible to grow livestock feed and such things as cantaloupes, tomatoes, lettuce, and cucumbers.

Rainier eastern Kansas is green with gently rolling hills and cottonwood trees beside streams. In the Flint Hills section, Indians once dug flint to make arrowheads. Now used for grazing, these grasslands are bright with wild flowers in the spring and summer. Here you can see what the prairie looked like before settlers came.

In the late 1800's, before railroads linked Texas with the East, cowboys drove longhorns to rail stops in Kansas. From these "cow towns"—Abilene, Dodge City, Wichita—the cattle were shipped to market.

These cow towns still dot Kansas' map, but they are cities today. In Wichita thousands of workers build planes, missiles, and parts for jets. Others make camping equipment, refine oil, and process grain. President Dwight D. Eisenhower spent his boyhood in Abilene, and many people now visit the Presidential library there. In Dodge City you can still see busy stockyards.

Remember Dorothy, the Kansas girl carried off by a cyclone in *The Wizard of Oz?* Many people call tornadoes "cyclones." The U. S. has more of these terrible winds than any other country, and most happen in such mid-continent states as Kansas.

Like a waving elephant's trunk, or a rope or funnel, a tornado screams across the land. Lightning zigzags inside its whirling core. Strange gassy smells arise. Where tornadoes touch the earth, destruction comes in an instant. Trees disappear. Houses explode into splinters. Straws are driven into boards like nails. Tornadoes can play other odd tricks—whisking away walls of a building without harming people inside, or leaving a farmer milking air where a moment before there had been a cow. No wonder many Kansans build storm cellars with their homes.

Mushrooms 15 feet (5 m) tall pop up near Carneiro. They're stone, worn by wind and water from layers of different hardness.

Area: the 14th largest state, 82,264 sq mi (213,063 sq km). **Population:** 2,326,000. Ranks 31st. **Major Cities:** Wichita, 264,901; Kansas City, 168,153; Topeka, 119,203. **Manufacturing:** aircraft, railroad equipment, automobiles, farm and garden equipment and non-electrical machinery, flour milling, meat packing, chemicals, printing and publishing, petroleum and coal products, products of stone, clay, glass, rubber, and plastic, and fabricated metal products. **Agriculture:** cattle, wheat, corn, hogs, sorghum, milk, soybeans. **Mining:** petroleum, natural gas, natural gas liquids, cement, stone, salt, sand and gravel, helium, coal. **Statehood:** 34th state. Admitted Jan. 29, 1861.

Buffalo grass

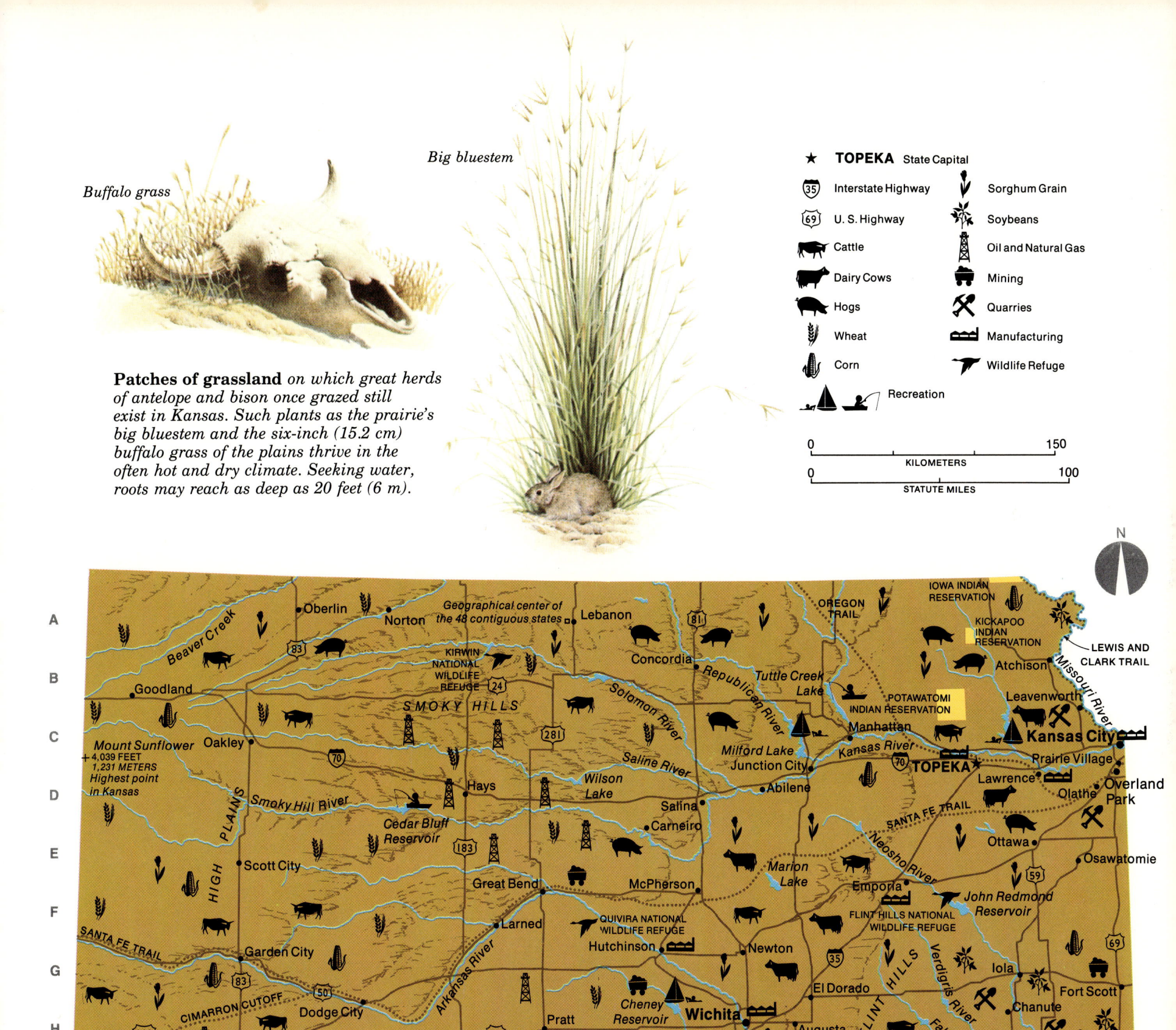

Big bluestem

★ **TOPEKA** State Capital
- (35) Interstate Highway
- (69) U.S. Highway
- Cattle
- Dairy Cows
- Hogs
- Wheat
- Corn
- Recreation
- Sorghum Grain
- Soybeans
- Oil and Natural Gas
- Mining
- Quarries
- Manufacturing
- Wildlife Refuge

0 — 150 KILOMETERS
0 — 100 STATUTE MILES

Patches of grassland on which great herds of antelope and bison once grazed still exist in Kansas. Such plants as the prairie's big bluestem and the six-inch (15.2 cm) buffalo grass of the plains thrive in the often hot and dry climate. Seeking water, roots may reach as deep as 20 feet (6 m).

N

Map of Kansas with labeled features:

- Oberlin, Norton, Geographical center of the 48 contiguous states, Lebanon
- IOWA INDIAN RESERVATION
- OREGON TRAIL
- KICKAPOO INDIAN RESERVATION
- Atchison, LEWIS AND CLARK TRAIL
- Beaver Creek, KIRWIN NATIONAL WILDLIFE REFUGE
- Concordia, Tuttle Creek Lake, POTAWATOMI INDIAN RESERVATION, Leavenworth, Missouri River
- Goodland, SMOKY HILLS, Solomon River, Republican River, Manhattan, Kansas City
- Mount Sunflower +4,039 FEET 1,231 METERS Highest point in Kansas, Oakley, Milford Lake, Kansas River, TOPEKA ★, Prairie Village
- Saline River, Junction City, Abilene, Lawrence, Overland Park, Olathe
- HIGH PLAINS, Smoky Hill River, Hays, Wilson Lake, Salina, SANTA FE TRAIL
- Cedar Bluff Reservoir, Carneiro, Ottawa
- Scott City, Marion Lake, Neosho River, Osawatomie
- Great Bend, McPherson, Emporia, John Redmond Reservoir
- Larned, QUIVIRA NATIONAL WILDLIFE REFUGE, FLINT HILLS NATIONAL WILDLIFE REFUGE
- SANTA FE TRAIL, Garden City, Hutchinson, Newton, Iola, Fort Scott
- CIMARRON CUTOFF, Dodge City, Arkansas River, Cheney Reservoir, Wichita, El Dorado, FLINT HILLS, Verdigris River, Chanute
- Pratt, Augusta, Fall River, Pittsburg
- RED HILLS, Elk River, Parsons
- Liberal, Cimarron River, Medicine Lodge, Winfield, Independence, Coffeyville
- Arkansas City

Cowboys and wheat fields go hand-in-hand in Kansas. Not the shoot-'em-up wranglers of movies and television, but rancher-farmers who grow cattle and grain together. When winter wheat—a kind planted in the fall—begins to grow, the cattle are allowed to munch on the young plants. In the spring the cattle go to feedlots, and the stalks can ripen.

Seas of wheat turn the Kansas prairies golden at harvesttime. And when the wind blows, the grain ripples like ocean waves. Wheat harvesting is the nation's biggest food-gathering operation. Machines roll through the fields cutting paths 20 feet (6 m) wide and producing 3 bushels (106 liters) of grain every minute. Elevators where the grain is stored reach so far toward heaven they are sometimes nicknamed "prairie cathedrals."

To lure tourists, Dodge City stages gunfights in a modern copy of its old Front Street. The original lured real cowboys, who drove a million cattle to the town's railroad in frontier days.

Bristly husks give wheat a bearded head. The grain also grows in beardless types—and colored ones.

Workers bike the half-mile hall atop this elevator at Hutchinson.

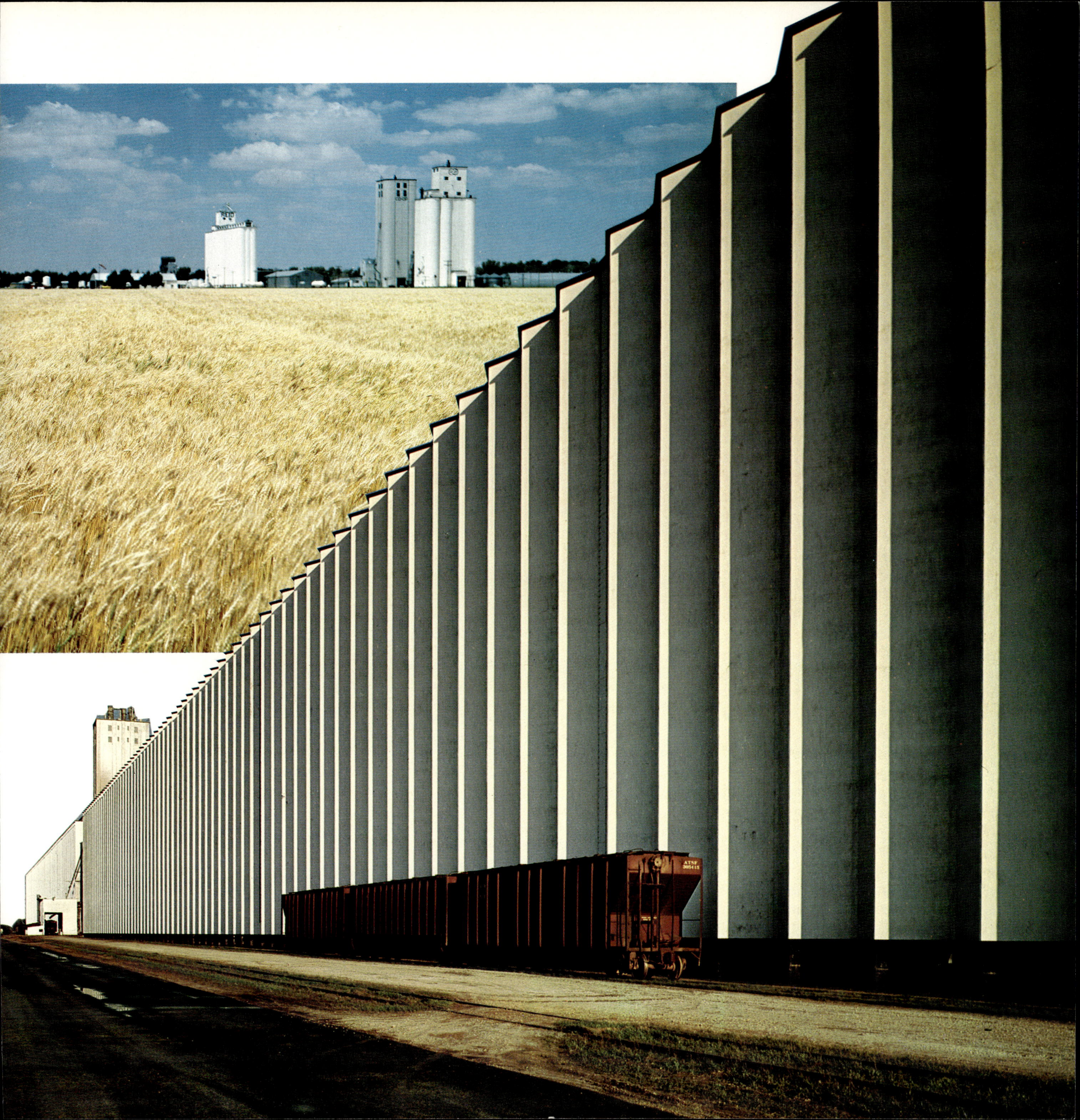

MINNESOTA

Showy Lady's Slipper

Common Loon

A trickle of water slides over pebbles.... Soon other streams join it and form Lake Itasca. Here, in northern Minnesota, the Mississippi River is born. It winds slowly across swamps and marshes, then heads south through pine forests and lakes. As it cuts by high limestone bluffs it gathers the flow of other streams for its journey to the gulf—and symbolizes Minnesota's ties to water.

The state got its name from *mni*, a Dakota Indian word for water. "Minnesota" means cloud-reflecting water. The name for the state's biggest city, Minneapolis, translates as "city of water." Many other towns are named for the falls, rapids, lakes, and river forks that sprinkle the map.

Minnesota calls itself the "land of 10,000 lakes," but actually there are more than 15,000. Some, like Lake of the Woods, were gouged out by glaciers long ago. Some, like Itasca, formed behind dams of rock and earth the ice sheets dropped. Also, huge chunks of ice that got stuck in thick layers of debris left hollows when they melted. Called "kettle holes," they account for many of Minnesota's small lakes and ponds.

One great body of water, Lake Superior, means a lot to the state commercially. It helps make Duluth one of the nation's major ports. Freighters from Duluth carry grain, iron ore, and manufactured goods to Great Lakes cities and overseas.

Even swamp water is important to Minnesota. It produces the sphagnum, or peat moss, that gardeners use for improving soils. Sphagnum is a kind of plant that likes acid shallows—often called bogs—where most trees and shrubs can't grow. Plants in bogs mat together in a cover that's springy to walk on, although you may also fall through. Harvesters dry and bale the moss

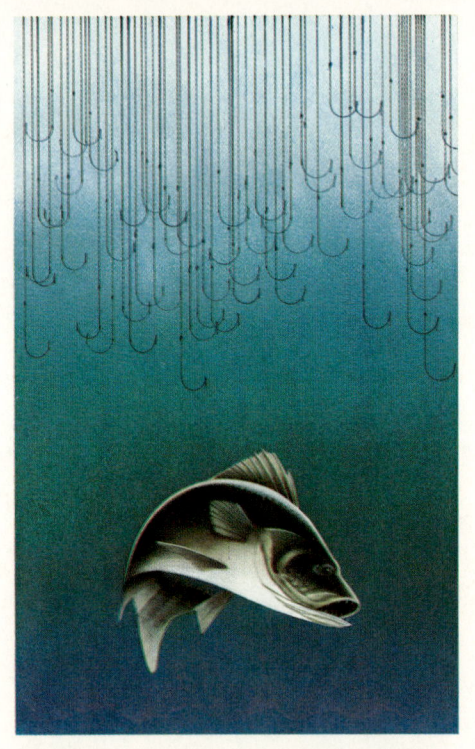

Pity the poor fish! Minnesota regularly ranks at or near the top among states in number of fishing licenses sold each year.

Area: the 12th largest state, 84,068 sq mi (217,735 sq km). **Population:** 3,975,000. Ranks 19th. **Major Cities:** Minneapolis, 378,112; St. Paul, 279,535; Duluth, 93,971; Bloomington, 79,210. **Manufacturing:** non-electrical machinery, food processing, fabricated metal products, electrical equipment, paper and paper products, printing and publishing, chemicals, industrial instruments, lumber and wood products, stone, clay, and glass products. **Agriculture:** dairy products, cattle, corn, soybeans, hogs, wheat, turkeys. Also eggs, barley, oats. **Mining:** iron ore, sand and gravel. **Other Important Activities:** shipping, tourism, fishing. **Statehood:** 32nd state. Admitted May 11, 1858.

for sale. Strange plants that eat insects—the pitcher plant and the sundew—also grow in bogs. Minnesota has 11,250 square miles (29,137 sq km) of these swamps.

But Minnesota's greatest natural resource is the soil. The glaciers brought in with them fine-ground stone called "drift," which makes rich soil. Minnesota grows corn and oats to feed beef cattle and about one million dairy cows. Their milk makes Minnesota a leading butter producer.

Under the ground are valuable resources too. Near Hibbing you can see one of the world's largest open-pit iron mines. The hole is about three miles long (4.8 km), a mile wide (1.6 km), and deep enough to bury a 50-story building. Its reddish, rusty colors may remind you of the Grand Canyon.

Southwest Minnesota has a special red stone that Indians prize. They carved calumets—peace pipes—from it. The place where it is found was considered sacred, and enemies faithfully kept a truce when they visited it. Now preserved as Pipestone National Monument, the area includes 160 acres (65 hectares) of prairie that looks the way it did when the first white men came.

Minnesota's major cities lie in the southeast. St. Paul, the capital, and Minneapolis sit on opposite sides of the Mississippi, grown there to a wide river. These Twin Cities, along with nearby smaller towns, create a metropolitan area of nearly two million persons. Here some 180 communities have gotten together in an interesting experiment in government. They have created a metropolitan council to tackle such common problems as water and sewer systems, transportation, and land use. The idea is that they can do better jointly than acting separately. It could be a pattern for other metropolitan areas in the nation.

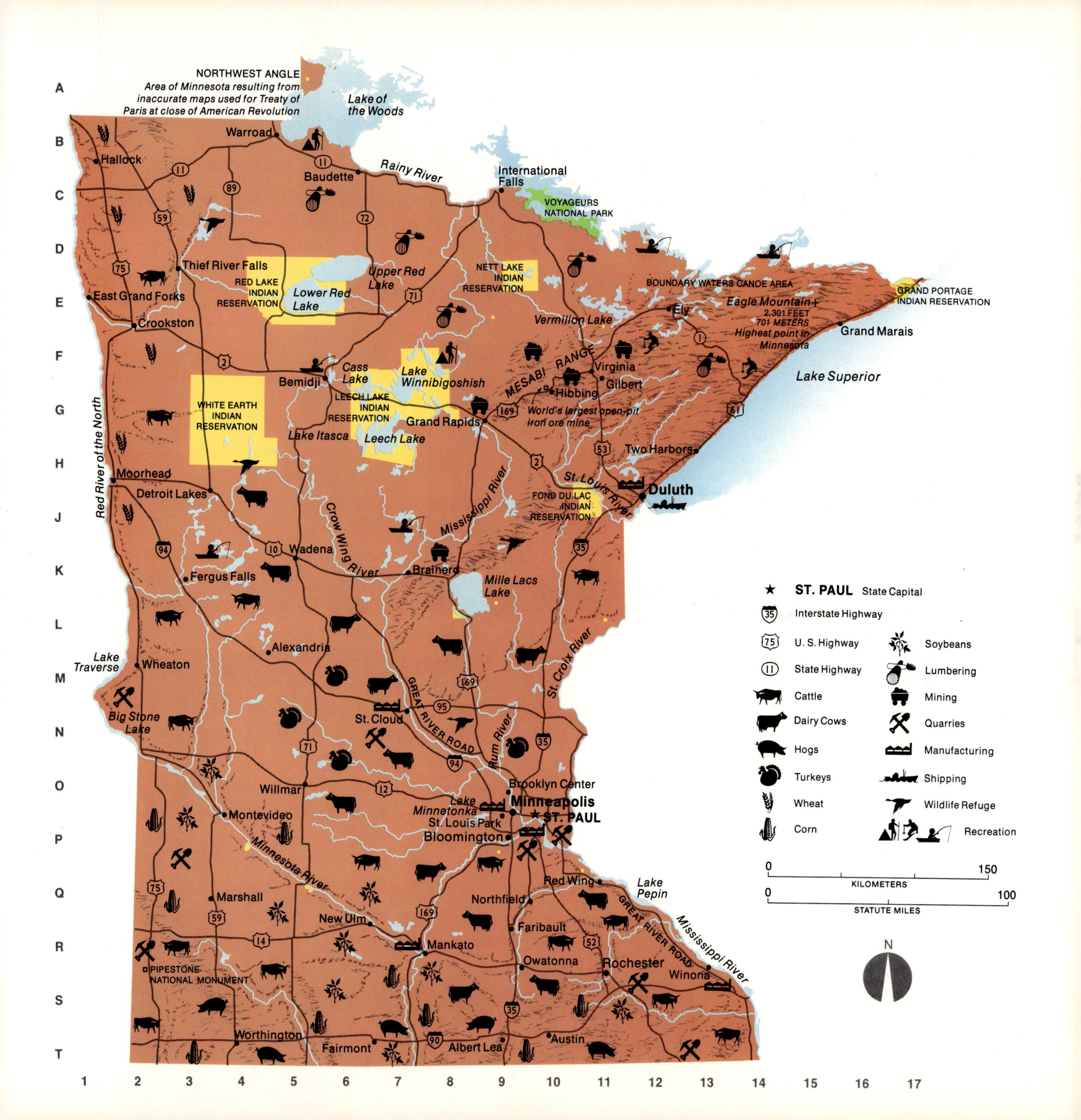

Minnesota

NORTHWEST ANGLE Area of Minnesota resulting from inaccurate maps used for Treaty of Paris at close of American Revolution

Map Labels

- Lake of the Woods
- Warroad
- Hallock
- Baudette
- Rainy River
- International Falls
- VOYAGEURS NATIONAL PARK
- Thief River Falls
- Upper Red Lake
- NETT LAKE INDIAN RESERVATION
- RED LAKE INDIAN RESERVATION
- Lower Red Lake
- East Grand Forks
- Crookston
- BOUNDARY WATERS CANOE AREA
- GRAND PORTAGE INDIAN RESERVATION
- Vermilion Lake
- Ely
- Eagle Mountain 2,301 FEET 701 METERS Highest point in Minnesota
- Grand Marais
- Bemidji
- Cass Lake
- Lake Winnibigoshish
- MESABI RANGE
- Virginia
- Gilbert
- Lake Superior
- WHITE EARTH INDIAN RESERVATION
- LEECH LAKE INDIAN RESERVATION
- Lake Itasca
- Leech Lake
- Grand Rapids
- Hibbing — World's largest open-pit iron ore mine
- Two Harbors
- Moorhead
- Red River of the North
- Detroit Lakes
- Crow Wing River
- Mississippi River
- St. Louis River
- FOND DU LAC INDIAN RESERVATION
- Duluth
- Wadena
- Fergus Falls
- Brainerd
- Mille Lacs Lake
- Lake Traverse
- Wheaton
- Alexandria
- St. Croix River
- Big Stone Lake
- St. Cloud
- GREAT RIVER ROAD
- Willmar
- Montevideo
- Rum River
- Brooklyn Center
- Lake Minnetonka
- Minneapolis ★ ST. PAUL
- St. Louis Park
- Bloomington
- Minnesota River
- Red Wing
- Lake Pepin
- Marshall
- New Ulm
- Northfield
- Faribault
- PIPESTONE NATIONAL MONUMENT
- Mankato
- Owatonna
- Rochester
- Winona
- Mississippi River
- Worthington
- Fairmont
- Albert Lea
- Austin

Legend

- ★ **ST. PAUL** State Capital
- 🛣 35 Interstate Highway
- 75 U.S. Highway
- 11 State Highway
- Cattle
- Dairy Cows
- Hogs
- Turkeys
- Wheat
- Corn
- Soybeans
- Lumbering
- Mining
- Quarries
- Manufacturing
- Shipping
- Wildlife Refuge
- Recreation

0 — 150 KILOMETERS
0 — 100 STATUTE MILES

N

Minnesota has an acre of water for each 20 acres (8 hectares) of land. Her lakes and forests make the northern and central parts of the state a magnet for people who like camping and canoeing. Exploring the wilderness of Voyageurs National Park or the Boundary Waters Canoe Area can let you feel like a voyageur, or fur trader. And with so much water for summer sports, perhaps it isn't surprising that waterskiing developed in Minnesota. Icy weather and heavy snows give the state great winter sports too.

Rivers drain Minnesota in three directions: the Mississippi to the gulf, the Red toward Hudson Bay, and others through the Great Lakes to the Atlantic.

Chippewas harvest wild rice in age-old ways—clubbing grain into poled canoes.

Indians still make pipes from soft red rock found at Pipestone National Monument. This 19th-century curio was cut from a single block.

Waterways thread Minnesota's Arrowhead area—the land tip aimed at Lake Superior.

Minnesota leads in raising turkeys. Benjamin Franklin wanted this native bird named our national symbol.

Quiet beauty in a million acres of wilderness—that's a camper's delight in the Boundary Waters Canoe Area.

Docks for oceangoing ships line 49 miles (79 km) of harbor in the neighboring cities of Duluth and Superior, Wisconsin.

Minnesotans—including "ice mice" at Gilbert—delight in winter sports.

MISSOURI

Rising like seats of a giant Ferris wheel, elevator cars in St. Louis's Gateway Arch take you higher and higher. At the top you get a breathtaking view of the countryside from more than 600 feet (183 m) above ground. You can look east toward the Mississippi River and the fields of Illinois. Looking west you see industrial buildings, suburbs, then the rolling Missouri prairie. This striking monument symbolizes St. Louis as the "Gateway to the West." The city earned that name because thousands of explorers, fur trappers, and pioneers funneled through it a century or so ago. They were leaving the civilized East to fan into the new lands across the Mississippi.

Rivers were main highways then, and a great stream leading toward the west joined the Mississippi a short way from St. Louis. Its name: the Missouri River. After crossing the state it turns north to form part of the western border. That bend became another pioneer jumping-off point, and there Kansas City grew. Now it too is the center of a great metropolitan area.

Kansas City is also a "buying and selling" town that even has a school for auctioneers. Here students practice how to sell anything from cattle to wheat to antique furniture. The wheat that's grown in neighboring Kansas moves in and out of the city every day by train, truck, or barge. Towboats push long strings of loaded barges down the Missouri to its confluence, or meeting place, with the Mississippi.

Missouri has always been important for transportation. It takes its name from an Indian phrase meaning "people with big canoes." In the 1800's, the white man's "big canoes"—steamboats—sailed the state's rivers. Children who grew up along the Mississippi dreamed of being steamboat pilots. One boy, Sam Clemens, lived in Hannibal, a small town north of St. Louis. Sam and his friends played pirate on the islands in the Mississippi and explored the caves along the shore. When Sam grew up he became a river pilot and a writer, and he signed his books "Mark Twain." In *Tom Sawyer* he tells how Tom and Becky got lost in a cave with "fantastic pillars...formed by the joining of great stalactites and stalagmites."

You can also find spooky caves and springs in the southern part of Missouri. This area, the "Ozark Plateau," is very different from the fields of soybeans and corn farther north. The Ozarks look like steep mountains, but they do not rise very high above sea level. The rugged hills seem high because rivers have cut sharp, deep valleys through the limestone. And underground streams have formed more than 3,500 caves. One room in the Meramec Caverns is large enough to park 300 automobiles.

The climate is milder in the Ozarks than in the northern part of the state, and the region's huge man-made lakes offer recreation to water-skiers, swimmers, and fishermen. Retired persons are moving there to enjoy the warm winters and cool summers. They need homes to live in and stores for shopping, so new businesses grow. This creates jobs for people who once farmed small patches of land with mules.

But Missouri keeps pieces of its rich past. Factory workers in the town of Washington make one of the state's trademarks, corncob pipes. Glassblowers, broom makers, and potters demonstrate craft skills in festivals at such places as Silver Dollar City near Branson. And you can still feel miles from civilization as you paddle down such backwoods streams as the Eleven Point River.

Ice-cream cones—and hot dogs and iced tea—first became well-known at the huge world's fair held in St. Louis in 1904.

Area: the 19th largest state, 69,686 sq mi (180,486 sq km). **Population:** 4,801,000. Ranks 15th. **Major Cities:** St. Louis, 524,964; Kansas City, 472,529; Springfield, 131,557; Independence, 111,481. **Manufacturing:** transportation equipment, food processing, chemicals, non-electrical machinery, printing and publishing, electrical equipment, fabricated metal products, primary metal products, apparel, paper and paper products, stone, clay, and glass products. **Agriculture:** cattle, soybeans, hogs, dairy products, corn, wheat. Also turkeys. **Mining:** lead, clay, cement, stone. **Other Important Activities:** tourism, fishing. **Statehood:** 24th state. Admitted Aug. 10, 1821.

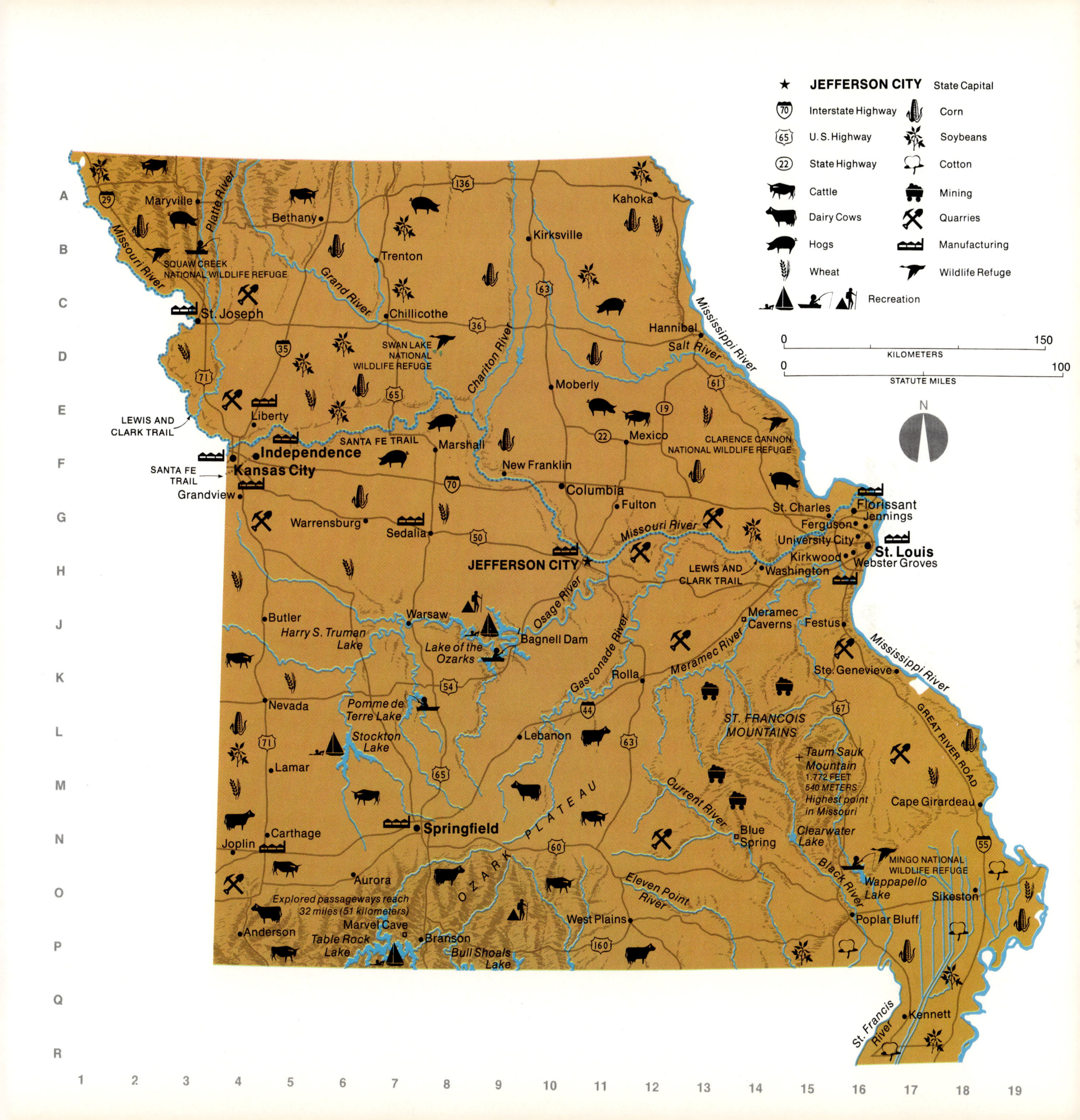

Missouri

Legend

- ★ **JEFFERSON CITY** State Capital
- 🛣 (70) Interstate Highway
- 🛣 (65) U.S. Highway
- 🛣 (22) State Highway
- 🐂 Cattle
- 🐄 Dairy Cows
- 🐖 Hogs
- 🌾 Wheat
- ⛵ Recreation
- 🌽 Corn
- ❀ Soybeans
- ☁ Cotton
- ⛏ Mining
- ⚒ Quarries
- 🏭 Manufacturing
- 🦅 Wildlife Refuge

Scale: 0 — 150 Kilometers / 0 — 100 Statute Miles

N

Labeled Places and Features

Row A–B: Maryville, Bethany, Kahoka, Platte River, Missouri River, (29), (136)

Row B–C: Squaw Creek National Wildlife Refuge, Trenton, Kirksville, Grand River

Row C–D: St. Joseph, Chillicothe, Hannibal, (36), Salt River, Mississippi River

Row D–E: Swan Lake National Wildlife Refuge, Moberly, (35), (71), (65), (61), Chariton River

Row E–F: Lewis and Clark Trail, Liberty, Marshall, Mexico, Clarence Cannon National Wildlife Refuge, (19), (22)

Row F–G: Santa Fe Trail, Independence, Kansas City, New Franklin, Columbia, St. Charles, Florissant, Jennings

Row G–H: Grandview, Warrensburg, Sedalia, Fulton, Missouri River, Ferguson, University City, Kirkwood, St. Louis, Webster Groves, (70), (50)

Row H–J: JEFFERSON CITY ★, Lewis and Clark Trail, Washington

Row J–K: Butler, Warsaw, Bagnell Dam, Osage River, Meramec Caverns, Festus, Harry S. Truman Lake, Lake of the Ozarks, Gasconade River, Meramec River

Row K–L: Nevada, Pomme de Terre Lake, Rolla, Ste. Genevieve, Mississippi River, (54), (67), Great River Road

Row L–M: Stockton Lake, Lebanon, ST. FRANCOIS MOUNTAINS, (71), (63)

Row M–N: Lamar, Taum Sauk Mountain 1,772 FEET 540 METERS Highest point in Missouri, Cape Girardeau, Current River

Row N–O: Joplin, Carthage, Springfield, Blue Spring, Clearwater Lake, (60), (55)

Row O–P: Aurora, OZARK PLATEAU, Eleven Point River, Black River, Wappapello Lake, Mingo National Wildlife Refuge, Sikeston

Row P–Q: Anderson, Marvel Cave, Branson, Table Rock Lake, Bull Shoals Lake, West Plains, Poplar Bluff, (160)

Explored passageways reach 32 miles (51 kilometers)

Row Q–R: St. Francis River, Kennett

Grid: columns 1–19, rows A–R

St. Louis's Gateway Arch—the nation's tallest man-made monument—carries 900 tons (818 metric tons) of stainless steel as its skin. That's the largest amount ever used in any project. The arch soars over a city that in recent years has torn down slums and rebuilt big chunks of its 61 square miles (158 sq km). But in its modernization it kept old landmarks. One is a courthouse where such famous people as Henry Clay and Ulysses S. Grant walked, and where a case involving a slave named Dred Scott helped lead to the Civil War.

All Missouri, like St. Louis, builds for today but is proud of its past. It cherishes its old mills, its touches of backwoods life and wilderness alongside busy waterfronts and bustling city scenes.

Animals at the St. Louis Zoo have starred in television's "Wild Kingdom" program.

Still working, this Ozark mill recalls days when mills were business and social centers. Its buhrs—grindstones—came from France a century ago.

188

Paddlers and pet glide an Ozark stream. The area's wrinkled landscape cradles wilderness beauty—and towns with such names as Truth, Harmony, Blue Eye.

Comic mountaineers, shaped by a whittler's skill, hint of days gone by. Ozark centers preserve such old-time handicrafts as carving.

Once cattle jammed stockyards like Kansas City's. Then packing plants moved closer to farms, causing empty pens.

Missouri River barges—this one is loading wheat at docks in Kansas City—can hold as much as 25 railroad cars.

Photographed from 73 feet (22 m) down, surface trees and divers take ghostly shape in the clear water of Blue Spring.

NEBRASKA

*"...The miles of fresh-plowed soil,
Heavy and black, full of strength and
   harshness;
The growing wheat, the ...weeds,
The toiling horses, the tired men."*

These words from a poem by Willa Cather, a writer who grew up in Nebraska, paint a picture of this great farming state as it was in the early 1900's. Although machines now do the work that horses did back then, the fresh-plowed soil of Nebraska is still "full of strength," fertile and black. It produces enough grain and grass to make Nebraska the third leading beef cattle state in the nation. Only Texas and Iowa rank higher.

Entering Nebraska from the east on Route 80, you first see miles of cornfields. Meat-packing plants have moved out to small towns near huge cattle feedlots. Here cattle from the range are penned and fattened before they are sent to market. Route 80 closely follows the Platte River, near the old Mormon and Oregon Trails which pioneers followed to Utah, California, and Oregon. Bearing north with the trails, along U.S. 26, you pass the tall spire of Chimney Rock. When the pioneers reached this landmark, they knew they would soon be crossing the Rockies. Many carved their names in the soft sandstone of the column.

The pioneers' movement west was the greatest overland migration in history. In one year alone, 1850, some 55,000 people crossed the plains. Their wagons wore wheel ruts you still can see today. At some spots the wagon tracks are deep enough for you to hide in—standing up!

Although most pioneers went farther west, many settled in Nebraska. It was here that Daniel Freeman received one of the first homesteads granted under an important law passed by Congress to encourage settlement. He got 160 acres (65 hectares) of farmland for only $10 in 1863. Early Nebraska homesteaders came from the eastern United States and nations in northern Europe. Because good land was cheap and plentiful, they put up with the blizzards in winter and the drought and grasshoppers that threatened their crops in summer.

They missed the trees they had at home, however. Cottonwoods and ash trees dotted the banks of rivers, but no forests grew on the flat, endless plains. Settlers began to plant orchards of fruit trees. They also set out rows of trees to make boundaries for their farms and to protect their fields from wind. Then J. Sterling Morton and a friend got an idea. Why not have a special day each year for planting trees?

Today Nebraskans celebrate Arbor Day close to April 22, the anniversary of Morton's birth. Tree planting became so popular in Nebraska that people even planted a forest. The national forests near Halsey and Valentine contain some 30,000 acres (12,141 hectares) of cone-bearing evergreens, planted in the dry, once-treeless Sand Hills region. This is the largest man-made forest area in the world.

Nebraska's wide-open spaces give it some unusual features. Great numbers of water birds nest in its lake-freckled Sand Hills region. Sandhill cranes, pausing on annual migrations, cover shallows like sprinkled pepper. And in these rural areas, some children still go to small country schools. They may study with only three or four other students and learn science from educational television. Nebraska was one of the first states to broadcast TV lessons to schools.

The mammoth, hunted for food by ancestors of Nebraska's Indians, had tusks about as long as it was tall—14 feet (4.3 m).

Area: the 15th largest state, 77,227 sq mi (200,017 sq km). **Population:** 1,561,000. Ranks 35th. **Major Cities:** Omaha, 371,455; Lincoln, 163,112. **Agriculture:** cattle, corn, hogs, wheat, sorghum, soybeans, milk. Also hay, sugar beets, eggs. **Manufacturing:** food processing, farm and garden machinery, electrical equipment, chemicals, printing and publishing, fabricated metal products. **Mining:** petroleum, natural gas, natural gas liquids, sand and gravel. **Statehood:** 37th state. Admitted March 1, 1867.

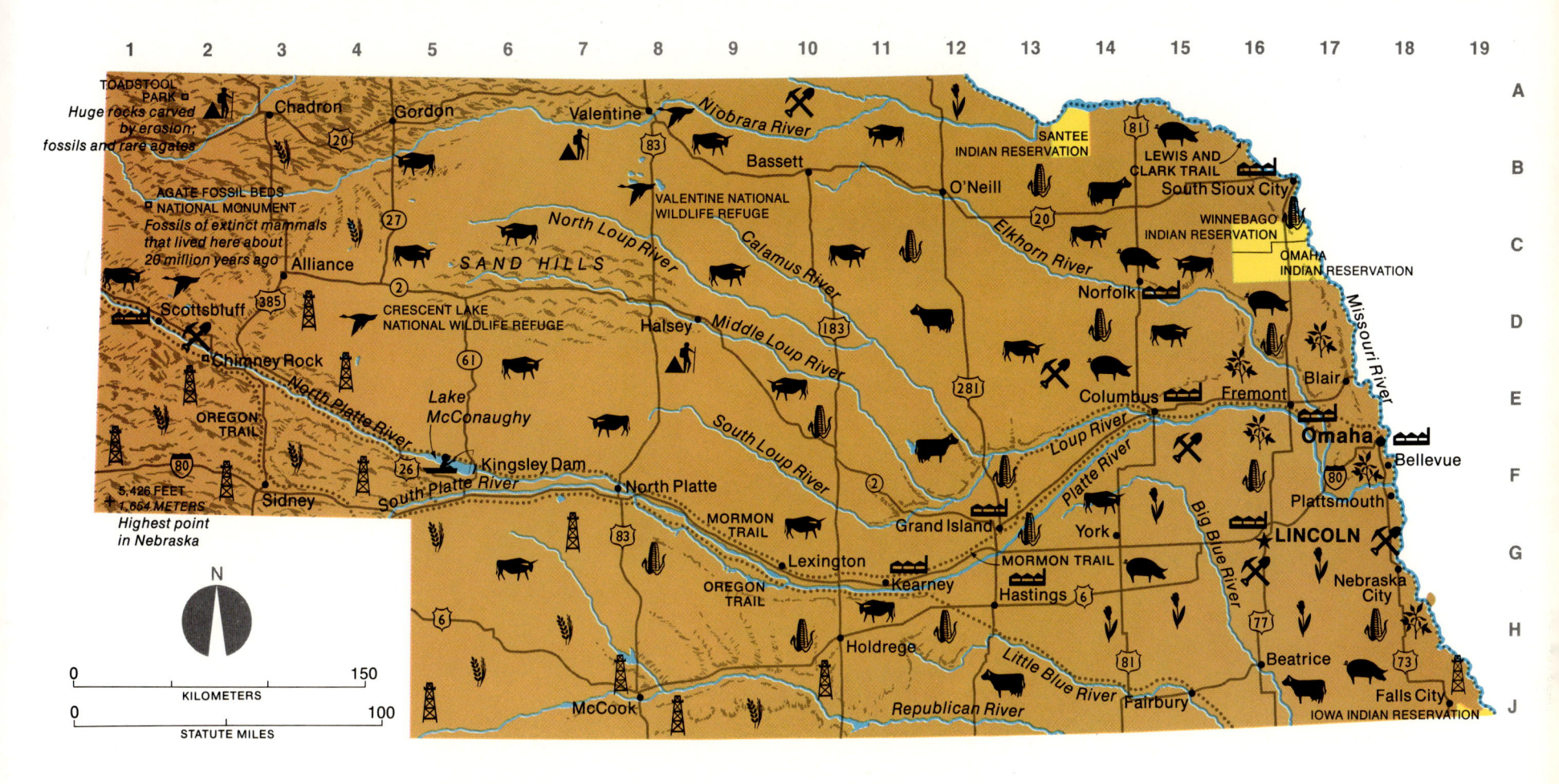

Steak, roasts, hamburger—*how much of a steer becomes cuts of meat? If you guess 50 percent, you're right. But the rest isn't wasted. It yields important by-products—extras we use in many ways. Hide for shoes, for example. Horn for buttons. Bone for bone-china dishes. And chemicals that go into hundreds of things—from marshmallows to tires, brushes to rugs, film to medicines.*

- ★ **LINCOLN** State Capital
- 80 Interstate Highway
- 83 U.S. Highway
- 27 State Highway
- Cattle
- Dairy Cows
- Hogs
- Wheat
- Sorghum Grain
- Corn
- Soybeans
- Oil and Natural Gas
- Quarries
- Manufacturing
- Wildlife Refuge
- Recreation

191

Playing grown-up on dad's old tractor comes naturally to many a Nebraska youngster. Farms cover the prairie that rolls right up to city doorsteps, and ranches spread over pasturelands dotted with windmills. About half the jobs in the state are tied in some way to agriculture. It's an oddity of history that at first pioneers ignored the region as they streamed through on their way to seek gold in the West. Now ripening wheat and corn bring gold to Nebraska's fields.

The state gets its name from an Omaha Indian word, *Nibdhathka*. It means "flat water." That's what the Omahas called the Platte River. Early settlers jokingly referred to the stream as "a mile wide and an inch deep," and said it was so muddy because it flowed upside down.

Pioneers carved their names on Chimney Rock. It soars 500 feet (152 m) above the plains.

Meat packing is an important Omaha industry. This plant mails frozen steaks; it can process 10,000 cattle a week.

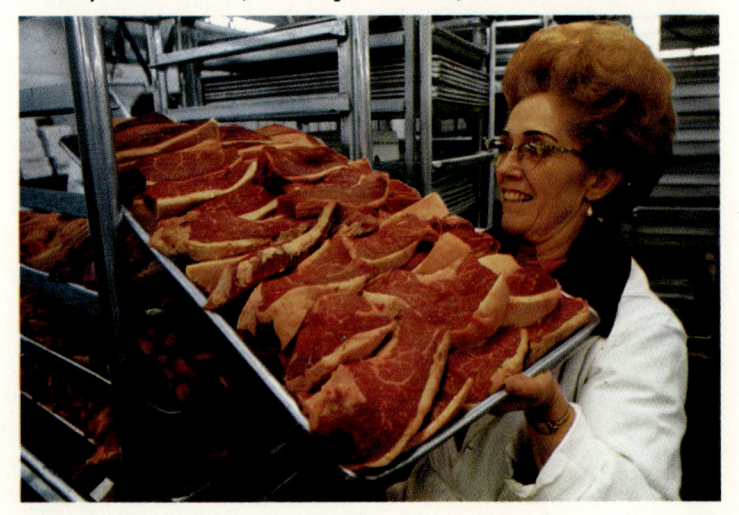

Gobbling two rows at a time, this corn picker cuts dried stalks and tosses ears into a trailer. Ears may be stored in cribs for feed, or processed in a sheller.

192

Windmills pump water for Nebraska Herefords. Ranching began in the state when cowboys drove longhorns north from Texas to feed on rich plains grasses.

Nebraska's lakes and cornfields play host to thousands of red-crowned sandhill cranes on their annual migrations.

Underground nerve center—that's this post at an Air Force base near Bellevue. From it the Strategic Air Command controls bombers and missiles protecting the nation.

193

NORTH DAKOTA

Wild Prairie Rose

Western Meadowlark

Want to stand at the very center of the North American continent? You'll find it near Rugby, a windswept prairie town 1,500 miles (2,414 km) from the Atlantic, Pacific, and Arctic oceans and from the Gulf of Mexico. You'll also find harsh winters and hot summers at Rugby. But that's typical of North Dakota's "continental" climate—a type that occurs where large landmasses lack the weather-easing benefits of great bodies of water. Television newsman Eric Sevareid, who grew up near Rugby, remembers the "frozen darkness of the winters, when a coyote's cry might seem at times to be the only sign of life."

Yet no other state depends so much on agriculture as does North Dakota. It grows more flax—important in making linen and linseed oil—and sunflower seed than any other state. Plants grow quickly because the state is so far north it gets long hours of sunshine in summer. Far from large cities and markets, North Dakota has found it hard to attract very many industrial plants. Most factories are small, employing fewer than 50 persons. They make farm machinery and process crops grown in the state.

Early settlers in the plains and prairie regions found the land covered with grass. They had to plow and "break the sod" before they could start to farm. Few trees grew, so there was little wood for building houses and barns. The settlers learned to use thick slabs of grass and soil to build homes they called "soddies." They cut and stacked the sod like bricks. Grass-topped roofs and walls three feet (.9 m) thick made houses that were warm in winter and cool in summer— though earth-loving bugs and leaks during heavy rains could be problems. Sod also went into sheds, barns, and corncribs.

Tallest structure in the United States, the television tower at Blanchard rises 2,063 feet (629 m) above the plains.

Area: the 17th largest state, 70,655 sq mi (182,996 sq km). **Population:** 653,000. Ranks 45th. **Major Cities:** Fargo, 56,058; Grand Forks, 41,909; Bismarck, 38,378. **Agriculture:** wheat, cattle, barley, milk, potatoes, hogs, sugar beets. Also flax, oats, hay. **Manufacturing:** non-electrical machinery, food processing, petroleum and coal products, printing and publishing, stone, clay, and glass products. **Mining:** petroleum, coal, sand and gravel, natural gas. **Statehood:** 39th state. Admitted Nov. 2, 1889.

Settlers likewise learned to use the steady winds that sweep across the land. The western part of the state gets little rain, but water lies under the ground. Farmers built windmills to pump the water to the surface for their horses, cattle, and sheep. Many farms in the Dakotas, Nebraska, and other Great Plains states still use the winds to turn the blades of their windmills. Rainfall is more plentiful in the eastern part of the state, where the fertile soil of the Red River Valley produces bumper crops.

The Missouri River, nicknamed "Big Muddy" because it carried so much silt, cuts across the western part of the state. There two-mile-wide (3.2 km) Garrison Dam produces electricity, provides irrigation for farms and ranches, and helps prevent the floods that brought disaster in past years.

North Dakotans tap other natural resources too. Oil comes from fields opened since 1951 in the western part of the state. The world's largest deposits of lignite, a brownish-black coal, also are found in the west. Other midwestern states buy electrical power from North Dakota plants that burn this coal. It is mined by huge machines that dig up—in a single bite—chunks of earth the size of a small house.

Years ago, beds of lignite near Amidon caught fire from campfires or lightning. They still are burning. Theodore Roosevelt wrote about the sulphur smells, the "lurid glow," and the "tongues of blue or cherry colored flame" that rise through cracks in the earth at such deposits.

At Theodore Roosevelt National Memorial Park you can see where the former President drove cattle and hunted game when he lived in the West. Nearby, at Little Missouri National Grasslands, bighorn sheep, buffalo, and deer still run free.

Production boom: *In 1860 a farmer could grow only enough to support himself and three other people. By 1940 it became himself and 11. Today it's 56.*

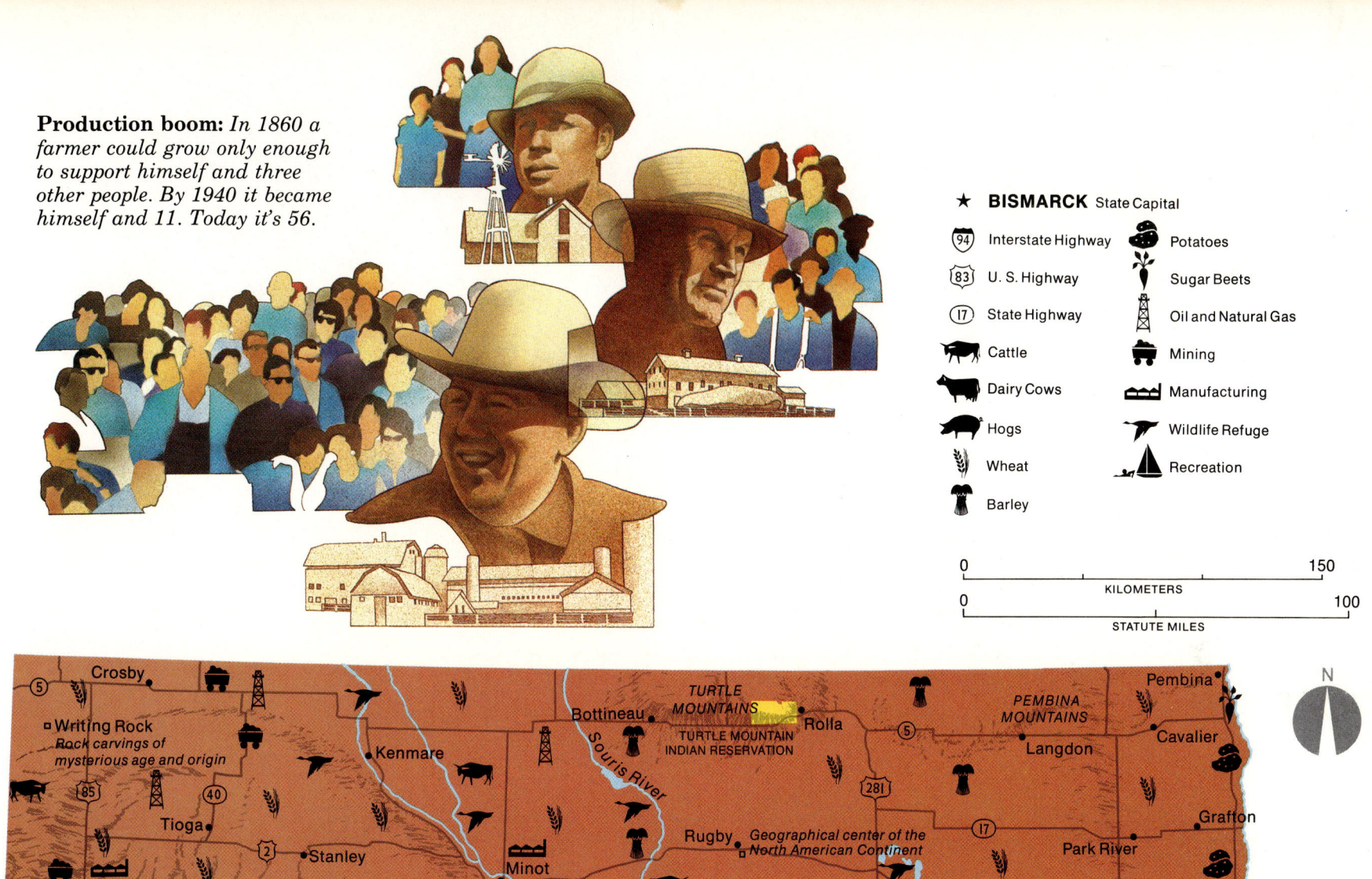

★ **BISMARCK** State Capital
- 94 Interstate Highway
- 83 U.S. Highway
- 17 State Highway
- Cattle
- Dairy Cows
- Hogs
- Wheat
- Barley
- Potatoes
- Sugar Beets
- Oil and Natural Gas
- Mining
- Manufacturing
- Wildlife Refuge
- Recreation

0 — 150 KILOMETERS
0 — 100 STATUTE MILES

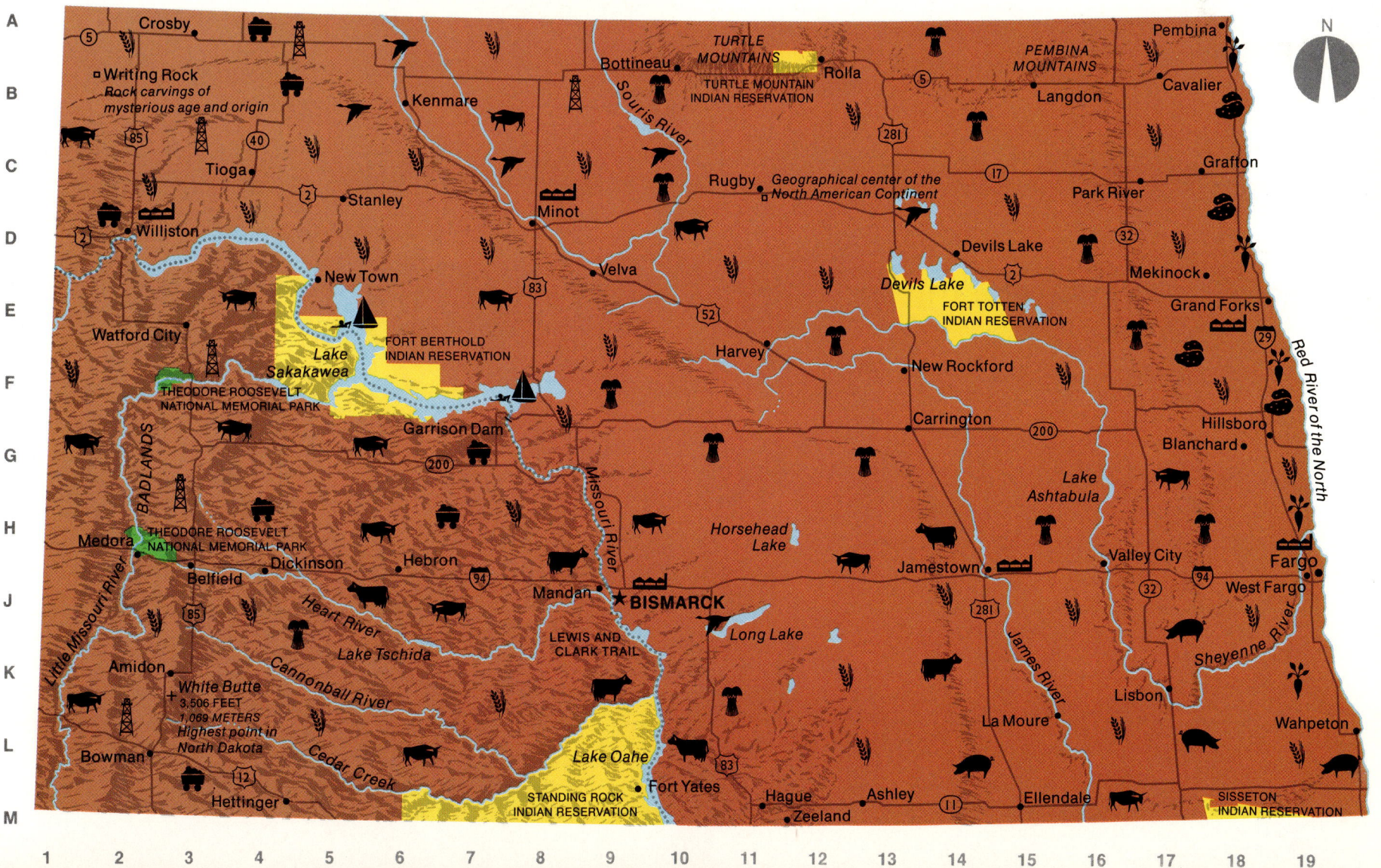

Homebound at day's end, "saddle busters" skirt a branch of Lake Sakakawea. North Dakota has been ranchland since the cattle drives of the 1880's.

Skating in streets or making a rink by sprinkling your yard means wintertime fun in North Dakota.

Fallow strips and golden grain edge fingers of land that poke into Lake Sakakawea. It has 1,600 miles (2,575 km) of shoreline—second to South Dakota's Oahe among the nation's largest man-made lakes.

Hillside lines bathed by a setting sun tell an ancient story. Inland seas once covered this region, now part of the Fort Berthold Indian Reservation. The shells and mud the seas left behind in time turned into layers of limestone and sandstone and shale. Then erosion carved the strata—layers—into the separated hills, or buttes, you see here. Fort Berthold Indians hope to turn the colorful area into a scenic recreation site.

North Dakota's dry land has other advantages. It's ideal for "spring" wheat—a kind planted in the spring and harvested in late August. This kind needs a growing season of only 100 days, and does best where yearly rainfall totals less than 30 inches (762 mm). The state meets both conditions.

Trim pintails flush from reedy shallows. North Dakota lies on one of the nation's main waterfowl flyways; its lakes and grainfields attract ducks and geese by the thousands.

Wheat spouting from the nation's combines goes into an amazing variety of products— some 350 sizes and shapes of macaroni alone, for example.

197

SOUTH DAKOTA

Suppose you were going to film a movie about the Old West. You might want a wide, raging river for covered wagons to cross, prairies for buffalo to roam, mountains and passes for gunmen to hide in, and gold mines and ghost towns. Many Western films are made in South Dakota because the state has those things, and more.

The Missouri River forms the southeast border between South Dakota and Nebraska, then veers west and north, dividing South Dakota into two almost equal parts. On the eastern side hot summer days, cool nights, rich prairie soil, and usually adequate rain help farmers grow corn and other grains. On the western side you find ranches and rolling plains. Some people say that if you want to know "where the West begins," look in the middle of the Missouri River!

If you drive west on Route 90 you will come to a land of weirdly shaped rock towers and cliffs. Few plants grow in this arid area, and you may feel like you are visiting the moon. Ages ago, lakes and swamps covered much of this land. Many strange animals lived there—one of them a three-toed horse only as big as a collie, another a rhino-like creature with forked horns growing out of its snout. Now scientists and rock collectors come to Badlands National Monument to study the fossils and formations.

Farther west the dome-shaped Black Hills rise like an island from the plains. Actually low mountains 3,000 to 4,000 feet high (914 to 1,219 m), they are covered with pine and spruce trees. Because the forests looked black from the plains, the Sioux Indians gave the hills their name.

In 1874 discovery of gold brought prospectors and adventurers swarming into the Black Hills. The region was sacred to

What will be the world's largest statue, a 563-foot (172 m) memorial to Chief Crazy Horse, takes shape near Custer.

Area: the 16th largest state, 77,047 sq mi (199,551 sq km). **Population:** 689,000. Ranks 44th. **Major Cities:** Sioux Falls, 73,925; Rapid City, 48,156; Aberdeen, 26,628. **Agriculture:** cattle, hogs, milk, wheat, corn, oats, soybeans, hay. Also eggs. **Manufacturing:** meat packing, flour and feed milling, farm equipment and other non-electrical machinery, lumber and wood products, stone, clay, and glass products, printing and publishing. **Mining:** gold, stone, sand and gravel, beryllium, cement. **Other Important Activities:** tourism, fishing. **Statehood:** the 40th state. Admitted Nov. 2, 1889.

the Sioux, and they fought to drive the intruders out. In turn, U. S. Army troops campaigned against the Indians. One of the resulting battles (in Montana) became famous as Custer's Last Stand.

Gold and other valuable minerals still are mined in the Black Hills. The Homestake Gold Mine, in the town of Lead, is the largest producing gold mine in the United States. Workers mine more than 1.5 million tons of ore each year. But from each ton comes only .2 of an ounce (5.7 gm) of gold.

Like the prospectors of long ago, tourists now swarm to the Black Hills. They visit gold mines and sawmills, ride an old railroad, and enjoy pageants of the Old West. They fish, hike, and watch the buffalo herds of Custer State Park. They explore such wonders as Wind Cave and Jewel Cave, whose underground passages sparkle with crystals. Water and chemicals seeping into limestone created these glittering caverns.

Nature used water and wind to carve the granite of the Black Hills. But man has also carved the formations. In 1927 Gutzon Borglum began a memorial to freedom and to the spirit of the American people. Using dynamite on the hard rock of Mount Rushmore, he and his crew worked 14 years to shape the huge faces of George Washington, Thomas Jefferson, Abraham Lincoln, and Theodore Roosevelt. Now a statue of Crazy Horse, a famous Sioux warrior, is being cut into Thunderhead Mountain nearby.

Less than 100 years ago the massacre by U. S. troops of Sioux in a camp at Wounded Knee brought an end to the Indian wars on the plains. Today some 32,000 descendants of the Indian tribes farm and raise livestock in the state. South Dakota has nine reservations. Only Arizona has more of its area set aside as Indian lands.

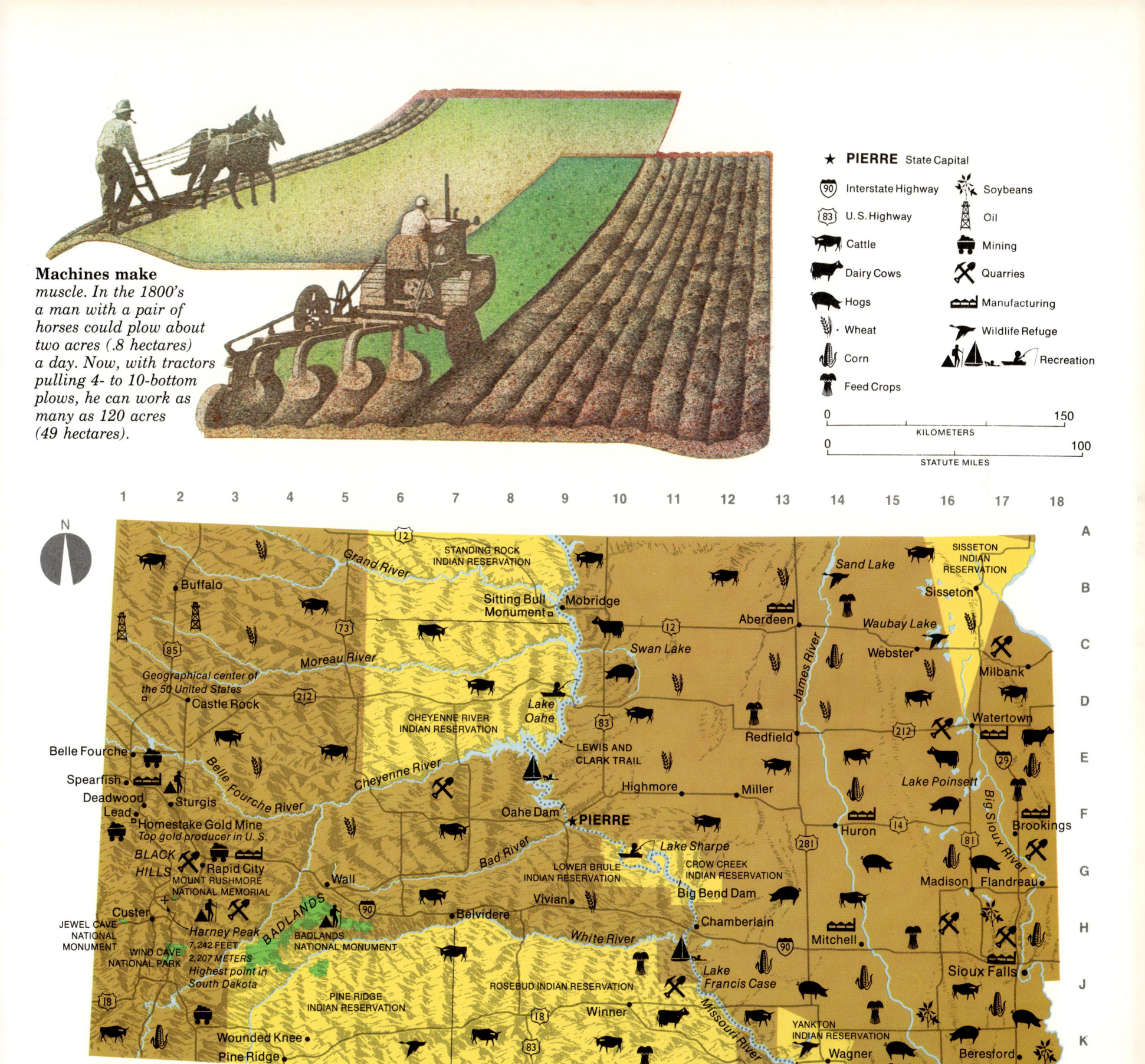

Machines make muscle. In the 1800's a man with a pair of horses could plow about two acres (.8 hectares) a day. Now, with tractors pulling 4- to 10-bottom plows, he can work as many as 120 acres (49 hectares).

★ **PIERRE** State Capital
- (90) Interstate Highway
- (83) U.S. Highway
- Cattle
- Dairy Cows
- Hogs
- Wheat
- Corn
- Feed Crops
- Soybeans
- Oil
- Mining
- Quarries
- Manufacturing
- Wildlife Refuge
- Recreation

0　　　　　　　150
KILOMETERS
0　　　　　　　100
STATUTE MILES

To Sioux Indians the tortured terrain was *mako sica*. French trappers called it *mauvaises terres*. We say the same thing with our "Badlands"—labeling the weirdly beautiful region that spills across part of South Dakota. Spires, knobs, gullies, sharp ridges, and deep colors mark the dry land. "Hell with the fires out," a gruff Army general called it.

Hills give South Dakota mineral riches and a reputation for being rugged. But the corn belt pokes into the state, and wheat and cattle ranches blanket the land.

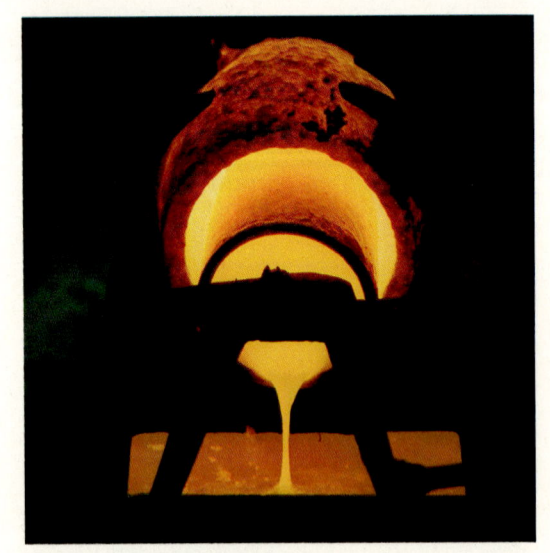

Gold—$68,000 worth—pours from pot to mold at Homestake Mining's plant in Lead.

Shells, mud laid down by rivers, ash from ancient volcanoes—all became the rock layers you see in the Badlands. Part of the region has been set aside as a national monument.

Protected buffalo make a comeback. Once 60 million roamed the plains; by 1900 only about 100 ran free.

Puppy love? No, just an identity check among prairie dogs. Their burrowing once served to plow the plains.

Intake towers dwarf Lake Oahe boaters at daybreak. The towers lead water to power generators in the dam.

Looking like flies on George Washington's nose, workers lend scale to the huge faces of Mount Rushmore's carvings. The granite will erode a mere hair's breadth in 1,000 years.

Energy and Its Uses

Did George Washington really chop down that cherry tree? No one knows. But if he did, we can guess what happened to the tree. It was probably cut up for firewood. In colonial America, people used wood to heat their houses and cook their food.

For light, they burned candles. Or they used lamps that burned oil made from whale blubber. Power for farm work was supplied by people or by animals—especially horses. The grain that farmers grew usually went to mills built beside fast-flowing rivers. There, the energy in falling water turned grinding wheels to make flour or cornmeal.

The wind did its share too. Ships traveling between Europe and the Colonies relied on wind to fill their great, billowing sails and push them across the Atlantic.

Today, most of us must go to museums to see an oil lamp or a horse-drawn plow. In the two hundred years since colonial days, several inventions and discoveries have greatly changed the American way of life.

Have you ever watched steam rattle the lid of a cooking pot when water is boiling inside? An invention called a steam engine put that power to work. Pressure from expanding steam pushes parts in the engine.

By 1850, steam engines had led the U.S. into the machine age. Steam-powered trains traveled the East Coast. Steam engines propelled some ships. And steam-driven machines in factories took over much work that had been done by hand. Wood, and later coal, provided fuel to make the steam.

A gas fuel manufactured from coal lit the streets of many cities. Whale oil had become very scarce. A fuel called kerosene—first made from coal and then from petroleum—provided most home lighting before electric lights came into use.

If you look through the glass of a clear light bulb, you can see a thin metal wire. When electric current passes through it, the wire glows white-hot and gives off light. Thomas Edison developed the first lamp of this kind in the late 1870's. Today, electricity provides power for many things. From toasters to television sets, you could count hundreds of them.

It's not easy to see where electricity comes from. The cord that plugs into the wall taps a convenient but expensive form of energy. Electricity comes by wire from power plants. And it takes a lot of falling water, or heat from a nuclear reactor, or coal, or natural gas, or petroleum to produce it.

Petroleum, a thick, black liquid also called oil, was known to the American Indians. But it was not until 1859 that the first commercial well gushed out "black gold" near Titusville, Pennsylvania.

Although Pennsylvania had the first well, Texas had the most oil. Vast quantities of it fueled a growing automobile industry. Model T Fords in the early 1900's started the American craze for cars. Today automobiles by the millions clog our highways.

Cars, trucks, buses, and airplanes create a huge demand for gasoline and other fuels made from oil. This energy source, along with natural gas and coal, now supplies more than 90 percent of our energy needs. These fuels are called "fossil fuels" because of the way they formed in the ground.

Imagine the earth hundreds of millions of years ago. There are no mammals, or dinosaurs, or even flowers. Shallow seas cover most of our planet. In the seas, tiny plants and animals float along, storing up energy from the sun. The plants and animals, so small they can fit through the eye of a needle, die and sink to the bottom. Layers of mud and sand cover them. The weight of the layers presses down, squeezing and heating the mass. Over the next several million years, the plant and animal fossils turn into petroleum or natural gas.

As time passes, geologic forces change the surface of the earth. The oil and gas collect in pools, trapped underground by layers of solid rock. There they lie hidden under deserts, hills, even under oceans—until people drill wells and pipe away the gas and oil.

Coal formed in a similar way. Ferns, rushes, and giant trees in ancient swamps died and were buried under mud and water. Over millions of years, the layers turned into a hard, black mineral—coal.

We burn most of our fossil fuels for energy. But about a tenth of the oil and natural gas goes into non-energy uses—to make such things as synthetic rubber and fabrics, chemicals, plastics, paints, and soaps.

Busy people using energy. *Americans consume more energy than people of any other nation—an amount equal to seven gallons (26 liters) of oil per day for every man, woman, and child.*

Uses electricity

Burns oil fuel

Burns natural gas

Made from oil or natural gas

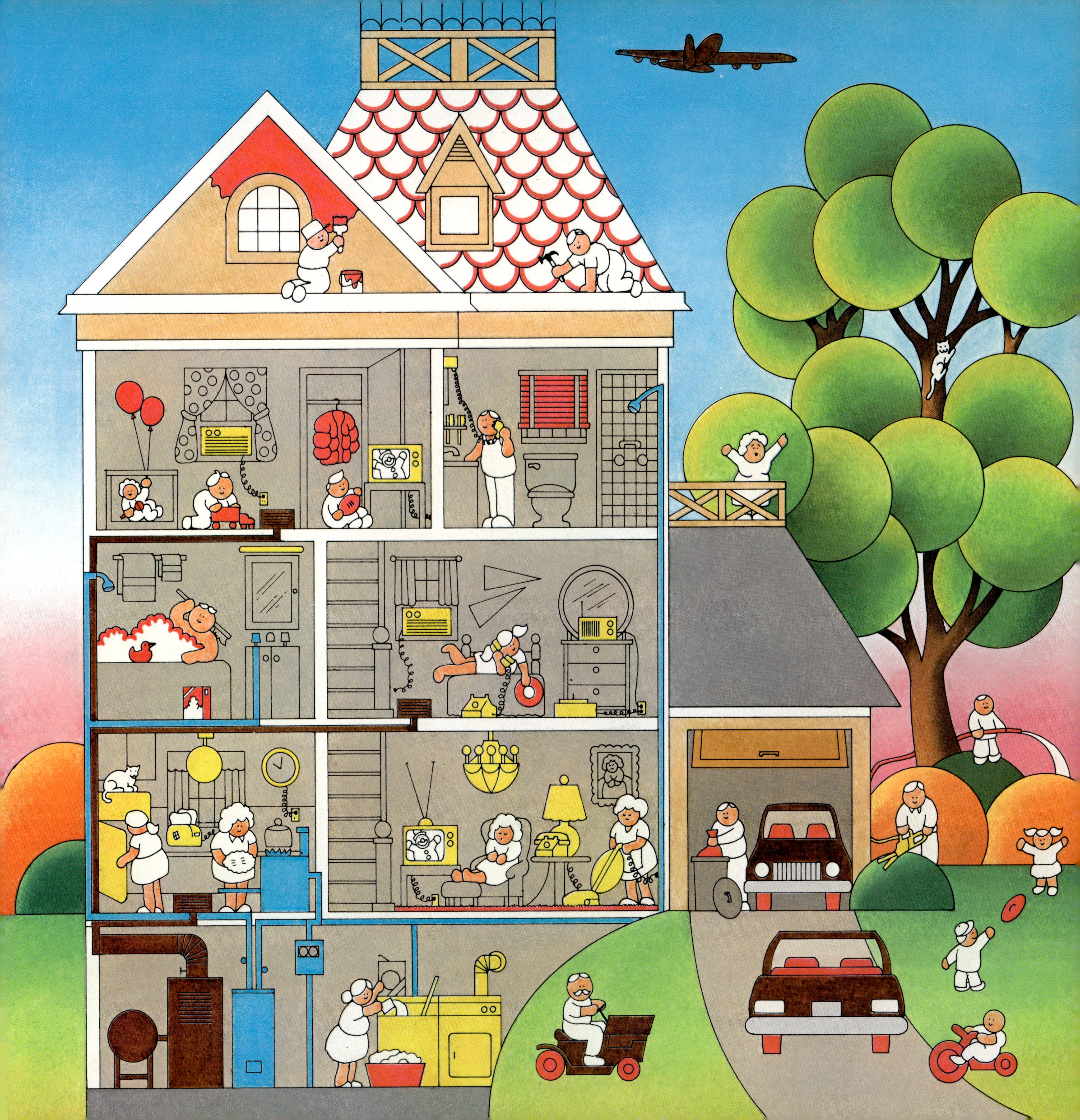

About three-quarters of our energy comes from oil and natural gas. Not many years ago these fuels seemed plentiful, and few people thought about saving energy.

But today, we cannot supply enough oil and gas from within our own borders. We buy nearly half our oil and some of our natural gas from other countries.

As the demand for energy grows, oil companies look for new deposits of oil and natural gas in Alaska and underwater, along America's shoreline. When it burns, natural gas causes less air pollution than either oil or coal. But because of gas shortages in recent years, many factories and electric plants will switch to coal.

Coal is our most abundant fossil fuel. But getting it out of the ground and burning it can damage the environment. Strip mining leaves scars to be filled, and coal-burning plants must install equipment to remove impurities that pollute the air.

Coal may eventually provide energy in a different way. We can make synthetic oil and gas from coal and some other fossil fuels. But the costs run high.

Deposits of shale rock in several states contain large amounts of oil that could be extracted. But what's to be done with the leftover rock? One scientist estimates that processing all the high-quality oil shale in Colorado would create enough spent rock to cover the entire state with a blanket ten feet (3 m) thick!

Tar-sand deposits in Utah also contain oil. But the cost of heating the sand underground and pumping the oil to the surface delays development of this resource.

Making electricity eats up a large amount of our total energy resources. Water tumbling over dams produces some electricity in the form of hydroelectric power.

Nuclear plants also contribute to our electricity supply. In a process called nuclear fission, uranium atoms split apart. This releases heat that makes steam to drive generators. Nuclear plants emit no smoke into the air, but radiation given off during the nuclear process can create hazards.

Our supplies of uranium may run low by the end of this century. In the meantime, scientists are working to perfect a "breeder" reactor that would use its fuel more efficiently. Another nuclear process called fusion holds promise for the more distant future. It would take its fuel from deuterium, a kind of hydrogen atom found in seawater.

We can stretch our fuel by using it wisely. We can save energy by making more efficient engines, insulating buildings, and turning down thermostats. But eventually, we will have to rely on renewable energy sources—those that can be replaced.

Geysers such as Old Faithful demonstrate a renewable source—heat inside the earth. Iceland has long used geothermal energy from hot springs to heat buildings. Italy boasts a large geothermal electric plant. The only large-scale geothermal plant in the United States—called The Geysers—is located in northern California. It could supply a city the size of San Francisco with nearly a quarter of its electricity.

As fossil fuels become more costly, many cities and factories are burning things that would otherwise go to waste. Orange rinds and milk cartons help to light up Ames, Iowa. The city's electric plant uses garbage as fuel. Some paper companies now burn scrap tree branches and bark as fuel for their electric plants.

Corn, sugarcane, and other vegetable material can be treated to make methane—a fuel similar to natural gas. Animal manure is a rich source of methane. If your family had six cows and equipment to turn the manure into gas, the cows could supply all the energy you needed for cooking, electric lighting, and household power.

Windmills once provided small amounts of electricity for hundreds of farms in the Midwest. Some energy experts favor plans to cover large areas with wind generators to make electricity for nearby cities.

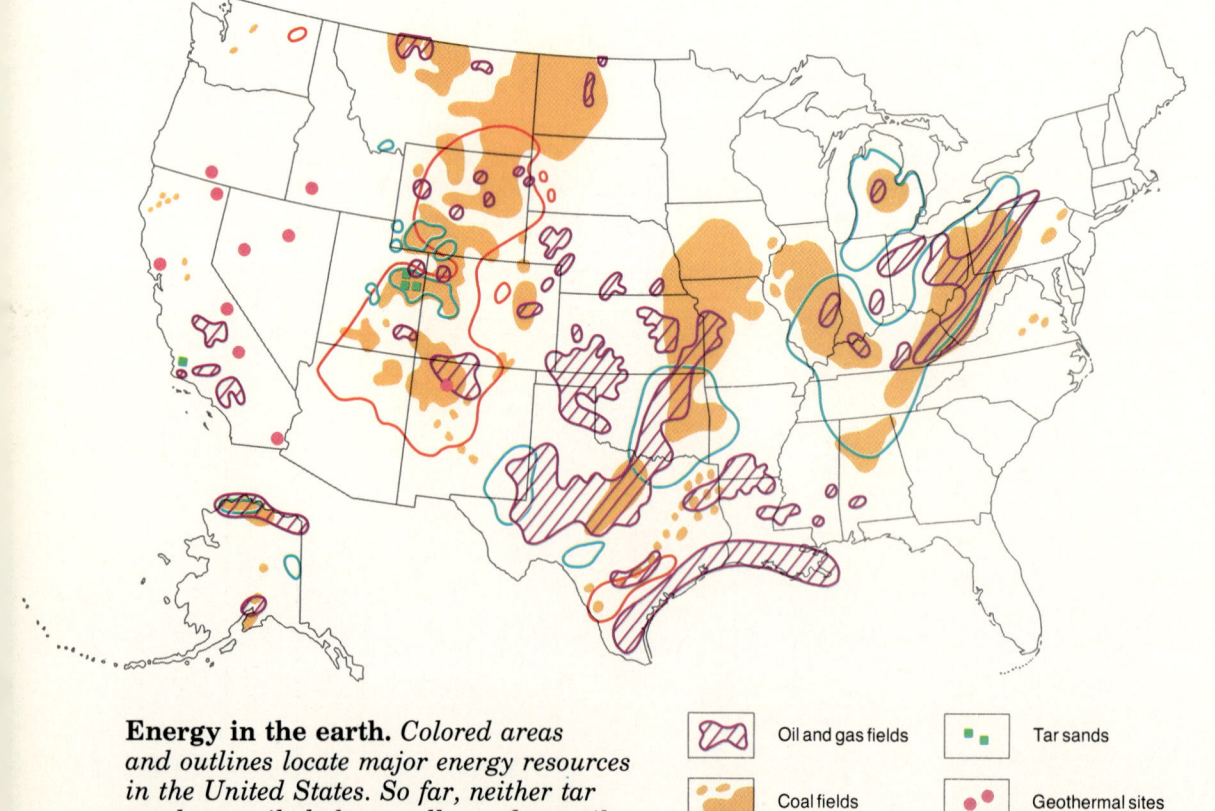

Energy in the earth. *Colored areas and outlines locate major energy resources in the United States. So far, neither tar sands nor oil shale actually produces oil. Pink dots mark The Geysers in California and other promising geothermal sites.*

ENERGY: WHERE IT COMES FROM...

Petroleum
domestic 26.5%
imported 20.0%

Natural Gas
domestic 25.5%
imported 1.2%

Coal 20.0%

Hydroelectric 4.0%

Nuclear 2.7%

Geothermal less than 0.1%

Solar less than 0.1%

Wood and Waste less than 0.1%

Electricity

Coal exports 2.1%

Products made from gas or oil 5.5%

Transportation uses 25.6%

Household and Commercial 23.1%

Industrial uses 24.7%

19%

WHERE IT GOES...

Energy that does useful work 45.3%

Lost or wasted energy 54.7%

Energy flows from sources to users in this chart. Orange bands trace the share of energy that goes into producing electricity. The U.S. imports petroleum and natural gas. But it exports coal to some foreign countries for their steelmaking industries. Of the three major consuming groups, **Transportation** takes the most energy—almost all as petroleum-based gasoline and other liquid fuels. **Household and Commercial** users include homes, schools, hospitals, stores, and offices. **Industrial uses** combine metalmaking, mining, and manufacturing. The gray bands represent energy that goes to waste. Producing and transmitting electricity is very inefficient. So are motor-vehicle engines: They waste about 80 percent of the energy in their fuel. And they cause more air pollution than all other energy users combined.

In the future, sunlight may replace fossil fuels as a major source of energy. Some people are installing special equipment on their roofs to trap the sun's heat with water. The water circulates through large panels tilted toward the sun. The solar-heated water can be used for washing, or it can flow through pipes to make rooms warm.

In hot climates, we need more energy for air cooling than for heating. In some buildings, solar hot water provides this as well.

You can observe a basic principle of air conditioning by dabbing a little rubbing alcohol on your arm. When the alcohol evaporates, it makes your skin feel cold. As the liquid turns into a gas, it is stealing heat from your arm.

In many solar air-conditioning systems, a liquid changes to gas, stealing heat from water inside metal coils. Air blown over the cold coils produces air conditioning.

Sunlight can produce electricity too. Some spacecraft take electric power directly from the sun. Groups of small cells mounted outside the craft change light energy in the sun's rays to electricity. One day, solar cells may also provide power for home use.

An experimental "power tower" near Albuquerque, New Mexico, will also make electricity. A field of 287 mirrors will focus sunlight onto a water boiler atop a tall tower. Heat from the concentrated sunlight will make steam to run a generator.

We can count on fossil fuels to supply our energy well into the 21st century. In the meantime, the sun and other renewable energy sources challenge us to put them to work for the future.

Built to save energy, *Terraset School (far right) nestles into a hillside near Reston, Virginia. The earth insulates Terraset, keeping it warmer in winter and cooler in summer. People and machines give off heat that usually goes to waste. But at Terraset, a recycling system puts that heat to work. Sunshine provides energy too. Held up by an orange grid, panels filled with water collect heat from the sun. The drawing shows how the hot water helps to heat and cool the building.*

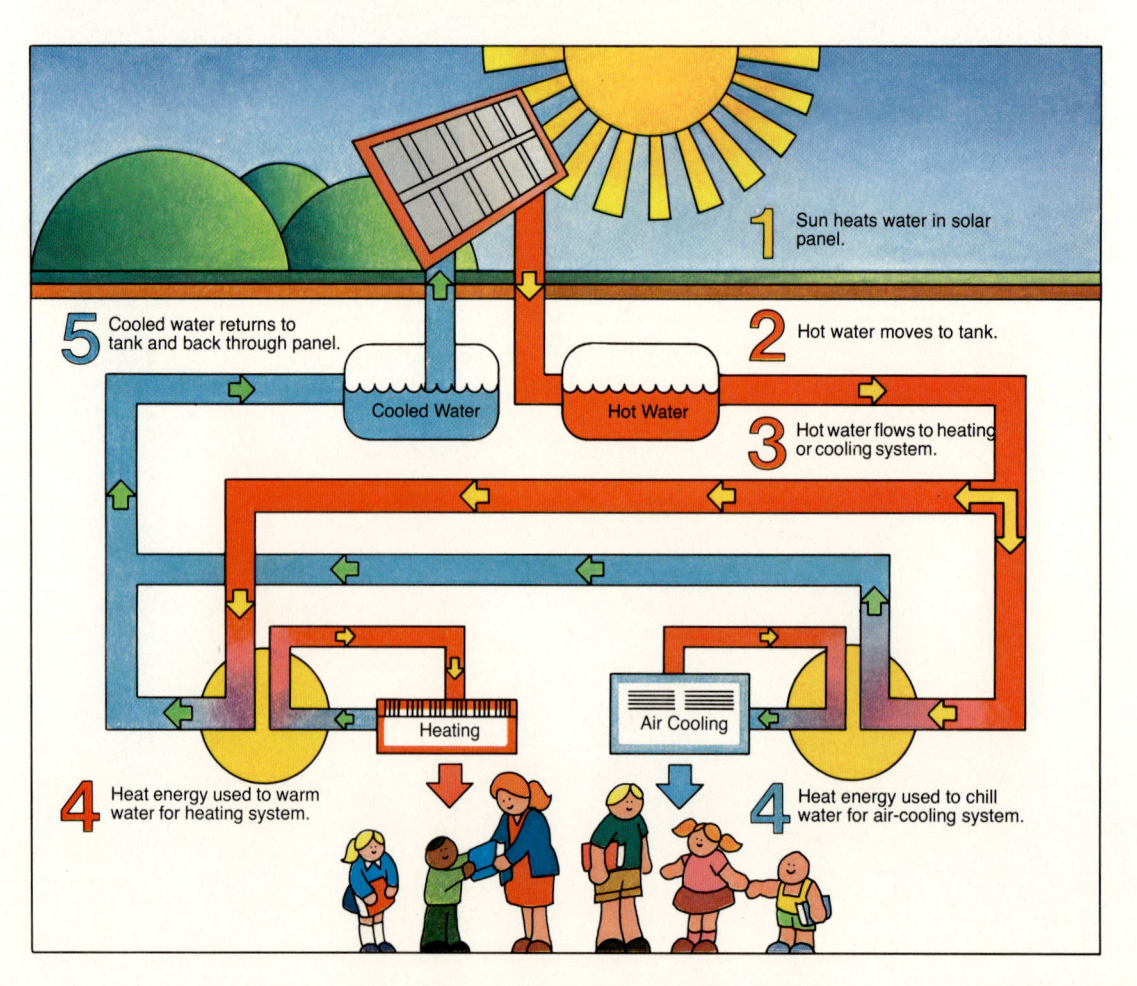

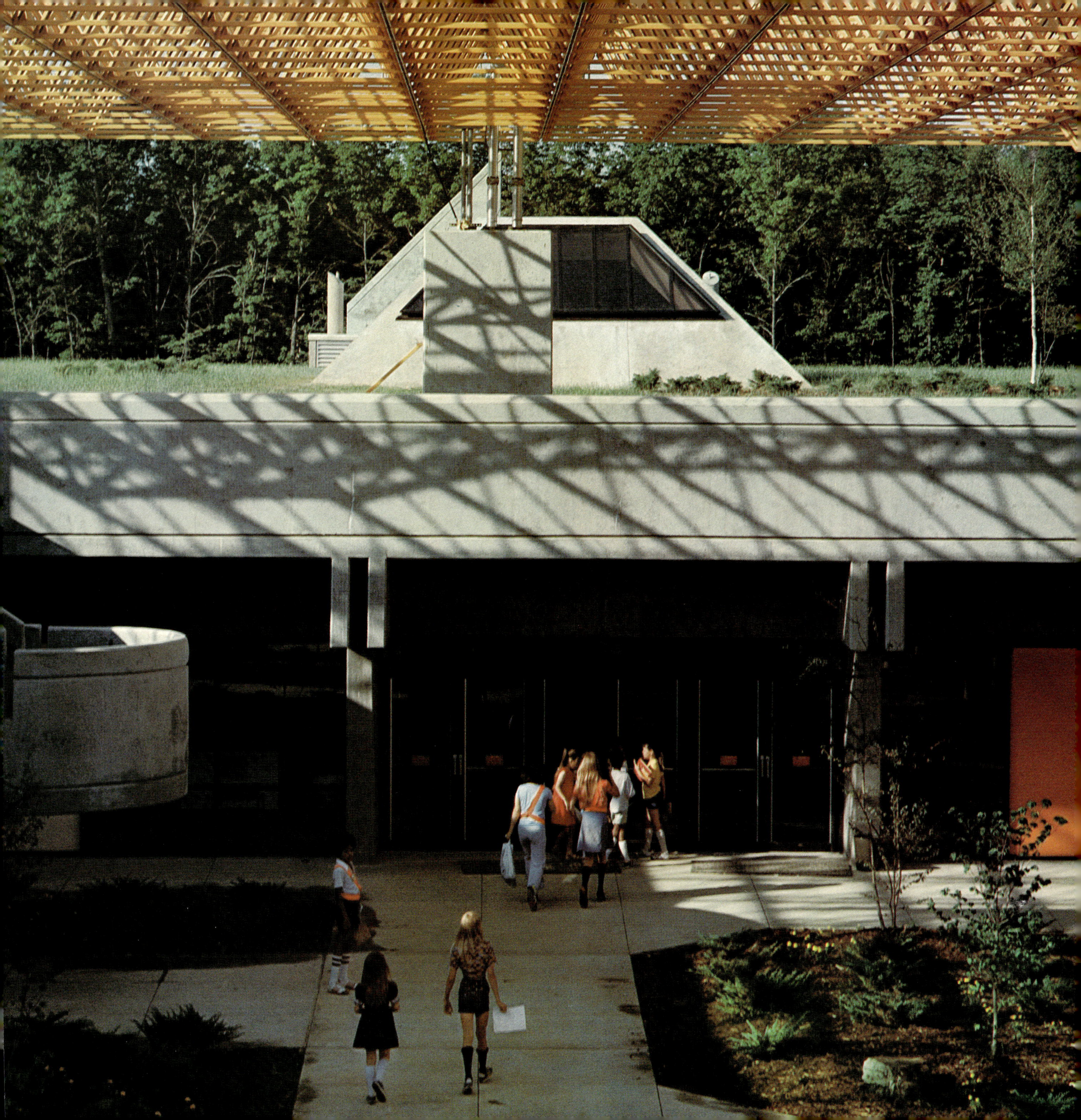

Ice Age horses and camels nibbled rich grasses on lands we know as desert today.

The Southwest

The Southwest has many landscapes—deserts, mountains, prairies, and plains. In desert country, glaring sun makes your mouth dry and your forehead wet. Temperatures may rise to 120°F (49°C), then drop by 40° (22°C) at night. Mountains rumple the land. The valleys in between would be lakes in a wetter climate, but high peaks to the west have robbed the winds of rain. Only 15 people live in a square mile (2.6 sq km) of this rugged land, shown on the western half of the map. Nearly three times as many people live east of the Rockies and other mountains that slope gently down to the Great Plains. Here we find oil, vast wheatfields, and grazing lands. The Rio Grande, outlining southwest Texas, flows into the Gulf of Mexico.

ARIZONA
NEW MEXICO
TEXAS
OKLAHOMA

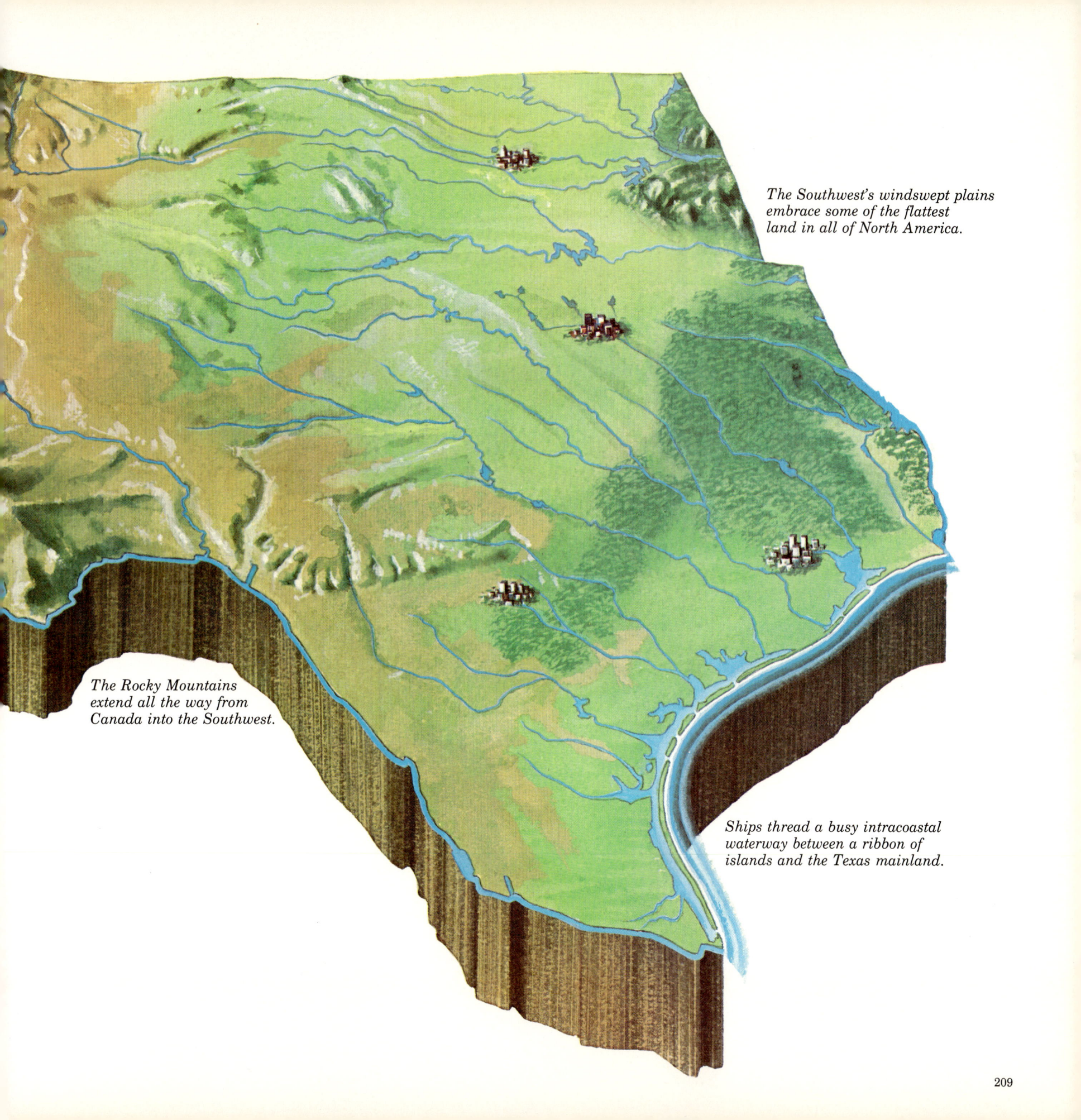

The Southwest's windswept plains embrace some of the flattest land in all of North America.

The Rocky Mountains extend all the way from Canada into the Southwest.

Ships thread a busy intracoastal waterway between a ribbon of islands and the Texas mainland.

ARIZONA

Have you ever seen an ocean in the desert? The city of Tempe, Arizona, has a swimming pool that makes giant waves. Pumped into a high wall, the water rushes out through underwater gates and splashes on a sandy beach. Surfers ride the waves in the middle of the desert!

If you lived in Tempe, you could surf in the morning and ski on the San Francisco Peaks in the afternoon. A belt of mountains begins where the desert ends. To the north are thick green pine forests and a highland gashed by deep canyons.

The Sonoran Desert claims most of southwestern Arizona. Near the city of Phoenix, you can see open canals bringing water from the Salt River. The water gurgles into swimming pools, lettuce fields, and groves of orange and lemon trees, sometimes following the same ditches that watered Indian cornfields centuries ago.

Arizonans worry about water. They know they're using it up faster than the rains can put it back. Someday water may be piped more than 300 miles (483 km) from the Colorado River to Phoenix, then to Tucson.

Not far from Tucson, you could visit the Saguaro National Monument, where prickly plants and strange animals survive with little water. More than 20 kinds of cacti, from tiny pincushions to giant ribbed saguaros, use their stems as storage tanks. The saguaro's shallow roots may soak up a half ton of water. By using it slowly, the cactus makes it last through long dry spells.

Bands of piglike peccaries roam the cactus forest, feeding on mesquite beans and prickly-pear cactus pads. Desert tortoises, scorpions, dragonlike lizards, and rattlesnakes scuttle through the brush. The Gila monster, our only poisonous lizard, appears sluggish but may whip its big head around to hiss a warning.

A shooting star collided with Arizona some 20,000 years ago, blasting a hole a mile (1.6 km) wide and 60 stories deep—earth's largest known meteorite crater.

Area: the sixth largest state, 113,909 sq mi (295,023 sq km). **Population:** 2,296,000. Ranks 32nd. **Major Cities:** Phoenix, 664,721; Tucson, 296,457; Mesa, 99,043. **Manufacturing:** non-electrical machinery, electric and electronic equipment, primary metals, transportation equipment (especially turbine aircraft engines). **Mining:** copper. Also molybdenum, sand and gravel, silver. **Agriculture:** beef cattle, cotton, vegetables, dairy products, hay, grains (feed crops and wheat), citrus fruits. **Other Important Activities:** tourism. **Statehood:** 48th state. Admitted Feb. 14, 1912.

Trails lead to the mountains, a different world from the desert. The higher you go, the cooler and wetter it is. You may see a deer, a bobcat, or the rare coatimundi—once described by an artist as "Coon and Monkey, with not a little dash of Pig."

In the early days, few settlers came to what is now Arizona. The heat and rugged mountains kept them out. Spanish soldiers explored the country, but the settlers who came later decided to live elsewhere—in a fertile valley in present-day New Mexico. As Americans began moving west, a few trappers and prospectors trickled into Arizona. Apache warriors, who were there first, swooped down on the intruders, taking food, horses, and sometimes scalps.

In 1877 a lone prospector set out to look for gold and silver in Apache country near the San Pedro River. "Instead of a mine, you'll find a tombstone," a friend warned him. He went anyway, struck it rich, and named the place "Tombstone." The mine turned out to be one of the biggest silver strikes in Arizona's history.

Mining is still important in Arizona—with a difference. Desert rocks yield gold and silver, but copper is king. More than half the copper produced in the United States comes from Arizona mines. Once, lonely prospectors dug with picks and shovels. Now, mining companies blast huge open pits with explosives, and trains transport the ore-bearing rock to copper mills.

Not long ago, hardly anyone loved the Arizona desert. In the last ten years or so, cities, farms, and industries have mushroomed. Half a million people—many of them tired of northern winters—moved to the land of almost continuous sunshine.

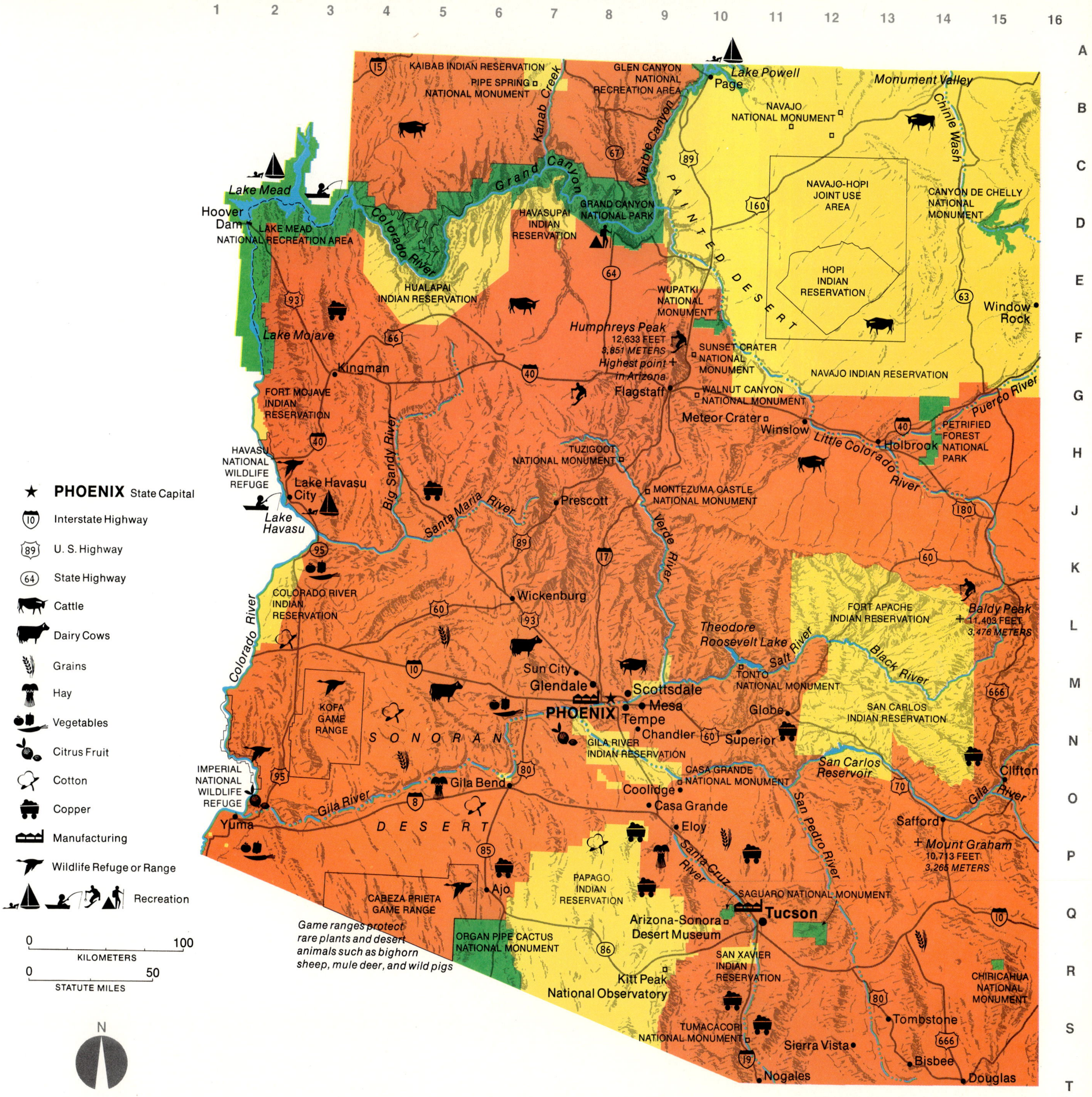

PHOENIX State Capital
Interstate Highway
U. S. Highway
State Highway
Cattle
Dairy Cows
Grains
Hay
Vegetables
Citrus Fruit
Cotton
Copper
Manufacturing
Wildlife Refuge or Range
Recreation
KILOMETERS
STATUTE MILES
N
KAIBAB INDIAN RESERVATION
PIPE SPRING NATIONAL MONUMENT
GLEN CANYON NATIONAL RECREATION AREA
Lake Powell
Page
Monument Valley
NAVAJO NATIONAL MONUMENT
Kanab Creek
Marble Canyon
Chinle Wash
Lake Mead
Hoover Dam
LAKE MEAD NATIONAL RECREATION AREA
Grand Canyon
Colorado River
HAVASUPAI INDIAN RESERVATION
GRAND CANYON NATIONAL PARK
PAINTED DESERT
NAVAJO-HOPI JOINT USE AREA
CANYON DE CHELLY NATIONAL MONUMENT
HOPI INDIAN RESERVATION
HUALAPAI INDIAN RESERVATION
WUPATKI NATIONAL MONUMENT
Window Rock
Lake Mojave
Humphreys Peak
12,633 FEET
3,851 METERS
Highest point in Arizona
SUNSET CRATER NATIONAL MONUMENT
NAVAJO INDIAN RESERVATION
Kingman
Flagstaff
WALNUT CANYON NATIONAL MONUMENT
Puerco River
FORT MOJAVE INDIAN RESERVATION
Meteor Crater
Winslow
PETRIFIED FOREST NATIONAL PARK
Big Sandy River
Holbrook
Little Colorado River
HAVASU NATIONAL WILDLIFE REFUGE
TUZIGOOT NATIONAL MONUMENT
Lake Havasu City
Lake Havasu
MONTEZUMA CASTLE NATIONAL MONUMENT
Santa Maria River
Prescott
Verde River
COLORADO RIVER INDIAN RESERVATION
Wickenburg
FORT APACHE INDIAN RESERVATION
Baldy Peak
11,403 FEET
3,476 METERS
Theodore Roosevelt Lake
Salt River
Black River
TONTO NATIONAL MONUMENT
Sun City
Glendale
Scottsdale
PHOENIX
Mesa
Tempe
Chandler
Globe
SAN CARLOS INDIAN RESERVATION
KOFA GAME RANGE
SONORAN DESERT
GILA RIVER INDIAN RESERVATION
Superior
IMPERIAL NATIONAL WILDLIFE REFUGE
CASA GRANDE NATIONAL MONUMENT
San Carlos Reservoir
Clifton
Gila Bend
Coolidge
Casa Grande
Gila River
San Pedro River
Yuma
Eloy
Safford
Santa Cruz River
Mount Graham
10,713 FEET
3,265 METERS
PAPAGO INDIAN RESERVATION
Ajo
CABEZA PRIETA GAME RANGE
SAGUARO NATIONAL MONUMENT
Tucson
Arizona-Sonora Desert Museum
Game ranges protect rare plants and desert animals such as bighorn sheep, mule deer, and wild pigs
ORGAN PIPE CACTUS NATIONAL MONUMENT
SAN XAVIER INDIAN RESERVATION
Kitt Peak National Observatory
CHIRICAHUA NATIONAL MONUMENT
Tombstone
TUMACACORI NATIONAL MONUMENT
Sierra Vista
Bisbee
Nogales
Douglas

Travel north from the desert cities. Drive the twisty roads of mountain and plateau country. Within a circle of 100 miles, you can ride a mule into the Grand Canyon, view an extinct volcano, see the gold-and-purple Painted Desert. About 85 percent of the state has been set aside as public land and Indian reservations. More Indians live here than in any other state. Dome-shaped houses called hogans dot the Navajo reservation, a dry, rocky land about the size of West Virginia. Navajo medicine men still sing ancient chants to cure the sick. But the children attend modern schools on the reservation.

Wind, rain, and frost shaped the Grand Canyon's dizzying spectacle. A mile (1.6 km) down, the Colorado River still carves the gorge after millions of years.

Young folks can visit but not live in Sun City, near Phoenix. The sprawling community for older people has golf courses, parks, man-made lakes, and shopping malls—but no schools.

Wood into stone: Colorful waterborne minerals replaced the wood in each cell of this petrified slab.

Fiery leftovers from a copper furnace pour down a steep ravine. Your house may have electric wiring or cooking pots made of copper mined in Arizona.

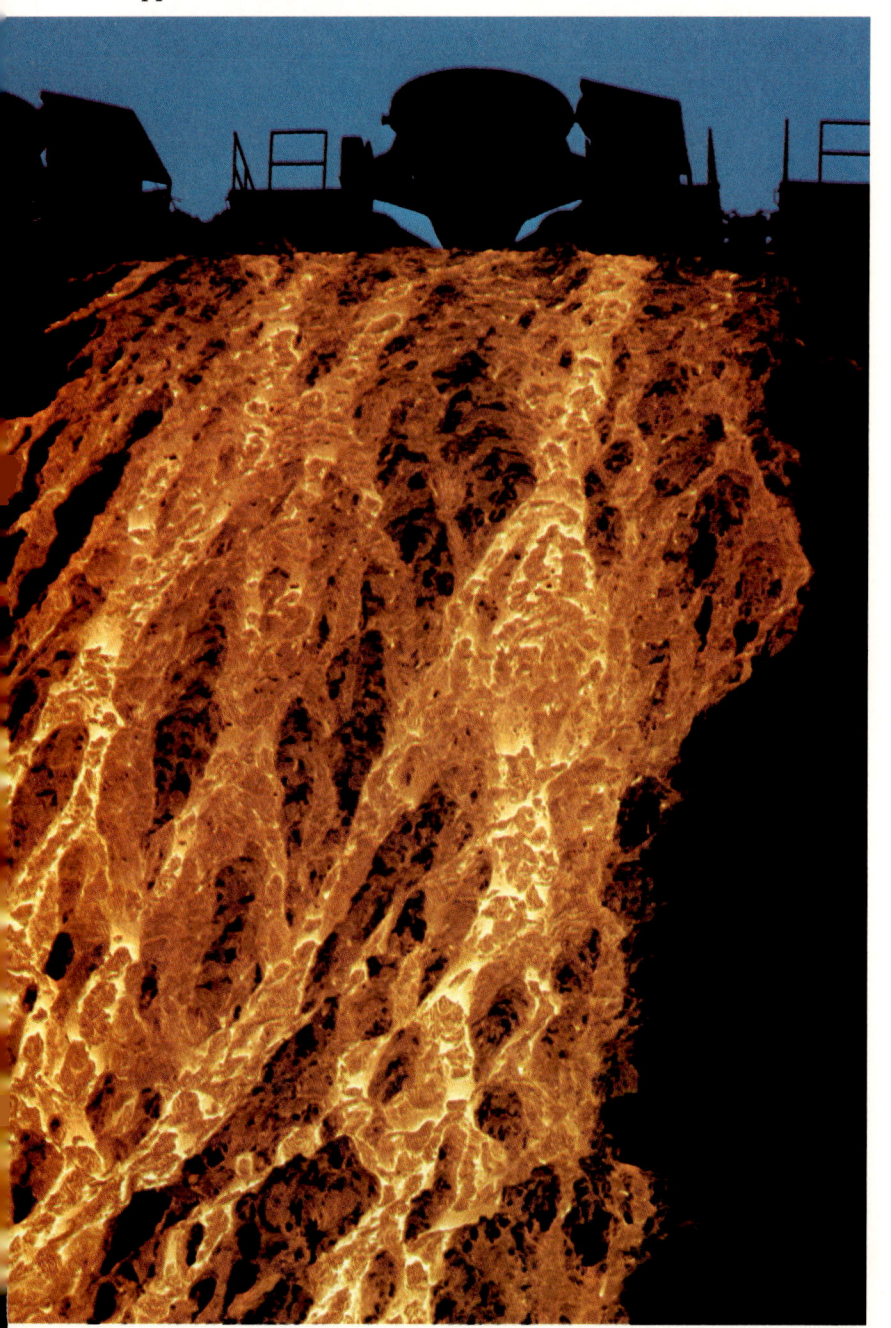

Spilling down the dunes in Navajo country, a flock of sheep may soon be shorn of their woolly coats. Indian women weave the fibers into fine rugs.

Home to a screech owl, the giant saguaro cactus may grow to 50 feet (15 m) and live 200 years.

Yucca Roadrunner

NEW MEXICO

High, wide, and dry. That's New Mexico. You may be surprised to learn how high it is. The capital, Santa Fe, sits at the foot of a mountain range; yet the city is still 7,000 feet (2,134 m) above sea level—higher than the tallest peak east of the Mississippi.

Only four states claim more land than New Mexico, and few have such a small population scattered over a large area. No other state has less of its surface in lakes and rivers—a tiny two-thousandths of one percent.

If you think of New Mexico as desert country, you're both right and wrong. In the eastern part of the state the wind blows free across flat plains rich in oil, wheat, and cattle. Forested mountains, high desert plateaus, and hot desert valleys wrinkle central and western New Mexico.

Ancient seas washed over this land again and again. The earth shifted. Volcanoes exploded, spilling hot lava. Thick piles of ash built up. Near the town of Grants, you'll find the "badlands"—miles of hard, black, twisted lava. You can hike the lava field, but the rocks will cut your shoes. And you'd better take a snakebite kit.

As the earth heaved, struggling to take its present shape, a rich treasure-house of minerals formed. Besides molybdenum (used to harden steel) and copper, New Mexico produces 47 percent of the nation's uranium, the chief source of atomic energy. It was here in this state that the first atomic bomb was exploded.

The test bomb went off in the same desert the Spanish crossed when they came up from Mexico to settle in 1598. The trip across the 90 miles (145 km) of hot sand and lava was so terrible the explorers called the desert *Jornada del Muerto,* Dead Man's Journey. During World War II, in 1945, this wasteland far from towns and cities was chosen for the bomb test. Now it's used to try out missiles and rocket launchers.

The Rocky Mountains extend stony fingers into northern New Mexico. The high country is a good place to camp and fish or ride a horse on wooded trails. Elk and marmots, mountain lions, quail and pheasant hide away on the slopes and in the woods.

The Rio Grande courses New Mexico from Colorado to the Mexican border. In places it's not grand at all, just a shallow, muddy stream. But human beings have lived in the Rio Grande Valley for thousands of years. Villages of today's Pueblo Indians cluster near the river. In little farming towns, Spanish-speaking Americans live much as their ancestors did.

Let's visit Santa Fe to see a blend of New Mexico's three cultures: Indian, Spanish-American, and Anglo (a word used in the Southwest to mean all other Americans).

Houses and shops built of adobe—sun-dried bricks—line the city's narrow streets. Doorways are hung with red chili peppers drying in the sun. In restaurants, diners can order an array of Mexican food, such as chicken with chocolate and pepper sauce, and *sopapillas,* a kind of fritter with butter and honey. Outside on the street, ranchers gather in groups, talking business. They're wearing high-heeled cowboy boots.

In front of the historic Palace of the Governors, built by the Spanish more than 300 years ago, Pueblo Indians sell fine handcrafted pottery and jewelry, just as they have since the building was new.

New Mexico has bustling cities, too. Space-age industry centers in Albuquerque, the largest city and home of a fourth of the state's people. And beyond the hubbub, there's still plenty of space to wander.

Autographed by travelers for centuries, Inscription Rock bears the name of a conquistador who passed by here in 1606.

Area: the fifth largest state, 121,666 sq mi (315,113 sq km). **Population:** 1,190,000. Ranks 37th. **Major Cities:** Albuquerque, 279,401; Santa Fe, 44,937. **Mining:** natural gas, oil, uranium, copper. Also potassium salts, coal, molybdenum. **Agriculture:** beef cattle. Also dairy products, hay, sorghum grains, wheat. **Manufacturing:** food processing, electric and electronic equipment, stone, clay, and glass products, printing and publishing, chemicals. **Other Important Activities:** tourism. **Statehood:** the 47th state. Admitted Jan. 6, 1912.

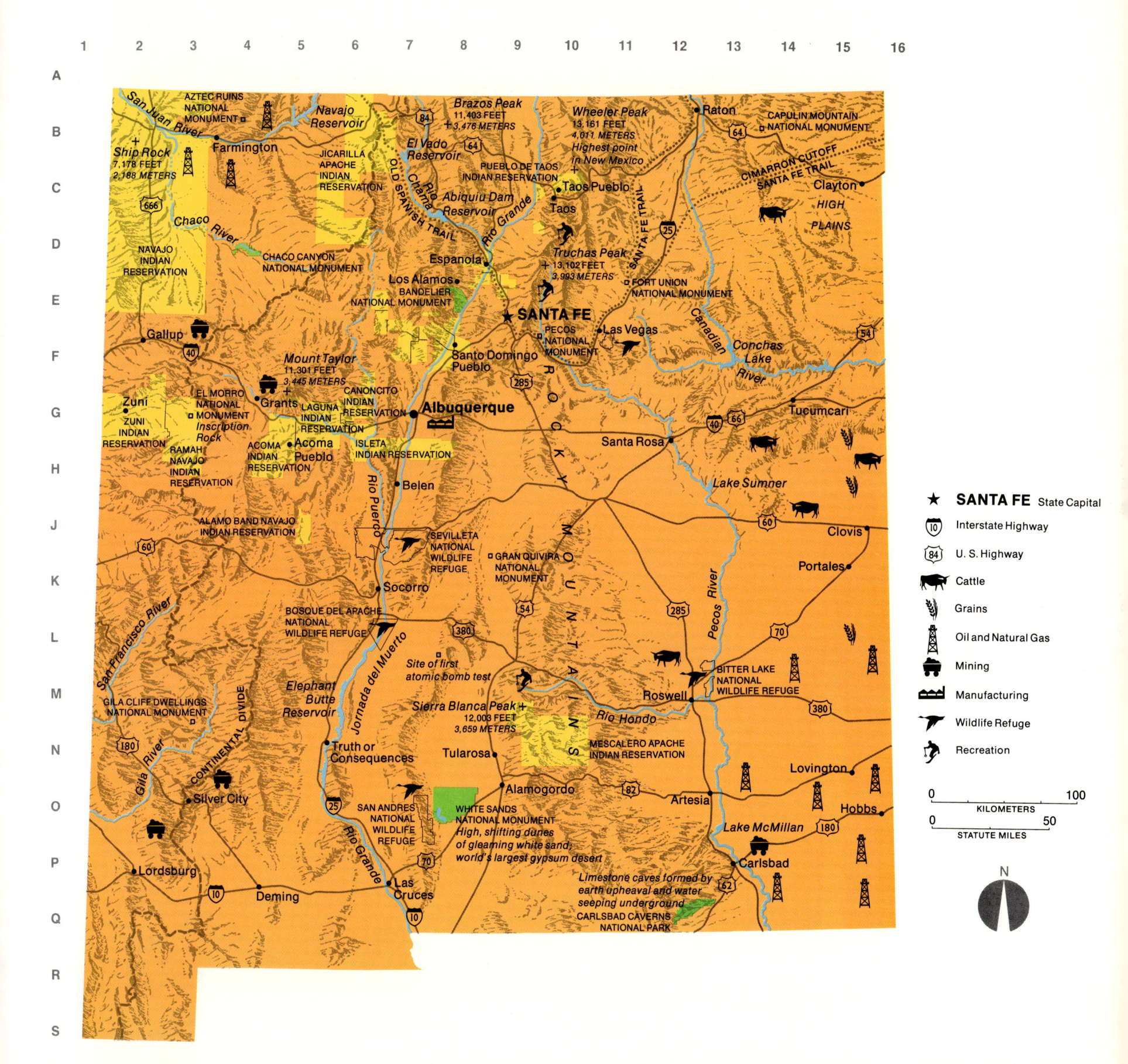

New Mexico Map

Grid Reference
Columns: 1–16
Rows: A–S

Cities and Towns
- Farmington
- Gallup
- Grants
- Zuni
- Los Alamos
- Española
- Taos
- Taos Pueblo
- Santo Domingo Pueblo
- **SANTA FE** (State Capital)
- Las Vegas
- Raton
- Clayton
- Albuquerque
- Belen
- Socorro
- Tucumcari
- Santa Rosa
- Clovis
- Portales
- Truth or Consequences
- Tularosa
- Alamogordo
- Roswell
- Artesia
- Lovington
- Hobbs
- Carlsbad
- Silver City
- Lordsburg
- Deming
- Las Cruces

Physical Features
- San Juan River
- Navajo Reservoir
- Ship Rock, 7,178 FEET / 2,188 METERS
- Chaco River
- El Vado Reservoir
- Brazos Peak, 11,403 FEET / 3,476 METERS
- Wheeler Peak, 13,161 FEET / 4,011 METERS — Highest point in New Mexico
- Abiquiu Dam Reservoir
- Rio Chama
- Rio Grande
- Truchas Peak, 13,102 FEET / 3,993 METERS
- Mount Taylor, 11,301 FEET / 3,445 METERS
- Inscription Rock
- Rio Puerco
- Canadian River
- Conchas Lake
- Pecos River
- Lake Sumner
- Rio Hondo
- Sierra Blanca Peak, 12,003 FEET / 3,659 METERS
- Jornada del Muerto
- Elephant Butte Reservoir
- Gila River
- San Francisco River
- Continental Divide
- Lake McMillan
- Rocky Mountains
- High Plains

National Monuments, Parks, and Reservations
- Aztec Ruins National Monument
- Jicarilla Apache Indian Reservation
- Pueblo de Taos Indian Reservation
- Capulin Mountain National Monument
- Navajo Indian Reservation
- Chaco Canyon National Monument
- Bandelier National Monument
- Fort Union National Monument
- Cimarron Cutoff Santa Fe Trail
- Old Spanish Trail
- Santa Fe Trail
- Pecos National Monument
- El Morro National Monument
- Zuni Indian Reservation
- Ramah Navajo Indian Reservation
- Canoncito Indian Reservation
- Laguna Indian Reservation
- Acoma Indian Reservation / Acoma Pueblo
- Isleta Indian Reservation
- Alamo Band Navajo Indian Reservation
- Sevilleta National Wildlife Refuge
- Gran Quivira National Monument
- Bosque del Apache National Wildlife Refuge
- Site of first atomic bomb test
- Gila Cliff Dwellings National Monument
- San Andres National Wildlife Refuge
- White Sands National Monument — High, shifting dunes of gleaming white sand; world's largest gypsum desert
- Mescalero Apache Indian Reservation
- Bitter Lake National Wildlife Refuge
- Carlsbad Caverns National Park — Limestone caves formed by earth upheaval and water seeping underground

Highways
- I-10, I-25, I-40
- US 54, 60, 62, 64, 66, 70, 82, 84, 180, 285, 380, 666

Legend
- ★ **SANTA FE** State Capital
- Interstate Highway
- U.S. Highway
- Cattle
- Grains
- Oil and Natural Gas
- Mining
- Manufacturing
- Wildlife Refuge
- Recreation

Scale: 0–100 Kilometers / 0–50 Statute Miles

215

Scientists at Los Alamos test a superhot metal drill, a tool they hope will reach the earth's interior heat—an energy source.

Indians stage rodeos, parades, and dances every year in the town of Gallup. Some 20 tribes pitch tents in the hills and take part. Tourists are welcome too at the red man's show.

216

Begun about 700 years ago, Taos Pueblo says no to electricity, running water, and telephones. Women sweep the dirt plaza and bake bread in beehive ovens.

A magic stone to the ancient Pueblo Indians, turquoise kept evil away. Set in silver, it brings fame to Zuni craftsmen today.

Yuccas bloom on the White Sands desert. Pioneers called the plants "Spanish bayonets."

Like icicles, stalactites drape a room called the King's Palace in Carlsbad Caverns National Park. Drop by drop, water from the ceiling left a trail of minerals. Stalagmites build from the floor up.

The Pueblo Indians live in America's oldest apartment houses. High-rise Taos Pueblo has four and five stories. In the old days it had no doors or windows. Ladders led to hatchways on the roof. If an enemy attacked, the ladders could be pulled up. Some of these Indians still have enemies to keep out. They believe the modern world will destroy their way of life. So the children learn the ancient religion in underground rooms called kivas, and buffalo and corn dancers honor the old gods. Legend says the Taos Indians' ancestors came up from the underworld through Blue Lake, high in the mountains. When this sacred place became part of a national forest, the Indians tried for 64 years to get it back. They did, in 1970.

OKLAHOMA

Oklahoma is so young there are a few oldtimers who remember every important event since the state entered the Union in 1907. Little more than a century ago, Oklahoma was Indian territory, a faraway wilderness little known to white people. The federal government used it as a kind of dumping ground for Eastern and other Indians living on lands the settlers wanted.

The state's name is an Indian word, from the Choctaw *okla,* "men," and *homma,* "red." Towns and cities with melodious Indian names sprinkle the eastern third of the state: Talhequah, Atoka, Tulsa, Eufaula. An eighth of our country's Indians live in Oklahoma. They hold a variety of jobs, such as farmer, businessman, scholar, or laborer. Many Cherokees live in the Ozark hill country and still speak Cherokee.

Oklahoma Territory became home for many Americans in 1889, when part of the Indian lands were opened for settlement. Thousands of people waited, then dashed in to claim a homestead. Busy tent cities sprang up. One of these was Oklahoma City. At noon the site was empty prairie. By nightfall it had 10,000 people!

Oil built Oklahoma. In 1897 the first profitable well spouted in Bartlesville. Soon after, the tough cowtown of Tulsa began calling itself the "oil capital of the world." Oklahoma City boomed. By leasing land to oilmen, members of the Osage tribe became the nation's richest Indians. Not all the Indians were lucky. Some were killed or had their oil-rich lands stolen from them.

Drillers have found oil or natural gas in all but five of the state's 77 counties. When wells go dry, new ones must be found and drilled, but known reserves won't last forever. Adventurous companies in search of more natural gas are drilling "superwells" nearly five miles (8 km) deep.

Cities have tried to attract new industries that will provide jobs. Thousands of Oklahomans work in aviation and aerospace. At Tinker Air Force Base in Oklahoma City, about 21,000 people are employed to repair planes and distribute supplies.

In the 19th century, wagon trains lumbered across the Oklahoma Panhandle on the Santa Fe Trail between Missouri and the Southwest. Today, huge feedlots fatten cattle for market. Fields of golden wheat wave on the western plains. In summer, big combines grind away around the clock, harvesting the grain before heavy rains, hail, or prairie fires can damage the valuable crop.

Oklahoma suffered from long dry spells in the 1930's. High winds churned up clouds of dust that ruined crops. John Steinbeck wrote a novel, *The Grapes of Wrath*. It tells about the "Okies"—farmers from Oklahoma and other plains states—who left their land and moved to California.

Water has often been a problem. The shallow Arkansas River winds through Oklahoma. In the old days when steamboats ran aground, their captains grumbled that the river had a "bottom too near its top." Recently, engineers dug channels in the Arkansas and Verdigris Rivers. Lashed to towboats, barges loaded with wheat and oil travel from a port near Tulsa to the Mississippi, and on to the Great Lakes or the Gulf of Mexico. The landlocked state has a lifeline to the sea. Today in eastern Oklahoma, there's water, water everywhere. Dozens of man-made lakes provide water for irrigation and flood control, for hydroelectric power, and for fun. "If we ever tip over," Oklahomans say, "Texas will be flooded."

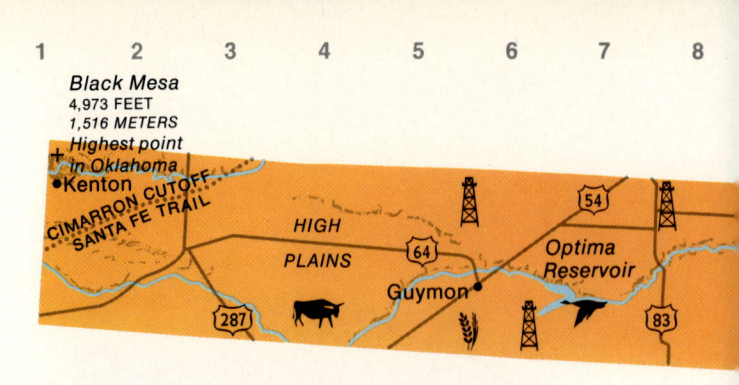

Like a sprinkling of diamonds, selenite crystals catch the sun's rays on the Glass Mountains' eroded buttes and mesas.

Area: the 18th largest state, 69,919 sq mi (181,089 sq km). **Population:** 2,811,000. Ranks 27th. **Major Cities:** Oklahoma City, 365,916; Tulsa, 331,726; Lawton, 76,421. **Mining:** natural gas, petroleum, coal, cement. **Manufacturing:** nonelectrical machinery (especially construction and oil-field machinery), food processing, fabricated metals, electric and electronic equipment, rubber and plastics (especially rubber tires and inner tubes). **Agriculture:** beef cattle, wheat, dairy products, cotton, peanuts. **Statehood:** the 46th state. Admitted Nov. 16, 1907.

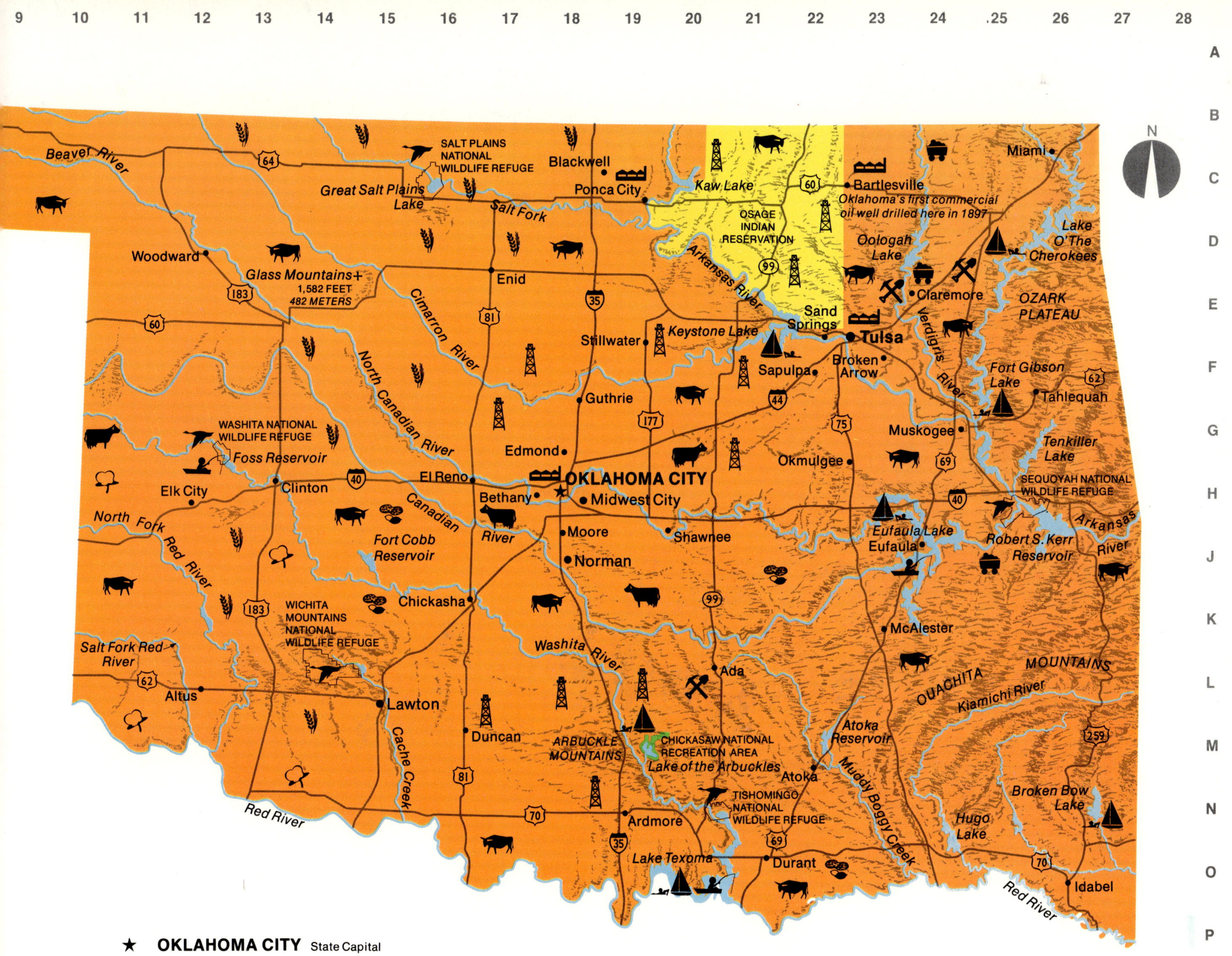
9 10 11 12 13 14 15 16 17 18 19 20 21 22 23 24 25 26 27 28
A B C D E F G H J K L M N O P
N
Beaver River
SALT PLAINS
NATIONAL
WILDLIFE REFUGE
Great Salt Plains
Lake
Blackwell
Ponca City
Salt Fork
Kaw Lake
OSAGE
INDIAN
RESERVATION
Bartlesville
Oklahoma's first commercial
oil well drilled here in 1897
Miami
Lake
O' The
Cherokees
Oologah
Lake
Claremore
OZARK
PLATEAU
Woodward
Glass Mountains+
1,582 FEET
482 METERS
Enid
Cimarron River
Arkansas River
Sand
Springs
Tulsa
Keystone Lake
Stillwater
Sapulpa
Broken
Arrow
Verdigris River
Fort Gibson
Lake
Tahlequah
North Canadian River
Guthrie
WASHITA NATIONAL
WILDLIFE REFUGE
Foss Reservoir
Edmond
Muskogee
Tenkiller
Lake
Okmulgee
Clinton
Elk City
El Reno
OKLAHOMA CITY
Bethany
Midwest City
SEQUOYAH NATIONAL
WILDLIFE REFUGE
North Fork Red River
Canadian River
Moore
Shawnee
Eufaula Lake
Eufaula
Robert S. Kerr
Reservoir
Arkansas River
Fort Cobb
Reservoir
Norman
Chickasha
WICHITA
MOUNTAINS
NATIONAL
WILDLIFE REFUGE
McAlester
Salt Fork Red
River
Washita River
Ada
MOUNTAINS
OUACHITA
Kiamichi River
Altus
Lawton
Duncan
Cache Creek
ARBUCKLE
MOUNTAINS
CHICKASAW NATIONAL
RECREATION AREA
Lake of the Arbuckles
Atoka
Reservoir
Atoka
Muddy Boggy Creek
Broken Bow
Lake
Hugo
Lake
Red River
Ardmore
TISHOMINGO
NATIONAL
WILDLIFE REFUGE
Lake Texoma
Durant
Idabel
Red River
64 60 183 60 81 35 177 44 75 62 69 40 40 183 62 99 81 70 35 69 70 259
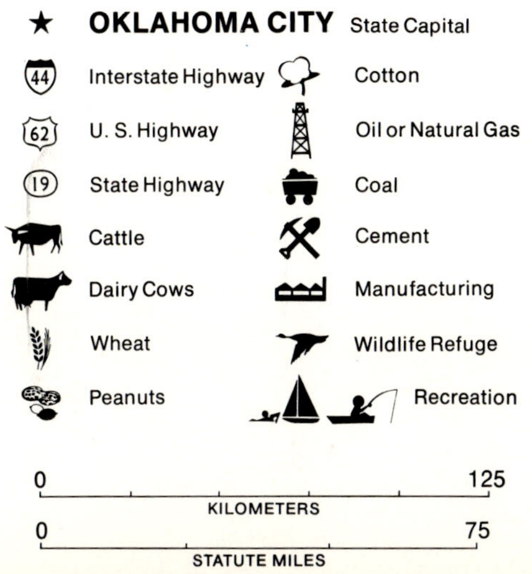
★ OKLAHOMA CITY State Capital
44 Interstate Highway
62 U. S. Highway
19 State Highway
Cattle
Dairy Cows
Wheat
Peanuts
Cotton
Oil or Natural Gas
Coal
Cement
Manufacturing
Wildlife Refuge
Recreation
0 125
KILOMETERS
0 75
STATUTE MILES

OKLAHOMA

Mistletoe
Scissor-tailed
Flycatcher

Oil rigs jab the skyline of Oklahoma City, where drillers sank 18 wells on the state capitol grounds. Half are still producing oil.

A pioneer's stone house stands near Kenton. On homesteads bare of rock and wood, building blocks were clumps of sod.

In summer, kids splash at Turner Falls, camp nearby in the Arbuckle Mountains.

Oklahoma got off to a running start back in 1889, when homesteaders gathered for the first big land rush. Men, women, and children came from all over the country. At noon, a soldier on high ground dropped a flag and blew a bugle. Thousands of settlers charged in on horses, in buckboards and prairie schooners. A few rode bicycles and snorting locomotives. Those who rushed in sooner than they should have gave Oklahoma its nickname—the "Sooner State." Families slept in covered wagons until crude houses were built. They planted corn and beans, hunted rabbits on the prairie, and lived through many a tornado. It was a hard life.

A tribal dancer leaps and whirls to the ancient rhythm of the drum. Festive powwows bring Indians together to share the old ways. About 125,000 Indians of at least 65 tribes live in Oklahoma.

Round 'em up! To preserve the grasslands of Wichita Mountains National Wildlife Refuge, a few buffalo are sold or sent to zoos every year.

TEXAS

Mockingbird
Bluebonnet

A steamboat captain named Richard King decided to go into the ranching business. He bought up land in south Texas, some for 15¢ an acre, none for more than a dollar an acre. His first land had belonged to a Spanish rancher killed by Indians. His first cattle were the scrawny, long-horned kind he could buy in Mexico.

From this beginning a hundred years ago, the King Ranch grew into a great cattle empire. At one time it covered 1¼ million acres (500,000 hectares) in six counties! Although the huge spread has shrunk a little, it's still one of the world's largest cattle ranches.

Since Captain King's day, ranching has changed. Some cattle still graze the open range, but many are penned in big feedlots, and the land used for growing feed. With scientific methods, Texas cattlemen raise nearly seven million beef animals a year. How much meat is that? Enough to make 18 billion hamburgers! In addition, herds of Texas dairy cows give 400 million gallons (1½ billion liters) of milk every year.

Texas is so big that when it entered the Union, Congress gave it the right to divide into five states. Since it didn't, the huge state has every kind of landscape besides the plains it's famous for. Comanche warriors once holed up in the desert and mountain country of west Texas. At Big Bend, where the Chisos Mountains are cradled in an arm of the Rio Grande, you can float down the river or ride rocky horse trails.

A big piney woods in the eastern part of the state gives way to rice-growing swamps on the Gulf of Mexico. Fruits and vegetables thrive in the fertile Rio Grande Valley; sheep and Angora goats graze the brushy hillsides of the Edwards Plateau.

In east Texas, a wedge of tangled growth

Goats in coats? Ranchers once put coats on newly shorn Angora goats to keep them dry in the freezing rains of Texas hill country.

Area: the second largest state, 267,338 sq mi (692,402 sq km). **Population:** 12,830,000. Ranks third. **Major Cities:** Houston, 1,326,809; Dallas, 812,797; San Antonio, 773,248; El Paso, 385,691. **Manufacturing:** chemicals, petroleum refining, non-electrical machinery, food processing, transportation equipment (aviation and aerospace, ships, motor vehicles). **Mining:** oil, natural gas. **Agriculture:** beef cattle, cotton, grains (sorghum and wheat), corn. **Other Important Activities:** tourism, shipping, shrimp fishing. **Statehood:** the 28th state. Admitted Dec. 29, 1845.

called the Big Thicket covers thousands of acres. A forest of trees, vines, and shrubs, the thicket once hid outlaws and Civil War deserters. Black bears and razorback hogs still roam there.

Orchids, cattails, and six-foot ferns mingle in the moist, jungly maze. The carnivorous pitcher plant grows there too. An insect that crawls into a pitcher plant will be dissolved by the plant's chemicals.

Under Texas soil lies a storehouse of oil. The first big strike came in 1901, when the town of Beaumont heard an earthshaking roar. A well called "Spindletop" exploded. It ran wild for nine days, gushing a lake of oil. Other producing wells followed, and today, pipelines and tankers carry Texas oil to many parts of the world.

Spindletop made Houston an oil center. The city grew and grew, and it's still growing. Many millionaires live there. From the harbor, the Houston Ship Channel winds through Galveston Bay. Oil refineries and petrochemical plants—where oil is made into everything from jet fuel to fertilizer—line the channel banks on both sides.

Houston now has a special hero—the astronaut. Outside the city, the Lyndon B. Johnson Space Center sprawls on rangeland where—not too long ago—cattle grazed and bounty hunters tracked wolves. Seconds after a spacecraft lifts off at Cape Canaveral, the world hears reports of its progress from Houston's Mission Control. Technicians there become the astronauts' eyes and ears, guiding the flight.

Visitors who tour the Johnson Space Center see recovered spacecraft, moon rocks, maybe even an astronaut. These days the astronaut could be a woman. Six women have been chosen to begin training at the center for the space shuttle of the 1980's.

222

Legend

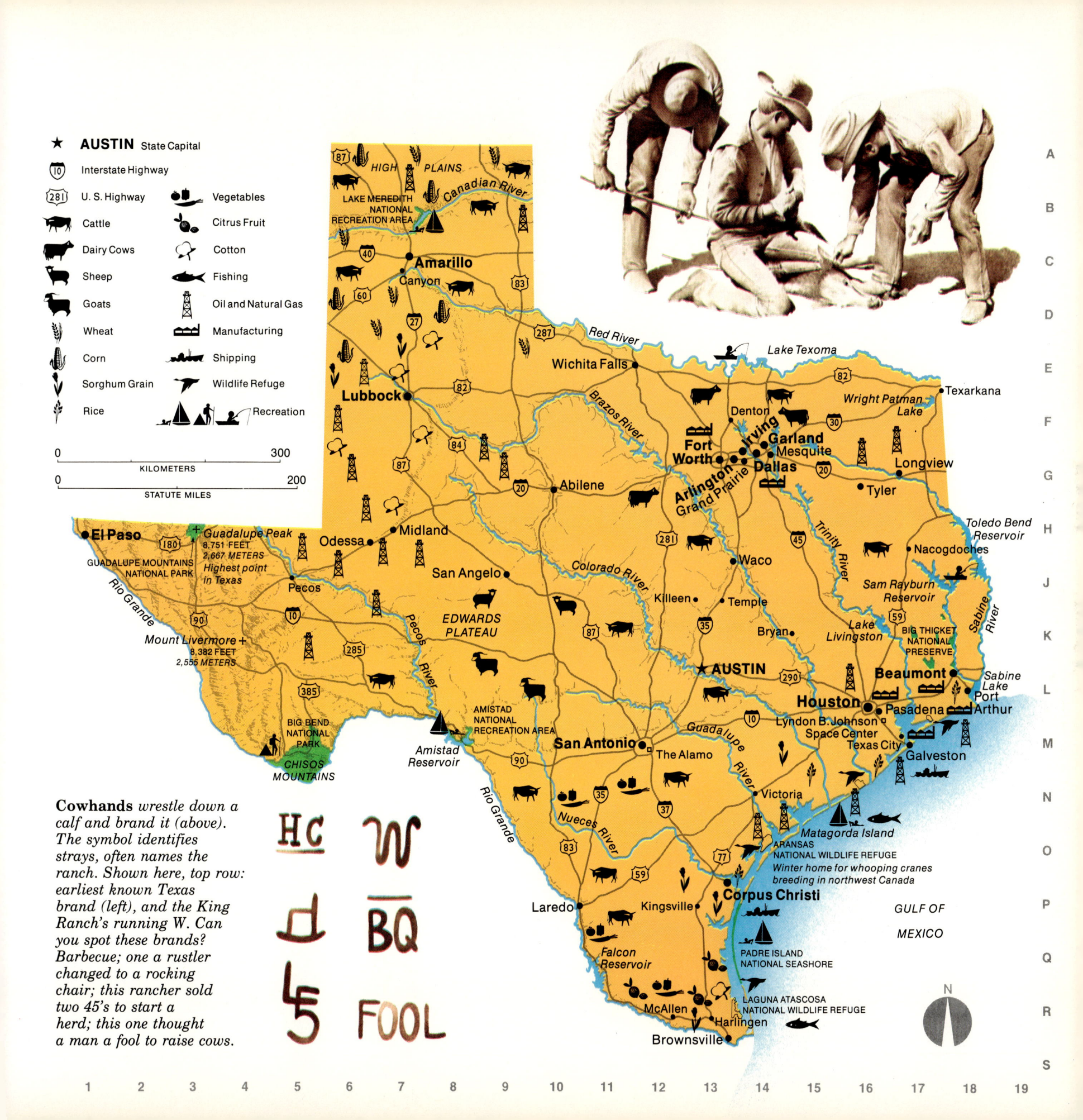

★ **AUSTIN** State Capital
🛣 Interstate Highway
🛣 U.S. Highway
🐄 Cattle
🐄 Dairy Cows
🐑 Sheep
🐐 Goats
🌾 Wheat
🌽 Corn
🌾 Sorghum Grain
🌾 Rice
🥕 Vegetables
🍊 Citrus Fruit
☁ Cotton
🐟 Fishing
🛢 Oil and Natural Gas
🏭 Manufacturing
🚢 Shipping
🦅 Wildlife Refuge
⛵ Recreation

0 — 300 KILOMETERS
0 — 200 STATUTE MILES

Cowhands wrestle down a calf and brand it (above). The symbol identifies strays, often names the ranch. Shown here, top row: earliest known Texas brand (left), and the King Ranch's running W. Can you spot these brands? Barbecue; one a rustler changed to a rocking chair; this rancher sold two 45's to start a herd; this one thought a man a fool to raise cows.

HC W
⊓ B̄Q
└5 FOOL

Map Labels

HIGH PLAINS
LAKE MEREDITH NATIONAL RECREATION AREA
Canadian River
Amarillo
Canyon
Lubbock
Red River
Lake Texoma
Wichita Falls
Wright Patman Lake
Texarkana
Brazos River
Denton
Fort Worth · Irving · Garland
Arlington · Dallas · Mesquite
Grand Prairie
Longview
Abilene
Tyler
El Paso
GUADALUPE MOUNTAINS NATIONAL PARK
Guadalupe Peak 8,751 FEET 2,667 METERS Highest point in Texas
Odessa · Midland
Rio Grande
Pecos
Mount Livermore 8,382 FEET 2,555 METERS
San Angelo
Colorado River
Waco
Trinity River
Toledo Bend Reservoir
Nacogdoches
Sam Rayburn Reservoir
Pecos River
EDWARDS PLATEAU
Killeen · Temple
Bryan
Lake Livingston
BIG THICKET NATIONAL PRESERVE
Sabine River
BIG BEND NATIONAL PARK
CHISOS MOUNTAINS
AMISTAD NATIONAL RECREATION AREA
Amistad Reservoir
★ AUSTIN
Beaumont
Houston
Pasadena
Sabine Lake
Port Arthur
San Antonio
The Alamo
Guadalupe River
Lyndon B. Johnson Space Center
Texas City
Galveston
Victoria
Nueces River
Matagorda Island
ARANSAS NATIONAL WILDLIFE REFUGE
Winter home for whooping cranes breeding in northwest Canada
Laredo
Kingsville
Corpus Christi
PADRE ISLAND NATIONAL SEASHORE
GULF OF MEXICO
Falcon Reservoir
LAGUNA ATASCOSA NATIONAL WILDLIFE REFUGE
McAllen · Harlingen
Brownsville

A city for cows, this giant feedlot pens 65,000 animals near Canyon, in the Texas Panhandle. Special feed fattens the cattle in three to six months, faster than grazing would. Then it's off to the slaughterhouse.

Whirling and swirling at fiesta time, Spanish dancers remind San Antonio of its colorful past.

On dusty trails the Texas cattle industry was born. Spanish explorers brought longhorn cattle up from Mexico. Wild herds ranged Texas, breeding with strays from pioneer wagon trains. Sometimes the longhorns were shot as game animals. Little by little, Texans rounded up and drove herds to railheads in Kansas. Drovers prodding the animals into cattle cars were called "cowpokes." But the skinny longhorns made tough steaks, and the ranchers began breeding better beef animals such as the Shorthorn and the white-faced Hereford. The King Ranch developed a hardy breed called the Santa Gertrudis. Texas leads the states in beef cattle—and also sheep and goats.

A bony shell protects the armadillo, native of the Big Thicket wilderness.

Coastal wells help Texas lead in oil production— three million barrels (477 million liters) a day.

Oil for the world's cars speeds by on a conveyor belt in one of the Gulf Coast's huge refineries.

Longhorns make a comeback on a Texas ranch. The horns may spread up to six feet (1.8 m).

Mountain States

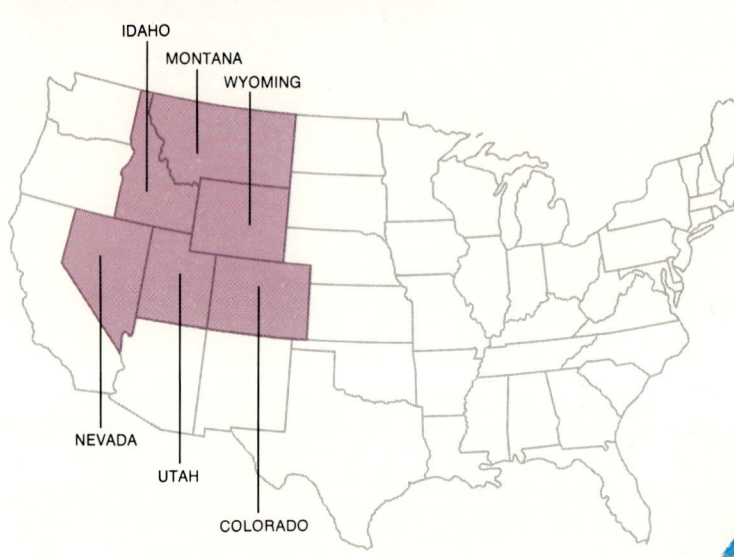

Pillars of lava pushing up under the earth's crust formed these mountains in Idaho.

Nevada's mountains were born when the land squeezed together and stretched apart—like an accordion.

Big, lonely, thirsty—and rumpled! That's the mountain states of the West you see here. Together they make up nearly one-fourth of the land area of the 48 connecting states. If you hiked across the widest part, as many pioneers did, you would cover almost a third of the distance between the Atlantic and Pacific oceans.

These states are not very crowded. Only 3 out of every 100 Americans live here—mostly in the Denver and Salt Lake City areas on either side of the white-tipped Rocky Mountains. That leaves a lot of places where you can walk for days without seeing another living person.

And the states are dry. An average of only 14 inches (355 mm) of rain falls here each year, while parts of Nevada and other states get even less.

The Rockies rose about 65 million years ago when the land here bent and folded.

COLORADO

Rocky Mountain Columbine

Lark Bunting

When David Lavender was a boy, he lived in the little mining town of Telluride, high in the Rocky Mountains of southern Colorado. He grew up and moved away and, many years later, wrote books in which he vividly remembered the scenes and adventures of those early years.

He recalled winters that seemed to drag on forever... the thrill of whizzing down a mountain slope seated on a miner's shovel... the danger of avalanches... and the never ending *brump! brump!* of giant machines that crushed rocks into powder.

Summer brought its own adventures. One of them was the family trip to Denver on a tiny train that wound through the mountains "wrapped in a swirling ball of its own smoke." The train ran on narrow tracks over a course so twisty the kids learned to chant:

It doubles in, it doubles out,
Leaving the traveler still in doubt
Whether the engine on the track
Is going on or coming back.

David Lavender's Colorado still exists. More roads cross the mountains now and many of the old mining camps have been turned into tourist and recreation resorts, but the snow still lies deep in winter and mountains still fill the sky. A little train like the one David Lavender rode even snorts and shuffles between Durango and Silverton during the summer.

Colorado is famous for its mountains. Some 50 peaks jut more than 14,000 feet (4,267 m) above sea level. With an average elevation of 6,800 feet (2,073 m), Colorado is easily the highest state in the U.S. Even its plains are high. They slope gently toward the Mississippi from a mile-high altitude along the eastern foot of the Rockies.

Stand in four states at once! The only place in the U.S. you can do this is in the Four Corners area of these western states.

Area: eighth largest state, 104,247 sq mi (269,999 sq km). **Population:** 2,619,000. Ranks 28th. **Major Cities:** Denver, 484,531; Colorado Springs, 179,584; Pueblo 105,312. **Manufacturing:** food products, instruments, fabricated metals, non-electrical machinery, transportation equipment. **Agriculture:** beef cattle, wheat, corn, milk, sheep. Also hay, sugar beets. **Mining:** oil, coal, molybdenum, natural gas, sand and gravel, zinc, silver, lead, stone, gold. **Other Important Activities:** tourism, banking, publishing. **Statehood:** the 38th state. Admitted Aug. 1, 1876.

Gold and silver—tons of it—brought settlers flocking to Colorado in the mid- and late-1800's. Those were wild days in places like Denver, Aspen, Leadville, and Central City. One undertaker even advertised group-rate burials for Saturday killings!

Miners still dig gold, silver, lead, and zinc from the mountains. The Climax Mine near Leadville produces much of the world's molybdenum, a metal added to steel to make it superstrong. But nowadays the real treasure lies in tourist gold—the millions of dollars spent each year by hordes of skiers and vacationers. Aspen alone has 30 ski lifts and 200 miles (322 km) of trails, more than any other ski resort in the nation.

Most Coloradans live in towns and cities along the eastern edge of the Rocky Mountains. Many of them work for Uncle Sam—as soldiers and airmen or in government agencies such as the FBI or the Department of Agriculture. Many others work in such industries as electronics and aerospace.

Farther east, farms and ranches spread across the plains. But water is sometimes scarce here—and has to be shared with several other states through which Colorado's rivers flow. You can imagine the squabbles over who gets how much water.

Colorado's Rockies are useful in still more ways: The North American Air Defense Command holes up deep inside Cheyenne Mountain near Colorado Springs. If an enemy nation suddenly attacked us, the defense command could seal itself behind bombproof doors and strike back with push-button missiles. And, in concrete vaults at Fort Collins, the Department of Agriculture preserves seeds from nearly every food plant we know. Thus, if all the world's spinach were to die off mysteriously, we would still have seeds enough to start over again.

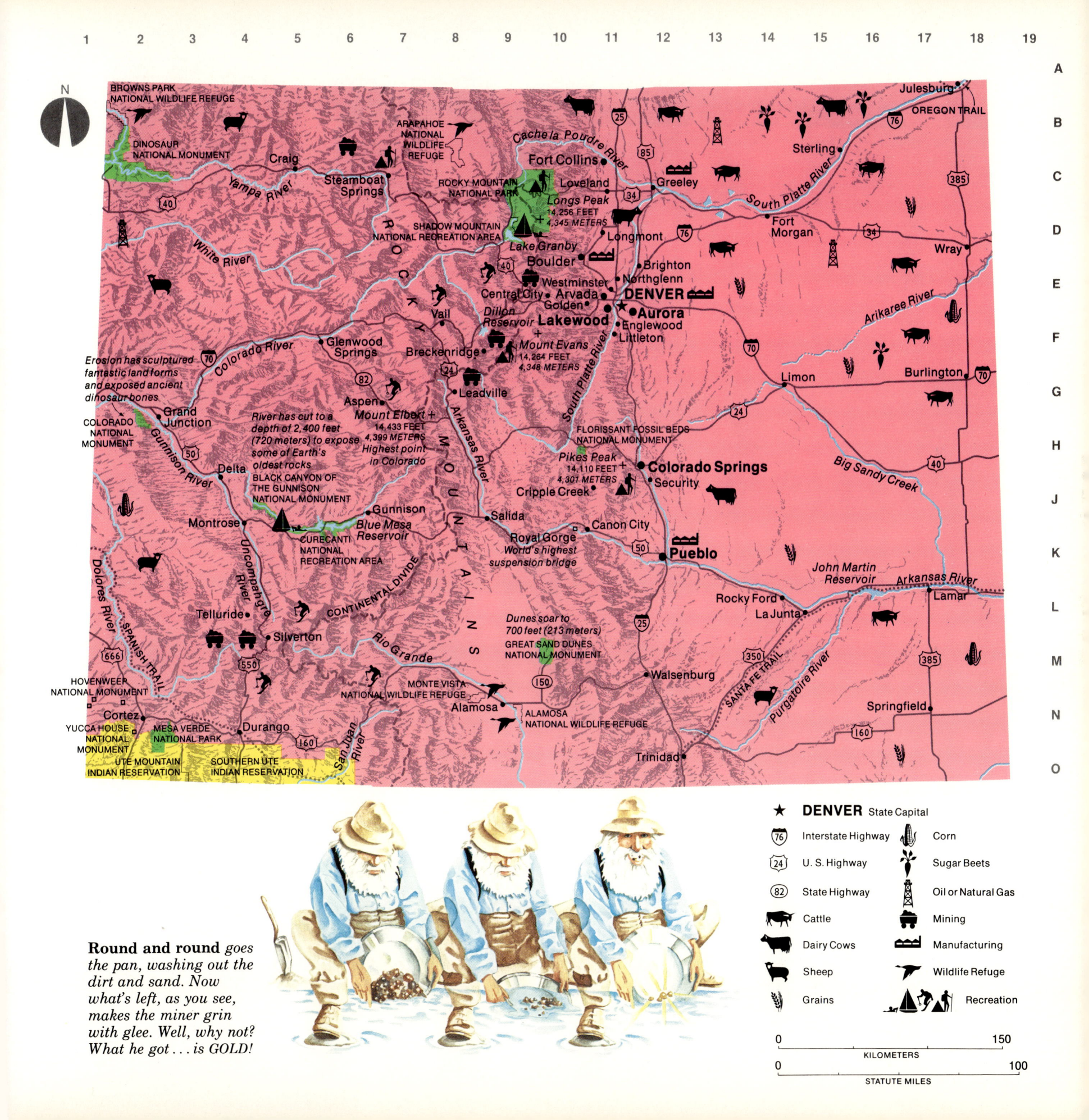

Round and round goes the pan, washing out the dirt and sand. Now what's left, as you see, makes the miner grin with glee. Well, why not? What he got... is GOLD!

Symbol	Legend	Symbol	Legend
★	**DENVER** State Capital		
76	Interstate Highway		Corn
24	U. S. Highway		Sugar Beets
82	State Highway		Oil or Natural Gas
	Cattle		Mining
	Dairy Cows		Manufacturing
	Sheep		Wildlife Refuge
	Grains		Recreation

0 — 150 KILOMETERS
0 — 100 STATUTE MILES

Long before Denver was dreamed of—in about the year 650—a group of Indians wandered onto the tablelands of southwestern Colorado, settled down, and began to farm. These ancient people built their first houses near their fields. Later, perhaps because of enemies, they moved to cliff houses where no enemy could reach them. Here, at Mesa Verde, they lived in peace for nearly 700 years. Then the climate turned dry. Year after year the crops died. Perhaps the Indians grew discouraged and moved away. Today thousands of visitors scramble up ladders and toeholds cut in the rock to see these ancient dwellings.

Mush, you huskies! A working team pulls a sled through a forest of cottonwood and aspen in the Rocky Mountains near Aspen.

Skiers weave wiggly trails through spruce trees growing near the timberline at Vail.

Only a few of these bighorn sheep still roam the high meadows of the Rockies.

230

An old-time locomotive, belching smoke and cinders, hauls sightseers between Durango and Silverton in the San Juan Mountains.

Sunrise lights the city of Denver and the majestic peaks of the nearby Rockies. Can you find the golden-domed state capitol?

Cliff Palace, sheltered beneath the stony arches of Mesa Verde, was home to a tribe of Indian farmers known only as Anasazi—Ancient Ones. The adobe fortress contains 200 rooms and was found by cowboys in 1888. Other cliff ruins lie at nearby Wetherill Mesa.

231

IDAHO

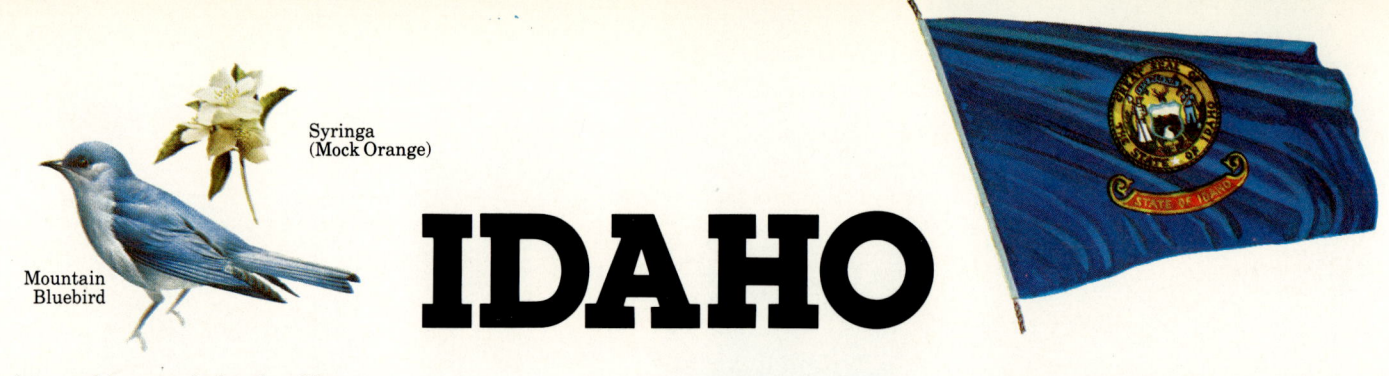

The big rubber raft bucks like a runaway bronco as it swirls and plunges into the roaring rapids of Idaho's Salmon River. Spray flies, soaking the passengers to the skin as they cling for dear life to the raft. Bounce!... Bump!... Splash! They shoot clear of the waves now and slide past canyon walls dark with forests of pine and fir. What an exciting way to see the biggest, wildest wilderness in the Rocky Mountain West.

Bighorn sheep live high on the slopes of mountains named Sawtooth, Lost River, and Bitterroot. So do elk and bear and mountain lions. You don't ride a car into *this* kind of country. No paved roads. You walk. Or ride a horse. Or float through with trusted guides. A few fishermen fly in, landing at tiny airstrips scratched into the high meadows. They fish for trout and salmon in the clear, fast-flowing streams.

A few of these streams hold some of the world's strangest frogs—voiceless kissing frogs. These creatures live in streams so swift and so noisy that, as tadpoles, they must "kiss" the rocks—hang onto them with lip suction—so they won't be washed away. Perhaps because the streams are too loud for the frogs' voices to be heard, they don't have any. They lead very quiet lives with nary a *croak!* or *garumph!* among them.

Idaho also has North America's deepest chasm—7,900-foot (2,408 m) Hells Canyon, formed where the Snake River cuts through the mountains along the border with Oregon. The chasm is deeper than the Grand Canyon—so deep that if you dropped a rock from a helicopter it would take more than half a minute to hit the river below.

Not all of Idaho is wilderness. The eastern part of the state contains cattle and sheep ranches. And more potatoes are grown in southern Idaho than anywhere else in the U.S. Factories in Idaho Falls, Blackfoot, and Burley turn whole potatoes into instant mashed potatoes and frozen French fries.

Mining is important, too. The Sunshine Mine near Kellogg makes Idaho the nation's leading producer of silver. And phosphate, a mineral that, among other things, puts the fizz into ice-cream sodas, is found near the town of Soda Springs.

Would you like to walk on the moon? Well, you can't, really. But the next best thing is to visit Craters of the Moon National Monument in southeastern Idaho. It's a fantastic, out-of-this-world place. Thousands of years ago, hot melted rock poured out of great cracks in the earth and flowed across the land. Underground explosions burped up cones, craters, and flat-topped hills of black and red and brown cinders. Very few plants grow here, so it's easy to feel that you've landed on another planet.

Hot gases in the lava also formed tunnels and caves. One of them, Boy Scout Cave, is so cold that water trapped inside has frozen into an underground river of ice. Visitors explore the low-ceilinged cave by scooting around on sleds! Even in the summer.

Pockets of deeply buried molten rock still heat water that seeps underground, giving parts of Idaho many hot springs. In Boise, the state capital, hot water piped from such springs heats some homes and office buildings during the winter.

Idaho is also the only state with a kidnapped capital. The northern city of Lewiston served as territorial capital until the 1860's. But one day a band of lawmakers from southern Idaho rode off with the territorial seal and official papers. They brought them to Boise—where records and seal remain to this day.

If piled in a heap, Idaho's 1977 potato crop would reach 550 feet (168 m) high, 100 feet (30 m) higher than Egypt's tallest pyramid.

Area: the 13th largest state, 83,557 sq mi (216,412 sq km). **Population:** 857,000. Ranks 41st. **Major Cities:** Boise, 99,771; Pocatello, 40,980; Idaho Falls, 37,042. **Agriculture:** potatoes, beef cattle, wheat, milk, hay, barley, sugar beets, wool. **Manufacturing:** food and food products, lumber and wood products, chemicals, stone, clay, and glass products, rubber and plastics, non-electrical machinery. **Mining:** silver, phosphate rock, lead, zinc, sand and gravel, stone, copper, gold, gemstones. **Statehood:** the 43rd state. Admitted July 3, 1890.

Mountain Bluebird

Syringa (Mock Orange)

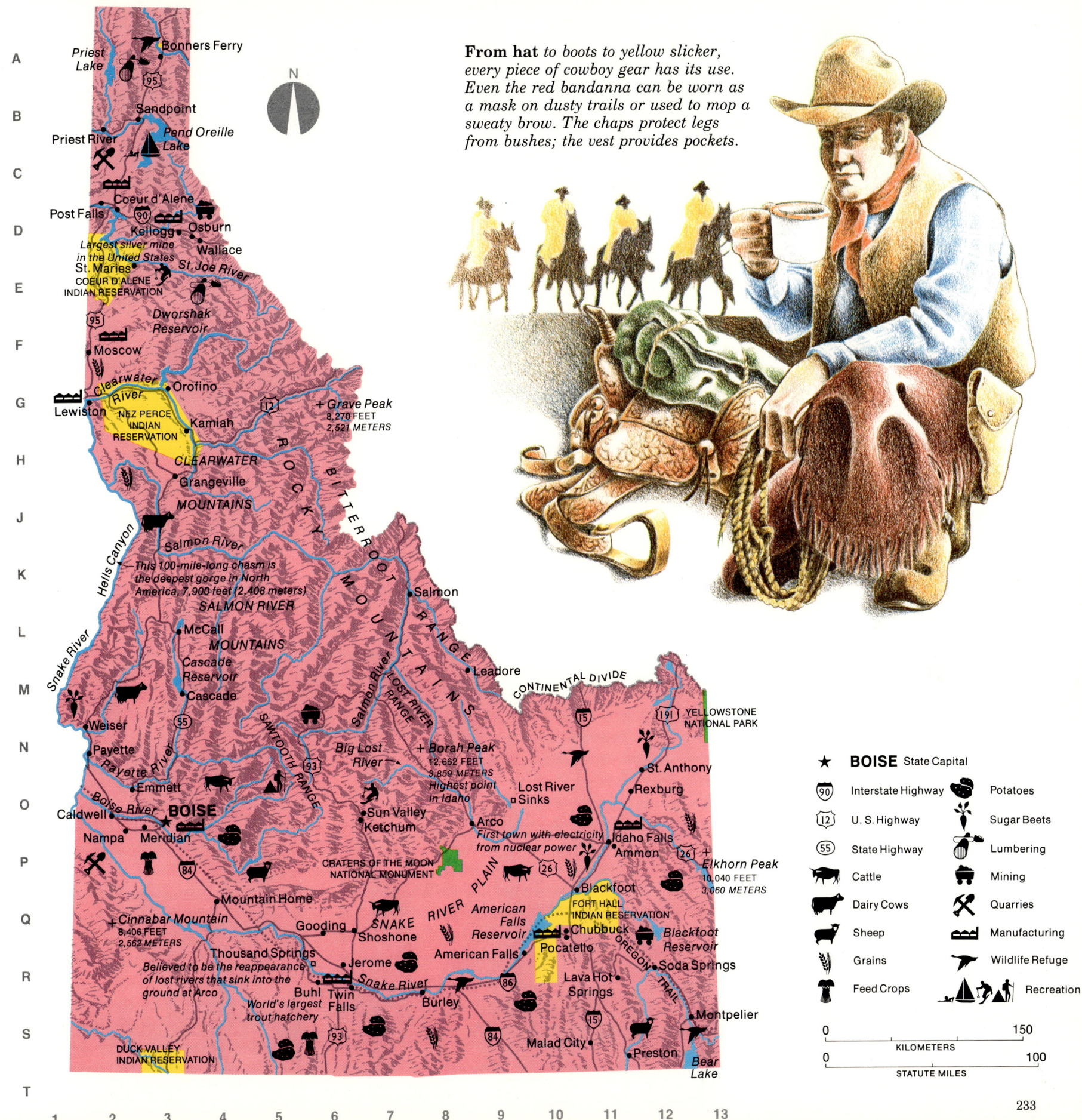

From hat to boots to yellow slicker, every piece of cowboy gear has its use. Even the red bandanna can be worn as a mask on dusty trails or used to mop a sweaty brow. The chaps protect legs from bushes; the vest provides pockets.

Map Features

Cities and Towns:
- Priest Lake, Bonners Ferry
- Sandpoint, Priest River
- Pend Oreille Lake
- Post Falls, Coeur d'Alene, Kellogg, Osburn, Wallace
- St. Maries, St. Joe River
- COEUR D'ALENE INDIAN RESERVATION
- Largest silver mine in the United States
- Dworshak Reservoir
- Moscow
- Clearwater River, Orofino
- Lewiston, Kamiah
- NEZ PERCE INDIAN RESERVATION
- Grave Peak 8,270 FEET / 2,521 METERS
- CLEARWATER MOUNTAINS
- Grangeville
- ROCKY MOUNTAINS
- BITTERROOT RANGE
- Hells Canyon — This 100-mile-long chasm is the deepest gorge in North America, 7,900 feet (2,408 meters)
- Salmon River
- SALMON RIVER MOUNTAINS
- Salmon, Leadore
- McCall
- Cascade Reservoir, Cascade
- LOST RIVER RANGE
- CONTINENTAL DIVIDE
- YELLOWSTONE NATIONAL PARK
- Snake River
- Weiser, Payette, Emmett
- Payette River
- SAWTOOTH RANGE
- Big Lost River
- Borah Peak 12,662 FEET / 3,859 METERS — Highest point in Idaho
- Lost River Sinks
- St. Anthony, Rexburg
- Caldwell, BOISE
- Nampa, Meridian
- Sun Valley, Ketchum
- Arco — First town with electricity from nuclear power
- Idaho Falls, Ammon
- CRATERS OF THE MOON NATIONAL MONUMENT
- Elkhorn Peak 10,040 FEET / 3,060 METERS
- Mountain Home
- Cinnabar Mountain 8,406 FEET / 2,562 METERS
- SNAKE RIVER PLAIN
- Gooding, Shoshone
- American Falls Reservoir
- FORT HALL INDIAN RESERVATION
- Chubbuck, Pocatello
- Blackfoot Reservoir
- Thousand Springs — Believed to be the reappearance of lost rivers that sink into the ground at Arco
- Jerome, American Falls
- OREGON TRAIL
- Lava Hot Springs, Soda Springs
- Buhl, Twin Falls — World's largest trout hatchery
- Burley
- Montpelier
- DUCK VALLEY INDIAN RESERVATION
- Malad City, Preston
- Bear Lake

Legend

- ★ **BOISE** State Capital
- 90 Interstate Highway
- 12 U.S. Highway
- 55 State Highway
- Cattle
- Dairy Cows
- Sheep
- Grains
- Feed Crops
- Potatoes
- Sugar Beets
- Lumbering
- Mining
- Quarries
- Manufacturing
- Wildlife Refuge
- Recreation

0 — 150 KILOMETERS
0 — 100 STATUTE MILES

The Snake River, sixth longest in the United States, is southern Idaho's liquid lifeline. Without its waters, most of the state's richest farming country would be empty, sunbaked desert. From its source in Wyoming, the Snake flows more than a thousand miles (1,600 km) before emptying into the still mightier Columbia River. If you saw the Snake from a satellite, it would look like a huge, upside-down question mark—flowing in every direction but east. Explorers called it the Accursed Mad River because of its wild, man-killing rapids. But dams have tamed the Snake and today most of Idaho's towns and cities lie close to its banks.

Vacationers ride the range near Leadore in the Bitterroot Mountains of eastern Idaho. Rabbit brush strews the valley with yellow blossoms.

The Snake River drains an area as big as New York and New England combined.

A mountain lion pauses for a streamside sip. Some 200 of the big cats prowl Idaho.

Each silver bar at this smelter near Kellogg weighs 69 pounds (31 kg) — and is worth nearly $14,500.

Potatoes, potatoes, potatoes. This machine carefully plucks them from the earth and plops them into the truck.

Sack racers hop a dusty course at a Fourth of July contest in Cascade.

MONTANA

Ever hear of Henry Plummer? He stood nearly six feet (183 cm) tall, had steel-gray eyes, and served as sheriff of Bannack and Virginia City, Montana, during the gold-rush days of the 1860's. The two towns were then rip-roaring mining camps and Henry, a lean, mean gunslinger, was the law.

But Henry kept a dreadful secret. While sheriff, he was also the leader of an outlaw gang that robbed and murdered travelers on lonely mountain trails.

When the good citizens of Bannack and Virginia City finally caught on to Henry's game, they hanged him from one of his own gallows. That same year (1864) they hanged 22 other outlaws—and each town started its first public school. Today, a marker along the highway south of Dillon recalls Sheriff Plummer's fate with the words: "It tamed him down considerably."

Montana, too, has tamed down considerably since those days. But it is still a high, wide, and lonesome state. If you placed its northern boundary along the Atlantic seacoast, it would stretch from Boston, Massachusetts, to Richmond, Virginia! Cities and towns of any size lie few and far between. A Montana rancher living far from town thinks nothing of driving a hundred miles (160 km) to the drugstore or to a dance. Ranch children may attend a one-room schoolhouse with six or eight other pupils or move into town to go to a bigger school. And, naturally, many a Montana youngster learns to ride a horse and drive a tractor not many years after learning to walk.

Because of its size, Montana is a land of many lands. The shining peaks of the Rocky Mountains plunge across its western skyline like waves during a storm. The Continental Divide, the imaginary line that separates east-flowing from west-flowing streams, zigzags crazily along the ridgetops. At a place called Triple Divide Pass in Glacier National Park, streams gushing from the mountains flow into the Atlantic and Pacific oceans—and Hudson Bay! This is Big Sky country—the land of the mountain goat, the grizzly bear, and the tourist. The high, snowy slopes of Glacier National Park are among the few places in the lower 48 states where you can get whomped in a snowball fight on the Fourth of July.

And Montana's mountains are still moving. Every year 20 to 40 small earthquakes rattle the hills. Once in a while a major jolt rocks the mountains—like the one in 1959 that tore the side off a peak in the Madison Range, near Wyoming's Yellowstone Park, and buried some two dozen campers.

Forests of fir and pine cover the lower mountain slopes. Lumbermen cut thousands of trees for fence posts, poles, and plywood sheets. From the forests around Eureka come more than two million Christmas trees a year.

East of the mountains, Montana's short-grass plains seem to roll endlessly toward the horizon—sheep and cattle country. And farther east, nodding fields of ripening wheat turn golden under the August sun. Here, too, lie vast underground deposits of oil, natural gas, and coal.

The discovery of gold and silver brought early settlers stampeding to Montana, but other minerals now are much more important. The town of Butte, which calls itself "the richest hill on earth," sits on top of one of the world's biggest copper deposits. Huge earth-crushing machines chew at the sides of the great open pit that may someday burrow 2,000 feet (600 m) into the ground—and swallow Butte.

How do you get to hard-to-reach forest fires? You jump—by parachute. The biggest smoke-jumper school is at Missoula.

Area: the fourth largest state, 147,138 sq mi (381,085 sq km). **Population:** 761,000. Ranks 43rd. **Major Cities:** Billings, 68,987; Great Falls, 60,868; Missoula, 29,569. **Agriculture:** beef cattle, wheat, barley, milk, hay. Also sheep, Christmas trees, seed potatoes. **Manufacturing:** lumber and wood products (paper, plywood, composition board), primary metals, oil and coal products, food and food products, stone. **Mining:** oil, coal, copper, natural gas, silver, gold. **Statehood:** 41st state. Admitted Nov. 8, 1889.

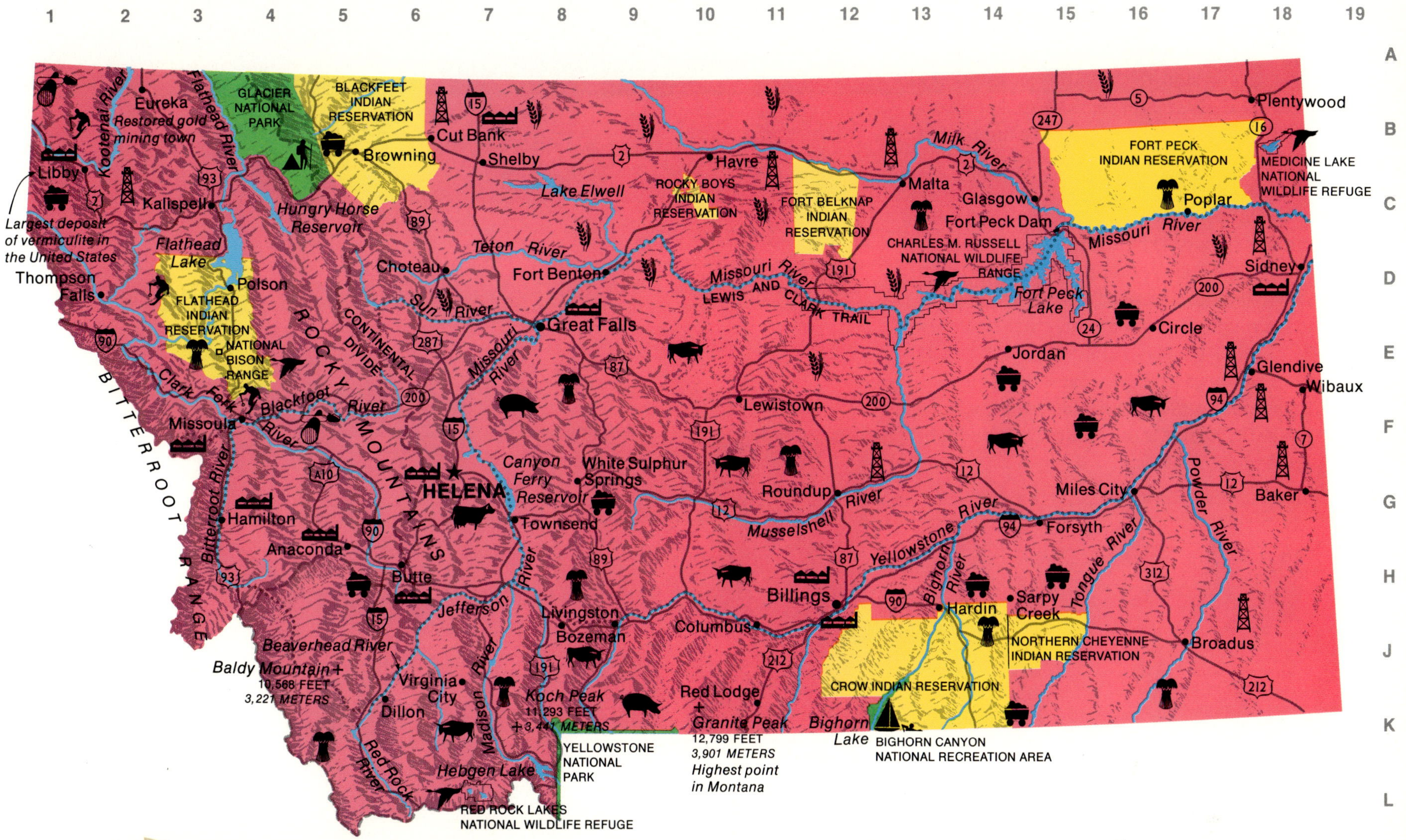

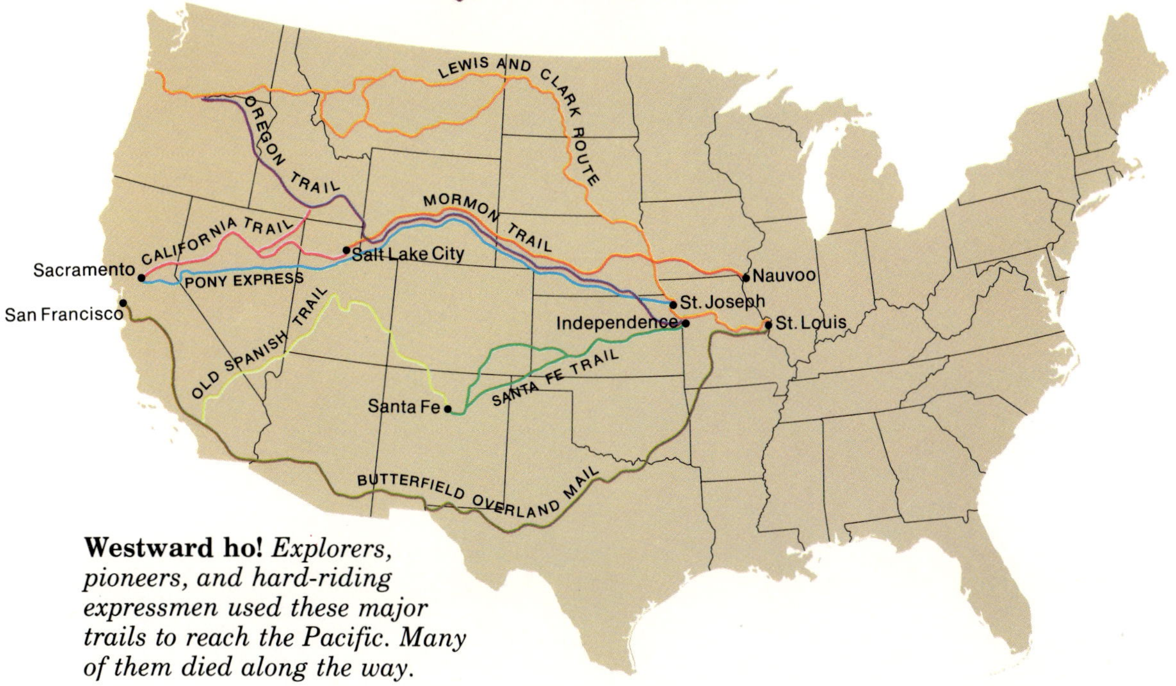

Westward ho! *Explorers, pioneers, and hard-riding expressmen used these major trails to reach the Pacific. Many of them died along the way.*

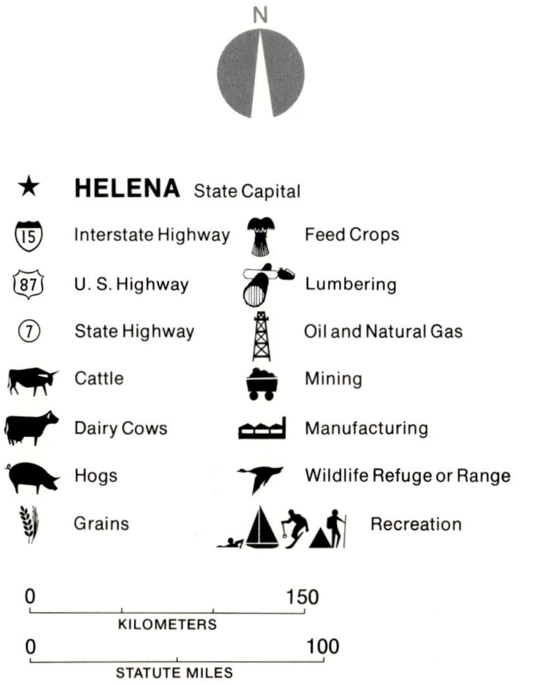

Look closely at the big picture on these pages. Notice how rounded and smooth the valley looks? That's because thousands of years ago glaciers covered most of the Rockies. Only the tops of the highest peaks poked above them—like islands in a frozen sea.

When ice piles up thick enough, gravity makes it move. As it moves, the ice bulldozes soil, rocks, trees, and anything else in the way. Boulders trapped in the moving ice grind rough, V-shaped gorges into smoothly rounded U-shaped valleys. These ancient rivers of ice gave Glacier Park its name. But today only a few small glaciers remain in the park, most of them tucked away in high, hard-to-reach places.

A golden eagle rides the wind near its nest in Livingston.

Autumn spreads its glory across Cut Bank Valley at Glacier National Park. Triple Divide Pass rises in the distance.

A 4-H club member grooms her hand-fed Hereford steer for the Chouteau County Fair in Fort Benton. Her entry won a blue ribbon; she won a showmanship prize.

Don't fall off the edge! A farmer's field reaches to the brink of a yawning coal pit near Sarpy Creek. A dragline gnaws away topsoil to get the coal.

Hundred-ton trucks, each with tires 12 feet (3.7 m) high, rumble toward the Anaconda Mine in Butte. The mine yields copper from a mile-wide (1.6 km) hole.

239

NEVADA

Spanish mapmakers had their own name for the place we know as Nevada. They called it "the northern mystery" because even the boldest explorers avoided its jagged mountains and desolate valleys. Many years later, the first United States Government geographer to explore the region wrote: "The appearance of the country was so forbidding that I was afraid to enter it."

Nevada, the seventh largest state, is also the driest state in the Union. Less than ten inches (254 mm) of rainfall a year sprinkle its parched countryside. Few trees grow there, except along streams and high in the mountains where melting snow provides water. Its long, flat valleys are covered with sagebrush and rabbit brush. Many salt and alkali flats dot the state, as well as shallow lakes that evaporate completely in the dry heat of summer. One of them, near the eastern foot of the Ruby Mountains, stretches about five miles (8 km) in length and serves as a haven for gulls, sandpipers, and other seashore birds. But you can walk across the lake, for nowhere is it much more than knee-deep! And if you poke around near its edge, you may be able to find fossil bones of woolly mammoths or saber-toothed tigers that roamed the area thousands of years ago.

Nevada is also a dusty state. Dust devils—small whirlwinds—skip across the flats during the summer. Local Indians say they are the restless spirits of dead tribesmen. Some of the larger funnels reach 1,000 feet (305 m) or more into the sky.

Driving is dusty business, too, because only the main highways are paved. Most people keep their car windows rolled up tight, but, even so, the bitter dust seeps in. Because drinkable water is so scarce, wise motorists often carry an extra supply—usually in heavy canvas water bags hung outside the car or truck.

Wherever you go in Nevada, you will see mountains, range after range of them, lined up like wrinkles in a washboard. Many peaks reach 5,000 to 8,000 feet (1,525 to 2,440 m) above the sagebrush-covered upland valleys. The mountains help make Nevada a spooky place, especially when dusk turns them into weird, fantastic shapes. Near Wendover stands an immense boulder. It looks ordinary enough by day, but at sundown the gathering shadows make it look like a huge skull grinning across the sun-reddened desert. And at night, when you're camped under the stars, the wails of coyotes and the screams of wildcats in the canyons are enough to chill your spine.

Nevada is also a land of ghost towns—places like Aurum, Arabia, Velvet, Midas, and Jungo. Gold and silver once brought miners, gamblers, gunmen, and dance-hall girls to these places. But most of the precious metals are gone now, and the buildings stand empty and creaking in the wind. Mining still plays a part in modern Nevada's economy, but nothing like in the days when the fabulous Comstock Lode yielded more than a billion dollars—and helped the North pay for the Civil War.

Cattle and sheep ranches spread across much of northern Nevada. In a few irrigated areas turkeys are raised, and wheat and other crops are grown.

But Nevada's biggest business is gambling, which has been legal, off and on, since 1869. Each year, some 15 million people crowd the plush casinos of Nevada's two biggest cities, Las Vegas and Reno. And more than a quarter of the state's citizens make their living from gambling, or feeding, housing, and entertaining tourists.

Two out of every five towns in Nevada (that's about 200 towns in all) are ghost towns—mostly deserted mining camps.

Area: seventh largest state, 110,540 sq mi (286,297 sq km). **Population:** 633,000. Ranks 46th. **Major Cities:** Las Vegas, 146,030; Reno, 78,097; North Las Vegas, 37,476. **Mining:** copper, gold, sand and gravel, barite, gypsum, stone, silver, pumice, gemstones, zinc, lead, mercury, magnesium, tungsten. **Manufacturing:** stone, clay, and glass products, food and food products, printing and publishing. **Agriculture:** beef cattle, milk, sheep, hay, potatoes, grain. **Other Important Activities:** legalized gambling, tourism, entertainment. **Statehood:** the 36th state. Admitted Oct. 31, 1864.

Nevada

Map Legend

- ★ **CARSON CITY** State Capital
- 🛣 Interstate Highway
- 🛣 U.S. Highway
- 🛣 State Highway
- Cattle
- Dairy Cows
- Sheep
- Grain
- Hay
- Potatoes
- Mining
- Quarries
- Manufacturing
- Wildlife Refuge or Range
- Tourism and Recreation

Scale: 0–150 Kilometers / 0–100 Statute Miles

N (north arrow)

Map Features

Grid columns 1–13, rows A–T

Indian Reservations & Protected Areas: Sheldon National Wildlife Refuge, Fort McDermitt Indian Reservation, Duck Valley Indian Reservation, Summit Lake Indian Reservation, Pyramid Lake Indian Reservation, Fallon Indian Reservation, South Fork Indian Reservation, Walker River Indian Reservation, Duckwater Indian Reservation, Goshute Indian Reservation, Lehman Caves National Monument, Death Valley National Monument, Desert National Wildlife Range, Lake Mead National Recreation Area, Department of Energy Nevada Test Site

Cities & Towns: Midas, Jungo, Winnemucca, Arabia, Velvet, Lovelock, Battle Mountain, Carlin, Elko, Wells, Wendover, Reno, Sparks, Virginia City, Fallon, Austin, Eureka, Aurum, McGill, Ely, Carson City, Minden, Yerington, Babbitt, Hawthorne, Tonopah, Goldfield, Pioche, Las Vegas, North Las Vegas, Henderson, Boulder City

Geographic Features: Pyramid Lake, Truckee River, Humboldt River, Humboldt Lake, Carson Sink, Reese River, Carson River, Walker Lake, Lake Tahoe, Great Basin, Ruby Dome 11,387 feet / 3,471 meters, Wheeler Peak 13,063 feet / 3,982 meters, Boundary Peak 13,143 feet / 4,006 meters — Highest point in Nevada, Lunar Crater — Volcanic action formed a pit 430 feet (131 meters) deep, Amargosa Desert, Spanish Trail, California Trail, Meadow Valley Wash, Virgin River, Lake Mead, Hoover Dam, Lake Mohave, Colorado River

Notes: Nuclear warheads tested underground

Wildlife Illustrations

Pack rat

Sidewinder rattlesnake

Roadrunner

Desert tortoise

Gila monster

Tarantula

Whether furry or scaly, fast or slow, most of these creatures prefer the hot, dry deserts of the Southwest. Two of them—the pack rat and tarantula—also live in Nevada's cool, high deserts.

Sourdough miners went after gold with pans and picks and shovels. Their gold was plainly visible—once they found where the deposit lay. But most of those old-time deposits have long since played out. Nowadays large mining companies employ scores of scientists and technicians to hunt "invisible" gold—gold so finely ground and scattered it can be seen only with super-powerful electron microscopes. A pile of ore as big as a house must be crushed and processed to get a pound or two of gold. Nearly 4,000 tons (3,600 metric tons) of ore—about the weight of a big U. S. Navy destroyer—had to be wrung out to get the 50-pound (22.6 kg) gold "button" shown below. It must undergo further refining and purifying before it can be cast into a bricklike ingot worth more than $100,000.

Glitter Gulch: A neon-lighted avenue of nightclubs and casinos lures millions of visitors to Las Vegas' famed "strip." Gamblers spend about a billion dollars a year here.

A smelterman holds gold from the Carlin mine, second-richest gold mine in the U. S. (The richest: South Dakota's Homestake).

Autumn snow clouds roll toward the desert over central Nevada's Toiyabe Range.

Mustangs take off in a blur of speed at the sight of humans. Ranchers hunted wild horses for pet-food factories until a 1971 law stopped the practice.

Giddap, Big Bird! A young jockey directs his steed with an upraised broom at Virginia City's annual ostrich race.

UTAH

Nowadays it seems heartless and cruel, but a hundred years ago the Shoshone Indians of northwestern Utah had little choice. It was the custom. The old and the sick would never survive the brutal, three-day hike across the Great Salt Lake Desert to the tribe's winter camp in the Deep Creek Mountains. So they were left near a water hole to starve, while the rest of the tribe pushed on across the desert.

To early settlers these Indians seemed to be among the poorest, most primitive people in America. They had no horses. Game often was scarce, so they ate lots of rabbits, roots, and roasted grasshoppers. And they slept in crude brush shelters.

In the spring, tribesmen returning to the water hole would gather the skulls of their dead and throw them into the pool. That's how Skull Valley, Utah, got its name.

But life here had not always been so harsh. Thousands of years before the Shoshones came, a huge lake—bigger than Lake Superior—covered most of northwestern Utah and parts of Nevada. Driving along the highways, you can see where the lapping waters of this ancient lake (scientists named it Bonneville) cut wide, flat shorelines—called terraces—along the mountainsides. People lived here, too. Stone Age hunters took shelter in caves snug and dry above the waves. The water is gone now, and so are the people. But if you walk onto the terraces, you can still find their caves—untouched since the dawn of history.

Utah is an amazing state. For one thing, its official bird is a sea gull, even though the state lies more than 500 miles (805 km) from the nearest ocean. Here's how it happened: In 1847 the first Mormon settlers, driven out of the East because of their religious beliefs, crossed the Wasatch Mountains and founded Salt Lake City. They watered the land and planted crops. But just as their wheat, corn, beans, and peas took hold, swarms of crickets arrived. Then, as if by miracle, great flocks of gulls soared over from nearby Great Salt Lake and ate the crickets. Enough of the crops were saved to keep the Mormons going. Ever since, the sea gull has reigned as Utah's official bird.

Modern Salt Lake City stretches between the foot of the Wasatch Mountains and the lakefront. Wide streets and tree-lined sidewalks give the city an airy, open feeling. Many of its people work in the 750 or so plants that produce chemicals, electronic equipment, food, steel, and other products.

Utah is a natural wonderland, too. Five national parks lie within its boundaries. Each one is more fantastic than the last—a goblin's delight of balancing boulders, hollowed-out places, and needle-shaped rocks. Giant archways bend like stone rainbows across hundreds of feet of empty space. Grumbling rivers chew canyons through thousands of feet of solid rock.

The state also shares Dinosaur National Monument with Colorado. Here you can see petrified bones of huge reptiles that roamed the countryside millions of years ago.

Mighty mountains—ideal for hiking, riding, camping, and skiing—wrinkle eastern Utah. Many of them yield copper, gold, zinc, and lead, and provide rich pastures for cattle and sheep. Unlike other Western states, where people spread themselves thinly over vast areas, most of Utah's people live on a fertile strip stretching 150 miles (240 km) along the Wasatch Mountains. They, like the cavemen of old, have found a home on the ancient beaches of Bonneville.

Fastest thing on wheels: The Blue Flame set a world record of 622 mph (1,001 kmph) at Bonneville flats in October 1970.

Area: the 11th largest state, 84,916 sq mi (219,931 sq km). **Population:** 1,268,000. Ranks 36th. **Major Cities:** Salt Lake City, 169,917; Ogden, 68,978; Provo, 55,593. **Manufacturing:** primary metals, non-electrical machinery, food and food products, transportation equipment, fabricated metals. **Mining:** oil, copper, coal, gold, natural gas, uranium, potassium salts, zinc, sand and gravel, silver, iron, salt, lead. **Agriculture:** beef cattle, dairy products, hay, turkeys, wheat. Also sheep. **Other Important Activities:** tourism. **Statehood:** the 45th state. Admitted Jan. 4, 1896.

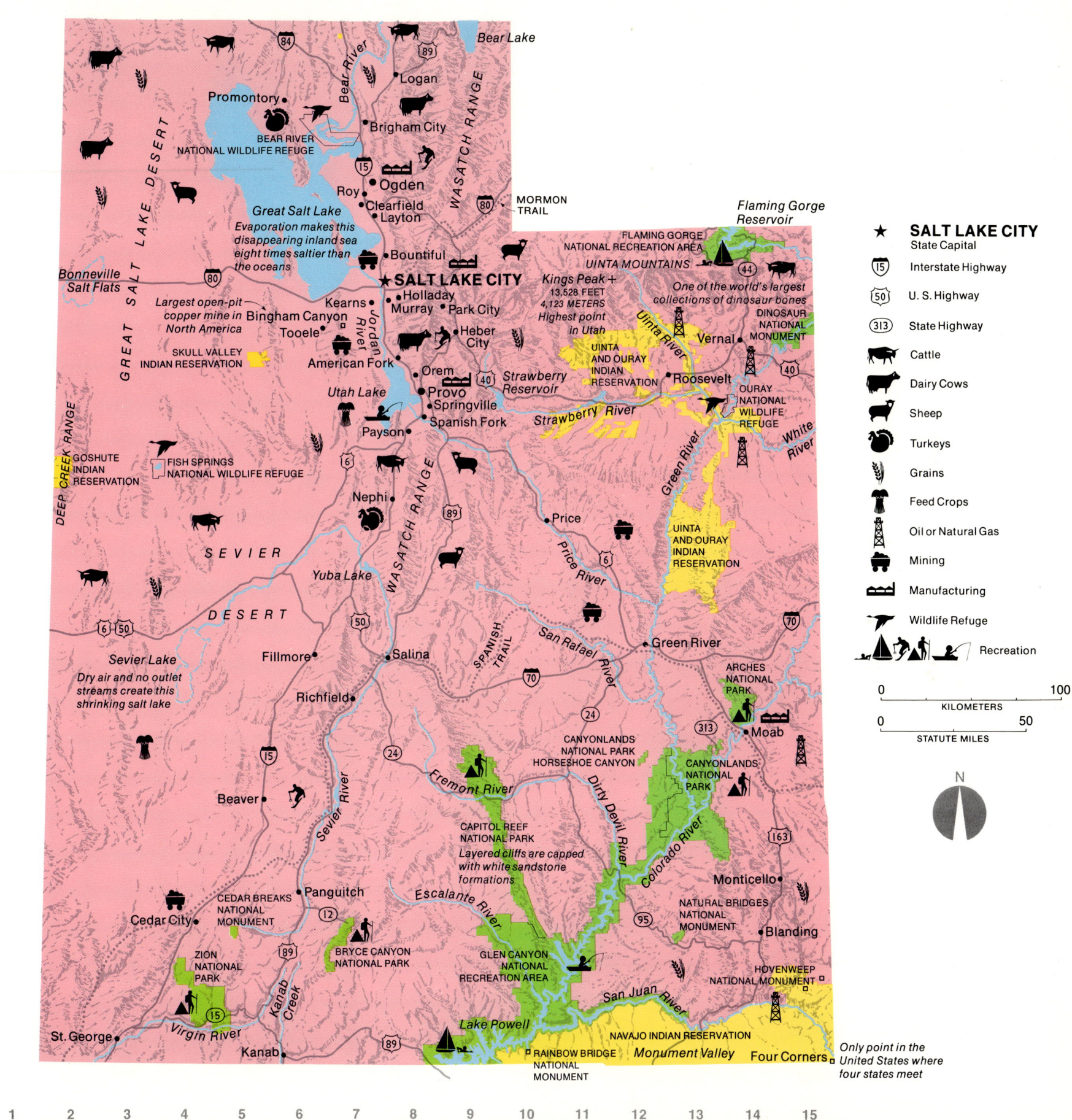

Utah

Map Legend

★ **SALT LAKE CITY** — State Capital
(15) Interstate Highway
(50) U.S. Highway
(313) State Highway
🐂 Cattle
🐄 Dairy Cows
🐑 Sheep
🦃 Turkeys
🌾 Grains
Feed Crops
Oil or Natural Gas
Mining
Manufacturing
Wildlife Refuge
Recreation

Map Features and Labels

Cities and Towns: Logan, Promontory, Brigham City, Ogden, Roy, Clearfield, Layton, Bountiful, Salt Lake City, Kearns, Holladay, Murray, Park City, Bingham Canyon, Tooele, Heber City, American Fork, Orem, Provo, Springville, Spanish Fork, Payson, Vernal, Roosevelt, Nephi, Price, Green River, Moab, Fillmore, Salina, Richfield, Beaver, Panguitch, Cedar City, Monticello, Blanding, St. George, Kanab, Four Corners

Physical Features: Bear Lake, Bear River, Great Salt Lake Desert, Great Salt Lake, Bonneville Salt Flats, Jordan River, Utah Lake, Uinta Mountains, Kings Peak +13,528 FEET / 4,123 METERS Highest point in Utah, Flaming Gorge Reservoir, Uinta River, White River, Strawberry Reservoir, Strawberry River, Green River, Wasatch Range, Deep Creek Range, Sevier Desert, Sevier Lake, Yuba Lake, Price River, San Rafael River, Spanish Trail, Fremont River, Escalante River, Dirty Devil River, Colorado River, Sevier River, Kanab Creek, Virgin River, Lake Powell, San Juan River, Monument Valley

Parks and Monuments: BEAR RIVER NATIONAL WILDLIFE REFUGE, SKULL VALLEY INDIAN RESERVATION, FISH SPRINGS NATIONAL WILDLIFE REFUGE, GOSHUTE INDIAN RESERVATION, FLAMING GORGE NATIONAL RECREATION AREA, DINOSAUR NATIONAL MONUMENT, UINTA AND OURAY INDIAN RESERVATION, OURAY NATIONAL WILDLIFE REFUGE, ARCHES NATIONAL PARK, CANYONLANDS NATIONAL PARK HORSESHOE CANYON, CANYONLANDS NATIONAL PARK, CAPITOL REEF NATIONAL PARK, NATURAL BRIDGES NATIONAL MONUMENT, CEDAR BREAKS NATIONAL MONUMENT, BRYCE CANYON NATIONAL PARK, ZION NATIONAL PARK, GLEN CANYON NATIONAL RECREATION AREA, HOVENWEEP NATIONAL MONUMENT, RAINBOW BRIDGE NATIONAL MONUMENT, NAVAJO INDIAN RESERVATION, MORMON TRAIL

Notes on Map

- *Great Salt Lake:* Evaporation makes this disappearing inland sea eight times saltier than the oceans
- Largest open-pit copper mine in North America
- One of the world's largest collections of dinosaur bones
- *Sevier Lake:* Dry air and no outlet streams create this shrinking salt lake
- *Capitol Reef National Park:* Layered cliffs are capped with white sandstone formations
- *Four Corners:* Only point in the United States where four states meet

Scale

0 — 100 KILOMETERS
0 — 50 STATUTE MILES

N (compass)

Candy corn? No. These are the Needles of Chesler Park in Canyonlands.

You can't sink in the Great Salt Lake—but you shouldn't swim there either. It's polluted.

Brachiosaurus, the world's largest plant eater, weighed as much as seven elephants. Fossils of other giant reptiles lie at Dinosaur Monument.

World's largest man-made hole: Kennecott Copper's mine in Bingham Canyon.

Hard rock cap protects a mushroom-shaped column at Canyonlands National Park.

People think of mountains as everlasting and unchanging. But they really aren't. Over thousands and millions of years, they crumble away—grain by grain, pebble by pebble, rock by rock. Water crumbles mountains whether it falls from the sky as raindrops, gushes down a slope as a torrent, or freezes and pries apart layers of rock. Wind crumbles mountains, too. It flings grains of sand that chip and nick and scratch exposed stone surfaces. And gravity makes the broken pieces tumble downward. Put all these forces together and they spell EROSION. And erosion is what carved the unusual rock shapes you see on these pages.

WYOMING

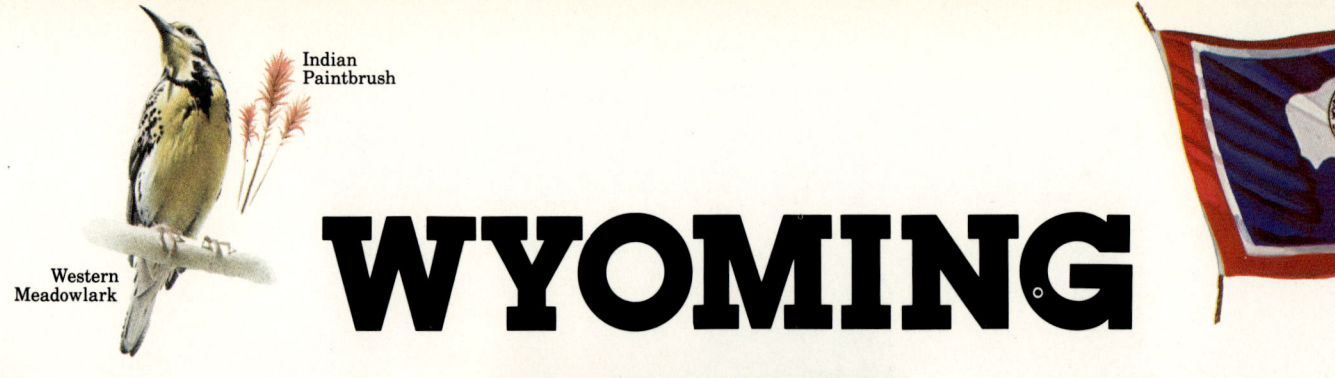

Wyoming has two nicknames: The Cowboy State and the Equality State. But did you know that as a producer of beef cattle Wyoming ranks behind such non-cowboy states as Alabama—and even Ohio and Indiana? As for equality, Wyoming did lead the nation in granting women the right to vote. Women were scarce there then, and the men hoped that the offer of the ballot would lure them into the territory. Besides, men outnumbered women 6 to 1 and had little to fear from being outvoted.

But when the women got into politics, the men got nervous. They tried to take away the women's vote—and would have succeeded if the territorial governor had not stopped them with a veto.

Wyoming then went on to elect the nation's first woman justice of the peace (1870), the first woman superintendent of schools (1894), and the first woman state representative (1910). And in 1924, it became the first state ever to elect a woman governor—Nellie Tayloe Ross.

Other nicknames, too, have been suggested for the state. One leading Wyoming citizen a few years ago said it should be called the Leftover State. When it entered the Union, he said, Wyoming "got what was left over—what the wheat farmers of Nebraska couldn't homestead, what the miners of Colorado didn't want, what the Mormons [of Utah] couldn't claim. So there was some plateau left over, and that became the square rectangle called Wyoming."

But what leftovers! The glorious mountains of the Teton Range rising like cathedrals against a deep blue sky. The marvels of Yellowstone Park with its whooshing geysers, thundering waterfalls, and 27 petrified forests buried in volcanic ash on top of one another! Even Wyoming's empty spaces hold enough underground coal, iron, oil, and gas to supply the nation for years.

Wyoming's oil riches have long been appreciated. Explorers and fur trappers found oil oozing from the ground near the Wind River Mountains and smeared it onto sore muscles, hoping to make the pain go away. Pioneers mixed oil with flour to grease the squeaking wheels of their wagons. The state's first commercial well started pumping in 1883, and today Wyoming ranks sixth among the nation's oil-producing states.

The state is also rich in tales of buried loot and "lost" mines. Eager treasure hunters still comb the mountains in search of the Lost Cabin, Lost Soldier, Lost Shovel, and Lost Dutchman mines. And they scour the wilds of Slade's Canyon and Cache Creek trying to find loot supposedly hidden by the James boys, Big Nose George, Teton Jackson, Butch Cassidy, and other desperadoes.

But much of Wyoming is high, dry, and windy country—and terribly lonely. Fewer than four people per square mile live there, less than any other state except Alaska! (By contrast, about 975 people per square mile pack themselves into New Jersey, our most thickly settled state.)

Perhaps because there are so few people, Wyoming also has very few ghosts. Aside from the pale rider of the mists in Big Horn Basin and the groans of men murdered in the mining tunnels beneath the old Cross Anchor Ranch, Wyoming has hardly any spooks to speak of.

But it does have lots of sheep, more than most other states of the Union. Even so, Wyoming is proudest of its cowboy past. You can see it on every license plate—the figure of a man on a bucking horse. But maybe the plates should show . . . a frisking lamb?

Wyoming was the first place in the United States to allow women to vote and hold office (in 1869, before it won statehood).

Area: the ninth largest state, 97,914 sq mi (253,596 sq km). **Population:** 406,000. Ranks 50th. **Major Cities:** Cheyenne, 46,677; Casper, 41,192; Laramie, 23,421. **Mining:** oil, sodium carbonate, coal, uranium, natural gas, bentonite, iron ore, sand and gravel, limestone. **Agriculture:** beef cattle, sugar beets, sheep, wheat, hay, barley, wool. **Manufacturing:** oil and coal products, chemicals, food and food products, stone and glass products, lumber and wood products, printing and publishing. **Statehood:** the 44th state. Admitted July 10, 1890.

Wyoming Map

Wapiti, or elk, once roamed much of North America. Only about 11,000 are left in the U.S. today, most of them around Yellowstone Park and the elk refuge near the Teton Range at Jackson Hole.

Map Features

Places and Landmarks
- YELLOWSTONE NATIONAL PARK — First national park in the United States
- Old Faithful
- Yellowstone Lake
- JOHN D. ROCKEFELLER, JR. MEMORIAL PARKWAY
- Jackson Lake
- GRAND TETON NATIONAL PARK
- Snake River
- NATIONAL ELK REFUGE
- Jackson
- ABSAROKA RANGE
- Powell
- Cody
- Lovell
- BIGHORN CANYON NATIONAL RECREATION AREA
- Greybull
- Sheridan
- BIGHORN MOUNTAINS
- Cloud Peak — 13,175 FEET, 4,016 METERS
- Buffalo
- Powder River
- Gillette
- DEVILS TOWER NATIONAL MONUMENT — Volcanic rock column 865 feet (264 meters) high
- BLACK HILLS
- Sundance
- Belle Fourche River
- New Castle
- Francs Peak — 13,153 FEET, 4,009 METERS
- Bighorn River
- Worland
- Thermopolis
- ROCKY MOUNTAINS
- WIND RIVER INDIAN RESERVATION
- Boysen Reservoir
- Hole in the Wall — Hideout of Butch Cassidy and the Sundance Kid
- Gannett Peak — 13,804 FEET, 4,028 METERS, Highest point in Wyoming
- Wind River
- Riverton
- Lander
- Pinedale
- Afton
- WIND RIVER RANGE
- Paradise Valley
- Casper
- Glenrock
- Douglas
- Lusk
- OREGON AND MORMON TRAILS
- South Pass — Discovered in 1812 as an easy pioneer route across the Rockies
- CONTINENTAL DIVIDE
- Pathfinder Reservoir
- Seminoe Reservoir
- Laramie Peak — 10,272 FEET, 3,131 METERS
- LARAMIE MOUNTAINS
- North Platte River
- Glendo Reservoir
- Torrington
- Wheatland
- OREGON TRAIL
- FOSSIL BUTTE NATIONAL MONUMENT
- Kemmerer
- SEEDSKADEE NATIONAL WILDLIFE REFUGE
- Green River
- GREAT DIVIDE BASIN
- Rawlins
- MEDICINE BOW MOUNTAINS
- Laramie River
- MORMON TRAIL
- Evanston
- Rock Springs
- Green River
- FLAMING GORGE NATIONAL RECREATION AREA
- Mammoth Kill Site — Well-preserved mammoth skeletons found here
- Saratoga
- Medicine Bow Peak — 12,013 FEET, 3,662 METERS
- Laramie
- Fox Farm
- Buford
- ★ CHEYENNE

Legend
- ★ **CHEYENNE** State Capital
- 90 Interstate Highway
- 16 U.S. Highway
- 24 State Highway
- Cattle
- Sheep
- Grains
- Feed Crops
- Sugar Beets
- Oil and Natural Gas
- Mining
- Manufacturing
- Wildlife Refuge
- Recreation

0 — 150 KILOMETERS
0 — 100 STATUTE MILES

A young rancher prepares for one of his chores; bottle-feeding a motherless lamb.

Pattern: Plowing across the slant of a hill helps save a farmer's field from erosion.

The Teton Mountains, discovered and named by French explorers, rise rough and jagged in the picture below. That's because they are very young mountains—barely ten million years old. (Most of the other mountains in the Rockies are 65 million years old.) Erosion has not yet worn the Tetons into old, smooth mountains like the Appalachians in the eastern states. What's more, the Tetons are still growing— about a foot (.3 m) every 300 years. The Tetons actually are a slab of rock that measures 40 miles (64 km) long by 15 miles (24 km) wide. The slab has been tilted upward along a crack in the earth's crust known as the Teton Fault. What you see here is the steep eastern front, or face, of the fault. The back side of the Teton Mountains slopes much more gently westward.

Young kayakers test their skill on the upper reaches of the Snake River in Wyoming. Beyond rise the snowy Teton Mountains.

250

Lower Falls of the Yellowstone River drops 308 feet (93.9 m) into the golden canyon that gave our first national park its name.

Yellowstone's Castle Geyser spouts steam and water 90 feet (27 m) into the air. The display lasts about 20 minutes.

Some 200 grizzlies roam Yellowstone. They are wild. Don't feed them!

251

City Places, Country Places

Every year, more people. There are more people to grow, live, work, and play on just about the same amount of land. Since 1917 we have added only specks of territory. The Virgin Islands were added in that year, and the Northern Mariana Islands will join us by 1981. In that same span of time we have doubled our population, adding more than 100 million people. Is the country getting crowded? Are we running out of land?

Simple arithmetic says no. If you divide the country's size by the number of people counted in 1970, it comes to 11 acres (4.45 hectares) for each person. It's a bit less now, because of the growth in population since 1970, but there's still a lot of elbow room. About three city blocks, or ten football fields, for each of us.

Of course, some of this acreage might as well be on the moon. But even if you subtract the frozen heights of Mount McKinley or the hot floor of Death Valley, there's plenty of good land left for farms and houses and factories and campgrounds.

Where should we put them? Now we're talking dollars and cents. The answers can make or lose a lot of money for some people. Until recently, the way we solved this kind of land problem was pretty easy. It resembled one of those playground games where the kid who brings the ball makes the rules. So it was with land. The owner could do pretty much what he pleased.

Things don't work that way anymore. What happens to a piece of land is important to the people who live around it. Sometimes it's important to the whole country. Our laws recognize those interests, and we fight hard to protect them. The residents of Oregon fight to keep new buildings and businesses from cluttering their beautiful seacoast. Is there a threat to the Florida Everglades? People across the country rise up to defend this bit of land, with its precious store of wildlife.

Alaska is full of wild treasure. How much shall we save? How much shall we open up for mining, oil drilling, timber cutting? The arguments grow bitter, and the bitterness shows in harsh slogans and bumper stickers up there.

The very fact that people argue about land use shows we've learned something from experience. It's a rough way to learn. Take the pine woods of central and northern Michigan, for example. If your roots are in the Midwest, chances are that the white pines of Michigan played a part in your family history. A century ago Michigan forests supplied the timber for most Midwestern houses. Not only for houses, but also for the spokes of wagon wheels and for the crossties of railroad tracks.

As the loggers chopped and sawed, the trees tumbled. They brought their owners three times as much money as the treasure dug from the California gold mines. What the loggers left standing, fire destroyed.

Remember the story of Mrs. O'Leary's cow? We don't know for sure, but the cow supposedly kicked over the lantern that sparked the great Chicago fire of 1871. On the very same day, a forest fire started in Michigan. It burned clear across the state, from Lake Michigan to Lake Huron. Land companies broke up the charred forest land and sold it for farming. A farmer for every 40 acres (16 hectares), went the slogan. People invested their sweat and their savings. But the soil was too sandy, the summers too short, the markets too far away. Farm families couldn't make a living, and abandoned the land.

By 1919, two-fifths of Michigan—15 million acres (6.1 million hectares)—was not being used for any productive purpose. Nature had set a pattern on the land. People had ignored nature's pattern, and paid for it in dollars and in misery.

How *could* the land be used? How could people stay in harmony with nature and still make a living? Michigan decided to ask the land itself. Surveyors walked the desolate counties, mapping the soil conditions, the hills and valleys, the plants and animals, the lakes and rivers. Here and there they spotted good patches of farmland. They found lovely streams waiting to be stocked with fish, and reviving woodland that could attract sport hunters. And the lakes, with

People don't *take much space. When we carve up America to show how we use our land, a tiny slice covers all the city places where most of us live. More than half goes for crop and stock farming. Wildlife refuge and park lands would double with new preserves planned in Alaska. We've found little use for the tundra and desert slice. Are they "wastelands" or nature's treasures?*

- **34%** Grazing, Pasture
- **21%** Cropland
- **24%** Forest Land
- **13%** Desert, Tundra, Swamp
- **4%** Parkland, Wildlife
- **3%** City Areas
- **1%** Military Sites

their quiet beauty, were great for cooling off in summer. Anyone lucky enough to have taken a vacation in northern Michigan knows the happy ending to this chapter in land-use history. The gutted, empty forest lands have become one of the famous resort regions of the United States.

Often, when we challenge nature, there is no happy ending. Ever hear of Old Kaskaskia, Illinois? It was settled in 1703, on a low peninsula between the Kaskaskia and Mississippi Rivers. Later it became the capital of Illinois Territory and then of the state. It was known as the oldest city in Illinois. You'd have to be a skindiver to find it today. It's at the bottom of the river. The Mississippi broke through the neck of land and gradually drowned the old town.

When Old Kaskaskia finally disappeared in 1910, Shawneetown became the oldest city in Illinois. It had been founded by pioneers who wanted to trade with the Shawnee Indians. Situated on the Ohio River, Shawneetown had the same problem as Old Kaskaskia. With melting snow, or heavy rain, a river rises. If the river rises high enough, it spills over its banks. The land covered by the spill is the river's floodplain. It can make good farmland or parkland. But if you build a city on it, watch out.

Like many another floodplain city, Shawneetown built walls, called levees, for protection. The Ohio overflowed those. Again and again the town built more levees, each one higher than the last high-water mark. Sooner or later the river rose above the levee. The people of Shawneetown got tired of watching their homes and barns float away. In the 1940's they did what townfolk had been thinking about doing for 130 years. The town moved three miles away from the river, up into the hills. There it sits today, high and dry.

Rapid City, South Dakota, put off moving day until 1972. Little wonder. Moving day is a headache even for a single family. Imagine what it takes to uproot whole sections of a modern city. For Rapid City the move took several years and cost about 400 million dollars. The job was so expensive that many experts doubt whether a move of this size could ever be done again.

In 1972 the city suffered one of the worst floods in our history. Swelled by a 14-inch (360 mm) rainstorm, Rapid Creek roared through the city. It ruined more than 1,000 homes, killed 238 people.

Flood control hadn't worked. The stricken city decided its people could no longer live nor work on land which could be flooded by Rapid Creek. With federal government help, families, schools, and businesses were relocated to higher ground. A seven-mile (11.3 km) stretch of land along the creek was marked off as a "floodway," the first one in the country. Today that scene of tragedy is a belt of green parks and ball fields. A nice place to visit, but you wouldn't—or shouldn't—try to live there.

Take a look at other nice places. Along the Atlantic seashore, for example... cool breezes, surf and suntan, gulls and Frisbees against the blue sky. The wind and ocean built those beaches and the sandhills behind the beaches. Wind and ocean are restless builders. They never seem satisfied with the shape of shore and dune.

On some of those dunes we build houses, roads, boardwalks. Each day's tides bring little changes. Hurricanes and winter's

Grow a City – Without Growing Pains

Many cities just grew, helter-skelter. This one started that way. Then we let an expert plan the rest. Growth was planned for pleasant living, with respect for the land. The numbered key tells where things are. Now erase the city for a moment. Lift the plastic.

There lies the land the settlers saw— mountains, foothills, a river flowing down to the sea. To serve the pioneer farmers, a city rose, near the falls of the river where ships had to stop. In time a railroad came.

The old central city was tightly built. The new one is open and airy; little parks surround office buildings, housing, and the educational center. The green riverside is reserved for fun and games. A flood would not swamp peoples' homes.

The smoke at the power plant blows away from the city. That's the usual wind pattern—so heavy industry lies off to the right. A beltway and transit system ease the traffic flow. With more growth come suburbs, an office building park, and a planned community of houses and businesses.

Nearby farms supply fresh milk and vegetables. There's protection for wildlife in marsh and forest—and places for people to relax, from the mountains to the ocean.

1 Old central city
2 Railroad station
3 New central city
4 High-rise apartments
5 Town houses
6 Educational center
7 Riverside greenbelt
8 Civic center
9 Power plant
10 Industrial park
11 Pulp mill
12 Commercial forest
13 Sewage treatment plant
14 Beltway
15 Mass transit with stations ▫
16 Athletic stadium
17 Airport
18 Suburbs
19 Office building park
20 Planned community
21 Dairy farms
22 Grain farms
23 Farm community
24 Vegetable farms
25 Marshland wildlife refuge
26 Woodland wildlife refuge
27 Campground and nature trails
28 Beach resort
29 Ski area

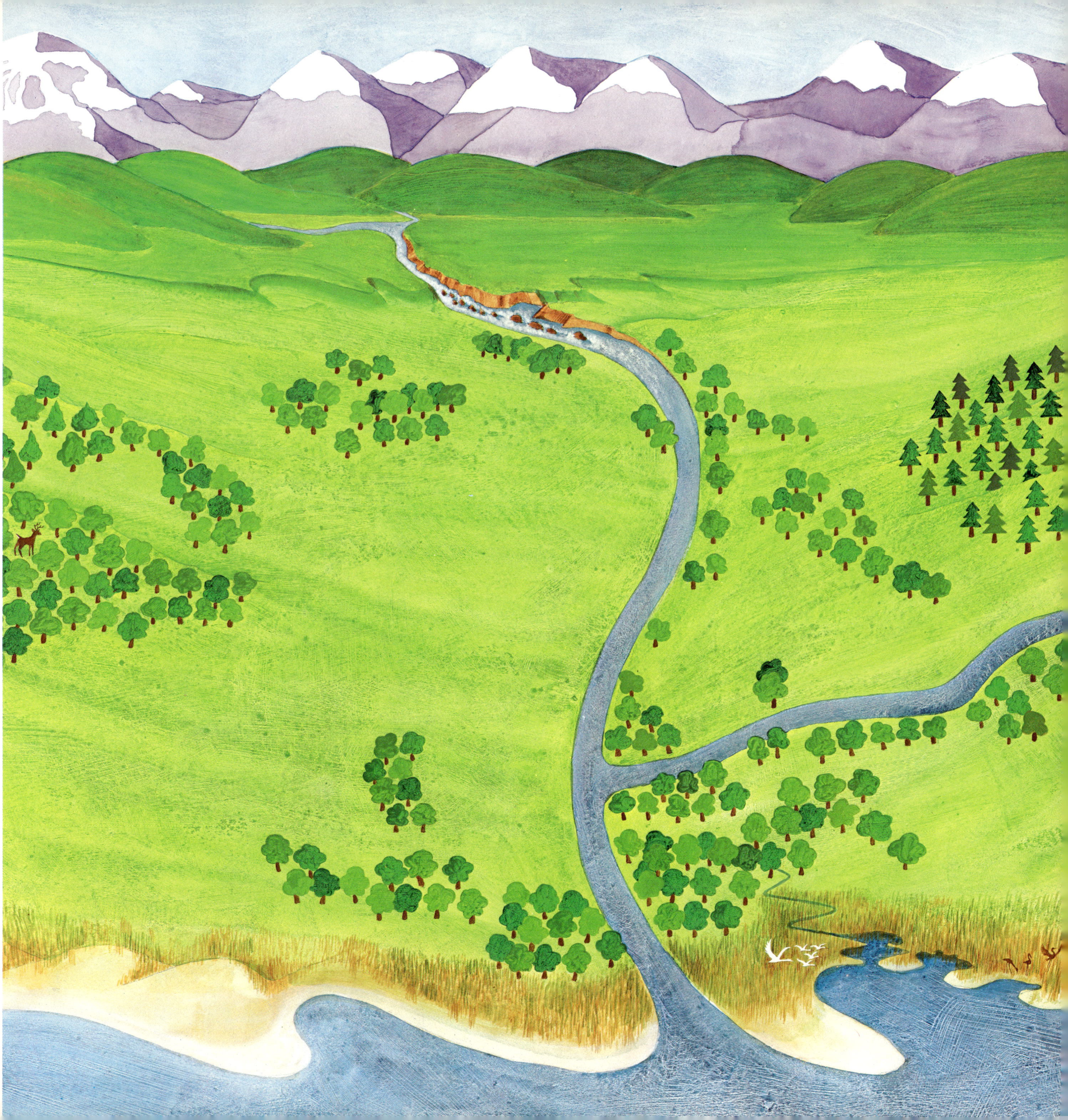

storms bring bigger ones. Beach communities build stone jetties to act as buffers against the waves. People plant fences on the dunes to pin down the drifting sands.

It works. The houses stand. The shore invites us, year after year. Until the year the big one hits, the storm you will tell your grandchildren about. Mile-a-minute winds. Waves four stories high. They come slamming in from the sea, over the beach, over the dunes. And the beach homes wash away like castles in the sand.

More nice places. The foothills and canyons of southern California. A house with a view. Life without winter. The hills are covered with brushy growth called chaparral. Often the hills are very dry and brushfires sweep across them. Sometimes heavy rains soak the hills, and the runoff floods the canyons. Fire and flood are part of nature's pattern in those hills and canyons.

People pour into southern California. They fill the lowlands and move up into the hills, higher and higher. They bring engineers, flood-control experts, fire fighters, safety rules. Nature's pattern remains. Brushfires crackle through the hills, destroying the thirsty mesh of plant growth that can soak up water. Then, when heavy rains follow the fires, the hills begin to move. Rivers of mud and gravel flow downhill, down on the houses.

Nice places. The suburbs, U.S.A. Every family with its own house, its own lawn, its own car (or two or three). New schools, shopping centers, swimming clubs. Need more room? Farther out the land is cheaper.

Farther and farther from the central cities the suburbs spread, with more roads, more roadside clutter, more cars, more fuel burned. Hardly anything is within walking distance. The green countryside shrinks. Metropolitan areas blur together. Where does Los Angeles finally end? Where does San Diego begin? People and cars jam up on the way to work, on the way to parks and beaches, at the shopping malls.

So even in this big, roomy country, many of us live in crowded places. They are likely to get more crowded, because the choice

Skimming Lake Erie algae. Pollution feeds it.

Land, water, and air—handle with care! This is the message in scenes such as these. Wastes dumped into Lake Erie (opposite page) made algae bloom, cut down the water's oxygen. A cleanup began after warnings that the life in the lake would soon die out. Swollen by storm, Lake Michigan chewed up the Indiana beach (left) and the community beside it. Sandbags didn't help. California's San Joaquin River spilled through a broken levee and into nearby homes. Where the tall redwoods stood, new trees must be planted to keep the soil from washing away.

Massive traffic jams make for foul tempers and foul air. In Los Angeles pollution hangs low and becomes smog. California fights back with tough laws against harmful fumes.

Lake Michigan home teeters after a storm.

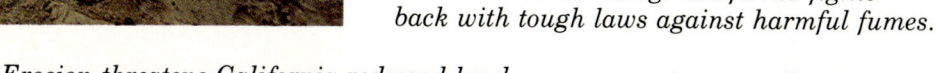

Erosion threatens California redwood land.

Rampaging river swamps a California house.

Los Angeles. It's called a "freeway." No joke.

open land around cities is getting scarce and very expensive. Letting the suburbs go on growing in big, shapeless blobs is a waste of land and energy, according to experts who study land use. They have thought up some promising ideas. These ideas seem brand new to us today, but our ancestors would recognize them.

Under one such plan, houses are built in clusters, as they were in so many New England villages. Building houses closer together saves space, leaving open land to be enjoyed by the whole community. It is the kind of pattern that produced the lovely village greens of New England towns.

The open land might be a bit of wild landscape left unspoiled. Hills and streams, rock formations, trees—untouched by the bulldozers. Places you can walk to and wander through. At one cluster community near Aspen, Colorado, homeowners left 300 acres (121 hectares) of open space as pasture land. Nibbling cattle or horses enlivened the land—and kept it mowed, for free.

Another idea is to build whole new towns and cities from the ground up. Everything is planned for in advance—homes, stores, schools, churches, movie theaters, clinics, office buildings, golf courses, boating lakes. Planning ahead, builders can put things where they make the most sense—for the land and for the people. The overall plan should result in a pleasing life-style.

Building new towns is a challenging job. The original plan may not work, and there's always the risk of losing a large amount of money. Some people don't care for the idea. They just don't see themselves fitting into a planned community. Still, new towns have created excitement across the land—from Reston, Virginia, and Columbia, Maryland, to Irvine in California.

We know the idea can work. Some of our most famous cities once were "new towns," carefully planned in advance on empty land. Washington, D. C., for example, and Austin, Texas, and Annapolis, Maryland, and quite a few others.

There's still another old idea the planners have freshened up to help solve today's problems. When this idea was new, more than a century ago, much of the country was a sweep of wilderness. Life for the settler was harsh, sometimes dangerous. It took money and time and very hard work to make a piece of wild land produce crops. If people were willing to take the risks, why not give them the land free?

In 1862 the Homestead Act made that idea the law of the land. A citizen over 21 could become the owner of 160 acres (65 hectares) after living on the land and farming it for five years. More than 1½ million settlers took advantage of the law, and turned some 270 million acres (109 million hectares) of wilderness into farmland.

We have no more good farmland for homesteading. But the idea is still useful. Today, life in the center of our big cities is often harsh, sometimes dangerous. People need homes and can't afford them. Yet thousands of city houses stand empty and brokendown. A new federal government program, still small in scale, has revived homesteading. A family willing to fix up one of those ramshackle houses and live in it can have it—in some cases for as little as a dollar.

There are homesteaders in Rockford and Chicago, Illinois; in Wilmington, Delaware; Baltimore, Maryland; and Washington, D. C. Today the pioneers are in the cities.

Welcome *to Arcosanti, a new kind of city. It's far from finished, but you can inspect a model, as these people are doing.*

Since 1970, Paolo Soleri, an architect and dreamer, has been trying to build it in the desert, 60 miles (97 km) north of Phoenix, Arizona. He has completed some residences, craft shops, and a restaurant. They would fit under the sloping overhang of the main structure. You're welcome to visit.

Soleri thinks cities should grow upward. Today's suburbs, spreading outward, waste miles of wiring and pipelines and paved streets. You need cars to shop or get to work, and also trucks and fire engines and ambulances. Arcosanti would ban the auto. You would take an elevator or a short stroll to school, to the movies, or to the vegetable garden. Moving belts would take trash to recycling stations. Soleri's dream city would capture the sun's energy, rise 25 stories high, and house 5,000 people.

Too small? Try the model opposite. Soleri designed a city of pyramids set on stilts. Its six sides give it the name "Hexahedron." A city for 170,000, reaching for the sky.

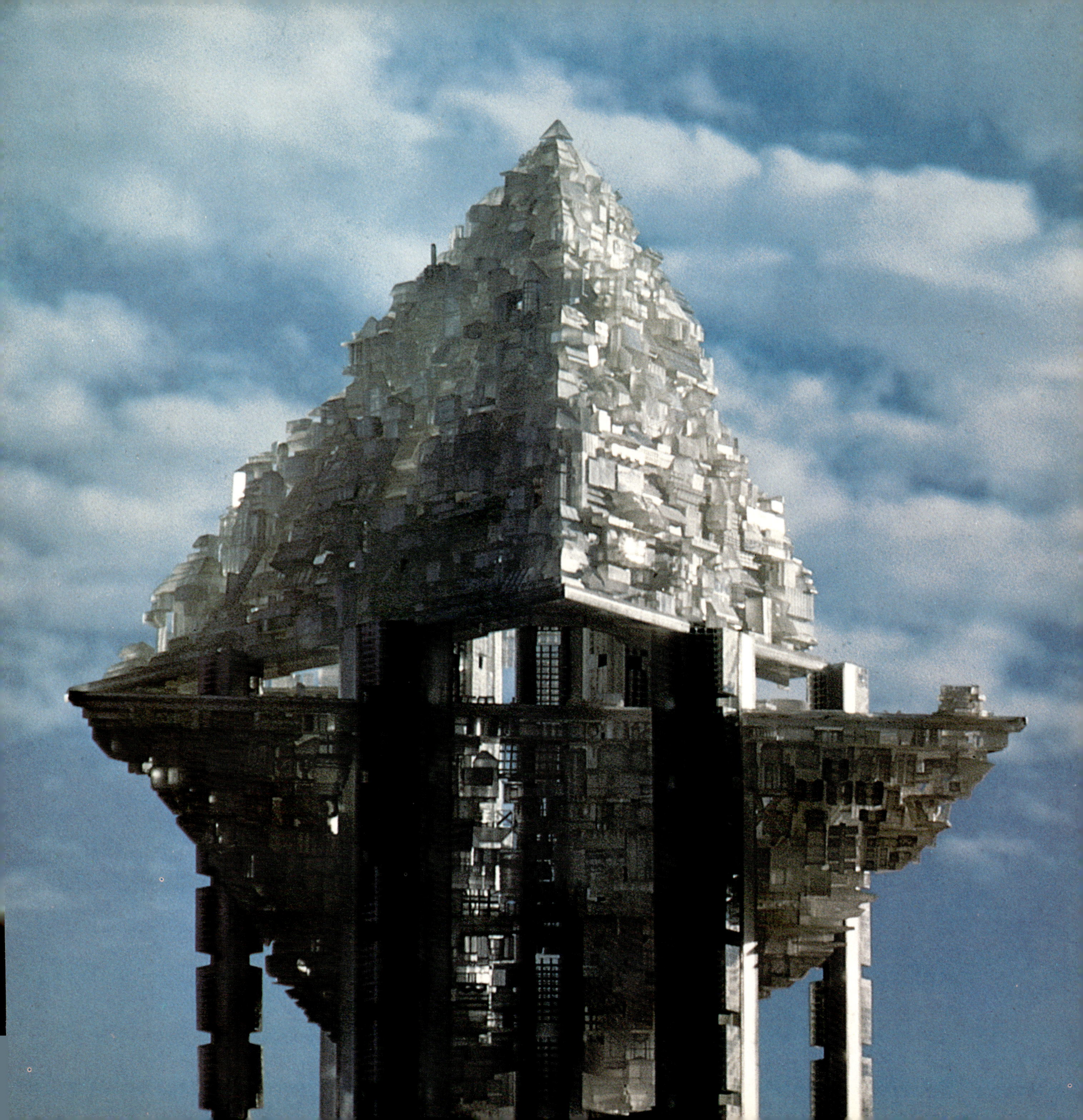

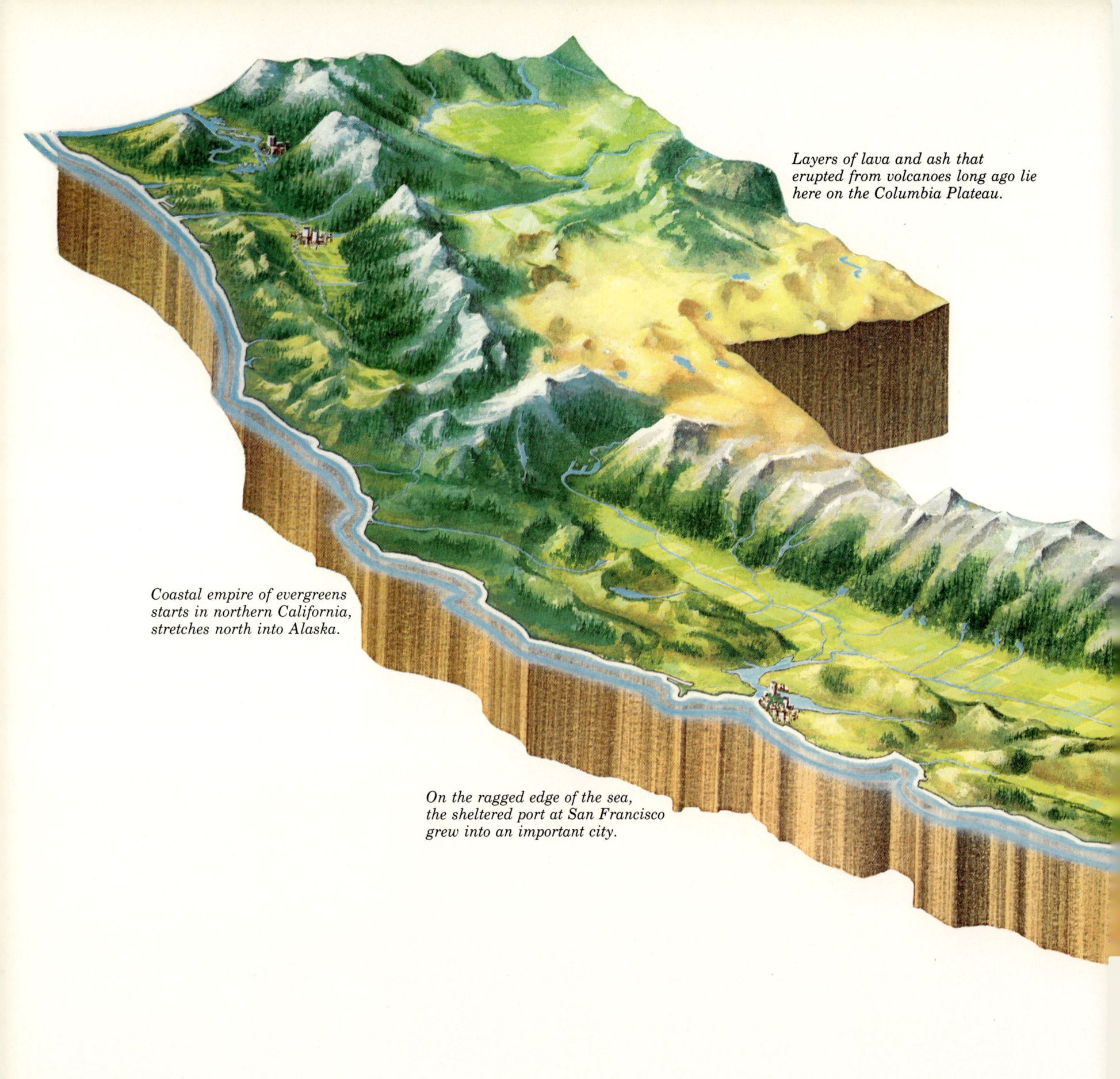

Layers of lava and ash that erupted from volcanoes long ago lie here on the Columbia Plateau.

Coastal empire of evergreens starts in northern California, stretches north into Alaska.

On the ragged edge of the sea, the sheltered port at San Francisco grew into an important city.

Pacific Coast States

For the coast with the most in scenic wonders, look west. Between sizzling desert at the toe and drizzly rain forest at the tip, the Pacific States span 1,200 miles (1,931 km) of sights to show and to know about: granite domes and spires and flowery meadows, lakes the color of the bluest gemstone, giant evergreens poking the sky.

Long mountain chains fence in rich valleys. Atop the Cascades, part of the higher chain, stand the snowy cones of volcanoes, mostly peaceful. They belong to a gang of volcanoes, the "Ring of Fire" around the Pacific.

Many people like to walk amid the quiet beauty of the mountains. Along the high peaks winds the Pacific Crest Trail—2,400 miles (3,842 km) long.

Think of the wonders you might see if you could walk the whole way.

Springs in California's blazing desert make an oasis where palm trees grow.

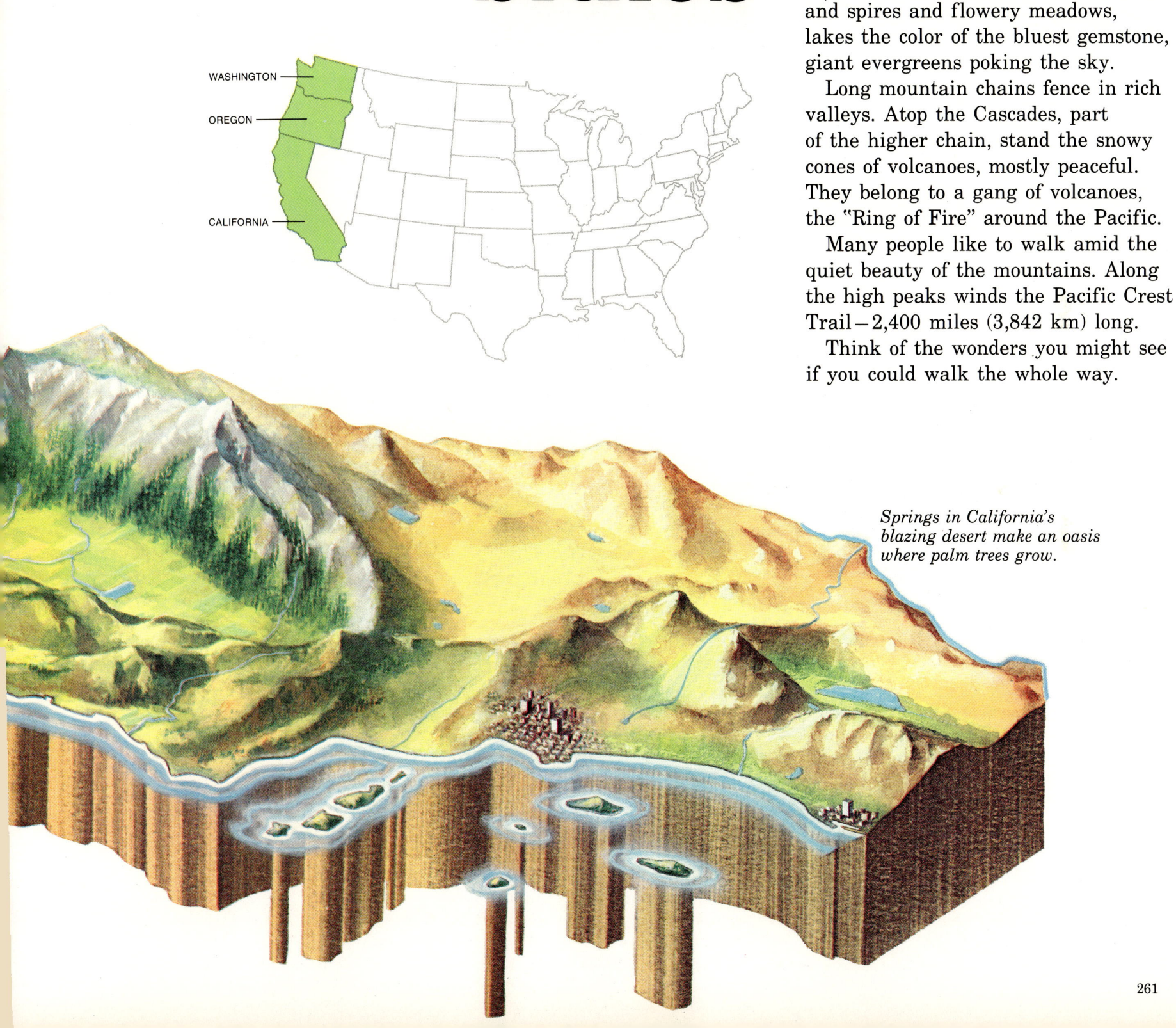

CALIFORNIA

Today, more people live in California than in any other state. They seem always on the move—rush to work, rush somewhere else to have fun—always thinking up ways to be different from other people. But the Golden State was not always such a busy, exciting place.

Poor California—all alone between a wall of high mountains and the deep sea. It had no farms, no cities, no factories, dams, or bridges. Indians, the first California people, lived on the fish, animals, acorns, and wild plants that nature gave them. The land was like a sleeping beauty.

It began to stir in 1769. Spanish explorers and priests came to start a chain of missions on the coast. Indians helped. The priests got Indians to leave their free life and settle at the missions, raising crops and tending cattle. In time, 21 missions stood between San Diego and Sonoma. Several towns and cities got their start as missions.

One was San Francisco. It stands on steep hills facing a fine, foggy harbor. In 1848 San Francisco was a sleepy little town of 500. One day a man raced into town shouting, "Gold! Gold from the American River!" As if by magic, the news spread. Rich California. Golden California. People wanted to come and get rich.

Ships brought gold-seekers from as far away as Australia. Others wrote "California or Bust!" on their ox-drawn wagons and began the long, hard trip by land. Plains, rivers, hills, deserts. And then high, snow-topped mountains, the Sierra Nevada, stood in their way. One group of pioneers was trapped by snow in Donner Pass, and about 40 died from hunger.

But more and more people kept coming to the Golden State. Those who did not find gold found other treasures. The warm sun and rich valley soils gave them visions of green things growing. They had problems to solve, but the vision came true.

Today huge farms in the valleys between the mountains grow mountains of vegetables, fruits, and other foods. The tomatoes, lettuce, walnuts, raisins, and strawberries you eat may have come from the Central Valley or Imperial Valley. Without irrigation, some of these farms would be desert.

California's plumbing system is one of the marvels of the state. Dams store the water of mountain rivers. Aqueducts, pipes, and ditches take it to farms and cities. The Los Angeles Aqueduct brings water 223 miles (359 km) from the Owens River.

Los Angeles spreads for miles in three directions. Freeways link its many parts. Most people drive cars to and from their jobs in the city or at aerospace factories, oil refineries, or steel mills. California has more cars than any other state—and a big share of the traffic jams and air pollution. Growth has its growing pains!

Even the earth has its "pains." Along the San Andreas Fault, huge rock plates of the earth's crust rub against each other like kids changing classes. Earthquakes result. Small ones knock pictures off the walls. Big ones can knock down the walls as well.

Some years, too much rain too fast causes floods and mud slides. Some years, it's too, too dry. Rivers and lakes run low. Thirsty hills and valleys turn brown. There is not enough water for plants, fish and animals, and for nearly 22 million people.

Farmers have to make the most of every drop in the ditches. With one hand on the water tap, a person has to think twice: Is this bath really necessary?

Poor rich California.

Palomar's giant telescope can track a star-like object as far away as 60,000,000,000,000,000,000,000 miles (more than ten billion light years).

Area: the third largest state, 158,693 sq mi (411,013 sq km). **Population:** 21,896,000. First in the nation. **Major Cities:** Los Angeles, 2,727,399; San Diego, 773,996; San Francisco, 664,520. **Manufacturing:** transportation equipment, food products, electrical equipment, machinery, fabricated metals, chemicals. **Agriculture:** cattle, milk, cotton, greenhouse and nursery products, grapes, tomatoes, hay, eggs, lettuce, rice, wheat. **Mining:** oil, natural gas. **Fishing:** tuna, anchovies, crabs, salmon. **Statehood:** the 31st state. Admitted Sept. 9, 1850.

California

Map Legend

★ **SACRAMENTO** State Capital

Symbol	Meaning	Symbol	Meaning
(10)	Interstate Highway		Fruit and Nuts
(50)	U.S. Highway		Cotton
(190)	State Highway		Greenhouse and Nursery
	Cattle		Fishing
	Dairy Cows		Lumbering
	Poultry and Eggs		Oil or natural gas
	Grains		Mining
	Feed Crops		Quarries
	Vegetables		Manufacturing
	Sugar Beets		Wildlife Refuge
	Citrus Fruit		Recreation
	Grapes		

Notable Features

- **Mount Shasta** 14,162 FEET / 4,317 METERS
- **Lassen Peak** 10,457 FEET / 3,187 METERS
- **Mount Whitney** 14,494 FEET / 4,418 METERS — Highest point in California
- **Lowest point in the Western Hemisphere** −282 FEET / −86 METERS
- **Palomar Mountain** 6,140 FEET / 1,871 METERS

National Parks and Monuments
- Redwood National Park
- Lower Klamath National Wildlife Refuge
- Tule Lake National Wildlife Refuge
- Lava Beds National Monument
- Clear Lake National Wildlife Refuge
- Whiskeytown-Shasta-Trinity National Recreation Area
- Lassen Volcanic National Park
- Point Reyes National Seashore
- Muir Woods National Monument
- Marshall Gold Discovery State Historic Park
- Yosemite National Park
- Devils Postpile National Monument
- Pinnacles National Monument
- Kings Canyon National Park
- Sequoia National Park
- Death Valley National Monument
- Channel Islands National Monument
- Joshua Tree National Monument
- Imperial National Wildlife Refuge

Indian Reservations
- Hoopa Valley Indian Reservation
- Round Valley Indian Reservation
- Tule River Indian Reservation
- Fort Mojave Indian Reservation
- Chemehuevi Indian Reservation
- Colorado River Indian Reservation
- Morongo Indian Reservation
- Agua Caliente Indian Reservation

Cities
Eureka, Redding, Santa Rosa, Sonoma, Napa, Vallejo, Berkeley, Oakland, Hayward, San Francisco, San Mateo, Palo Alto, Sunnyvale, Santa Clara, San Jose, SACRAMENTO, Stockton, Modesto, Merced, Monterey, Salinas, Fresno, Visalia, San Luis Obispo, Santa Maria, Lompoc, Santa Barbara, Ventura, Oxnard, Bakersfield, Barstow, Needles, Simi Valley, Burbank, Hollywood, Glendale, Pasadena, San Bernardino, Riverside, Palm Springs, Blythe, Los Angeles, Torrance, Long Beach, Garden Grove, Anaheim, Disneyland, Costa Mesa, San Diego, El Cajon, Chula Vista, El Centro

Rivers and Water Features
Klamath River, Eel River, Sacramento River, Feather River, Shasta Lake, Clear Lake, Folsom Lake, Lake Tahoe, Mono Lake, Tuolumne River, San Joaquin River, Kings River, Kern River, Owens River, Salinas River, Monterey Bay, Gulf of Santa Catalina, Salton Sea, Colorado River, Los Angeles Aqueduct, California Aqueduct, Colorado River Aqueduct, All American Canal

Other Features
- Klamath Mountains
- Sierra Nevada
- San Andreas Fault
- Pacific Crest Trail
- California Trail
- Donner Pass
- Spanish Trail
- Mojave Desert
- San Joaquin Valley
- Imperial Valley
- Big Sur
- Goose Lake
- Channel Islands
- Pacific Ocean

Scale: 0–250 KILOMETERS / 0–150 STATUTE MILES

N (compass)

Shadows tag along as a girl walks on waves of sand. Dunes also "walk," taking new shapes. Windy sides have the gentler slope.

Pounding ocean waves play a rock concert. Scuba divers explore a beach of shiny pebbles scoured by the surf.

Sea otter wears a fur wet suit. It uses a rock to crack shellfish from the dive-and-dine.

People look like mini-people among the giant sequoias of the Sierra Nevada. A taller, thinner cousin, the coast redwood, grows near the sea.

Workers pile a cargo of carrots onto a truck. A canal brings Colorado River water to farms in the dry Imperial Valley.

Most anything goes and anything grows somewhere in California. It has hot deserts; it has foggy shores where sea animals live and trees grow 300 feet (91 m) tall. The state trees—two kinds of redwoods—grow the tallest and biggest of all.

If you don't like the climate one place, try another. The state has all types from subtropical to arctic, a place to suit 200 different crops. Its big farms lead the nation in 44 crops and in total food production. In fact, not many *nations* of the world grow more food than our Golden State. Its people have many reasons to sing "I love you, California. You're the greatest...."

Grapevines take a shower from the sprinkler. California grows most of the nation's grapes—for raisins, wine, or eating fresh.

Ripe grapes are picked gently by hand. Harvest workers move from farm to farm.

Special machines move, wash, peel, and pack foods to be canned. Tomatoes get an easy ride, but end up in cans of soup.

OREGON

Lightning has struck. Wind whips the flames through timberlands of Oregon. By land and air, an army of trained fire fighters goes into battle. Planes fly low to wet the trees with chemicals. Land crews use bulldozers to clear a strip of ground around the fire so it cannot leap from bush to bush.

Oregonians know how destructive fire can be. In 1933 flames roared through hilly Tillamook County, turning 400 square miles (1,036 sq km) of prime timber into black skeletons. People look at a tall tree in different ways. You may see it as a living work of art, a home for birds, an anchor for the soil. Or you may see it as so many board feet of lumber for houses and piles of chips to make paper. But a fine forest ruined by fire is a sad sight to all.

On the ashes of the Tillamook Burn, Oregon kids 30 years ago helped plant seedlings. Those tiny trees are growing up, turning a wasteland into new forest.

Oregon leads the nation in lumber and wood products. Forests cover half the state. Douglas fir and hemlock thrive in the moist Coast Ranges and on the west side of the Cascades. Ponderosa pine grows on drier slopes east of the Cascades.

At Portland and Coos Bay logs and lumber are loaded onto ocean freighters for export, mainly to Japan. Trains and trucks haul forest products to inland markets. Plywood, chipboard, paper, mulch for gardens—such products use up nearly all parts of a tree, even the bark and sawdust.

Most of Oregon's people live and work in Portland and smaller cities and towns in the Willamette Valley. Forest-products plants cluster around Eugene. Albany refines rare metals used in nuclear reactors. Salem, the capital, specializes in canning and freezing fruits and vegetables grown nearby.

Back in the 1840's the Willamette Valley's rich soil and mild, moist climate sounded like paradise to farmers from harsh places. Fed up with plowing poor soil in spring and shoveling snow in winter, thousands packed up and headed their covered wagons west on the Oregon Trail.

If you enter the state from the east, as they did, you meet a high, dry plateau. Amid sagebrush and lava rocks, herds of cattle range. Vast fields of wheat ripple over much of north central Oregon's high desert.

The state may have taken its name from *Ouragan*—Hurricane—the French trappers' name for the Columbia River. Huge dams now tame the powerful river that drowned many a pioneer. A scenic highway threads the deep gorge where the Columbia cuts through the Cascades.

Today Oregon has many modern trails. One of the most beautiful roads winds up and down the hilly coast. It lets you see the sea clash with the land. The sea erodes cliffs, caves, arches, and rocky islets. You can dig clams on sandy beaches, fish or splash in the surf with gulls and barking sea lions, or bike, hike, picnic.

Hundreds of state parks and campgrounds help attract ten million visitors each year from other states. Visit, yes—but please don't move here, say Oregonians. Like the hardworking, furry loggers that gave the state its nickname, "Beaver State" people like to keep their home in shape. Floods of newcomers might mar the sense of order and space that Oregonians value.

To keep mobs of moving vans off the trail to Oregon, some folks spread fibs about it. They just might tell you it *never* stops raining, that the earthworm is the state animal, and the state bird is the mosquito.

Call them superfish. Pacific salmon are able to leap waterfalls, swim upstream hundreds of miles, and find—by its smell—the brook where they were born.

Area: the 10th largest state, 96,981 sq mi (251,180 sq km). **Population:** 2,376,000. Ranks 30th. **Major Cities:** Portland, 356,732; Eugene, 92,451; Salem, 78,168. **Manufacturing:** lumber and wood products, food products, paper products, primary metals, instruments. **Agriculture:** wheat, cattle, dairy products, potatoes, greenhouse and nursery products, hay, grass seed. **Fishing:** salmon, shrimp, crabs, tuna. **Mining:** stone, sand and gravel, nickel. **Other Important Activities:** tourism. **Statehood:** the 33rd state. Admitted Feb. 14, 1859.

Dams too high for a single bound blocked the way. Sockeye salmon couldn't get home to spawn. They needed help: fish ladders, a staircase of small bypass dams. Now superfish is on its way over Bonneville—leaping ladders.

★	**SALEM** State Capital		
5	Interstate Highway		Fruit and Nuts
95	U. S. Highway		Plants and Flowers
78	State Highway		Fish and Shellfish
	Cattle		Lumbering
	Dairy Cows		Mining
	Poultry and Eggs		Quarries
	Wheat		Manufacturing
	Feed Crops		Wildlife Refuge or Range
	Vegetables		Recreation

Mount Hood is a white gleam in the eye of Portland, 50 miles (80 km) away. The snowy cone atop the Oregon Cascades offers a favorite place to hike, climb, and ski.

Born in the Cascades, bedded softly between two mountain ranges, the Willamette River flows north to meet the Columbia River beyond Portland. In its 187 miles (301 km) the Willamette takes the runoff of orchards, gardens, dairy farms, canneries, metal refineries, plywood plants, paper mills, and 70 percent of Oregon's people. Fifteen years ago, the Willamette stank. By summer's end, salmon wouldn't touch it. And they did not spawn. Then the people and industries did a costly cleanup of their favorite rotten river. The salmon count says it worked. In 1965 only 79 fall chinook salmon came; now they average more than 30,000. What's good for salmon is good for Oregon.

Willamette River makes lazy loops in a green quilt of farms. This fertile valley was the end of the trail for many pioneer families.

Strawberries are ripe, and many hands help. Boys and girls earn pocket money. Trucks rush ripe fruit to a freezing plant.

The ocean has eroded the shore near Bandon, leaving sea stacks—islands of hard rock.

Huge knives peeled these thin slices of wood from the trunk of the big fir tree. They will be dried, spread with glue, and stacked like a sandwich, making sheets of plywood.

Waterfalls earn the Cascade Range its name. This one is in Three Sisters Wilderness.

WASHINGTON

If water had its way it would never stay still. Round and round it cycles: sea to air to land and back to sea. In the Olympic Mountains of Washington you can stand in a high spot and trace this whole life-giving circle that water makes.

Above the glint of the Pacific you see clouds formed of rising vapors. Winds sail the clouds inland where tall, cool mountains make them rise and drop the moisture. On peaks you see it as snow. Mount Olympus, the kingpin, gets a whopping 200 inches (5,080 mm) of wetness a year. On slopes, you see pools of meltwater, streams, waterfalls. In the valleys, rushing rivers that speed the water home to the sea.

Western river valleys like the Hoh average 140 inches (3,556 mm) of rain yearly. All that moisture, added to rich soil and mild climate, works the green magic of a rain forest. Spruce, hemlock, fir, cedar, and bigleaf maple trees grow close together. Club moss hangs like green beards from the branches. Ferns, vines, and mosses grow thick on the forest floor. It seldom freezes. The lush greenery makes living easy for animals from huge elk to tiny jumping mice.

The coastal mountains shelter Olympia the capital and other Puget Sound cities from this very heavy rainfall. The Sound, a deep arm of the sea, lets ships from Seattle sail to Asia and Alaska. Shipping zoomed when supplies were needed to build the oil pipeline across Alaska. Now tankers come into Puget Sound bringing some of Alaska's oil to refineries near Ferndale.

As in Oregon, the Cascades divide the state into a moist, forested west and a dry eastern plateau. The mighty Columbia River rules Washington's arid east. Born in Canada, it zigzags down across the state from the northeast, slices the Cascades, and runs west, forming the border with Oregon.

In the 1930's the federal government began taming the wild Columbia with dams, the first at Bonneville. The biggest, Grand Coulee, took eight years to build. It stands 550 feet (168 m) high, seven times as wide, and backs water to the Canada border 150 miles (241 km) away.

Grand Coulee and dozens of other Columbia dams created new farmlands east of the Cascades. Under the magic wand of irrigation, the sagebrush desert—plowed, planted, and cared for—now yields potatoes, sugar beets, fruits, and other crops.

Falling water also spins turbines to make low-cost electricity. The aluminum industry is the biggest customer for this hydro power. Smelters at Spokane, Vancouver, Longview, and other cities make the lightweight metal. Washington is No. 1 in aluminum. Some of the aluminum takes wing as jetliners, including the giant Boeing 747, made in Seattle and Everett. More aluminum goes into the silvery web of cables that feed power through the northwest and, in times of surplus, to other states.

At the Hanford Works, Columbia water flows into another kind of powerhouse. During World War II, 55,000 people worked here on a secret project: making plutonium for the atomic bomb. Later, the Hanford Works began making electricity at one of the world's largest nuclear power plants. Hanford has built up one of the world's largest nuclear garbage dumps. Scientists are trying to agree on the safest way to get rid of millions of gallons of radioactive waste. One plan is to bury it half a mile deep, far below the level of the Columbia River. Unlike kitchen garbage that can be rotted and recycled to help gardens grow, nuclear wastes can pose a danger to life for 500,000 years.

Does the ruffed grouse, Bonasa umbellus,
Like its rain forest house? They tell us
That the bugs taste sweeter
Where it rains by the liter,
Though a nest with a moat needs a boat.

Area: the 20th largest state, 68,192 sq mi (176,616 sq km). **Population:** 3,658,000. Ranks 22nd. **Major Cities:** Seattle, 487,091; Spokane, 173,698; Tacoma, 151,267. **Manufacturing:** transportation equipment, lumber and wood products, food products, paper products, primary metals, fabricated metals, chemicals. **Agriculture:** wheat, milk, cattle, potatoes, hay, apples, eggs, greenhouse and nursery products. **Mining:** cement, sand and gravel, stone, coal. **Fishing:** salmon, oysters, tuna, crabs. **Statehood:** the 42nd state. Admitted Nov. 11, 1889.

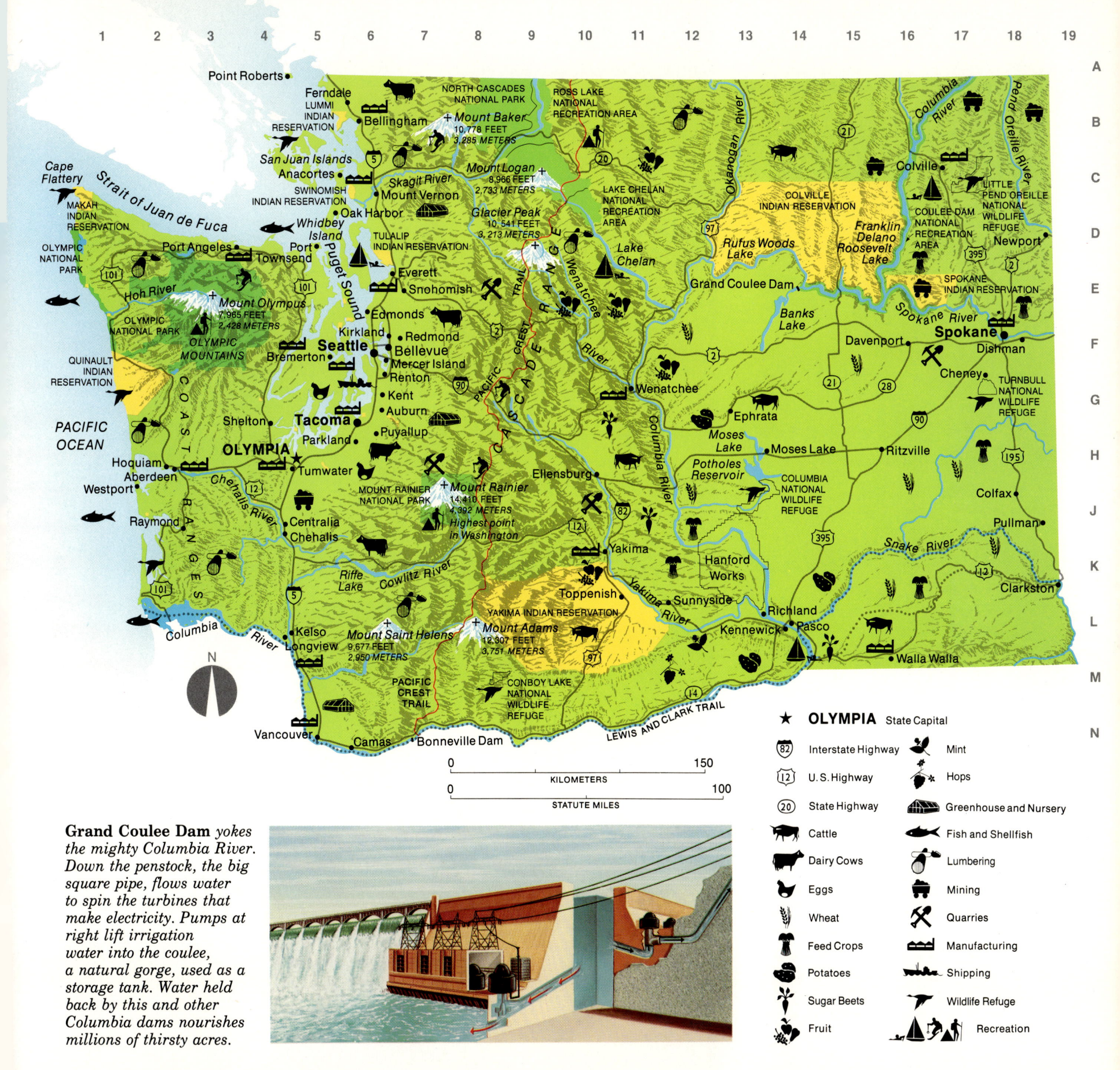

Washington

Map grid columns: 1–19 (top); rows: A–N (right side)

Map Labels

Water Features:
- Pacific Ocean
- Strait of Juan de Fuca
- Puget Sound
- Columbia River
- Snake River
- Spokane River
- Pend Oreille River
- Okanogan River
- Wenatchee River
- Yakima River
- Skagit River
- Cowlitz River
- Chehalis River
- Hoh River
- Ross Lake National Recreation Area
- Lake Chelan
- Lake Chelan National Recreation Area
- Rufus Woods Lake
- Franklin Delano Roosevelt Lake
- Banks Lake
- Moses Lake
- Potholes Reservoir
- Riffe Lake
- Conboy Lake National Wildlife Refuge
- Columbia National Wildlife Refuge
- Turnbull National Wildlife Refuge
- Little Pend Oreille National Wildlife Refuge
- Coulee Dam National Recreation Area
- Grand Coulee Dam
- Bonneville Dam

Geographic Features:
- Cape Flattery
- Point Roberts
- San Juan Islands
- Whidbey Island
- Olympic Mountains
- Olympic National Park
- North Cascades National Park
- Mount Rainier National Park
- Cascade Range
- Coast Ranges
- Pacific Crest Trail
- Lewis and Clark Trail

Mountains:
- Mount Baker 10,778 FEET / 3,285 METERS
- Mount Logan 8,966 FEET / 2,733 METERS
- Glacier Peak 10,541 FEET / 3,213 METERS
- Mount Olympus 7,965 FEET / 2,428 METERS
- Mount Rainier 14,410 FEET / 4,392 METERS — Highest point in Washington
- Mount Saint Helens 9,677 FEET / 2,950 METERS
- Mount Adams 12,307 FEET / 3,751 METERS

Indian Reservations:
- Makah Indian Reservation
- Quinault Indian Reservation
- Lummi Indian Reservation
- Swinomish Indian Reservation
- Tulalip Indian Reservation
- Yakima Indian Reservation
- Colville Indian Reservation
- Spokane Indian Reservation

Cities and Towns:
- Ferndale, Bellingham, Anacortes, Mount Vernon, Oak Harbor, Port Angeles, Port Townsend, Everett, Snohomish, Edmonds, Kirkland, Redmond, Seattle, Bellevue, Mercer Island, Renton, Bremerton, Kent, Auburn, Shelton, Tacoma, Parkland, Puyallup, Olympia, Tumwater, Hoquiam, Aberdeen, Westport, Raymond, Centralia, Chehalis, Kelso, Longview, Vancouver, Camas, Ellensburg, Yakima, Toppenish, Sunnyside, Richland, Kennewick, Pasco, Walla Walla, Colfax, Pullman, Clarkston, Ritzville, Moses Lake, Ephrata, Davenport, Wenatchee, Cheney, Dishman, Spokane, Colville, Newport, Hanford Works

Highways: 5, 90, 82, 101, 12, 2, 14, 97, 20, 21, 28, 195, 395

Legend

★ **OLYMPIA** State Capital
- (82) Interstate Highway
- (12) U.S. Highway
- (20) State Highway
- Cattle
- Dairy Cows
- Eggs
- Wheat
- Feed Crops
- Potatoes
- Sugar Beets
- Fruit
- Mint
- Hops
- Greenhouse and Nursery
- Fish and Shellfish
- Lumbering
- Mining
- Quarries
- Manufacturing
- Shipping
- Wildlife Refuge
- Recreation

Scale: 0–150 Kilometers / 0–100 Statute Miles

Grand Coulee Dam yokes the mighty Columbia River. Down the penstock, the big square pipe, flows water to spin the turbines that make electricity. Pumps at right lift irrigation water into the coulee, a natural gorge, used as a storage tank. Water held back by this and other Columbia dams nourishes millions of thirsty acres.

271

Loggers trim a fallen giant. The Douglas fir is our most valuable timber species.

Lummi Indian, a fish rancher in Puget Sound, traps a coho salmon returning from the sea.

"A" for its apples, says Washington's report card. Orchards thrive under irrigation in the valleys around Wenatchee.

Steepest ups and downs in the West tell you that the North Cascades are young mountains—lifted about five million years ago. More recently, during the Ice Age, glaciers covered all but the tips of the range. And newer glaciers still grind, sharpening the ridges. North Cascades National Park was created in 1968 to preserve the wild beauty of these mountains for people to enjoy. Its thundering rivers and deep lakes stay clean but icy cold. Some are good to fish in, but you probably wouldn't want to swim there unless you're first cousin to a grizzly bear. In summer, wild flowers decorate the trails, and larch trees turn a bright green. As for peaks, the park has climbs to try your soles on. But Mount Sahale, right, is strictly for goats and super experts, sound of leg and lung—and very, very careful.

272

Lady of the Lake *ferries summer passengers up Lake Chelan to Stehekin. Mail and supplies also come by boat.*

Where yellow wallflowers spread, mountain goats gather. Summer brings a sweet-smelling bouquet to Mount Angeles in Olympic National Park.

Peaks sharp as cougar fangs test climbers in North Cascades National Park. Their reward: a top-of-the-world view.

273

Alaska, Hawaii
and Distant Shores

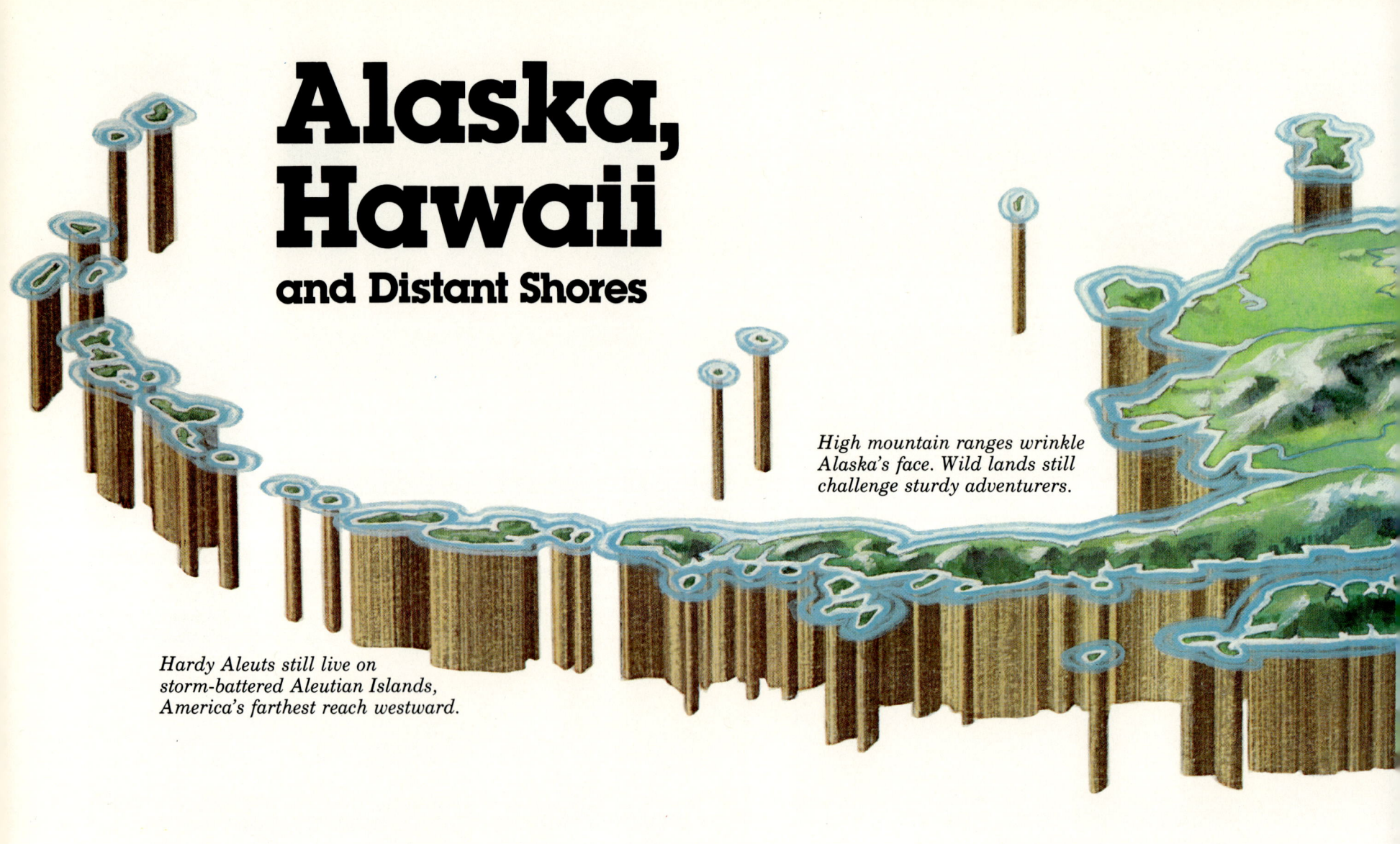

High mountain ranges wrinkle Alaska's face. Wild lands still challenge sturdy adventurers.

Hardy Aleuts still live on storm-battered Aleutian Islands, America's farthest reach westward.

Some of America's most unusual lands lie far beyond the shores of the 48 "contiguous" states—the states that touch each other. To the northwest sprawls Alaska, twice as big as the next largest state, Texas. To the southwest lies tiny Johnston Atoll, site of a military outpost and little else. With a population of about 300 and an area of less than a square mile (2.6 sq km), Johnston is the smallest inhabited United States possession. From Guam in the Pacific to the Virgin Islands in the Caribbean, American flags fly more than 10,000 miles (16,093 km) apart.

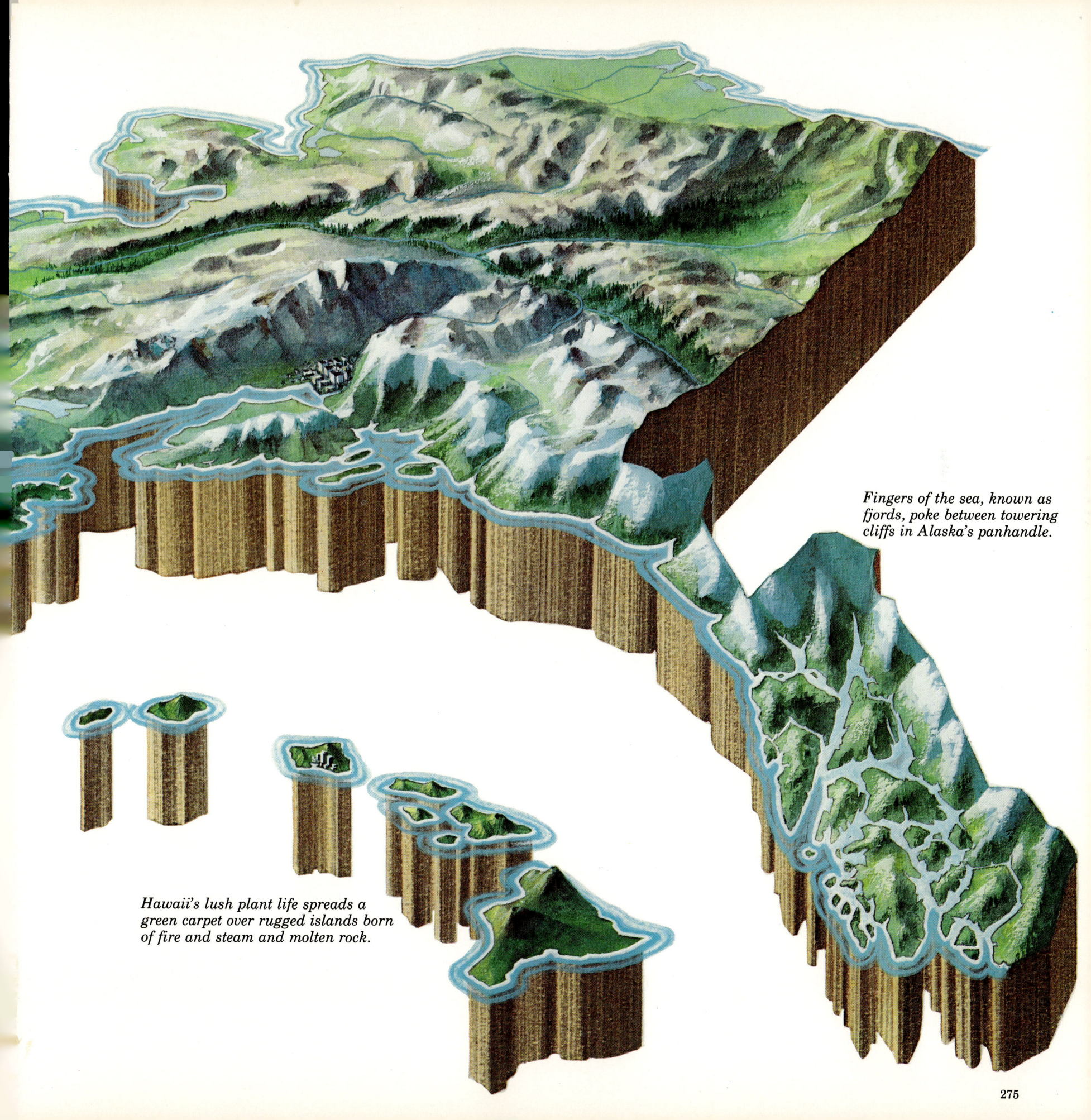

Fingers of the sea, known as fjords, poke between towering cliffs in Alaska's panhandle.

Hawaii's lush plant life spreads a green carpet over rugged islands born of fire and steam and molten rock.

ALASKA

Willow Ptarmigan

Forget-Me-Not

If you were a fisherman, Alaska would be a great place to spread your nets. Alaska ranks last among the states in the value of its farm products, but first in commercial fishing. Big factories on the southern coast and islands keep busy freezing and canning a shimmering treasure of salmon, crabs, halibut, and shrimp as fast as the boats can haul them in. But "fishermen's luck" is tricky, and sometimes the boats come back nearly empty.

If you were a lumberjack, Alaska would be a great place to swing your ax. Today most lumbermen prefer a growling chain saw that can topple many forest giants in the time it would take to chop down only one. In dense evergreen forests along the panhandle—that strip of islands and coastal mountains curving down from the state's southeastern corner—the saws and machinery reap a timber harvest that rivals fish processing in dollar value.

If you were a farmer, Alaska would be a great place to sink your roots—providing you chose land around Anchorage. In that tiny part of the state, you would enjoy a comfortable summer of breezes cooled by ocean currents offshore. And you'd see vegetables such as lettuce and cabbages grow to enormous size. That's because this state is so far north on our spinning globe. Here, in summer, the sun can be seen all day and most of the night—and the more sun your cabbages get, the better they grow.

But in spite of all those hours of daylight, most of Alaska is too cold and the land too poorly suited to farming. In fact, there are fewer than 400 farms in the whole state. So the biggest state in the nation must import about 90 percent of the food it needs.

In Barrow, the most northern town in the nation, the sun doesn't set for almost three months in summer and doesn't rise for two months in winter. It's like one day stretched out to last a season! If you have a world globe in your home or classroom, you and a friend can see for yourselves how this happens. Make a chalk mark (or something else you can easily erase afterward) on a city such as New York or San Francisco, and another on Point Barrow, Alaska. Next, you be the sun; stand across the room with your eyes at about the same level as the globe, with the globe's axis tilted slightly ($23\frac{1}{2}°$) toward you, as it would be in summer. Now watch what happens when your friend slowly turns the globe. New York and San Francisco come and go as you "rise" and "set." But you can always see Point Barrow as it circles the North Pole, day after day.

If you were a tourist, Alaska would be a great place to spend a vacation. Here you might click snapshots of snowcapped peaks such as Mount McKinley, highest in North America... of moose and bear and caribou roaming the nearly empty interior... of boats, airplanes, and snowmobiles that link towns scattered over long stretches of roadless wilderness... of Eskimos and Aleuts and Indians whose ancestors lived here for thousands of years.

If you were one of these native Alaskans, you'd enjoy something not many American Indians have won: ownership of the land your forefathers trod. In the 1960's, Alaskan native groups claimed ancestral rights to many millions of acres. About that time, oil was discovered on the North Slope and a pipeline across Alaska was proposed—but who owned the land it would cross and the oil fields it would serve? It took a historic act of Congress to decide. Today, native groups own huge tracts of Alaska, and oil interests pay them for exploration rights.

Area: the largest state, 586,412 sq mi (1,518,800 sq km). **Population:** 407,000. Ranks 49th. **Major Cities:** Anchorage, 161,018; Fairbanks, 29,920. **Mining:** oil, sand and gravel, natural gas, coal. **Manufacturing:** seafood processing, wood pulp, lumber and wood products. **Fishing:** salmon, crabs, halibut, shrimp, herring. **Agriculture:** fur trapping, dairy products. Also greenhouse and nursery products, hay, vegetables. **Other Important Activities:** military and government operations, tourism. **Statehood:** the 49th state. Admitted Jan. 3, 1959.

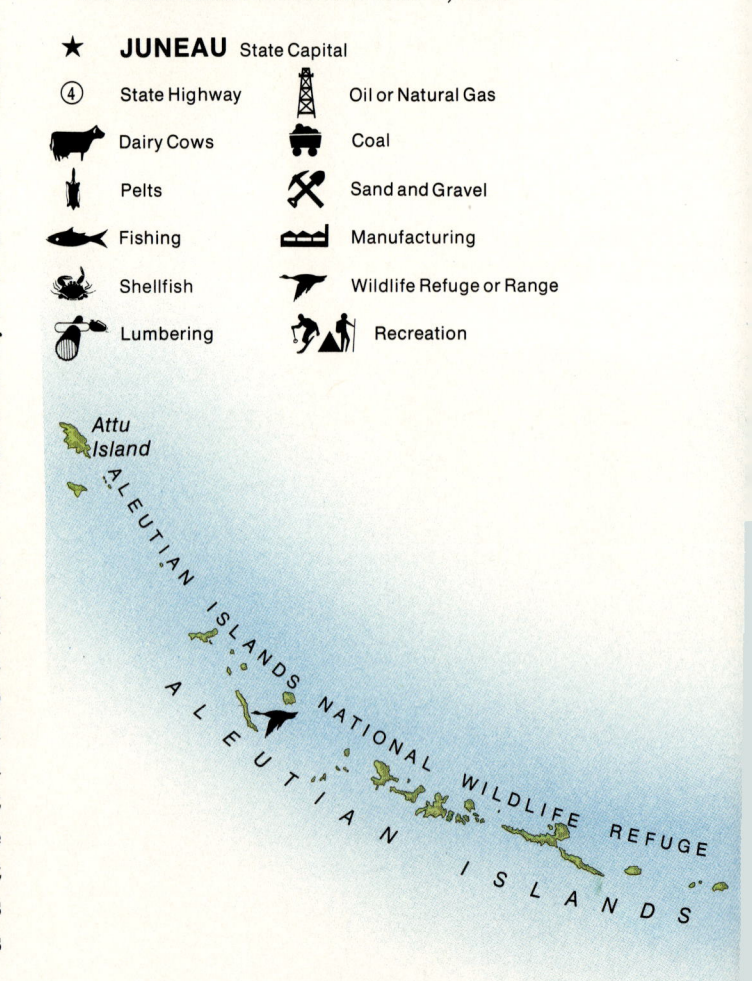

★ **JUNEAU** State Capital
- State Highway
- Dairy Cows
- Pelts
- Fishing
- Shellfish
- Lumbering
- Oil or Natural Gas
- Coal
- Sand and Gravel
- Manufacturing
- Wildlife Refuge or Range
- Recreation

Attu Island

ALEUTIAN ISLANDS NATIONAL WILDLIFE REFUGE

ALEUTIAN ISLANDS

At home on the ice, *the walrus lives in no other state but Alaska. A full-grown male may outweigh 15 men. From its built-in "blanket" of blubber, hunters of the 1800's obtained an oil used in lamps. Others killed walruses for their ivory tusks or just for trophies. Saved by laws, herds are now increasing.*

Point Barrow
Northernmost point • Barrow
of the United States

BEAUFORT SEA

Vast oil deposit
discovered in 1968
Prudhoe Bay

ARCTIC OCEAN

NORTH SLOPE

CHUKCHI SEA

Colville River

BROOKS RANGE

Noatak River

ARCTIC NATIONAL WILDLIFE RANGE

Little Diomede Island

Bering Strait

Kotzebue
Kotzebue Sound

Kobuk River

CONTINENTAL DIVIDE

TRANS-ALASKA PIPELINE

SEWARD PENINSULA

ARCTIC CIRCLE

Koyukuk River

Yukon River

• Nome

Livengood • Circle
Manley
Hot Springs • College
Fairbanks
ALASKA HIGHWAY
Eagle

St. Lawrence Island

BERING SEA

Norton Sound

Yukon Delta

Yukon River

Tanana River

St. Matthew Island
BERING SEA NATIONAL WILDLIFE REFUGE

CLARENCE RHODE NATIONAL WILDLIFE RANGE

Highest point in United States
Mount McKinley
20,320 FEET; 6,194 METERS

MOUNT McKINLEY NATIONAL PARK

Nunivak Island
NUNIVAK NATIONAL WILDLIFE REFUGE

Kuskokwim River

Bethel

ALASKA

Mount Foraker
17,400 FEET
5,304 METERS

RANGE

WRANGELL MOUNTAINS

Mount Bona
16,421 FEET
5,005 METERS

KUSKOKWIM MOUNTAINS

Susitna River

Matanuska River

Copper River

McCarthy

Pribilof Islands

CAPE NEWENHAM NATIONAL WILDLIFE REFUGE

Iliamna Lake

Anchorage
Spenard
Kenai • Valdez
Soldotna • Whittier
Seward • Cordova

ST. ELIAS MOUNTAINS

Mount St. Elias
18,008 FEET; 5,489 METERS

Cook Inlet
Homer
KENAI NATIONAL MOOSE RANGE

Bristol Bay

Malaspina Glacier
Largest glacier in North America

ALASKA MARINE HIGHWAY SYSTEM

Becharof Lake
KATMAI NATIONAL MONUMENT

Skagway
Haines
Mendenhall Glacier

ALASKA PENINSULA

• Kodiak

GLACIER BAY NATIONAL MONUMENT
Sixteen glaciers

★ **JUNEAU**

Kodiak Island
KODIAK NATIONAL WILDLIFE REFUGE

GULF OF ALASKA

PANHANDLE

COAST MOUNTAINS

ALEUTIAN RANGE

Sitka
Petersburg
Wrangell

AUEUTIAN ISLANDS NATIONAL WILDLIFE REFUGE

Unimak Island

ALEXANDER ARCHIPELAGO

Unalaska Island

Ketchikan
METLAKATLA INDIAN RESERVATION

PACIFIC OCEAN

N

0   500
KILOMETERS
0   300
STATUTE MILES

Out of a land of long and severe winters come glaciers like great tongues of ice. In high valleys where snow builds up faster than it can melt, its own weight squeezes it into ice. As the pressure builds, the ice creeps downhill. At the sea's edge, chunks break off to become icebergs.

Generations of Indians carved totem poles, not to worship them but to portray figures from life and legend. This one honors a Tlingit tribal hero, the raven.

Warm currents circling the North Pacific help keep the Gulf of Alaska nearly ice-free. There, fisherfolk keep busy when salmon come to spawn.

Stilts help to protect a fur trapper's catch from gnawing animals. Here in the lonely Alaskan wilds, trappers still follow a rugged life-style.

Crude oil crosses Alaska in this new pipeline. It was one of the biggest construction jobs in history—and many young women worked on it.

Our largest state—and one of our most beautiful—might still be a part of Russia if not for the foresight of William Seward. Sea captain Vitus Bering, a Dane sailing for the Russians, discovered Alaska's shore and the Aleutian Islands in 1741, but Russia did little with her vast new realm. In 1867, Secretary of State Seward arranged for the United States to buy Alaska from Russia for $7,200,000. Some said he had bought a wasteland—"Seward's Folly," they sneered. But today, Alaska is a frontier of defense—and a harsh homeland for trappers, prospectors, fishermen, and families building a future for themselves in a still raw and untamed land.

Alaska's one big city, Anchorage, spills into suburbs between the mountains and the sea. In this aerial view, you're looking at the hometown of about four out of every ten Alaskans.

The Alaska brown bear is the largest meat-eating land animal in the world.

279

HAWAII

Ahead of you, great blue-green waves roll in from beyond the horizon and dash themselves to froth on the rocks at your feet. Behind you, the living volcano of Mauna Loa lifts its head into a crown of clouds. Here at South Cape on the "Big Island" named Hawaii, you become a very special person: You're standing farther south than anyone else in the 50 United States!

Hawaii—the name of both the Big Island and the whole chain of islands—is very special too. It is the newest state, and the only one surrounded by ocean. It has seasons, but you'd hardly notice the changes between them; all year round the temperature seldom rises above 85° F (29° C) or drops below 60° F (16° C) in the seaside lowlands where most of the people live. On Mauna Kea, Mauna Loa's slightly higher twin, you can ski on real snow in winter months while your friends splash in the warm surf 20 miles (32 km) away.

If you could drain the Pacific, you would see that the people of the Hawaiian Islands are living on the slopes of mountains. From their peaks to their bases on the ocean floor, Mauna Loa and Mauna Kea stand about six miles (9.7 km) tall. Many of the world's mountains are *higher,* because they start out on higher ground. But if you could move them all onto the same flat plain, you would see that none of them is *taller* than the half-submerged giant, Mauna Kea.

It took the past 25 million years for volcanic eruptions to build up these islands. Gradually some of the hard lava wore into soft, fertile soil. By the time the first Polynesians arrived in huge, twin-hulled canoes more than a thousand years ago, the islands had become lush and green.

In 1778, Capt. James Cook sailed here under the English flag. His discovery began a steady stream of newcomers. Ranchers, planters, and businessmen put together vast estates that still lock up most of Hawaii's private land. Half the state is owned by government—but seven-eighths of the rest belongs to less than 40 owners! A single family owns all of Niihau; sorry, no visitors. Lanai has one owner, too, but you're welcome to visit this largest pineapple plantation in the world. Both of these islands put together could be swallowed up by the huge Parker Ranch on Hawaii; it blankets 291 square miles (754 sq km)!

In Cook's day this land was home to some 300,000 natives. Today their descendants number about half that, and only one in 17 claims to be pure Hawaiian. For many years they have watched other groups win dominance—the Japanese in politics and education, for example. But now they press toward a fairer share of Hawaii's bounty. And so do Filipinos and other groups. Compromise and "live-and-let-live" have kept things neighborly in the past. More compromise may now be needed in this state where every group is a minority.

People live on the seven largest islands. But there are 132 in all, some no more than a jutting rock or a wave-washed reef. They span 388 miles (624 km) from the eastern edge of Hawaii northwestward to Niihau, then another 1,135 miles (1,827 km) to tiny, uninhabited Kure Island.

Dependable trade winds—avenues of trade in days of sailing ships—blow from the northeast, laden with moisture from the sea. Mountains force the winds upward; this cools the air and squeezes out the water as rain. On Kauai's Waialeale peak there is more rain than anywhere else on earth—about 460 inches (11,684 mm) a year.

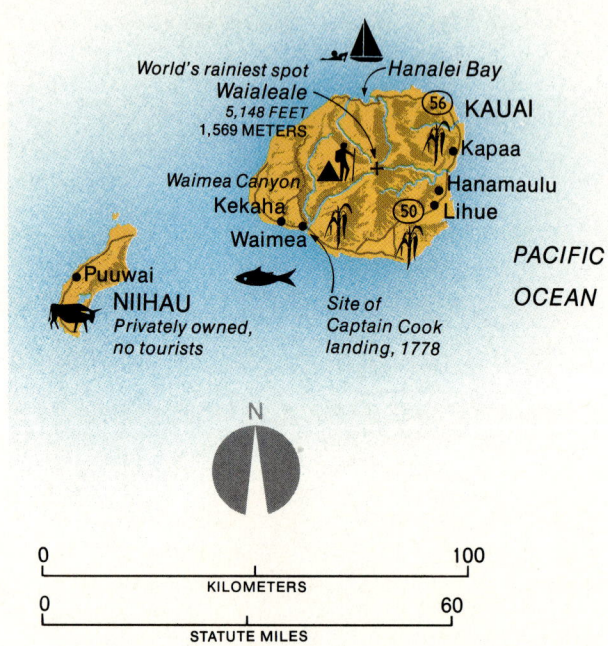

Area: 47th largest state, 6,450 sq mi (16,705 sq km). **Population:** 895,000. Ranks 40th. **Major Cities:** Honolulu, 705,381; Hilo, 29,000. **Manufacturing:** food processing (especially sugarcane and pineapples), printing and publishing, fabricated metals, stone, clay, and glass products, clothing and textiles. **Agriculture:** sugarcane, pineapples, dairy products, beef cattle, flowers (especially orchids) and foliage plants, tropical fruits (papayas, bananas, and others), macadamia nuts, coffee. **Mining:** stone, cement. **Fishing:** tuna, deep-sea gamefish (especially marlin). Also prawns, oysters, and clams by aquaculture or "sea-farming." **Other Important Activities:** tourism, government and military operations, shipping, banking and finance. **Statehood:** the 50th state. Admitted Aug. 21, 1959.

★ **HONOLULU** State Capital
(HI) Interstate Highway
(31) State Highway
🐂 Cattle
🐄 Dairy Cows
🍍 Pineapples
🥥 Tropical Fruit
Macadamia Nuts
🎋 Sugarcane
☕ Coffee
🌸 Flowers and Plants
🐟 Fishing
⛏ Quarries
🏭 Manufacturing
🚢 Shipping
⛵🏄🏕 Tourism and Recreation

OAHU
- Wahiawa
- Waipahu
- Pearl City
- Kaneohe
- Kailua
- ★ HONOLULU
- Pearl Harbor
- Diamond Head
- Waikiki Beach
- (83)

MOLOKAI
- Kalaupapa
- Kaunakakai
- *Kamakou* 4,970 FEET 1,515 METERS
- (450)

LANAI
- Lanai City

MAUI
- Lahaina
- Wailuku
- Kahului
- Pukalani
- *Haleakala Crater* 10,023 FEET 3,055 METERS
- HALEAKALA NATIONAL PARK
- (31)

PACIFIC OCEAN

KAHOOLAWE
Uninhabited island used as target by Navy and Air Force

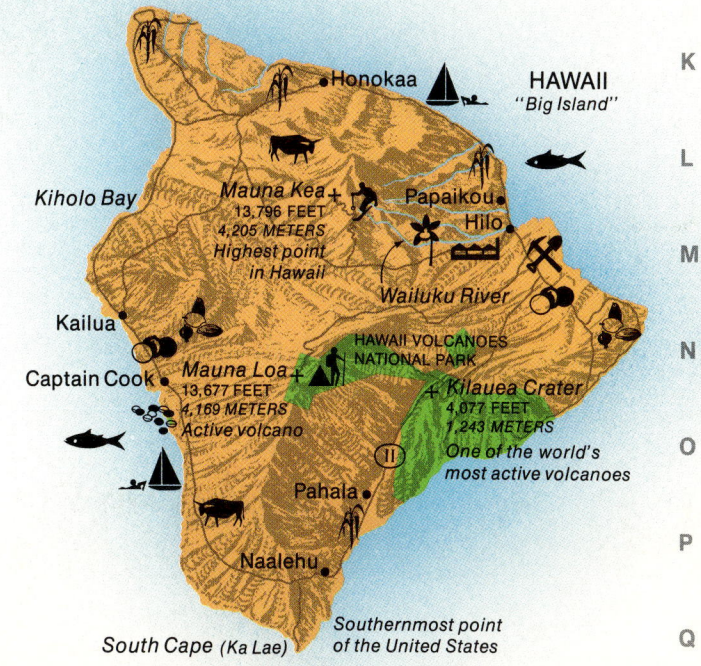

Built from the bottom up, *islands such as the Hawaiian chain begin with lava eruptions on the ocean floor—shown here without the water. Volcanoes still shake the "Big Island" with lava flows (above) so thick they may take years to cool down.*

HAWAII "Big Island"
- Honokaa
- *Kiholo Bay*
- *Mauna Kea* 13,796 FEET 4,205 METERS Highest point in Hawaii
- Papaikou
- Hilo
- *Wailuku River*
- Kailua
- Captain Cook
- *Mauna Loa* 13,677 FEET 4,169 METERS Active volcano
- HAWAII VOLCANOES NATIONAL PARK
- *Kilauea Crater* 4,077 FEET 1,243 METERS One of the world's most active volcanoes
- Pahala
- (11)
- Naalehu
- *South Cape (Ka Lae)* Southernmost point of the United States

In old Hawaiian, still spoken by some, Oahu is said to mean "gathering place." Here the chieftains of the islands held their councils. Oahu is still a gathering place for many races and beliefs. Some call the Hawaiian population a "melting pot," but it's more like a salad bowl, where things mix but don't melt together. Surfing and the hula recall ancient Hawaiians who invented surfboards but had no writing; they used dances and chants to preserve their traditions. In sailing ships came the Yankee whalers, preachers, and merchants. Chinese and Japanese workers came to grow sugarcane; their descendants built graceful temples and launched many businesses. Each newcomer helped give Hawaii a richer blend of peoples than any other state.

A fierce war god made of feathers, shells, and dog teeth recalls the religion of old Hawaii. Some Hawaiians still practice it.

Sprawling Honolulu and gently curving Waikiki Beach lie beyond Diamond Head, whose crater long ago boiled with lava.

Giant waves test the world's best surfers in championships held at Oahu every year.

As in old Hawaii, hula dancers often tell a story with their hands.

Pineapples, brought from Jamaica in the 1880's, now help Hawaii prosper.

A performer leaps for lunch at Oahu's Sea Life Park. The animal is a false killer whale.

DISTANT SHORES

There is more to the United States than just the united states. The nation's family also includes millions of people who live on islands near and far (see page 274). In many ways their homelands are linked with the 50 states, for they too fly the American flag and are part of "the republic for which it stands...."

A string of islands divides the Atlantic Ocean from the Caribbean Sea. They curve to the southeast from the waters off southern Florida. When Columbus sighted land here, he thought he had circled the globe and reached India. The islands have been called the West Indies ever since. Among them are the island of Puerto Rico and a group named the American Virgin Islands.

Puerto Rico, whose name means "rich port," rules itself. Once it was a colony of Spain, then a territory of the United States. Today it is a commonwealth with its own flag and government, but it has chosen to keep some of its ties with the United States.

Though its people speak Spanish and trace much of their culture to Spain, they are United States citizens. Thus, many were able to move to mainland states from their crowded island when jobs became scarce after World War II. Others have stayed on the island to work in factories, construction projects, sugarcane fields, coffee and pineapple plantations, and tourist resorts.

Tourists also flock to the **Virgin Islands.** More than a million visitors a year swim and tan themselves on the beaches of American-owned St. Croix, St. Thomas, and St. John. About 47 smaller islets help make the American Virgin Islands a scenic paradise for vacationing boaters.

To sail from these waters to the Pacific Ocean a century ago, sea captains had to brave the stormy Cape Horn at the southern tip of South America. Many a stout ship perished on the long journey. But since 1914 there's been a shortcut: the Panama Canal that slices across Central America. Treaties with Panama allowed the United States to build and own the canal and to control the Canal Zone, a strip of land about ten miles (16 km) wide that served as a corridor for the canal and a home for Americans working there. In recent years, the canal has been the subject of many meetings as the two nations worked out treaties to abolish the Canal Zone in 1979 and to make Panama the canal's owner in the year 2000.

If you were aboard a ship sailing from Puerto Rico or the Virgin Islands, you'd cross more than a thousand miles of ocean before reaching the Panama Canal. And once you passed through the 40-mile-long (64 km) waterway, you'd still have to sail a third of the way around the world to visit the most distant members of America's family. They live on Pacific islands and island groups with names such as **Guam, American Samoa,** and the **Marianas**—names that echoed in the grim reports of battle as World War II swept through the Pacific. At the war's end, some of these islands were placed in America's care by the United Nations. Others had been part of the nation for many years before that. Tourists and a military base provide jobs on Guam. On other islands people work at fishing, native crafts, and drying coconut meat into copra that later yields coconut oil.

More and more, America's outposts move toward self-rule and a greater voice in their own affairs. See them on the map in the pocket of this atlas; learn more about them from the list on page 289.

Faraway isles add new faces to the nation's family portrait. This macaw's home is the Virgin Islands, where green hills overlook glassy bays (lower). Waves challenge Puerto Rico's shore (upper) as surefooted kids in Samoa challenge a palm tree.(center).

U.S. Virgin Islands, Puerto Rico, American Samoa, Northern Mariana Islands, Guam

U.S. VIRGIN ISLANDS
- ATLANTIC OCEAN
- CARIBBEAN SEA
- Crown Mountain 1,556 FEET / 474 METERS — Highest point in the Virgin Islands
- St. Thomas
- **CHARLOTTE AMALIE**
- St. John — VIRGIN ISLANDS NATIONAL PARK
- BUCK ISLAND REEF NATIONAL MONUMENT
- Frederiksted
- Christiansted
- St. Croix

PUERTO RICO
- ATLANTIC OCEAN
- CARIBBEAN SEA
- Aguadilla
- Arecibo
- Vega Baja
- Cataño
- ★ **SAN JUAN**
- Bayamón
- Guaynabo
- Carolina
- Fajardo
- Culebra — CULEBRA NATIONAL WILDLIFE REFUGE
- Mayagüez
- El Yunque 3,494 FEET / 1,065 METERS
- Caguas
- Isabel Segunda
- Vieques
- San Germán
- CORDILLERA CENTRAL
- Cerro de Punta 4,390 FEET / 1,338 METERS — Highest point in Puerto Rico
- Humacao
- Cayey
- Coamo
- CABO ROJO NATIONAL WILDLIFE REFUGE
- Ponce
- Guayama
- Phosphorescent Bay

Legend
- ★ CAPITAL CITY
- (30) Highway
- Copra
- Fruit and Vegetables
- Coffee
- Tobacco
- Sugarcane
- Fishing
- Quarries
- Manufacturing
- Wildlife Refuge
- Tourism and Recreation
- N

AMERICAN SAMOA
- PACIFIC OCEAN
- Manua Islands
- Ofu
- Olosega
- Tau — Faleasao, Luma, Siufaga, Maia, Leusoalii
- Lata Mountain 3,056 FEET / 932 METERS — Highest point in American Samoa
- Tutuila
- **PAGO PAGO** ★
- Fagatogo
- Aua
- Fagaitua
- Alao
- Aunuu
- Matafao Peak 2,142 FEET / 653 METERS
- Pago Pago Harbor
- Nuuuli
- Leone
- Iliili

NORTHERN MARIANA ISLANDS
- Rota
- Shinapaaru
- Songsong 1,611 FEET / 491 METERS
- Capitol Hill — Administrative center for the Trust Territory of the Pacific Islands
- Kalabera
- Tanapag 1,526 FEET / 465 METERS
- Susupe
- Chalan Kanoa
- Saipan
- Tinian
- Aguijan
- PACIFIC OCEAN

GUAM
- Ritidian Point
- PHILIPPINE SEA
- **AGANA** ★
- Yigo
- Dededo
- Tamuning
- Apra Harbor
- Mongmong
- Barrigada
- Sinajana
- Yona
- Agat
- Umatac
- Mount Lamlam 1,329 FEET / 405 METERS — Highest point in Guam
- Merizo
- Inarajan
- PACIFIC OCEAN

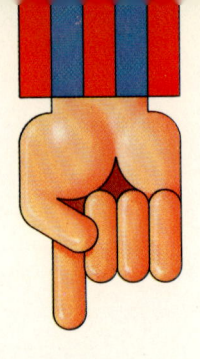

Facts at Your Fingertips

Populations of U.S. Cities

The U.S. is becoming more and more a nation of city dwellers. The Census Bureau says that six cities have more than one million people within their city limits. These pages list all the legally incorporated cities in the U.S. with more than 37,000 residents. Populations here, and those given for cities in the state stories, are the Census Bureau's most recent estimate, made in 1975.

ALABAMA
Birmingham 276,273
Decatur 39,377
Dothan 44,256
Gadsden 50,357
Huntsville 136,419
Mobile 196,441
Montgomery 153,343
Prichard 39,319
Tuscaloosa 69,425

ALASKA
Anchorage 161,018

ARIZONA
Glendale 65,671
Mesa 99,043
Phoenix 664,721
Scottsdale 77,529
Tempe 92,014
Tucson 296,457

ARKANSAS
Fort Smith 66,663
Hot Springs 38,207
Little Rock 141,143
North Little Rock 61,768
Pine Bluff 54,631

CALIFORNIA
Alameda 72,017
Alhambra 60,715
Anaheim 193,616
Arcadia 46,697
Bakersfield 77,264
Baldwin Park 45,712
Bellflower 51,145
Berkeley 110,465
Buena Park 61,840
Burbank 86,001
Carson 78,671
Cerritos 43,153
Chula Vista 75,497
Compton 75,143
Concord 95,114
Costa Mesa 76,058
Culver City 38,211
Cypress 39,518
Daly City 72,741
Downey 85,812
El Cajon 60,404
El Monte 67,698
Escondido 49,815
Fairfield 50,264
Fountain Valley 52,377
Fremont 117,862
Fresno 176,528
Fullerton 93,692
Gardena 45,202
Garden Grove 118,454
Glendale 132,360
Hawthorne 53,953
Hayward 92,802
Huntington Beach 149,706
Inglewood 86,610
La Habra 43,037
Lakewood 81,802
La Mesa 42,587
La Mirada 39,447
Livermore 49,850
Long Beach 335,602
Los Angeles 2,727,399
Lynwood 38,039
Modesto 83,540
Montebello 46,665
Monterey 49,179
Mountain View 55,143
Napa 46,557
National City 44,289
Newport Beach 61,853
Norwalk 86,826
Oakland 330,651
Oceanside 56,003
Ontario 63,140
Orange 82,157
Oxnard 86,506
Pacifica 39,531
Palo Alto 52,277
Pasadena 108,220
Pico Rivera 51,495
Pomona 82,275
Redondo Beach 62,400
Redwood City 54,160
Richmond 69,713
Riverside 150,612
Rosemead 41,514
Sacramento 260,822
Salinas 70,438
San Bernardino 102,076
San Bruno 37,693
San Buenaventura 63,441
San Diego 773,996
San Francisco 664,520
San Jose 555,707
San Leandro 66,953
San Mateo 77,878
San Rafael 45,219
Santa Ana 177,304
Santa Barbara 72,125
Santa Clara 82,822
Santa Monica 92,115
Santa Rosa 65,087
Simi Valley 70,086
South Gate 56,560
South San Francisco 48,947
Stockton 117,600
Sunnyvale 102,462
Thousand Oaks 55,523
Torrance 139,776
Upland 37,487
Vallejo 70,681
Walnut Creek 46,321
West Covina 75,783
Westminster 66,758
Whittier 72,059

COLORADO
Arvada 74,254
Aurora 118,060
Boulder 78,560
Colorado Springs 179,584
Denver 484,531
Fort Collins 55,984
Greeley 47,362
Lakewood 120,350
Pueblo 105,312

CONNECTICUT
Bridgeport 142,960
Bristol 58,560
Danbury 54,512
East Hartford 54,132
Enfield 46,932
Fairfield 58,084
Greenwich 59,566
Groton 39,764
Hamden 50,168
Hartford 138,152
Manchester 50,417
Meriden 57,697
Middletown 39,694
Milford 49,704
New Britain 78,556
New Haven 126,845
Norwalk 76,688
Norwich 41,060
Stamford 105,151
Stratford 50,656
Wallingford 37,357
Waterbury 107,065
West Hartford 66,605
West Haven 53,002

DELAWARE
Wilmington 76,152

DISTRICT OF COLUMBIA
Washington 712,000

FLORIDA
Boca Raton 42,363
Clearwater 67,069
Coral Gables 43,370
Daytona Beach 48,037
Fort Lauderdale 152,959
Gainesville 72,236
Hialeah 117,682
Hollywood 119,002
Jacksonville 535,030
Lakeland 49,705
Largo 39,064
Melbourne 39,821
Miami 365,082
Miami Beach 94,063
North Miami 42,135
North Miami Beach 37,705
Orlando 113,179
Panama City 38,031
Pensacola 64,168
Pompano Beach 48,821
St. Petersburg 234,389
Sarasota 47,089
Tallahassee 83,725
Tampa 280,340
West Palm Beach 61,471

GEORGIA
Albany 73,373
Athens 49,457
Atlanta 436,057
Augusta 54,019
Columbus 159,352
Macon 121,157
Savannah 110,348
Warner Robins 39,696

HAWAII
Honolulu 705,381

IDAHO
Boise 99,771
Idaho Falls 37,042
Pocatello 40,980

ILLINOIS
Arlington Heights 70,019
Aurora 76,955
Belleville 43,762
Berwyn 49,618
Bloomington 41,509
Calumet City 37,974
Champaign 58,398
Chicago 3,099,391
Chicago Heights 39,527
Cicero 63,444
Danville 41,603
Decatur 89,604
Des Plaines 55,828
Downers Grove 38,597
East St. Louis 57,929
Elgin 59,754
Elmhurst 45,020
Evanston 76,665
Granite City 39,790
Joliet 74,401
Moline 44,568
Mount Prospect 49,140
North Chicago 42,639
Oak Lawn 62,317
Oak Park 59,773
Park Ridge 42,957
Peoria 125,983
Quincy 43,784
Rockford 145,459
Rock Island 49,031
Schaumburg 39,882
Skokie 67,674
Springfield 87,418
Waukegan 65,133
Wheaton 37,932

INDIANA
Anderson 69,486
Bloomington 48,955
East Chicago 44,186
Elkhart 43,959
Evansville 133,566
Fort Wayne 185,299
Gary 167,546
Hammond 104,892
Indianapolis 714,878
Kokomo 52,022
Lafayete 48,894
Marion 40,574
Michigan City 41,166
Muncie 78,329
New Albany 37,492
Richmond 43,898
South Bend 117,478
Terre Haute 63,998

IOWA
Ames 43,412
Cedar Rapids 108,998
Council Bluffs 58,660
Davenport 99,941
Des Moines 194,168
Dubuque 61,754
Iowa City 47,899
Sioux City 85,719
Waterloo 77,681

KANSAS
Hutchinson 40,925
Kansas City 168,153
Lawrence 50,887
Overland Park 81,013
Salina 38,960
Topeka 119,203
Wichita 264,901

KENTUCKY
Covington 44,467
Lexington 186,048
Louisville 335,954
Owensboro 50,788

LOUISIANA
Alexandria 49,481
Baton Rouge 294,394
Bossier City 46,565
Kenner 43,781
Lafayette 75,430
Lake Charles 76,087
Monroe 61,016
New Orleans 559,770
Shreveport 185,711

MAINE
Lewiston 41,045
Portland 59,857

MARYLAND
Baltimore 851,698
Bowie 37,323
Hagerstown 37,233
Rockville 44,299

286

MASSACHUSETTS
Arlington 49,815
Beverly 37,180
Boston 636,725
Brockton 95,878
Brookline 52,590
Cambridge 102,420
Chicopee 57,771
Everett 39,473
Fall River 100,430
Fitchburg 38,976
Framingham 65,540
Haverhill 44,377
Holyoke 46,435
Lawrence 67,390
Lowell 91,493
Lynn 79,327
Malden 55,778
Medford 60,769
New Bedford 100,133
Newton 88,559
Peabody 45,200
Pittsfield 54,893
Quincy 91,494
Revere 41,078
Salem 38,957
Somerville 80,798
Springfield 170,790
Taunton 41,935
Waltham 56,251
Weymouth 56,815
Worcester 171,566

MICHIGAN
Allen Park 39,511
Ann Arbor 103,542
Battle Creek 43,338
Bay City 47,215
Dearborn 98,986
Dearborn Heights 79,239
Detroit 1,335,085
East Detroit 42,693
East Lansing 50,425
Farmington Hills 54,124
Flint 174,218
Garden City 40,361
Grand Rapids 187,946
Jackson 43,994
Kalamazoo 79,542
Lansing 126,805
Lincoln Park 49,514
Livonia 114,881
Midland 37,434
Muskegon 44,176
Pontiac 82,318
Portage 38,641
Roseville 58,141
Royal Oak 79,191
Saginaw 86,202
St. Clair Shores 85,934
Southfield 75,978
Sterling Heights 86,932
Taylor 76,626
Troy 55,169
Warren 172,755
Westland 92,689
Wyandotte 38,508
Wyoming 57,918

MINNESOTA
Bloomington 79,210
Duluth 93,971
Edina 47,989
Minneapolis 378,112
Minnetonka 42,202
Richfield 43,186
Rochester 56,211
St. Cloud 40,621
St. Louis Park 46,665
St. Paul 279,535

MISSISSIPPI
Biloxi 46,407
Greenville 42,449
Gulfport 43,126
Hattiesburg 38,490
Jackson 166,512
Meridian 46,256

MISSOURI
Columbia 63,227
Florissant 70,465
Independence 111,481
Joplin 40,139
Kansas City 472,529
St. Joseph 77,679
St. Louis 524,964
Springfield 131,557
University City 45,061

MONTANA
Billings 68,987
Great Falls 60,868

NEBRASKA
Lincoln 163,112
Omaha 371,455

NEVADA
Las Vegas 146,030
North Las Vegas 37,476
Reno 78,097

NEW HAMPSHIRE
Manchester 83,417
Nashua 61,002

NEW JERSEY
Atlantic City 43,969
Bayonne 73,574
Belleville 37,137
Bloomfield 52,162
Camden 89,214
Clifton 79,467
East Orange 73,420
Elizabeth 104,405
Hoboken 39,124
Irvington 58,196
Jersey City 243,756
Kearny 39,202
Linden 40,170
Montclair 42,859
Newark 339,568
New Brunswick 47,420
Passaic 50,132
Paterson 136,098
Plainfield 43,910
Trenton 101,365
Union City 52,648
Vineland 53,637
West New York 37,021
West Orange 43,342

NEW MEXICO
Albuquerque 279,401
Las Cruces 40,336
Roswell 37,980
Santa Fe 44,937

NEW YORK
Albany 110,311
Binghamton 60,666
Buffalo 407,160
Elmira 37,320
Freeport 39,585
Hempstead 39,452
Jamestown 37,637
Mount Vernon 67,687
New Rochelle 71,841
New York 7,481,613
Niagara Falls 80,773
North Tonawanda 39,798
Rochester 267,173
Rome 49,014
Schenectady 74,995
Syracuse 182,543
Troy 60,312
Utica 82,443
Valley Stream 39,405
White Plains 48,327
Yonkers 192,509

NORTH CAROLINA
Asheville 59,591
Burlington 37,586
Charlotte 281,417
Durham 101,224
Fayetteville 65,915
Gastonia 49,343
Greensboro 155,848
High Point 61,330
Raleigh 134,231
Rocky Mount 38,947
Wilmington 53,818
Winston-Salem 141,018

NORTH DAKOTA
Bismarck 38,378
Fargo 56,058
Grand Forks 41,909

OHIO
Akron 251,747
Canton 101,852
Cincinnati 412,564
Cleveland 638,793
Cleveland Heights 51,141
Columbus 535,610
Cuyahoga Falls 46,804
Dayton 205,986
East Cleveland 38,144
Elyria 52,474
Euclid 63,307
Garfield Heights 38,206
Hamilton 66,469
Kettering 69,949
Lakewood 65,395
Lancaster 37,952
Lima 51,372
Lorain 84,907
Mansfield 56,916
Marion 39,719
Mentor 39,523
Middletown 48,004
Newark 39,123
North Olmsted 37,420
Parma 98,883
Springfield 77,317
Toledo 367,650
Warren 60,486
Youngstown 132,203

OKLAHOMA
Enid 48,030
Lawton 76,421
Midwest City 50,105
Muskogee 37,313
Norman 59,948
Oklahoma City 365,916
Tulsa 331,726

OREGON
Corvallis 38,502
Eugene 92,451
Portland 356,732
Salem 78,168

PENNSYLVANIA
Allentown 106,624
Altoona 59,692
Bethel Park 37,946
Bethlehem 73,827
Chester 48,529
Erie 127,895
Harrisburg 58,274
Johnstown 40,044
Lancaster 56,669
Philadelphia 1,815,808
Pittsburgh 458,651
Reading 81,592
Scranton 95,884
State College 39,067
Wilkes-Barre 57,040
York 48,587

RHODE ISLAND
Cranston 74,381
East Providence 49,636
Pawtucket 72,024
Providence 167,724
Warwick 85,875
Woonsocket 46,888

SOUTH CAROLINA
Charleston 57,470
Columbia 111,616
Greenville 58,518
North Charleston 58,544
Spartanburg 46,929

SOUTH DAKOTA
Rapid City 48,156
Sioux Falls 73,925

TENNESSEE
Chattanooga 161,978
Clarksville 51,910
Jackson 43,357
Johnson City 39,325
Knoxville 183,383
Memphis 661,319
Nashville 423,426

TEXAS
Abilene 96,459
Amarillo 138,743
Arlington 110,543
Austin 301,147
Baytown 48,191
Beaumont 113,696
Brownsville 72,157
Bryan 37,160
Corpus Christi 214,838
Dallas 822,451
Denton 43,499
El Paso 385,691
Fort Worth 358,364
Galveston 60,125
Garland 111,322
Grand Prairie 56,842
Harlingen 40,423
Houston 1,357,394
Irving 103,703
Killeen 49,307
Laredo 76,998
Longview 52,034
Lubbock 163,525
McAllen 48,563
Mesquite 61,933
Midland 62,950
Odessa 84,476
Pasadena 97,561
Plano 37,486
Port Arthur 53,557
Richardson 59,190
San Angelo 66,099
San Antonio 773,248
Temple 39,518
Texas City 40,939
Tyler 61,434
Victoria 44,842
Waco 97,607
Wichita Falls 95,008

UTAH
Ogden 68,978
Provo 55,593
Salt Lake City 169,917

VERMONT
Burlington 37,133

VIRGINIA
Alexandria 105,220
Charlottesville 41,655
Chesapeake 104,459
Danville 45,563
Hampton 125,013
Lynchburg 63,066
Newport News 138,760
Norfolk 286,694
Petersburg 45,245
Portsmouth 108,674
Richmond 232,652
Roanoke 100,585
Suffolk 49,210
Virginia Beach 213,954

WASHINGTON
Bellevue 65,365
Bellingham 41,789
Bremerton 37,206
Everett 48,371
Seattle 487,091
Spokane 173,698
Tacoma 151,267
Vancouver 47,742
Yakima 49,264

WEST VIRGINIA
Charleston 67,348
Huntington 68,811
Parkersburg 38,882
Wheeling 44,369

WISCONSIN
Appleton 59,182
Eau Claire 47,852
Green Bay 91,189
Janesville 48,660
Kenosha 80,727
La Crosse 49,082
Madison 168,196
Milwaukee 665,796
Oshkosh 50,107
Racine 94,744
Sheboygan 49,431
Waukesha 45,767
Wauwatosa 56,514
West Allis 69,084

WYOMING
Casper 41,192
Cheyenne 46,677

More Facts at Your Fingertips

U.S. Super Facts

DRIEST SPOT
Death Valley, California; annual average rainfall 1.35 inches (34.3 mm)

HIGHEST TEMPERATURE
134°F (56.7°C) at Death Valley, California; recorded July 10, 1913

LOWEST TEMPERATURE
-80°F (-62.2°C) at Prospect Creek, Alaska; recorded January 23, 1971

LONGEST RIVER
Mississippi–Missouri; 3,710 miles (5,971 km) long

HIGHEST POINT
Mount McKinley, Alaska; 20,320 feet (6,194 m) high

LOWEST POINT
Death Valley, California; 282 feet (86 m) below sea level

HIGHEST WATERFALL
Yosemite, California; 2,425 feet (739 m) high

HIGHEST CITY
Leadville, Colorado; 10,200 feet (3,109 m) high

LOWEST TOWN
Calipatria, California; 183 feet (56 m) below sea level

LARGEST STATE
Alaska; 586,412 sq mi (1,518,800 sq km)

SMALLEST STATE
Rhode Island; 1,214 sq mi (3,144 sq km)

MOST CROWDED STATE
New Jersey; 935.3 people per sq mi (361.1 people per sq km)

LEAST CROWDED STATE
Alaska; 0.7 person per sq mi (0.3 per sq km)

World Super Facts

RAINIEST SPOT
Mt. Waialeale, Hawaii; annual average rainfall 460 inches (11,684 mm)

LARGEST GORGE
Grand Canyon, Colorado River, Arizona; 217 miles (349 km) long, 4 to 18 miles (6.4 to 29 km) wide, 1 mile (1.6 km) deep

DEEPEST GORGE
Hells Canyon, Snake River, Idaho; 7,900 feet (2,408 m)

STRONGEST SURFACE WIND
231 mph (372 kmph), Mount Washington, New Hampshire; recorded 1934

OLDEST LIVING PLANT
Bristlecone pine in California, about 4,600 years old

TALLEST LIVING PLANT
Howard Libbey redwood tree in California, 365 feet (111 m) tall

LARGEST LIVING PLANT
General Sherman sequoia in California; 275 feet (84 m) tall, 83 feet (25 m) around

LONGEST NATURAL ARCH
Landscape Arch in Arches National Park, Utah, spans 291 feet (89 m)

MOST EXTENSIVE CAVE SYSTEM
Flint-Mammoth Cave System in Kentucky; total mapped passageway length of 191 miles (307 km)

SHORTEST RIVER
D River in Lincoln City, Oregon; flows 440 feet (134 m) from Devil's Lake to the Pacific

U.S. Forest Areas

Our forest areas include more than 700 million acres (283,279,950 hectares), such as national and state forests, wilderness areas, timberland, parks, privately owned woods.

State	Area Forested
Alabama	67%
Alaska	33%
Arizona	26%
Arkansas	55%
California	42%
Colorado	34%
Connecticut	70%
Delaware	31%
Florida	51%
Georgia	69%
Hawaii	48%
Idaho	41%
Illinois	11%
Indiana	17%
Iowa	7%
Kansas	3%
Kentucky	47%
Louisiana	53%
Maine	90%
Maryland	47%
Massachusetts	70%
Michigan	53%
Minnesota	37%
Mississippi	56%
Missouri	34%
Montana	24%
Nebraska	2%
Nevada	11%
New Hampshire	89%
New Jersey	51%
New Mexico	24%
New York	57%
North Carolina	66%
North Dakota	1%
Ohio	25%
Oklahoma	21%
Oregon	49%
Pennsylvania	62%
Rhode Island	65%
South Carolina	65%
South Dakota	21%
Tennessee	50%
Texas	14%
Utah	29%
Vermont	74%
Virginia	64%
Washington	54%
West Virginia	79%
Wisconsin	43%
Wyoming	16%

15 Largest U.S. Metropolitan Areas

Why do we look at metropolitan areas? Because many city places spread beyond the city limits. The U.S. Census Bureau defines a metropolitan area as one which includes a central city or two cities with a population of 50,000 or more. It may also include nearby communities which have economic and social ties with the main city. Some metropolitan areas include several towns and spread into two or three states. Of the 277 metropolitan areas in the nation, 15 have over two million people. Another 21 have more than one million. The metropolitan area populations listed here are Census Bureau estimates for July 1, 1976.

	Metropolitan Area	Location	Population
1.	New York	New York-New Jersey	9,526,800
2.	Chicago	Illinois	7,006,400
3.	Los Angeles-Long Beach	California	7,004,400
4.	Philadelphia	Pennsylvania-New Jersey	4,822,400
5.	Detroit	Michigan	4,389,900
6.	Boston-Lowell-Brockton-Lawrence-Haverhill	Massachusetts-New Hampshire	3,905,600
7.	San Francisco-Oakland	California	3,158,900
8.	Washington, D.C.	Maryland-Virginia-District of Columbia	3,033,900
9.	Nassau-Suffolk	New York	2,675,300
10.	Dallas-Fort Worth	Texas	2,585,300
11.	Houston	Texas	2,392,100
12.	St. Louis	Missouri-Illinois	2,386,300
13.	Pittsburgh	Pennsylvania	2,306,300
14.	Baltimore	Maryland	2,152,400
15.	Minneapolis-St. Paul	Minnesota-Wisconsin	2,033,400

Top Products / Top States

Here, in order of their dollar value, are major crops, minerals, and fish, and the states that led in their production for 1976. Nationwide leaders in agriculture, mining, and fishing are at right. Rank may change from year to year.

Farm Products | Leaders

1. Cattle and calves—*Texas, Iowa, Nebraska, Kansas*
2. Dairy products—*Wisconsin, California, New York, Minnesota*
3. Corn—*Illinois, Iowa, Indiana, Nebraska*
4. Soybeans—*Illinois, Iowa, Indiana, Ohio*
5. Hogs—*Iowa, Illinois, Indiana, Minnesota*
6. Wheat—*Kansas, North Dakota, Washington, Montana*
7. Cotton—*Texas, California, Mississippi, Arizona*
8. Eggs—*California, Georgia, Arkansas, North Carolina*
9. Broiler chickens—*Arkansas, Georgia, Alabama, North Carolina*
10. Tobacco—*North Carolina, Kentucky, Virginia, South Carolina*
11. Greenhouse and nursery—*California, Florida, Ohio, New York*
12. Hay—*California, Arizona, Washington, Idaho*
13. Potatoes—*Idaho, Maine, Washington, California*
14. Sorghum grain—*Texas, Nebraska, Kansas, Oklahoma*
15. Rice—*Arkansas, California, Texas, Louisiana*
16. Tomatoes—*California, Florida, Ohio, New Jersey*
17. Turkeys—*Minnesota, North Carolina, California, Arkansas*
18. Peanuts—*Georgia, Alabama, Texas, North Carolina*
19. Oranges—*Florida, California, Texas, Arizona*
20. Barley—*North Dakota, California, Montana, Minnesota*
21. Grapes—*California, New York, Washington, Pennsylvania*
22. Sugar Beets—*California, Minnesota, Idaho, Colorado*
23. Forest products—*North Carolina, Georgia, Wisconsin, Washington*
24. Lettuce—*California, Arizona, Florida, New Mexico*
25. Sugarcane—*Florida, Hawaii, Louisiana, Texas*

Leaders:
1. California
2. Iowa
3. Texas
4. Illinois
5. Minnesota
6. Nebraska
7. Kansas
8. Indiana
9. Wisconsin
10. North Carolina

Minerals | Leaders

1. Petroleum—*Texas, Louisiana, California, Oklahoma*
2. Coal—*Kentucky, West Virginia, Pennsylvania, Illinois*
3. Natural gas—*Texas, Louisiana, Oklahoma, New Mexico*
4. Natural gas liquids—*Texas, Louisiana, Oklahoma, New Mexico*
5. Cement—*California, Texas, Pennsylvania, Michigan*
6. Copper—*Arizona, Utah, New Mexico, Montana*
7. Stone—*Pennsylvania, Illinois, Texas, Missouri*
8. Iron ore—*Minnesota, Michigan, California, Wyoming*
9. Sand and gravel—*California, Alaska, Texas, Michigan*
10. Phosphate rock—*Florida, Idaho, North Carolina, Tennessee*
11. Lime—*Ohio, Pennsylvania, Missouri, Michigan*
12. Salt—*Louisiana, Texas, New York, Ohio*
13. Uranium—*New Mexico, Wyoming, Utah, Colorado*
14. Zinc—*Missouri, Tennessee, New York, Colorado*
15. Sulfur—*Texas, Louisiana*
16. Lead—*Missouri, Idaho, Colorado, Utah*
17. Sodium carbonate—*Wyoming, California*
18. Potassium salts—*New Mexico, Utah, California*
19. Boron minerals—*California*
20. Silver—*Idaho, Arizona, Colorado, Montana*
21. Gold—*South Dakota, Nevada, Utah, Arizona*
22. Bromine—*Arkansas, Michigan*
23. Magnesium compounds—*Michigan, California, New Jersey, Florida*
24. Vanadium—*Arkansas, Colorado, Idaho, Utah*
25. Gypsum—*Michigan, California, Texas, Iowa*

Leaders:
1. Texas
2. Louisiana
3. West Virginia
4. California
5. Kentucky
6. Pennsylvania
7. Oklahoma
8. New Mexico
9. Wyoming
10. Arizona

Fish | Leaders

1. Shrimp—*Texas, Louisiana, Florida, Alabama*
2. Salmon—*Alaska, Washington, Oregon, California*
3. Tuna—*California, Oregon, Washington, Hawaii*
4. Crabs—*Alaska, Virginia, Maryland, Louisiana*
5. Menhaden—*Louisiana, Virginia, Mississippi, New Jersey*

Leaders:
1. Alaska
2. California
3. Louisiana
4. Texas
5. Massachusetts

U.S. Territories and Outlying Areas

The United States Government controls many outlying lands under different arrangements. Two recent territories—Alaska and Hawaii—are now states. Puerto Rico is a commonwealth and governs itself. Soon the Northern Mariana Islands will become a commonwealth.

American Samoa
U. S. territory; seven islands in the Pacific; area, 76 sq mi (197 sq km); population, 31,500

Guam
U. S. territory; one of the Mariana Islands in the Pacific; area, 212 sq mi (549 sq km); population, 100,000

Howland, Baker, and Jarvis Islands
U. S. possession; islands in the Pacific; area, 2.77 sq mi (7.17 sq km); uninhabited

Johnston Atoll
U. S. possession; reef around four islets in the Pacific; area, .92 sq mi (2.38 sq km); population, 300

Kingman Reef
U. S. possession; reef in the Pacific; area, .01 sq mi (.026 sq km); uninhabited

Midway Islands
U. S. possession; reef around two islets in the Pacific; area, 1.9 sq mi (4.9 sq km); population, 2,000

Navassa Island
U. S. possession; island in the Caribbean; area, 2 sq mi (5.2 sq km); uninhabited

Palmyra Island
U. S. possession; atoll of more than 50 islets in the Pacific; area, 3.85 sq mi (9.97 sq km); uninhabited

Panama Canal Zone
Under U. S. jurisdiction until 1979; strip of land five miles on either side of the Panama Canal; area, 647 sq mi (1,676 sq km); population, 45,000

Puerto Rico
Commonwealth associated with the U. S.; island in the Caribbean; area, 3,435 sq mi (8,897 sq km); population, 3,200,000

Trust Territory of the Pacific
U. N. trust territory administered by the U. S.; more than 2,000 islands and atolls in the Pacific; three major groups: the Carolines, the Marshalls, and the Marianas (except Guam); total land area, 700 sq mi (1,813 sq km); also called Micronesia; population, 120,000

Virgin Islands
U. S. territory; island group in the Caribbean; area 130 sq mi (337 sq km); population, 110,000

Wake Island
U. S. possession; island in the Pacific; area, 2.5 sq mi (6.5 sq km); population, 150

Books to Know About

This list will help you find out more about the subjects in your *Atlas*. Even though a few of the books (marked *) are for older readers, you can enjoy them all. We hope that our suggestions will lead you to the many other good books we haven't space to mention.

For general information, see *The States of the Nation* series, published by Coward, McCann, and Geoghegan, Inc.; the *Enchantment of America* series from Childrens Press; and many excellent state atlases.* Time-Life's *Library of America** and *American Wilderness** series are fully illustrated. National Geographic books,* such as *Our Continent, America's Wonderlands, Vanishing Wildlife of North America,* and *We Americans,* abound with pictures and information, as do the magazines, *National Geographic* and *National Geographic World.*

Maps and Your Atlas: James F. Madden's *The Wonderful World of Maps* shows how to read maps. *The Story of Maps* by Monroe Schere gives a history of mapmaking.

America's Many Faces: Peter Farb surveys land, plants, and animals in *The Face of North America.* Charlton Ogburn Jr.'s *The Forging of Our Continent** shows how our land was formed. *Tales of the Elders* by Carol Ann Bales is "a memory book" with photographs of American immigrants.

America at Work: A lively introduction, *Industry: Man and the Machine,* comes from the Educational Research Council of America. Ernst S. Marzell shows how *Great Inventions* affect our everyday life.

Weather and Climate: *American Weather Stories** by Patrick Hughes is fun. James P. Hall takes you *Exploring and Understanding Weather and Climate.*

The Wonders of Agriculture: *Wheat Country* by Grant Heilman has lots of pictures. Peter and Mike Stevenson's *Farming in Boxes* tells how to grow your own crops. *The Farm Book* by Charles E. Roth and R. Joseph Froehlich explains farm ecology.

Energy and Its Uses: *Energy* by Irving Adler answers basic questions. The *Man and Materials* series edited by Ian Ridpath has volumes on coal, gas, and oil. Albert Hinkelbein explains and illustrates *Energy and Power.*

City Places, Country Places: *Old Cities and New Towns* and *Central City/Spread City* are honest, lively discussions of urban problems by Alvin Schwartz. Betty Miles's *Save the Earth!* is subtitled *An Ecology Handbook for Kids.*

Our Nation's Capital: *Beautiful Washington, D.C.* by Gene Gurney, and Dolphin G. Thompson's *A Picture Guide to Black America in Washington, D.C.* show you the city and the people who live and work there.

New England: *New England Country* by Dorothy Wood offers a sweeping picture. In *Saltmarshes and Shifting Dunes,* John F. Waters focuses on the animals and plants of Cape Cod. Robert Frost's poems in *You Come Too* will show you New England in a different way.

Mid-Atlantic States: Dorothy Wood explores *Hills and Harbors. Today in Old New York* by ElvaJean Hall and Beatrice H. Criner tells an exciting history. David Macaulay takes you *Underground* in a big city.

Appalachian Highlands: Betty L. Toone pictures *Appalachia: The Mountains, the Place, and the People.* The University Press of Kentucky gives us *Kentucky, A Pictorial History.** You can plan a trip on the Appalachian Trail with *The First Book of Hiking* by C. William Harrison.

The Southeast: *The Mississippi* by Corinne J. Naden describes life on the river. The coral reefs of Florida are illustrated in *These Islands are Alive* by Julian May. Jo Polseno tells *The Secrets of a Cypress Swamp.*

Great Lakes States: Allan Carpenter describes *Illinois, Land of Lincoln.* In *The Great Lakes,* James P. Barry discusses history, geography, and trade. You can take *A Walk in the Forest* with Ilka List and Albert List, Jr.

The Heartland: *The Treeless Plains* by Glen Rounds is about pioneering. The Department of Agriculture's *The Face of Rural America* shows farm life in photographs. Paintings illustrate the harshness of *A Prairie Boy's Winter* by William Kurelek.

The Southwest: *The Beautiful Southwest,** a *Sunset* book gives a wide view. Laurence Pringle gives a close-up in *The Gentle Desert. The Hole in the Mountain* by Mabel Otis Robison is the story of Carlsbad Caverns.

Mountain States: Herbert S. Zim surveys *The Rocky Mountains. The Cowboy Trade* by Glen Rounds realistically presents the cowboy life. Tony Gibbs writes about *Backpacking.*

Pacific Coast States: *National Parks of the West** is a *Sunset* book full of beautiful pictures. Rebecca B. Markus gives us *The First Book of Volcanoes and Earthquakes* and C. William Harrison, *The First Book of Modern California.*

Alaska, Hawaii, and Distant Shores: Vivian L. Thompson tells *Hawaiian Tales of Heroes and Champions. Dwellers of the Tundra* by Aylette Jenness shows life in an Eskimo village. In *We All Come From Someplace: Children of Puerto Rico,* Julia Singer describes children at work and play.

We'd like to thank...

We are grateful to many people and organizations for their help in preparing this book. Special thanks go to our consultants Harry Perry and Marion Clawson, Resources for the Future; Walter Arensberg of Skidmore, Owings, and Merrill; and Walter Cottrell of the National Weather Service. We are indebted to the following teachers and many of their students for advising us: Charlotte Kovach, Violet Tibbetts, Ann B. Knox, and Posy Mendoza in Washington, D.C.; Ann McKay, Cathy Davis, and Nancy Beach in Falls Church, Virginia.

We thank the National Park Service, the Bureau of Mines, the National Marine Fisheries Service, the Fish and Wildlife Service, the Bureau of Indian Affairs, the Office of Territorial Affairs, the Forest Service, and the Smithsonian Institution, particularly Stanwyn G. Shetler, for providing information and statistics. We received help from George Coffman and Wayne D. Rasmussen at the Department of Agriculture; Arthur Mielke and Beulah Land at the Bureau of the Census; Charles Readling at the Department of Energy; Linnea Hazen at the Bureau of Economic Analysis; and Jim Lynch of the Goddard Space Flight Center. We are indebted to William Griffith, who worked on our weather map. Many state agencies, especially the departments of agriculture, were also helpful.

We thank the staffs of many public and private libraries. Books and pamphlets we found most useful include many publications of the U.S. government, particularly the *National Atlas;* Neal R. Peirce's series on the United States (*The Mid-Atlantic States of America* was written with Michael Barone); the *American Guide Series,* written during the Great Depression but still invaluable today; Ben. J. Wattenberg's *The Real America;* and *Science* magazine.

The editors gratefully acknowledge permission to reprint extracts from the following: *Red Hills and Cotton: An Upcountry Memory* by Ben Robertson, © 1960 by the University of South Carolina Press; *The Flash of a Firefly* by the Fifth Grade Class, St. Joseph's School, Keshena, Wis., © 1973 by Robin Butterfield; "Prairie Spring" by Willa Cather from *O Pioneers!,* © 1913 by Houghton-Mifflin Co.

Illustration Credits

Maps by the Geographic Art and Cartographic Divisions, NGS.
State Flowers and State Birds by Robert Hynes.
State Flags by Marilyn Dye Smith.
Fact Box Illustrations by Dennis Luzak.

The following abbreviations are used in this list:
NGP – National Geographic Photographer
NGS – National Geographic Staff

2, 3 – Fabric Sculpture by Carol Inouye. Photograph by Joseph D. Lavenburg and Robert S. Oakes, both NGS. 6 (top) – Library of Congress. (bottom) – Victor R. Boswell, Jr., NGP. 9 (top left) – David M. Seager, Sanders & Noe, Inc. (center left) – Richard Krepel. (bottom left) – NOAA, Satellite Photo.

The Land and the People: 10, 11 – Heinz Kleutmeier, Sports Illustrated, Time, Inc. 12 (left) – Dan Guravich. (right) – A. Durand Jones. 13 (left) – David Muench. (center) – Patricia Caulfield. (right) – Farrell Grehan. 16 (top left) – E. R. Degginger. (top right) – Larry B. Jennings, NAS, Photo Researchers. (center left & right) – Ronald A. Helstrom. (bottom left) – Lowell Georgia. 17 – Stephen J. Krasemann. 18, 19 – Jeff Foott. 19 (right) – Thomas C. Dunstan. 20, 21 – David M. Seager, Sanders & Noe, Inc. 22 (left) – David Hiser. (top) – James L. Amos, NGP. (bottom) – Martin Rogers. 22, 23 (center) – William Albert Allard. 23 (top) – Dewitt Jones. (bottom left) – B. Anthony Stewart. (bottom right) – LeRoy Woodson, Jr. 24, 25 – David M. Seager, Sanders & Noe, Inc. 29 – William S. Weems. (center left) – James L. Stanfield, NGP.

New England: 30, 31 – William H. Bond, NGS. 33 – Sue Levin. 34 (top) – Farrell Grehan. (left) – William R. Curtsinger. (right) – David L. Arnold, NGS. 35 (top & right) – B. Anthony Stewart. (bottom) – David L. Arnold, NGS. 37 – Sue Levin. 38 (top) – Marc A. Johnson. (left) – Steve Raymer, NGP. (right) – David Hiser. 39 – David Hiser. (bottom right) – Frederick Kent Truslow. 41 – Dennis Luzak. 42 – James P. Blair, NGP. 43 (top left) – Ira Block. 43 (top right) – Farrell Grehan. (bottom right) – Ted Spiegel, Black Star. 45 – Howard S. Friedman. 46 – Kathleen Reevis Judge. (left) – Clyde H. Smith. 47 – Clyde H. Smith. 49 – Howard S. Friedman. 50, 51 – Fred Ward, Black Star. 50 (bottom) – Paul Beaver. 51 (right) – James L. Amos, NGP. 53 – Robert Hynes. 54 – Nathan Benn. (bottom) – B. Anthony Stewart. 55 – Nathan Benn. (center) – Emory Kristof, NGP. (bottom) – B. Anthony Stewart.

America At Work: 56 – Steve Karchin. 57 – Dennis Luzak. 58 – Michael David Brown. 60, 61 – David M. Seager, Sanders & Noe, Inc.

Mid-Atlantic States: 62, 63 – William H. Bond, NGS. 66 (top) – Bates Littlehales, NGP. (center left) – John E. Fletcher, NGS. (center right) – DuPont. (bottom) – Robert de Gast. 67 – Fred Maroon. 69 – Robert Hynes. 70, 71 – Robert W. Madden, NGP. 70 (top) – Emory Kristof, NGP. 71 (top left) – James P. Blair, NGP. (bottom left) – Ted Spiegel, Black Star. 73 – Howard S. Friedman. 74 – William R. Curtsinger. (top) – James P. Blair, NGP. 74, 75 (top) – Ernest Baxter, Black Star. (bottom) – T. W. Putney. 75 (right) – James L. Amos, NGP. 78 (top) – James L. Amos, NGP. (left) – Ted Spiegel, Black Star. (right) – Bruce Dale, NGP. 78, 79 – William Albert Allard. 79 (top) – Thomas J. Abercrombie, NGS. (bottom) – Ed Cooper. 82 – William Albert Allard. (left) – Martin Rogers. 83 (top left) – Clyde Hare. (top right) – Marie-Louise Brimberg. (bottom left) – Janis K. Wheat. (bottom right) – Ted Spiegel, Black Star.

Appalachian Highlands: 84, 85 – William H. Bond, NGS. 87 – Howard S. Friedman. 88, 89 – J. Bruce Baumann. 88 (bottom) – David Alan Harvey, NGP. 89 (top) – Bruce Dale, NGP. (right) – James P. Blair, NGP. 91 – Dennis Luzak. 92 (top) – B. Anthony Stewart. (bottom left) – Dick Durrance II. (bottom center) – Ronald A. Helstrom. (bottom right) – Bruce Roberts, Photo Researchers. 93 (top left) – NASA. (right) – Emory Kristof, NGP. (bottom left) – Manuel Lopez. 95 – William H. Bond, NGS. 96 (top left) – Emory Kristof, NGP. (top right) – Martin Rogers. (bottom left) – Jodi Cobb, NGP. (bottom right) – James L. Stanfield, NGP. 97 – Emory Kristof, NGP. 99 – Sue Levin. 100 (top) – David Alan Harvey, NGP. (bottom) – Thomas Anthony DeFeo. 101 – Farrell Grehan. (bottom left) – James L. Stanfield, NGP. (bottom right) – William R. Curtsinger. 103 – Sue Levin. 104 – Linda Bartlett. (left) – James L. Stanfield, NGP. 105 (left) – Jodi Cobb, NGP. (top right) – Bruce Dale, NGP. (bottom right) – Linda Bartlett.

Weather and Climate: 106 – Steve Karchin. 107 – Paul Hogarth. 109 – NOAA, Satellite Photo. 110 (left) – Lowell Georgia. (right) – Wayne C. Carlson. 111 (top) – Jim Brandenburg. (bottom left) – Ric Ferro. (bottom right) – Ira Block. 112, 113 – Paul Hogarth.

The Southeast: 114, 115 – William H. Bond, NGS. 117 – Sue Levin. 118 (top left) – Alabama Travel Department. (top center) – Dick Durrance II. (top right) – Allan Roberts. 118, 119 (bottom) – Jill Durrance. 119 (top) – Dick Durrance II. (right) – Gulf States Paper Corp. 122 – Bruce Dale, NGP. (top right) – Matt Bradley. 122, 123 (bottom) – Walter Meayers Edwards. 123 (top left) – Crater of Diamonds State Park. (right) – Matt Bradley. 125 – Robert Hynes. 126 (top) – Otis Imboden, NGP. (left) – James L. Amos, NGP. 126, 127 (bottom) – Frederick Kent Truslow. 127 (top left & center right) – James L. Amos, NGP. (top center) – Steve Raymer, NGP. (top right) – Paul A. Zahl. (bottom right) – Frederick Kent Truslow. 130 (left) – Thomas Nebbia. (top) – Howell Walker. (center) – U. S. Department of Agriculture. (bottom) – David Alan Harvey, NGP. 131 (top) – Wendell D. Metzen. (bottom) – Dick Durrance II. 134, 135 – James L. Stanfield, NGP. 135 (center right) – Charles Harbutt, Magnum. 137 – Howard S. Friedman. 138 (left) – Dick Durrance II. (top) – B. Anthony Stewart. (bottom) – Stephen Green-Armytage. 139 – James P. Blair, NGP. (bottom) – Eugene Fisher. 141 – Robert Hynes. 142 – Jessie O'Connell Gibbs. (top left) – J. Bruce Baumann. (top right) – Ronald A. Helstrom. 143 (top & left) – J. Bruce Baumann. (right) – William S. Weems.

Great Lakes States: 144, 145 – William H. Bond, NGS. 148 (top) – Joseph J. Scherschel, NGP. (top right) – Frederick Kent Truslow. (bottom) – James L. Stanfield, NGP. 149 (left) – James L. Amos, NGP. (top & bottom right) – James L. Stanfield, NGP. 151 – Howard S. Friedman. 152, 153 – J. Bruce Baumann. 152 (top) – Fred Maroon 153 (bottom left) – Robert W. Madden, NGP. (bottom right) – Bruce Dale, NGP. 156 (left) – Martin Rogers. (right) – Anthony Boccaccio. 157 – Robert W. Madden, NGP. (top) – Charles Steinhacker. (left) – Frederick Kent Truslow. 160 (left) – Robert S. Oakes, NGP. (top right) – Georg Gerster. (bottom left) – Corson Hirschfeld. (bottom right) – Martin Rogers. 161 – Robert W. Madden, NGP. (top right) – James L. Amos, NGP. 164 – Cary Wolinsky, Stock, Boston. (bottom) – Steve Raymer, NGP. 165 – Donald N. Emmerich. (right) – Cary Wolinsky, Stock, Boston.

The Wonders of Agriculture: 166 – Dennis Luzak. 167 – Richard Newton. 168, 169 – Ned Seidler, NGS. 170, 171 – Richard Krepel.

The Heartland: 172, 173 – William H. Bond, NGS. 175 – Dennis Luzak. 176, 177 – James A. Sugar. 177 (top three) – Albert Moldvay. (center left) – Steve Raymer, NGP. 179 – Robert Hynes. 180 – Nick Kelsh. (right) – Lowell Georgia. 181 (top) – George J. Schwartz, FPG. (right) – Alan Pitcairn, Grant Heilman. 184 (left) – David S. Boyer, NGS. (right) – James L. Stanfield, NGP. (bottom) – Victor R. Boswell, Jr., NGP. 185 – David S. Boyer, NGS. (top right) – Robert W. Madden, NGP. (bottom right) – James L. Amos, NGP. 188 (top left) – Tom Hooper. (bottom left) – James L. Stanfield, NGP. (right) – Bruce Dale, NGP. 189 (top left) – Larry Nicholson. (top right & center) – Ted Spiegel, Black Star. (bottom left & right) – Bruce Dale, NGP. 191 – Richard Krepel. 192, 193 – Lowell Georgia. 193 (right) – Jen and Des Bartlett. 195 – Richard Krepel. 196 (left) – Jim Brandenburg. (bottom right) & 196, 197 (top) – David Hiser. 197 – Leo P. La Londe. 199 – Richard Krepel. 200 (top left) – Homestake Mining Co. (bottom left) – Bates Littlehales, NGP. (right) – Grant Heilman. 201 (top) – Jim Brandenburg. (bottom) – U. S. Army. (right) – W. L. Highton.

Energy and Its Uses: 202 – Steve Karchin. 203 – David M. Seager, Sanders & Noe, Inc. 205 – Beverage & Associates. 206 (top) – Jim Mendenhall. (bottom) – Beverage & Associates. 207 – James P. Blair, NGP.

The Southwest: 208, 209 – William H. Bond, NGS. 212 (top) – Emory Kristof, NGP. (bottom) – Farrell Grehan. 213 – Robert F. Sisson, NGP. (top left) – Walter Meayers Edwards. (bottom center) – Farrell Grehan. (bottom right) – David Muench. 216, 217 – Adam Woolfitt. 216 (top right) – Emory Kristof, NGP. 217 (top right) – Victor R. Boswell, Jr., NGP. 220, 221 – Robert W. Madden, NGP. 224 (top) – William Albert Allard. (left) – Dean Conger, NGP. 224, 225 (bottom) – Lowell Georgia. 225 (top left) – Blair Pittman. (top & bottom right) – William Albert Allard.

Mountain States: 226, 227 – William H. Bond, NGS. 229 – Sue Levin. 230 (top) – Dean Conger, NGP. (left) – Veronica Smith, NGS. (bottom) – James K. Morgan. 231 (top left) – James L. Amos, NGP. (top right) – Dick Durrance II. (bottom) – Farrell Grehan. 233 – Sue Levin. 234, 235 – Dean Conger, NGP. 234 (left) – William Albert Allard. (bottom center) – Maurice G. Hornocker. 235 (bottom right) – Kurt E. Smith. 238 (left) – David Hiser. 238, 239 (top) – Charles and Derek Craighead. (bottom) – David S. Boyer, NGS. 239 – Nicholas DeVore III. 241 – Howard S. Friedman. 242 (top) – Walter Meayers Edwards. (left) – J. Bruce Baumann. 242, 243 (bottom) – Sam Abell. 243 – J. Bruce Baumann. 246 (top left) – David Hiser. (bottom left) – Jay H. Matternes. (bottom right) & 247 (top) – Walter Meayers Edwards. 247 (bottom left) – James L. Amos, NGP. (bottom right) – David Hiser. 250 (top) – Robert Hynes. 250 (top) – Emory Kristof, NGP. (left) – Georg Gerster. 250 (bottom) & 251 (bottom) – Frank and John Craighead. 251 (top left) – Joseph J. Scherschel, NGP. (right) – Jonathan Blair.

City Places, Country Places: 252 – Steve Karchin. 253 – Michael David Brown. 255 – Beverage & Associates. 256 – O. Louis Mazzatenta, NGS. 257 (top) – Martin Rogers. (center left) – Richard Stacks. (center right) – Tom Myers. (bottom) – James P. Blair, NGP. 258, 259 – Ivan Pintar.

Pacific Coast States: 260, 261 – William H. Bond, NGS. 264 (top left) – Thomas Nebbia. (center) – Dick Durrance II. (bottom) – James A. Mattison, Jr. (right) – David Muench. 265 (top) – Thomas Nebbia. (center) – Harry Cullum. (bottom) – Earl Roberge. (right) – Charles O'Rear. 267 – Howard S. Friedman. 268 – David S. Boyer, NGS. 269 (top left) – David Muench. (top center) – Lowell Georgia. (top right) – Bates Littlehales, NGP. (bottom left) – Ed Cooper. (bottom right) – Bruce Dale, NGP. 271 – Howard S. Friedman. 272 (top left) – Washington Apple Commission. (top center) – Lowell Georgia. (top right) – David Alan Harvey, NGP. 272, 273 (bottom) & 273 (top) – James P. Blair, NGP. 273 (right) – Farrell Grehan.

Alaska, Hawaii and Distant Shores: 274, 275 – William H. Bond, NGS. 277 – Robert Hynes. 278 – Steve McCutcheon. (left) – George F. Mobley, NGP. (right) – Jim Rearden. 279 (top left) – Thomas J. Abercrombie, NGS. (top right) – Steve Raymer, NGP. (bottom left) – Bruce Dale, NGP. (bottom right) – Allan L. Egbert. 281 (top) – Robert W. Madden, NGP. (bottom) – Tony Chen. 282, 283 – Bates Littlehales, NGP. (top center) – Robert B. Goodman. 284 (top two) – B. Anthony Stewart. (bottom two) – James L. Stanfield, NGP.

291

Index

Map pages are in **boldface type** (133). Letters and numbers following in lightface (M8) will locate the place named. See page 8 for help in using them.

Illustrations are in *italic (250)*. Text references are in lightface type (178).

Abbreviations Used In This Book

bbl—*barrel*
°C—*degrees Celsius*
cm—*centimeter*
CO$_2$—*carbon dioxide*
°F—*degrees Fahrenheit*
gm—*gram*
ha—*hectare*
IR—*Indian Reservation*
kg—*kilogram*
km—*kilometer*
kmph—*kilometers per hour*
kw—*kilowatt*
l—*liter*
m—*meter*
mi—*mile*
mm—*millimeter*
mph—*miles per hour*
NECMA—*New England County and Metropolitan Area*
NL—*National Lakeshore*
NM—*National Monument or Memorial*
NMP—*National Memorial Park*
NP—*National Park*
NRA—*National Recreation Area*
NS—*National Seashore*
NWR—*National Wildlife Refuge*
pop—*population*
SMSA—*Standard Metropolitan Statistical Area*
sq km—*square kilometer*
sq m—*square meter*
sq mi—*square mile*
SP—*State Park*
t—*metric ton*
U. S.—*United States*

A

Abbeville, La. **133** M8
Aberdeen, Md. **69** C20
Aberdeen, Wash. **271** H2
Abert, Lake, Oreg. **267** M10
Abilene, Kans. **179** D13; 178
Abilene, Texas **223** G10
Abiquiu Dam Reservoir, N. Mex. **215** C8
Absaroka Range, Wyo. **249** C5
Acadia NP, Maine **37** P10
Acoma IR, N. Mex. **215** H5
Acoma Pueblo, N. Mex. **215** H5
Adams, Mount, Wash. **271** L8
Adirondack Mountains, N. Y. **77** F15
Adirondack Park, N. Y. **77** F14; 79
Adrian, Mich. **155** T13
Agana, Guam **285** R17
Agat, Guam **285** S16
Agate Fossil Beds NM, Nebr. **191** C1
Agriculture 166-171; contour plowing *250*; dry farming 178; erosion control *88*; fair 174, *177*; food production 195; grain elevators *181*; insect control 169; insect damage 116, 140, 244; leading crops and producers 289; research 169, 171, 174; tree farms 169, 236; truck farming 72, 150; U. S. Department of *71*; weather 106, *110-111*, 168, 169; *see also* Crops; Dairy farming; Farm machinery; Fruit and fruit growing; Irrigation; Livestock; Poultry; Ranches and ranching
Agua Caliente IR, Calif. **263** S13
Aguadilla, Puerto Rico **285** B8
Aguijan, Northern Mariana Islands **285** N16
Aiken, S. C. **141** J7
Akron, Ohio **159** F13; tire factory *161*
Alabama 116-119
Alabama River, Ala. **117** P4; 118
The Alamo, Texas **223** M12
Alamo Band Navajo IR N. Mex. **215** J5
Alamogordo, N. Mex. **215** O9
Alamosa NWR, Colo. **229** N9
Alao, American Samoa **285** Q11
Alaska **274**; 16, 24, 170, 252, 270, 274-279, 288; oil reserves 204; population density 248
Alaska, Gulf of **277** O20; fishing *278*
Alaska Highway **277** H20
Alaska Peninsula **277** N15-O12
Albany, Ga. **129** O5
Albany, N. Y. **77** L17; 76
Albany, Oreg. **267** F4; 266
Albemarle Sound, N. C. **91** C24
Albert Lea, Minn. **183** T9
Albuquerque, N. Mex **215** G7; 206, 214
Aleutian Islands, Alaska **276-277** K1-O12; 274

Aleutian Islands NWR, Alaska **276-277**
Aleutian Range, Alaska **277** N15
Alexander Archipelago, Alaska **277** P26
Alexandria, La. **133** G7
Alexandria, Va. **99** C21; 98
All American Canal, Calif. **263** T17-U15
Allagash, Maine **37** B8
Allagash River, Maine **37** D7
Allagash Wilderness Waterway, Maine **37** D7; 36
Allatoona Lake, Ga. **129** D4
Allegany IR, N. Y. **76** N3
Allegheny Mountains **68, 81, 99, 103**; Seneca Rocks *105*
Allegheny Reservoir, Pa. **81** B6
Allegheny River, Pa. **81** G4; 80
Allentown, Pa. **81** H17
Alliance, Ohio **159** G14
Alligator *127, 131*
Alligator Bayou, La. *135*
Altamaha River, Ga. **129** O14
Alton, Ill. **147** N4
Altoona, Pa. **81** H8
Alum Creek Lake, Ohio **159** K8
Aluminum 120, 270
Amana, Iowa **175** G14; 174, 177
Amargosa Desert, Nev. **241** P8
Amarillo, Texas **223** C7
American Falls Reservoir, Idaho **233** Q10
American Revolution 40, 43, 52, 80; treaty 65
American Samoa **274, 285**; 284, 289
Americus, Ga. **129** M5
Ames, Iowa **175** F9; 204
Amherst, Mass. **40** F9
Amidon, N. Dak. **195** K3; 194
Amistad NRA, Texas **223** M8
Amistad Reservoir, Texas **223** M8
Ammonoosuc River, N. H. **45** J5
Amory, Miss. **137** E11
Amsterdam, N. Y. **77** J16
Anaconda, Mont. **237** H5
Anaheim, Calif. **263** R11
Anchorage, Alaska **277** L19; 106, 276, *279*
Anderson, Ind. **151** J9
Anderson, S. C. **141** D3; 140
Andersonville, Ga. **129** L5
Androscoggin River, Maine–N. H. **37** P4; **45** F8; 36
Angeles, Mount, Wash. *273*
Animals: cave-dwelling *87*; desert *241*; endangered 18, 19; extinct 198, dinosaurs 12, mammoth *190*, 240; *see also* Birds; Fish; Livestock; Poultry; *and* animals by name
Ann Arbor, Mich. **155** S14; 154
Anna, Lake, Va. **99** F19
Annandale, Va. **99** C21
Annapolis, Md. **69** G18; 68, 258
Anniston, Ala. **117** F10
Apalachicola River, Fla. **125** C6

Apopka, Lake, Fla. **125** G14
Apostle Islands, Wis. **163** B7
Apostle Islands NL, Wis. **163** B7
Appalachian Mountains **45, 53, 77, 81, 87, 90, 95, 99, 103, 117, 129**; 18-19, 84, 86, 94, 116, 250
Appalachian Trail **33, 37, 40, 45, 53, 69, 73, 77, 81, 90, 95, 99, 103, 129**; *92*, 131; marker *37*
Appleton, Wis. **163** M13
Appomattox, Va. **99** J16
Appomattox River, Va. **99** J18
Apra Harbor, Guam **285** R15
Aquifer 74, 124
Aransas NWR, Texas **223** O14
Arapaho NWR, Colo. **229** C8
Arbuckle Mountains, Okla. **219** M18; 220
Arches NP, Utah **245** M14; 288
Arcosanti, Ariz. *258*
Arctic NWR, Alaska **277** D22
Ardmore, Okla. **219** N19
Arecibo, Puerto Rico **285** B10
Arikaree River, Colo. **229** F16
Arizona 25, 210-213, 258; desert *13*; Indian lands 198
Arizona-Sonora Desert Museum, Ariz. **211** Q10
Arkabutla Lake, Miss. **137** B6
Arkansas 120-123
Arkansas City, Kans. **179** K14
Arkansas River **121, 179, 219, 229**; 120, 218
Arlington, Texas **223** G13
Arlington, Va. **99** C21; 98
Arlington Heights, Ill. **147** C10
Armadillo *225*
Aroostook (county), Maine 36
Aroostook River, Maine **37** D10
Artesia, N. Mex. **215** O13
Arvada, Colo. **229** E11
Asbury Park, N. J. **73** K10
Asheville, N. C. **90** D6
Ashland, Ky. **87** C24
Ashtabula, Ohio **159** B15
Aspen, Colo. **229** G7; 228, 230
Assateague Island, Md.-Va. 98
Assateague Island NS, Md.-Va. **69** O26; **99** F26; 68
Assawompset Pond, Mass. **41** L20
Astoria, Oreg. **267** A3
Atchafalaya Bay, La. **133** O10
Atchafalaya River, La. **133** L10
Atchafalaya Swamp, La. 135
Atchison, Kans. **179** B18
Athens, Ga. **129** D8; 128
Athens, Ohio **159** O11
Atlanta, Ga. **129** E4; 128
Atlantic City, N. J. **73** R7; 72, *74-75*
Atlantic Ocean, Ga. **129** P17
Atoka, Okla. **219** M22; 218
Atoka Reservoir, Okla. **219** M22
Attleboro, Mass. **41** K17
Attu Island, Alaska **276** K1
Atwood, Lake, Ohio **159** H14
Au Sable River, Mich. **155** L14
Aua, American Samoa **285** R7

Auburn, Mass. **41** H13
Auburn, N. Y. **77** J9
Aucilla River, Fla. **125** C9
Augusta, Ga. **129** F12
Augusta, Kans. **179** H14
Augusta, Maine **37** P6
Aunuu, American Samoa **285** R11
Aurora, Colo. **229** E11
Aurora, Ill. **147** D9
Austin, Texas **223** L13; 258
Automobiles: Blue Flame *244*; imported *71*; manufacturing 56, *57*, 59, 150, 154, *157*, 202; racing 150
Avery Island, La. **133** N9
Aztec Ruins NM, N. Mex. **215** B4

B

Babylon, N. Y. **77** T18
Backbone Mountain, Md. **68** E1
Bad River, S. Dak. **199** G8
Bad River IR, Wis. **163** D7
Badlands, N. Dak. **196** G2
Badlands NM, S. Dak. **199** H4; 198, *200*
Bagnell Dam, Mo. **187** J9
Baker, Oreg. **267** E16
Baker, Mount, Wash. **271** B8
Bakersfield, Calif. **263** O9
Baldy Mountain, Mont. **237** J5
Baldy Peak, Ariz. **211** L14
Baltimore, Md. **69** E17; 68, *71*
Bamberg, S. C. **141** K10
Bandelier NM, N. Mex. **215** E8
Bandon, Oreg. **267** L2; coastal erosion *269*
Bangor, Maine **37** N9
Banks Lake, Wash. **271** F13
Bannack, Mont. 236
Bantam Lake, Conn. **33** E5
Bar Harbor, Maine **37** P10
Baraboo, Wis. **163** P9; 162
Barataria Bay, La. **133** O15
Bardstown, Ky. **87** G14
Barkhamsted Reservoir, Conn. **33** B8
Barkley, Lake, Ky.-Tenn. **86** M6; **95** A8
Barnegat Bay, N. J. **73** N9
Barnegat NWR, N. J. **73** O9
Barnstable, Mass. **41** M25
Barre, Vt. **53** H7; 52
Barren River, Ky. **87** L11
Barren River Lake, Ky. **87** L12
Barrigada, Guam **285** R18
Barrington, R. I. **49** G10
Barrow, Alaska **277** B18; 276
Bartlesville, Okla. **219** C23; 218
Bastrop, La. **133** A8
Bath, Maine **37** R5
Baton Rouge, La. **133** K11; 132
Batten Kill River, Vt. **53** R3
Battle Creek, Mich. **155** S11; 154
Battle Mountain, Nev. **241** E7
Baxter SP, Maine **37** G8; moose *38*
Bay City, Mich. **155** O13
Bay Mills IR, Mich. **155** F13
Bayamón, Puerto Rico **285** B14
Bayonne, N. J. **73** G9
Bayou Bartholomew, Ark. **121** N11

Bayou D'Arbonne, La. **133** B5-6
Bayou Dorcheat, La. **133** A3
Bayou La Batre, Ala. **117** T2; 116
Bayou Macon, La. **133** C10
Beanblossom, Ind. **151** N7; 152
Bear Lake, Idaho–Utah **233** T12; **245** A9
Bear River, Utah **245** B7
Bear River NWR, Utah **245** C6
Bears: black *92*; brown *279*; grizzly *14, 251*; polar *16*
Beaufort, S.C. **141** O11
Beaufort Sea, Alaska **277** B20
Beaumont, Texas **223** L18; 222
Beaver Island, Mich. **155** H10
Beaver Lake, Ark. **121** B4
Beaver River, Okla. **219** C10
Beaver River, Pa. **81** G2
Beaverhead River, Mont. **237** J6
Beaverton, Oreg. **267** C5
Becharof Lake, Alaska **277** N16
Beckley, W. Va. **103** O7; 102
Belle Fourche River, S. Dak.–Wyo. **199** F3; **249** D15
Belleville, Ill. **147** P5
Bellevue, Nebr. **191** F18; 193
Bellevue, Wash. **271** F6
Bellingham, Wash. **271** B6
Beloit, Wis. **163** T11
Beltsville, Md. **69** G16; 71
Bemidji, Minn. **183** F6
Bennington, Vt. **53** T3
Benton Harbor, Mich. **155** T8
Berea, Ky. **87** H18
Bering Sea NWR, Alaska **277** J10
Berkeley, Calif. **263** J4
Berkeley Springs, W. Va. **103** F17; 102
Berkshire Hills, Mass. **40** F5; *19, 30, 40*
Berlin, N. H. **45** G8
Bessemer, Ala. **117** G7
Bethany Beach, Del. **65** S8
Bethel, Conn. **33** K4
Bethel Park, Pa. **81** J3
Bethesda, Md. **69** G14
Bethlehem, Pa. **81** G17; 80
Bettendorf, Iowa **175** H17
Beverly, Mass. **41** D20
Big Bay de Noc, Mich. **155** H7
Big Bend Dam, S. Dak. **199** G11
Big Bend NP, Texas **223** M5; 222
Big Black River, Miss. **137** J6
Big Blue River, Nebr. **191** G15
Big Cypress National Preserve, Fla. **125** O16; swamp *124, 126*
Big Cypress Seminole IR, Fla. **125** N16
Big Eau Pleine Reservoir, Wis. **163** L9
Big Horn Basin, Wyo. 248
Big Lake NWR, Ark. **121** D17
Big Lost River, Idaho **233** N7
Big Muddy River, Ill. **147** R7
Big Sandy Creek, Colo. **229** H16
Big Sandy River, Ariz. **211** H4
Big Sandy River, Ky.–W. Va. **87** E24; **103** M1

Big Sioux River, Iowa–S. Dak. **175** C1; **199** F17
Big South Fork National River and Recreation Area, Ky.–Tenn. **87** M17; **95** B18
Big Stone Lake, Minn. **183** N2
Big Sur, Calif. **263** M5
Big Thicket National Preserve, Texas **223** K17; 222
Bighorn, Lake, Mont. **237** K12
Bighorn Canyon NRA, Mont.–Wyo. **237** K12; **249** A8
Bighorn Mountains, Wyo. **249** C10
Bighorn River, Mont.–Wyo. **237** H13; **249** E8
Bighorn sheep *17, 230, 232*
Billings, Mont. **237** H12
Biloxi, Miss. **137** S10
Bingham Canyon, Utah **245** F7; copper mine *247*
Binghamton, N.Y. **77** N11
Birds *16, 126-127*; blackbirds *66*; cranes, sandhill *190, 193*; ducks *34, 79*; eagles *18-19, 238-239*; egrets *16*; geese *148*; grouse *270*; gulls *42, 93*; heron chick *101*; macaw *284*; owl *213*; pintails *197*; puffins *39*; roadrunner *241*; swan, mute *51*; wintering areas *114, 120*
Birmingham, Ala. **117** G7; 116
Biscayne Bay, Fla. **125** P19
Biscayne NM, Fla. **125** P18
Bismarck, N. Dak. **195** J9
Bistineau, Lake, La. **133** C3
Bitter Lake NWR, N. Mex. **215** M13
Bitterroot Range, Idaho–Mont. **233** J7; **237** F2; *232, 234-235*
Bitterroot River, Mont. **237** G3
Black Canyon of the Gunnison NM, Colo. **229** J4
Black Hills, S. Dak.–Wyo. **199** G2; **249** C17; *172, 198*
Black Lake, Mich. **155** J13
Black Mesa, Okla. **218** B1
Black Mountain, Ky. **87** L23
Black River, Ariz. **211** M13
Black River, Ark.–Mo. **121** D13; **187** O16
Black River, La. **133** G9
Black River, S.C. **141** H15
Black River, Wis. **163** M6
Black Warrior River, Ala. **117** J4
Blackbeard Island NWR, Ga. **129** O15; 19
Blackfeet IR, Mont. **237** B5
Blackfoot, Idaho **233** Q10; 232
Blackfoot Reservoir, Idaho **233** Q12
Blackfoot River, Mont. **237** E5
Blackstone River, R. I. **49** B7
Blackwater NWR, Md. **69** M20
Blakely, Ga. **129** O3
Blanchard, N. Dak. **195** G18; television tower *194*
Blanchard River, Ohio **159** F4
Block Island, R.I. **49** T5; *48, 50, 51*
Block Island Sound, R.I. **49** Q5

Bloomfield, Conn. **33** D10
Bloomfield, N. J. **73** F9
Bloomington, Ill. **147** H7
Bloomington, Ind. **151** N6; 153
Bloomington, Minn. **183** P9
Blue Mesa Reservoir, Colo. **229** K6
Blue Mountain, Ark. **121** J3
Blue Mountain, N. H. **45** E7
Blue Mountains, Oreg. **267** C15-F14
Blue Ridge Mountains **91** B9; **99** G15; **129** B8; 128
Blue Spring, Mo. **187** N14; diver *189*
Bluegrass region, Ky. *86, 88-89*
Bluestone Lake, W. Va. **103** Q8
Bluestone River, W. Va. **103** Q7
Boats and ships: barges *186, 189*; canoes *39, 70*; colonial *101*; containership *73*; iceboats *54*; kayak *104*; *Mayflower II 43*; sailboats *43, 50-51*; steamboats *135, 186*; tanker *66*; towboats *148*; whaling *34-35*
Bobcat *131*
Boca Raton, Fla. **125** N18
Bogalusa, La. **133** J15
Bois Blanc Island, Mich. **155** H12
Bois Brule River, Wis. **163** D5
Boise, Idaho **233** O3; 232
Boise River, Idaho **233** O2
Bombay Hook NWR, Del. **65** H5; 66
Bomoseen, Lake, Vt. **53** N2
Bonneville Dam, Oreg.–Wash. **267** C7; **271** N7; 270; fish ladders *267*
Bonneville Salt Flats, Utah **245** E2; 244
Booneville, Miss. **137** B11
Boothbay Harbor, Maine **37** R6
Borah Peak, Idaho **233** N8
Borgne, Lake, La. **133** M17
Bosque del Apache NWR, N. Mex. **215** L6
Bossier City, La. **133** B2
Boston, Mass. **41** F19; *40, 43, 72*
Boston Mountains, Ark. **121** E5
Boulder, Colo. **229** D10
Boundary Peak, Nev. **241** M4
Boundary Waters Canoe Area, Minn. **183** E13; *185*
Bow Lake, N. H. **45** Q8
Bowie, Md. **69** G17
Bowling Green, Ky. **87** L11
Bowling Green, Ohio **159** E6
Boyer River, Iowa **175** F4
Boysen Reservoir, Wyo. **249** G8
Bozeman, Mont. **237** J8
Bradford Mountain, Conn. **33** B5
Brandon, Miss. **137** L6
Branson, Mo. **187** P7; 186
Brasstown Bald, Ga. **129** A7; 128
Brattleboro, Vt. **53** T7
Brazos Peak, N. Mex. **215** B8
Brazos River, Texas **233** F11
Breaks Interstate Park, Ky.–Va. **87** J25; **98** K5
Bremerton, Wash. **271** F5

Breton NWR, La. **133** N19
Breton Sound, La. **133** O17
Bridgeport, Conn. **33** M6
Bridges *47, 67, 68, 98*; Mackinac Bridge *156*
Bridgeville, Pa. **81** J2; steel plant *83*
Brigantine NWR, N. J. **73** Q7
Brigham City, Utah **245** C7
Brighton Seminole IR, Fla. **125** L16
Bristol, Conn. **33** F8
Bristol, R. I. **49** H10
Bristol, Tenn. **95** A25
Bristol, Va. **98** M5
Bristol Bay, Alaska **277** M14
Broad River, S. C. **141** D8
Brockton, Mass. **41** J19
Broken Bow Lake, Okla. **219** N27
Bromley Mountain, Vt. **53** Q4
Brookhaven, Miss. **137** O5
Brookline, Mass. **41** F18
Brooks Range, Alaska **277** D15-22
Brookville Lake, Ind. **151** M11
Browns Park NWR, Colo. **229** B2
Brownsville, Texas **223** S13
Brule River, Mich.–Wis. **155** G4; **163** F13
Bryan, Texas **223** K15
Bryce Canyon NP, Utah **245** R7
Buck Island Reef NM, U. S. Virgin Islands **285** G5
Buffalo, N. Y. **76** K3; *76*; snow *111*
Buffalo *16, 18, 200, 220-221*
Buffalo National River, Ark. **121** D6; *120, 122-123, 123*
Buffalo River, Tenn. **95** E8
Buggs Island Lake, Va. **99** N17
Bull Shoals Lake, Ark.–Mo. **121** B7; **187** P9
Bulls Bay, S. C. **141** L16
Burbank, Calif. **263** R10
Burley, Idaho **233** R8; 232
Burlington, Iowa **175** L16
Burlington, N. C. **91** C15
Burlington, Vt. **53** F3; 52
Burt Lake, Mich. **155** J12
Butte, Mont. **237** G6; copper mine *236, 239*
Buzzards Bay, Mass. **41** O21

Cabeza Prieta Game Range, Ariz. **211** Q4
Cabin Creek, W. Va. **103** M6
Cabo Rojo NWR, Puerto Rico **285** E8
Cabot, Mount, N. H. **45** G7
Cache Creek, Okla. **219** M15
Cache la Poudre River, Colo. **229** B10
Caddo Lake, La. **133** B2
Cadillac Mountain, Maine **37** P11
Caguas, Puerto Rico **285** C15
Cahaba River, Ala. **117** H6; 118
Caillou Bay, La. **133** Q12
Cairo, Ill. **147** T7; 146
Calamus River, Nebr. **191** C9
Calcasieu Lake, La. **133** N4

Calcasieu River, La. **133** K5
Calhoun, Ga. **129** B3
California *23, 25, 168, 171, 257, 262-265*; cotton *136*
California Aqueduct, Calif. **263** J5-R12
California Trail, Calif.–Nev. **241** D10; **263** G6
Caloosahatchee River, Fla. **125** M15
Calumet City, Ill. **147** D11
Cambridge, Md. **69** L21
Cambridge, Mass. **41** F18
Camden, Maine **37** P8
Camden, N. J. **73** M3
Cameron, La. **133** N4
Camp David, Md. **69** B12
Canaan, Conn. **33** A4
Canaan Valley, W. Va. **103** H13
Canadian River, N. Mex.–Okla.–Texas **215** F13; **219** H16; **223** B8
Canaveral NS, Fla. **125** G17
Candlewood Lake, Conn. **33** H3
Cannonball River, N. Dak. **195** K5
Canoncito IR, N. Mex. **215** G6
Canton, Ohio **159** G13
Canyon, Texas **223** C7; feedlots *224*
Canyon de Chelly NM, Ariz. **211** D15
Canyon Ferry Reservoir, Mont. **237** G7
Canyonlands NP, Utah **245** O13; Chesler Park *246-247*; Horseshoe Canyon **245** O12
Cape Ann, Mass. **41** C22
Cape Canaveral, Fla. **125** D9; *127*
Cape Charles, Va. **99** K25
Cape Cod, Mass. **41** M26; *31, 40, 42*
Cape Cod Bay, Mass. **41** L24
Cape Cod Canal, Mass. **41** M23
Cape Cod NS, Mass. **41** J27; *42*
Cape Elizabeth, Maine **37** S4
Cape Fear, N.C. **91** L20
Cape Fear River, N. C. **91** H17; 143
Cape Flattery, Wash. **271** C1
Cape Girardeau, Mo. **187** M18
Cape Hatteras, N.C. **91** F27; lighthouse *93*
Cape Henlopen, Del. **65** O8; *64, 66*
Cape Henry, Va. **99** L25; 98
Cape Lookout, N. C. **91** H24
Cape May, N. J. **73** T5; *64*
Cape Newenham NWR, Alaska **277** M13
Cape Romain NWR, S. C. **141** L16; turtle *142*
Cape Romano, Fla. **125** O14
Cape Sable, Fla. **125** Q16
Cape San Blas, Fla. **125** D6
Capitals, state *26-27*
Capitol Hill, Northern Mariana Islands **285** G19
Capitol Reef NP, Utah **245** P10
Captain Cook, Hawaii **281** N21
Capulin Mountain NM, N. Mex. **215** B14
Caribou, Maine **37** C11
Carlin, Nev. **241** D9; gold mine *242*
Carlisle, Pa. **81** J11
Carlsbad, N. Mex. **215** P13

293

Carlsbad Caverns NP, N. Mex. **215** P12; King's Palace *216-217*
Carneiro, Kans. **179** E11; 178
Carolina, Puerto Rico **285** B15
Carolina Sandhills NWR, S. C. **141** C-D13
Caroline Islands **274**, 289
Carson City, Nev. **241** H1
Carson River, Nev. **241** H3
Carson Sink, Nev. **241** G4
Carters Lake, Ga. **129** B4
Carthage, Miss. **137** J8
Carthage, Mo. **187** N5
Casa Grande NM, Ariz. **211** O9
Cascade, Idaho **233** M3; 235
Cascade Range, Oreg.-Wash. **267** L6; **271** G9; 17, 261, 266, 270; Mount Hood *268;* waterfall *269*
Cascade Reservoir, Idaho **233** M3
Casper, Wyo. **249** H12
Cass Lake, Minn. **183** F6
Cass River, Mich. **155** O15
Castle Rock Lake, Wis. **163** O9
Cataño, Puerto Rico **285** B14
Cataract Lake, Ind. **151** M5
Catawba River, S. C. **141** C10
Catoctin Mountain Park, Md. **69** B12
Catskill Mountains, N. Y. **77** O15
Catskill Park, N. Y. **77** N15
Cattaraugus IR, N. Y. **76** L2
Cave-in-Rock, Ill. 146
Cave Run Lake, Ky. **87** E21
Caves 86, 88, 186, *216-217*, 232; cave-dwelling animals *87;* crystal formations 198
Cayey, Puerto Rico **285** D14
Cecil M. Harden Lake, Ind. **151** L4
Cedar Bluff Reservoir, Kans. **179** D7
Cedar Breaks NM, Utah **245** Q5
Cedar Creek, N. Dak. **195** L5
Cedar Falls, Iowa **175** E12
Cedar Island NWR, N. C. **91** F25
Cedar Keys NWR, Fla. **125** F11
Cedar Point NWR, Ohio **159** C6
Cedar Rapids, Iowa **175** F14
Cedar River, Iowa **175** G15
Celina, Ohio **159** H2
Center Hill Lake, Tenn. **95** C14
Central City, Colo. **229** E10; 228
Central Falls, R. I. **49** C9
Central Valley, Calif. 262
Centralia, Ill. **147** O7
Centralia, Wash. **271** J4
Cerro de Punta, Puerto Rico **285** D11
Chaco Canyon NM, N. Mex. **215** D4
Chaco River, N. Mex. **215** D3
Chalan Kanoa, Northern Mariana Islands **285** J18
Chalmette, La. **133** M15
Chamberlain Lake, Maine **37** F7
Chambersburg, Pa. **81** K10
Champaign, Ill. **147** J9

Champlain, Lake, Canada-U.S. **53** E2; **77** B18; 30, 52, *54*, 78
Chandeleur Sound, La. **133** M19
Chandler, Ariz. **211** N9
Channel Islands, Calif. **263** R7-T10
Channel Islands NM, Calif. **263** R-S9
Chapel Hill, N. C. **91** C16; 90
Chappaquiddick Island, Mass. **41** Q24
Chargoggagoggmanchauga-goggchaubunagungamaugg, Lake (Lake Webster), Mass. **41** J13
Chariton River, Mo. **187** D9
Charles M. Russell NWR, Mont. **237** D13
Charles Mound, Ill. **147** A4
Charles River, Mass. **41** H16; 40, *43*
Charles Town, W. Va. **103** G19; 102
Charleston, S. C. **141** M14; 140, *142-143*
Charleston, W. Va. **103** M5
Charlestown, R. I. **49** O4
Charlotte, N. C. **97** F11
Charlotte Amalie, U. S. Virgin Islands **285** B2
Charlotte Harbor, Fla. **125** M14
Charlottesville, Va. **99** G17
Chassahowitzka NWR, Fla. **125** G12
Chatsworth, N. J. **73** N7; 72
Chattahoochee River, Ala.-Ga. **117** Q13; **129** D6-R3
Chattanooga, Tenn. **95** G16; 96, 97
Chattooga River, S. C. **141** C1
Chautauqua Lake, N. Y. **76** M1
Cheaha Mountain, Ala. **117** G10
Cheat River, W. Va. **103** F12; 102
Chehalis, Wash. **271** J4
Chehalis River, Wash. **271** J4
Chelan, Lake, Wash. **271** E11; *273*
Chelsea, Mass. **41** F19
Chemehuevi IR, Calif. **263** Q17
Cheney Reservoir, Kans. **179** H11
Cherokee IR, N. C. **90** E4
Cherokee Lake, Tenn. **95** B22
Chesapeake, Va. **99** L24
Chesapeake and Delaware Canal, Del.-Md. **65** D2; *66*
Chesapeake Bay, Md.-Va. **69** K18; **99** H24; 68, *70*, 98
Chesapeake Bay Bridge-Tunnel, Va. **99** K25; 98
Chester, Conn. **33** J13
Chester, Pa. **81** L17
Chester River, Md. **69** E22
Chesterfield, S. C. **141** C13
Chesuncook Lake, Maine **37** G7
Cheyenne, Wyo. **249** O16
Cheyenne River, S. Dak. **199** E6
Cheyenne River IR, S. Dak. **199** D7
Chicago, Ill. **147** C11; 25, 146;

beach *149;* fire (1871) 252; immigrants 23; steelmaking 81; world's fair (1893) 146
Chicago Heights, Ill. **147** E11
Chickamauga, Ga. **129** A2
Chickamauga Lake, Tenn. **95** F17
Chickasaw NRA, Okla. **219** M19
Chickasawhay River, Miss. **137** P11
Chicopee, Mass. **40** J8
Chicot, Lake, Ark. **121** P13
Chillicothe, Ohio **159** O8
Chimney Rock, Nebr. **191** E2; 190, *192*
Chincoteague Island, Va. **99** G26
Chinle Wash, Ariz. **211** B14
Chippewa, Lake, Wis. **163** F6
Chippewa Falls, Wis. **163** K5
Chippewa River, Wis. **163** L3
Chiricahua NM, Ariz. **211** R15
Chisos Mountains, Texas **223** M5; *222*
Chocorua, Mount, N. H. **45** L8
Choctaw IR, Miss. **137** J9
Choctaw NWR, Ala. **117** N3
Choctawhatchee River, Fla. **125** A5
Choptank River, Md. **69** H22
Christiansted, U. S. Virgin Islands **285** G4
Chukchi Sea, Arctic Ocean **277** D14
Chula Vista, Calif. **263** U13
Churchill Lake, Maine **37** E7
Cicero, Ill. **147** D10
Cimarron Cutoff, Kans. **179** H3
Cimarron Cutoff, Santa Fe Trail, N. Mex. **215** C14
Cimarron River, Kans.-Okla. **179** J4; **219** E16
Cincinnati, Ohio **159** P3; 158; chemist *161*
Cinnabar Mountain, Idaho **233** Q2
Circle, Alaska **277** G21
Cities 252-259; city planning 254, *255;* planned cities 98, 258, models of *258*, *259;* populations and density 20-21, 23, 286, 288
Civil War 52, 94, 97, 100, 102, 116, 139, 188
Clarence Cannon NWR, Mo. **187** E14
Clarence Rhode NWR, Alaska **227** J13
Clark Fork River, Mont. **237** F3
Clark Hill Lake, Ga.-S. C. **129** E11; **141** G5
Clarksburg, W. Va. **103** G10
Clarksdale, Miss. **137** D4
Clarksville, Tenn. **95** B9
Clear Lake, Calif. **263** G3
Clear Lake, Iowa **175** B9
Clear Lake NWR, Calif. **263** B6
Clearwater, Fla. **125** J12
Clearwater Lake, Mo. **187** N15
Clearwater Mountains, Idaho **233** H-J4
Clearwater River, Idaho **233** G2
Clemson, S. C. **141** C3; 140

Cleveland, Ohio **159** D12; 158; immigrants 23
Cleveland, Tenn. **95** G17
Cleveland Heights, Ohio **159** D12
Clifton, N. J. **73** E9
Clinch River, Tenn.-Va. **95** A22; **98** M4
Clingmans Dome, Tenn. **95** E21
Clinton, Iowa **175** F18
Clinton, Miss. **137** L5
Cloud Peak, Wyo. **249** C10
Clouds *107*, 108, *109*, 110, 112
Clovis, N. Mex. **215** J15
Coal 204-205; bituminous 80, 102; distribution center 158; formation of 89, 202; leading producers 289; lignite 194; reserves 102, 116, 146, 236, 248; steelmaking 56, 80, 81, 116
Coal mining 89, 146; coal cars *105;* coal pit *239;* machinery 86, 102; mines *105, 118;* strip mining 94, 204, land restored *95*
Coamo, Puerto Rico **285** D13
Coast Ranges **263**, **267**, **271**, **277**; 266
Cocoa Beach, Fla. **125** H17
Cody, Wyo. **249** C6
Coeur d'Alene, Idaho **233** D2
Coeur d'Alene IR, Idaho **233** E2
Coffeyville, Kans. **179** K17
Coinage *83*
Coldwater River, Miss. **137** A7
Colfax, Wash. **271** J18
College Park, Md. **69** G15
Colonists and settlers 65, 237; 48, 64, 74, 86, 94, 99, 140, 194, 202, 244, 280, 282; British 98, 100, 101; French 116, 132; French Canadians 132, 174; homesteaders 218, 220; immigrants 23, 40, 124, 158, 178; Pennsylvania Dutch 82; Pilgrims 40, 43; Puritans 32, 48; Russians 178; Spanish 116, 132, 214, 262; *see also* Pioneers
Colorado 25, 228-231; cluster community 258
Colorado NM, Colo. **229** H2
Colorado River **211**, **223**, **229**, **241**, **245**, **263**; 14, 210, 212
Colorado River Aqueduct, Calif. **263** Q17-R12
Colorado River IR, Ariz.-Calif. **211** L2; **263** R17
Colorado Springs, Colo. **229** H12; 228
Columbia, Md. **69** F16; 258
Columbia, Miss. **137** P7
Columbia, Mo. **187** F10
Columbia, S. C. **141** F10
Columbia NWR, Wash. **271** J13
Columbia River, Oreg.-Wash. **267** A2-B13; **271** B17-L2; 234, 266, 269, 270; dams 266, *267*, 270, *271*
Columbus, Ga. **129** K3
Columbus, Ind. **151** N8
Columbus, Miss. **137** F11

Columbus, Nebr. **191** E14
Columbus, Ohio **159** L8; 158
Colville IR, Wash. **271** D14
Colville River, Alaska **277** D18
Combahee River, S. C. **141** N11
Conanicut Island, R. I. **49** L9
Conboy Lake NWR, Wash. **271** M8
Conchas Lake, N. Mex. **215** F13
Concord, Mass. **41** E17; 40
Concord, N. H. **45** Q7
Concord, N.C. **91** E11
Conecuh River, Ala. **117** O9
Conemaugh River, Pa. **81** H5
Congaree Swamp NM, S. C. **141** G11
Connecticut 32-35
Connecticut River **33**, **40**, **45**, **53**; 32, *34*
Connecticut River Valley: tobacco 32, *35*
Connorsville, Ind. **151** L10
Constitution, U. S. 20, 64, 65
Continental Divide **215**, **229**, **233**, **237**, **249**, **277**; 14, 236
Conway, Lake, Ark. **121** H9
Cook Inlet, Alaska **277** M17
Cooper River, S. C. **141** K14
Cooperstown, N. Y. **77** K14
Coos Bay, Oreg. **267** K2; 266
Coosa River, Ala.-Ga. **117** H8; **129** C2
Copper Harbor, Mich. **155** C5
Copper: leading producers 289; mine *239, 247;* mining 157, 210, 214, 236, 244; smelting: slag *213*
Copper River, Alaska **277** K21
Coral reefs 115, 124
Coralville Lake, Iowa **175** G14
Cordillera Central, Puerto Rico **285** D10-13
Corinth, Miss. **137** A11
Corning, N. Y. **77** N7
Corpus Christi, Texas **223** P13
Corvallis, Oreg. **267** F4
Coshocton, Ohio **159** K12
Costa Mesa, Calif. **263** S11
Coulee Dam NRA, Wash. **271** D16
Council Bluffs, Iowa **175** J3
Covington, Ky. **87** A17
Cowboys: branding *223;* cattle drives 178, 180; clothing *233;* gunfights *180*
Cowlitz River, Wash. **271** K7
Crab Orchard Lake, Ill. **147** R7; 148
Crab Orchard NWR, Ill. **147** R7
Cranberry Isles, Maine **37** Q10
Crane Prairie Reservoir, Oreg. **267** J7
Cranston, R. I. **49** F8
Crater Lake, Oreg. **267** L6
Crater Lake NP, Oreg. **267** L6
Crater of Diamonds SP, Ark. **121** M4; 120
Craters of the Moon NM, Idaho **233** P8; 232
Crawfordsville, Ind. **151** J4
Crescent Lake NWR, Nebr. **191** D4
Cripple Creek, Colo. **229** J11
Crisfield, Md. **69** Q22

294

Crops *166-171;* leading 289; and weather 106, *110-111;* corn *166,* 170, *176,* 190, *192,* popcorn *174,* products from *157, 175;* cotton 94, 116, 118, 120, 132, 136, *139,* 140, *168,* 170; peanuts 98, 116, 128, *130,* 168, 171; potatoes 36, *39, 168,* 232, *234-235;* rice 120, 132, 168, 170, 222; soybeans 90, 98, 120, 132, 146, 150; tobacco 32, *35,* 86, *88,* 98, 171, auction 90, *92,* harvest 90; vegetables 50, *74, 265,* 276; wheat 166, 168, 170, 178, *180-181,* 197, 218, processing *167,* products from 197; wild rice 165, *184; see also* Fruit and fruit growing
Cross Creeks NWR, Tenn. **95** B8
Crow Creek IR, S. Dak. **199** G11
Crow IR, Mont. **237** I13
Crow Wing River, Minn. **183** J6
Crown Mountain, U. S. Virgin Islands **285** B2
Crystal Springs, Miss. **137** M5
Culebra, Puerto Rico **285** C20
Culebra NWR, Puerto Rico **285** C19
Cumberland, Md. **68** B5
Cumberland, Lake, Ky. **87** L15
Cumberland Gap, Ky.-Tenn.-Va. **87** M20; **95** A21; **98** M1
Cumberland Island NS, Ga. **129** Q15
Cumberland Mountain, Ky. **87** M21
Cumberland Plateau, Ky.-Tenn. **87, 95**
Cumberland River, Ky.-Tenn. **86-87** K5-L21; **95** B14
Curecanti NRA, Colo. **229** K5
Current River, Mo. **187** M13
Curwood, Mount, Mich. **155** E4
Custer, S. Dak. **199** H2; 198
Custer SP, S. Dak. 198
Cut Bank Valley, Mont. *238-239*
Cuyahoga Falls, Ohio **159** F13
Cuyahoga River, Ohio **159** E13; fire 158
Cuyahoga Valley NRA, Ohio **159** E13
Cypress Swamp, Del. **65** S6

Dahlonega, Ga. **129** B6
Dairy farming 52, 162, *164,* 182, 222; leaders 289
Dale Hollow Lake, Ky.-Tenn. **87** M15; **95** A16
Dallas, Oreg. **267** E4
Dallas, Texas **223** G14
The Dalles, Oreg. **267** C9
Dalton, Ga. **129** A3
Dalton, Mass. **40** E4; 40
Dams 17, 94, 96, *97,* 194, 201; Columbia River 270; diagram *271;* fish ladders *267;* Snake River 234; *see also* Energy
Danbury, Conn. **33** J3
Danby, Vt. **53** P4; quarry *54*
Danville, Ill. **147** J11
Danville, Va. **99** N14

Dardanelle, Lake, Ark. **121** F5
Darien, Conn. **33** N3
Dauphin Island, Ala. **117** U2
Davenport, Iowa **175** H17
Davenport, Wash. **271** F16; 8
Daviess County, Ind. 150
Davis, Mount, Pa. **81** L5
Dawson, Ga. **129** N5; 128
Dayton, Ohio **159** M4; 161
Daytona Beach, Fla. **125** E16
De Gray Lake, Ark. **121** L6
De Kalb, Ill. **147** C8
De Soto Falls, Ga. *131*
Deadwood, S. Dak. **199** F1
Dearborn, Mich. **155** S16; 154, 157
Dearborn Heights, Mich. **155** S15
Death Valley NM, Calif.-Nev. **241** O7; **263** N13; 288
Decatur, Ga. **129** E5
Decatur, Ill. **147** K7
Dedham, Mass. **41** G18
Deep Creek Lake, Md. **68** C2
Deep Creek Range, Utah **245** J2; 244
Deer *16, 142*
Deer Isle, Maine **37** Q9
Deer Park, N. Y. **77** T19
Deerfield, Mass. **40** D8; 40
Defiance, Ohio **159** E3
Delaware 64-67
Delaware, Ohio **159** K8
Delaware and Raritan Canal, N. J. **73** J6
Delaware Bay, Del.-N. J. **65** J6; **73** S4; 64
Delaware Lake, Ohio **159** J8
Delaware Memorial Bridge, Del. 67
Delaware River **65, 73, 77, 81**
Delaware Water Gap NRA, N. J.-Pa. **73** B5; **81** F18
Delmarva Peninsula, Del.-Md.-Va. **65** M3; **69** N23; **99** G26; 64, 68, 98
Delray Beach, Fla. **125** N18
Delta NWR, La. **133** P18
Demopolis, Ala. **117** L4; 119
Denison, Iowa **175** F4
Denton, Texas **223** F13
Denver, Colo. **229** E11; 228, 231
Department of Energy Nevada Test Site, Nev. **241** O8
Derby, Conn. **33** K7
Des Moines, Iowa **175** H9; 174
Des Moines River, Iowa **175** L14
Des Plaines, Ill. **147** C10
Deschutes River, Oreg. **267** E9
Desert NWR, Nev. **241** O10
Deserts *13,* 17, 208, 261, 270; climate *112-113,* 208; plants 14, 210, *217;* wildlife *16,* 17, 210, *241*
Detroit, Mich. **155** S16; 56, 59, 154; salt mine *154*
Detroit Lakes, Minn. **183** J3
Detroit River, Mich. **155** T16; 154
Devils Lake, N. Dak. **195** E14
Devils Postpile NM, Calif. **263** K9

Devils Tower NM, Wyo. **249** B16
Dewey Beach, Del. **65** Q8
Diamond Head, Hawaii **281** F11; *282*
Diamonds 120, *123*
D'Iberville, Miss. **137** S10
Dickson Mounds, Ill. **147** H5
Dillon, Mont. **237** K6; 236
Dillon Lake, Ohio **159** L11
Dillon Reservoir, Colo. **229** F9
Dinosaur NM, Colo.-Utah **229** B-C2; **245** F15; 244, *246*
Dinosaur SP, Conn. **33** F11
Dirty Devil River, Utah **245** O11
Disneyland, Calif. **263** S11
District of Columbia *see* Washington, D. C.
Dixville Notch, N. H. **45** D8
Dodge City, Kans. **179** H6; 178, Front Street *180*
Dolores River, Colo. **229** L1
Donner Pass, Calif. **263** G7; 262
Door Peninsula, Wis. **163** K16; cherry harvest *165*
Dothan, Ala. **117** Q12
Douglas Lake, Tenn. **95** C22
Dover, Del. **65** J4
Dover, N. H. **45** Q10
Downers Grove, Ill. **147** D10
Driskill Mountain, La. **133** C5
Drought: crop damage 106, *111*
Drummond, Lake, Va. **99** M23
Drummond Island, Mich. **155** G14
Dry Tortugas, Fla. **125** S12
Du Bay, Lake, Wis. **163** L10
Du Quoin, Ill. **147** Q7; 149
Dubuque, Iowa **175** D17; 174
Duck River, Tenn. **95** D9
Duck Valley IR, Idaho-Nev. **233** S3; **241** A8
Duckwater IR, Nev. **241** J9
Duluth, Minn. **183** J12; 182
Durango, Colo. **229** N4; 228, 231
Durham, N. C. **91** C16; 90
Dust Bowl era 18, 218
Dust storms 240
Dworshak Reservoir, Idaho **233** F4

Eagle, Alaska **277** H22
Eagle Mountain, Minn. **183** E15
Earthquakes 94, 236, 262
East Chicago, Ind. **151** B3
East Cleveland, Ohio **159** D12
East Cote Blanche Bay, La. **133** O10
East Detroit, Mich. **155** S16
East Fork White River, Ind. **151** P7
East Hartford, Conn. **33** E11
East Lansing, Mich. **155** R13
East Lyme, Conn. **33** J15
East Okoboji Lake, Iowa **175** A5
East Orange, N. J. **73** F9
East Point, Ga. **129** F5
East Providence, R. I. **49** E9
East Ridge, Tenn. **95** G16
East St. Louis, Ill. **147** O4

Eastern Neck NWR, Md. **69** G20
Eastern Shore, Md.-Va. 68, 98
Easton, Md. **69** J21
Easton, Pa. **81** G18
Eastport, Maine **37** M15; fishermen *39*
Eau Claire, Wis. **163** K5
Eau Claire River, Wis. **163** K11
Edgartown, Mass. **41** P23
Edisto River, S. C. **141** K11
Edmonds, Wash. **271** E6
Educational institutions 40, 90, 186, 236
Edwards Plateau, Texas **223** K8; 222
Eel River, Calif. **263** D2
Eel River, Ind. **151** L4
Effigy Mounds NM, Iowa **175** B15; 174
El Cajon, Calif. **263** U13
El Centro, Calif. **263** T15
El Dorado, Ark. **121** Q7
El Morro NM, N. Mex. **215** G3
El Paso, Texas **223** H1
El Vado Reservoir, N. Mex. **215** B7
Elbert, Mount, Colo. **229** G8
Electricity 202, 205; power plants 204, 254; *see also* Energy
Elephant Butte Reservoir, N. Mex. **215** M6
Eleven Point River, Mo. **187** O12; 186
Elgin, Ill. **147** C9
Elizabeth, N. J. **73** G9
Elizabeth City, N. C. **91** B25
Elizabeth Islands, Mass. **41** P21
Elizabethton, Tenn. **95** B25
Elk 249
Elk Lake, Mich. **155** L11
Elk River, Kans. **179** J16
Elk River, Tenn. **95** G11
Elk River, W. Va. **103** K8
Elkhart, Ind. **151** B8; band instruments *153*
Elkhorn Peak, Idaho **233** P13
Elkhorn River, Nebr. **191** C13
Elko, Nev. **241** D9
Elmhurst, Ill. **147** C10
Elmira, N. Y. **77** N8
Elwell, Lake, Mont. **237** C8
Ely, Minn. **183** E12
Elyria, Ohio **159** E11
Emporia, Kans. **179** F16
Energy 202-207; geothermal 204, 216; hot springs 204, 232; hydroelectric power 17, 38, 76, 94, 96, 140, 194, 204, 218, 270, 271; natural gas 218, 236; nuclear power 94, *96,* 204, 214, 270; resources **204;** use *203, 205;* water power 36, 202; windmills *49, 99,* 124, *192-193,* 194, 204; *see also* Coal; Dams; Electricity; Oil industry; Solar energy
Enfield, Conn. **33** B11
Enid, Okla. **219** E17
Enid Lake, Miss. **137** D7
Enka, N. C. **90** E5; textile mill *92*

Enterprise, Ala. **117** P10; 116
Equinox, Mount, Vt. **53** Q3
Erie, Pa. **81** A3; 80
Erie, Lake **76, 81, 155, 159;** 158; algae *256;* depth 145; pollution 158; *see also* Great Lakes
Erie Canal, N. Y. **77** J7, *147;* 76
Erie NWR, Pa. **81** C3
Erling, Lake, Ark. **121** Q4
Erosion 12, 50, 94, 140, *178,* 197, 201, *246-247,* 250, *257;* coastal 266, *269;* control 88, *95, 250*
Escalante River, Utah **245** Q9
Escanaba, Mich. **155** H7
Escanaba River, Mich. **155** G6
Eskimos 276
Essex, Md. **69** E18
Estuary 70
Euclid, Ohio **159** D13
Eufaula, Okla. **219** J24; 218
Eufaula Lake, Okla. **219** J24
Eufaula NWR, Ala.-Ga. **117** M13; **129** M3
Eugene, Oreg. **267** H4; 266
Eureka, Calif. **263** D2
Eureka, Mont. **237** B2; 236
Eureka Springs, Ark. **121** B4; 120
Evans, Mount, Colo. **229** F10
Evanston, Ill. **147** C10
Evansville, Ind. **151** T2
Everett, Wash. **271** E6; 270
Everett, Mount, Mass. **40** J1
Everglades NP, Fla. **125** P16; 124, *126-127,* 252
Explorers and discoverers 6, 50, 131, 279, 280

Fairbanks, Alaska **277** H20
Fairfax, Va. **99** C20; 98
Fairfield, Conn. **33** M5
Falcon Reservoir, Texas **223** Q11
Fall River, Kans. **179** H16
Fall River, Mass. **41** N18
Fallon IR, Nev. **241** H4
Falmouth, Maine **37** R4
Falmouth, Mass. **41** O22
Fargo, N. Dak. **195** J19
Faribault, Minn. **183** R9
Farm machinery 166, 171, 180, *192,* 194, *199, 234-235;* cherry pickers *165,* 171; combines *176, 178, 197*
Farmington, Conn. **33** E9
Farmington, N. Mex. **215** B3
Fayetteville, Ark. **121** C3
Fayetteville, N. C. **91** G17
Feather River, Calif. **263** G5
Felsenthal NWR, Ark. **121** Q9
Fergus Falls, Minn. **183** K3
Ferguson, Mo. **187** G16
Fern Ridge Lake, Oreg. **267** H4
Ferndale, Wash. **271** B6; 270
Findlay, Ohio **159** F6
Finger Lakes, N. Y. **77** K8
Fire Island NS, N. Y. **77** T20
First Connecticut Lake, N. H. **45** B8
Fish *125, 127,* 136; leading

295

289; salmon *156, 272, 278,* migration 266, 267; shellfish *51, 69, 70,* 135
Fish Springs NWR, Utah **245** J4
Fishing industry 36, *39,* 42, 51, 68, 69, *70,* 135, 276, 278; fish farms 136, *272;* leaders 289
Fitchburg, Mass. **41** D13
Flagstaff, Ariz. **211** G9
Flagstaff Lake, Maine **37** L4
Flambeau River, Wis. **163** G6
Flaming Gorge NRA, Utah–Wyo. **245** E13; **249** O4
Flaming Gorge Reservoir, Utah **245** E14
Flathead IR, Mont. **237** E3
Flathead Lake, Mont. **237** D3
Flathead River, Mont. **237** B3
Flint, Mich. **155** Q14
Flint Hills, Kans. **179** H15; 178
Flint Hills NWR, Kans. **179** F16
Flint River, Ga. **129** P5
Flint River, Mich. **155** Q15
Floods 136, 254; control 96, 194, 254
Florence, Ala. **117** B4
Florence, S. C. **141** E15
Florida 14, 25, 124-127, 131, 171; freeze (1977) *111;* thunderstorms 112
Florida, Straits of, Fla. **125** S17
Florida Bay, Fla. **125** R16
Florida Keys, Fla. **125** R17; 115, 124
Florissant, Mo. **187** G16
Florissant Fossil Beds NM, Colo. **229** H10
Fond du Lac, Wis. **163** O13
Fond du Lac IR, Minn. **183** J11
Fontana Lake, N. C. **90** E2
Food consumption 166
Food processing 154; dairy products 162, *164;* fish 276; fruit 124, 266, 269; maple syrup 52, *55;* meat *149,* 190, *192;* peanuts 128; vegetables 74, 174, 232, *265,* 266; wheat *167*
Foraker, Mount, Alaska **277** J18
Ford Motor Company: assembly plant 154, *157*
Forest products 38, *130,* 266; leading producers 289; furniture 90; plywood *269;* rayon 98; *see also* Papermaking
Forests 190, 248, 253, 255, 264, 270; areas of U. S. 288; coniferous 14; deciduous *13,* 15; fires 236, 252, 266; vegetation zones *45*
Fort Apache IR, Ariz. **211** L13
Fort Belknap IR, Mont. **237** C12
Fort Benton, Mont. **237** D9; county fair *238*
Fort Berthold IR, N. Dak. **195** F6; *196-197*
Fort Cobb Reservoir, Okla. **219** J15
Fort Collins, Colo. **229** C11; 228
Fort Dodge, Iowa **175** E7

Fort Gibson Lake, Okla. **219** F25
Fort Hall IR, Idaho **233** Q11
Fort Knox, Ky. **87** G12
Fort Lauderdale, Fla. **125** N18; 124
Fort McDermitt IR, Nev.–Oreg. **241** A6; *267* O16
Fort Madison, Iowa **175** L15
Fort Mojave IR, Ariz.–Calif. **211** G2; **263** P16
Fort Morgan, Colo. **229** D14
Fort Myers, Fla. **125** M14
Fort Peck Dam, Mont. **237** C15
Fort Peck Lake, Mont. **237** D15
Fort Peck IR, Mont. **237** B16
Fort Pierce, Fla. **125** K18
Fort Randall Dam, S. Dak. **199** K13
Fort Scott, Kans. **179** G19
Fort Smith, Ark. **121** F2; 120
Fort Totten IR, N. Dak. **195** E14
Fort Union NM, N. Mex. **215** E11
Fort Wayne, Ind. **151** E10
Fort Worth, Texas **223** G13
Fort Yates, N. Dak. **195** M9
Foss Reservoir, Okla. **219** H12
Fossil Butte NM, Wyo. **249** L1
Fossils 72, 198, 240, 244, *246*
Four Corners, Utah **245** T15
Four Corners area 228
Fox River, Ill.–Wis. **147** E8; **163** N11
Foxfire 128
Framingham, Mass. **41** G16
Francis, Lake, N. H. **45** C8
Francis Case, Lake, S. Dak. **199** J12
Franconia Notch, N. H.: bridge *47*
Francs Peak, Wyo. **249** E5
Frankfort, Ind. **151** H6
Frankfort, Ky. **87** E16
Franklin, Ind. **151** M7
Franklin, Tenn. **95** D11
Franklin Delano Roosevelt Lake, Wash. **271** D16
Frederick, Md. **69** D13
Fredericksburg, Va. **99** E20
Frederiksted, U. S. Virgin Islands **285** H3
Freedom Trail, Boston, Mass. 40
Freeman, Lake, Ind. **151** G5
Freeport, Ill. **147** B6
Freeport, Maine **37** R5
Fremont, Mich. **155** P9; 154
Fremont, Ohio **159** E7
Fremont River, Utah **245** O9
French Broad River, N. C. **90** F5
Frenchman Bay, Maine **37** O11
Fresno, Calif. **263** M8
Frissell, Mount, Conn. **33** A3
Frogs, voiceless kissing 232
Front Royal, Va. **99** C17; 98
Fruit and fruit growing *39,* 130, 154, 158, *165,* 168, 171, *265;* leaders 289; apples 52, *78, 100,* 102, *272;* citrus 124, *127,* freeze *111;* cranberries *42,* 168; peaches 90, 128, 130, 140; pineapples 280, *283;* strawberries *168, 269*
Fulton, Mo. **187** G11

Gadsden, Ala. **117** E10
Gaffney, S. C. **141** A7
Gaillard, Lake, Conn. **33** K10
Gainesville, Fla. **125** D13
Gainesville, Ga. **129** C7
Galesburg, Ill. **147** F4
Galilee, R. I. **49** O7; 51
Gallatin, Tenn. **95** B12
Gallup, N. Mex. **215** F2; 216
Galveston, Texas **223** M17
Galveston Bay, Texas 222
Gannett Peak, Wyo. **249** G4
Garden Grove, Calif. **263** S11
Gardner, Mass. **41** D12
Garfield Heights, Ohio **159** D12
Garland, Texas **223** F14
Garrison Dam, N. Dak. **195** G8; 194
Gary, Ind. **151** C3; steelmaking 81, 150
Gary, W. Va. **103** Q5; coal cars *105*
Gas, natural: leading producers 289; *see also* Energy
Gasconade River, Mo. **187** K11
Gaston, Lake, N. C.–Va. **91** A19; **99** M18
Gastonia, N. C. **91** F10
Gateway NRA, N. J.–N. Y. **73** H10; **77** T17
Gatlinburg, Tenn. **95** D21
Gavins Point Dam, S. Dak. **199** L16
Geist Reservoir, Ind. **151** K8
Genesee River, N. Y. **77** J5
Geneva, N. Y. **77** K8
Geographical centers: contiguous 48 states **179** A10; 50 states **199** D1; North America **195** C11
Geology 10, 12; coal formation 89, 202; historical 198, 208, 214, 244, ancient seas 12, 173, 197, 214; marble formation 54; mountain formation 18-19, 114, 172, 186, 272, 280, erosion 247, 250; rock layers *89, 197,* 200; *see also* Glaciers; Landforms; Volcanoes
George, Lake, Fla. **125** E15
George, Lake, N. Y. **77** F18
Georgetown, S. C. **141** J16; 140
Georgia 128-131, 168, 171; Indians 126
Geothermal energy *see* Energy
Gettysburg, Pa. **81** L11
Gila Cliff Dwellings NM, N. Mex. **215** M3
Gila River, Ariz.–N. Mex. **211** O3-15; **215** O2
Gila River IR, Ariz. **211** N8
Gilbert, Minn. **183** F11; 185
Glacier Bay NM, Alaska **277** N24
Glacier NP, Mont. **237** B4; 236, *238-239*
Glacier Peak, Wash. **271** D9
Glaciers *278;* Ice Age 19, 30, 42, 145, 146, 148, 162, 182, 238, 272, Great Lakes 151
Glass Mountains, Okla. **219** E14; 218

Glastonbury, Conn. **33** E11
Glen Canyon NRA, Ariz.–Utah **211** B10; **245** R10
Glen Cove, N. Y. **77** S18
Glendale, Ariz. **211** M8
Glendale, Calif. **263** R11
Glendo Reservoir, Wyo. **249** J16
Glens Falls, N. Y. **77** H17
Gloucester, Mass. **41** C21
Gnaw Bone, Ind. **151** N7; 152
Gogebic, Lake, Mich. **155** F2
Gogebic Range, Mich. **155** E1
Gold mining 198, 228, *229,* 236, 240, 242; leading producers 289; panning *229;* refining *200,* 242
Gold rush 198, 228, 236, 262
Golden, Colo. **229** E10
Goldsboro, N. C. **91** E19
Goose Creek, S. C. **141** L14
Goose Lake, Calif.–Oreg. **263** A7; **267** O10
Gore Mountain, Vt. **53** B11
Goshen, Ind. **151** C8
Goshute IR, Nev.–Utah **241** G12; **245** J2
Graham, Mount, Ariz. **211** P14
Gran Quivira NM, N. Mex **215** K9
Granby, Lake, Colo. **229** D9
Grand Canyon, Ariz. **211** C7; 17, *212,* 232, 288
Grand Canyon NP, Ariz. **211** D8
Grand Coulee Dam, Wash. **271** E14; 270, *271*
Grand Forks, N. Dak. **195** E18
Grand Island, N. Dak. **155** F8
Grand Isle, La. **133** P15
Grand Isle County, Vt. 52
Grand Junction, Colo. **229** G2
Grand Lake, La. **133** N6
Grand Lake, Maine **37** L12
Grand Lake, Ohio **159** J3
Grand Portage IR, Minn. **183** E17
Grand Prairie, Texas **223** G13
Grand Rapids, Mich. **155** Q10; 154
Grand River, Mich. **155** Q12
Grand River, Mo. **187** C6
Grand River, S. Dak. **199** B6
Grand Teton NP, Wyo. **249** E2; *250-251*
Grand Traverse Bay, Mich. **155** K10
Grandview, Mo. **187** G4
Granite Peak, Mont. **237** K10
Grants, N. Mex. **215** G4; 214
Grants Pass, Oreg. **267** N4
Grasslands *13,* 15, 18, 168, 173, *179,* 194; Bluegrass 86, *88*
Grave Peak, Idaho **233** G6
Great Basin, Nev. **241** F8
Great Bay, N. H. **45** R10
Great Bay, N. J. **73** Q8
Great Bend, Kans. **179** E9
Great Dismal Swamp, N. C. **91** A24
Great Dismal Swamp NWR, Va. **99** M23
Great Divide Basin, Wyo. **249** M8

Great Egg Harbor River, N. J. **73** P5
Great Falls, Mont. **237** E8
Great Lakes 144-145; fish *156;* formation of *151;* shipping 80, 146, *147,* 182, *185*
Great Miami River, Ohio **159** K4
Great Quittacas Pond, Mass. **41** M20
Great River Road **147,** *163,* **175, 183,** *187*
Great Sacandaga Lake, N. Y. **77** J16
Great Salt Lake, Utah **245** D6; *246*
Great Salt Lake Desert, Utah **245** C4-G3; 244
Great Salt Plains Lake, Okla. **219** C16
Great Sand Dunes NM, Colo. **229** M10
Great Serpent Mound, Ohio **159** P6; *160*
Great Smoky Mountains, N. C.–Tenn. 19, 90, 94; trail *92;* waterfalls *96*
Great Smoky Mountains NP, N. C.–Tenn. **90** D3; **95** E20; 19
Great Stone Face, N. H. *46*
Great Swamp NWR, N. J. **73** F7
Great White Heron NWR, Fla. **125** R15
Greeley, Colo. **229** C12
Green Bank, W. Va. **103** L12
Green Bay, Mich. **155** J7
Green Bay, Wis. **163** L14
Green Bay, Wis. **163** K15; waterskiers *165*
Green Mountains, Vt. **53** B8-U4; 30, 52
Green River, Utah–Wyo. **245** H13-M12; **249** L3
Green River Lake, Ky. **87** J15
Green Swamp, N. C. **91** K18
Greenbrier River, W. Va. **103** P8
Greeneville, Tenn. **95** B23
Greenfield, Mass. **40** C8
Greensboro, N. C. **91** C14; 90
Greenville, Miss. **137** G3
Greenville, N. C. **91** D21
Greenville, S. C. **141** B4; 140
Greenwich, Conn. **33** O2
Greenwood, Miss. **137** F5
Greenwood, S. C. **141** F6
Greenwood, Lake, S. C. **141** E6
Greers Ferry Lake, Ark. **121** F10
Greeson, Lake, Ark. **121** L4
Grenada Lake, Miss. **137** E7
Gretna, La. **133** M15
Greylock, Mount, Mass. **40** D3
Griffin, Ga. **129** G5
Groton, Conn. **33** K16; 35
Guadalupe Mountains NP, Texas **223** H3
Guadalupe Peak, Texas **223** H3
Guadalupe River, Texas **223** M13
Guam **274, 285** S17; 274, 284, 289
Guayama, Puerto Rico **285** E14

Guaynabo, Puerto Rico **285** B14
Gulf Islands NS, Fla.–Miss. **125** C2; **137** T10
Gulfport, Miss. **137** S9
Gunnison River, Colo. **229** H3
Gunpowder River, Md. **69** C17
Guyandotte River, W. Va. **103** N3

Hackensack, N. J. **73** E9
Haddonfield, N. J. **73** M4; 72
Hagerstown, Md. **69** B11
Haleakala Crater, Hawaii **281** G19
Haleakala NP, Hawaii **281** G19
Hallandale, Fla. **125** O18
Halsey, Nebr. **191** D9; 190
Hamden, Conn. **33** J8
Hamilton, Ohio **159** O3
Hammonasset Point, Conn. **33** L12
Hammond, Ind. **151** C3; steel mill *152*
Hampton, Va. **99** K24; 98
Hampton Harbor Inlet, N. H. **45** T10
Hampton Roads, Va. **99** K24; 98
Hanalei Bay, Hawaii **280** B4
Hancock, Md. **69** A8
Hanford Works, Wash. **271** K13; 270
Hannibal, Mo. **187** C13; 186
Hanover, Pa. **81** L12
Harlingen, Texas **223** R13
Harney Basin, Oreg. **267** K11
Harney Lake, Oreg. **267** K13
Harney Peak, S. Dak. **199** H2
Harpers Ferry, W. Va. *7*, **103** G19; *6*
Harris Neck NWR, Ga. **129** N15
Harrisburg, Pa. **81** J12
Harrisonburg, Va. **99** E15
Harrodsburg, Ky. **87** G16
Harry S. Truman Lake, Mo. **187** J6
Hart Mountain National Antelope Range, Oreg. **267** M12
Hartford, Conn. **33** E10; 32
Hartwell Lake, Ga.–S. C. **129** C9; **141** D3
Harvey, Ill. **147** D10
Hastings, Nebr. **191** H12
Hatchie NWR, Tenn. **94** F4
Hatchie River, Tenn. **94** E3
Hattiesburg, Miss. **137** P8
Havasu, Lake, Ariz. **211** J2
Havasu NWR, Ariz. **211** H2
Havasupai IR, Ariz. **211** D7
Haverhill, Mass. **41** B18
Hawaii **274**; 70, 275, 280-283
Hawaii (island), Hawaii **281** K25; 280
Hawaii Volcanoes NP, Hawaii **281** N23
Hays, Kans. **179** D8
Haystack Mountain, Vt. **53** T4
Hayward, Calif. **263** K5
Hazard, Ky. **87** J22
Hazleton, Pa. **81** F15
Heart River, N. Dak. **195** J5

Hebgen Lake, Mont. **237** L8
Helena, Mont. **237** G7
Hells Canyon, Idaho–Oreg. **233** K2; **267** D18; *232, 288*
Hempstead, N. Y. **77** T18
Henderson, Ky. **86** G7
Henderson, Nev. **241** R10
Henderson, N. C. **91** B18
Hershey, Pa. **81** J13; *80*
"Hexahedron" (model city) *259*
Hialeah, Fla. **125** O18
Hibbing, Minn. **183** G10; *182*
Hickory, N.C. **91** D9; *90*
Higgins Lake, Mich. **155** M12
High Plains, Kans. **179** D4-F3
High Point, N. J. **73** A6
High Point, N. C. **91** C13; *90*
High Rock Lake, N. C. **91** D12
Highland, Ind. **151** C2
Highland Park, Ill. **147** B10
Highways and roads *138, 139, 150, 240, 255, 266*; freeways *257, 262*; pioneer trails *20, 138, 139, 150, 190, 218, 237, 266*; toll roads *72, 76, 80*
Hillside NWR, Miss. **137** H5
Hilo, Hawaii **281** M25
Hilton Head Island, S. C. **141** P11
Hingham, Mass. **41** G20
Hiwassee Lake, N. C. **90** F1
Hiwassee River, Tenn. **95** F18
Hobart, Ind. **151** C3
Hobbs, N. Mex. **215** O16
Hoboken, N. J. **73** F10
Hocking River, Ohio **159** N11
Hoh River, Wash. **271** E2; valley *270*
Hole in the Wall, Wyo. **249** G12
Holla Bend NWR, Ark. **121** G6
Holland, Mich. **155** R9
Hollywood, Calif. **263** R11
Hollywood, Fla. **125** O18
Holyoke, Mass. **40** H8
Homestake Gold Mine, S. Dak. **199** F1; *198, 200, 242*
Homesteading *190, 218, 220, 258*
Homochitto River, Miss. **137** O3
Honokaa, Hawaii **281** K23
Honolulu, Hawaii **281** E11; *282*
Hood, Mount, Oreg. **267** D7; *268*
Hoopa Valley IR, Calif. **263** C2
Hoover Dam, Ariz.–Nev. **211** D2; **241** R12
Hoover Reservoir, Ohio **159** K8
Hopatcong, Lake, N. J. **73** D6
Hopewell, Va. **99** J21
Hopi IR, Ariz. **211** E12
Hoquiam, Wash. **271** H2
Horicon NWR, Wis. **163** P12
Horsehead Lake, N. Dak. **195** H12
Horses: breeds *53*; horse farms *71, 86, 88-89*; wild horses *243*
Horseshoe Point, Fla. **125** E10
Hot springs *see* Thermal springs
Hot Springs, Ark. **121** K6; *120*
Hot Springs, Va. **99** G12
Hot Springs NP, Ark. **121** K6
Houghton Lake, Mich. **155** M12

Houma, La. **133** O13
Housatonic River, Conn.–Mass. **33** J5; **40** H2
Houses *22-23, 138, 212, 255*; energy use *203*; adobe *214, 217*; cliff dwellings *230, 231*; colonial *101*; hogans *212*; log cabins *64, 86*; sod *194*; stone *220*
Houston, Texas **223** L16; *222*
Houston Ship Channel, Texas *222*
Hovenweep NM, Colo.–Utah **229** N1; **245** R15
Hualapai IR, Ariz. **211** E5
Hubbard Lake, Mich. **155** L14
Hudson River, N. Y. **77** N17; **147**; *76*
Hugo Lake, Okla. **219** N24
Humboldt Lake, Nev. **241** F4
Humboldt River, Nev. **241** D7
Humphreys Peak, Ariz. **211** G9
Hungry Horse Reservoir, Mont. **237** C4
Huntington, Ind. **151** F9
Huntington, W. Va. **103** L2
Huntington Lake, Ind. **151** F10
Huntsville, Ala. **117** B8; space museum *117*
Huron, Lake, **155** L15; depth *145; see also* Great Lakes
Hurricanes *112, 116, 136*; control project *112-113*
Hutchinson, Kans. **179** G11; grain elevator *181*
Hyannis, Mass. **41** N25
Hyde Park, N. Y. **77** O17
Hydroelectric power *see* Energy; Dams

Idaho *17, 226, 232-235*
Idaho Falls, Idaho **233** P11; *232*
Iliamna Lake, Alaska **277** M16
Illinois *146-149, 254*
Illinois and Mississippi Canal, Ill. **147** E5
Illinois River, Ill. **147** J4
Illinois River, Oreg. **267** N3
Illinois Waterway **147**, *148*
Imperial NWR, Ariz.–Calif. **211** N1; **263** T17
Imperial Valley, Calif. **263** T15; *262, 265*
Independence, Kans. **179** J17
Independence, Mo. **187** F4
Indian Lake, Ohio **159** J5
Indian River Bay, Del. **65** R7-8
Indiana *150-153*
Indiana Dunes NL, Ind. **151** B4; *150*
Indianapolis, Ind. **151** L7; *150, 152*
Indians *102, 104, 178, 182, 192, 197, 198, 200, 218, 240, 262*; ancient peoples *157, 160, 174, 190, 230*; cliff dwellings *231*; harvesting rice *184*; hunter *164*; mounds *160*; peace pipes *182, 184*; rodeo *216*; sports *138*; totem pole *278*; tribal costume *126*; tribal dance *221*; tribes *17, 94, 165, 198, 200,*

210, 213, 214, 217, 218, 244, 276
International Falls, Minn. **183** C9
Inventors and inventions *32, 33, 48, 56, 59, 60-61, 150, 161*; flying machine *91*; light bulb *202*; steam engine *202*
Iowa *171, 174-177, 190*; prairie *13*
Iowa City, Iowa **175** H15
Iowa IR, Kans.–Nebr. **179** A17; **191** J19
Iowa River, Iowa **175** G12
Ipswich, Mass. **41** C20
Iron Mountain, Mich. **155** H5
Iroquois NWR, N. Y. **76** J4
Irrigation *170, 194, 210, 234, 240, 262, 265, 270, 271, 272*; wells *178*
Irving, Texas **223** G14
Irvington, N. J. **73** F8
Isle Au Haut, Maine **37** Q9
Isle La Motte, Vt. **53** B2
Isle of Palms, S. C. **141** M15
Isle Royale, Mich. **155** B3
Isle Royale NP, Mich. **155** B2; *156, 157*
Isles of Shoals, N. H. **45** S12
Isleta IR, N. Mex. **215** H6
Istokpoga, Lake, Fla. **125** K15
Itasca, Lake, Minn. **183** G5; *182*
Ithaca, N. Y. **77** M9

J. N. "Ding" Darling NWR, Fla. **125** N14
J. Percy Priest Lake, Tenn. **95** C12
Jackson, Mich. **155** S13
Jackson, Miss. **137** L5; *136*
Jackson, Tenn. **94** E5
Jackson Hole, Wyo. *249*
Jackson Lake, Wyo. **249** E2
Jacksonville, Ark. **121** J10
Jacksonville, Fla. **125** B14
Jacksonville, Ill. **147** K4
Jacksonville, N. C. **91** G21
James River, N. Dak.–S. Dak. **195** K15; **199** D13
James River, Va. **99** H16; *98, 100*
Jamestown, N. Dak. **195** J14
Jamestown, N. Y. **76** N1
Jamestown, Va. **99** K22; *98*; reconstruction *101*
Janesville, Wis. **163** S11
Jay Peak, Vt. **53** B7
Jefferson, Mount, Oreg. **267** F7
Jefferson City, Mo. **187** H10
Jefferson River, Mont. **237** H7
Jeffersonville, Ind. **151** R9
Jekyll Island, Ga. **129** P15
Jennings, Mo. **187** G16
Jerimoth Hill, R. I. **49** D2
Jersey City, N. J. **73** F10
Jewel Cave NM, S. Dak. **199** H1; *198*
Jicarilla Apache IR, N. Mex. **215** C6
Jocassee, Lake, S. C. **141** B2
John Day River, Oreg. **267** E10

John F. Kennedy Space Center, Fla. **125** G17
John H. Kerr Reservoir, N. C. **91** A18
John Martin Reservoir, Colo. **229** L16
John Pennekamp Coral Reef SP, Fla. **125** Q19
John Redmond Reservoir, Kans. **179** F17
Johnson City, Tenn. **95** B25
Johnston, R. I. **49** E7
Johnston Atoll, Pacific Ocean **274**; *289*
Johnstown, Pa. **81** J6
Joliet, Ill. **147** E10; nail factory *149*
Jonesboro, Ark. **121** D15
Joplin, Mo. **187** N4
Jordan River, Utah **245** F7
Jornada del Muerto, N. Mex. **215** M6
Joshua Tree NM, Calif. **263** R15
Juan de Fuca, Strait of, Wash. **271** D2
Julesburg, Colo. **229** A18
Junction City, Kans. **179** D14
Juneau, Alaska **277** N25
Juniata River, Pa. **81** H10

Kahoolawe, Hawaii **281** J17
Kaibab IR, Ariz. **211** A7
Kailua, Hawaii **281** N20
Kailua, Oahu, Hawaii **281** E11
Kalamazoo, Mich. **155** S10; *154*
Kalamazoo River, Mich. **155** S10
Kalispell, Mont. **237** C3
Kamakou, Hawaii **281** F15
Kanab, Utah **245** S6
Kanab Creek, Ariz.–Utah **211** B7; **245** S6
Kanawha River, W. Va. **103** K4; *102*
Kaneohe, Hawaii **281** E11
Kankakee River, Ill.–Ind. **147** F10; **151** D3
Kannapolis, N. C. **91** E11
Kansas *178-181*
Kansas City, Kans. **179** C19
Kansas City, Mo. **187** F4; *186, 189*
Kansas River, Kans. **179** C15
Kaskaskia River, Ill. **147** N7
Katahdin, Mount, Maine **37** H9; *30, 36*
Katmai NM, Alaska **277** N16
Kauai, Hawaii **280** B5; *280*
Kaukauna, Wis. **163** M13
Kaw Lake, Okla. **219** C20
Kearney, Nebr. **191** G11
Kearns, Utah **245** F7
Keene, N. H. **45** S3
Kelleys Island, Ohio **159** D9
Kellogg, Idaho **233** D3; silver mine *232*; smelter *235*
Kenai National Moose Range, Alaska **277** M18
Kennebec River, Maine **37** K5; log drives *36, 38-39*
Kenner, La. **133** M14
Kennett Square, Pa. **81** L16
Kennewick, Wash. **271** L14

297

Kenosha, Wis. **163** S15
Kent, Ohio **159** F13
Kent Island, Md. **69** H19
Kenton, Okla. **218** B1; 220
Kentucky 86-89; coal 102
Kentucky Lake, Ky.–Tenn. **86** M6; **94** B7
Kentucky River, Ky. **87** G20
Kentwood, Mich. **155** Q10
Keokuk, Iowa **175** M15
Keowee, Lake, S. C. **141** C2
Kern River, Calif. **263** N10
Keshena, Wis. **163** K12
Ketchikan, Alaska **277** Q27
Ketchum, Idaho **233** O7
Kettering, Ohio **159** M4
Keweenaw Peninsula, Mich. **155** D4
Key Largo, Fla. **125** Q18
Key West, Fla. **125** S15
Key West NWR, Fla. **125** S14
Keystone Lake, Okla. **219** F21
Kiamichi River, Okla. **219** L25
Kiawah Island, S. C. **141** N14
Kickapoo IR, Kans. **179** A17
Kiholo Bay, Hawaii **281** L21
Kilauea Crater, Hawaii **281** N24
Killcohock NWR, N. J. **73** P1
Killeen, Texas **223** J13
Killington Peak, Vt. **53** N5; 52
King Ranch, Texas 222, 225; brand 223
Kings Canyon NP, Calif. **263** L10
Kings Peak, Utah **245** E12
Kings River, Calif. **263** M8
Kingsley Dam, Nebr. **191** F6
Kingsport, Tenn. **95** A24; 94
Kingston, N. Y. **77** O17
Kingston, R. I. **49** M6
Kingsville, Texas **223** P13
Kinston, N. C. **91** F21
Kirkland, Wash. **271** F6
Kirksville, Mo. **187** B9
Kirkwood, Mo. **187** H16
Kirwin NWR, Kans. **179** B8
Kissimmee, Lake, Fla. **125** J15
Kissimmee River, Fla. **125** K16
Kitt Peak National Observatory, Ariz. **211** R9
Kittatinny Mountains, N. J. **73** D4
Kitts Hammock, Del. **65** K5; 66
Kitty Hawk, N. C. **91** B26; 91
Klamath Falls, Oreg. **267** N7
Klamath Mountains, Calif. **263** C3
Klamath River, Calif.–Oreg. **263** B3; **267** O7
Knoxville, Tenn. **95** C20; 94
Kobuk River, Alaska **277** E17
Koch Peak, Mont. **237** K8
Kodiak, Alaska **277** N17
Kodiak Island, Alaska **277** O17
Kodiak NWR, Alaska **277** O17
Kofa Game Range, Ariz. **211** N3
Kokomo, Ind. **151** H7; 150
Kootenai River, Mont. **237** B2
Koshkonong, Lake, Wis. **163** R11
Kotzebue Sound, Alaska **277** F15

Koyukuk River, Alaska **277** F18
Kure Island, Hawaii 280
Kuskokwim Mountains, Alaska **277** H17-L14
Kuskokwim River, Alaska **277** K15
Kutztown, Pa. **81** H16; 82

La Crosse, Wis. **163** O5
La Grange, Ga. **129** H3
La Porte, Ind. **151** B5
Lac Court Oreilles IR, Wis. **163** F5
Lac des Allemands, La. **133** M13
Lac du Flambeau IR, Wis. **163** F9
Lacassine NWR, La. **133** M5
Lackawanna, N. Y. **76** K3
Laconia, N. H. **45** O7
Lafayette, Ind. **151** H5
Lafayette, La. **133** L8; 132
Lafitte, La. **133** N15
Laguna Atascosa NWR, Texas **223** R13
Laguna IR, N. Mex. **215** G5
Lake Ashtabula, N. Dak. **195** G16
Lake Charles, La. **133** L4
Lake Chelan NRA, Wash. **271** D10
Lake Havasu City, Ariz. **211** J2
Lake Mead NRA, Ariz.–Nev. **211** D2; **241** Q12
Lake Meredith NRA, Texas **223** B7
Lake of the Arbuckles, Okla. **219** M20
Lake O' The Cherokees, Okla. **219** D26
Lake of the Ozarks, Mo. **187** J9
Lake of the Woods, Minn. **183** A6; 182
Lake Providence, La. **133** A11
Lake Woodruff NWR, Fla. **125** F15
Lake Worth, Fla. **125** M19
Lakeland, Fla. **125** J14
Lakes: ancient 198, 244; glacial origins 19, 30, 151, 162, 182; man-made 97, 196, 218; see also Great Lakes
Lakewood, Colo. **229** F11
Lakewood, N. J. **73** L9
Lakewood, Ohio **159** D12
Lamlam, Mount, Guam **285** S16
Lamoille River, Vt. **53** D4
Lanai, Hawaii **281** H15; 280
Lancaster, Ohio **159** M9
Lancaster, Pa. **81** K14; 80; farm 82
Land Between the Lakes, Ky. **86** L6
Land O' Lakes, Wis. **163** E11
Land reclamation 95
Land use 252-258; city planning 254, 255; diagram 253; forest areas 288
Landforms: badlands 198, 200; bluffs 50; buttes 196-197; dome mountains 172; hammock 66; kettle holes

182; moraine 42; origins see Glaciers; Volcanoes; sand dunes 66, 150, 153, 154, 254, 256, 264
L'Anse IR, Mich. **155** E4
Lansing, Mich. **155** R12
Laramie, Wyo. **249** N14
Laramie Mountains, Wyo. **249** M15
Laramie Peak, Wyo. **249** K15
Laramie River, Wyo. **249** M14
Laredo, Texas **223** P10
Largo, Fla. **125** J12
Las Cruces, N. Mex. **215** P7
Las Vegas, Nev. **241** Q11; 240, 242
Las Vegas, N. Mex. **215** F11
Lassen Peak, Calif. **263** D5
Lassen Volcanic NP, Calif. **263** D6
Lata Mountain, American Samoa **285** N9
Laurel, Miss. **137** N9
Lava Beds NM, Calif. **263** B6
Lava Hot Springs, Idaho **233** R11
Lawrence, Kans. **179** D18
Lawrence, Mass. **41** B18
Lawton, Okla. **219** L15
Lead, S. Dak. **199** F1; gold 198, 200
Lead Mountain, Maine **37** M11
Leadore, Idaho **233** M8; range 234
Leadville, Colo. **229** G8; 228, 288
Leavenworth, Kans. **179** B19
Lebanon, Kans. **179** A10
Lebanon, Pa. **81** J14
Leech Lake, Minn. **183** H7
Leech Lake IR, Minn. **183** G6
Leesburg, Va. **99** B19
Leesville Lake, Ohio **159** J14
Lehigh River, Pa. **81** G16; 80
Lehman Caves NM, Nev. **241** J12
Leipsic River, Del. **65** H3
Lenoir, N. C. **91** C8
Levittown, N. Y. **77** T18
Lewes, Del. **65** P8; 64, 66
Lewis and Clark Trail **175, 179, 187, 191, 195, 199, 237, 267, 271**
Lewis Smith Lake, Ala. **117** E6
Lewiston, Idaho **233** G2; 232
Lewiston, Maine **37** Q4
Lexington, Ky. **87** F17; 86; horse farm near 88
Lexington, Mass. **41** E17; 40
Lexington, Nebr. **191** G10
Lexington, N. C. **91** D12
Liberal, Kans. **179** K4
Liberty, Mo. **187** E4
Liberty Reservoir, Md. **69** D16
Licking River, Ky. **87** C18
Lima, Ohio **159** H4
Lincoln, Nebr. **191** G16
Litchfield, Conn. **33** E6
Little Bay, N. H. **45** R10
Little Blue River, Nebr. **191** J14
Little Colorado River, Ariz. **211** H13
Little Diomede Island, Alaska **277** E13

Little Kanawha River, W. Va. **103** H6
Little Miami River, Ohio **159** N4
Little Missouri National Grasslands, N. Dak. 194
Little Missouri River, N. Dak. **195** J2
Little Pee Dee River, S. C. **141** F16
Little Pend Oreille NWR, Wash. **271** C17
Little Red River, Ark. **121** G11
Little Rock, Ark. **121** J9; 120
Little Sioux River, Iowa **175** D3
Little Tallahatchie River, Miss. **137** C6
Little Traverse Bay, Mich. **155** J11
Little Wabash River, Ill. **147** O9
Littleton, Colo. **229** F11
Livengood, Alaska **277** G20
Livermore, Mount, Texas **223** K4
Livestock 116, 119, 120, 174, 213, 232, 236, 240, 248; branding 223; cattle 136, 189, 190, 193, 222, 224-225, by-products 191, leading producers 289; feed 120, 136, 176, 182; feedlots 218, 222, 224; goats 222; lambs 250; pigs 177; see also Horses; Poultry
Livingston, Mont. **237** J9; 238
Livingston, Lake, Texas **223** K16
Livonia, Mich. **155** S15
Lockport, N. Y. **76** H3
Logan, Utah **245** B8
Logan, Mount, Wash. **271** C9
Logansport, Ind. **151** F6
Lompoc, Calif. **263** Q7
Long Beach, Calif. **263** S11
Long Beach, Miss. **137** S9
Long Branch, N. J. **73** J10
Long Island, N. Y. **77** S20; duck farm 79
Long Island Sound, Conn.–N.Y. **33** M9; **77** R20; 32
Long Lake, N. Dak. **195** J11
Long Pond, Mass. **41** M20
Long Trail, Vt. **53** C6
Longfellow Mountains, Maine **37** H8-L5
Longmont, Colo. **229** D11
Longs Peak, Colo. **229** D10
Longview, Texas **223** G17
Longview, Wash. **271** L4; 270
Lookout, Point, Md. **69** P19
Lookout Mountain, Tenn. **95** G16; 97
Lorain, Ohio **159** D10; steel mill 161
Los Alamos, N. Mex. **215** E8; laboratory 216
Los Angeles, Calif. **263** R11; freeway 257
Los Angeles Aqueduct, Calif. **263** N11-Q10; 262
Lost River Range, Idaho **233** M7; 232
Lost River Sinks, Idaho **233** O9

Louisiana 114, 132-135, 171; Mississippi River delta 12
Louisville, Ky. **87** E13; 86
Loup River, Nebr. **191** E14
Loveland, Colo. **229** C11
Lowell, Mass. **41** C17
Lower Brule IR, S. Dak. **199** G10
Lower Klamath NWR, Calif. **263** A5
Lower Red Lake, Minn. **183** E5
Loxahatchee NWR, Fla. **125** M18
Lubbock, Texas **223** F7
Lumber industry 98, 119, 136, 162, 169, 236, 252, 266, 276; log drives 36, 38-39; logging 119, 272
Lummi IR, Wash. **271** B5
Lums Pond, Del. **65** D2
Lunar Crater, Nev. **241** L9
Lutherville-Timonium, Md. **69** D17
Lynchburg, Va. **99** J15
Lyndon B. Johnson Space Center, Texas **223** M16; 222
Lynn, Mass. **41** E19

McAlester, Okla. **219** K2
McAllen, Texas **223** R12
McConaughy, Lake, Nebr. **191** F5
Machias Bay, Maine **37** N13
Mackay Island NWR, N. C. **91** A26
McKeesport, Pa. **81** J3
Mackinac, Straits of, Mich. **155** H11
Mackinac Bridge, Mich. 156
Mackinac Island, Mich. **155** H12
McKinley, Mount, Alaska **277** J19; 276, 288
McMillan, Lake, N. Mex. **215** O13
Macomb, Ill. **147** H3
Macon, Ga. **129** J7
Madeline Island, Wis. **163** C7
Madison, Wis. **163** R10
Madison Range, Mont.: earthquake 236
Madison River, Mont. **237** K7
Magazine Mountain, Ark. **121** G4
Maia, American Samoa **285** M10
Maine 36-39, 51; coast 31; forest 13
Makah IR, Wash. **271** C1
Malaspina Glacier, Alaska **277** M22
Malden, Mass. **41** E19
Malheur Lake, Oreg. **267** K14
Malheur NWR, Oreg. **267** L14
Mammoth Cave, Ky. 86, 88, 288
Mammoth Cave NP, Ky. **87** K12
Mammoth Kill Site, Wyo. **249** N9
Mammoth Spring, Ark. **121** B12
Manassas, Va. **99** C20
Manchester, Conn. **33** D12
Manchester, N. H. **45** S7; 44
Manchester, Vt. **53** R3
Mandan, N. Dak. **195** J9
Manhattan, Kans. **179** C15

Manistee, Mich. **155** N8
Manistee River, Mich. **155** M10
Manistique, Mich. **155** G8
Manistique Lake, Mich. **155** G9
Manitou Islands, Mich. **155** K9
Manitowoc, Wis. **163** N15
Mankato, Minn. **183** R8
Manley Hot Springs, Alaska **277** H19
Mansfield, Ohio **159** G9
Mansfield, Mount, Vt. **53** E5; 52
Mansfield Hollow Lake, Conn. **33** D15
Manua Islands, American Samoa **285** M4
Manufacturing 52, 56-61, 72, 76, 120, 174, 186, 213; aerospace industry 154, 161, 178, 218, 270; automobiles 56, *57, 59*, 150, 154, *157*; chemicals 64, 75; glassmaking 102, *103*, marbles *102*; guns 32, 40; history 32, 33, 56, 59; industrial areas *59, 255*; labor force *58*; machinery 59, 102, 194; metalworking 32, *35*; musical instruments *153*; petroleum products 132, 202, factory *134*; products, number of 56; products, principal *58*; shipbuilding 98, 136; soapmaking *161*; tires *161*; whiskey 86; *see also* Food processing; Forest products; Steelmaking; Textiles
Mapmaking 6-9, 32
Maquoketa River, Iowa **175** E16
Marble Canyon, Ariz. **211** C9
Marblehead, Mass. **41** D20
Marcy, Mount, N.Y. **77** E17
Mariana Islands **274, 285**; 252, 284, 289
Marietta, Ga. **129** E4
Marietta, Ohio **159** N13
Marion, Ind. **151** G9
Marion, Iowa **175** F14
Marion, Ohio **159** H7
Marion, Lake, S.C. **141** H12
Marion Lake, Kans. **179** E13
Mark Twain NWR, Ill.-Iowa **147** N3; **175** J16
Marlborough, Mass. **41** F15
Marquesas Keys, Fla. **125** S14
Marquette, Mich. **155** F6
Marshall, Mo. **187** F8
Marshall Gold Discovery State Historic Park, Calif. **263** H7
Marshall Islands **274**; 289
Marshalltown, Iowa **175** F11
Marshfield, Wis. **163** L8
Martha's Vineyard, Mass. **41** Q22
Martin, Lake, Ala. **117** K10
Martin NWR, Md. **69** P20
Martinsburg, W. Va. **103** F18
Martinsville, Va. **99** M12
Marvel Cave, Mo. **187** P7
Mary, Lake, Miss. **137** P1
Maryland 64, 68-71
Maryville, Tenn. **95** D20
Mason City, Iowa **175** B10
Mason-Dixon Line 68

Massabesic Lake, N.H. **45** S8
Massachusetts 23, 40-43, 51, 168
Massachusetts Bay, Mass. **41** E21
Massena, N.Y. **77** A14
Massillon, Ohio **159** G13
Matafao Peak, American Samoa **285** R6
Matagorda Island, Texas **223** O15
Matanuska River, Alaska **277** K19
Mattamuskeet NWR, N.C. **91** E25
Mattaponi River, Va. **99** G21
Mattoon, Ill. **147** L9
Maui, Hawaii **281** G18
Maumee, Ohio **159** D5
Maumee River, Ind.-Ohio **151** E11; **159** E3
Maumelle, Lake, Ark. **121** J8
Mauna Kea, Hawaii **281** L23; 280
Mauna Loa, Hawaii **281** N22; 280
Maurepas, Lake, La. **133** L14
Maurice River, N.J. **73** R4
Mayagüez, Puerto Rico **285** C8
Mayflower: replica *43*
Mead, Lake, Ariz. **211** D2
Meadow Valley Wash, Nev. **241** N12
Medford, Mass. **41** E18
Medford, Oreg. **267** N5
Medicine Bow Mountains, Wyo. **249** M12-O13
Medicine Bow Peak, Wyo. **249** N12
Medicine Lake NWR, Mont. **237** B18
Medicine Lodge, Kans. **179** J10
Melbourne, Fla. **125** H17
Melrose, Mass. **41** E19
Memphis, Tenn. **94** G1; *94, 96*, 136
Memphremagog, Lake, Vt. **53** B8
Menasha, Wis. **163** M13
Mendenhall Glacier, Alaska **277** N25
Mendota, Lake, Wis. **163** R10
Menominee Falls, Wis. **163** Q14
Menominee IR, Wis. **163** K12
Menominee River, Mich.-Wis. **155** J5; **163** H14
Menomonie, Wis. **163** K3
Mentor, Ohio **159** C13
Meramec Caverns, Mo. **187** J14; 186
Meramec River, Mo. **187** K13
Merced, Calif. **263** L7
Mercer Island, Wash. **271** F6
Meriden, Conn. **33** G9
Meridian, Miss. **137** L10
Merrimack River, Mass.-N.H. **41** C17; **45** P6; 44
Merritt Island, Fla. **125** H17
Mesa, Ariz. **211** M9
Mesa Verde NP, Colo. **229** N2; cliff dwellings *230, 231*
Mesabi Range, Minn. **183** F11-G9

Mescalero Apache IR, N. Mex. **215** N10
Mesquite, Texas **223** G14
Metals: primary and fabricated defined 154
Meteor Crater, Ariz. **211** G11; *210*
Methuen, Mass. **41** B17
Metlakatla IR, Alaska **277** Q27
Mexico, Mo. **187** E11
Miami, Fla. **125** O18; 106, 124
Miami Beach, Fla. **125** O18; *126*
Michigan 23, 154-157; history 252; land use 252, 254
Michigan, Lake **147, 151, 155, 163**; beach erosion *257*; Chicago beach *149*; coho salmon *156*; depth 145; Indiana dunes *153*; *see also* Great Lakes
Michigan City, Ind. **151** B5
Middle Loup River, Nebr. **191** D9
Middlebury, Vt. **53** J3
Middletown, Conn. **33** G11
Middletown, Ohio **159** N3
Middletown, R.I. **49** L10
Midland, Mich. **155** O13
Midland, Texas **223** H7
Midwest City, Okla. **219** H18
Milford, Conn. **33** L7
Milford, Mass. **41** H15
Milford Lake, Kans. **179** C14
Milk River, Mont. **237** B13
Mille Lacs Lake, Minn. **183** K8
Millington, Tenn. **94** F2
Millinocket, Maine **37** J9; 36
Mills, grist 98, *188*, 202
Millville, N.J. **73** Q4
Millwood Lake, Ark. **121** N3
Milton, Mass. **41** G19
Milwaukee, Wis. **163** R14; immigrants 23
Milwaukee River, Wis. **163** P13
Mineral Point, Wis. **163** R8; 162
Mines and mining 214, 228, 232; ghost towns 240; iron 116, 182, reserves 248; lead 162, 174, 228; leaders 289; salt mine *154*; *see also* Coal mining; Copper; Gold mining; Quarrying; Silver mining
Mingo NWR, Mo. **187** N16
Minot, N. Dak. **195** D8
Minneapolis, Minn. **183** O9; 182
Minnesota 23, 56, 114, 132, 173, 182-185
Minnesota River, Minn. **183** P5
Minnetonka, Lake, Minn. **183** P9
Miramar, Fla. **125** O18
Mishawaka, Ind. **151** B7
Missisquoi River, Vt. **53** B5
Mississinewa Lake, Ind. **151** G8
Mississinewa River, Ind. **151** H9
Mississippi 136-139
Mississippi Palisades, Ill. 146
Mississippi Petrified Forest, Miss. **137** K5

Mississippi River **86, 94, 121, 133, 137, 147, 163, 175, 183, 187**; *134, 139*, 145, 173, 184, 186, 288; delta *12*; floods 254; oxbow lake 136, *137*; path 132, 139; sediment 114; source 132, 182
Mississippi Sound, Ala.-Miss. **117** T2; **137** T10
Missoula, Mont. **237** F4; 236
Missouri 186-189
Missouri River **175, 179, 187, 191, 195, 199, 237**; 173, 186, 194, 198, 288
Mitchell, S. Dak. **199** H14
Mitchell, Mount, N.C. **90** D7
Moab, Utah **245** N14
Mobile, Ala. **117** S3; 116
Mobile Bay, Ala. **117** T3; 116
Mobile River, Ala. **117** R3
Modesto, Calif. **263** K6
Mohave, Lake, Nev. **241** S12
Mohawk River, N.Y. **77** J14; 76
Mohawk Trail, Mass. **40** D6
Mohican River, Ohio **159** J11
Mojave, Lake, Ariz. **211** F2
Mojave Desert, Calif. **263** P14
Moline, Ill. **147** E4
Molokai, Hawaii **281** E15
Monadnock, Mount, N.H. **45** T3; 44
Monhegan Island, Maine **37** R7
Mono Lake, Calif. **263** J10
Monocacy River, Md. **69** C13
Monomoy Island, Mass. **41** N27
Monongahela River, Pa.-W.Va. **81** L3; **103** F11; 80, 102
Monroe, La. **133** B8
Monroe, Mich. **155** T15
Monroe Lake, Ind. **151** O6
Monroeville, Pa. **81** H3
Montana 16, 198, 236-239
Montauk Point, N.Y. **77** R23
Montclair, N.J. **73** E8
Monte Vista NWR, Colo. **229** N8
Monterey, Calif. **263** M5
Monterey Bay, Calif. **263** M5
Montevideo, Minn. **183** P4
Montezuma Castle NM, Ariz. **211** J9
Montgomery, Ala. **117** L9; 116
Montpelier, Vt. **53** G6
Monument Valley, Ariz.-Utah **211** B14; **245** S12
Moon Lake, Miss. **137** C4
Moore, Okla. **219** J18
Moorhead, Minn. **183** H2
Moose *38*, 156, *157*
Moosehead Lake, Maine **37** J6; log drive *38-39*
Mooselookmeguntic Lake, Maine **37** M2
Moreau River, S. Dak. **199** C5
Morgan Horse Farm, Vt. **53** J3
Morgan Point, Conn. **33** L9
Morgantown, W. Va. **103** F11
Mormon Trail **175, 191, 245, 249**; 190
Morristown, N.J. **73** F7
Morristown, Tenn. **95** B22
Morse Reservoir, Ind. **151** J7
Moscow, Idaho **233** F2
Moses Lake, Wash. **271** H13

Mosquito Creek Lake, Ohio **159** D15
Moss Point, Miss. **137** S11
Moultrie, Ga. **129** P7
Moultrie, Lake, S.C. **141** K14
Mound City Group NM, Ohio **159** O8
Mound State Monument, Ala. **117** J4
Moundsville, W.Va. **103** D8
Mount Desert Island, Maine **37** P10
Mount Hope Bay, R.I. **49** H11
Mount McKinley NP, Alaska **227** J19
Mount Pleasant, Mich. **155** O12
Mount Pleasant, S.C. **141** M14
Mount Rainier NP, Wash. **271** J7
Mount Rushmore NM, S. Dak. **199** H2; 198, *201*
Mount Sterling, Ky. **87** F19
Mount Vernon, Ill. **147** P8
Mount Vernon, N.Y. **77** S17
Mount Vernon, Ohio **159** J10
Mount Vernon, Va. 98
Mount Vernon, Wash. **271** C6
Mountain Brook, Ala. **117** G7
Mountain goats *273*
Mountain lions 232, *234*
Mountain View, Ark. **121** D9; *123*; Ozark Folk Center 123
Mountains: formation of 172, 226, 227
Muddy Boggy Creek, Okla. **219** N23
Muir Woods NM, Calif. **263** J4
Mullett Lake, Mich. **155** J12
Mullica River, N.J. **73** O6
Muncie, Ind. **151** J10
Murfreesboro, Ark. **121** M4; 123
Murfreesboro, Tenn. **95** D12
Murray, Lake, S.C. **141** F8
Murray, Utah **245** F8
Muscatatuck NWR, Ind. **151** O8
Muscatatuck River, Ind. **151** O9
Muscatine, Iowa **175** H16; 174
Museums 48, 117, 123
Muskegon, Mich. **155** Q9
Muskegon Lake, Mich. **155** Q9
Muskegon River, Mich. **155** O10
Muskingum River, Ohio **159** M12
Muskogee, Okla. **219** G24
Musselshell River, Mont. **237** G11
Myrtle Beach, S.C. **141** G18
Mystic Seaport, Conn. **33** J17; *34-35*

Nacogdoches, Texas **223** H17
Namekagon River, Wis. **163** F4
Nampa, Idaho **233** P2
Nanticoke River, Del.-Md. **65** R2; **69** M22
Nantucket Island, Mass. **41** R26
Nantucket Sound, Mass. **41** P25
Napa, Calif. **263** J4
Naples, Fla. **125** O14
Narragansett Bay, R.I. **49** H9; 48, 50

299

Narragansett Pier, R. I. **49** N7
Nashua, N. H. **45** U7
Nashville, Tenn. **95** C11; 94; Grand Ole Opry *96*
Natchez, Miss. **137** O2; *139*
Natchez Trace Parkway, Ala.–Miss.–Tenn. **95** G8; **117** A3; **137** B11-O2; *138*, *139*
Natchitoches, La. **133** E4
National Bison Range, Mont. **237** E3
National Elk Refuge, Wyo. **249** F2
Natural Bridges NM, Utah **245** Q13
Naugatuck, Conn. **33** H7
Naugatuck River, Conn. **33** J7
Nauvoo, Ill. **147** H1
Navajo-Hopi Joint Use Area, Ariz. **211** D12
Navajo IR, Ariz.–N. Mex.–Utah **211** G12; **215** D2; **245** S11-15
Navajo NM, Ariz. **211** B11
Navajo Reservoir, N. Mex. **215** B5
Nebraska 171, 178, 190-193
Necedah NWR, Wis. **163** N8
Needham, Mass. **41** G17
Needles, Calif. **263** P17
Neenah, Wis. **163** N13
Neosho River, Kans. **179** E15
Nepaug Reservoir, Conn. **33** D8
Neptune, N. J. **73** K9
Nett Lake IR, Minn. **183** D9
Neuse River, N. C. **91** E19
Nevada 226, 240-243
New Albany, Ind. **151** R8
New Bedford, Mass. **41** N20
New Berlin, Wis. **163** R14
New Bern, N. C. **91** F22
New Britain, Conn. **33** F9
New Brunswick, N. J. **73** H7
New Canaan, Conn. **33** M3
New Castle, Del. **65** C4; *64*
New Castle, Ind. **151** K10
New Castle, Pa. **81** F2
New City, N. Y. **77** R17
New Concord, Ohio **159** L12; *158*
New Hampshire 44-47
New Haven, Conn. **33** K8; *32*
New Hope, Pa. **81** J18
New Iberia, La. **133** M9
New Jersey 72-75; population density 248, 288
New Jersey Turnpike, N. J. **73** L6; *72*
New London, Conn. **33** K16; *35*
New Mexico 214-217
New Orleans, La. **133** M15; 114, 132, *134*
New Philadelphia, Ohio **159** J13
New River, N. C. **91** G21
New River, Va.–W. Va. **99** L9; **103** N7; 102, *104*
New Rochelle, N. Y. **77** S17
New Ulm, Minn. **183** R6
New York 25, 76-79
New York City, N. Y. **77** T17; 25, 72, 76, *78*; immigrants *23*
New York State Barge Canal (Erie Canal), N. Y. **76-77** G18-J2

New York State Thruway, N. Y. **76-77** J2-S17; route *76*
Newark, Del. **65** C2
Newark, N. J. **73** F9; *72*
Newark, Ohio **159** L10
Newburgh, N. Y. **77** P16
Newburyport, Mass. **41** A20
Newfound Lake, N. H. **45** N5
Newington, Conn. **33** E10
Newport, Ky. **87** A17
Newport, R. I. **49** M10; *48*, *50*, *51*
Newport News, Va. **99** L23; *98*
Newton, Mass. **41** F18
Nez Perce IR, Idaho **233** G3
Niagara Falls, Canada–N. Y. **76** J2; *79*
Niagara River, N. Y. **76** H2
Niantic Bay, Conn. **33** K15
Niihau, Hawaii **280** D2; *280*
Niles, Ohio **159** E15
Niobrara River, Nebr. **191** A9
Noatak River, Alaska **277** E17
Nogales, Ariz. **211** T11
Nolin River Lake, Ky. **87** J11
Nomans Land Island, Mass. **41** R21
Nome, Alaska **277** G14
Nonquit Pond, R. I. **49** K12
Norfolk, Va. **99** L24; *98*
Norfolk Lake, Ark. **121** B9
Normal, Ill. **147** H7
Norman, Okla. **219** J18
Norman, Lake, N. C. **91** E10
Norris Lake, Tenn. **95** B20; *97*
Norristown, Pa. **81** K17
North Adams, Mass. **40** C4
North Branch Potomac River, W. Va. **103** G14
North Canadian River, Okla. **219** G15
North Carolina 90-93
North Cascades NP, Wash. **271** B8; *272-273*
North Charleston, S. C. **141** L14
North Chicago, Ill. **147** B10
North Dakota 23, 168, 171, 194-197
North Fork Red River, Okla. **219** J11
North Fork River, W. Va.: kayaker *104*
North Haven, Conn. **33** J9
North Las Vegas, Nev. **241** Q11
North Little Rock, Ark. **121** J9
North Loup River, Nebr. **191** C8
North Olmsted, Ohio **159** E11
North Platte River, Nebr.–Wyo. **191** E4; **249** J15
North Providence, R. I. **49** D7
North Slope, Alaska **277** C17-20; *276*
North Tonawanda, N. Y. **76** J3
Northampton, Mass. **40** G7
Northern Cheyenne IR, Mont. **237** J15
Northern Mariana Islands *see* Mariana Islands
Northwest Angle, Minn. **183** A5
Norton Sound, Alaska **277** G14
Norwalk, Conn. **33** N4
Norwalk Islands, Conn. **33** N4

Norwich, Conn. **33** G16
Norwood, Mass. **41** H18
Norwood, Ohio **159** P3
Nottoway River, Va. **99** L18
Noxontown Pond, Del. **65** F2
Noxubee NWR, Miss. **137** G10
Nuclear energy 94, *96*, 204, 214, 270; *see also* Energy
Nueces River, Texas **223** O11
Nunivak Island, Alaska **277** K12
Nunivak NWR, Alaska **277** K12
Nuuuli, American Samoa **285** S6

Oahe, Lake, N. Dak.–S. Dak. **195** L10; **199** D9; *196*, *201*
Oahe Dam, S. Dak. **199** F9
Oahu, Hawaii **281** D11; *282*, *283*
Oak Park, Ill. **147** C10
Oak Ridge, Tenn. **95** C19; National Laboratory 94, *96*
Oakland, Calif. **263** K4
Ocala, Fla. **125** F13
Ocean City, Md. **69** N27; *68*
Ocheyedan Mound, Iowa **175** A4
Ochlockonee River, Fla. **125** B8
Ocmulgee NM, Ga. **129** J8
Ocmulgee River, Ga. **129** M9
Oconee River, Ga. **129** J9
Ocracoke, N. C. **91** F25; *93*
Odessa, Texas **223** H6
Ofu, American Samoa **285** L2
Ogden, Utah **245** D7
Ogeechee River, Ga. **129** J12
Ohio 158-161
Ohio River **81**, 86-87, **103**, **147**, **151**, **159**; 80, 102, 145; commerce 86, 146, 148, 158; flooding *254*
Oil City, Pa. **81** D4
Oil industry 56, 59-60; leaders *289*; pipeline 56, 276, *279*; refineries 72, *74-75*, 136, 178, *225*, largest 132, process 59-60; reserves 116, 120, 194, 202, 218, 222, 236, 248, sources 204; rigs *220-221*, *225*; wells 222, first *80*, *202*
Okanogan River, Wash. **271** C13
Okatibbee Lake, Miss. **137** K10
Okeechobee, Lake, Fla. **125** L17; 124, 126
Okefenokee NWR, Ga. **129** Q12
Okefenokee Swamp, Ga. **129** R12; *131*
Oklahoma 56, 218-221; tornado *110*
Oklahoma City, Okla. **219** H18; 218; oil rigs *220-221*
Okmulgee, Okla. **219** H23
Olathe, Kans. **179** D19
Old Faithful, Wyo. **249** C2; *12*, *204*
Old Kaskaskia, Ill. 254
Old Man of the Mountains, N. H. **45** J6
Old Prentiss, Miss. 136
Old Saybrook, Conn. **33** K13
Old Spanish Trail, N. Mex. **215** C7

Old Speck Mountain, Maine **37** O2
Old Sturbridge Village, Mass. **41** J11
Olentangy River, Ohio **159** H8
Olosega, American Samoa **285** L4
Olympia, Wash. **271** H5; *270*
Olympic Mountains, Wash. **271** F3; *270*
Olympic NP, Wash. **271** E1; *273*
Olympus, Mount, Wash. **271** E3; *270*
Omaha, Nebr. **191** F18; meat packing *192*
Omaha IR, Nebr. **191** C17
Oneida, N. Y. **77** J11
Oneida IR, Wis. **163** L13
Oneida Lake, N. Y. **77** H11
Onondaga IR, N. Y. **77** K10
Onslow Bay, N. C. **91** J22
Ontario, Lake **77** F8; *see also* Great Lakes
Ontonagon River, Mich. **155** F2
Oologah Lake, Okla. **219** D24
Opelika, Ala. **117** K12
Opelousas, La. **133** K8
Opossum *118*
Optima Reservoir, Okla. **218** C7
Oregon 17, 232, 252, 266-269
Oregon Caves NM, Oreg. **267** O4
Oregon Dunes NRA, Oreg. **267** H2
Oregon Territory *65*
Oregon Trail *179*, *191*, *229*, *233*, *249*, *267*; 190, 266
Orem, Utah **245** G8
Organ Pipe Cactus NM, Ariz. **211** R6
Orlando, Fla. **125** G15
Osage IR, Okla. **219** D21
Osage River, Mo. **187** J10
Oskaloosa, Iowa **175** J12
Oshkosh, Wis. **163** N13
Ossabaw Island, Ga. **129** N16
Ossipee Lake, N. H. **45** M9
Oswego, N. Y. **77** G9
Ottawa, Ill. **147** E8
Ottawa NWR, Ohio **159** D7
Ottawa River, Ohio **159** G4
Otter, sea *264*
Otter Creek, Vt. **53** L3
Ottumwa, Iowa **175** K12
Ouachita, Lake, Ark. **121** K5
Ouachita Mountains, Ark.–Okla. **121** J2-5; **219** L24-26
Ouachita River, Ark.–La. **121** O7; **133** D8
Ouray NWR, Utah **245** G14
Outer Banks, N. C. **91** F26; *92*, *93*
Overland Park, Kans. **179** D19
Owatonna, Minn. **183** R9
Owens River, Calif. **263** L11; *262*
Owensboro, Ky. **87** G8
Owosso, Mich. **155** Q13
Owyhee, Lake, Oreg. **267** J17
Owyhee River, Oreg. **267** M17
Oxford, Miss. **137** C8
Oxnard, Calif. **263** R9

Ozark Plateau (Mountains), Ark.–Mo.–Okla. **121** D4-7; **187** N9; **219** E26; *122-123*, 146, 173, 188, 189, 218; geology 114, 186

Pachaug Pond, Conn. **33** G17
Pacific Crest Trail, Calif.–Oreg.–Wash. **263** F7; **267** K7; **271** A10-N7; length *261*
Padre Island NS, Texas **223** Q14
Paducah, Ky. **86** K4
Pago Pago, American Samoa **285** R6
Pahala, Hawaii **281** P23
Painted Desert, Ariz. **211** C9-F11; *212*
Palm Beach, Fla. **125** M19; *124*
Palm Springs, Calif. **263** R14
Palo Alto, Calif. **263** K4
Palomar Mountain, Calif. **263** S13; telescope *262*
Pamlico River, N. C. **91** E23
Pamlico Sound, N. C. **91** F25; *92*
Pamunkey River, Va. **99** H21
Panama Canal *274*; 158, 284, 289
Panama City, Fla. **125** C5
Papago IR, Ariz. **211** Q8
Papermaking 40, *78*, 128, 130, 154; process *36*; pulp 98, 162
Paradise Valley, Wyo. **249** J12
Paramus, N. J. **73** D9
Park Forest, Ill. **147** E10
Parkersburg, W. Va. **103** G5
Parkland, Wash. **271** H6
Parkville, Md. **69** D18
Parma, Ohio **159** E12
Parris Island, S. C. **141** O11
Parsons, Kans. **179** J18
Pasadena, Calif. **263** R11
Pasadena, Texas **223** L16
Pascagoula, Miss. **137** S11; *136*
Pascagoula River, Miss. **137** R11
Pasco, Wash. **271** L14
Passaic, N. J. **73** E9
Passamaquoddy Bay, Maine **37** M15; tides *38*
Patapsco River, Md. **69** F18
Paterson, N. J. **73** E9
Pathfinder Reservoir, Wyo. **249** K11
Patoka River, Ind. **151** R3
Patuxent River, Md. **69** M17
Pawcatuck River, R. I. **49** N4
Pawleys Island, S. C. **141** J17
Pawtucket, R. I. **49** D9; Old Slater Mill *48*, 56
Pawtuxet River, R. I. **49** G7
Payette River, Idaho **233** N2
Pea Island NWR, N. C. **91** D27
Peabody, Mass. **41** D20
Peace River, Fla. **125** L14
Pearl City, Hawaii **281** E10
Pearl Harbor, Hawaii **281** E10
Pearl River, La.–Miss. **133** K16; **137** H9-T7
Pecos, Texas **223** J5
Pecos NM, N. Mex. **215** F9
Pecos River, N. Mex.–Texas **215** L13; **223** K7

Pee Dee NWR, N. C. **91** G13
Pee Dee River, N. C.–S. C. **91** F13; **141** F16
Peekskill, N. Y. **77** Q17
Pekin, Ill. **147** H6
Pelican Island NWR, Fla. **125** J17
Pembina Mountains, N. Dak. **195** A15
Pemigewasset River, N. H. **45** K6
Pend Oreille Lake, Idaho **233** B3
Pend Oreille River, Wash. **271** B18
Pendleton, Oreg. **267** C13
Pennsauken, N. J. **73** M4
Pennsylvania 25, 56, 64, 68, 80-83
Pennsylvania Dutch 80, *82*
Pennsylvania Turnpike, Pa. **81** K5; 80
Penobscot Bay, Maine **37** P9
Penobscot River, Maine **37** K10; 36
Pensacola, Fla. **125** B2
Peoria, Ill. **147** G6
Pepin, Lake, Minn.–Wis. **163** L2; **183** Q12
Perdido River, Fla. **125** A1
Pere Marquette River, Mich. **155** O9
Perth Amboy, N. J. **73** H8
Peru, Ind. **151** F7
Peshtigo River, Wis. **163** H13
Petenwell Lake, Wis. **163** N9
Peterborough, N. H. **45** T4
Petersburg, Va. **99** K20
Petrified Forest NP, Ariz. **211** H14
Petrified wood *213*, 248
Petroleum *see* Oil industry
Phelps Lake, N. C. **91** D24
Phenix City, Ala. **117** L13
Philadelphia, Miss. **137** J9; 138
Philadelphia, Pa. **81** K18; 19, 25, 80, *83*
Phillipsburg, N. J. **73** F3
Phoenix, Ariz. **211** M8; 210
Phosphorescent Bay, Puerto Rico **285** E8-F10
Pickwick Lake, Miss.–Tenn. **94** H7; **137** A12
Pictured Rocks NL, Mich. **155** F8
Piedmont NWR, Ga. **129** H7
Pierre, S. Dak. **199** F9
Pikes Peak, Colo. **229** H11
Pikesville, Md. **69** D17
Pine Barrens, N. J. **73** N7-R5; 72, *74*
Pine Bluff, Ark. **121** L10
Pine Creek Gorge, Pa. **81** C11
Pine Hill, Ala. **117** N4; 119
Pine Island, Fla. **125** M14
Pine Mountain, Ky. **87** K23
Pine Ridge IR, S. Dak. **199** J5
Pinellas Park, Fla. **125** J12
Pinnacles NM, Calif. **263** M6
Pioneers 12, 20, 86, 190; pioneer trails 20, *138*, 139, 150, 190, 218, **237**, 266; *see also* trails by name
Pipe Spring NM, Ariz. **211** B7

Pipestone NM, Minn. **183** R2; 182, 184
Piqua, Ohio **159** K4
Piscataqua River, N. H. **45** Q10
Pittsburg, Kans. **179** J19
Pittsburgh, Pa. **81** H3; 56, 80, 81
Pittsfield, Maine **37** N7
Placid, Lake, N. Y. **77** D16
Plainfield, N. J. **73** G7
Plains, Ga. **129** M5
Plantation, Fla. **125** N18
Plaquemine, La. **133** L11
Platte River, Mo. **187** A4
Platte River, Nebr. **191** F14; 190, 192
Plattsburgh, N. Y. **77** B18
Pleasant Bay, Maine **37** O12
Pleasure Ridge Park, Ky. **87** E13
Plimoth Plantation, Mass. **41** K22; 40
Plum Island, Mass. **41** B21
Plymouth, Mass. **41** K22; 40; port *43*
Plymouth Bay, Mass. **41** K22
Pocatello, Idaho **233** Q10
Pocomoke River, Md. **69** O24
Pocono Mountains, Pa. **81** E17
Poinsett, Lake, S. Dak. **199** E17
Point Barrow, Alaska **277** B18; 276
Point Judith, R. I. **49** P7; 48
Point Reyes NS, Calif. **263** J3
Point Roberts, Wash. **271** A4
Pollution 56; air 72, 113, 205, 257, control of 64, 116; water 32, 94, 158, 246, 269
Pomme de Terre Lake, Mo. **187** K7
Pompano Beach, Fla. **125** N18
Ponca City, Okla. **219** C19
Ponce, Puerto Rico **285** E11
Ponce de Leon Bay, Fla. **125** Q16
Pontchartrain, Lake, La. **133** L15
Pontiac, Ill. **147** G8
Pontiac, Mich. **155** R15
Population: by age groups *24*; by occupation *24-25*; censuses 20, 23-24; density *20-21*, 208, 226, 248, greatest 72; distribution *22-23*; growth 24, 25, graph *21*; highest 262; labor force *58, 60-61*; tables 286-287, 288; total, U. S. 166
Port Angeles, Wash. **271** D3
Port Arthur, Texas **223** L18
Port Chester, N. Y. **77** S18
Port Huron, Mich. **155** Q17
Port Royal Sound, S. C. **141** P12
Portage, Mich. **155** T10
Portage Lake, Mich. **155** D4
Portland, Maine **37** S4
Portland, Oreg. **267** C5; 266, *268*
Ports 48, *71, 73, 78*, 96, 98, *134*,
136, 140, 146, 182, *185*, 189; four largest 71; restoration *34-35*
Portsmouth, N. H. **45** R11
Portsmouth, Ohio **159** R8
Portsmouth, Va. **99** L24; 98
'Possum *118*
Potawatomi IR, Kans. **179** B16
Potholes Reservoir, Wash. **271** H13
Potomac River, Md.–Va.–W.Va. *7;* 69 E11; **99** F22; **103** E18; *6, 98*
Pottstown, Pa. **81** J16
Poughkeepsie, N. Y. **77** P17
Poultry: leading producers 289; chickens 64, 116, 120, *122*, 128, 174, rooster *177*; ducks *79*; turkeys 150, *185*, 240
Powder River, Mont.–Wyo. **237** G17; **249** C13
Powell, Lake, Ariz.–Utah **211** B10; **245** S10
Poygan, Lake, Wis. **163** N12
Prairie *see* Grasslands
Prairie dogs 18, *201*
Prairie du Chien, Wis. **163** R6
Prairie Village, Kans. **179** C19
Pratt, Kans. **179** H9
Prattville, Ala. **117** L8
Prescott, Ariz. **211** J7
Presidential Range, N. H. **45** H7; 19
Presidents 102, 146, 178, 194; Mount Rushmore, S. Dak. 198, *201*
Presque Isle, Maine **37** D11
Prettyboy Reservoir, Md. **69** B17
Pribilof Islands, Alaska **277** M10
Price River, Utah **245** K11
Prichard, Ala. **117** S3
Priest Lake, Idaho **233** A2
Priest River, Idaho **233** B2
Prime Hook NWR, Del. **65** O6-7
Prince William Forest Park, Va. **99** D20
Princeton, N. J. **73** J6
Prineville, Reservoir, Oreg. **267** H10
Promontory, Utah **245** B6
Providence, R. I. **49** E8; 48
Providence River, R. I. **49** F9
Provincetown, Mass. **41** J25
Provo, Utah **245** G8
Prudence Island, R. I. **49** J10
Prudhoe Bay, Alaska **277** C20
Pueblo, Colo. **229** K12
Pueblo de Taos IR, N. Mex. **215** C10
Puerco River, Ariz. **211** G15
Puerto Rico 274, **285** C12; *284*, 289
Puget Sound, Wash. **271** E6; 270
Pullman, Wash. **271** J19
Pumpkin Center, Ind. **151** Q6
Purgatoire River, Colo. **229** N14
Puyallup, Wash. **271** H6
Pymatuning Reservoir, Pa. **81** C1
Pyramid Lake, Nev. **241** F2
Pyramid Lake IR, Nev. **241** F2

Quabbin Reservoir, Mass. **41** F10
Quarrying: leaders 289; granite 52, 128; limestone 52, 116, *152*; marble 52, 54, 128
Queen River, R. I. **49** L6
Quinault IR, Wash. **271** G1
Quincy, Ill. **147** K1
Quincy, Mass. **41** G19
Quinebaug River, Conn. **33** E17
Quivira NWR, Kans. **179** F10
Quoddy Head, Maine **37** N15

Rabun Gap, Ga. **129** A8; *128*
Raccoon *89*
Raccoon River, Iowa **175** F7
Racine, Wis. **163** S15; 162
Radford, Va. **99** K10
Railroads: in planned community *255;* cog railway *46*; narrow-gauge 228, *231*; steam engine *140*, 202
Rainbow Bridge NM, Utah **245** S10
Rainier, Mount, Wash. **271** J7
Rainy River, Minn. **183** C7
Raisin River, Mich. **155** T14
Raleigh, N. C. **91** D17; 90
Raleigh Bay, N. C. **91** F26
Ramah Navajo IR, N. Mex. **215** H3
Ranches and ranching 193, 196, 198, 200, 228, 232, 236, 240, 248, 250; King Ranch 222, 225, brand *223;* Parker Ranch 280
Randolph, Mass. **41** H19
Rangeley Lake, Maine **37** M3
Rantoul, Ill. **147** J9
Rapid City, S. Dak. **199** G2; flooding *254*
Rapidan River, Va. **99** E18
Rappahannock River, Va. **99** G22; 98
Raritan River, N. J. **73** G6
Rathbun Lake, Iowa **175** L11
Raystown Lake, Pa. **81** J9
Reading, Pa. **81** J15
Red Bank, N. J. **73** J9
Red Cliff IR, Wis. **163** C7
Red Hills, Kans. **179** J7
Red Lake IR, Minn. **183** E5
Red River 121, 133, 219, 223
Red River of the North, Canada–U. S. **183** H1; **195** F19; *184*; valley 194
Red Rock River, Mont. **237** K6
Red Rock Reservoir, Iowa **175** J10
Red Rocks Lakes NWR, Mont. **237** L7
Red Wing, Minn. **183** Q11
Redding, Calif. **263** D4
Redwood NP, Calif. **263** B2
Reelfoot Lake, Tenn. 94
Reelfoot NWR, Tenn. **94** B3
Reese River, Nev. **241** F7
Rehoboth Bay, Del. **65** Q8
Rehoboth Beach, Del. **65** P8
Reidsville, N. C. **91** B14

Rend Lake, Ill. **147** Q7
Reno, Nev. **241** G1; *240*
Renton, Wash. **271** G6
Republican River, Kans.–Nebr. **179** B12; **191** J12
Reston, Va. **99** B20; 98, 258; Terraset School *206-207*
Revere, Mass. **41** E19
Revolutionary War *see* American Revolution
Reynoldsburg, Ohio **159** L8
Rhinelander, Wis. **163** G10
Rhode Island 48-51, 288
Rhode Island (island), R. I. **49** L10
Rhode Island Sound, R. I. **49** O11; 51
Rib Mountain, Wis. **163** K9; 162
Rice Lake, Wis. **163** H4
Richland, Wash. **271** L13
Richmond, Ind. **151** K11
Richmond, Ky. **87** G18
Richmond, Va. **99** H20; 72, 98
Ridgefield, Conn. **33** L3
Ridgewood, N. J. **73** D9
Riffe Lake, Wash. **271** K6
Rio Chama, N. Mex. **215** C7
Rio Grande, Colo.–N. Mex.–Texas **215**, **223**, **229**; 208, 214, 222
Rio Hondo, N. Mex. **215** M11
Rio Puerco, N. Mex. **215** J7
Ripon, Wis. **163** O12
Ritidian Point, Guam **285** O18
Riverhead, N. Y. **77** S21; duck farm *79*
Riverside, Calif. **263** R12
Riviera Beach, Fla. **125** M18
Roads *see* Highways
Roanoke, Va. **99** K12; 98
Roanoke Island, N. C. **91** C26
Roanoke Rapids, N. C. **91** A20
Roanoke River, N. C. **91** B21
Robert S. Kerr Reservoir, Okla. **219** J26
Rochester, Minn. **183** R11
Rochester, N. Y. **77** J6; 76
Rock formations 46, 128, 198, *200, 240, 246-247;* "mushrooms" *178;* sandstone *105;* sea stacks *269*
Rock Hill, S. C. **141** B10
Rock Island, Ill. **147** E4
Rock River, Ill.–Wis. **147** C6; **163** R12
Rockford, Ill. **147** B7
Rockland, Maine **37** Q8
Rockville, Md. **69** G14
Rocky Boys IR, Mont. **237** C10
Rocky Fork Lake, Ohio **159** P6
Rocky Hill, Conn. **33** F11
Rocky Mount, N. C. **91** C20
Rocky Mountain NP, Colo. **229** C9
Rocky Mountains **215, 229, 233, 237, 249;** *12, 31, 112-113,* 173, 209, 214, 228, *231*, 236; age 227, 250; extent 14; glaciers, Ice Age 238; wildlife *17*, 230
Rogers, Mount, Va. **98** M7
Rogue River, Oreg. **267** M2
Rolla, Mo. **187** K12

301

Rome, Ga. **129** C2
Rome, N. Y. **77** H12
Rosebud IR, S. Dak. **199** J8
Roseburg, Oreg. **267** K4
Roseville, Mich. **155** R16
Ross Lake NRA, Wash. **271** B10
Ross R. Barnett Reservoir, Miss. **137** K6
Roswell, N. Mex. **215** M12
Rota, Northern Mariana Islands **285** J14
Rotterdam, N. Y. **77** K16
Rough River, Ky. **87** H9
Round Valley IR, Calif. **263** E3
Roundup, Mont. **237** G12
Royal Gorge, Colo. **229** K10
Royal Oak, Mich. **155** R16
Ruby Mountains, Nev. 240; Ruby Dome **241** E10
Rufus Woods Lake, Wash. **271** E13
Rugby, N. Dak. **195** C11; 194
Rum River, Minn. **183** N9
Rumford, Maine **37** O3; 36
Rushmore, Mount, S. Dak. 198, *201*
Russell Cave NM, Ala. **117** A10
Ruston, La. **133** B6
Rutland, Vt. **53** N4

Sabine Lake, La.–Texas **133** N2; **233** L18
Sabine NWR, La. **133** N3
Sabine River, La.–Texas **133** J3; **223** K18
Sac and Fox IR, Iowa **175** H12
Sacajawea Peak, Oreg. **267** D17
Saco River, Maine **37** Q2
Sacramento, Calif. **263** H6
Sacramento River, Calif. **263** F5
Sag Harbor, N. Y. **77** R22
Saginaw, Mich. **155** P14
Saginaw Bay, Mich. **155** O14
Saginaw River, Mich. **155** O14
Saguaro NM, Ariz. **211** Q10-12; 210
Sahale, Mount, Wash. *272-273*
St. Albans, Vt. **53** C3; 52
St. Andrew Sound, Ga. **129** Q15
St. Augustine, Fla. **125** D15
St. Charles, Mo. **187** G15
St. Clair, Lake, Mich. **155** R17
St. Clair River, Mich. **155** Q17; 154
St. Clair Shores, Mich. **155** R16
St. Cloud, Minn. **183** N7
St. Croix, U. S. Virgin Islands **285** H4; 284
St. Croix River, Maine **37** K13
St. Croix River, Minn.–Wis. **163** J1; **183** M10
St. Elias Mountains, Alaska **277** L22-N24
St. Francis, Ark. **121** B17; 120
St. Francis River, Ark.–Mo. **121** G15; **187** Q16
St. Francois Mountains, Mo. **187** L14
St. Helena Island, S. C. **141** O12
St. Helens, Mount, Wash. **271** L6
St. Joe River, Idaho **233** E4
St. John, U. S. Virgin Islands **285** B4; 284
St. John River, Maine **37** D6
St. Johns River, Fla. **125** C14
St. Joseph, Mich. **155** T8
St. Joseph, Mo. **187** C3
St. Joseph River, Ind.–Mich. **151** D11; **155** T11
St. Lawrence Island, Alaska **277** G12
St. Lawrence River, N. Y. **77** C11
St. Lawrence Seaway, Canada–U. S. 76, *147*, 154
St. Louis, Mo. **187** G16; 186, *188*
St. Louis Park, Minn. **183** P9
St. Louis River, Minn. **183** H10
St. Marks NWR, Fla. **125** C8
St. Marys River, Fla.–Ga. **125** A14; **129** Q13
St. Marys River, Ind. **151** F11
St. Marys River, Mich. **155** F13; 154
St. Matthew Island, Alaska **277** J10
St. Michaels, Md. **69** J20
St. Paul, Minn. **183** P10; 182
St. Petersburg, Fla. **125** J12
St. Regis IR, N. Y. **77** A14
St. Simons Island, Ga. **129** P15
St. Thomas, U. S. Virgin Islands **285** B2; 284
St. Vincent NWR, Fla. **125** E6
Saipan, Northern Mariana Islands **285** J19
Sakakawea, Lake, N. Dak. **195** F5; *196;* branch *196-197*
Sakonnet River, R. I. **49** K11
Salamonie Lake, Ind. **151** F9
Salamonie River, Ind. **151** G10
Salem, Mass. **41** D20
Salem, N. H. **45** T8
Salem, Oreg. **267** E5; 266
Salem, Va. **99** K12
Salina, Kans. **179** D12
Salinas, Calif. **263** M5
Salinas River, Calif. **263** O7
Saline Lake, La. **133** E5
Saline River, Ark. **121** N9
Saline River, Kans. **179** D11
Salisbury, Md. **69** M23
Salisbury, N. C. **91** D12
Salkehatchie River, S. C. **141** L10
Salmon *see* Fish
Salmon River, Idaho **233** K4-M7; 232
Salmon River Mountains, Idaho **233** L4
Salt Fork Red River, Okla. **219** K11
Salt Fork River, Okla. **219** D17
Salt Lake City, Utah **245** E8; 244
Salt Plains NWR, Okla. **219** C16
Salt River, Ariz. **211** M11; 210
Salt River, Mo. **187** D12
Salton Sea, Calif. **263** S15
Saluda River, S. C. **141** F7
Salvador, Lake, La. **133** N15
Sam Rayburn Reservoir, Texas **223** J17
San Andreas Fault, Calif. **263** E1-U15; 262
San Andres NWR, N. Mex. **215** O7
San Angelo, Texas **223** J9
San Antonio, Texas **223** M12; fiesta *224*
San Bernardino, Calif. **263** R12
San Carlos IR, Ariz. **211** N13
San Carlos Reservoir, Ariz. **211** N12
San Diego, Calif. **263** U13; 262
San Francisco, Calif. **263** K4; 260, 262
San Francisco River, N. Mex. **215** L2
San Joaquin River, Calif. **263** L7; flood *257*
San Joaquin Valley, Calif. **263** M7-P10
San Jose, Calif. **263** L5
San Juan, Puerto Rico **285** B14
San Juan Islands, Wash. **271** C5
San Juan Mountains, Colo. *231*
San Juan River, Colo.–N. Mex.–Utah **215** B2; **229** O6; **245** S12
San Luis Obispo, Calif. **263** P7
San Mateo, Calif. **263** K4
San Pedro River, Ariz. **211** P12; 210
San Rafael River, Utah **245** L11
San Xavier IR, Ariz. **211** R11
Sand Hills region, Nebr. **191** C6; 190
Sand Lake, S. Dak. **199** B14
Sand Springs, Okla. **219** F22
Sandusky, Ohio **159** D9
Sandusky River, Ohio **159** F7
Sandwich, Mass. **41** M23
Sandy Hook Bay, N. J. **73** H9
Sanford, Maine **37** T2
Sangamon River, Ill. **147** K7
Sanibel Island, Fla. **125** N14; *127*
Santa Barbara, Calif. **263** Q8
Santa Catalina, Gulf of, Calif. **263** T11
Santa Clara, Calif. **263** K5
Santa Claus, Ind. **151** S4
Santa Cruz River, Ariz. **211** P10
Santa Fe, N. Mex. **215** E9; *214*
Santa Fe Trail *179, 187, 215, 218, 229*
Santa Maria, Calif. **263** P7
Santa Maria River, Ariz. **211** J6
Santa Rosa, Calif. **263** H4
Santa Rosa Island, Fla. **125** C3
Santee IR, Nebr. **191** B13
Santee NWR, S. C. **141** J13-K14
Santee Point, S. C. **141** K17
Santee River, S. C. **141** J15
Santo Domingo Pueblo, N. Mex. **215** F8
Sapelo Sound, Ga. **129** N15
Saranac Lake, N. Y. **77** D16
Sarasota, Fla. **125** K13
Saratoga Springs, N. Y. **77** J17
Sardis Lake, Miss. **137** C7
Sarpy Creek, Mont. **237** H14; coal pit *239*
Sassafras Mountain, S. C. **141** B3
Satellite maps 9, *109;* supplement in back of book
Satilla River, Ga. **129** O10
Saugatuck Reservoir, Conn. **33** L4
Saugus, Mass. **41** E19
Sault Ste. Marie, Mich. **155** F12
Saunderstown, R. I. **49** L8
Savannah, Ga. **129** L16
Savannah NWR, S. C. **141** P10
Savannah River, Ga.–S. C. **129** H14; **141** N9; *128*
Sawtooth Range, Idaho **233** N5; 232
Sayreville, N. J. **73** H8
Schenectady, N. Y. **77** K17; 76
Schuylkill River, Pa. **81** G15
Scioto River, Ohio **159** H6
Scituate Reservoir, R. I. **49** F5
Scotlandville, La. **133** K11
Scottsbluff, Nebr. **191** D1
Scottsdale, Ariz. **211** M8
Scranton, Pa. **81** D16
Sea Island, Ga. **129** P15; Spanish moss *130*
Seas, ancient 12, 173, 202, 214
Seattle, Wash. **271** F6; *270*
Sebago Lake, Maine **37** R3
Sebring, Fla. **125** K15
Second Lake, N. H. **45** B9
Sedalia, Mo. **187** G8
Seedskadee NWR, Wyo. **249** M4
Seekonk River, R. I. **49** D9
Selma, Ala. **117** L6
Seminoe Reservoir, Wyo. **249** L11
Seminole, Lake, Ga. **129** R3
Seneca Rocks, W. Va. **103** J13; *105*
Seney NWR, Mich. **155** G9; 154
Sequoia NP, Calif. **263** M10
Sequoyah NWR, Okla. **219** H25
Severn River, Md. **69** G18
Sevier Desert, Utah **245** K5
Sevier Lake, Utah **245** M4
Sevier River, Utah **245** O7
Sevilleta NWR, N. Mex. **215** J7
Seward, Alaska **277** M19
Seward Peninsula, Alaska **277** F14
Shadow Mountain NRA, Colo. **229** D9
Shafer, Lake, Ind. **151** F5
Shaker Heights, Ohio **159** D12
Sharon, Pa. **81** E1
Sharpe, Lake, S. Dak. **199** G11
Sharpsburg, Md. **69** C10
Shasta, Mount, Calif. **263** B5
Shasta Lake, Calif. **263** D4
Shawnee, Okla. **219** J20
Shawneetown, Ill. **147** R9; *146, 254*
Sheboygan, Wis. **163** O15
Shelby, Mont. **237** B7
Shelbyville, Lake, Ill. **147** L8
Sheldon NWR, Nev. **241** B3
Shellrock River, Iowa **175** C11
Shelton, Conn. **33** K7
Shenandoah NP, Va. **99** D17; 98
Shenandoah River, Va.–W. Va. **99** B18; **103** H19
Shenandoah Valley, Va. **99** D16; *100-101*
Shenipsit Lake, Conn. **33** C13
Shepaug River, Conn. **33** F4
Shepherdstown, W. Va. **103** F19
Sheridan, Wyo. **249** B11
Shetucket River, Conn. **33** F16
Sheyenne River, N. Dak. **195** K18
Ship Rock, N. Mex. **215** B2
Shively, Ky. **87** E13
Shreveport, La. **133** B2
Shrewsbury, Mass. **41** G14
Sidney Lanier, Lake, Ga. **129** D6
Sierra Blanca Peak, N. Mex. **215** M9
Sierra Nevada, Calif. **263** E6-O11; *12, 17, 112-113,* 262, 264
Silver City, N. Mex. **215** O3
Silver Dollar City, Mo. 186
Silver mining 210, 228, 232, 236, 240; leading producers 289; smelter *235*
Silver Spring, Md. **69** G15
Silverton, Colo. **229** M4; 228, 231
Simi Valley, Calif. **263** R10
Sinclair, Lake, Ga. **129** G8
Sioux City, Iowa **175** D2; 174
Sioux Falls, S. Dak. **199** J17
Sipsey River, Ala. **117** G4
Sisseton IR, N. Dak.–S. Dak. **195** M18; **199** B16
Sitka, Alaska **277** O25
Sitting Bull Monument, S. Dak. **199** C9
Six Mile Lake, La. **133** N11
Skagit River, Wash. **271** C7
Skagway, Alaska **277** M25
Skull Valley, Utah 244
Skull Valley IR, Utah **245** G5
Skunk River, Iowa **175** K14
Skyline Drive, Va. **99** E16; 98
Skyscraper, tallest 146
Slaves 116, 118, 128, 140
Sleeping Bear Dune, Mich. 154
Sleeping Bear Dunes NL, Mich. **155** L9
Smith Island, Md.–Va. **69** Q21; **99** F25
Smith Mountain Lake, Va. **99** L13
Smithfield, Va. **99** L23; 98
Smoky Hill River, Kans. **179** D5
Smugglers Notch, Vt. **53** E5
Smyrna, Ga. **129** E4
Snake River **233, 249, 267, 271;** *232, 234, 250-251;* Hells Canyon 232, 288
Snake River Plain, Idaho **233** Q8
Snakes *16, 241*
Snow, Mount, Vt. **53** S4
Soda Springs, Idaho **233** R12; phosphate 232
Solar energy 206; diagram *206*
Solomon River, Kans. **179** C11
Somerville, Mass. **41** F18
Songsong, Northern Mariana Islands **285** J13

Sonoma, Calif. **263** J4; 262
Sonoran Desert, Ariz. **211** N4-P4; 210
Soo Canals, Canada–U. S. **155** F13; 154
Souris River, N. Dak. **195** B9
South Bend, Ind. **151** B7
South Branch Potomac River, W. Va. **103** H15
South Cape (Ka Lae), Hawaii **281** Q22; 280
South Carolina 140-143
South Dakota 168, 171, 198-201
South Fork IR, Nev. **241** E10
South Hero Island, Vt. **53** D2
South Holston Lake, Tenn. **95** A26
South Loup River, Nebr. **191** F10
South Milwaukee, Wis. **163** R14
South Pass, Wyo. **249** K6
South Platte River, Colo.–Nebr. **191** F5; **229** A18-F8
South Portland, Maine **37** S4
Southampton, N. Y. **77** S22
Southern Ute IR, Colo. **229** O4
Spanish Trail **229, 241, 245, 263**
Spartanburg, S. C. **141** B6; 140
Spenard, Alaska **277** L19
Spirit Lake, Iowa **175** A5
Spokane, Wash. **271** F18; 270
Spokane IR, Wash. **271** E16
Spokane River, Wash. **271** E16
Sponges *124*
Spoon River, Ill. **147** H4
Springer Mountain, Ga. **129** B5
Springfield, Ill. **147** K6
Springfield, Mass. **40** J8; 40
Springfield, Mo. **187** N7
Springfield, Ohio **159** L5
Springfield, Oreg. **267** H5
Springfield, Vt. **53** P7; 52
Spruce Knob, W. Va. **103** K13
Squam Lake, N. H. **45** M7
Squaw Creek NWR, Mo. **187** B2
Stamford, Conn. **33** N3
Standard Metropolitan Statistical Areas (SMSA) 25-26, 288
Standing Rock IR, N. Dak.–S. Dak. **195** M9; **199** B7
State College, Pa. **81** G9
Staten Island, N. Y. **77** T16
Statesville, N. C. **91** D10
Statues: boll weevil 116; Paul Revere *43*; Statue of Liberty 23, *78-79*; war god *282*
Staunton, Va. **99** F15
Steelmaking: auto industry 59, 150, 154; furnaces 56, 59, 102; largest producer 146; mills *83, 152, 161;* products 59, nails *149;* raw materials 56, 80, *81,* 116
Stehekin, Wash. 273
Sterling Heights, Mich. **155** R16
Steubenville, Ohio **159** J16
Stevens Point, Wis. **163** L10
Stillwater, Okla. **219** F19
Stockbridge IR, Wis. **163** K12
Stockton, Calif. **263** J6

Stockton Lake, Mo. **187** L6
Stone Mountain, Ga. **129** E6; 128
Stoney Lonesome, Ind. **151** N7; 152
Stonington, Conn. **33** K18
Stony Creek, Pa. **81** J6
Stoughton, Mass. **41** H18
Stowe, Vt. **53** F6
Strafford, Vt. **53** L7; *55*
Stratford, Conn. **33** M6
Stratford Point, Conn. **33** M7
Stratton Mountain, Vt. **53** R4
Strawberry Reservoir, Utah **245** G10
Strawberry River, Utah **245** H11
Streeter Pond, N. H. *47*
Sturgeon Bay, Wis. **163** K16
Stuttgart, Ark. **121** K12; 120
Suffolk, Va. **99** M23
Sugar Creek, Ind. **151** J5
Sugarbush Valley, Vt. **53** H4
Sugarloaf Mountain, Maine **37** M4
Suitland, Md. **69** H15
Sullivans Island, S. C. **141** M14
Sulphur, La. **133** L3
Summer Lake, Oreg. **267** L9
Summersville Lake, W. Va. **103** M8
Summit Lake IR, Nev. **241** B3
Sumner, Lake, N. Mex. **215** H13
Sumter, S. C. **141** G12
Sun City, Ariz. **211** M8; *212*
Sun Valley, Idaho **233** O7
Sunapee, Lake, N. H. **45** P4
Sunapee, Mount, N. H. **45** Q4
Sundance, Wyo. **249** C17
Sunflower, Mount, Kans. **179** C1
Sunnyvale, Calif. **263** L5
Sunset Crater NM, Ariz. **211** F10
Sunshine Mine, Idaho 232
Supawna Meadows NWR, N. J. **73** P1
Superior, Wis. **163** C3; 185
Superior, Lake **155, 163, 183;** 182, depth 144; *see also* Great Lakes
Susitna River, Alaska **277** K19
Susquehanna River, Md.–N. Y.–Pa. **69** B20; **77** M12; **81** C-L14
Sutton Lake, W. Va. **103** K9
Suwannee River, Fla.–Ga. **125** D11; **129** R11
Swan Lake, S. Dak. **199** C10
Swan Lake NWR, Mo. **187** D8
Swans Island, Maine **37** Q10
Swinomish IR, Wash. **271** C6
Syracuse, N. Y. **77** J10

Table Rock Lake, Mo. **187** P7
Tacoma, Wash. **271** G6
Tahlequah, Okla. **219** F26; 218
Tahoe, Lake, Calif.–Nev. **241** J1; **263** G8
Tahquamenon River, Mich. **155** F10
Taliesin, Wis. **163** Q8
Talladega, Ala. **117** G9

Tallahassee, Fla. **125** B8
Tallahatchie River, Miss. **137** E5
Tallapoosa River, Ala. **117** L10
Tampa, Fla. **125** J13; 23
Tampa Bay, Fla. **125** K12
Tanana River, Alaska **277** J21
Tangier Island, Va. **99** G25
Tanglewood, Mass. **40** G2
Taos, N. Mex. **215** C10
Taos Pueblo, N. Mex. **215** C10; *217*
Tar River, N. C. **91** B18
Tarpon Springs, Fla. **125** H12; 124
Taum Sauk Mountain, Mo. **187** L15
Taunton, Mass. **41** K19
Taunton River, Mass. **41** M18
Taylor, Mount, N. Mex. **215** F5
Telluride, Colo. **229** L4; 228
Tempe, Ariz. **211** N8; 210
Temple, Texas **223** J13
Ten Thousand Islands, Fla. **125** P15
Tenkiller Lake, Okla. **219** G26
Tennessee 94-97
Tennessee NWR, Tenn. **95** D8
Tennessee River, Ala.–Ky.–Tenn. **86, 94, 95, 117;** *94, 96, 116*
Tennessee Valley Authority 96; dams *97*
Tensas River, La. **133** E10
Terre Haute, Ind. **151** M3
Terrebonne Bay, La. **133** Q13
Teton Mountains, Wyo. 248, *250-251*
Teton River, Mont. **237** D7
Texarkana, Ark. **121** P3; 120
Texarkana, Texas **223** E17
Texas 17, 18, 25, 56, 171, 178, 208, 209, 222-225, 274; cattle 190; cotton 136; oil 132, 202
Texas City, Texas **223** M17
Texoma, Lake, Okla.–Texas **219** O20; **223** E14
Textiles 90, 140; history 44, 48, 56; synthetic fiber 64, 66, *92,* 98
Thames River, Conn. **33** J16
Theodore Roosevelt Lake, Ariz. **211** M10
Theodore Roosevelt NMP, N. Dak. **195** F-H3; *194*
Thermal springs 12, 14, 102, 120, 232; energy source **204,** 232; *see also* Energy
Thibodaux, La. **133** N12
Thief River Falls, Minn. **183** D3
The Thimbles, Conn. **33** L10
Third Lake, N. H. **45** A8
Thomasville, Ga. **129** R6
Thomasville, N.C. **91** C13
Thompson Falls, Mont. **237** D2
Thousand Islands, N. Y. **77** D10
Thousand Springs, Idaho **233** R6
Three Sisters, Oreg. **267** H7; waterfall *269*
Thunderhead Mountain, S. Dak. 198
Thunderstorms 110, 112

Ticonderoga, N. Y. **77** F18; 78
Tiffin, Ohio **159** F7
Tillamook Bay, Oreg. **267** C3
Timbalier Bay, La. **133** P14
Time zones **26-27**
Timms Hill, Wis. **163** H8; 162
Tims Ford Lake, Tenn. **95** G13
Tinian, Northern Mariana Islands **285** L17
Tippecanoe River, Ind. **151** D7
Tishomingo NWR, Okla. **219** N21
Titusville, Fla. **125** G16
Titusville, Pa. **81** C4; 80, 202
Toadstool Park, Nebr. **191** A2
Toiyabe Range, Nev. *242-243*
Toledo, Ohio **159** C6
Toledo Bend Reservoir, La.–Texas **133** G3; **223** H18
Tom, Mount, Mass. **40** H7
Tombigbee River, Ala.–Miss. **117** M3; **137** F11
Tombstone, Ariz. **211** S13; 210
Toms River, N. J. **73** L8
Tonawanda IR, N. Y. **76** J4
Tongue River, Mont. **237** H15
Tonto NM, Ariz. **211** M11
Topeka, Kans. **179** D17
Torch Lake, Mich. **155** K11
Tornadoes *110, 112,* 178
Torrance, Calif. **263** S11
Torrington, Conn. **33** D6
Towson, Md. **69** D17
Trans-Alaska Pipeline, Alaska **277** E20
Transportation *see* Automobiles; Great Lakes; Highways; Pioneers; Railroads; *and* canals by name
Traverse, Lake, Minn. **183** M2
Traverse City, Mich. **155** L10
Tree, world's tallest 265, 288
Trenton, Mich. **155** T 16
Trenton, N. J. **73** K5
Trinity River, Texas **223** H15
Triple Divide Pass, Mont. 236, *238*
Troy, Mich. **155** R16
Troy, N. Y. **77** K17
Truchas Peak, N. Mex. **215** D10
Truckee River, Nev. **241** G2
Trumbull, Conn. **33** L6
Truro, Mass. **41** J26
Truth or Consequences, N. Mex. **215** N6
Tsala Apopka Lake, Fla. **125** F13
Tschida, Lake, N. Dak. **195** K6
Tucson, Ariz. **211** Q11; 210
Tucumcari, N. Mex. **215** G14
Tug Fork (river), Ky.–W. Va. **87** F25; **103** P3
Tulalip IR, Wash. **271** D6
Tule Lake NWR, Calif. **263** A6
Tule River IR, Calif. **263** N10
Tullahoma, Tenn. **95** F13
Tulsa, Okla. **219** F23; 218
Tumacacori NM, Ariz. **211** S11
Tuolumne River, Calif. **263** J8
Tupelo, Miss. **137** C10
Tupper Lake, N. Y. **77** D15
Turnbull NWR, Wash. **271** G18

Turtle Mountain IR, N. Dak. **195** B12
Turtle Mountains, N. Dak. **195** A11
Turtles *142, 241*
Tuscaloosa, Ala. **117** H5; coal mine *118*
Tuscarawas River, Ohio **159** G13
Tuscarora IR, N. Y. **76** H3
Tuskegee, Ala. **117** L11
Tuttle Creek Lake, Kans. **179** B14
Tutuila, American Samoa **285** R4
Tuzigoot NM, Ariz. **211** H8
Twelve Mile, Ind. **151** F7; 150
Twin Falls, Idaho **233** R6
Two Rivers, Wis. **163** N15
Tygart Lake, W. Va. **103** G11
Tyler, Texas **223** G16

Uinta and Ouray IR, Utah **245** G11, K13
Uinta Mountains, Utah **245** E11-13
Uinta River, Utah **245** F12
Umatilla IR, Oreg. **267** C14
Umbagog Lake, N. H. **45** E9
Unalaska Island, Alaska **277** P10
Uncompahgre River, Colo. **229** K4
Unimak Island, Alaska **277** P11
Union City, N. J. **73** F10
Union City Reservoir, Pa. **81** B3
Union Slough NWR, Iowa **175** B7
Uniontown, Pa. **81** L3
U. S. Weather Service: National Hurricane Center 112; National Meteorological Center 106; weather map *109*
University City, Mo. **187** G16
Upper Arlington, Ohio **159** L8
Upper Darby, Pa. **81** K18
Upper Klamath Lake, Oreg. **267** N7
Upper Mississippi River Wildlife and Fish Refuge, Ill.–Iowa–Wis. **147** C5; **163** P5; **175** D17
Upper Red Lake, Minn. **183** D6
Urbana, Ill. **147** J9
Utah 244-247
Utah Lake, Utah **245** G8
Ute Mountain IR, Colo. **229** O2
Utica, N. Y. **77** J13

Vail, Colo. **229** F8; 230
Valdez, Alaska **277** L20
Valdosta, Ga. **129** Q9
Valentine, Nebr. **191** A8; 190
Valentine NWR, Nebr. **191** B8
Vallejo, Calif. **263** J4
Valley Falls, R. I. **49** C9
Valley Forge, Pa. **81** K17; 80
Valley Station, Ky. **87** F12
Valparaiso, Ind. **151** C4
Van Wert, Ohio **159** G2
Vancouver, Wash. **271** N5; 270

303

Vegetation zones **14-15**; *see also* Forests; Plants
Ventura, Calif. **263** R9
Verde River, Ariz. **211** K9
Verdigris River, Kans.-Okla. **179** G16; **219** F24; 218
Vermilion Lake, Minn. **183** E11
Vermont 52-55
Vernon, Conn. **33** D12
Vero Beach, Fla. **125** J18
Vicksburg, Miss. **137** L3; 136
Victoria, Texas **223** N14
Vieques, Puerto Rico **285** D19
Vinalhaven Island, Maine **37** Q9
Vincennes, Ind. **151** Q2
Vineland, N. J. **73** Q4
Vineyard Haven, Mass. **41** P22
Virgin Islands **274, 285**; 252, 274, 284, 289
Virgin Islands NP, U. S. Virgin Islands **285** B4
Virgin River, Nev.-Utah **241** P13; **245** S4
Virginia 64, 98-101
Virginia Beach, Va. **99** L25
Virginia City, Mont. **237** J7; 236
Virginia City, Nev. **241** H2; 243
Visalia, Calif. **263** N9
Volcanoes 261; ancient 120, 214, 260; crater *282*; landforms from 232, 280, 281; lava flows 280, *281*
Voyageurs NP, Minn. **183** C10; 184

Wabash, Ind. **151** F8
Wabash River, Ill.-Ind. **147** P10; **151** H3-R1; 146
Waccamaw, Lake, N. C. **91** J18
Wachusett Reservoir, Mass. **41** F14
Waco, Texas **223** J13
Wahiawa, Hawaii **281** D10
Waialeale, Hawaii **280** B4; 288
Waikiki Beach, Hawaii **281** F11; *282*
Wailuku River, Hawaii **281** M24
Waimea Canyon, Hawaii **280** C3
Walker Lake, Nev. **241** K3
Walker River IR, Nev. **241** J4
Walla Walla, Wash. **271** M16
Wallenpaupack, Lake, Pa. **81** D18
Wallingford, Conn. **33** H9; silversmith *35*
Walnut Canyon NM, Ariz. **211** G10
Walrus *277*
Walt Disney World, Fla. **125** H15
Walter F. George Reservoir, Ala.-Ga. **117** N13; **129** N3
Wanaque Reservoir, N. J. **73** C8
Wapack NWR, N. H. **45** S5
Wapakoneta, Ohio **159** H4; 158
Wapanocca NWR, Ark. **121** F16
Wappapello Lake, Mo. **187** O16
Wapsipinicon River, Iowa **175** F15

Warm Springs, Ga. **129** J4
Warm Springs IR, Oreg. **267** E7
Warm Springs Reservoir, Oreg. **267** J15
Warner Robins, Ga. **129** K7
Warren, Mich. **155** R16
Warren, Ohio **159** E15
Warren, R. I. **49** G10
Warwick, R. I. **49** G7
Wasatch Range, Utah **245** B9-K8; 244
Washington 270-273
Washington, D. C. **28**; 28-29, 68, 98, 258; Census Clock 24
Washington, Mo. **187** H14; 186
Washington, Pa. **81** J2
Washington, Mount, N. H. **45** H8; 44, *46*, 288; plant life *45*
Washington Crossing, Pa. **81** J19
Washington Island, Wis. **163** G16
Washita NWR, Okla. **219** G12
Washita River, Okla. **219** L18
Watauga Lake, Tenn. **95** B26
Watchaug Pond, R. I. **49** O4
Waterbury, Conn. **33** G7
Wateree Lake, S. C. **141** D11
Wateree River, S. C. **141** F11
Waterford, Conn. **33** K15
Waterloo, Iowa **175** E12
Waterpower *see* Energy
Watertown, Conn. **33** G6
Watertown, N. Y. **77** E11
Watertown, S. Dak. **199** D16
Waterville, Maine **37** O6
Watts Bar Lake, Tenn. **95** D18
Waubay Lake, S. Dak. **199** C16
Waukegan, Ill. **147** B10
Waukesha, Wis. **163** R13
Wausau, Wis. **163** K10
Wauwatosa, Wis. **163** R14
Waycross, Ga. **129** P12
Weather and climate 106-113; agriculture 106, 110-111, 168-169; changes in 108, 113; control 112-113; desert temperatures 208; drought 106, *111;* factors influencing 106, *107*, 110, 194; mountains 17, *112-113*, 173; forecasting 106; rainfall 173, 174, 270, greatest 280, scarce 17, 178, 226, 240; records 288; satellite map **109**; snow 52, 106, *111*, 236; storms *110*, 112, 116, 136, 178, Great Lakes 145, 149; winds 44, 108, 110, 280; winter 1977 106, *111*
Webster Groves, Mo. **187** H16
Weirton, W. Va. **103** B9; 102
Weiss Lake, Ala. **117** D11
Wellesley, Mass. **41** G17
Wenatchee, Wash. **271** G11; 272
Wenatchee River, Wash. **271** E10
Wendover, Nev. **241** D13; 240
Wentworth, Lake, N. H. **45** N9
West Allis, Wis. **163** R14
West Branch Farmington River, Conn. **33** B7

West Branch Susquehanna River, Pa. **81** E9
West Cote Blanche Bay, La. **133** N9
West Chester, Pa. **81** K16
West Hartford, Conn. **33** E10
West Haven, Conn. **33** L8
West Lafayette, Ind. **151** H4
West Memphis, Ark. **121** G16
West Palm Beach, Fla. **125** M19
West Point, N. Y. **77** Q17
West Point Lake, Ga. **129** H3
West River, Vt. **53** S6
West Virginia 102-105
West Warwick, R. I. **49** G6
Westbrook, Maine **37** S4; 36
Westfield, Mass. **40** J7
Westminster, Colo. **229** E11
Westport, Conn. **33** M4
Wetherill Mesa, Colo. 231
Wethersfield, Conn. **33** E11
Weymouth, Mass. **41** G19
Whale, false killer *283*
Wheaton, Ill. **147** C9
Wheaton, Md. **69** G14
Wheeler Lake, Ala. **117** B6
Wheeler NWR, Ala. **117** C7
Wheeler Peak, Nev. **241** J12
Wheeler Peak, N. Mex. **215** C10
Wheeling, W. Va. **103** C8
Whidbey Island, Wash. **271** D5
Whiskeytown-Shasta-Trinity NRA, Calif. **263** D4
White Butte, N. Dak. **195** K3
White Earth IR, Minn. **183** G3
White Lake, La. **133** N6
White Mountains, N. H. **45** J8; 31, 44, 47
White Plains, N. Y. **77** S17
White River, Ark. **121** B8-M13
White River, Colo.-Utah **229** D3; **245** H15
White River, Ind. **151** N5
White River, S. Dak. **199** H10
White River, Vt. **53** L6
White River Junction, Vt. **53** M8
White River NWR, Ark. **121** M13; 120
White Sands NM, N. Mex. **215** O8; *217*
White Sulphur Springs, Mont. **237** G8
White Sulphur Springs, W. Va. **103** O10
Whiteface Mountain, N. Y. **77** C17
Whitefish Bay, Mich. **155** E11
Whitefish Bay, Wis. **163** Q14
Whitehall, Ohio **159** L8
Whitewater River, Ind. **151** M11
Whitney, Mount, Calif. **263** M11
Wichita, Kans. **179** H13; 178
Wichita Falls, Texas **223** E12
Wichita Mountains NWR, Okla. **219** L14; buffalo roundup *220-221*
Wickiup Reservoir, Oreg. **267** J7
Wickliffe, Ohio **159** D13
Wicomico River, Md. **69** N16
Wilkes-Barre, Pa. **81** E15
Willamette River, Oreg. 267

G4; *269;* valley 266
Williamsburg, Va. **99** K23; *101*
Williamsport, Pa. **81** E12; 80
Willimantic River, Conn. **33** D14
Willingboro, N. J. **73** L5
Wilmette, Ill. **147** C10
Wilmington, Del. **65** B4; 64
Wilmington, N. C. **91** K20; 90
Wilson, N. C. **91** D20; tobacco auction *92*
Wilson Lake, Ala. **117** B5
Wilson Lake, Kans. **179** D10
Winchester, Va. **99** B18
Wind Cave NP, S. Dak. **199** J2; 198
Wind River, Wyo. **249** G7
Wind River IR, Wyo. **249** F6
Wind River Range, Wyo. **249** H5; 248
Windham, Conn. **33** E15
Windmills *see* Energy
Window Rock, Ariz. **211** E16
Windsor, Conn. **33** D11
Windsor, Vt. **53** O8; 52
Winfield, Kans. **179** J14
Winnebago, Lake, Wis. **163** N13; 162
Winnebago IR, Nebr. **191** C16
Winnibigoshish, Lake, Minn. **183** F7
Winnipesaukee, Lake, N. H. **45** O8
Winnisquam Lake, N. H. **45** O6
Winona, Miss. **137** F7
Winooski River, Vt. **53** G6
Winston-Salem, N. C. **91** C12
Winter Park, Fla. **125** G15
Wisconsin 42, 56, 162-165, 168
Wisconsin Dells, Wis. **163** P9
Wisconsin Rapids, Wis. **163** M9
Wisconsin River, Wis. **163** H9
Wissota, Lake, Wis. **163** K5
Withlacoochee River, Fla. **125** F13
Woburn, Mass. **41** E18
Wolf River, Wis. **163** J12
Wood, petrified 213, 248
Wood River, R. I. **49** J3
Woodall Mountain, Miss. **137** A12
Woods Hole, Mass. **41** O22
Woonasquatucket River, R. I. **49** C6
Woonsocket, R. I. **49** A7
Worcester, Mass. **41** G13
Worden Pond, R. I. **49** N5
Worthington, Ohio **159** L8
Wounded Knee, S. Dak. **199** K4; 198
Wrangell, Alaska **277** P26
Wrangell Mountains, Alaska **277** K21
Wright Brothers NM, N. C. **91** C26
Wright Patman Lake, Texas **223** F17
Writing Rock, N. Dak. **195** B2
Wupatki NM, Ariz. **211** F10
Wyandotte, Mich. **155** S16
Wylie Lake, S. C. **141** A10
Wyoming 234, 248-251
Wyoming, Mich. **155** R10

Xenia, Ohio **159** M5

Yadkin River, N. C. **91** C9
Yakima, Wash. **271** K10
Yakima IR, Wash. **271** L9
Yakima River, Wash. **271** L11
Yalobusha River, Miss. **137** E6
Yampa River, Colo. **229** C4
Yankton IR, S. Dak. **199** K14
Yazoo NWR, Miss. **137** H3
Yazoo River, Miss. **137** G5
Yellow River, Fla. **125** B2
Yellowstone Lake, Wyo. **249** C3
Yellowstone NP, Idaho-Mont.-Wyo. **233** N13; **237** K8; **249** B2; 12, 14, 248, 249; geysers 204, *251*
Yellowstone River, Mont. **237** H13; Lower Falls *251*
Yockanookany River, Miss. **137** H7
Yonkers, N. Y. **77** S17
York, Pa. **81** K13
York River, Va. 98
Yosemite NP, Calif. **263** J9; 288
Youghiogheny River, Md.-Pa. **68** C1; **81** K4
Youngstown, Ohio **159** F16
Ypsilanti, Mich. **155** S15
Yuba Lake, Utah **245** K7
Yucca House NM, Colo. **229** N2
Yukon Delta, Alaska **277** H14
Yukon River, Canada-U. S. **277** F22-H14
Yuma, Ariz. **211** P1

Zanesville, Ohio **159** L11
Zion, Ill. **147** B10
Zion NP, Utah **245** R4
Zuni IR, N. Mex. **215** G2

Type composition by National Geographic's Photographic Services. Color separations by Colorgraphics, Inc., Forestville, Md.; Graphic Color Plate, Inc., Stamford, Conn.; Chanticleer Company, Inc., New York, N. Y.; Beck Engraving Co., Inc., Philadelphia, Pa. Transvision by Milprint, Milwaukee, Wisc. Printed and bound by Fawcett Printing Corp., Rockville, Md. Paper by Westvaco Corp., New York, N. Y.

Library of Congress CIP Data

National Geographic Society, Washington, D. C. Book Service

Picture atlas of our fifty States

At head of title: National Geographic.
Bibliography: p.
Includes index.
SUMMARY: Includes maps and other pertinent information about the geography, climate, and population of each of the 50 states.
1. United States—Maps.
[1. United States—Maps. 2. Atlases]
I. Title. II. Title: Our fifty States.
G1200.N34 1978 912′.73 78-10385
ISBN 0-87044-216-3